Interpretation and Application of UK GAAP for Accounting Periods Commencing on or After 1 January 2015

Interpretation and Application of UK GAAP for Accounting Periods Commencing on or After 1 January 2015

Steven Collings

This edition first published 2015
© 2015 Steven Collings

Registered office

John Wiley & Sons Ltd, The Atrium, Southern Gate, Chichester, West Sussex, PO19 8SQ, United Kingdom

For details of our global editorial offices, for customer services and for information about how to apply for permission to reuse the copyright material in this book please visit our website at www.wiley.com.

Wiley publishes in a variety of print and electronic formats and by print-on-demand. Some material included with standard print versions of this book may not be included in e-books or in print-on-demand. If this book refers to media such as a CD or DVD that is not included in the version you purchased, you may download this material at http://booksupport.wiley.com. For more information about Wiley products, visit www.wiley.com.

A catalogue record for this book is available from the Library of Congress.

A catalogue record for this book is available from the British Library.

ISBN 978-1-118-81927-2 (paperback)   **ISBN 978-1-118-81925-8 (ebk)**
ISBN 978-1-118-81926-5 (ebk)   **ISBN 978-1-119-05294-4 (ebk)**

Set in 11/12pt TimesLTStd by Laserwords Private Limited, Chennai, India

Printed in Great Britain by TJ International Ltd, Padstow, Cornwall, UK

CONTENTS

Contents

ABOUT THE AUTHOR

Steve Collings FMAAT FCCA is the audit and technical partner at Leavitt Walmsley Associates Ltd, a firm of Chartered Certified Accountants based in Sale, Cheshire, in the United Kingdom, where Steve trained and qualified. Steve was admitted as a member of the Association of Accounting Technicians (AAT) in 2001 and went on to qualify as a Chartered Certified Accountant (ACCA) in 2005. He was admitted as a Fellow Member of the AAT in 2006 and became a Fellow Member of ACCA in 2010. Steve also holds ACCA's Diploma in International Financial Reporting Standards, Diploma in International Financial Reporting Standards for Small–Medium Entities as well as ACCA's Certificates in IFRS and International Auditing Standards and holds Senior Statutory Auditor status in the UK.

Steve is the author of several books on the subjects of accounting and auditing, including *Interpretation and Application of International Standards on Auditing* (Wiley, March 2011), *IFRS For Dummies* (Wiley, March 2012), *Frequently Asked Questions in IFRS* (Wiley, April 2013), *Financial Accounting for Dummies* (Wiley, April 2013) and *Corporate Finance for Dummies* (Wiley, October 2013). He has had many articles published in the professional accounting media, most notably AccountingWEB.co.uk and much of Steve's work can be seen on his website at www.stevecollings.co.uk.

Steve lectures professionally qualified accountants on the areas of accounting, auditing and Solicitors Accounts Rules and was named *Accounting Technician of the Year* at the British Accountancy Awards in 2011. He was also awarded *Outstanding Contribution to the Accountancy Profession* by the Association of International Accountants in 2013. In 2014 he was shortlisted for *Practitioner of the Year* at the 2014 British Accountancy Awards.

FOREWORD

When thinking about new UK GAAP the Chinese curse comes to mind, 'May you live in interesting times', because applying new UK GAAP will be interesting times. Many people will underestimate the size of the learning curve ahead of them. Yes, the standards are much shorter, easier to read and there are many exemptions but that does not mean that there are not many differences from the previous UK standards.

In my professional career there have been lots of changes to the UK accounting standards; indeed I trained under SSAP 2! The difference this time is that everything is changing at the same time. This is a 'big bang' move to a new you approach. There are lots of exciting headline changes in areas such as financial instruments and investment properties but perhaps more importantly there is plenty of 'devil in the detail'.

Ultimately, this is not a change to old UK GAAP, it is a move to something completely different, based upon standards written by a standard setting committee based outside of the UK. The new standards are not a 'copy and paste' job from what went before, so concentrating on what has changed can be futile. Instead, focus on the new standards in their entirety.

I say all of this not to spread doom and gloom but to calibrate your expectations of the journey ahead.

However, having said that, I have assumed that you are only familiar with old UK GAAP. If you are a child of IFRS then your learning curve will be much shorter and less steep. After all, new UK GAAP is based upon IFRS. Luckily for you, your author is an IFRS man. Because new UK GAAP is so brief, knowledge of full IFRS is very useful indeed to interpret standards like FRS 102. Sometimes the standard in new UK GAAP only gives you half the story and in this book Steve uses his understanding of IFRS to fill in the GAAPs (excuse the accounting pun).

I always tell accountants to 'read the standards' and this remains true for new UK GAAP. However, the aforementioned brevity of the standards means that this will sometimes raise as many questions as it answers. That is why books like this will be more essential than ever under new UK GAAP. Sometimes people use textbooks as a short cut to find out what the standard says. This book does more than that. It does what the standard sometimes does not do; it helps you understand what the standard means and how it applies in practice.

I have admired the clarity of Steve's writing for some time, particularly on the subject of IFRS, where many writers assume that the only business that exists is big business. More recently I have had the pleasure of working with Steve on joint projects writing on new UK GAAP and I was honoured to be asked to write this foreword. I like the way that Steve starts with the basics and uses clear examples to build on this and illustrate how new UK GAAP works.

I hope that you find Steve's wisdom useful on your journey up the new UK GAAP learning curve. I have been speaking about and writing about new UK GAAP for what seems like a long time now and as I write this I think I am starting to get towards the top of that learning curve, but I am not there yet. So as a fellow traveller on the journey to understanding new UK GAAP, I wish you the best of luck and I finish as I started with a Chinese proverb, albeit this time a more positive one. 'Be not afraid of going slowly, be only afraid of standing still.'

John Selwood ACA
Lecturer and writer

PREFACE

This is the first edition of *Interpretation and Application of UK GAAP for Accounting Periods Commencing on or After 1 January 2015*. The focus of this book is to provide preparers of financial statements in the UK and Republic of Ireland with concise and transparent information that will allow a clear understanding of how the UK GAAP works.

The publication of FRS 102 *The Financial Reporting Standard applicable in the UK and Republic of Ireland* was the biggest change that the UK GAAP has seen in its history. Previous UK GAAP had become overly complex and voluminous and the issuance of FRS 102 marked the end of a long process of consultation by the Financial Reporting Council (FRC). FRS 102 replaces all Financial Reporting Standards (FRSs), Statements of Standard Accounting Practice (SSAPs) and Urgent Issues Task Force Abstracts (UITFs) for accounting periods commencing on or after 1 January 2015 (although earlier adoption is permissible).

The FRC are to be commended on their efforts in scaling down the UK GAAP from some 3,000+ pages down to approximately 360. FRS 102 brings with it a much more user-friendly set of standards, organised by Section numbers as opposed to FRS/SSAP/UITF numbers, as was previously the case in the UK GAAP. Certain accounting treatments have been modernised, reflecting the ways in which businesses operate in today's climate as well as serving to reduce diversity in the ways in which preparers will account for, and disclose, certain items within the financial statements.

At the time of writing the small companies regime had been exposed for consultation by both the Department for Business Innovation and Skills and the FRC following the introduction of the EU Accounting Directive (Chapter 4 looks in more detail about this issue). Relevant chapters in this publication have incorporated the consultations but no decision had been made as to how the small companies regime will take effect in the UK at the time this book went to print and hence readers are encouraged to keep up to date with developments in this area by regularly reviewing the Department for Business Innovation and Skills website and the FRC website.

Most chapters in this book contain real-life practical examples in order to aid understanding.

My wish is that readers find this book informative and helpful in their day-to-day dealing with the new UK GAAP. As a practitioner myself, I recognise the needs of accountants and appreciate the complexities that we face within the profession. Financial reporting has evolved considerably over recent years and more emphasis is placed on producing high-quality financial information that meets users' needs. I hope that this book serves to meet those needs and feedback is welcome via the publishers that can be incorporated in any future editions.

Steve Collings, FMAAT FCCA
September 2014

ACKNOWLEDGEMENTS

Writing a book is a huge project and one in which an author needs to have a strong and supportive team behind them. I would like to offer my sincere thanks to Gemma Valler, the commissioning editor for this title, for the support offered during the writing process and also extending the deadline so I could take account of sweeping changes currently taking place with the small companies regime.

I would also like to thank my technical editor Caroline Fox, BA FCA, who has, once again, done a remarkable job on ensuring the technical accuracy of this publication.

Finally, I would like to thank you the reader, who has picked up this book, and I hope that it offers a helpful insight into the world of the UK GAAP and aids in the application of the new reporting regime.

INTRODUCTION

INTRODUCTION

Interpretation and Application of UK GAAP for Accounting Periods Commencing on or After 1 January 2015 is aimed at providing preparers of financial statements with comprehensive guidance and information that will allow financial statements prepared under the new UK GAAP to conform to the new regime. This publication brings to life much of the theory contained in UK GAAP and offers a practical approach to understanding the requirements of UK GAAP from a real-life perspective.

Standard-setting around the world has evolved considerably over recent years and International Financial Reporting Standards (IFRS) have gathered faster pace, with many countries adopting an international-based framework. At the time of writing the introduction of FRS 102 *The Financial Reporting Standard applicable in the UK and Republic of Ireland* was part of a significant overhaul of UK GAAP. At the time of going to print, the UK and Republic of Ireland were about to have a four-tiered structure to financial reporting, which is shown in the following table:

Class of entity	*EU-endorsed IFRS*	*Mainstream UK GAAP (FRS 102)*	*Small companies regime (the FRSSE)**	*Micro-entities regime (the FRSME)*
Listed and AIM listed	√			
Medium and unlisted	√	√		
Small	√	√	√	√

*At the time of writing the FRSSE was being tentatively withdrawn by the Financial Reporting Council (FRC) for accounting periods commencing on or after 1 January 2016 and companies reporting under the small companies regime are to be brought under the scope of FRS 102 (as amended for smaller companies). Consultations issued by the Department for Business Innovation and Skills and the FRC on 29 August 2014 outline the proposed new structure. The way forward for the small companies regime was to be outlined in Exposure Drafts to be issued towards the end of 2014/early 2015, with final standards expected in the summer of 2015. For 'micro-entities', which are dealt with in Chapter 4, such entities can apply the micro-entities legislation if they so wish.

The main objective of standard-setters around the globe is to enhance transparency. Adopting an international-based financial reporting framework has the intended objective of producing financial statements that are based on high-quality financial reporting standards, which, in turn, strengthens understandability and transparency across all entities. Accounting has evolved considerably over the years, with the concept of fair value accounting moving higher up the ranks and as such there was a need to introduce a new UK GAAP.

HISTORY OF THE UK AND REPUBLIC OF IRELAND STANDARD-SETTING BODY

The Financial Reporting Council (FRC) was established by the government back in 1990 and was charged with the promotion of good-quality financial reporting. This objective was to be achieved through two subsidiary bodies:

- Accounting Standards Board (ASB) and
- The Financial Reporting Review Panel (FRRP).

Prior to the establishment of the ASB, standards were issued by the Accounting Standards Council (ASC). The standards issued by the ASC were known as *Statements of Standard Accounting Practice* (SSAPs) and between 1971 and 1990, 34 SSAPs were issued by the ASC. A number of these SSAPs were adopted by the newly formed ASB in 1990, although going forward the ASB would not issue further SSAPs; rather they would be charged with issuing Financial Reporting Standards (FRSs).

In 1991, a new department was formed to assist the ASB in carrying out their work, known as the *Urgent Issues Task Force* (UITF). This department was set up to undertake investigations in areas where conflicts with accounting standards existed or where interpretative guidance was needed following ambiguous points, or clarification was sought by financial statement preparers. The first UITF Abstract was issued on 24 July 1991 titled *Convertible bonds – supplemental interest/premium.*

Due to well-publicised corporate collapses in the United States, the government decided in 2004 that the regulatory system in the UK needed to be further strengthened in an attempt to restore confidence. This resulted in the FRC becoming the UK's single independent regulator of the accounting and auditing profession, which would be solely responsible for issuing accounting standards and enforcing their application.

The ASB survived a 22-year lifespan that ended on 2 July 2012 when it was integrated with the FRC's new Codes and Standards Division. This restructuring was brought about because of the need for enhanced independence and the need to ensure effective governance of the regulatory activities under the responsibility of the FRC board. During this 22-year lifespan, the ASB issued 29 FRSs; however, it had become clear that due to the intention by the ASB to aid a smooth transition to an international-based financial reporting framework, the ASB had essentially become more of an advisory body as opposed to a standard-setting body. This was due to the fact that many of the later FRSs were merely IFRSs/IASs that had been rebadged in the UK. For example, FRS 20 *Share-based Payment* was a UK version of IFRS 2 *Share-based Payment*, FRS 21 *Events after the Balance Sheet Date* was IAS 10 *Events after the Reporting Period* and FRS 22 *Earnings per Share* was essentially IAS 33 *Earnings per Share*. In addition to this, many of the later FRSs had hardly any impact on private companies that make up the vast majority of the UK and Republic of Ireland business market (such as FRS 24 *Financial Reporting in Hyperinflationary Economies*, FRS 27 *Life Assurance*, FRS 29 *Financial Instruments: Disclosures* and FRS 30 *Heritage Assets*).

The Codes and Standards Committee was formed during this restructuring exercise and the objective of this committee was to advise the board of the FRC on the maintenance of an effective framework of UK codes and standards. The ASB was replaced with the Accounting Council, which provides an advisory role to the Codes and Standards Committee and the board of the FRC. In addition, the UITF was disbanded as a result of the reforms. Accounting standards previously issued by the ASB became the responsibility of the board of the FRC on 2 July 2012 when the restructuring was finalised.

ISSUANCE OF THE NEW UK GAAP

The process of modernising the old UK GAAP was a long and arduous one. The ASB had already acknowledged prior to the issuance of Exposure Drafts that the UK GAAP in its old form had become overly complex and voluminous. They had also expressed a desire for the UK and Republic of Ireland to adopt an international-based financial reporting framework to provide consistency in the way financial reporting works but within a high-quality and 'fit for purpose' framework. This intention was further accentuated in 2009 when the ASB announced that to essentially dispose of old FRSs/SSAPs and UITF Abstracts would be a significant task, but they viewed the project as an opportunity to simplify UK GAAP with the intention of ensuring that UK GAAP produced more relevant, comparable and understandable information.

FREDs 43 to 45 were published outlining the proposed changes to UK GAAP and these FREDs were based on the International Accounting Standard Board's *IFRS for SMEs* that was planned to become (and was exposed as) the *Financial Reporting Standard for Mid-Sized Entities* in the UK. The name of the proposals was coined the 'FRSME'.

This Exposure Draft caused a significant amount of outcry amongst the accountancy profession as it was based around the concept of 'public accountability', which was a very difficult concept to apply or define in the UK and Republic of Ireland. In addition, the Exposure Draft eliminated some of the more common accounting practices that have become established in the UK and Republic of Ireland (such as the withdrawal of the revaluation method for fixed assets, the writing-off of borrowing costs directly to profit or loss with no option to capitalise such costs and the requirement to calculate deferred tax using a 'temporary difference' approach rather than a 'timing difference' approach, as was the case in FRS 19 *Deferred Tax*).

Having listened to feedback on FREDs 43 to 45, the ASB went back and redrafted the proposals that became FREDs 46 to 48 and were exposed for comment. The revised Exposure Drafts:

- Eliminated the tier system for large, small–medium and micro-companies,
- Introduced accounting treatments permitted under the old UK GAAP and
- Incorporated guidance for public benefit entities into FRED 48.

FREDs 46 to 48 were to become FRSs 100, 101 and 102 respectively. FRS 103 *Insurance Contracts* is an industry-specific FRS, which was published in March 2014 and which deals with insurance contracts. Due to its specialist nature, FRS 103 is outside the scope of this book.

FRS 102 is part of a 'family' of standards, with the others being:

- FRS 100 *Application of Financial Reporting Requirements*,
- FRS 101 *Reduced Disclosure Framework* and
- FRS 103 *Insurance Contracts*.

FRS 100 and FRS 101 were both issued on 22 November 2012. FRS 100 outlines which entities can use which standard. Smaller companies will still continue to use the FRSSE (or the relevant small companies regime following the changes to small company financial reporting in 2015/16). The FRSSE (effective April 2008) was updated for the consequential effects of FRS 102 (see later in the chapter) and therefore the FRSSE was re-issued as the FRSSE (effective January 2015), which is effective for accounting periods commencing on or after 1 January 2015, with earlier adoption permissible.

FRS 101 is basically EU-endorsed IFRS, but with reduced disclosure requirements for qualifying entities. The standard outlines the reduced disclosure framework, which is available for qualifying entities that report under EU-adopted IFRS. When FRS 100 and 101 were both issued, they were set with an effective from date for accounting periods commencing on or after 1 January 2015, although earlier adoption is permissible. Legislation was introduced in the UK for year-ends ending on or after 1 October 2012, which allowed companies that are not required to apply IFRS by the 'IAS Regulation' more flexibility to change their accounting framework to FRS 101 or FRS 102. The advantage here was in relation to groups with a 31 December 2012 year-end who were being encouraged to adopt the standard early and take advantage of the reduced disclosures available, given that the disclosure requirements in EU-adopted IFRS are fairly vast.

In the press release, the FRC announced that they planned for FRS 102 to become effective for accounting periods commencing on or after 1 January 2015, with earlier adoption permissible (which did occur). There were two limited amendments that the FRC had recognised which related to:

- Accounting for multi-employer pensions and
- Service concession arrangements.

In relation to the accounting for multi-employer pensions, the amendments related to the situations where there was an agreement to fund a deficit in a multi-employer pension plan. The FRC issued the proposed amendment following them, obtaining evidence of diversity in practice where the previous FRS 17 *Retirement Benefits* was applied.

FRS 17 permitted entities who were not able to identify their share of the underlying assets and liabilities of a multi-employer pension plan on a 'consistent and reasonable basis' to account for such a scheme as if it were a defined contribution scheme and make additional disclosures within the financial statements. Where the scheme was a defined contribution scheme, FRS 17 required contributions to be recognised as an expense in the profit and loss account. As a consequence, FRS 17 did not explicitly require entities that were involved in a multi-employer scheme, which was accounted for as a defined contribution scheme and which had not entered into a funding agreement for future payments, to recognise a liability on the balance sheet (statement of financial position) that represented obligations to pay pension benefits in their financial statements.

The FRC took the decision not to amend FRS 17 to require entities that accounted for a multi-employer scheme as a defined contribution scheme to recognise a liability to pay pension benefits in their financial statements on the grounds that FRS 17 was to have a very short life going forward. Instead, the FRC decided to amend draft FRS 102 in order to clarify that a liability should be recognised in such situations to represent a requirement to make payments to fund a deficit relating to past service where the entity has entered into an agreement to make those payments.

In addition, the FRC also acknowledged that paragraph 9(b) (v) in FRS 17 will be applicable in the period prior to FRS 102 becoming effective. This paragraph requires disclosure of any implications for an employer of a deficit in a multi-employer scheme. The FRC said that where a reporting entity has an agreed schedule for the funding of a deficit, they will need to give careful consideration to this requirement and that they consider that information about an agreement with the multi-employer scheme that determines how it will fund a deficit should be disclosed with this requirement and would more than likely include:

- The existence of the agreement,
- The period over which the payments will be made and
- Any available information about the expected amount of the payments.

The FRC clarified in the Exposure Draft that the above will not apply to individual employers that participate in a group scheme due to the fact that different accounting requirements apply to the recognition of a surplus or deficit in a group scheme.

The second amendment related to service concession arrangements and the accounting, by grantors, for service concession arrangements. Draft FRS 102 only included requirements for operators of service concessions and it was flagged that grantors may also be within the scope of FRS 102. As a result, the amendment requires grantors to recognise the infrastructure assets and liabilities for service concession arrangements, with the accounting requirements based on a finance lease liability model.

Following this Exposure Draft containing the two limited amendments, FRS 102 was finally issued as a standard by the FRC on 5 March 2013 and marked the end of a long and arduous project to overhaul accounting standards in the UK. The end result was a standard that was clear, transparent and much less voluminous (a total of 335 pages including the Appendices as opposed to 3,000+ in old UK GAAP).

FRS 102 was re-published in August 2014 to take account of the changes in relation to financial instruments and hedge accounting as well as dealing with some typographical issues.

STRUCTURE OF THE NEW UK GAAP

The old UK GAAP was structured by FRS number order – for example, FRS 1 *Cash Flow Statements*, FRS 2 *Accounting for Subsidiary Undertakings*, FRS 3 *Reporting Financial Performance* and so forth. SSAPs and UITF Abstracts also followed a numerical sequence.

The structure of the new UK GAAP is markedly different in that it is structured as a series of FRSs (FRS 100, 101, 102 and 103).

FRS 100 *Application of Financial Reporting Requirements*

This is structured as follows:

- Summary
- Financial Reporting Standard 100
- Application of Financial Reporting Requirements
  - Objective
  - Scope
  - Abbreviations and definitions
  - Basis of preparation of financial statements
  - Application of statements of recommended practice
  - Statement of compliance
  - Date from which effective and transitional arrangements
  - Withdrawal of current accounting standards
  - Consequential amendments to the FRSSE
- Application Guidance
  - The interpretation of equivalence
- Approval by the FRC
- The Accounting Council's Advice to the FRC to Issue FRS 100
- Appendices
  - Glossary
  - Note on legal requirements
  - Previous consultations
  - Republic of Ireland (RoI) legal references

FRS 101 *Reduced Disclosure Framework*

- Summary
- Financial Reporting Standard 101
- Reduced Disclosure Framework
  - Objective
  - Scope
  - Abbreviations and definitions
  - Reduced disclosures for subsidiaries and ultimate parents
  - Statement of compliance
  - Date from which effective and transitional arrangements
- Application Guidance
  - Amendments to International Financial Reporting Standards as adopted in the European Union for compliance with the Act and the Regulations
- Approval by the FRC
- The Accounting Council's Advice to the FRC to Issue FRS 101
- Appendices
  - Glossary
  - Note on legal requirements
  - Previous consultations
  - Republic of Ireland (RoI) legal references

FRS 102 *The Financial Reporting Standard applicable in the UK and Republic of Ireland*

- Summary
- Financial Reporting Standard 102
- Financial Reporting Standard applicable in the UK and Republic of Ireland
  1. Scope
  2. Concepts and Pervasive Principles
  3. Financial Statement Presentation
  4. Statement of Financial Position
  5. Statement of Comprehensive Income and Income Statement
     Appendix: Example showing presentation of discontinued operations
  6. Statement of Changes in Equity and Statement of Income and Retained Earnings
  7. Statement of Cash Flows
  8. Notes to the Financial Statements
  9. Consolidated and Separate Financial Statements
  10. Accounting Policies, Estimates and Errors
  11. Basic Financial Instruments
  12. Other Financial Instruments Issues
  13. Inventories
  14. Investments in Associates
  15. Investments in Joint Ventures
  16. Investment Property
  17. Property, Plant and Equipment
  18. Intangible Assets other than Goodwill

SMALLER COMPANIES AND THE FINANCIAL REPORTING STANDARD FOR SMALLER ENTITIES

Chapter 4 looks in more detail at the specific financial reporting requirements for companies at the smaller end of the scale. At the time of writing, small company financial reporting was undergoing a significant period of change and consultations had been issued by both the BIS and the FRC on 29 August 2014 as a consequence of the EU Accounting Directive. Consultations closed in November 2014 and final standards relating to the small companies regime are expected in the summer of 2015 with an 'effective from' date of 1 January 2016 (although at the time of writing this had not yet taken place).

Smaller companies are eligible to use the Financial Reporting Standard for Smaller Entities (the FRSSE). The FRSSE has been amended because of FRS 102 and the latest version (at the time of writing) issued by the FRC was the FRSSE (effective January 2015), which is effective for accounting periods commencing on or after 1 January 2015, with earlier adoption permissible.

The *Small Companies (Micro-Entities Accounts) Regulations 2013* (SI 2013/3008) brought the European Union's directive on 'micro-company' reporting into effect in November 2013. For the purposes of this statutory instrument, an entity can qualify as a micro-entity if two, or more, of the following are not exceeded in a year:

* Turnover   £632,000
* Balance sheet total   £316,000
* Employee head count   10

Companies that fail to meet two out of the above three criteria for two consecutive years will fail to meet the qualifying criteria for micro-entities.

Under the micro-entities regime, a micro-entity will prepare a balance sheet, which will present (where applicable):

Format 1 balance sheet

* Called up share capital not paid
* Fixed assets
* Current assets
* Prepayments and accrued income
* Creditors due within one year
* Net current assets (liabilities)
* Total assets less current liabilities
* Creditors due after more than one year
* Provisions for liabilities
* Accruals and deferred income
* Capital and reserves

Format 2 balance sheet

Assets:

* Called up share capital not paid
* Fixed assets
* Current assets
* Prepayments and accrued income

Liabilities:

- Capital and reserves
- Provisions for liabilities
- Creditors (those due within and more than one year are separated)
- Accruals and deferred income

Profit and loss account:

- Turnover
- Other income
- Cost of raw materials and consumables
- Staff costs
- Depreciation and other amounts written off assets
- Other charges
- Tax
- Profit or loss

Notes to the micro-entity's financial statements

Notes will be placed at the foot of the balance sheet and will merely consist of:

- Guarantees and other financial commitments and
- Directors' benefits: advances, credits and guarantees.

The micro-entities regulations are effective for financial years ending on or after 30 September 2013 for companies filing their accounts on or after 1 December 2013. An important point to emphasise is the fact that the new regime will not affect the recognition or measurement of amounts included in a micro-entity's financial statements. In addition, the reduced disclosure regime will only affect companies who apply the FRSSE. Companies that will qualify to report under the micro-entities regulations will still apply the FRSSE but are eligible to apply the reduced disclosures in the new Regulations.

As part of the overhaul of the small companies regime, the FRC announced their intention to issue a separate standard for micro-entities, namely the *Financial Reporting Standard for Micro-Entities* (FRSME), which will also offer further simplifications to micro-entity accounts. Companies not eligible to apply the FRSME or who choose not to apply the FRSME may have the option of applying FRS 102 'Light', which will be an amended version of FRS 102 for small companies, and the FRC have suggested including a Section 1A *Small Entities* in FRS 102 that will set out the framework and presentation and disclosure requirements for small entities.

Financial reporting has developed considerably over the last few years and it is likely to be further developed as new accounting practices emerge or existing practices are amended to keep up with the ways in which entities conduct their business.

1 GENERAL REQUIREMENTS OF THE COMPANIES ACT 2006

INTRODUCTION

In the United Kingdom and Republic of Ireland (RoI), financial statements are prepared using Generally Accepted Accounting Practice (GAAP) and legislation prescribed in the form of the Companies Act 2006. Additional legislation also applies to certain financial statements (for example, the Charities Act) but this publication will only consider the Companies Act 2006 in relation to accounting by companies. At the outset of this chapter it is important to emphasise that the small companies regime in the UK is planned for significant change and these changes are discussed in more detail in Chapter 4. Readers are advised to keep up to date with all developments in this area by regularly reviewing the Department for Business Innovation and Skills' website as well as the Financial Reporting Council's website, as consultation documents were issued in September 2014 outlining proposals to overhaul the small companies regime in the light of the EU Accounting Directive. This chapter examines some of the proposals, with more detail being examined in Chapter 4, but at the time of writing, no final framework had been issued by the Department for Business Innovation and Skills nor the Financial Reporting Council.

Accounting standards are issued and amended by the Financial Reporting Council (FRC). The Regulations consist of the *Small Companies and Groups (Accounts and Directors' Report) Regulations 2008* (SI 2008/409) and the *Large and Medium-sized Companies and Groups (Accounts and Reports) Regulations 2008* (SI 2008/410). The application of accounting standards and the requirements of the Companies Act 2006 have the objective of enabling financial statements to give a true and fair view of the state of a company's financial affairs as at the reporting date, satisfying the directors' duty.

The Consultative Committee of Accountancy Bodies (CCAB) are committed to the promotion and compliance with accounting standards by their members, whether they are auditors or preparers of financial information. The CCAB is made up of:

- The Association of Chartered Certified Accountants (ACCA)
- The Chartered Institute of Public Finance and Accountancy (CIPFA)
- The Institute of Chartered Accountants in England and Wales (ICAEW)
- The Institute of Chartered Accountants in Ireland (ICAI)
- The Institute of Chartered Accountants in Scotland (ICAS)

Whilst the Chartered Institute of Management Accountants (CIMA) is no longer part of the CCAB, it also expects conformance and compliance with accounting standards by its members.

Significant departures from accounting standards and the requirements of the Companies Act 2006 must be adequately disclosed within the financial statements in order that the users can have an understanding of the reasons why the departure is considered to be appropriate. This can arise in certain issues where fair value accounting is concerned. Investment properties, for example, are required to be carried in a company's balance sheet (statement of financial position) at fair value at each reporting date under GAAP. The Companies Act 2006 requires fixed assets to be depreciated on a systematic basis; however, where investment properties are concerned the requirement to depreciate such properties is overridden (known as the 'true and fair override') because to carry such properties in the balance sheet at open market value as at the balance sheet date is considered to give more relevant and reliable information. Such a departure from the requirements of the Companies Act 2006 should be disclosed within the notes to the financial statements (often within the Accounting Policies section). An example of such a disclosure is as follows:

Example – Illustrative disclosure when the true and fair override is invoked

No depreciation is provided for in respect of investment properties as they are accounted for under the provisions in Section 16 of FRS 102. Such properties are held for their investment potential and not for consumption within the business. This is a departure from the Companies Act 2006 which requires all properties to be depreciated and the directors consider that to depreciate them would not enable the financial statements to give a true and fair view. Investment properties are stated at their market value at the reporting date.

ACCOUNTING REQUIREMENTS UNDER THE COMPANIES ACT 2006

Part 15 of the Companies Act 2006 deals with Accounts and Reports related to a company's financial statements. It outlines the distinction between companies that are subject to the small companies regime and those that are not.

Every company prepares financial statements to a reporting date (a financial year). The Companies Act 2006 says that a company's financial year:

- Begins with the first day of its first accounting reference period and
- Ends with the last day of that period or such other date, not more than seven days before or after the end of that period, as the directors may determine.

For subsequent financial years, these will:

- Begin with the day immediately following the end of the company's previous financial year and
- End with the last day of its next accounting reference period or such other date, not more than seven days before or after the end of that period, as the directors may determine.

The requirement to prepare annual financial statements is laid down in Chapter 4 to Part 15 of the Companies Act 2006. Section 394 requires the directors of every company to prepare financial statements for the company for each of its financial years, unless the company is exempt from that requirement under section 394A. These financial statements are referred to as the company's 'individual accounts'. Under section 394A, a company is exempt from the requirement to prepare individual accounts for a financial year if:

- It is itself a subsidiary undertaking,
- It has been dormant throughout the whole of that year and
- Its parent undertaking is established under the law of an EEA state.

The section then goes on to say that exemption is conditional upon compliance with all of the following conditions:

- All members of the company must agree to the exemption in respect of the financial year in question,
- The parent undertaking must give a guarantee under section 394(C) in respect of that year,
- The company must be included in the consolidated accounts drawn up for that year or to an earlier date in that year by the parent undertaking in accordance with:
  - The provisions of the Seventh Directive (83/349/EEC) or
  - International Accounting Standards,
- The parent undertaking must disclose in the notes to the consolidated accounts that the company is exempt from the requirement to prepare individual accounts by virtue of this section and
- The directors of the company must deliver to the registrar within the period for filing the company's accounts and reports for that year:
  - A written notice of the agreement referred to in subsection (2) (a),
  - The statement referred to in section 394(C) (1),
  - A copy of the consolidated accounts referred to in subsection (2) (C),

- A copy of the auditor's report on those accounts and
- A copy of the consolidated annual report drawn up by the parent undertaking.

The filing requirements are also laid down in the Companies Act. Private companies must file their financial statements with the Registrar of Companies (Companies House) within nine months after the financial year-end (although different filing requirements apply to a newly incorporated entity). Public companies must file their financial statements within six months after the financial year-end.

Thresholds for small and medium-sized companies and groups

A company is deemed to be 'small' and hence can apply the small companies regime if it satisfies the small company thresholds for two out of three consecutive years. The thresholds are as follows **(note that these thresholds are planned to be changed in 2015 – see Chapter 4 for further details of these changes)**.

Size	Turnover	Balance sheet total	Employees
Small company	£6.5m	£3.26m	50
Small group	£6.5m net	£3.26m net	50
	£7.8m gross	£3.9m gross	
Medium company	£25.9m	£12.9m	250
Medium group	£25.9m net	£12.9m net	250
	£31.1m gross	£15.5m gross	

Where reference to 'net' or 'gross' is made this relates to intra-group trading. 'Net' means that intra-group trading (and the effects thereof) have been eliminated, whilst 'gross' means that intra-group trading (and the effects thereof) have not been eliminated. A point to note is that a company may satisfy the qualifying criteria using gross or net figures and it is permissible to mix the use of gross and net figures in any year. Rather than eliminating intra-group transactions, the gross criteria should be checked first and the net size criteria checked only if required.

Financial statement content

A small company has a choice of preparing full UK GAAP financial statements without taking advantage of any of the concessions. In reality this is uncommon as small companies will often take advantage of the small companies regime in the Companies Act 2006. Where advantage is taken to prepare financial statements in accordance with the small companies regime, the company will use the Financial Reporting Standard for Smaller Entities (FRSSE) (or another alternative regime if the FRSSE is withdrawn following the overhaul of the small companies regime). Small companies must also file abbreviated financial statements with the Registrar of Companies. The fact that a company may file abbreviated financial statements with Companies House does not absolve them from any other responsibility for preparation of full financial statements for the shareholders or any other regulatory body to whom the financial statements may be submitted (for example, the Charities Commission).

Where the financial statements contain an auditor's report, the audit report is the special audit report contained in section 449 of the Companies Act 2006. This auditor's report states that in the auditor's opinion:

- The company is entitled to deliver abbreviated accounts in accordance with the section in question and
- The abbreviated accounts to be delivered are properly prepared in accordance with regulations on that section.

If the auditor's report is qualified, section 449(3) (a) requires the special report to set out the qualified auditor's report in full as well as outlining any further material deemed necessary so that users are able to understand the reasons for the audit qualification. In addition, where the auditor's report contains a statement under:

- Section 498(2) (a) or (b) (accounts, records or returns inadequate or accounts not agreeing with records and returns) or
- Section 498(3) (failure to obtain necessary information and explanations),

the special report must set out that statement in full.

A table outlining the financial statement requirements is shown below:

	Full financial statements	*Full balance sheet only*	*Abbreviated financial statements*	*Abbreviated balance sheet only*
Formats under Companies Act 2006	Schedule 1	Schedule 1	Schedule 4	Schedule 4
Companies Act 2006 accounts or IAS accounts	Option available for both	Option available for both	Option not available for IAS accounts	Option available for both
Statement in a prominent position on balance sheet	Yes – Companies Act 2006, section 414(3)	Yes – Companies Act 2006, section 444(5)	Yes – SI 2008/409 Schedule 4, paragraph 2	Yes – Companies Act 2006, section 444(5)
Copy of profit and loss account	Yes	No	No	No
Copy of directors' report	Yes	No	No	No
Audit report (where audit exemption does not apply)	Yes – Companies Act 2006, section 495	Yes – Companies Act 2006, section 495	Yes – Companies Act 2006, section 449 (special auditors' report)	Yes – Companies Act 2006, section 495
Notes to the financial statements	Yes	Yes	Yes, although limited to those referred to under SI 2008/409 Schedule 4	Yes, although limited to those referred to under SI 2008/409 Schedule 4

The balance sheet formats are set out in Schedule 1 to SI 2008/409 and take the form of Format 1 and Format 2. Format 1 is the most commonly used format for the balance sheet and is referred to below, although Format 2 permits identical combinations of headings.

Format 1 balance sheet (Large and Medium Companies and Groups (Accounts and Directors' Report) Regulations 2008)	*Format 1 balance sheet (Small Companies and Group (Accounts and Directors' Report) Regulations 2008)*
A. Called up share capital not paid	A. Called up share capital not paid
B. Fixed assets	B. Fixed assets
B I. Intangible assets	B I. Intangible assets
1. Goodwill	1. Goodwill
2. Development costs	2. Other intangible assets
3. Concessions	
4. Payments on account	
B II. Tangible assets	B II. Tangible assets
1. Land and buildings	1. Land and buildings
2. Plant and machinery	2. Plant and machinery, etc.
3. Fixtures and fittings	
4. Payments on account	
B III. Investments	B III. Investments
1. Shares in group undertakings	1. Shares in group undertakings and participating interests
2. Participating interests	2. Loans to group undertakings and undertakings in which the company has a participating interest
3. Loans to group undertakings	
4. Loans to undertakings, etc.	
5. Other investments other than loans	3. Other investments other than loans
6. Other loans	4. Other investments
7. Own shares	
C. Current assets	C. Current assets
C I. Stocks	C I. Stocks
1. Raw materials, etc.	1. Stocks
2. Work in progress	2. Payments on account
3. Finished goods/goods for resale	
4. Payments on account	
C II. Debtors	C II. Debtors
1. Trade debtors	1. Trade debtors
2. Amounts owed by group undertakings	2. Amounts owed by group undertakings and undertakings in which the company has a participating interest
3. Amounts owed by undertakings in which the company has a participating interest	
4. Other debtors	3. Other debtors
5. Called up share capital not paid	
6. Prepayments and accrued income	
C III. Investments	C III. Investments
1. Shares in group undertakings	1. Shares in group undertakings
2. Own shares	2. Other investments
3. Other investments	
C IV. Cash at bank and in hand	C IV. Cash at bank and in hand
D. Prepayments and accrued income	D. Prepayments and accrued income

E. Creditors: amounts falling due within one year
  1. Bank loans and overdrafts
  2. Trade creditors
  3. Amounts owed to group undertakings
  4. Amounts owed to undertakings in which the company has a participating interest
  5. Debenture loans
  6. Payments received on account
  7. Bills of exchange payable
  8. Other creditors including taxation and social security
  9. Accruals and deferred income

F. Net current assets (liabilities)

G. Total assets less current liabilities

H. Creditors: amounts falling due after one year
  1. Bank loans and overdrafts
  2. Trade creditors
  3. Amounts owed to group undertakings
  4. Debenture loans
  5. Payments received on account
  6. Bills of exchange payable
  7. Other creditors including taxation and social security
  8. Accruals and deferred income

I. Provisions for liabilities
  1. Pensions and similar obligations
  2. Taxation, etc.
  3. Other provisions

J. Accruals and deferred income

K. Capital and reserves

K I. Called up share capital

K II. Share premium account

K III. Revaluation reserve

K IV. Other reserves
  1. Capital redemption reserve
  2. Reserves for own shares
  3. Reserves provided for by articles
  4. Other reserves

K V. Profit and loss account

E. Creditors: amounts falling due within one year
  1. Bank loans and overdrafts
  2. Trade creditors
  3. Amounts owed to group undertakings and undertakings in which the company has a participating interest
  4. Other creditors

F. Net current assets (liabilities)

G. Total assets less current liabilities

H. Creditors: amounts falling due after one year
  1. Bank loans and overdrafts
  2. Trade creditors
  3. Amounts owed to group undertakings and undertakings in which the company has a participating interest
  4. Other creditors

I. Provisions for liabilities

J. Accruals and deferred income

K. Capital and reserves

K I. Called up share capital

K II. Share premium account

K III. Revaluation reserve

K IV. Other reserves

K V. Profit and loss account

The formats above will remain relevant under FRS 102 because the Financial Reporting Council decided that company law formats could continue to apply under the new regime and hence preparers will not see much change in the overall format of the financial statements themselves under FRS 102.

The Companies Act 2006 allows small companies to adopt the use of any of the four alternative formats of the profit and loss account, which are set out in Schedule 1 to SI 2008/409.

Format 1 profit and loss account

Turnover	X
Cost of sales	X
Gross profit or loss	X
Distribution costs	X
Administrative expenses	X
Other operating income	X
Income from shares in group undertakings	X
Income from participating interests	X
Income from other fixed asset investments	X
Other interest receivable and similar income	X
Amounts written off investments	X
Interest payable and similar charges	X
Tax on profit or loss on ordinary activities	X
Profit or loss on ordinary activities after taxation	X
Extraordinary income	X
Extraordinary charges	X
Extraordinary profit or loss	X
Tax on extraordinary profit or loss	X
Other taxes not shown under the above items	X
Profit or loss for the financial year	X

Format 2 profit and loss account

Turnover	X
Change in stocks of finished goods and in work in progress	X
Own work capitalised	X
Other operating income	X
Raw materials and consumables	X
Other external charges	X
Staff costs	
Wages and salaries	X
Social security costs	X
Other pension costs	X
Depreciation and other amounts written off tangible and intangible fixed assets	X

Exceptional amounts written off current assets	X
Other operating charges	X
Income from shares in group undertakings	X
Income from participating interests	X
Income from other fixed asset investments	X
Other interest receivable and similar income	X
Amounts written off investments	X
Interest payable and similar charges	X
Tax on profit or loss on ordinary activities	X
Profit or loss on ordinary activities after taxation	X
Extraordinary income	X
Extraordinary charges	X
Extraordinary profit or loss	X
Tax on extraordinary profit or loss	X
Other taxes not shown under the above items	X
Profit or loss for the financial year	X

Format 3 profit and loss account

Charges

Cost of sales	X
Distribution costs	X
Administrative expenses	X
Amounts written off investments	X
Interest payable and similar charges	X
Tax on profit or loss on ordinary activities	X
Profit or loss on ordinary activities after taxation	X
Extraordinary charges	X
Tax on extraordinary profit or loss	X
Other taxes not shown under the above items	X
Profit or loss for the financial year	X

Income

Turnover	X
Other operating income	X
Income from shares in group undertakings	X
Income from participating interests	X
Income from other fixed asset investments	X
Other interest receivable and similar income	X
Profit or loss on ordinary activities after taxation	X
Extraordinary income	X
Profit or loss for the financial year	X

Format 4 profit and loss account

Charges
 Reduction in stocks of finished goods and work-in-progress   X
 Raw materials and consumables   X
 Other external charges   X
 Staff costs
  Wages and salaries   X
  Social security costs   X
  Other pension costs   X
 Depreciation and amounts written off tangible and intangible fixed assets   X
 Exceptional amounts written off current assets   X
 Other operating charges   X
 Amounts written off investments   X
 Interest payable and similar charges   X
 Tax on profit or loss on ordinary activities   X
 Profit or loss on ordinary activities after taxation   X
 Extraordinary charges   X
 Tax on extraordinary profit or loss   X
 Other taxes not shown under the above items   X
 Profit or loss for the financial year   X
Income
 Turnover   X
 Increase in stocks of finished goods and work-in-progress   X
 Own work capitalised   X
 Other operating income   X
 Income from shares in group undertakings   X
 Income from participating interests   X
 Income from other fixed asset investments   X
 Other interest receivable and similar income   X
 Profit or loss on ordinary activities after taxation   X
 Extraordinary income   X
 Profit or loss for the financial year   X

At the time of writing, the Department for Business Innovation and Skills were consulting on only having Format 1 and Format 2 for the profit and loss account as Formats 3 and 4 are rarely used, although no final decision had been made.

TRUE AND FAIR AND ADEQUATE ACCOUNTING RECORDS

The directors of a company are required, in law, to prepare financial statements that give a true and fair view of the state of the company's affairs as at the reporting date. The concept of true and fair has been enshrined in company law for many years and the directors are prohibited from approving financial statements that do not give a true and fair view.

Section 396 of the Companies Act 2006 outlines that financial statements must:

- In the case of the balance sheet, give a true and fair view of the state of affairs of the company as at the end of the financial year and, in the case of the profit and loss account, give a true and fair view of the profit or loss of the company for the financial year.
- Comply with the provisions made by the Secretary of State by regulations as to the form and content of the balance sheet and profit and loss account and additional information to be provided by way of notes to the accounts.

In many cases, companies will achieve compliance with both sections 396(2) and (3) by the application of accounting standards and compliance with legislation. However, there are some instances where the requirements of the Companies Act 2006 may be overridden (the true and fair override). Section 396(4) says:

- If compliance with the regulations and any other provision made by or under this Act as to the matters to be included in a company's individual accounts or in notes to those accounts, would not be sufficient to give a true and fair view, the necessary additional information must be given in the accounts or in a note to them.

Section 396(5) also requires the particulars of such departures from the Companies Act 2006, together with the reasons for such a departure and its effect. The majority of departures from the requirements of the Companies Act 2006 derive from the provisions laid down in accounting standards where the applicable accounting standard is inconsistent with the requirements of the Companies Act 2006. An example of such a departure would be the non-depreciation of investment properties that are carried in the balance sheet (statement of financial position) at open market value (fair value) at each reporting date; hence no depreciation would be charged on such properties despite the Companies Act 2006 requiring depreciation to be charged against fixed assets.

The term 'adequate accounting records' is derived from the Companies Act 2006 and it is the duty of every company to keep adequate accounting records. Section 396(2) defines the constitution of adequate accounting records and says that adequate accounting records means records that are sufficient:

- To show and explain the company's transactions,
- To disclose with reasonable accuracy, at any time, the financial position of the company at that time and
- To enable the directors to ensure that any accounts required to be prepared comply with the requirements of this Act (and, where applicable, of Article 4 of the IAS Regulation).

Companies are required to maintain accounting records that record the company's assets and liabilities as well as containing records that detail the day-to-day transactions (monies received and expended by the company) and the matters in respect of which the receipt and expenditure takes place. When a company is involved in the buying and selling of goods, the accounting records must contain:

(a) A statement of stock held by the company at the end of each financial year of the company,

(b) All statements of stocktakings from which any statement of stock as is mentioned in paragraph (a) has been or is to be prepared and

(c) Except in the case of goods sold by way or ordinary retail trade, statements of all goods sold and purchased, showing the goods and the buyers and sellers in sufficient detail to enable all these to be identified.

When it is evident that a company has failed to maintain adequate accounting records, every officer of the company is guilty of an offence under section 387(1). Where an officer(s) of a company is proved guilty, the punishments outlined in section 387(3) (a) and (b) are:

- On conviction on indictment, to imprisonment for a term not exceeding two years or a fine (or both).
- On summary conviction:
  - In England and Wales, to imprisonment for a term not exceeding twelve months or to a fine not exceeding the statutory maximum (or both);
  - In Scotland or Northern Ireland, to imprisonment for a term not exceeding six months or to a fine not exceeding the statutory maximum (or both).

Retention of accounting records

Accounting records have to be kept either at the company's registered office or at an alternative location as the directors think fit. Wherever these accounting records are held, provisions exist in the Companies Act 2006 at section 388(b), which says that these records must be open to inspection by the company's officers. If such accounting records are retained at a place that is outside the United Kingdom, it is mandatory under legislation for accounts and returns in relation to the business dealt with in those accounting records to be sent to, and kept at, a place in the United Kingdom and for such information to be available for inspection. This requirement is embellished in section 388(3) (a) and (b), which says that the accounts and returns to be sent to the United Kingdom must be such as to:

- Disclose with reasonable accuracy the financial position of the business in question at intervals of not more than six months and
- Enable the directors to ensure that the accounts required to be prepared under this Part comply with the requirements of this Act (and, where applicable, Article 4 of the IAS Regulation).

Accounting records in respect of a private company are to be retained for a period of three years from the date on which they are made. For public companies, accounting records must be retained for a period of six years from the date on which they are made.

The officers of a company will be committing a criminal offence if they fail to maintain adequate accounting records for the prescribed levels of time and in a place required under the Companies Act 2006. An offence is committed by an officer if he:

- Fails to take all reasonable steps for securing compliance by the company with subsection (4) of that section (period for which records to be preserved) or
- Intentionally causes any default by the company under that subsection.

Section 389(4) outlines the punishments to be levied by the courts in the event that a person is found guilty:

- On conviction on indictment, to imprisonment for a term not exceeding two years or a fine (or both);
- On summary conviction:
  - In England and Wales, to imprisonment for a term not exceeding twelve months or to a fine not exceeding the statutory maximum (or both);
  - In Scotland and Northern Ireland, to imprisonment for a term not exceeding six months or to a fine not exceeding the statutory maximum (or both).

An important point to emphasise is that where a company has not kept adequate accounting records, ALL officers of the company will be guilty of an offence under the Companies Act 2006. Adequate accounting records are also required to be kept for the purposes of taxation and auditors of companies must also report by exception if, in the auditor's opinion, adequate accounting records have not been kept or returns adequate for the audit have not been received from branches that have not been visited by the auditor.

INTERNATIONAL FINANCIAL REPORTING STANDARDS

International financial reporting standards (IFRS) have become more widespread over recent years. Many countries have chosen to adopt IFRS as their financial reporting framework on the grounds that such standards offer consistency in financial reporting for reporting entities. Many commentators also believe that the adoption of IFRS opens up wider potential to access more capital markets. The International Accounting Standards Board (IASB) is very keen to promote the adoption of IFRS across the globe and their stated goal is to develop, in the public interest, a single set of high-quality, understandable, enforceable and globally accepted financial reporting standards based upon clearly articulated principles.

IFRS began to gather pace in 2005 as 27 European Union member states and many other countries adopted the use of IFRS. Countries such as Argentina, Brazil and Canada have since followed suit and adopted IFRS as their financial reporting framework.

In the United Kingdom, listed companies were mandated to present their financial statements under EU-adopted IFRS for accounting periods commencing on or after 1 January 2005. This was closely followed by companies listed on the Alternative Investment Market (AIM) in 2007.

The adoption of IFRS around the world has not been without controversy. Indeed, in the UK, the legality of IFRS in the UK was brought into question and a legal opinion was given by George Bompas QC on 8 April 2013 who concluded that since the true and fair view is paramount, company directors have a duty to override IFRS in order to comply with it. In his opinion, Bompas took issue with an earlier legal opinion on the same issue, which was commissioned by the Financial Reporting Council (FRC), and this opinion was provided by Martin Moore QC. This acknowledged the FRC's approach, which is that the true and fair requirement is integral to the preparation of financial statements in the UK, whether they are prepared under UK GAAP or IFRS. Moore also said that companies could depart from the relevant standard but only in 'extremely rare' or 'exceptional' circumstances.

On 3 October 2013, the Department for Business Innovation and Skills released a government response to the concerns raised in which it states:

> *'The Department for Business has given serious consideration to concerns raised by some stakeholders that accounts prepared over the past 30 years, in accordance with UK or international financial reporting standards, have not been properly prepared under UK and EU law.*
>
> *However, it is entirely satisfied that the concerns expressed are misconceived and that the existing legal framework, including international financial reporting standards, is binding under European law.'*

On the same day as the Department for Business issued this response, the FRC issued a press release confirming that it shared the view of the Department for Business.

Smaller companies and IFRS

In the UK, listed companies are required to report under EU-endorsed IFRS and it is rare to find any smaller companies (other than listed companies) reporting under the IFRS framework. This is due, in large part, to the significant disclosure requirements that IFRS mandates and such disclosure requirements are not considered to be 'fit for purpose' for companies at the smaller end of the scale.

In July 2009, the IASB issued the *IFRS for SMEs*. The overall objective of the *IFRS for SMEs* is essentially to provide a framework under IFRS, but with a much less burdensome disclosure regime. The standard itself is a stand-alone document, which only contains one optional cross-reference to mainstream IFRS in relation to financial instruments (which provides a choice concerning the treatment of financial instruments). The IASB issued *IFRS for SMEs* for those entities that do not have 'public accountability'. The concept of public accountability has been extremely difficult to define in the UK and Republic of Ireland and the concept was withdrawn in the second round of Exposure Drafts that the FRC issued to explain their intention to replace UK GAAP. The *IFRS for SMEs* was not compatible with UK companies' legislation and this is the reason why it was never adopted in its entirety in the UK. Notwithstanding its incompatibility with UK company law, FRS 102 is based on *IFRS for SMEs*, which has been amended to be compatible with UK legislation and EU Directives.

List of current IFRS and IAS in extant

At the time of writing, the following international accounting standards (IAS) and international financial reporting standards (IFRS) and interpretations (SIC/IFRIC) were in issue:

IAS 1	Presentation of Financial Statements
IAS 2	Inventories
IAS 7	Statement of Cash Flows
IAS 8	Accounting Policies, Changes in Accounting Estimates and Errors
IAS 10	Events after the Reporting Period
IAS 11	Construction Contracts
IAS 12	Income Taxes
IAS 16	Property, Plant and Equipment
IAS 17	Leases
IAS 18	Revenue
IAS 19	Employee Benefits
IAS 20	Accounting for Government Grants and Disclosure of Government Assistance
IAS 21	The Effects of Changes in Foreign Exchange Rates
IAS 23	Borrowing Costs
IAS 24	Related Party Disclosures
IAS 26	Accounting and Reporting by Retirement Benefit Plans
IAS 27	Separate Financial Statements
IAS 28	Investments in Associates and Joint Ventures
IAS 29	Financial Reporting in Hyperinflationary Economies
IAS 32	Financial Instruments: Presentation
IAS 33	Earnings per Share
IAS 34	Interim Financial Reporting
IAS 36	Impairment of Assets
IAS 37	Provisions, Contingent Liabilities and Contingent Assets
IAS 38	Intangible Assets
IAS 39	Financial Instruments: Recognition and Measurement (superseded by IFRS 9: Financial Instruments where IFRS 9 is applied)
IAS 40	Investment Property
IAS 41	Agriculture
IFRS 1	First-time Adoption of IFRS
IFRS 2	Share-based Payment
IFRS 3	Business Combination
IFRS 4	Insurance Contracts

IFRS 5	Non-current Assets Held for Sale and Discontinued Operations
IFRS 6	Exploration for and Evaluation of Mineral Assets
IFRS 7	Financial Instruments: Disclosures
IFRS 8	Operating Segments
IFRS 9	Financial Instruments
IFRS 10	Consolidated Financial Statements
IFRS 11	Joint Arrangements
IFRS 12	Disclosure of Interests in Other Entities
IFRS 13	Fair Value Measurement
IFRS 14	Regulatory Deferral Accounts
IFRS 15	Revenue from Contracts with Customers
IFRIC 1	Changes in Existing Decommissioning, Restoration and Similar Liabilities
IFRIC 2	Members' Shares in Co-operative Entities and Similar Instruments
IFRIC 4	Determining Whether an Arrangement Contains a Lease
IFRIC 5	Rights to Interests Arising from Decommissioning, Restoration and Environmental Rehabilitation Funds
IFRIC 6	Liabilities Arising from Participating in a Specific Market – Waste Electrical and Electronic Equipment
IFRIC 7	Applying the Restatement Approach under IAS 29 Financial Reporting in Hyperinflationary Economies
IFRIC 9	Reassessment of Embedded Derivatives
IFRIC 10	Interim Financial Reporting and Impairment
IFRIC 12	Service Concession Arrangements
IFRIC 13	Customer Loyalty Programmes
IFRIC 14	IAS 19 – The Limit on a Defined Benefit Asset, Minimum Funding Requirements and their Interaction
IFRIC 15	Agreements for the Construction of Real Estate
IFRIC 16	Hedges of a Net Investment in a Foreign Operation
IFRIC 17	Distributions of Non-cash Assets to Owners
IFRIC 18	Transfers of Assets from Customers
IFRIC 19	Extinguishing Financial Liabilities with Equity Instruments
IFRIC 20	Stripping Costs in the Production Phase of a Surface Mine
IFRIC 21	Levies
SIC-7	Introduction of the Euro
SIC-10	Government Assistance – No Specific Relation to Operating Activities
SIC-15	Operating Leases – Incentives
SIC-25	Income Taxes – Changes in the Tax Status of an Enterprise or its Shareholders

SIC-27	Evaluating the Substance of Transactions in the Legal Form of a Lease
SIC-29	Disclosure – Service Concession Arrangements
SIC-31	Revenue – Barter Transactions Involving Advertising Services
SIC-32	Intangible Assets – Web Site Costs

GENERALLY ACCEPTED ACCOUNTING PRACTICE

The way in which company accounts are prepared is governed by the requirements of generally accepted accounting practice (GAAP). UK GAAP includes accounting standards and companies legislation and is also frequently cited in tax legislation because HM Revenue and Customs require financial statements used in the calculation of taxable profit or loss to be prepared under GAAP.

The prescribed GAAP in the UK is as follows:

- EU-endorsed IFRS,
- UK GAAP (FRSs 100, 101, 102 and 103),
- Financial Reporting Standard for Smaller Entities (note the planned changes above and in Chapter 4) and
- Micro-entities legislation.

Statements of Recommended Practice (SORPs) are publications issued to certain industries or sectors, which recommend accounting practices and go to supplement accounting standards and other legal and regulatory requirements; for example, Limited Liability Partnerships have a SORP titled *Accounting by Limited Liability Partnerships*. SORPs are not issued by the Financial Reporting Council, but are instead issued by a SORP-making body. At the time of writing, seven out of the eight SORPs were being updated as a result of the new UK GAAP. The remaining SORP not being updated was that of the insurance sector SORP, which is expected to be withdrawn because of the introduction of FRS 103 *Insurance Contracts* (issued by the FRC on 20 March 2014), which specifies the accounting and disclosure requirements for entities dealing with such contracts.

To achieve a true and fair view, financial statements must comply with UK GAAP. Auditors are also specifically required to report in their auditors' report if the financial statements comply with UK GAAP (or not).

SUBSTANCE OF TRANSACTIONS

Financial statements prepared under UK GAAP must report the 'substance' of transactions and not merely the legal form. The term 'substance of a transaction' is taken to mean the commercial reality of a transaction and the section in FRS 102 that can illustrate this concept extremely well is that of Section 20 *Leases*. In a leasing transaction, the lessor may continue to hold the legal ownership of an asset subject to a finance lease; however, the characteristics of the transaction are such that the lessee enjoys the rights to use the asset in order to generate economic benefits for the entity leasing the asset. This, in substance, gives rise to an asset. This concept can also be accentuated when it can be demonstrated that the 'risks and rewards' of ownership of the asset have substantially been transferred from lessor to lessee (for example, where the lessee is required to carry out maintenance of the asset at its own cost or where the lessee is required to pay early termination fees in the event the lease is cancelled before its maturity date).

Paragraph 2.8 to FRS 102 refers specifically to substance over form and says that transactions as well as other events and conditions should be accounted for and presented in accordance with their substance and not merely their legal form. When a company applies this concept, the reliability of their financial statements is enhanced.

The concept of substance over form was initially identified back in the early 1980s and emerged due to the ways in which entities were financing their operations. It became apparent that financing transactions were becoming more complex and this complexity often led to a separation of the legal title to an asset from access to its economic benefits and risk. Certain financing arrangements were being entered into which, in some instances, were deliberately engineered to achieve a desired outcome (which was to keep financing arrangements off the balance sheet). This practice was coined 'off balance sheet finance' and the concept is still as much a problem today as it was back in the early 1980s. At the time of writing, standard-setters across the world (in particular the IASB and the US Financial Accounting Standards Board) are trying to overhaul the ways in which certain financing arrangements (namely leases) are accounted for so as to reduce the instances where entities achieve off balance sheet finance.

The problem with off balance sheet finance, and the non-reporting of the substance of a transaction, is the fact that not only can it have a significant effect on the balance sheet of a company but it can also have a significant effect on a company's reported profit (or loss). This is particularly the case in a sale and leaseback arrangement, which may not have been accounted for as such; the arrangement could have been reported as a fixed asset disposal, and hence a profit could be recorded, when, in fact, the transaction was (in substance) a financing arrangement (a secured loan).

In determining the substance of a transaction and when an asset or a liability should be recognised on the balance sheet, it is necessary to determine whether an asset or a liability has, in fact, been created. Entities falling under the scope of FRS 102 will be pointed to the *Concepts and Pervasive Principles* in Section 2 of FRS 102. An asset is a resource that is controlled by the reporting entity that derives economic benefit for the entity itself. The point to emphasise where assets are concerned is the concept of 'control'. To meet the definition of an asset, an entity must have control over that asset.

Conversely, a liability is an obligation on the part of the entity that creates an expectation that the entity will experience an outflow of funds (or depletions of other assets) in order to settle the obligation.

In assessing whether an asset or a liability has been created, the characteristics of the transaction should be scrutinised and not simply the legal form. The term 'risks and rewards' is often cited when determining the substance of transactions and some factors that may be considered are as follows.

Risks

- Which party to the transaction will bear the risks of unfavourable (or favourable) changes to the value of the asset?
- Who will bear the risk of obsolescence of the asset?
- Who will bear the risk that the asset may be damaged or lost?

Rewards

- Who benefits from any increases in the fair value of the asset?
- Who will benefit from the income streams associated with the asset?
- Who will benefit from the use of the asset?

The above lists are not exhaustive and there are many other factors that may need consideration when determining the substance of a transaction. The important aspect where substance over form is concerned is not to merely rely on the legalities of the transaction – the commercial reality of the transaction will determine whether an asset or a liability has been created, which will then determine the relevant accounting treatment.

DIRECTORS' REPORTS

In addition to preparing financial statements, the directors of a company are also required under the Companies Act 2006 to prepare a directors' report. Where the company is the parent of a group and the directors prepare consolidated financial statements, the directors must prepare a group directors' report. The group directors' report will cover all the undertakings that have been dealt with in the consolidation process.

Small companies are permitted to prepare a directors' report, although the content of these directors' reports are very minimal and merely outline the principal activity of the company during the year and the names of the directors who served on the board during the year. There is also reference to the fact that the directors' report of a small company has been prepared in accordance with the small companies regime in the Companies Act 2006.

Companies that will not be eligible to apply the FRSSE (or other small companies regime, which may come into effect following the EU Accounting Directive) and who must report under FRS 102 are required to prepare a directors' report that complies with the following requirements in the Companies Act 2006:

- General matters (section 416) including SI 2008/410 disclosures;
- Matters relating to the company and subsidiaries (SI 2008/410) (relating to a parent company preparing consolidated financial statements);
- A statement as to disclosure of information to auditors as per section 418.

Strategic reports

For financial years ending on or after 30 September 2013, the Companies Act 2006 (Strategic Report and Directors' Report) Regulations 2013 will apply. Companies should review the guidance that has been issued by the FRC, although the majority of the FRC's guidance relates to quoted companies, other public companies, large companies and medium-sized companies. Companies that qualify as small or that would also qualify as small except for being, or having been, a member of an ineligible group are exempted from the requirement to prepare a strategic report. Parent companies that prepare consolidated financial statements must also prepare a 'group strategic report', which relates to all the undertakings that have been included in the consolidation.

For financial years ending on or after 30 September 2013, the directors of a company that qualifies as large or medium-sized must prepare a strategic report in addition to the directors' report and this requirement has been introduced by new sections 414(A) to 414(D) to the Companies Act 2006. At the same time as introducing these new sections, section 417 of the Companies Act 2006, which required a directors' report to include a business review of the company, was repealed. The consequence for unquoted companies is that the strategic report will essentially mirror the requirements of the business review.

The main difference between the strategic report and the business review is that the strategic report must be presented separately in the financial statements from the directors' report. In addition, section 414(D) to the Companies Act 2006 requires the strategic report to be separately approved by the board of directors and signed on behalf of the board by a director or the company secretary.

Content of the strategic report

The overarching objective of the strategic report is to inform the shareholders and help them to assess how the directors have discharged their duty to promote the success of the company. To achieve this objective, the strategic report must:

- Contain a fair review of the company's business, that is, a balanced and comprehensive analysis of the development and performance of the company's business in the period and of its position at the end of it.
- Contain a description of the principal risks and uncertainties facing the company.
- To the extent necessary for an understanding of the development, performance or position of the company's business include analysis using key financial performance indicators and, where appropriate, analysis using other key performance indicators, including information relating to environmental and employee matters. 'Key performance indicators' are factors by reference to which the development, performance or position of the company's business can be measured effectively. A company qualifying as medium-sized for a financial year does not need to include non-financial information.

- Where appropriate, include references to, and additional explanations of, amounts included in the company's annual accounts.
- Contain matters otherwise required by Regulations, like the Large and Medium-sized Companies and Group Accounting Regulations (SI 2008/410), to be disclosed in the directors' report, that the directors consider to be of strategic importance to the company. However, when a company chooses to disclose in the strategic report information that is required to be included in the directors' report, it should state in the directors' report that it has done so and so should indicate which information has been disclosed elsewhere.

For quoted companies, the strategic report must contain additional information as follows:

- The main trends and factors likely to affect the future development, performance and position of the company's business and information about environmental matters (including the impact of the company's business on the environment), the company's employees, social, community and human rights issues, including information about any policies of the company in relation to those matters and the effectiveness of those policies. If the report does not contain the information on environmental matters, employees and social, community and human rights issues, it must state which of those kinds of information it does not contain.
- A description of the company's strategy and the company's business model.
- A breakdown showing at the end of the financial year the number of persons of each sex who were directors of the company, the number of persons of each sex who were senior managers of the company (other than those who were directors) and the number of each person of each sex who were employees of the company.
- A company is not required to disclose information in the strategic report about impending developments or matters in the course of negotiation if the disclosure would, in the opinion of the directors, be seriously prejudicial to the interests of the company.

The amendments to the Companies Act 2006 have resulted in some disclosures no longer being required in the directors' report, in particular:

- A description of the principal activities of the company during the year,
- Details of charitable donations,
- Policy and practice on payment of creditors and
- The acquisition of own shares by private companies.

GROUP ACCOUNTS

Under the Companies Act 2006, the parent of a group (other than a small group) is required to prepare consolidated financial statements (with certain exceptions). The objective of such financial statements is to show the results of the group as if the group structure did not exist, that is, the trading results of all companies within the group with the outside world. To achieve this objective, the following accounting is required for consolidated financial statements:

- Elimination of intra-group balances and transactions,
- Provisions for acquisitions and merger accounting,
- The treatment and disclosure of non-controlling interests (minority interests),
- Non-consolidated subsidiary undertakings,
- Associates and joint ventures and
- The preparation of the financial statements as if the group structure did not exist.

Group financial statements are considered in more detail in Chapter 6.

APPROVAL OF FINANCIAL STATEMENTS

Before their issuance, the directors' report, financial statements and auditor's report all need to be approved and signed off. The board of directors are required to approve the financial statements (usually, but not always, in a general meeting). The company secretary *or* a director is required to sign the directors' report and at least one director is required to sign the balance sheet and the name of the signatory must be stated.

The report of the auditors must state the names of the auditor(s) and be signed and dated. Where the auditor is an individual, section 503 of the Companies Act 2006 says the report must be signed by the individual. Where the auditor is a firm, the report of the auditors must be signed by the senior statutory auditor in his/her own name, for and on behalf of the firm of auditors.

For small companies that are subject to the small companies regime, a statement must be made (in a prominent position) that the financial statements have been prepared in accordance with the special provisions for companies subject to the small companies regime above the signature. In addition, the balance sheet must contain a statement to that effect in a prominent position above the signature.

INTERACTION OF FRS 102 TERMINOLOGY WITH COMPANIES ACT 2006 TERMINOLOGY

As mentioned earlier in this chapter, IFRS has gathered faster pace around the globe and the use of international terminology has also gathered faster pace. FRS 102 is based on *IFRS for SMEs* (with certain amendments to *IFRS for SMEs*, which are outlined in Chapter 5).

The following table outlines the key terminology differences in FRS 102 as compared to the Companies Act 2006:

Company law terminology	FRS 102 terminology
Accounting reference date	Reporting date
Accounts	Financial statements
Associated undertaking	Associate
Balance sheet	Statement of financial position
Capital and reserves	Equity
Cash at bank and in hand	Cash
Debtors	Trade receivables
Diminution in value [of assets]	Impairment
Financial year	Reporting period
Group [accounts]	Consolidated [financial statements]
IAS	EU-adopted IFRS
Individual [accounts]	Individual [financial statements]
Interest payable and similar charges	Finance costs
Interest receivable and similar income	Finance income/investment income
Minority interests	Non-controlling interest
Net realisable value [of any current asset]	Estimated selling price less costs to complete and sell
Parent undertaking	Parent
Profit and loss account	Income statement (under the two-statement approach)
	Part of the statement of comprehensive income (under the single-statement approach)
Related undertakings	Subsidiaries, associates and joint ventures
Stocks	Inventories
Subsidiary undertaking	Subsidiary
Tangible assets	Includes: property, plant and equipment; investment property
Trade creditors	Trade payables

A point worth noting is that as entities will be complying with the company law formats (even under the FRS 102 regime), a reporting entity may select to use the same terminology throughout their financial statements as under the previous UK GAAP (hence 'debtors' rather than 'receivables' and 'stocks' rather than 'inventories').

For Limited Liability Partnerships (LLPs), the Statement of Recommended Practice (SORP) that gives guidance on the accounting and disclosure requirements for LLPs has also been updated to reflect the new financial reporting regime under FRS 102.

MICRO-ENTITIES LEGISLATION

This section of the chapter examines the new micro-entities legislation and Chapter 4 also considers the issue concerning micro-entities in more detail.

On 1 December 2013, legislation was introduced in the form of SI 2013/3008, the Small Companies (Micro-Entities' Accounts) Regulations 2013, which was brought in by the European Union with the objective of reducing costs for small and medium-sized entities. The legislation is effective for financial years ending on or after 30 September 2013 and where the company's financial statements are filed with the Registrar of Companies (Companies House) on or after 1 December 2013.

Under SI 2013/3008, a company qualifies as a micro-entity if it meets at least two of the following three conditions:

- Turnover of not more than £632,000;
- Gross assets (balance sheet total) of not more than £316,000;
- Average number of employees not exceeding ten.

Where a company has a short accounting period, then the turnover figure must be adjusted proportionately to decipher if the company does qualify as a micro-entity.

> **Example – Company with a short period-end**
>
> A company with a year-end date of 31 December 2016 has been trading since 1 April 2016 (a nine-month accounting period).
>
> Where an accounting period is not one year, the turnover figure must be adjusted proportionately. In this case, the company will use 9/12 × £632,000 to determine whether the entity qualifies as a micro-entity.

For companies that are parent companies, the company will qualify as a micro-entity in the year only if:

- The company qualifies as a micro-entity in that year,
- The group headed up by the company qualifies as a small group (as defined in the Companies Act 2006 section 383(2) to (7)) and
- The company has not voluntarily elected to prepare consolidated accounts.

A key point to emphasise where groups are concerned is that care must be taken in assessing whether each company within the group qualifies as a micro-entity. The exemptions available under the micro-entities regime will not be available for subsidiary companies that are included in consolidated financial statements for the year. In addition, the micro-entities regime is not applicable to:

- Investment undertakings,
- Financial holding undertakings,
- Credit institutions,
- Insurance undertakings and
- Charities.

At the time of writing, there were also no plans to allow Limited Liability Partnerships (LLPs) to take advantage of the micro-entity exemptions. In addition, at the time of writing, there was no legislation in place in the Republic of Ireland in respect of micro-entities, although the legislation was in the consultation stage.

Financial statements prepared under the Companies Act 2006 must give a true and fair view and this concept has been enshrined in companies legislation for many years. Under the micro-entities regime, such entities will only be required to disclose minimal amounts of information at the foot of the balance sheet and additional disclosures will not be required; hence the financial statements are therefore presumed to give a true and fair view as per the legislation applied to micro-entities (known as the 'deeming provisions'). The amounts in the financial statements themselves will continue to be prepared to UK GAAP and hence recognition and measurement issues are not affected; it is only the additional disclosures that will not be required.

In addition, a micro-entity will not be able to:

- Use the revaluation model for tangible fixed assets.
- Measure fixed asset investments at market value.
- Account for investment properties using the fair value model in the small companies regime. Therefore, a micro-entity applying the small companies regime will account for such property under the normal fixed asset rules as opposed to fair value.

The reason for the prohibitions above is that the legislation does not recognise any provisions of the alternative accounting rules. It will also not be possible, for example, to use a previous GAAP revaluation amount as deemed cost for assets that have been subjected to the revaluation model under GAAP (for example, investment property).

The profit and loss account under the micro-entities legislation will be prepared under Format 2 as follows:

(a) Turnover
(b) Other income
(c) Cost of raw materials and consumables
(d) Staff costs
(e) Depreciation and other amounts written off assets
(f) Other charges
(g) Tax
(h) Profit or loss

The balance sheet will be prepared using either Format 1 or Format 2 as follows:

Balance sheet – Format 1

(a) Called up share capital not paid
(b) Fixed assets
(c) Current assets
(d) Prepayments and accrued income
(e) Creditors: amounts falling due within one year
(f) Net current assets (liabilities)
(g) Total assets less current liabilities
(h) Creditors: amounts falling due after more than one year

(i) Provisions for liabilities
(j) Accruals and deferred income
(k) Capital and reserves

Balance sheet – Format 2

Assets

(a) Called up share capital not paid
(b) Fixed assets
(c) Current assets
(d) Prepayments and accrued income

Liabilities

(a) Capital and reserves
(b) Provisions for liabilities
(c) Creditors
(d) Accruals and deferred income

It is to be noted that under Format 2, aggregated amounts of creditors and accruals and deferred income that fall due within one year and after more than one year must be shown separately.

The balance sheet must also contain, in a prominent position above the signature, a statement that the accounts are prepared in accordance with the micro-entity provisions.

Notes to the financial statements

Under the micro-entities legislation, limited notes are required to be made underneath the balance sheet, which contain disclosures relating to:

(a) Guarantees and other financial commitments and
(b) Any directors' benefits: advances, credits and guarantees.

Illustrative financial statements prepared under the micro-entities legislation are shown in Chapter 4.

2 THE STATUTORY AUDIT REQUIREMENT AND ACCOUNTING PRINCIPLES

INTRODUCTION

There is still a statutory audit requirement in the UK and Republic of Ireland despite the introduction of a new financial reporting regime and this chapter will consider the statutory audit requirements together with the relaxations of the audit requirements introduced into legislation in the UK in 2012.

The auditing profession has been in the headlines a lot over recent years and in the majority of cases for all the wrong reasons. Auditors have been subjected to significant amounts of criticism due to the financial crisis that started in 2007/8, and in many cases have even been blamed for allowing certain institutions to 'get away' with issues that they would otherwise not have been allowed to.

Regulators are keen to ensure that the value of audit is restored and that the general public have confidence in auditors and the reports that they issue on entities' financial statements. For this reason, the regulators such as the Financial Reporting Council (FRC) have been carefully scrutinising the financial statements of various entities, and professional bodies have also been carefully regulating audit firms to ensure that the appropriate standards of audit work are met. Auditors and regulators both have a significant role to play in ensuring that the value of audit is maintained and this will mean auditors ensuring that they comply, at all times, with the requirements of International Standards on Auditing (UK and Republic of Ireland).

Auditing and financial reporting go 'hand in hand' and auditors of companies applying the new UK GAAP must have a thorough understanding of FRSs 100, 101, 102 and (where applicable) 103 – particularly the transitional aspects to ensure that accounting policies and principles have been followed.

This chapter will take a look at the statutory audit requirement in the UK and also the implications that the relaxation of audit thresholds has had on firms and, indeed, certain companies together with the accounting principles that must be complied with that are dealt with in Section 2 of FRS 102, *Concepts and Pervasive Principles*.

THE STATUTORY AUDIT REQUIREMENT

Many small, privately-owned companies will be able to take advantage of audit exemption and not have their financial statements audited. An exception to this is where the company's Articles of Association say that the company must be subject to audit or where enough shareholders ask for one. The reality is that in the UK and Republic of Ireland, most small companies will not be subjected to statutory audit.

However, if the company's financial year ends *on or after 1 October 2012*, a company may qualify for audit exemption if it meets *two* out of the following criteria:

- The company has annual turnover of not more than £6.5 million,
- The company has gross assets (fixed *plus* current assets) of not more than £32.6 million and
- The company has 50 or fewer employees (on average).

The Department for Business Innovation and Skills (BIS) have said that they may issue a consultation on raising the audit exemption thresholds, although at the time of writing no such consultation had been issued and readers are therefore advised to keep abreast of developments by regularly reviewing the BIS website.

Where the company qualifies for audit exemption based on meeting at least two of the criteria above, the following statement must be included on the balance sheet:

For the year ending [insert financial year-end date] the company was entitled to exemption from audit under section 477 of the Companies Act 2006 relating to small companies.

The members have not required the company to obtain an audit of its accounts for the year in question in accordance with section 476.

The directors acknowledge their responsibilities for complying with the requirements of the Act with respect to accounting records and the preparation of accounts.

These accounts have been prepared in accordance with the provisions applicable to companies subject to the small companies regime.

Prior to the reform of audit in 2012, a company had to have an audit if it had a turnover of more than £6.5 million or gross assets of more than £3.26 million.

THE REFORM OF AUDIT IN 2012 AND THE IMPLICATIONS

In September 2012, the government announced changes to the statutory audit requirement for a range of companies based in the UK. These changes took effect for accounting periods commencing on or after 1 October 2012 and the government said the reforms could exempt 36,000 UK companies and Limited Liability Partnerships, 83,000 subsidiaries and 67,000 dormant companies from the requirement to have a mandatory audit. The reforms were borne out of the UK's commitment to end the goldplating of EU rules as well as helping to reduce 'red tape' on small and growing businesses. The review that was undertaken by BIS identified potential costsavings of some £390 million to UK businesses.

The reforms were announced and the following changes were made to the statutory audit requirement:

- Companies qualifying as small under the Companies Act 2006 can now take audit exemption. Under the old regime, companies had to have an audit if turnover was more than £6.5 million or gross assets (balance sheet total) were more than £3.26 million. A statutory audit under the old regime was required regardless of whether the company qualified as small.
- Subsidiaries of the European Economic Area (EEA) parents may take audit exemption regardless of their size, depending on them meeting certain criteria. The main criterion that subsidiaries have to meet is that the parent company must issue a guarantee in respect of the liabilities of the subsidiary, which is enforceable, until the liabilities are discharged.

There were many questions asked as to whether these reforms would affect the way in which companies choosing to take advantage of the new audit exemption opportunities do business. The main question being asked was whether banks and financiers would still require a company to have a statutory audit, despite them qualifying for exemption under the new rules. The likelihood is that some banks and financiers do require audited financial statements in certain situations to offer comfort that the company is financially viable; however, the reality was that many companies were able to (and so did) take advantage of the new audit exemption regime with no detrimental effect.

At the time of the announcement, BIS did acknowledge that HM Revenue and Customs (HMRC) *could* potentially increase the number of enquiries into company accounts that have not been audited. BIS did, however, confirm that the likely impact of HMRC increasing enquiries into unaudited financial statements could not be quantified.

The alignment of the audit thresholds with the small company qualification thresholds (see Chapter 1) is clearly welcome news for many companies – particularly those companies who failed the audit exemption test previously because of a property held in the balance sheet that then took the company's balance sheet total over the £3.26 million benchmark (for example, a small investment property company). The obvious reason for companies in these sorts of sectors welcoming the news is that they are often closely-owned companies with relatively straightforward transactions. Further increases in the audit exemption limits could take place in the future.

Notwithstanding that many companies in the UK welcome the alignment, and thus dispensing of the annual requirement, there are some companies in the UK that may be much slower in taking up the exemption. These companies often have a much higher level of transactions and shareholders may also voluntarily choose to continue with the annual audit requirement because of the value it adds to the company's financial statements. Enquiries into a company's corporation tax return by HMRC are likely to be much less for audited financial statements than those enquiries into unaudited financial statements (though it is true to say that audited financial statements do, also, get inspected by HMRC). In addition to this, some smaller companies are still mandated by the terms of their loan or financing agreements to have their financial statements independently audited and it has been acknowledged that those companies who are still mandated by the terms of their financing arrangements are reluctant to approach their financiers to request dispensation of the annual audit on the grounds that to amend restrictive covenants could well expose the company to more onerous lending criteria.

Where subsidiary companies are concerned, many of these are also eligible for audit exemption, regardless of whether they qualify as small, on the condition that their liabilities are guaranteed by the parent company. In addition, dormant subsidiaries will no longer be required to prepare and file annual financial statements, provided they, too, obtain a guarantee from their parent company regarding their liabilities.

An important point to note is that parent companies need to carefully consider the guarantee they give on their subsidiary's liabilities. Guarantees cannot be withdrawn and are in force until all liabilities under the guarantee have been settled or discharged (this also applies to contingent liabilities). As a consequence of these requirements, parent companies will need to carefully consider their position, particularly where a parent company may dispose of a subsidiary (or plans to dispose of a subsidiary) and there are still undischarged liabilities guaranteed by the parent company. It is also worth pointing out that as audit exemption is taken on an annual basis, the guarantee must also be given on an annual basis – one guarantee does not cover all subsequent years' audit exemption.

Notwithstanding the exemption of qualifying subsidiary companies from the requirement to have a statutory audit, some audit work will need to be undertaken at subsidiary level in order for the group auditor to form a group audit opinion. In this respect, BIS have estimated that subsidiary companies that take advantage of the audit exemption may see a reduction in their audit fees of between 10 and 25%. At the time of writing, these savings were yet to be corroborated (as were potential savings of £390 million). Whilst many companies may not elect to have a formal statutory audit, the use of accountants to prepare the financial statements (or carry out limited checks on the accounts) will still be needed in the vast majority of cases.

THE CONCEPTS AND PERVASIVE PRINCIPLES

The *Concepts and Pervasive Principles* relating to financial statements is dealt with in Section 2 *Concepts and Pervasive Principles* of FRS 102. This particular section outlines the overall objective of financial statements that are prepared in accordance with FRS 102 and outlines the qualities that must be contained within financial statements in order that they are useful to users. Certain characteristics must be present within the financial statements, and a notable difference between FRS 102 where the *Concepts and Pervasive Principles* is concerned and mainstream IFRS (including *IFRS for SMEs*) is the inclusion in FRS 102 of the 'prudence' concept, which is currently absent from IFRS (although there have been calls by some respondents to include the prudence concept in the revised *Conceptual Framework for Financial Reporting*, which the International Accounting Standards Board (at the time of writing) is currently in the process of redrafting).

A key principle in the *Concepts and Pervasive Principles* is its authority in relation to other areas of FRS 102. If there is a conflict, or inconsistency, between the *Concepts and Pervasive Principles* in Section 2 and the requirements of any other section in FRS 102, the requirements in the relevant section of FRS 102 will take precedence. The *Concepts and Pervasive Principles*, therefore, does not have the force of a section of FRS 102. It is there to assist preparers in developing specific accounting policies (in rare situations that FRS 102 does not deal with a transaction or event) and assists the UK and Republic of Ireland standard-setting body to amend and create accounting standards.

The *Concepts and Pervasive Principles* outlines the *objective* of what the financial statements aim to achieve as well as the *qualitative characteristics* that they must possess in order to comply with the requirements of FRS 102. It gives guidance on recognition, measurement and offsetting and is essentially a condensed version of the IASB's *Conceptual Framework* and its underlying principles are much in accordance with the previous *Statement of Principles for Financial Reporting* and FRS 5 *Reporting the Substance of Transactions*.

Objective of financial statements

The *Concepts and Pervasive Principles* says that the objective of financial statements it to provide information relating to the financial position, performance and cash flows of a reporting entity that is useful to aid the decision-making of the users of those financial statements. The financial position relates to the balance sheet (statement of financial position) of the company and the assets, liabilities and equity at the reporting date. The performance of the company is dealt with in the profit and loss account (income statement/statement of comprehensive income) and the ways in which the reporting entity has generated and spent cash is dealt with in the cash flow statement (statement of cash flows). Notes to the financial statements contain additional breakdown of information contained in the primary financial statements as well as narrative disclosures, which help to aid understanding and enable the financial statements to give a true and fair view.

The *Concepts and Pervasive Principles* goes on to say that the financial statements also show the results of the stewardship of management, which relates to the resources made available for management in the day-to-day running of the company and the accountability by management of those resources.

An underlying principle where the objective of financial statements is concerned relates to the difference between internal management accounts and financial statements that are intended to give a true and fair view. Paragraph 2.2 to the *Concepts and Pervasive Principles* refers to those users that are not in a position to demand tailored reports that meet their particular information needs. This particular paragraph refers to the fact that general purpose financial statements (i.e. year-end financial statements that are intended to give a true and fair view) should possess the *qualitative characteristics* outlined in the *Concepts and Pervasive Principles* and not be tailored to meet the needs of parties such as management or directors. For this reason, general purpose financial statements are presented using prescribed formats and information is not omitted on the grounds that it may be too complex for the user to understand.

QUALITATIVE CHARACTERISTICS

When general purpose financial statements are prepared, they must possess certain qualitative characteristics that will enhance their credibility and give users the required understanding in order to make rational, economic decisions about the company as a whole. There are ten qualitative characteristics that general purpose financial statements must possess. A notable difference between the qualitative characteristics in FRS 102 and the qualitative characteristics in the old UK GAAP laid down in the *Statement of Principles* issued by the previous Accounting Standards Board is that FRS 102 contains more characteristics, as follows:

- Understandability
- Relevance
- Materiality
- Reliability
- Substance over form
- Prudence
- Completeness
- Comparability
- Timeliness
- Balance between benefit and cost

The old *Statement of Principles* only contained five characteristics and the ones that have been brought forward into FRS 102 are:

- Understandability
- Relevance
- Materiality
- Reliability
- Comparability

Understandability

Financial statement information should be presented in such a way that users, who have a reasonable knowledge of business, accounting and economic activities, can comprehend the information being conveyed. Users are expected to study the financial information with a certain degree of due diligence and this characteristic confirms that information should not be left out of the financial statements simply on the grounds that it may be too complex for users to understand.

Relevance

Information provided in general purpose financial statements must be relevant to the decision-making requirements of the users. The *Concepts and Pervasive Principles* outlines the fact that information is relevant to the financial statements when it has the ability to influence the decision-making of users by helping them to evaluate past, present or future events or correct past evaluations (this is often referred to as 'confirmatory' or 'predictive' characteristics).

Because relevant information has the ability to influence the decision-making of users, there is a subset to this qualitative characteristic, which is that of *materiality*.

Materiality

Information is material (and therefore has relevance) if the omission or mis-statement of that information (both individually and collectively) has the ability to influence the decision-making abilities of users taken on the basis of the financial statements. In other words, a potential investor may choose to invest in a company on the basis of the financial statements, but where information has been omitted (either intentionally or by way of error), the inclusion of such information may make the investor choose not to invest in the company.

There is no predetermined 'one-size-fits-all' level of materiality – it is judged wholly on the size and nature of the omission or misstatement depending on the company's individual circumstances. For example, an understated accrual of £10,000 may be material to a small owner-managed business, but may be immaterial (both in isolation and when combined with other misstatements) in a multi-million pound turnover business. In reflection of this, the *Concepts and Pervasive Principles* acknowledges that the size or nature of the item (or a combination of both) may be the determining factor in deciphering whether an omission or misstatement is, or is not, material.

An important point to note where materiality is concerned is that information that is immaterial should NOT be left uncorrected (even though it may not have a material impact on the financial statements) to achieve a particular presentation of the financial position, performance or cash flows of an entity.

Reliability

Clearly, to enable the financial statements to achieve the objective laid down in the *Concepts and Pervasive Principles*, financial statement information must be reliable. This qualitative characteristic recognises that information is reliable when it is free from material error and bias and faithfully represents that which it either purports to represent or could reasonably be expected to represent. The term 'error' is taken to mean omissions and misstatements of information within the financial statements. In addition, an error can arise because of the failure to use, or misuse of, information that was available at the time when the financial statements were authorised for issue.

The presentation of information within the financial statements that aims to influence the decision-making or judgement of a user is said not to be reliable on the grounds that it is not neutral or free from bias. Auditors of financial information must pay particular attention to this characteristic, particularly where financial statements contain a lot of accounting estimates or management judgement.

Substance over form

The concept of 'substance over form' was looked at briefly in Chapter 1. This par-ticular characteristic requires transactions and other events to be reported in the finan-cial statements in accordance with their substance (i.e. in line with their commercial reality) as opposed to their legal form. A typical transaction where this characteristic is particularly relevant is that of a finance lease. Whilst the lessee may not legally own the asset that is subject to the finance lease, the substance of the transaction is that the lessee does have an asset (which is reported on the statement of financial position/ balance sheet) for which a corresponding liability is also recognised on the statement of financial position/balance sheet (which represents the obligations to pay rentals to the lessee). Another example would be where consolidated financial statements are prepared by management. The objective of consolidated financial statements is to show the group in line with its economic substance, which is that of a single, economic entity. To achieve this, the cost of the investment recorded in the parent's individual financial statements is replaced by adding in 100%, line-by-line, the subsidiary's assets, liabilities, income and expenses to show control. When the substance of transactions is reported (rather than merely the legal form of such), this is said to enhance the reliability of financial statements.

Prudence

The concept of prudence is a long-established concept and is the inclusion of a degree of caution in the exercise of judgements that are required when making estimates that involve a degree of uncertainty. When prudence is exercised, the objective is that assets and income are not overstated, whilst liabilities and expenses are not understated. One of the main themes flowing through the concept of prudence is that it does not permit bias. In other words, the exercising of prudence will not permit the deliberate misstatement of assets, liabilities, income and expense.

A typical scenario where the exercising of prudence is often seen is in relation to construction contract accounting (which is covered in Chapter 8). When a contract is expected to make a loss, the loss is recognised immediately and is usually accounted for by recognising an appropriate amount of revenue and then recognising an expense to the extent that the expenditure generates the required loss. For example, if a contract is expected to make a loss of £1,000 and the amount of revenue to be recognised at a certain stage of completion has been calculated to be £2,000, then the cost of sales (or expenses as the case may be) will be £3,000 to generate a loss of £1,000. In other words, the expense amount to be recognised in a loss-making contract is a 'balancing figure'. This is because the concept of prudence requires losses in contract accounting to be recognised immediately.

Completeness

General purpose financial statements prepared under UK GAAP must be complete within the boundaries of both materiality and cost. There is a close interaction between 'completeness' and 'relevance' because information that is omitted can cause the information in the financial statements to be false and/or misleading and therefore render the information both unreliable and irrelevant, which will cause the user to make inappropriate conclusions regarding the entity.

Comparability

The idea behind this concept is that the users of a set of general purpose financial statements should be able to compare the financial statements of a reporting entity through time to identify trends in its financial position and performance. This is the main reason why the measurement and presentation of the effects of similar transactions and other events and conditions have to be carried out in a consistent manner. If two entities both operating in the same industry were to report similar transactions in differing ways, the concept of comparability would not be achieved because there is no consistency. In addition, to also achieve comparability, the accounting policies of the reporting entity should be disclosed within the financial statements so that users are aware of them. When an entity changes an accounting policy, there should be adequate disclosure as to the effects of those changes so that users can understand the impact the change has had on the financial statements.

Timeliness

The concept of timeliness also overlaps with the concept of 'relevance'. This is because if information is provided beyond a decision timeframe, that information may lose its relevance and hence the concept of timeliness involves preparing financial information within a decision timeframe so that there is no undue delay in the reporting of information. The concept of timeliness does acknowledge that in attempting to achieve a balance between relevance and reliability, the major consideration is how best to satisfy the needs of users in making economic decisions.

Balance between benefit and cost

The costs of providing information should not exceed the benefits derived from that information and the manner in which a cost/benefit analysis is undertaken is purely a judgemental process. The concept of balance between benefit and cost does acknowledge that the costs are not necessarily borne by those users who enjoy the benefits of the information and it is often the case that the benefits of the information are enjoyed by a broad range of external users.

THE FINANCIAL STATEMENT ELEMENTS AND THE RECOGNITION AND MEASUREMENT OF THOSE ELEMENTS

Section 2 *Concepts and Pervasive Principles* outlines the objective of financial statements. Paragraphs 2.2 and 2.3 outline the objective of financial statements that essentially say that the overall objective of the financial statements is to provide information relating to the financial position, financial performance and cash flows of the reporting entity. The financial statements will be used by users to reach economic decisions. In addition, the general purpose financial statements will also show the results of the stewardship of management including the accountability of management for the resources that the shareholders have entrusted to management.

The information contained in financial statements is communicated through a complete set of financial statements, which provide information about an entity's:

- Assets,
- Liabilities,
- Equity,
- Income and
- Expenses.

These five classifications are known as the financial statement 'elements'. Assets, liabilities and equity are reported through the statement of financial position (balance sheet), which shows the financial position. Income and expenses are reported through the income statement/statement of comprehensive income (profit and loss account), which shows the financial performance of the entity. The reporting entity's cash flows are reported through the statement of cash flows (cash flow statement), which enables the user to identify how the entity has generated cash and how it has used that cash in the reporting period.

Assets

An asset is a resource that the entity has at its disposal and uses to generate future economic benefit. In order to meet the recognition criteria, the entity must be able to 'control' that asset (see below).

Reference to the 'future economic benefits' means the asset's potential to contribute directly to the cash and cash equivalents of the entity.

Example – Asset contributing to the cash flows of the company

A manufacturing company is plant-intensive and own lots of machinery to manufacture the products that it sells on to its customers, all of which are reported on the entity's balance sheet as fixed assets. The machinery makes the products that will contribute to stock/inventory, which will then be sold to customers, which will turn the stock into debtors and sales. The debtor will eventually pay the company, which will then turn the debtor into cash.

This example highlights how items of machinery can be recognised as an asset because it meets the recognition criteria of such.

The key point to note in the definition of an asset is the term 'controlled by the entity'. A reporting entity must be able to exercise control over an asset and therefore one of the reasons why employees, for example, are not recognised as assets is because an organisation cannot exercise control over its workforce – they could leave at any time. The ability to control the asset is therefore pivotal in recognising an asset within the financial statements.

The term 'future economic benefits' could be viewed as future revenue or a reduction in future costs. In addition, the cash flows that an entity receives from an asset may not necessarily come simply from the continued use of the asset – cash flows can also be derived when the entity disposes of the asset. The proceeds from the disposal of an asset are not recognised within turnover, but instead the profit or loss on disposal of the asset is recognised in the profit and loss account.

Example – Disposal of an asset

An entity has an item of machinery with a net book value as at 31 December 2014 of £40,000 (made up of £80,000 cost less £40,000 accumulated depreciation). The entity's accounting policy for depreciation of such an asset is to charge a full year's depreciation in the year of acquisition and none in the year of disposal. On acquisition of the machine, the directors assumed a residual value of nil as the entity, at the time, expected to keep the machine in use for its entire useful economic life of four years. However, because of the company's decision to stop manufacturing a certain type of product, the machine has become redundant and has been sold on to an unconnected third party for £25,000.

The entity will not report the £25,000 within the revenue/turnover figure in its income statement (profit and loss account). The sales proceeds will, instead, form part of the calculation of profit or loss on disposal of the machine, which will be reported in the income statement (profit and loss account). This can be calculated as follows:

Net book value of the machine on disposal	£40,000
Less proceeds	£25,000
Loss on disposal of the machine	£15,000

Liabilities

One of the main characteristics of a liability is that a reporting entity must have a 'present obligation' to act or perform in a certain way. There are two types of 'obligation' where liabilities are concerned:

1. A 'legal' obligation and
2. A 'constructive' obligation.

Legal obligation

A legal obligation is an obligation that is enforceable by way of a binding contract or a statutory requirement (for example, a court order). It is usually fairly clear when a reporting entity has a legal obligation.

Constructive obligation

A constructive obligation can be slightly more subjective. A constructive obligation is an obligation that derives from an entity's actions, including:

1. Through an established pattern of the entity's past practice, published policies or a statement made by the entity, the entity has indicated to other parties that it will accept certain responsibilities and
2. Because of the above, the entity has created a valid expectation on the part of those other parties that it will discharge those responsibilities.

Example – Constructive obligation

Entity A has a year-end date of 31 December 2015 and is in the process of preparing its financial statements under FRS 102 for the year then ended. On 4 April 2016, the draft figures have been finalised and the annual general meeting is to take place on this date. In that meeting the shareholders have decided to declare a dividend in the financial statements for the year-end date of 31 December 2015 amounting to £4 per share and the directors wish for the dividend to be included in those financial statements.

Entity B also has a year-end date of 31 December 2015 and produces monthly management accounts, which the board discuss in general meeting. The November 2015 management accounts showed a healthy profit and the shareholders decided on

10 December 2015 that a dividend should be proposed amounting to £4 per share as there would be more than sufficient profit to meet the payment of the dividend to the shareholders. The dividend was subsequently paid to the shareholders on 10 January 2016.

ENTITY A

Entity A has approved the payment of a dividend after the year-end. The problem with this scenario is that there was no *constructive obligation* at the year-end to pay the dividend (a constructive obligation arises by way of a board resolution that is documented and approved). Therefore, in this scenario, as there is no constructive obligation, Entity A cannot go back and retrospectively recognise the dividend as a liability in the 31 December 2015 financial statements. The dividend must be recognised in the 2016 financial statements.

ENTITY B

Entity B has foreseen that profitability is more than sufficient in order to pay a dividend and the shareholders have passed a resolution in the general meeting on 10 December 2015 (which is well before the year-end date of 31 December 2015). A constructive obligation has arisen because the passing of the resolution in general meeting gives rise to a liability to the shareholders. As a result, Entity B is able to include the dividend in the financial statements as a liability as at 31 December 2015 and this liability will be cleared in the subsequent financial year as it was paid to the shareholders on 10 January 2016.

Equity

Equity is the residual interest in the assets of an entity after all of its liabilities have been deducted. It can be put into a form of equation as follows:

Assets *minus* Liabilities = Equity

In the statement of financial position (balance sheet), equity may be made up of a number of items, for example:

- Issued share capital
- Share premium account
- Revaluation reserve
- Retained earnings (profit and loss reserves)

All these items will be found within the equity section at the bottom half of the statement of financial position (balance sheet). However, whilst some elements of equity may be distributable to shareholders in the form of a dividend, the Companies Act 2006 may prohibit other elements being distributed (such as the share premium account).

Income

Income is reported within the performance statement, which is that of the income statement/statement of comprehensive income (referred to as the profit and loss account). Income is primarily increased in the entity's economic benefits (such as sales or increases in cash) or the decreasing of liabilities. Income is essentially enhancements of assets with the exception of contributions from shareholders (or other equity investors).

Income can arise primarily from two forms:

- Income from revenue and
- Income from gains.

Income from revenue

The company's day-to-day revenue-producing activities will be classified as income from revenue. For example, a clothing retailer will derive income from revenue from the sale of clothes; a car dealership will derive income from revenue from the sale of motor vehicles.

Income from gains

Gains are items of income that do not meet the definition of revenue. This concept was looked at in the above example where a manufacturing company had disposed of an item of machinery (see Example – Disposal of an asset). Gains are usually disclosed separately and not included in income as they are generally 'one-off' transactions that have not been derived from the principal activities of the company.

Expenses

Likewise with income, expenses can be divided into two separate components:

- Expenses that arise in the ordinary course of business and
- Losses.

Expenses that arise in the ordinary course of business

These are an entity's day-to-day running costs such as cost of sales, payroll costs, advertising costs, depreciation and amortisation and such like. Expenses that arise in the ordinary course of business take the form of an outflow of cash or a depletion of assets (for example, depreciation will reduce the net book value of fixed assets and items recognised in the cost of sales will reduce the value of inventory).

Losses

Losses are other items that meet the definition of expenses and may also arise in the ordinary course of business. Losses are usually reported separately so as to aid the decision-making process of the users. Typical losses are:

- Losses on disposal of property, plant and equipment
- Impairment losses
- Losses on disposal of investments

Recognition and measurement of assets, liabilities, income and expenses

Recognition is the means by which an item is incorporated within an entity's financial statements as either an asset, liability, item of equity, item of income or item of expense. There are two criteria that have to be met in order to recognise this, which are:

- It is probable that the entity will receive future economic benefit associated with the item and
- The item has a cost or value that can be measured reliably.

The term 'probable' is taken to mean 'more likely than not'.

Recognition and measurement of assets

Property, plant and equipment are recognised in the statement of financial position (balance sheet) as a long-term asset. For financial reporting purposes, the phrase 'long term' is taken to mean for more than 12 months from the reporting date. Any items of expenditure that are not expected to flow to the entity beyond the current reporting period will not be recognised on the statement of financial position (balance sheet) as a fixed (non-current) asset, but will instead be recognised as an expense in the statement of comprehensive income (or income statement/profit and loss account) as this expenditure is incurred.

Example – Non-contingent asset

> A firm of solicitors has been sued by one if its clients for negligent advice and it has been proved that the firm was negligent. The courts have awarded the client damages and costs as a result of the claim. The firm of solicitors have contacted their professional indemnity insurers concerning the claim and the insurers have agreed to meet the costs of the claim. At the year-end of 31 December 2015, the claim had not been received, but correspondence received from the insurers confirmed the claim was still being processed and that it should be paid out by 28 February 2016. The company's financial controller has recognised a contingent asset within the financial statements of the company as at 31 December 2015.
>
> Contingent assets cannot be recognised in the financial statements as per paragraph 2.38. However, in this instance, the flow of future benefits to the entity is virtually certain (by way of the correspondence received from the insurers confirming receipt by 28 February 2016). Therefore the proceeds from the insurers will not fall to be classified as a contingent asset as the recognition of the asset is appropriate in the circumstances.

FRS 102 at paragraph 2.38 prohibits the recognition of contingent assets because they fail to meet the recognition criteria. For the purposes of FRS 102, a *contingent asset* is only a possible asset that has arisen because of past events. It is 'contingent' because the crystallisation of the asset will only be confirmed by the occurrence (or non-occurrence) of one, or more, uncertain future events, which are not within the control of the entity.

Assets are initially recognised at cost (unless FRS 102 requires initial measurement to be on another basis – such as fair value). Non-financial assets are subsequently measured under two methods:

- Property, plant and equipment can be measured using the cost model or the revaluation model. If the revaluation model is used it must be applied to all assets within the same class.

- Inventories are measured at the lower of cost and selling price less costs to complete and sell.

There are certain types of assets that FRS 102 permits, or requires, to be valued at fair value, including:

- Investments in associates and joint ventures that an entity chooses to measure at fair value,
- Investment property that an entity measures at fair value,
- Biological assets that an entity measures at fair value less estimated costs to sell,
- Agricultural produce that an entity measures, at the point of harvest, at fair value less estimated costs to sell,
- Property, plant and equipment when the entity chooses to measure such assets under the revaluation model and
- Intangible assets that an entity chooses to measure under the revaluation model.

Financial assets are measured at amortised cost less amounts in respect of impairment. The exceptions to this rule are:

- Investments in non-convertible preference shares and non-puttable ordinary and preference shares that are traded on a public market or whose fair value can be reliably estimated. These are measured at fair value with fluctuations in fair value going through profit or loss and
- Any financial instruments that, on initial recognition, were designated by the entity as at fair value through profit or loss.

Recognition and measurement of liabilities

On initial recognition, an entity will recognise non-financial liabilities at historical cost unless FRS 102 requires initial measurement on another basis, such as fair value. However, most liabilities will be measured using a best estimate of the amount that will be required to be settled by the entity at the reporting date. For trade payables (trade creditors) this is usually the amount outstanding to suppliers at the reporting date and accruals are usually best estimates of the amounts of goods/services received at the year-end for which no invoice has been received. Provisions are generally best estimates of the amounts required to be settled and other liabilities are either best estimates or actual monetary amounts that have been settled after the year-end, or a combination of both.

Financial liabilities are measured at amortised cost less amounts in respect of impairment. The exceptions are:

- Investments in non-convertible preference shares and non-puttable ordinary and preference shares that are traded on a public market or whose fair value can be reliably estimated. These are measured at fair value with fluctuations in fair value going through profit or loss and
- Any financial instruments that, on initial recognition, were designated by the entity as at fair value through profit or loss.

Offsetting assets and liabilities

Assets and liabilities, income and expenses cannot be offset against one another unless FRS 102 requires, or permits, such offsetting. There is a difference between offsetting and the use of allowances against assets.

- When an entity makes an allowance against a potential bad debt, this is not offsetting – it is merely reducing an asset to a recoverable amount. The same applies when a reporting entity makes a provision for slow or obsolete items of inventory.
- When a reporting entity whose principal activity is not that of the purchase and sale of fixed assets sells such a fixed asset, the gain or loss on disposal of that asset is calculated by deducting the net book value of the fixed asset at the date of disposal against the sales proceeds. This gain or loss is then reported separately within the income statement. It is not reported within revenue or cost of sales as the principal activity of the entity is not that of a business that regularly buys or sells such fixed assets.

Example – Disposal of an item of plant

Zedcolour Trading Co. Limited manufactures plastic masterbatches for the plastics industry. It is a plant-intensive company and has a year-end of 31 December. The declared accounting policy for Zedcolour Trading Co. Ltd in respect of depreciation of plant and machinery is to charge a full year's depreciation in the year of acquisition (on a non-pro-rata basis) and no depreciation in the year of disposal. On 1 November 2014 the company disposed of an item of machinery that had a net book value on this date of £17,000. The company sold this machine for £14,500.

The company has made a loss on disposal amounting to (£14,500 less £17,000) £2,500. This amount will be reported as a loss on disposal of an asset in the profit and loss account.

Had the company made a profit of £2,500, this would be reported as a profit on disposal within the profit and loss account.

3 THE PRIMARY FINANCIAL STATEMENTS AND DISCLOSURE NOTES

INTRODUCTION

The financial statements and associated disclosure notes are one of the most important pieces of documentation that a company produces. The financial statements can influence lending decisions, tax liabilities (or refunds), creditworthiness of the company, staff numbers and the way in which stakeholders generally perceive the company. They can also influence valuations for buying or selling a company. The financial statements play a vital part in the running of a company and it is of paramount importance, therefore, that the financial statements are prepared in accordance with the relevant financial reporting framework, whether this is mainstream UK GAAP, the small companies regime, EU-endorsed IFRS or the micro-entities regime.

FRS 102 at Section 3 *Financial Statement Presentation* specifically outlines how an entity will achieve *fair presentation* of financial statements. It goes on to explain how an entity reporting under FRS 102 achieves compliance with the Standard and then explains what constitutes a 'complete' set of financial statements.

The underlying theme in Section 3 is to ensure that reporting entities that fall under the scope of FRS 102 report financial information in a consistent manner. In other words, the reports that FRS 102 requires in order to achieve compliance cannot be tailored to specific (internal) needs. For example, if the directors of a reporting entity refuse to include a statement of cash flows (cash flow statement) within the primary financial statements, the company cannot state they have complied with FRS 102, because the Standard requires a statement of cash flows (cash flow statement) to be included as part of the primary financial statements, subject to exemptions in the small companies regime or FRS 101 *Reduced Disclosure Framework*.

The term 'primary financial statements' means the income statement/statement of comprehensive income (profit and loss account), statement of financial position (balance sheet), statement of cash flows (cash flow statement), statement of changes in equity and statement of income and retained earnings and the related notes. Each one of these primary statements is given equal prominence, so the balance sheet does not take precedence over, say, the statement of cash flows. Each statement in its own right conveys different (and equally essential) information about the state of the company's affairs at the reporting date or for the period then ended.

Section 3 of FRS 102 has a close interaction to Section 2 *Concepts and Pervasive Principles*. This is because in order to achieve 'fair presentation', a reporting entity must ensure that the financial statements faithfully represent the effects of transactions, other events and conditions in accordance with the recognition and measurement criteria for assets, liabilities, income and expenses. If this is not achieved, the entity cannot say it has complied with FRS 102, so to that end it is important that reporting entities carefully consider the effects of transactions and events and ensure that they appropriately classify them as assets, liabilities, income and expenses accordingly. In the event that a relevant Section of FRS 102 does not deal with the accounting for a transaction or event, then management are required to develop an accounting policy, in accordance with the *Concepts and Pervasive Principles* in Section 2 having regard to the faithful representation of the transaction(s) or event(s).

PRESENTATION OF FINANCIAL STATEMENTS FAIR PRESENTATION

Financial statements have to be presented fairly in all material respects. This is essentially the same concept as the 'true and fair view' principle that has been enshrined in UK companies legislation for many years. In order to achieve fair presentation, reporting entities that correctly apply the relevant provisions of FRS 102 that are applicable to them are presumed to achieve a fair presentation of the financial position, financial performance and cash flows of entities that fall under the scope of FRS 102.

Additional disclosures will be necessary when a reporting entity complies with the provisions in FRS 102, but such compliance is insufficient to enable the users of the financial statements to fully understand the effects of certain transactions, other events and conditions on the entity's financial position and performance. The underlying theme, therefore, is conveying relevant and reliable information to users of the financial statements that is understandable. Financial statement preparers must keep in mind that information cannot simply be left out of the financial statements because it may be too complex for the user to understand.

COMPLIANCE WITH FRS 102

Reporting entities applying FRS 102 are required to make an *explicit and unreserved* statement of compliance with FRS 102 in the notes to the financial statements. An entity will not be able to make such a statement if its financial statements do not comply with all the requirements in FRS 102.

An example of how the explicit and unreserved statement of compliance may look is as follows.

> **Example – Accounting convention and statement of compliance with FRS 102 (first set of FRS 102 financial statements)**

Accounting convention and statement of compliance with FRS 102

The financial statements have been prepared under the historical cost convention as modified by the revaluation of certain assets. The financial statements of the company for the year ended 31 December 2015 have been prepared in accordance with the Financial Reporting Standard applicable in the UK and Republic of Ireland (FRS 102) issued by the Financial Reporting Council. These are the company's first set of financial statements prepared in accordance with FRS 102 (see note X for an explanation of the transition).

Where the entity is a 'public benefit entity', it is also required to make an explicit and unreserved statement of compliance but must state that it is a public benefit entity.

There may be very rare occasions when management may deem it necessary to depart from a relevant provision in FRS 102 because to comply with the relevant provision would be so misleading that it would essentially conflict with the objective of financial statements. In practice, such situations will be extremely rare, but if the situation is justifiable and departure from a relevant provision in FRS 102 is required to achieve the objective of financial statements, management must ensure that the following disclosures are made:

- That management has concluded that the financial statements present fairly the entity's financial position, financial performance and cash flows,
- That the entity has complied with FRS 102 or applicable legislation (for example, the Companies Act 2006), except that it has departed from a particular requirement of FRS 102 or applicable legislation in order to achieve a fair presentation and
- The nature of the departure, including the treatment that FRS 102 or applicable legislation would require, the reason why that treatment would be so misleading in the circumstances that it would conflict with the objective of financial statements set out in Section 2 and the treatment that the entity has adopted to achieve a true and fair view.

FREQUENCY AND CONSISTENCY

Financial statements must be prepared by entities at least once a year (together with the previous period/year comparatives). However, it is not uncommon for companies to change their year-end dates for various reasons – for example, to suit their reporting needs or to align their year-end to a parent company. A change in reporting date will result in a longer or shorter period and the financial statements for that particular date must disclose:

- That fact,
- The reason the entity has used a longer or shorter period and
- The fact that comparative amounts presented in the financial statements (including the related notes) are not entirely comparable.

When preparing the financial statements, an entity must present separately each material class of similar items. In addition, FRS 102 also requires items of a dissimilar nature of function to be separately presented (unless such items are immaterial).

COMPLETE SET

A 'complete' set of financial statements must include all of the following:

(a) A statement of financial position (balance sheet) at the reporting date,
(b) Either:
>   i. A single statement of comprehensive income for the accounting period which displays all items of income and expense recognised during the reporting period including those items the entity has recognised in determining its resulting profit or loss (which is a subtotal in the statement of comprehensive income) and items of other comprehensive income or
>   ii. A separate income statement (profit and loss account) and a separate statement of comprehensive income. If the reporting entity chooses to present both an income statement and a statement of comprehensive income, the statement of comprehensive income must begin with profit or loss for the financial year and then disclose the items of other comprehensive income,

(c) A statement of changes in equity for the reporting period,
(d) A statement of cash flows (cash flow statement) for the reporting period and
(e) Notes, which comprise a summary of significant accounting policies together with other explanatory information.

STATEMENT OF FINANCIAL POSITION

The statement of financial position (commonly referred to as the 'balance sheet' in the UK and Republic of Ireland) is the primary statement that shows what the company owns and what it owes. It is a snapshot of the financial *position* of the company at the close of business on the last day of the reporting period. The statement of financial position is split between an entity's assets, liabilities and equity. The format of the statement of financial position is laid down in the Companies Act 2006 and Section 4 *Statement of Financial Position* says that an entity must present a statement of financial position in accordance with one of the following four requirements for a balance sheet:

• Part 1 *General Rules and Formats* of Schedule 1 to the Regulations
• Part 1 *General Rules and Formats* of Schedule 2 to the Regulations
• Part 1 *General Rules and Formats* of Schedule 3 to the Regulations
• Part 1 *General Rules and Formats* of Schedule 1 to the LLP Regulations

A parent company preparing consolidated financial statements will be required to prepare a consolidated statement of financial position in accordance with Schedule 6 to the Regulations or Schedule 3 to the LLP Regulations.

Chapter 1 *General Requirements of Companies Act 2006* goes into a lot of detail regarding the format of the statement of financial position.

Long-term debtors

Prior to the issuance of FRS 102, there was UITF Abstract 4 *Presentation of Long-term Debtors in Current Assets*. This Abstract was issued to clarify the position regarding debtors that fall due after more than one year. Long-term creditors are separately disclosed on the face of the balance sheet, as well as in the notes to the financial statements. The provisions in UITF 4 said that where debtors due after more than one year are so material in the context of the total net current assets that in the absence of disclosure of debtors due after more than one year on the face of the balance sheet readers may misinterpret the accounts, the amount of long-term debtors should be disclosed on the face of the balance sheet. This principle has been carried over into FRS 102 and where the amount of debtors due after more than one year from the reporting date is so material in the context of the entity's total net current assets that, in the absence of disclosure of the debtors falling due after more than one year on the face of the balance sheet, readers may not interpret the financial statements correctly, the amount of debtors falling due after more than one year should be disclosed on the face of the balance sheet within current assets. It will also be permissible to disclose the amount due after more than one year in the notes to the financial statements.

Example – Disclosure of long-term debtor (balance sheet extract)

	31/12/2015	*31/12/2014*
	£	*£*
Current assets		
Stock	X	X
Debtors: amounts falling due within one year	X	X
Debtors: amounts falling due after more than one year	X	X
Cash at bank and in hand	X	X

Long-term creditors

Creditors that fall due after more than one year are also shown separately on the face of the statement of financial position (balance sheet) as well as in the notes to the financial statements. A key point to note is that bank overdrafts do not fall to be classified as a long-term creditor, despite the fact that the overdraft may not be 'called in' by the bank within 12 months from the reporting date. This is because bank overdrafts are ordinarily repayable 'on demand' and as such are always shown within current liabilities. Other forms of finance such as loans and finance lease obligations are always split between the portion of the loan that will be repaid within 12 months from the reporting date and the portion that falls due in more than 12 months from the reporting date.

Example – Disclosure of long-term creditors (balance sheet extract)

	Note	31/12/2015 £	31/12/2015 £	31/12/2014 £	31/12/2014 £
CREDITORS Amounts falling due within one year	7	X		X	
Net current assets (liabilities)			X		X
TOTAL ASSETS LESS CURRENT LIABILITIES			X		X
Creditors: amounts falling due after more than one year	8		X		X
NET ASSETS			X		X

Share capital

FRS 102 mandates certain disclosures to be made in respect of share capital, either on the face of the statement of financial position or within the notes to the financial statements. For each class of share capital an entity must disclose the following:

- The number of shares issued and fully paid.
- The number of shares issued but not fully paid.
- Par value per share or the fact that the shares have no par value.
- A reconciliation of the number of shares outstanding at the beginning and at the end of the period (note that this reconciliation does not need to be presented for prior periods).
- The rights, preferences and restrictions attaching to that class including restrictions on the distribution of dividends and the repayment of capital.
- Shares in the entity held by the entity or by its subsidiaries, associates or joint ventures.
- Shares reserved for issue under options and contracts for the sale of shares, including the terms and amounts.

In addition, reporting entities must also disclose a description of each reserve within equity.

Where an entity reports under FRS 102 but does not have share capital (for example, a trust or a Limited Liability Partnership), it must disclose the equivalent to the above, showing changes during the accounting period in each category of equity, and the rights, preferences and restrictions that are attached to each category of equity.

Disposal of asset(s) or disposal group(s)

When the entity has entered into a binding sale agreement for a major disposal of assets, or a disposal group, the following disclosures must be made within the notes to the financial statements:

- A description of the asset(s) or the disposal group,
- A description of the facts and circumstances surrounding the sale and
- The carrying value of the assets or, for a disposal group, the carrying values of the underlying assets and liabilities.

STATEMENT OF COMPREHENSIVE INCOME AND THE INCOME STATEMENT

The statement of comprehensive income and the income statement is essentially the profit and loss account and the statement of total recognised gains and losses combined or shown separately and is dealt with in Section 5 *Statement of Comprehensive Income and Income Statement*. This particular Section offers reporting entities a choice of presentation in that it can present its total comprehensive income for a period, either:

- In a single statement of comprehensive income. When the entity opts for this choice it will present all of its income and expense recognised in the period (including those items taken directly to reserves) or
- In two statements – an income statement (the profit and loss account) and a statement of comprehensive income – in which case the income statement presents all items of income and expense recognised in the period except those items of income and expense that are recognised in equity or as required by FRS 102.

Please note – any change from the single-statement approach to the two-statement approach (or vice versa) is a change in accounting policy and therefore the provisions in Section 10 *Accounting Policies, Estimates and Errors* will be triggered (these are covered in Chapter 7). This will mean that the prior period must also be restated as if the single-statement approach or the two-statement approach had always been adopted.

Single-statement approach

The Companies Act 2006 specifies the relevant presentation layouts and paragraph 5.5 of FRS 102 requires the income statement (prepared as a single statement) to follow one of the following:

(a) Part 1 *General Rules and Formats* of Schedule 1 to the Regulations
(b) Part 1 *General Rules and Formats* of Schedule 2 to the Regulations
(c) Part 1 *General Rules and Formats* of Schedule 3 to the Regulations
(d) Part 1 *General Rules and Formats* of Schedule 1 to the LLP Regulations

When consolidated financial statements are prepared, the consolidated statement of comprehensive income is presented in accordance with the requirements laid down in respect of a consolidated profit and loss account in Schedule 6 to the Regulations or Schedule 3 to the LLP Regulations.

There are certain line items that the statement of comprehensive income must include as follows:

(a) Classified by nature (excluding amounts in (b)), the components that make up other comprehensive income that are recognised as part of total comprehensive income outside profit or loss as permitted or required by FRS 102. The Standard permits reporting entities to present components of other comprehensive income either:
   i. Net of the related tax effects or
   ii. Before the related tax effects show one amount representing the aggregate amount of income tax relating to those components.

(b) The entity's share of other comprehensive income of associates and jointly controlled entities that have been accounted for using the equity method.

(c) Total comprehensive income for the period.

If the reporting entity has interests in other companies (for example, a subsidiary), the entity must present additional disclosures at the foot of the statement of comprehensive income which show:

(d) Profit or loss for the period attributable to:
   i. The non-controlling interest and
   ii. Owners of the parent.

(e) Total comprehensive income for the period attributable to:
   i. Non-controlling interest and
   ii. Owners of the parent.

Example – Single statement approach – profit and loss account Format 1

	31.12.15	31.12.14
	£	£
Turnover	X	X
Cost of sales	(X)	(X)
Gross profit	X	X
Distribution costs	(X)	(X)
Administrative expenses	(X)	(X)
Other operating income	X	X
Operating profit	X	X
Income from shares in group undertakings	X	X
Income from participating interests	X	X
Income from other fixed asset investments	X	X
Other interest receivable and similar income	X	X
Amounts written off investments	(X)	(X)
Interest payable and similar charges	(X)	(X)
Profit on ordinary activities before taxation	X	X
Tax on profit on ordinary activities	(X)	(X)
Profit on ordinary activities after taxation for the financial year	X	X

Two-statement approach

Under this approach, a reporting entity presents an income statement (as illustrated above), but then continues with the items taken to other comprehensive income during the reporting period immediately after 'profit after taxation' to arrive at 'total comprehensive income for the year'. Paragraph 5.7 of FRS 102 says that the items that must be included in the income statement (profit and loss account) must conform to one of the following requirements:

- Part 1 *General Rules and Formats* of Schedule 1 to the Regulations
- Part 1 *General Rules and Formats* of Schedule 2 to the Regulations
- Part 1 *General Rules and Formats* of Schedule 3 to the Regulations
- Part 1 *General Rules and Formats* of Schedule 1 to the LLP Regulations

Where the parent produces consolidated financial statements, these must conform to the requirements for a consolidated income statement (profit and loss account) in Schedule 6 to the Regulations, or Schedule 3 to the LLP Regulations.

Example – Statement of comprehensive income

	31.12.15	31.12.14
	£	£
Turnover	X	X
Cost of sales	(X)	(X)
Gross profit	X	X
Distribution costs	(X)	(X)
Administrative expenses	(X)	(X)
Other operating income	X	X
Operating profit	X	X
Income from shares in group undertakings	X	X
Income from participating interests	X	X
Income from other fixed asset investments	X	X
Other interest receivable and similar income	X	X
Amounts written off investments	(X)	(X)
Interest payable and similar charges	(X)	(X)
Profit on ordinary activities before taxation	X	X
Tax on profit on ordinary activities	(X)	(X)
Profit on ordinary activities after taxation for the financial year	X	X
Other comprehensive income:		
Actuarial losses on defined benefit pension plans	(X)	(X)
Deferred tax movement relating to actuarial loss	X	X
Total comprehensive income for the year	X	X

Where an entity has discontinued operations during the year, it must disclose (on the face of the income statement or statement of comprehensive income if prepared) an amount that shows the total of:

(a) The after-tax profit or loss of discontinued operations and
(b) The after-tax gain or loss attributable to the impairment or on the disposal of the assets or disposal group(s) that constitute discontinued operations.

Paragraph 5.7D also requires a reporting entity to present a line-by-line analysis in the income statement (or statement of comprehensive income if prepared) using a columnar format showing those items that relate to discontinued operations (separately from continuing operations) and a total column is presented. The previous periods that have also been presented in the financial statements relating to discontinued operations must also be re-presented so that disclosures for all discontinued operations relating to the current and previous accounting period are presented.

Operating profit

The above illustrations showing the single- and two-statement approach disclose 'operating profit'. This illustration is reflective of the fact that many companies in the UK and Republic of Ireland choose to show operating profit on the face of the income statement/profit and loss account. However, paragraph 5.9B of FRS 102 does not require operating profit to be disclosed. This paragraph does acknowledge that some companies may choose to show operating profit on the face of the income statement/profit and loss account and, where the entity chooses to do so, it must ensure that the amount disclosed as operating profit is representative of activities that would be regarded as 'operating'. Paragraph 5.9B offers examples of what it considers not to be operating activities, such as inventory write-downs and restructuring and relocation expenses.

Other issues relevant to the income statement/statement of comprehensive income

When management conclude that additional line items, headings and subtotals should be presented in the income statement/statement of comprehensive income on the grounds that such presentation is relevant to an understanding of the entity's financial performance, it must ensure that this is undertaken to ensure that the financial statements achieve the objectives laid down in the *Concepts and Pervasive Principles* and that relevant and reliable information is conveyed to the users.

In addition, to ensure that the objective of financial statements is achieved, items that are included in total comprehensive income and that are considered material are also disclosed separately (both the nature of the items and their amount) in the statement of comprehensive income (income statement, if presented) or in the notes to the financial statements. This includes 'extraordinary items', which are items that possess a high degree of abnormality and arise from events or transactions that fall outside the ordinary activities of the reporting entity and which are not expected to recur.

An entity can choose to present expenses using classifications based on either the nature, or function, of the expenses within the entity. If an entity chooses to analyse expenses by 'nature' it will show the expenses according to their nature (for example, depreciation, raw materials and consumables and staff costs). If the entity chooses to analyse costs by function it will adopt the same style as illustrated above (cost of sales, distribution costs, administrative expenses, etc.).

STATEMENT OF CHANGES IN EQUITY AND STATEMENT OF INCOME AND RETAINED EARNINGS

The statement of changes in equity and the statement of income and retained earnings are dealt with in FRS 102 in Section 6 *Statement of Changes in Equity and Statement of Income and Retained Earnings*. This particular section is a fairly brief section within FRS 102 (spanning just under one and a half pages) but it outlines some important concepts relating to these primary financial statements.

Statement of changes in equity

The statement of changes in equity presents an entity's profit or loss for an accounting period together with items that it has taken to other comprehensive income (for example, the revaluation of an item of property, plant and equipment or actuarial gains and losses on a defined benefit pension plan). It also presents amounts that the entity has taken to the statement of changes in equity in relation to the correction of material errors and the effects of changes in accounting policy during the period as well as amounts invested by, and distributions to, equity investors during the period.

Paragraph 6.3 of FRS 102 outlines the information that is to be presented within the statement of changes in equity, showing:

(a) The total amount of comprehensive income for the period, showing separately the total amounts attributable to owners of the parent and the amount attributable to non-controlling interests,

(b) In relation to each component of equity, the effects of retrospective application or retrospective restatement recognised in accordance with Section 10 *Accounting Policies, Estimates and Errors* and

(c) For each component of equity, a reconciliation between the carrying value at the beginning and the end of the period, separately disclosing changes that have arisen from:
   i. Profit or loss,
   ii. Other comprehensive income and
   iii. The amounts of investments by, and dividends and other distributions to, owners. Separate disclosure is required relating to issues of shares, purchase of own share transactions, dividends and other distributions to the entity's owners, as well as changes in ownership interests in subsidiaries where loss of control has not taken place.

Example – Statement of changes in equity

	Note	Share capital	Share premium account	Profit and loss reserves	Total
		£	£	£	£
Balance at 1 January 2014		X	X	X	X
Profit for the year				X	X
Other comprehensive income				X	X
Dividends paid	3			(X)	(X)
Issue of share capital		X	X		X
Balance at 31 December 2014		X	X	X	X
Profit for the year				X	X
Other comprehensive income				X	X
Dividends paid	3			(X)	(X)
Issue of share capital		X	X		X
Balance at 31 December 2015		X	X	X	X

Statement of income and retained earnings

The statement of income and retained earnings can be presented in place of a statement of comprehensive income and a statement of changes in equity where the only changes in equity during the period are due to:

- Profit or loss,
- Payment of dividends,
- Corrections of prior period material errors and
- Changes in accounting policy.

The objective of the statement of income and retained earnings is to show an entity's profit or loss and changes in retained earnings for an accounting period.

Paragraph 6.5 of FRS 102 requires the following to be presented:

(a) Retained earnings (profit and loss reserves) at the beginning of the reporting period,
(b) Dividends declared and paid or payable during the period,
(c) Restatements of retained earnings for corrections of prior period material errors,
(d) Restatements of retained earnings for changes in accounting policy and
(e) Retained earnings at the end of the reporting period.

Example – Statement of income and retained earnings

	31.12.2015
	£
Profit for the year	X
Retained earnings brought forward	X
Dividends	(X)
Retained earnings carried forward	X

STATEMENT OF CASH FLOWS

The statement of cash flows (cash flow statement) is dealt with in Section 7 *Statement of Cash Flows* in FRS 102. The purpose of this primary financial statement is to show how the reporting entity has generated and spent cash during the accounting period. It is the only primary statement that is not prepared under the accruals basis of accounting and also provides information about an entity's changes in cash and cash equivalents.

Cash equivalents

Cash equivalents are investments that are short-term and are highly liquid. They are amounts that are readily convertible to known amounts of cash and that are not exposed to significant risk of changes in value. Paragraph 7.2 of FRS 102 says that an investment would normally qualify to be classed as a cash equivalent when it has a short maturity and places a timespan of three months or less from the acquisition date.

A bank overdraft would normally be considered to be a financing activity of the entity (similar to borrowings). The entity must consider if an overdraft repayable on demand forms an integral part of its cash management, because if the overdraft is repayable on demand and does form an integral part of the entity's cash management then it will form a component of the entity's cash and cash equivalents.

Short-term deposit accounts might also be classified as cash equivalents depending on the circumstances. In comparison with previous FRS 1 *Cash Flow Statements*, some of the items that would have been classified within 'management of liquid resources' may now be included in cash and cash equivalents.

Section 7 requires the statement of cash flows to be presented using three cash flow classifications, those that arise from an entity's:

- Operating activities,
- Investing activities and
- Financing activities.

Cash flow statements prepared under FRS 102 will therefore be notably different in appearance to those under previous UK GAAP at FRS 1.

Operating activities

These are an entity's day-to-day revenue-producing activities. Some examples of cash flows from operating activities are:

(a) Cash receipts from the sale of goods and/or the rendering of services,
(b) Cash receipts from royalties, fees, commissions and other revenue,
(c) Cash payments made to suppliers for goods and services,
(d) Cash payments to and on behalf of employees (payroll),
(e) Cash payments or refunds of tax to HMRC, unless such payments/receipts can be specifically identified with the entity's financing and investing activities,

(f) Cash receipts and payments from investments, loans and other contracts that are held for dealing or trading purposes, which are similar to inventory acquired specifically for resale, and

(g) Cash advances and loans made to other parties by entities operating as financial institutions.

Example – Sale of a machine

The Bury Corporation is a company that manufactures outdoor garden furniture and is plant-intensive due to the nature of its activities. The financial year-end is 31 December 2015 and on 30 November 2015 the company sold an item of machinery that had a net book value of £40,000 for sales proceeds of £45,000 (hence a gain on disposal of £5,000). The Bury Corporation raised an invoice for the sale of this machine and the bookkeeper has included this amount within turnover for the accounting period.

The company's principal activity is not that of a retailer of plant and machinery – it is a manufacturing company and therefore the disposal proceeds of £45,000 will form part of the gain on disposal and be reported as such on disposal of property, plant and equipment within the company's income statement (profit and loss account) rather than in revenue. In the statement of cash flows, such proceeds will be reported within investing activities and not operating activities.

The example above highlights the provisions in paragraph 7.4, which acknowledges that a company may enter into certain transactions, such as the disposal of an item of plant by a manufacturing company, which may give rise to a gain or loss on disposal of the plant that is included within profit or loss. However, such cash flows relating to transactions like this are reported in investing and not operating activities due to the company's principal activity (that of a manufacturer).

Investing activities

Investing activities are activities that involve the acquisition and disposal of long-term assets. Paragraph 7.5 of FRS 102 gives a comprehensive list of examples of what it considers to be investing activities, including:

(a) Payments made in cash to acquire fixed assets (i.e. property, plant and equipment). This also includes self-constructed assets, intangible assets and other long-term assets for use in the business. In addition, cash payments include those relating to capitalised development costs.

(b) Cash receipts from the sale of intangible and tangible fixed assets and other long-term assets.

(c) Cash payments to acquire debt or equity instruments of other entities and interests in joint ventures. (The exception to this relates to payments other than for those instruments classified as cash equivalents or held for dealing or trading.)

(d) Cash receipts from sales of debt or equity instruments of other entities and interests in joint ventures. (The exception to this relates to receipts for those instruments classified as cash equivalents or held for dealing or trading.)

(e) Cash advances and loans made to third parties with the exception of those made by financial institutions.

(f) Cash receipts from the repayment of advances and loans made to third parties.

(g) Payments of cash for future contracts, forward contracts, option contracts and swap contracts. (The exception is when such contracts are held for dealing or trading or the payments are classified as financing activities.)

(h) Receipts of cash from futures contracts, forward contracts, option contracts and swap contracts. (The exception is when the contracts are held for dealing or trading, or the receipts are classified as financing activities.)

Financing activities

These are the activities that change the borrowing and equity structure of the company and paragraph 7.6 of FRS 102 gives some useful examples of what it considers to be financing activities as follows:

(a) Cash proceeds from a share issue or the issuance of other equity instruments,

(b) Cash payments to the entity's shareholders to acquire or redeem the entity's shares,

(c) Cash proceeds from issuing debentures, loans, notes, bonds, mortgages and other short-term or long-term borrowings,

(d) Cash repayments of loans and amounts borrowed and

(e) Cash payments made by a lessee for the reduction of the outstanding finance lease liability.

Presentation of cash and cash equivalents

Ordinarily the amount of cash and cash equivalents that are presented at the end of the statement of cash flows will be in agreement to with the cash and cash equivalents reported in the entity's statement of financial position (balance sheet) at the end of the accounting period. Therefore, if this is the case, then reporting entities will not be required to present a reconciliation of the amounts reported in the statement of cash flows to the equivalent items that are reported in the company's statement of financial position (balance sheet).

Presentation of the statement of cash flows

There are two methods of presentation for the statement of cash flows under Section 7:

(a) The direct method and

(b) The indirect method.

The *direct method* is generally the preferred option, because this presents information about major classes of gross cash receipts and gross cash payments, which can be extracted directly from the accounting records (hence the word 'direct' being included in the name). The reality is that this method is not as common as the indirect method, but both methods are equally available for adoption.

The *indirect method* is a method whereby the profit or loss for the accounting period is adjusted for the effects of:

- Changes in working capital from one period to the next (changes in inventory, receivables and payables),
- Non-cash items such as depreciation, provisions, accrued income and expenses, unrealised foreign currency gains and losses, undistributed profits of associates and non-controlling interests and
- All other items for which the cash effects relate to investing or financing activities.

Example – Cash flow statement prepared using the indirect method

	Note	2015 £'000	2014 £'000
Operating activities			
Profit before tax		X	X
Adjustments	1	X	X
Net changes in working capital	2	X	X
Income tax paid		(X)	(X)
Interest paid		(X)	(X)
Cash flow from operating activities		X	X
Investing activities			
Purchase of fixed assets		(X)	(X)
Proceeds from disposal of fixed assets		X	X
Acquisition of subsidiary (net of cash)		(X)	(X)
Interest received		X	X
Cash flow from investing activities		(X)	(X)
Financing activities			
Proceeds from issue of share capital		X	X
New loan raised		X	X
Capital repayments		(X)	(X)
Interest paid		(X)	(X)
Dividends paid to equity holders		(X)	(X)
Cash flow from financing activities		(X)	(X)
Net changes in cash and cash equivalents		X	X
Cash and cash equivalents at start of year		X	X
Cash and cash equivalents at end of year	3*	X	X

*A note reconciling the cash and cash equivalents reported in the statement of cash flows to the cash and cash equivalents reported in the statement of financial position (balance sheet) will not be required if these amounts are identical to the amount similarly described in the statement of financial position (balance sheet).

Reporting cash flows on a net basis

Paragraph 7.10A of FRS 102 does make allowances for certain types of cash flows to be reported in the statement of cash flows on a net basis. These are:

(a) Receipts and payments of cash on behalf of customers when the cash flows reflect the activities of the customer rather than those of the entity. An example might include the acceptance and repayment of demand deposits of a bank or rents collected on behalf of, and subsequently paid over to, the property owners.

(b) Receipts and payments of cash for items where there is a quick turnaround of turnover, the amounts are large and the maturities are short. An example could be a short-term borrowing with a maturity of three months or less.

Foreign currency cash flows

When the entity has cash flows denoted in a foreign currency, it must apply the exchange rate between the functional currency and the foreign currency at the date of the cash flow. Paragraph 7.11 also allows an entity to use an exchange rate that approximates the actual rate, such as a weighted average exchange rate for the period.

Any unrealised gains and losses that arise from changes in the foreign currency exchange rates are not cash flows of the entity. However, in recognition of this, paragraph 7.13 of FRS 102 does say that in order to reconcile cash and cash equivalents at the beginning and end of the accounting period, the effect of exchange rate changes on cash and cash equivalents held or due in a foreign currency is to be presented in the statement of cash flows. To achieve this, the reporting entity must re-measure cash and cash equivalents held during the reporting period at period-end exchange rates and the resulting unrealised gain or loss must be shown separately from cash flows arising from operating, investing and financing activities.

Interest and dividends

Section 7 of FRS 102 considers both dividends and interest as either operating or financing cash flows. In general, paragraph 7.14 requires a company to present cash flows from interest and dividends both paid and received separately and consistently from one period to the next as either operating, investing or financing cash flows.

Interest paid and interest and dividends received could be classified by a reporting entity as operating cash flows because they are included within profit or loss. Alternatively, they may be classified as financing cash flows if they are costs of obtaining financial resources or are returns on investments.

Dividends paid to shareholders may be classified as financing activities (as shown in the illustrative statement of cash flows above) because they are a cost of obtaining financial resources. However, FRS 102 does permit an entity to classify dividends paid as a component of cash flows from operating activities on the grounds that they are paid out of operating cash flows.

Non-cash transactions

Because of the nature of the statement of cash flows and the basis on which it is prepared (a cash basis rather than an accruals basis), paragraph 7.18 requires reporting entities to exclude from the statement of cash flows any investing and financing cash flows that do not require the use of cash and cash equivalents. Where an entity has such transactions, these must be disclosed elsewhere in the financial statements and disclose all the required information about those investing and financing activities.

Paragraph 7.19 gives three examples of non-cash transactions that may be encountered by a reporting entity in the preparation of their statement of cash flows:

(a) The entity acquires assets either by assuming directly related liabilities or by means of a finance lease,

(b) The entity acquires another entity through an equity issue and

(c) The entity converts existing debt to equity (a convertible loan).

Whilst Section 7 mandates the need for an entity to produce a cash flow statement, not all entities need to do so. For example, a company applying the small companies regime need not prepare a cash flow statement. In addition, FRS 101 *Reduced Disclosure Framework* allows qualifying entities exemption from preparing a cash flow statement provided the equivalent disclosure is made in the consolidated financial statements.

NOTES TO THE FINANCIAL STATEMENTS

The notes to the financial statements are an integral part of a set of general purpose financial statements and essentially break down the amounts reported in the primary statements into more detail. In addition, some disclosures will be required under FRS 102 that were not previously required under old UK GAAP and so preparers of FRS 102 financial statements are encouraged to ensure that a disclosure checklist reflects the disclosure requirements of the new accounting regime. The disclosure notes also offer narrative disclosures to users relating to information that is relevant to the accounting period and the disclosure notes are dealt with in Section 8 *Notes to the Financial Statements*, which also acknowledges that nearly every other section in FRS 102 requires disclosures that are usually presented in the notes to the financial statements.

Several of the disclosure notes pertinent to a reporting entity are usually produced automatically by automated accounts production software programs. However, care must be taken with such software programs because they often only generate the bare minimum 'template' disclosures. Disclosure notes must be entity-specific and present the notes in a systematic manner. The amounts reported in the primary financial statements are always cross-referenced to the relevant disclosure note in the financial statements, which offers further information concerning such amounts.

Paragraph 8.2 requires the notes to the financial statements to:

(a) Present information concerning the basis of preparation of the financial statements. The entity must also make disclosure about the specific accounting policies used in the preparation of their financial statements.

(b) Disclose the information required by FRS 102 that is not presented elsewhere in the entity's financial statements.

(c) Disclose information that is not presented elsewhere in the financial statements but which is considered to be relevant to an understanding of the financial statements.

Paragraph 8.3 of FRS 102 requires the notes to be presented in a 'systematic manner'. To that end, the order of the notes should be as follows:

1. A statement that the financial statements have been prepared in accordance with FRS 102,
2. The entity's significant accounting policies that have been applied in the preparation of the financial statements,
3. Supporting information for each item presented in the primary financial statements in the same sequence that each line item is presented and
4. Any other disclosures that are considered to be relevant to an understanding of the financial statements.

The accounting policies that need disclosure are those that are 'significant' in the preparation of the financial statements. There is little to be achieved by disclosing every conceivable accounting policy for an entity that is not applicable – for example, if the entity does not have assets subjected to leasing arrangements, there is no requirement to disclose an accounting policy for hire purchase and leasing arrangements because the information is irrelevant and will dilute the meaningfulness of the financial statements. FRS 102 is clear that only the significant accounting policies should be disclosed in the notes to the financial statements and these policies should also disclose the measurement basis (or bases) used in the preparation of the financial statements as well as the other accounting policies that have been used that are relevant to an understanding of the financial statements.

Judgements and estimates

The accounting policies section of the notes to the financial statements must also disclose information concerning the judgements made by management in the process of applying the entity's accounting policies that have the most significant effect on the amounts reported in the financial statements. There are new disclosures that management will need to carefully think about in order to distinguish and disclose where necessary.

It is also widely acknowledged that all financial statements will contain some degree of estimations when it comes to monetary amounts. For example, inventory and work-in-progress will have some degree of estimation attached to them as will general bad debt provisions, accruals and such like. Whilst many monetary estimations will be immaterial to the financial statements as a whole, paragraph 8.7 of FRS 102 requires an entity to disclose information relating to the key assumptions concerning the future of the entity and other key sources of estimation uncertainty that may give rise to a significant risk of causing a material adjustment to the carrying amounts in the succeeding financial year. Specific disclosures include:

(a) Their nature and
(b) Their carrying value as at the end of the reporting period.

GOING CONCERN

In their preparation of financial statements, management must make an assessment of the entity's ability to continue as a going concern. This is a fundamental principle in the preparation of financial statements and an entity is presumed to be a going concern unless management either intends to liquidate the entity, or to cease trading, or has no realistic alternative but to do so. Going concern is considered to be a material issue in all entities, both large and small.

The issue relating to going concern has moved up the ranks over recent years, due in large part to the recent economic crisis. Management have a responsibility to take into account all available information about the future in assessing the entity's ability to continue as a going concern and this assessment must be at least (but not limited to) 12 months from the date the financial statements are authorised for issue. The important part management must understand here is the timeframe; many financial reporting frameworks require a going concern assessment to be undertaken for a period of 12 months from the date of the financial statements (i.e. the year- or period-end). In the UK and Republic of Ireland it is 12 months from the date the financial statements are authorised for issue.

Assessing going concern

The problem with assessing going concern is that it is very much subjective and involves a lot of judgement on the part of management. These problems are also accentuated by the fact that management may well make judgements relating to going concern, and thus prepare the financial statements on the going concern basis, but that is not a guarantee that the company will necessarily be in existence 12 months after those financial statements have been approved.

Companies that are financially sound and that have a tight control over the budgets and cash flows are in a much better position to assess the appropriateness of the going concern basis than companies that have a very tight cash flow and operate to a very restricted budget with no real available information to hand to assist them in making their assessment of going concern.

Companies that prepare budgets and forecasts may look at where their profitability and cash flows will be at certain times in the future. These are particularly useful where companies may suffer from seasonal declines in cash flow or where the business is of a certain cyclical nature.

If borrowing facilities are coming up for renewal with no indications that the financier is prepared to renew the borrowings, this is more than likely going to cast significant doubt on the company's ability to continue as a going concern. Management must assess the likelihood that the company's borrowing facilities will be renewed and, if not, consider how likely it is that they can secure borrowing facilities from other financiers.

Assessing going concern is often not overly complicated and smaller, owner-managed companies should be able to do their going concern assessment more easily than larger companies who have complex operations.

The following are some examples of potential indicators that a company might not be a going concern. The list is not exhaustive and other additional factors may give rise to going concern difficulties:

- Recurring losses with no real indicators that the company is going to return to profitability,
- An insolvent statement of financial position (balance sheet),
- Negative operating cash flows in cash flow forecasts,
- Inability to stick to credit terms imposed by suppliers or loss of credit from suppliers,
- Breach of loan agreements,
- Loss of key employees, customers and suppliers,
- Pending litigation issues,
- Loss of a major contract (or the impending loss of a major contract),
- Technical obsolescence of goods and
- Withdrawal of borrowing facilities or indicators that borrowing facilities will not be renewed.

When management becomes aware of material uncertainties that may cast doubt on the entity's ability to continue as a going concern, those uncertainties must be disclosed within the financial statements. If management concludes that the going concern presumption is not appropriate, the financial statements must disclose the basis on which they have been prepared (usually on the 'break-up' basis) and the reason why the entity is not considered to be a going concern.

4 FINANCIAL REPORTING FOR SMALLER COMPANIES

INTRODUCTION

Financial reporting has to be proportionate to the needs of users of the financial statements. To require a company at the smaller end of the scale to report the same level of detail as that of a blue-chip PLC would clearly be unreasonable and would result in financial information that is not relevant or appropriate to the company in question.

Companies (and groups) are classed as small or medium depending on the levels of turnover, gross assets and number of employees and these current levels (which are set for change in 2015) are summarised as follows:

	Turnover	Balance sheet total	No. of employees
Small company	£6.5m	£3.26m	50
Small group	£6.5m net	£3.26m net	50
	£7.8m gross	£3.9m gross	
Medium-sized company	£25.9m	£12.9m	250
Medium-sized group	£25.9m net	£12.9m net	250
	£31.1m gross	£15.5m gross	

The size limits above determine whether a business is deemed as 'small' in the eyes of the Companies Act 2006 and thus eligible to take advantage of reduced disclosure requirements in its financial statements. A company must satisfy two out of the three criteria above for two consecutive years before they can be classed as small. Financial statement preparers must keep in mind that in the event that the government increases the size limits, they must apply the new limits to the comparative year to see if the company does, in fact, qualify as small. *At the time of writing, it was proposed that the size limits were to increase in 2015.* These changes are planned to take effect for accounting periods commencing on or after 1 January 2016 (see the later section 'Changes to the Small Companies Regime').

In January 2014, an announcement was made by the Department for Business, Skills and Innovation that a further classification of company was to be formed, which is discussed further in this chapter (see the section 'Micro-Entities').

To overcome the hurdle of excessive reporting for companies that are not large or medium sized, there is a standard known as the *Financial Reporting Standard for Smaller Entities* (the FRSSE), which was originally developed in 1997. Since its birth, the FRSSE has seen five updates as a result of changes in accounting standards and the new Companies Act 2006.

The popularity of the FRSSE has grown considerably since 1997, largely because of its ease of use and the reduced disclosure requirements that companies that are eligible to use it can take advantage of. The latest version of the FRSSE, following the issuance of FRS 102 *The Financial Reporting Standard applicable in the UK and Republic of Ireland,* is the FRSSE (effective January 2015), which was issued in July 2013 and contains fairly minimal changes from the previous version, which was the FRSSE (effective April 2008). Whilst the FRSSE (effective January 2015) is effective for accounting periods commencing on or after 1 January 2015, it is permissible to early-adopt this standard.

At the time of writing, the Financial Reporting Council (FRC) had recently announced plans to withdraw the FRSSE in its entirety following the introduction of the EU Accounting Directive and to bring small companies that are not applying the micro-entities legislation in their financial statements under FRS 102. If the FRC go ahead with these proposals, a new Section 1A *Small Entities* will be introduced into FRS 102, which will set out the framework and presentation and disclosure requirements for small entities.

FINANCIAL REPORTING STANDARD FOR SMALLER ENTITIES VERSUS FRS 102

The FRSSE (effective April 2008) was amended and re-issued as the FRSSE (effective January 2015) in July 2013. A new reporting regime brings with it a host of changes and FRS 102 brings in some new accounting practices due to the evolvement of financial reporting over the years. Not all of these new accounting practices in FRS 102 are applicable to the FRSSE (effective January 2015) and hence the original intention was to make future amendments to the FRSSE to align it more with FRS 102; however, the tentative plans by the FRC to withdraw the FRSSE in its entirety will mean no further changes to the FRSSE will be made.

There are some notable differences between the FRSSE and FRS 102, which are discussed below.

Investment properties

In FRS 102, Section 18 *Intangible Assets other than Goodwill* deals with all intangible assets, whilst Section 19 *Business Combinations and Goodwill* deals with goodwill. Paragraphs 6.11 to 6.17 in the FRSSE (effective January 2015) deals with other intangible assets and goodwill.

FRS 102 says that all intangible assets will have a finite useful life and there is a default period of amortisation for both goodwill and intangible assets of five years where management of a company cannot reliably estimate the useful economic life.

The FRSSE (effective January 2015) at paragraph 6.13 also considers capitalised goodwill and intangible assets to have a finite useful life and requires such assets to be written off to profit or loss on a straight-line (or more appropriate) basis over their useful economic lives. Paragraph 6.13 does follow the same stance as FRS 102 in that this useful economic life will be presumed not to exceed five years where an entity is unable to make a reliable estimate of the useful life of goodwill or intangible assets. However, paragraph 6.15 does say that useful economic lives shall be reviewed at the end of each reporting period and revised if necessary, subject to the constraint that the revised life shall not exceed 20 years from the date of acquisition.

Also it is worth pointing out that in the FRSSE (effective January 2015), the period chosen for amortising goodwill (together with the reasons for choosing that period) must be disclosed by way of a note to the financial statements.

Deferred tax

FRS 102 introduces a timing difference plus approach to the calculation of deferred tax balances, which aligns the concept of deferred tax more to an international outcome (i.e. IAS 12 *Income Taxes*). In addition, FRS 102 at Section 29 *Income Tax* requires the calculation of deferred tax on non-monetary assets that are subjected to the revaluation model (for example, investment properties). The FRSSE (effective January 2015) continues with the same principles as previous UK GAAP in that deferred tax is NOT recognised on:

- Revaluation gains and losses unless, by the balance sheet date, the entity has entered into a binding agreement to sell the asset and has revalued the asset to the selling price or
- Taxable gains arising on revaluations or sales if it is more likely than not that the gain will be rolled over into a replacement asset.

FRS 102 places a prohibition on entities discounting deferred tax balances to present day values. The reality is that, in practice, hardly any entity discounts such balances to take account of the time value of money. However, the FRSSE (effective January 2015) acknowledges that whilst the discounting of deferred tax balances is not required, where an entity does discount deferred tax balances, then all deferred tax balances that have been measured by reference to undiscounted cash flows and for which the impact of discounting is material should also be discounted.

Revenue recognition

FRS 102 at Section 23 *Revenue* is slightly more relaxed in its wording in that revenue is recognised at the fair value of the consideration 'received or receivable'. Under the FRSSE (effective January 2015), the wording continues from the previous

Application Note G to FRS 5 *Reporting the Substance of Transactions* (also known as 'UITF 40') in that a seller recognises revenue when, and to the extent that, it obtains the 'right to consideration' in exchange for its performance.

Leases

Section C *Definitions* to the FRSSE (effective January 2015) defines a finance lease. Within this definition is a presumption that the risks and rewards of ownership of the leased asset are transferred to the lessee if, at the inception of a lease, the present value of the minimum lease payments, including any initial payment, amounts to substantially all (normally 90% or more) of the fair value of the leased asset. Hence, reference is made to a 90% benchmark in the FRSSE (effective January 2015) which was the case in the previous UK GAAP at SSAP 21 *Accounting for Leases and Hire Purchase Contracts* in the Guidance Notes.

There is no reference to a 90% benchmark in FRS 102 and this is where more judgement will be needed on the part of the accountant. FRS 102 instead refers to 'substantially all' of the fair value of the leased asset, but does give some useful examples of indicators that a lease falls to be classified as a finance lease.

Short-term employee benefits

Section 28 to FRS 102 *Employee Benefits* requires an accrual to be made for short-term employee benefits that have been accrued, but not paid, by the reporting date (for example, unpaid holiday entitlement). There is no specific requirement to make such accruals under the FRSSE (effective January 2015).

Related parties

FRS 102 at Section 33 *Related Party Disclosures* (specifically paragraph 33.9) does not explicitly require the names of related parties to be disclosed (only the nature of the related party relationship, outstanding balances and commitments necessary for an understanding of the effect on the financial statements). In addition, Section 33 requires the following to be disclosed:

- The amount of the transactions,
- The amount of outstanding balances and
  - Their terms and conditions, including whether they are secured and the nature of the consideration to be provided in settlement,
  - Details of any guarantees given or received,
  - Provisions for uncollectible receivables related to the amount of outstanding balances and
  - The expense recognised during the period in respect of bad or doubtful debts due from related parties.

The FRSSE (effective January 2015) does require the names of the transacting relating parties at paragraph 15.1(c) (i).

It is also worth pointing out that paragraph 33.7 of FRS 102 requires key management personnel compensation to be disclosed in total.

Grants

Under FRS 102 at Section 24 *Government Grants*, there is a new 'performance model' in addition to the existing 'accrual model' that has been introduced. Under the performance model there are certain conditions relating to the recognition of a grant and which says that:

- A grant that imposes specific performance conditions is recognised in income when the performance conditions are met.
- Where a grant does not specify performance conditions, it is recognised in income when the proceeds are received or receivable.
- Grants that are received before the recognition criteria are satisfied are recognised as a liability.

The FRSSE (effective January 2015) does not include the performance model. Grants are recognised in profit and loss so as to match them with the expenditure to which they are intended to contribute. However, a grant will not be recognised in income under the FRSSE (effective January 2015) until the conditions for its receipt have been complied with and there is reasonable assurance that the grant will be received.

New introductions to the FRSSE (effective January 2015)

Whilst there are still some existing practices that remain in the FRSSE (effective January 2015) such as fair value changes in investment property going through a revaluation reserve, the FRSSE (effective January 2015) contains references to *The Financial Reporting Standard applicable in the UK and Republic of Ireland* and removes references to FRSs/SSAPs and UITF Abstracts.

Where the FRSSE (effective January 2015) does not deal with an accounting policy for a new transaction or event, it states that entities should have regard to FRS 102, not as a mandatory document, but as a means of establishing current practice.

The Financial Reporting Council has also removed reference to standards that apply to consolidated financial statements on the grounds that the general requirements in the FRSSE (effective January 2015), which relate to the development of accounting policies for transactions or events that are not covered in the FRSSE (effective January 2015), apply equally to consolidated financial statements.

As well as introducing the five-year presumed useful life for goodwill or intangible assets, the FRSSE (effective January 2015) also requires reporting entities to carry out an assessment (at each reporting date) of whether there is any indication that an asset is carried in the balance sheet (statement of financial position) at more than the recoverable amount and, where such an indication exists, the recoverable amount will be estimated and the asset written down to that recoverable amount. This is to essentially prevent reporting entities from carrying assets in the balance sheet at inflated values and the paragraphs that users of the FRSSE (effective January 2015) should comply with are at 6.45A to 6.45C.

CONSEQUENTIAL AMENDMENTS TO THE FRSSE (EFFECTIVE APRIL 2008) DUE TO FRS 102

Due to the introduction of FRS 102, the FRSSE (effective April 2008) saw some consequential amendments that resulted in the issuance of the FRSSE (effective January 2015). These amendments are noted as follows.

Status of the FRSSE

- The Status of the FRSSE has been changed to become the FRSSE (effective January 2015) and paragraph 1 has also been changed to remove inapplicable text.
- Paragraph 2 has been changed to include reference to FRS 100 *Application of Financial Reporting Requirements* and also to remove reference to the previous UK GAAP.
- Paragraph 4 has been changed to refer to the new UK GAAP and acknowledges the consequential amendments to the FRSSE, where it previously referred to standards or Abstracts that are now withdrawn.
- Paragraph 5 is amended in respect of transactions and events that are not covered by the FRSSE. In the previous UK GAAP, if a transaction or event was not covered by the FRSSE, the accountant would default back to mainstream GAAP or an alternative financial reporting framework (for example, IFRS) to decipher the appropriate accounting treatment. Paragraph 5 is amended so that entities must first have regard to their own existing accounting policies and then go back to FRS 102 to develop a new accounting policy (but not as a mandatory document).
- Public benefit entities are now referred to in paragraph 5A.
- Paragraph 6 was amended requiring entities that are not eligible to apply the FRSSE to report under EU-adopted IFRS, apply FRS 101 in the individual financial statements of qualifying entities or apply FRS 102 in accordance with the requirements of FRS 100.
- Paragraph 11 is amended to remove reference to the first issuance of the FRSSE in November 1997.

Main body of the FRSSE

- The footnote to paragraph 2.6 is amended to include provisions 'applicable' rather than 'relating' to small companies.
- Capitalised goodwill and intangible assets having a finite useful life are amended so that the useful economic life is now five, rather than 20, years.
- Paragraph 6.45 is amended to remove the suggestion of obsolescence or fall in demand for a product.
- Paragraph 6.45 is removed as there is now paragraph 6.45A, which specifically requires an entity applying the FRSSE (effective January 2015) to undertake an assessment of whether there is any indication of asset impairment and, when there is, to write down the asset to its recoverable amount. Paragraphs 6.45B and 6.45C also deal with asset impairment issues.

- Paragraph 15.7 is amended so as to include paragraph (d), which says that related party transactions entered into between two or more members of a group, provided that any subsidiary that is a party to the transaction is wholly owned by such a member, does not require disclosure as a related party transaction.

Changes to Part C *Definitions*

- The definition of *close family* is amended and now includes the person's children, spouse or domestic partner, children of that person's spouse or domestic partner and dependents of that person or that person's spouse or domestic partner.
- The definition of *key management personnel* is now included.
- The definition of *public benefit entities* is inserted.
- The definition of a related party is replaced as follows:

  A related party is a person or entity that is related to the entity that is preparing its financial statements (in this Standard referred to as the 'reporting entity').

  (a) A person or a close member of that person's family is related to a reporting entity if that person:
    i. Has control or joint control over the reporting entity,
    ii. Has significant influence over the reporting entity or
  (b) *Is a member of the key **management personnel** of the reporting entity or of a parent of the reporting entity. An entity is related to a reporting entity if any of the following conditions applies:*
    i. The entity and the reporting entity are members of the same group (which means that each parent, subsidiary and fellow subsidiary is related to the others).
    ii. One entity is an associate or joint venture of the other entity (or an associate or joint venture of a member of a group of which the other entity is a member).
    iii. Both entities are joint ventures of the same entity.
    iv. One entity is a joint venture of a third entity and the other entity is an associate of the third entity.
    v. The entity is a retirement benefit scheme for the benefit of employees of either the reporting entity or an entity relating to the reporting entity. If the reporting entity itself is such a scheme, the sponsoring employers are also related to the reporting entity.
    vi. The entity is controlled or jointly controlled by a person identified in (a).
    vii. A person identified in (a) (i) has significant influence over the entity or is a member of the key management personnel of the entity (or of a parent of the entity).

- The final sentence in paragraph 35 to Appendix IV *Development of the FRSSE* has been deleted, which referred to Appendix V. Appendix V to the FRSSE (effective April 2008) has also been deleted.

- Paragraphs 38 and 39 to Appendix IV have been renumbered paragraphs 41 and 42, which refer to the relationship of the FRSSE with other documents issued by the Financial Reporting Council (FRC). New paragraphs 38, 39 and 40 have been included, which make reference to the new UK GAAP and consequential amendments to the FRSSE (effective April 2008).
- Paragraphs 41 and 42 have been changed to remove reference to the old UK GAAP and replace the word 'Board' with 'FRC'.
- Paragraph 42 has been amended to make reference to FRS 102 and remove reference to 'auditors', 'the board' and citation of an example of marking to market fixed interest instruments.

MICRO-ENTITIES

The issues relating a company that falls to be classed as a 'micro-entity' is also examined in Chapter 1.

On 1 December 2013, legislation was introduced in the form of SI 2013/3008 *The Small Companies (Micro-Entities Accounts) Regulations 2013*, which was brought in by the European Union with the objective of reducing costs for small and medium-size companies. The legislation is effective for financial years ending on or after 30 September 2013 and where the company's financial statements are filed with the Registrar of Companies on or after 1 December 2013.

Whilst the micro-entities legislation does reduce the disclosure requirements for very small companies, the option to adopt the micro-entities regime may not be the right choice for small entities. For example, creditors or lenders may require more information to be included within the financial statements and also, in the light of the new EU Accounting Directive, disclosures under the small companies regime will also experience reduction.

Although micro-entity accounts are simpler there is less flexibility; for example, micro-entities cannot alter headings in their financial statements because line items must follow the formats in the legislation.

Eligibility

The definition of a micro-entity is contained in sections 384A and 384B of the Companies Act 2006 and the qualifying conditions are met by an entity in a year where it does not exceed two, or more, of the following criteria:

- Turnover £632,000
- Balance sheet total £316,000
- Number of employees 10

Example – Short accounting period

A company with a year-end date of 31 December 2013 has been trading since 1 April 2013 (i.e. a nine-month accounting period). Are there any additional considerations that the company must take into account if the accounting period is less than one year?

Yes. Where an accounting period is not one year, the turnover figure must be adjusted proportionately. In this case the company will use 9/12 × £632,000 to determine whether the entity qualifies as a micro-entity.

Example – Group member

A company is the parent of a group of companies and is trying to establish if it qualifies as a micro-entity under the regime.

For companies that are parent companies, the company will qualify as a micro-entity in the financial year only if:

- The company qualifies as a micro-entity individually in that year,
- The group headed up by the company qualifies as a small group (as defined in the Companies Act 2006 section 383(2) to (7)) and
- The company has not voluntarily elected to prepare consolidated accounts.

The important point to emphasise where groups are concerned is that care must be taken in assessing whether each company within the group qualifies as a micro-entity. The exemptions available under the micro-entities regime will NOT be available for subsidiary companies that are included in consolidated financial statements for the year.

Exclusions

Although it is called the 'micro-entities regime', it in fact only applies to companies. In addition, the micro-entities regime is not applicable to:

- Investment undertakings,
- Financial holding undertakings,
- Credit institutions,
- Insurance undertakings,
- Charities,
- Limited Liability Partnerships and
- Companies in Ireland (although at the time of writing a consultation had been opened in the Republic of Ireland regarding the micro-entities legislation).

Compliance with the true and fair concept

Financial statements prepared under the Companies Act must give a true and fair view and this concept has been enshrined in legislation for many years. Micro-entities will only be required to disclose minimal amounts of information at the foot of the balance sheet and additional disclosures will not be required; thus the accounts are presumed to give a true and fair view as per the legislation applied to micro-entities (these are often referred to as the 'deeming provisions'). The amounts in the financial statements themselves will continue to be prepared under GAAP – it is only the additional disclosures that will not be required, so recognition and measurement issues will continue as normal.

Accounting issues for micro-entities

The recognition and measurement principles in the micro-entities legislation will remain largely unchanged, but the legislation essentially:

- Withdraws the use of the revaluation model for tangible fixed assets.
- Withdraws the choice to measure fixed asset investments at market value.
- Requires micro-entities to account for investment properties under normal fixed asset rules (i.e. at cost less depreciation and impairment) and not under the alternative accounting rules.

The legislation does not recognise any of the alternative accounting rules and hence a micro-entity cannot use the revaluation model for its fixed assets; nor can a micro-entity use a previous revaluation as deemed cost when applying the micro-entities legislation for the first time.

Financial Reporting Standard for Micro-Entities

At the time of writing, the FRC had issued proposals to introduce a separate standard for micro-entities, being the *Financial Reporting Standard for Micro-Entities* (FRSME).

The proposed FRSME is going to be based on the recognition and measurement requirements of FRS 102 with further simplifications. As a consequence, regardless of whether small companies apply the FRSME or the simplified FRS 102 regime, they will apply accounting treatments that are consistent with the new UK GAAP (i.e. full FRS 102).

The FRC have acknowledged that the consistency within accounting treatments will result in a reduction in the number of accounting changes necessary as entities grow.

The micro-entities regime is optional and a company that would otherwise qualify to apply the FRSME could choose not to and apply the simplified FRS 102 (if the changes being consulted upon go ahead), full FRS 102 or EU-endorsed IFRS (although it is expected to be relatively rare for a micro-entity to choose full FRS 102 or EU-endorsed IFRS to prepare its financial statements). Companies in the Republic of Ireland cannot use the micro-entities regime because no legislation currently exists, but this has been consulted on as part of the DJEI Consultation Document.

The FRSME will be developed from FRS 102 and will be adapted so as to reflect the requirements of the micro-entities legislation but with further simplifications as follows:

- Presentation and disclosure requirements as set out in legislation.
- FRS 102-specific recognition and measurement requirements except for:
  - Financial instruments, which will only be measured at amortised or historical cost,
  - No requirement to account for deferred tax,
  - No requirement to account for equity-settled share-based payments prior to the issue of shares,
  - Simplified accounting for post-employment benefits, where a micro-entity will be able to account for a defined benefit pension plan as a defined contribution plan,
  - Withdrawal of the option to capitalise borrowing costs and

- No requirement to apply sections of FRS 102 that will not generally apply to micro-entities (e.g. Section 19 Business Combinations and Goodwill, Section 31 Hyperinflation and most of Section 34 Specialised Activities (although the subsection Agriculture will be retained)).

If a micro-entity has derivative financial instruments, the FRSME will not allow these to be accounted for at fair value or require disclosure of the existence and nature of such instruments because the legislation prohibits this (the micro-entities regime does not recognise any provisions of the alternative accounting rules). However, the FRC have mentioned that the FRSME will clarify when a derivative instrument becomes onerous and hence the obligation will be recognised at present value.

A sample set of illustrative financial statements prepared under the micro-entities regime are shown below.

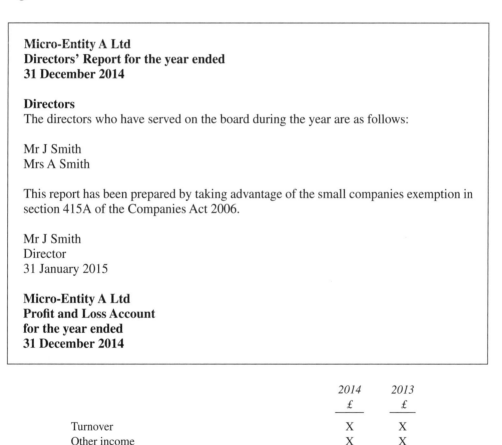

Micro-Entity A Ltd
Directors' Report for the year ended
31 December 2014

Directors
The directors who have served on the board during the year are as follows:

Mr J Smith
Mrs A Smith

This report has been prepared by taking advantage of the small companies exemption in section 415A of the Companies Act 2006.

Mr J Smith
Director
31 January 2015

Micro-Entity A Ltd
Profit and Loss Account
for the year ended
31 December 2014

	2014 £	2013 £
Turnover	X	X
Other income	X	X
Cost of raw materials and consumables	(X)	(X)
Staff costs	(X)	(X)
Depreciation and other amounts written off assets	(X)	(X)
Other charges	(X)	(X)
Tax	(X)	(X)
Profit	X	X

Micro-Entity A Ltd
Balance Sheet
as at 31 December 2014

	2014		2013	
	£	£	£	£
Called up share capital not paid		X		X
Fixed assets		X		X
Current assets	X		X	
Prepayments and accrued income	X		X	
Creditors: amounts falling due within one year	(X)		(X)	
Net current assets (liabilities)		X		X
Total assets less current liabilities		X		X
Creditors: amounts falling due after more than one year		(X)		(X)
Provisions for liabilities		(X)		(X)
Accruals and deferred income		(X)		(X)
Net assets		X		X
Capital and reserves		X		X

Notes to the financial statements

1. Directors' benefits: advances, credits and guarantees

During the year the company made an advance of £X to a director of the company in respect of a personal loan. This amount was fully repaid by the year-end.

2. Guarantees and other financial commitments

The company is currently defending itself in a legal claim brought against it by one of its suppliers who are claiming damages for breach of contract amounting to £X. No provision has been made in the financial statements for this amount on the grounds that the legal advisers are uncertain as to whether the company will be successful in its defence.

The company had capital commitments contracted, but not provided for, amounting to £X.

The company is entitled to exemption from audit under Section 477 of the Companies Act 2006 for the year ended 31 December 2014. The members have not required the company to obtain an audit of its financial statements for the year ended 31 December 2014 in accordance with section 476 of the Companies Act 2006.

The directors acknowledge their responsibilities for:

(a) Ensuring that the company keeps accounting records that comply with the Companies Act 2006 and

(b) Preparing financial statements that give a true and fair view of the state of the affairs of the company as at the end of each financial year and of its profit or loss for each financial year in accordance with the requirements of the micro-entity provisions.

Filing requirements for micro-entities

The concept of abbreviated financial statements does not apply to micro-entities and therefore a micro-entity can file the 'full' micro-entity accounts with the Registrar of Companies. Alternatively, the micro-entity can simply file the balance sheet with the associated notes at the bottom of the balance sheet (i.e. no filing of the directors' report or profit and loss account).

CHANGES TO THE SMALL COMPANIES REGIME

On 29 August 2014, the Department for Business Innovation and Skills (BIS) announced details of how it intends to transpose the new EU Accounting Directive into UK law. BIS has until 20 July 2015 to enact the Accounting Directive, with the intention of the new regime taking effect for financial years beginning on or after 1 January 2016. This consultation in turn resulted in the Financial Reporting Council (FRC) issuing a consultation document for a new *Financial Reporting Standard for Micro-Entities* (FRSME) in place of the FRSSE and providing a reporting template that will be able to accommodate some of the EU reforms.

The EU Directive is going to replace the 4th and 7th Accounting Directives and establish minimum legal requirements for financial statements in the EU as well as providing 100 Member State options. These options will enable approximately 11,000 additional companies to use the 'lighter touch' financial reporting framework, which is available under the small companies accounting regime.

The main objectives of the new Accounting Directive are to:

- Simplify accounting requirements to reduce the administrative burden on companies – particularly smaller companies.
- Increase the clarity and comparability of financial statements. This should reduce the cost of capital and increase the level of cross-border trade and merger and acquisition activity.
- Protect essential user needs by retaining necessary accounting information for users.

In order to achieve these objectives, the Directive:

- Introduces a 'building block' approach to the statutory accounts where disclosure levels increase depending on the size of the undertaking.
- Reduces the number of options available to the preparers in respect of recognition, measurement and presentation.
- Creates a largely harmonised small company regime and, for the first time, limits the amount of information that Member States can demand from small undertakings in their financial statements.

The most notable changes relate to the size criteria for companies. The proposals only increase the size criteria for accounting purposes; they do not have any effect on the limits for audit exemption as the BIS will consider audit exemption proposals separately at a later date. Readers are advised to keep abreast of developments by regularly reviewing the BIS website.

The Directive sets out mandatory thresholds for micro (see later section on 'Micro-Entities'), small, medium and large companies based on:

- The average number of employees,
- Balance sheet total/gross assets (fixed + current assets) and
- Net turnover at the reporting date.

A micro or a medium company comes under the relevant size if it does not exceed the limits of at least two out of the three criteria. Large undertakings (or groups) are those that on their reporting date exceed at least two of the three criteria for medium-sized undertakings (or groups).

At the time of writing, the proposed regime was as follows.

	Balance sheet £	Net turnover £	Average no. of employees
For individual company accounts			
Micro-entity	≤316,000	≤632,000	≤10
Medium-sized company	≤18,000,000	≤36,000,000	≤250
Large company	≥18,000,000	≥36,000,000	≥250
For group/consolidated accounts			
Medium-sized group	≤18,000,000 net	≤36,000,000 net	≤250
	≤21,600,000 gross	≤43,200,000 gross	
Large group	≥18,000,000 net	≥36,000,000 net	≥250
	≥21,600,000 gross	≥43,200,000 gross	

The Directive also sets out a mandatory minimum threshold for small companies and a company will qualify as small if it does not exceed the limits of at least two of the three criteria. There is an added concession for small companies only in the Directive, which allows Member States to increase the balance sheet total and net turnover values by up to 50% so as to allow more companies to access the less burdensome small companies regime if they so wish.

The table below outlines the minimum and maximum thresholds permitted under the proposed small companies regime.

	Balance sheet £	Net turnover £	Average no. of employees
For individual company accounts			
Small company (using minimum mandatory threshold values)	≤3,500,000	≤7,000,000	≤50
Small company (using maximum threshold values permitted)	≤5,100,000	≤10,200,000	≤50

For group/consolidated accounts

Small group (using minimum mandatory threshold values)	≤3,500,000 net	≤7,000,000 net	
	≤4,200,000 gross	≤8,400,000 gross	≤50
Small group (using maximum threshold values permitted)	≤5,100,000 net	≤10,200,000 net	
	≤6,100,000 gross	≤12,200,000 gross	≤50

The proposals acknowledge that if BIS were to adopt the minimum thresholds that define a small company, this would only offer a small increase of around 7% over the current thresholds and hence just 1,000 medium-sized companies would then fall into the small companies regime. BIS therefore proposes to adopt the *maximum small company thresholds* so as to allow an additional 11,000 companies access to the small companies regime.

The Directive adopts a 'think small first' approach and it has created a small companies regime that allows qualifying companies to prepare income statements (profit and loss accounts), statements of financial position (balance sheets) and notes to the accounts, which are proportionate to their size and achieve the information needs of users whilst at the same time imposing a largely harmonised small company regime.

In the light of the 'think small first' approach, the Directive restricts Member States' ability to require statutory disclosures from small companies within national reporting regimes and so in the UK this restriction extends to the accounting standards, which are published by the Financial Reporting Council taken alongside the provisions of the Companies Act 2006 and Regulations. Notwithstanding these restrictions, the company would still be under a duty to consider if the financial statements give a true and fair view and therefore directors of reporting entities may need to provide additional notes in order to achieve a true and fair view where the mandatory notes are considered insufficient for this purpose. This was a concern of the FRC who viewed this requirement as being somewhat burdensome for directors of small companies.

The Directive permits that Member States may only require small companies to provide the following 13 disclosure notes:

- Accounting policies adopted
- Fixed assets revaluation table
- Fair valuation note
- Financial commitments, guarantees or contingencies not included in the balance sheet
- The amount of advances and credits granted to members of the administrative managerial and supervisory bodies (with supporting information)
- Exceptional items
- Amounts due or payable after more than five years and entire debts covered by valuable security
- Average number of employees during the financial year

- Fixed asset note (in addition to the mandatory revaluation table)
- Name and registered office of the undertaking drawing up the consolidated financial statements of the smallest body of undertakings of which the undertaking forms part
- Nature and business purpose of arrangements not included in the balance sheet
- Nature and effect of post balance sheet events
- (Limited) related party transactions.

In relation to the above, Member States need not include five of the above notes as mandatory disclosures, which are the:

- Fixed asset note (in addition to the mandatory revaluation table)
- Name and registered office of the undertaking drawing up the consolidated financial statements of the smallest body of undertakings of which the undertaking forms part
- Nature and business purpose of arrangements not included in the balance sheet
- Nature and effect of post balance sheet events
- (Limited) related party transactions

BIS considers that provision of all 13 notes to be important for a proper understanding of the company's accounts and are not viewed by BIS as being overly burdensome for companies and hence it is proposed that all 13 notes should continue to be disclosed in the notes by small companies. As mentioned above, a company would still be required to provide additional notes should it be necessary for the financial statements to give a true and fair view.

In respect of abbreviated financial statements, BIS proposes to take up the option and allow eligible small companies to prepare and publish abbreviated accounts if they wish. The Directive provides an option for small companies to prepare both an abbreviated balance sheet and an abbreviated profit and loss account and this option has previously not been taken up in the UK (small companies generally only publish an abbreviated balance sheet if they so wish) and so BIS sought views on whether small companies should have the choice of preparing an abbreviated balance sheet and profit and loss account if they wish.

The consultation paper outlines many more changes and proposals for the small companies regime, including:

- Reducing the number of Formats for the profit and loss account from four to two.
- A potential for greater flexibility within layouts of profit and loss accounts and balance sheets.
- Accounting for participating interests using the equity method (rather than cost-based and fair value methods).
- Changes to the maximum period over which goodwill and development costs can be written off. The proposals require that the period must not be shorter than five years and must not exceed ten years. This will only apply where the useful life cannot be reliably estimated.

- Information on subsidiaries included within consolidated accounts. The UK currently permits companies to provide this information when submitting the Annual Return to Companies House and this option is proposed to be withdrawn; hence the consolidated accounts would provide information relating to subsidiaries and BIS considers the Annual Return option as diluting the meaningfulness of the consolidated accounts.
- Removing the requirement for micro-entities to prepare a directors' report, although the proposals do include a requirement that the note on any acquisition of a micro-entity's own shares appears as a footnote to the abbreviated balance sheet.

As mentioned earlier in the chapter, readers are encouraged to keep abreast of developments in this area so that clients and directors of companies can be advised appropriately and the financial statements are prepared correctly.

Proposed changes to the accounting of small companies

Given the above proposals issued by BIS, the FRC have had to issue proposals in respect of the accounting requirements for small companies.

On 29 August 2014, the FRC outlined their proposed framework as follows:

(a) Micro-entities will apply the Financial Reporting Standard for Micro-Entities (FRSME).

(b) Small entities that are not micro-entities will apply FRS 102 *The Financial Reporting Standard applicable in the UK and Republic of Ireland*. The FRC are proposing to insert a new section in FRS 102 (Section 1A *Small Entities*), which will outline the presentation and disclosure requirements that will apply to small companies and will be based on the new legal provisions. In all other respects FRS 102 will remain unchanged.

(c) Entities that apply EU-endorsed IFRS in the preparation of their financial statements will continue to do so.

(d) Qualifying entities will continue to have the option to prepare financial statements in accordance with the provisions in FRS 101 *Reduced Disclosure Framework*.

(e) An entity can still have the option to apply a more comprehensive accounting standard if they so wish. For example, a micro-entity could choose between the new FRSME, FRS 102 applying the small companies regime, full FRS 102 or EU-endorsed IFRS.

The FRSSE is proposed to be withdrawn with small companies being brought under the scope of FRS 102 (as in (b) above).

The proposals are anticipated to take effect for accounting periods commencing on or after 1 January 2016. The FRC comment period on the consultation was open until 30 November 2014; the FRC then plan to issue Exposure Drafts following the consultation period, outlining their revised framework with final standards expected to be issued in the summer of 2015.

5 SUMMARY OF THE KEY DIFFERENCES BETWEEN FRS 102 AND 'OLD' UK GAAP

INTRODUCTION

UK GAAP has been in existence for many years and financial reporting has evolved considerably over those years. The prevalence of International Financial Reporting Standards (IFRS) has gathered faster pace with many jurisdictions seeing the benefits of uniform financial reporting and hence the adoption of IFRS. In the UK and Republic of Ireland, it had been the intention by the (now defunct) Accounting Standards Board (now the Accounting Council of the Financial Reporting Council) that the UK and Republic of Ireland would adopt the use of an international-based financial reporting framework. This transition started in 2005 when all listed entities in the UK were mandated to apply EU-endorsed IFRS to their financial statements, closely followed in 2007 by those companies listed on the Alternative Investment Market. The decision to introduce an international-based framework in the UK was based on the fact that IFRS itself was becoming more widespread and the promotion of uniform accounting policies to give companies access to wider capital markets as well as improving consistency in the way entities report financial information has moved up the ranks considerably over the last decade.

In March 2013, the Financial Reporting Council (FRC) issued FRS 102 *The Financial Reporting Standard applicable in the UK and Republic of Ireland*. FRS 102 applies to unlisted entities and the publication of this FRS marked the end of a lengthy period of uncertainty within the accountancy profession as to the direction that UK GAAP was to take. FRS 102 was re-published in August 2014 to take account of changes to the financial instruments sections of the standard.

Based on the International Accounting Standards Board's *IFRS for SMEs*, FRS 102 brings about a simplified reporting regime for entities that will fall under its scope as well as introducing more up-to-date and relevant accounting requirements, which had fallen behind in the old UK GAAP. The Accounting Standards Board acknowledged some years ago that old UK GAAP had become far too complex and preparers of financial statements in the UK often complained about the onerous requirements imposed on them and their clients due to the voluminous nature of the old UK GAAP.

FRS 102 (August 2014) is 360 pages long (including the Appendices) in contrast to the old UK GAAP, which was in excess of 3,000 pages long, and this reduction in volume was hugely welcomed in the UK and Republic of Ireland. Roger Marshall, an FRC board member and Chairman of its Accounting Council, said that FRS 102 *'modernises and simplifies financial reporting for unlisted companies and subsidiaries of listed companies as well as public benefit entities such as charities'*.

FRS 102 is largely a set of 35 stand-alone chapters. However, the FRC have included some cross-referencing for EU-endorsed IFRS to be consulted (for example, with regards to financial instruments).

The standard becomes mandatory for accounting periods commencing on or after 1 January 2015, although earlier adoption is permissible. In reality it is unlikely that the take-up for early adoption will be significant.

A point worth emphasising is that rules in FRS 102 are retrospective and hence the comparative year must be restated to conform to the requirements of FRS 102. Therefore, assuming a 31 December 2015 year-end, it is the balance sheet as at 31 December 2013 that will form the backdrop for the new FRS 102 financial statements. This is because the *date of transition* is the *start date of the earliest period reported in the financial statements*.

FRS 102 was originally exposed as FRED 48 and brought with it some welcome changes that were not previously incorporated into the previous Exposure Draft (for example, the option to capitalise borrowing costs as part of the cost of a self-constructed asset). It also removed the concept of 'public accountability', which is contained within *IFRS for SMEs* and (if mandated in the UK and Republic of Ireland) would have resulted in some entities having to apply EU-endorsed IFRS, which would have been wholly inappropriate given the vast disclosure requirements contained in full EU-endorsed IFRS that would have applied to, for example, small pension schemes. It was difficult to define the concept of 'public accountability' in the eyes of legislation and so this concept was dropped in FRS 102.

As the UK standard-setters had always foreseen that the UK and Republic of Ireland would eventually report under an international-based financial reporting framework, they did, wherever possible, try to align old UK GAAP to its international counterpart. However, with a new financial reporting regime comes some new accounting practices and methodologies and FRS 102 does bring about some notable changes to old UK GAAP, which are covered in the next sections. FRS 102 also introduces terminology that is found in international GAAP and that differs from the terminology used in the Companies Act 2006. The following table outlines the differences in this terminology.

Company law terminology	*FRS 102 terminology*
Accounting reference date	Reporting date
Accounts	Financial statements
Associated undertaking	Associate
Balance sheet	Statement of financial position
Capital and reserves	Equity
Cash at bank and in hand	Cash
Debtors	Trade receivables
Diminution in value [of assets]	Impairment
Financial year	Reporting period
Group [accounts]	Consolidated [financial statements]
IAS	EU-adopted IFRS
Individual [accounts]	Individual [financial statements]
Interest payable and similar charges	Finance costs
Interest receivable and similar income	Finance income/investment income
Minority interests	Non-controlling interest
Net realisable value [of any current asset]	Estimated selling price less costs to complete and sell
Parent undertaking	Parent
Profit and loss account	Income statement (under the two-statement approach)
	Part of the statement of comprehensive income (under the single-statement approach)
Related undertakings	Subsidiaries, associates and joint ventures
Stocks	Inventories
Subsidiary undertaking	Subsidiary
Tangible assets	Includes: property, plant and equipment; investment property
Trade creditors	Trade payables

ACCOUNTING POLICIES AND ERRORS

Accounting policies and errors are dealt with in Section 10 *Accounting Policies, Estimates and Errors*. Paragraph 10.4 of FRS 102 tells financial statement preparers that if FRS 102 does not specifically address a transaction, or other event or condition, an entity's management must develop and apply an accounting policy, which is:

- **Relevant** – information is relevant to aid the decision-making process of users.
- **Reliable** – will result in the financial statements faithfully representing the financial position, performance and cash flows. In addition, the policy must also reflect the economic substance of the transaction(s)/event(s)/condition(s) rather than reflecting the legal form. To achieve reliability the policy adopted must be neutral, prudent and complete in all material respects.

FRS 18 *Accounting Policies* was very similar, but in some cases the end result and impact on profit or loss would not necessarily be the same.

Under the previous GAAP, FRS 3 *Reporting Financial Performance* required the correction of 'fundamental' errors by way of a prior-year adjustment. The term 'fundamental error' was described in FRS 3 as an error that essentially destroys the truth and fairness of the financial statements. Section 10 requires an error to be corrected by way of a prior-year adjustment if it is 'material' and therefore it is likely that there will be more errors corrected by way of a prior-year adjustment under FRS 102 than was the case under the old UK standards.

STATEMENT OF CASH FLOWS (CASH FLOW STATEMENT)

The statement of cash flows is a mandatory statement under FRS 102 and there are no situations exempting companies under the scope of FRS 102 from preparing such a statement, although small companies are exempt from preparing a cash flow statement and a company applying FRS 101 *Reduced Disclosure Framework* is also exempt from preparing such a statement, provided the cash flow statement is included in the consolidated financial statements prepared by the parent.

FRS 1 *Cash Flow Statements* required a cash flow statement to be prepared using the following standard cash flow classifications:

- Operating activities
- Dividends from joint ventures and associates
- Returns on investments and servicing of finance
- Taxation
- Capital expenditure and financial investments
- Acquisitions and disposals
- Equity dividends paid
- Management of liquid resources
- Financing

Section 7 *Statement of Cash Flows* of FRS 102 requires the statement of cash flows to be prepared using three types of cash flow classification – those arising from:

- Operating activities,
- Investing activities and
- Financing activities.

Operating activities are the day-to-day revenue-producing activities that are not investing or financing activities. This category is essentially a 'default' category, encompassing all cash flows that do not fall within investing or financing classifications.

Investing activities are those activities that involve the acquisition and disposal of long-term assets, for example monies used for the purchase of fixed assets and cash receipts from the disposal of fixed assets.

Financing activities are those activities that change the equity and borrowing composition of the company. For example, if a client issues shares in the year to raise cash, the proceeds from the issue would be a financing activity. Similarly, where an entity raises a loan, such proceeds would be classified as a financing activity.

FRS 102 is going to require a lot more reclassifications of cash flows due to the reduced number of cash flow classifications. For example, corporation tax paid would have appeared under the 'Taxation' heading under FRS 1. Taxation is now incorporated within operating activities and only included within investing or financing activities if any of the corporation tax paid can be specifically attributed to investing or financing activities.

CONSOLIDATED FINANCIAL STATEMENTS

Consolidated (and separate) financial statements are dealt with in Section 9 *Consolidated and Separate Financial Statements*. There are not many significant changes between Section 9 and FRS 2 *Accounting for Subsidiary Undertakings*. However, FRS 102 does allow an accounting policy choice for subsidiaries that are held for resale and these can be measured at cost less impairment or at fair value. These elements of the investment portfolio must be excluded and measured at fair value, which will result in more subsidiaries being excluded.

There is no impact on profit or loss where there is a change in non-controlling (minority) interests but the parent still retains control of the subsidiary. Such transactions are accounted for as a transaction with equity holders. Although the changes are not likely to impact a large range of business – where they do have an impact there are some important differences that entities need to take on board.

The definition of a subsidiary is slightly different from previous UK GAAP but any practical impact is likely to be unusual.

DEFERRED TAXATION

Deferred tax is dealt with in Section 29 *Income Tax* of FRS 102 and this Section requires deferred tax to be recognised in respect of all timing differences at the end of the accounting period. This is a similar concept to the previous FRS 19 *Deferred Tax*. However, FRS 102 uses a timing difference 'plus' approach for deferred tax, which will result in larger deferred tax balances being recognised because Section 29 brings in three additional situations that will trigger deferred tax considerations:

1. Revaluations including investment property (this includes *all* revaluations rather than only when there is an agreement to sell the revalued asset).
2. Fair values on business combinations (which result in adjustment to the goodwill recognised).
3. Unremitted earnings on overseas subsidiaries or associates (rather than only to the extent that the distribution has been agreed).

FRS 102 also combines all aspects of taxation into Section 29, whereas the old UK GAAP had a separate FRS 19 for deferred tax, FRS 16 *Current Tax*, SSAP 5 *Accounting for Value Added Tax* and tax issues relating to retirement benefit plans were also mentioned in FRS 17 *Retirement Benefits*.

FRS 102 also contains a prohibition preventing entities discounting deferred tax assets and liabilities down to present day values. In practice, hardly any entities discount deferred tax balances down to take account of the time value of money, so this prohibition is going to go largely unnoticed.

DEFINED BENEFIT PENSION PLANS

FRS 102 deals with defined benefit pension plans in Section 28 *Employee Benefits* and paragraph 28.18 provides a number of simplifications where the valuation basis (the Projected Unit Credit Method) would require undue cost or effort. Section 28 does not require the use of an independent actuary to provide a valuation as FRS 17 *Retirement Benefits* did. However, the entity must be able to measure its obligation and cost under a defined benefit pension plan without undue cost or effort. Therefore, unless the reporting entity employs an actuary, companies are going to have to use the services of an actuary to arrive at the valuation required to incorporate the defined benefit pension plan into the financial statements and also to provide necessary disclosure notes for the plan. In addition, Section 28 does not require a comprehensive actuarial valuation to be carried out annually. In periods between comprehensive actuarial valuations, and provided the principal actuarial assumptions have not changed significantly, Section 28 recognises that the defined benefit obligation can be measured by adjusting the prior period measurement for changes in employee demographics (for example, the number of employees and their salary levels).

There is also a change in FRS 102 relating to the net interest on the net defined benefit plan liability that may have a significant impact, depending on the assets held by the plan. This is calculated as a single item by multiplying the net defined benefit plan's liability by the discount rate used to determine the present value of the plan's liabilities. Under the previous FRS 17, a reporting entity would have calculated an expected return on plan assets and an interest cost relating to the plan's liabilities and so the revised approach in Section 28 is likely to have a potential impact on an entity's earnings.

This could also impact group planning, in terms of whether to introduce a contractual agreement or stated policy of charging the costs of defined benefit pension plans to individual group entities.

EMPLOYEE BENEFITS

The main issue surrounding this area in Section 28 *Employee Benefits* is the fact that the Section requires accruals for holiday pay (as well as other short-term benefits provided to employees that have accrued, but have not been paid at the reporting date). Under the previous UK GAAP, many companies did not make accruals for such transactions (despite FRS 12 *Provisions, Contingent Liabilities and Contingent Assets* citing an example of unpaid holiday pay accrued, but not paid by the entity until the subsequent accounting period as meeting the definition of a liability). The difficulty under FRS 102 is potentially going to be in the calculation of holiday pay that is to be carried over for future use and the pulling together of this information for the very first time, which is likely to be cumbersome and time-consuming – especially for larger organisations where there is no central record kept of this information.

FAIR VALUE ACCOUNTING

FRS 102 places an increased amount of emphasis on the use of fair values as well as introducing a number of accounting policy choices that will be available to entities reporting under the Standard. This increased emphasis affects a number of areas of the financial statements, such as:

- *Biological assets* – living animals and plants that can be measured using fair values provided such fair values can be obtained reliably. Changes in the fair values of biological assets are taken through profit or loss. However, the fair value model is not a mandatory model and reporting entities can still carry such assets at cost.
- *Business combinations* – intangible assets acquired in a business combination that are separate from goodwill at acquisition and whose fair value can be measured reliably are measured at fair value.
- *Financial instruments* – certain financial instruments, such as derivatives (forward foreign currency contracts, interest rate swaps and options and commodity contracts) and investments in certain equity shares, are carried at fair value with changes in fair value going through profit or loss.
- *Investments in subsidiaries* – are carried at fair value (where such fair values can be reliably estimated) with changes in fair value going through profit or loss. Alternatively, the parent can carry the investment in the subsidiary at cost less impairment.
- *Investment property* – is valued at fair value when such values can be measured reliably with changes in fair value going through profit or loss (not a revaluation reserve).
- *Property, plant and equipment* – can be measured using either the revaluation model (for all assets in the same class) or under the depreciated historic cost model. On transition to FRS 102, an entity can elect to use an old UK GAAP valuation as 'deemed cost' and carry the asset under the cost model going forward.

FIXED ASSETS

Old UK GAAP at FRS 15 *Tangible Fixed Assets* went into a lot of detail concerning the capitalisation criteria for 'subsequent expenditure'. As a general rule, FRS 15 required subsequent expenditure to be written off to profit or loss unless the expenditure:

- Provided an enhancement of the economic benefits of the asset that were in excess of the previously assessed standard of performance.
- Related to a component of a tangible fixed asset that had been treated separately for depreciation purposes, which was replaced or restored.
- Related to a major inspection or overhaul of the tangible fixed asset that restored the economic benefits of the asset(s) that had been used up by the entity and that had already been reflected in the depreciation charge.

Paragraphs 34 to 41 of FRS 15 went into a lot of detail where subsequent expenditure was concerned. FRS 102 does not specifically cover subsequent expenditure, but merely states at paragraph 17.15 that day-to-day servicing of property, plant and equipment must be recognised in profit or loss in the periods in which the costs are incurred. Preparers of financial statements under FRS 102 would be directed to the *Concepts and Pervasive Principles* in Section 2 of FRS 102 to determine whether any subsequent expenditure does, in fact, meet the definition and recognition criteria of an asset outlined in paragraphs 2.15(a) and 2.27(a) and (b).

Paragraph 17.5 of FRS 102 deals with 'spare parts and servicing equipment'. Under the previous UK GAAP, these would have been ordinarily carried in the financial statements as inventory, with recognition taking place as and when such parts/equipment were used in the business. FRS 102 at paragraph 17.5 requires 'major' spare parts and standby equipment to be included within the cost of the fixed asset(s) to which it relates when the business is expected to use them for more than one accounting period. The main difference here is that FRS 15 did not make specific reference to 'major spare parts/standby equipment'. The treatment under FRS 102 essentially means that the cost of major spare parts/standby equipment would be recognised within the depreciation charge rather than in profit and loss through consumption of stock (i.e. cost of sales). This would also potentially have an impact on an entity's gross profit margins.

Where fixed assets are acquired under a deferred payment arrangement (i.e. deferred beyond normal credit terms), the cost of the asset must be the present value of all future payments in accordance with paragraph 17.13 of FRS 102. Such issues were not specifically covered in FRS 15 and this would mean that under FRS 15, the value of assets that were capitalised would essentially be understated, giving rise to a lower depreciation charge. FRS 102 addresses this issue so that the net book value of fixed assets under FRS 102 is higher, but this would also have a consequential increase on the depreciation charge, thus reducing profitability or increasing losses.

There is a difference with regard to residual values. Under previous UK GAAP such values were based on prices prevailing at the date of acquisition and an upward adjustment was only permitted in limited circumstances. Under FRS 102, estimates are based on current prices and thus can be adjusted upwards or downwards in certain circumstances.

GOODWILL AND INTANGIBLE ASSETS

Intangible assets (other than goodwill) are dealt with in Section 18 *Intangible Assets other than Goodwill* with goodwill being dealt with in Section 19 *Business Combinations and Goodwill*. The key difference in FRS 102 as opposed to FRS 10 *Goodwill and Intangible Assets* is in relation to the presumed maximum life of goodwill where management are unable to make a reliable estimate of such a useful life. Old UK GAAP presumed a maximum life of 20 years, with an option to rebut this presumption if a longer or indefinite useful life could be justified. FRS 102 says that intangible assets and goodwill will always have a finite life and where no reliable estimate can be made of such intangible assets or goodwill, the presumed useful life is deemed to be a maximum of five years. At the time of writing, the Department for

Business Innovation and Skills (BIS) were consulting on whether this presumed useful life should be increased from five years up to ten years, but no decision had yet been made as it was only at the consultation stage. Readers are advised to regularly check BIS's website to keep abreast of developments in this area.

The impact of the reduction from 20 years to five years is the potential for large write-downs of goodwill and intangible assets as well as accelerated write-offs over a shorter period of time, which will affect reported profit or loss.

INVESTMENT PROPERTIES

SSAP 19 *Accounting for Investment Properties* required investment properties to be classified in the statement of financial position (balance sheet) at market value, with changes in this market value going through the revaluation reserve account and reported through the statement of total recognised gains and losses.

Investment properties are dealt with in Section 16 *Investment Property* and paragraph 16.7 essentially extinguishes the use of the revaluation reserve and requires all changes in fair value to be recognised in profit or loss. The upshot of this treatment would be that reported profit or loss would be different than would otherwise be the case under SSAP 19, although there would not be a tax effect until such time as the property was disposed of. The accounting treatments can be compared as follows.

Example – Fair value changes in investment property

SSAP 19

Company A Limited has an investment property on its balance sheet with a carrying value as at 31 December 2015 of £125,000 with an associated revaluation surplus of £40,000*. On 31 December 2016, a professionally qualified, reputable valuation agent confirmed that the value of this investment property had increased to £130,000.

Under SSAP 19, the entries as at 31 December 2016 would be:

DR	Investment property	£5,000
CR	Revaluation reserve	£5,000

Being fair value increase in investment property.
There would be no impact on profit or loss for the year.

FRS 102

Under FRS 102, the £5,000 would be reported through profit or loss within operating profit; hence profitability under FRS 102 would be £5,000 higher than it would be under SSAP 19.

*On transition to FRS 102, the revaluation reserve would be moved into retained earnings (profit and loss account reserves) as there is no concept of a revaluation reserve for investment properties under FRS 102.

It is also worth noting that FRS 102 requires fair values to be obtained where such values can be obtained without 'undue cost or effort'. SSAP 19 did not make this exception and in FRS 102 if obtaining fair values would result in undue cost or effort, the entity instead accounts for the investment property in accordance with Section 17 *Property, Plant and Equipment* until a reliable measure of fair value becomes available. In reality, the entity would commission a surveyor to undertake the valuation and it is very difficult to see how obtaining such values for investment property would cause undue cost or effort.

Many in the profession argue about the accounting treatment in relation to fair value changes for investment property. Whilst accounting standards do not give specific reasoning behind their methodologies, investment property carried at fair value is not subjected to depreciation or impairment testing as such properties are valued at fair value at each reporting date; hence any changes in fair value are taken directly to profit or loss. This treatment is consistent with IAS 40 *Investment Property* and *IFRS for SMEs*. An important point to emphasise, however, is that any fair value gains on investment property are **not** distributable to shareholders in the form of a dividend because they are not a realised profit for dividend purposes. Reporting entities will need to keep a record of the value of undistributable reserves relating to investment properties and it might be worthwhile accumulating such reserves in a separate component of equity to distinguish undistributable reserves from those that are distributable (although there is no requirement to do this in company law).

LEASES

SSAP 21 *Accounting for Leases and Hire Purchase Contracts* sets out a specific benchmark when determining whether a lease is a finance or an operating lease as demonstrated in paragraph 22 to the Guidance Notes, which were contained in SSAP 21. This benchmark is where the minimum lease payments amount to 90% or more of the fair value of the asset subjected to the lease (often referred to as the 'bright line test').

The classification under FRS 102 does not refer to a 90% benchmark, but instead offers examples of the various situations that individually, or in combination, could give rise to a lease being classified as a finance lease. These classifications are as follows:

1. Ownership of the asset is transferred to the lessee at the end of the lease term.
2. The lessee can purchase the asset at a price sufficiently lower than fair value at the date such an option becomes exercisable and it is reasonably certain that the option will be exercised.
3. The term of the lease is for the major part of the economic life of the asset. Title does not have to be transferred at the end of the lease.
4. At the start of the lease term the present value of the minimum lease payments the lessee is committed to make is equivalent to at least substantially all of the fair value of the leased asset.
5. The assets subjected to the lease are of such a specialised nature that only the lessee can use them without major modifications being made.

Section 20 also contains three other indicators that the lease could be a finance lease as follows:

(a) Should the lessee cancel the lease before the agreed termination date, the lessor's losses associated with the cancellation are borne by the lessee.
(b) Gains or losses from changes in the residual value of the leased asset accrue to the lessee.
(c) The lessee could continue the lease for a secondary period at a rent that is substantially lower than market rent.

The classification criteria above are based upon the risks and rewards of ownership of the associated asset and which party retains those risks and rewards. There are a number of factors that can determine whether risks and rewards have, or have not, been transferred from lessor to lessee and therefore paragraph 20.7 of FRS 102 acknowledges that the examples of indicators contained in paragraphs 20.5 to 20.6 will not be conclusive in every respect and consideration must therefore be given to other indicators that risks and rewards may (or may not) have transferred from lessor to lessee. There is more judgement required under FRS 102 than in SSAP 21.

In some cases, lessees may receive an incentive payment to take up a lease. Paragraph 20.15A says that any incentive should be allocated on a straight-line basis over the term of the lease (unless another systematic basis is representative of the time pattern of the lessee's benefit).

REVENUE RECOGNITION

There are some slight variations in the wording relating to the measurement of revenue. Revenue recognition is dealt with in Section 23 *Revenue* and paragraph 23.3 of FRS 102 refers to revenue being the fair value of the consideration *'received or receivable'*. Application Note G to FRS 5 *Reporting the Substance of Transactions* at paragraph G4 said that a seller recognises revenue under an exchange transaction with a customer when, and to the extent that, it obtains 'the right to consideration' in exchange for its performance.

This subtle difference in wording could potentially allow for later recognition of profit that would result in a potentially different tax treatment as the tax treatment follows the accounting treatment. The Financial Reporting Council (FRC) have suggested that if there is abuse of the wording then they will issue an Abstract to clarify the treatment.

Paragraph 23.15 to FRS 102 also refers to a 'specific act' and a 'significant act'. This paragraph says that when a specific act is much more significant than any other act, the entity postpones revenue recognition until the significant act is executed. UITF 40 (Application Note G to FRS 5) was much more prohibitive in that it required revenue to be recognised in line with performance (passing a 'milestone' or the occurrence of a 'critical event') and thus earning the right to consideration. There is the potential here for the possibility of later revenue recognition due to the interpretation aspect of the wording and reporting entities must be extremely careful not to disproportionately delay revenue recognition or accelerate revenue recognition as this will not only impact on the financial statements but will also have a tax impact. Again, if there is any abuse of Section 23 by reporting entities, the FRC are likely to issue an Abstract to clarify the appropriate treatment.

Paragraph 23.16 of FRS 102 says that if a client cannot estimate the outcome of a service contract (more likely to be the case where construction contracts are concerned), the entity should only recognise revenue to the extent of the costs incurred. In contrast, paragraph 10 to SSAP 9 *Stocks and Long-Term Contracts* said that where the outcome of a long-term contract could not be assessed with reasonable certainty, no profit should be reflected in the profit and loss account and suggested showing as turnover a proportion of the total contract value using a zero estimate of profit.

INVENTORY (STOCK) VALUATIONS

Under SSAP 9 *Stocks and Long-Term Contracts*, inventory (stock) could be valued using the last-in first-out method (LIFO); however, SSAP 9 did not favour this method because it resulted in the valuation of current assets that had little relationship to actual cost and where the reporting entity adopted the use of LIFO the directors had to justify its use.

Paragraph 13.18 follows the same stance of its international counterpart, IAS 2 *Inventories* and *IFRS for SMEs*, and outlaws the use of the LIFO method. The only permissible methods are the first-in first-out (FIFO) and average cost (although a different cost formula can be used where inventories are different in nature or use) and so this will have an impact on the valuation of inventories (and resulting profit or loss).

DIFFERENCES BETWEEN FRS 102 AND *IFRS FOR SMES*

Whilst FRS 102 is largely based on the IASB's *IFRS for SMEs*, it has had to be amended in certain areas to be compatible with the Companies Act 2006 and EU Directives and so there are some differences between FRS 102 and *IFRS for SMEs*, which are outlined below.

Section 1: Scope

IFRS for SMEs applies to small and medium entities that do not have public accountability. The concept of public accountability was removed by the FRC and FRS 100 *Application of Financial Reporting Requirements* sets out the scope of entities that apply FRS 102.

Section 2: Concepts and Pervasive Principles

No significant differences.

Section 3: Financial Statement Presentation

Paragraph 3.7 of *IFRS for SMEs* outlines the disclosures required when management conclude that compliance with a requirement of *IFRS for SMEs* would be so misleading that it would conflict with the objective of financial statements of SMEs.

This paragraph has been deleted in FRS 102 and the requirements of the Companies Act 2006 are instead referred to for the use of the true and fair override.

Paragraph 3.16 of *IFRS for SMEs* defines the concept of 'materiality' and says that omissions or misstatements of items are material if they could, individually or collectively, influence the economic decisions of users made on the basis of the financial statements. This paragraph goes on to say that materiality depends on the size and nature of the omission or misstatement judged in the surrounding circumstances with the size or nature of the item, or a combination of both, being the determining factor. FRS 102 at paragraph 3.16 amends this and instead clarifies the role of materiality.

An additional paragraph 3.16A is incorporated in FRS 102, which confirms that disclosures will not be required if the information is not material to the financial statements.

Section 4: Statement of Financial Position

FRS 102 removes the requirements in Section 4 of *IFRS for SMEs* and replaces them by the requirements of the Companies Act 2006.

Section 5: Statement of Comprehensive Income and Income Statement

Again, like with Section 4, the requirements of Section 5 to *IFRS for SMEs* have been removed and replaced by the requirements of the Companies Act 2006. Paragraph 5.10 to *IFRS for SMEs* says that an entity shall not present or describe any items of income and expense as 'extraordinary items' in the statement of comprehensive income (or in the income statement, if presented) or in the notes. This paragraph has been amended in FRS 102 to deal with 'ordinary activities' and a separate paragraph (5.10A) has been incorporated in FRS 102 that deals with 'extraordinary items'.

Section 6: Statement of Changes in Equity and Statement of Income and Retained Earnings

FRS 102 includes an additional paragraph 6.3A that requires entities to present, for each component of equity, an analysis of other comprehensive income by item. This can be presented either within the notes or in the statement of changes in equity.

Section 7: Statement of Cash Flows

The scope of Section 7 to FRS 102 specifically excludes mutual life assurance companies, pension funds and certain investment funds. In addition, paragraphs 7.10A to 7.10E are included in FRS 102 and these paragraphs require cash flows to be reported on a net basis in certain situations.

IFRS for SMEs at paragraphs 7.11 and 7.12 deals with the translation of cash flows from foreign currency into the entity's functional currency. Specifically paragraph 7.11 requires an entity to apply (to the foreign currency amount) the exchange rate between the functional currency and the foreign currency at the date of the cash flows. Paragraphs 7.11 and 7.12 in FRS 102 have been amended to relax the exchange rates permitted to be used.

Section 8: Notes to the Financial Statements

No significant differences.

Section 9: Consolidated and Separate Financial Statements

FRS 102 offers further clarification in the Scope paragraph to confirm that Section 9 applies to all parent entities that present consolidated financial statements that are intended to give a true and fair view. In addition, the requirements to present consolidated financial statements have been amended to comply with the Companies Act 2006.

Paragraph 9.9 of *IFRS for SMEs* says that a subsidiary is not excluded from consolidation because it operates in a jurisdiction that imposes restrictions on transferring cash or other assets out of the jurisdiction. This paragraph is amended in FRS 102 to say that a subsidiary that is held exclusively with a view to subsequent resale because it is held as part of an investment portfolio is to be excluded from consolidation. Such subsidiaries are to be measured at fair value with changes going through profit or loss. This exemption will be required regardless of whether the subsidiary was previously consolidated under FRS 2 *Accounting for Subsidiary Undertakings* prior to the transition to FRS 102.

Paragraph 14.4B and 15.9B have been incorporated within FRS 102 and these paragraphs require an investor that has investments in associates or jointly controlled entities held as part of an investment portfolio to measure those investments at fair value with changes in fair value going through profit or loss in the consolidated financial statements.

Paragraph 9.10 is amended in FRS 102 to confirm that Employee Share Ownership Plans and similar arrangements are Special Purpose Entities.

Schedule 6 to the Regulations in the UK requires a subsidiary's financial statements that are included in the consolidated financial statements to be for the same reporting period (financial year) as that of the parent. Paragraph 9.16 in FRS 102 has been amended to reflect this requirement. In addition, the paragraph has also been amended to take into consideration circumstances when it would not be practicable to align the subsidiary's reporting date with the parent's and goes on to specify which financial statements of the subsidiary can be used in the consolidation.

Further paragraphs 9.18A and 9.18B are included in FRS 102, which clarify the treatment of a disposal of a subsidiary when the parent loses control. In addition, paragraph 9.19A is included in FRS 102 when the parent may dispose of ownership interest in a subsidiary but still retains control of that subsidiary. Paragraph 9.19B is included in FRS 102 to confirm the accounting treatment of a step acquisition (an acquisition made in stages).

Paragraphs 9.19C and 9.19D are included in FRS 102, which deal with the treatment of non-controlling interests (minority interests) when a parent's ownership interest in a subsidiary changes, but control is retained by the parent.

Paragraphs 9.23A to 9.25 distinguish between individual financial statements and separate financial statements and also confirm that it is the Companies Act 2006 that specifies when individual financial statements must be prepared.

IFRS for SMEs at paragraphs 9.28 and 9.29 deals with 'combined financial statements'. Paragraph 9.28 to *IFRS for SMEs* confirms that combined financial statements are a single set of financial statements of two or more entities controlled by a single investor and confirms that under *IFRS for SMEs* such financial statements are not required. FRS 102 has deleted paragraphs 9.28 to 9.30 (paragraph 9.30 in *IFRS for SMEs* deals with the disclosures in combined financial statements).

Paragraphs 9.31 to 9.32 are inserted in FRS 102, which provide guidance on exchanges of businesses or other non-monetary assets for an interest in a subsidiary, joint venture or associate (previously this guidance was contained in UITF 31 *Exchanges of businesses or other non-monetary assets for an interest in a subsidiary, joint venture or associate*).

Paragraphs 9.33 to 9.38 are included in FRS 102, which outline the accounting treatment for intermediate payment arrangements that were previously contained in UITF 32 *Employee benefit trusts and other intermediate payment arrangements*.

Section 10: Accounting Policies, Estimates and Errors

Paragraph 10.5 in FRS 102 has been amended to clarify when an entity is required to refer to SORPs in developing an accounting policy.

Paragraph 10.10A has been inserted, which deals with changes in accounting policies relating to property, plant and equipment (dealt with in Section 17 *Property, Plant and Equipment*). This paragraph brings Section 17 and Section 18 *Intangible Assets other than Goodwill* in line with Section 10 *Accounting Policies, Estimates and Errors* in *IFRS for SMEs*.

Section 11: Basic Financial Instruments

The Scope paragraph in FRS 102 at Section 11 is amended to outline the fact that certain financial statements do not fall within the scope of Section 11.

Paragraph 11.9(c) is amended and outlines the fact that contractual prepayment provisions, which are contingent future events, exclude those that protect the holder from credit deterioration or tax changes.

Paragraph 11.14(b) is inserted in FRS 102 to confirm that entities can choose to designate debt instruments as fair value through profit or loss in certain situations.

Paragraph 11.38A is included in FRS 102, which allows the offsetting of certain financial assets and financial liabilities in the statement of financial position.

Paragraph 11.48A is included in FRS 102 to require entities to disclose information required under Regulations for financial instruments that are not held as part of a trading portfolio and that are not derivative financial instruments.

Paragraphs 11.48B and 11.48C in *IFRS for SMEs* require disclosure of total interest income and total interest expense for financial assets or financial liabilities that are not measured at fair value through profit or loss and the amount of any impairment loss for each class of financial asset. In FRS 102 the disclosure requirements are extended and paragraph 11.48B requires a financial institution (other than a retirement benefit plan) to apply the requirements in paragraph 34.17 to FRS 102. Paragraph 11.48C to FRS 102 requires a retirement benefit plan to apply the requirements in paragraphs 34.39 to 34.48.

Section 12: Other Financial Instruments Issues

The Scope section in FRS 102 excludes financial instruments issued by an entity with a discretionary participation feature, reimbursement assets and financial guarantee contracts.

Paragraph 12.24 confirms that the cumulative amount of foreign exchange differences that relate to a hedge of a net investment in a foreign operation are not reclassified to profit or loss on disposal (or partial disposal).

FRS 102 includes an additional paragraph 12.25B that permits the offsetting of certain financial assets and financial liabilities in the statement of financial position.

Paragraph 12.26 is amended in FRS 102 so that it complies with the requirements of the Companies Act 2006.

Section 13: Inventories

Further paragraphs 13.4A and 13.20A are included in FRS 102, which deal with inventories held for distribution at no or nominal consideration.

Paragraph 13.5A is included in FRS 102 to provide guidance on inventory that is acquired through non-exchange transactions.

Paragraph 13.8A is included in FRS 102, which clarifies the treatment for provisions against dismantling and restoration costs of property, plant and equipment in the cost of inventory.

Paragraph 13.15 has been amended in FRS 102 and this amendment allows for the inclusion of the cost model for agricultural produce in Section 34 *Specialised Activities*.

Section 14: Investments in Associates

The Scope section has been amended in FRS 102, which now clarifies the section's application to consolidated financial statements and to the financial statements of an entity that is not a parent but which holds investments in associates.

Paragraph 14.4(b) in *IFRS for SMEs* says that an investor shall account for all of its investments using the equity method in paragraph 14.8. As this method is not compliant with company legislation in the UK and Republic of Ireland, this paragraph has been deleted in FRS 102. Paragraph 14.4(d) has been inserted to allow non-parent investors to account for investments in associates at fair value with changes in fair value going through profit or loss.

Paragraph 14.4B has been inserted in FRS 102, which requires an investor that is a parent and has investments in associates held as part of an investment portfolio to measure those investments at fair value with changes in fair value going through profit or loss in their consolidated financial statements.

Paragraph 14.9 to *IFRS for SMEs* says that when an investment in an associate is recognised initially, an investor shall measure it at the transaction price that excludes transaction costs. This paragraph is amended in FRS 102 to require transaction costs to be included as part of the transaction price on initial recognition.

Paragraph 14.10 to *IFRS for SMEs* says that at each reporting date an investor shall measure its investments in associates at fair value with changes in fair value recognised in profit or loss, using the fair valuation guidance in paragraphs 11.27 to 11.32.

This paragraph has been amended in FRS 102 to require changes in fair value to be recognised through other comprehensive income to accord with paragraphs 17.15E and 17.15F to FRS 102, where the entity adopts the use of the fair value model as opposed to recognising changes in fair value through profit or loss.

A further paragraph 14.15A has been included in FRS 102 to provide information about associates held by entities that are not parents.

Section 15: Investments in Joint Ventures

The Scope section in FRS 102 has been amended to clarify the application of Section 15 to the consolidated financial statements and to the financial statements of a venturer that is not a parent.

Paragraph 15.9(b) to *IFRS for SMEs* says that a venturer shall account for all of its interests in jointly controlled entities using the equity method in paragraph 15.13. This has been deleted in FRS 102 because such a method is not compliant with companies legislation. Paragraph 15.9(d) is inserted, which allows non-parent investors to account for investments in jointly controlled entities using the fair value model with changes being recognised in profit or loss.

Paragraph 15.9B has been included in FRS 102 to allow an investor that is also a parent that has investments in jointly controlled entities that are held as part of an investment portfolio to measure those investments using the fair value model with changes being recognised in profit or loss in their consolidated financial statements.

Paragraph 15.14 has been amended in FRS 102 to require transaction costs to be included as part of the transaction price on initial recognition.

Paragraph 15.15 is amended to require changes in the fair value of investments in joint ventures to be recognised in other comprehensive income to comply with paragraphs 17.15E and 17.15F when the fair value model is used rather than through profit or loss.

A further paragraph 15.21A is included in FRS 102 to provide information concerning associates held by entities that are not parents.

Section 16: Investment Property

No significant differences.

Section 17: Property, Plant and Equipment

This Section now permits the use of the revaluation model as a means of measurement after initial recognition rather than restricting the measurement to the cost model as *IFRS for SMEs* at paragraph 17.15 does.

Section 18: Intangible Assets other than Goodwill

Section 18 in FRS 102 permits entities to recognise intangible assets that result from expenditure incurred on the internal development of intangible assets, although there are certain criteria that must be met before an entity can recognise an internally developed intangible asset. Section 18 in FRS 102 also provides guidance on what constitutes the cost of an internally generated intangible asset and specifies the criteria for initial recognition.

In addition, Section 18 has also been amended in FRS 102 to allow reporting entities to use either the cost model or revaluation model.

Section 19: Business Combinations and Goodwill

Section 19 of FRS 102 has been amended to reflect the use of the merger accounting method for group reconstructions. This method is outlined in paragraphs 19.23 to 19.33.

Section 19 of FRS 102 includes additional paragraphs 19.15A to 19.15C, which provide guidance on the treatment of deferred tax assets or liabilities, employee benefit arrangements and share-based payments of a subsidiary on acquisition.

Paragraph 19.23(a) in *IFRS for SMEs* says that where an entity is unable to make a reliable estimate of the useful life of goodwill, the life is presumed to be ten years. This is amended in FRS 102 to be five years (although the Department for Business Innovation and Skills is consulting on increasing the presumed useful economic life to ten years).

Paragraph 19.24 covers the issue of goodwill in a bargain purchase (negative goodwill). This paragraph in *IFRS for SMEs* has been amended in FRS 102 so that it complies with the requirements of the Companies Act 2006.

Section 20: Leases

The Scope section of Section 20 has been amended in FRS 102 so that it covers operating leases that are onerous.

Further paragraphs 20.15A and 20.25A are included in FRS 102, which clarifies the treatment of operating lease incentives for lessees and lessors.

Paragraph 20.15B is included in FRS 102 so as to provide guidance on the treatment of onerous operating lease contracts.

Section 21: Provisions and Contingencies

Section 21 in FRS 102 also covers financial guarantee contracts and a further paragraph 21.17A has been inserted in FRS 102 to outline the accounting treatment of such contracts.

Section 22: Liabilities and Equity

FRS 102 at Section 22 includes an additional paragraph 22.3A to clarify that a financial instrument where the issuer does not have the unconditional right to avoid settling in cash or by delivery of another financial asset (or otherwise to settle it in such a way that would be a financial liability) and where settlement is dependent on the occurrence or non-occurrence of uncertain future events beyond the control of the issuer and the holder, is a financial liability of the issuer unless specific circumstances apply.

Paragraph 22.18 to *IFRS for SMEs* says that when an entity has an obligation to distribute non-cash assets to its owners as a dividend, it must recognise a liability and this liability is measured at the fair value of the assets to be distributed. This paragraph is removed and paragraph 22.18 to FRS 102 only requires disclosure of the fair value of such assets to be distributed.

Section 23: Revenue

No significant differences.

Section 24: Government Grants

FRS 102 introduces the 'accrual' model of accounting for grants, which is not covered in *IFRS for SMEs*. This model is dealt with in paragraphs 24.5C to 24.5G in FRS 102 and essentially allows entities to recognise grant income on a systematic basis over the period in which the entity recognises the related costs for which the grant is intended to compensate.

Section 25: Borrowing Costs

Entities are permitted to capitalise borrowing costs that are directly attributable to the acquisition, construction or production of a qualifying asset in FRS 102, which is outlawed in *IFRS for SMEs*.

Section 26: Share-based Payment

FRS 102 has re-defined 'equity-settled share-based payments' so that it is more aligned to the definition contained in IFRS 2 *Share-based Payment*. In addition, FRS 102 clarifies the fact that option pricing models do not have to be applied in all situations.

Section 27: Impairment of Assets

An additional paragraph 27.20A is included in FRS 102, which provides guidance on the treatment of impairments on assets that are held for their service potential.

Paragraph 27.31 in FRS 102 also allows the reversal of impairment losses against goodwill and paragraph 27.33A is inserted, which includes a descriptive disclosure requirement of the events and circumstances that have led to the recognition (or reversal) of an impairment loss.

Section 28: Employee Benefits

FRS 102 is consistent with the amended IAS 19 *Employee Benefits* issued in 2011 in respect of the presentation of the cost of a defined benefit plan and the accounting for group plans.

An additional paragraph 28.11A is included in FRS 102 that requires the recognition of a liability on a defined benefit multi-employer plan that is accounted for as a defined contribution scheme where the funding of a deficit on the plan has been agreed.

The option to use a simplified valuation method in measuring the liability in a defined benefit plan has been removed in paragraph 28.19 to FRS 102.

Section 29: Income Tax

The entire section has been replaced with UK-specific requirements.

Section 30: Foreign Currency Translation

No significant differences.

Section 31: Hyperinflation

No significant differences.

Section 32: Events after the End of the Reporting Period

Further paragraphs 32.7A and 32.74B are included in FRS 102 that provide guidance on the impact of changes in an entity's going concern status.

Section 33: Related Party Disclosures

An additional paragraph 33.1A is included in FRS 102, which includes the exemption from disclosure of related party transactions for wholly owned entities that is available in the Companies Act 2006.

Section 34: Specialised Activities

The agriculture subsection is amended in FRS 102 to allow entities to adopt the use of the cost model.

The extractives subsection has been amended in FRS 102 to require application of IFRS 6 *Exploration for and Evaluation of Mineral Resources*.

The service concession arrangements subsection has been amended in FRS 102, which clarifies the accounting by operators and provides guidance to grantors.

FRS 102 contains additional subsections to that of *IFRS for SMEs*, which now include:

- Financial Institutions,
- Retirement Benefit Plans: Financial Statements,
- Heritage Assets,
- Funding Commitments,
- Incoming Resources from Non-Exchange Transactions,
- Public Benefit Entity Combinations and
- Public Benefit Entity Concessionary Loans.

Section 35: Transition to this FRS

This Section has been amended in FRS 102 to reflect all the other changes brought in by FRS 102.

6 CONSOLIDATED AND SEPARATE FINANCIAL STATEMENTS

INTRODUCTION

In the broadest terms, when a business controls another business it is required to prepare consolidated financial statements (often referred to as 'group financial statements'). The requirement to prepare consolidated financial statements is contained in the Companies Act 2006 and in Section 9 *Consolidated and Separate Financial Statements*. Both the Companies Act 2006 and Section 9 set out the manner in which consolidated financial statements are prepared. The overarching objective of consolidated financial statements is to show the results of a group of companies in line with its economic substance, which is that of a single reporting entity (in other words, as if the group structure never existed). This is down to a variety of requirements, but in general many companies operate through complex structures for a variety of reasons under the control of a parent company. For that reason, the parent company's financial statements alone will not give the complete picture of its economic activities or financial position. The objective, therefore, of consolidated financial statements is to show the extended business unit that conducts activities under the control of the parent company.

Section 9 (and this chapter) is only concerned with a parent–subsidiary relationship (i.e. where there would be a requirement to prepare group financial statements). The requirement to prepare group financial statements only applies to groups that are not eligible to apply any exemptions from consolidation (for example, small groups that are covered later in this chapter) and only where the parent company is a parent at the year-end.

Consolidated financial statements are prepared with the intention of showing the results of the group as if it were a single company in its own right with one group of shareholders. As a result, balances and profits in a set of consolidated financial statements are only those that arise as a result of transactions with third parties;

any balances and transactions with companies in the group structure are eliminated as consolidation adjustments, the concept of which is covered later in this chapter (see 'Principles of Consolidation').

There is some terminology contained in the Companies Act 2006 and in Section 9 that should be understood where consolidated financial statements are concerned.

Term	Meaning
Consolidated financial statements	The financial statements of a group prepared by consolidation
Consolidation	The process of adjusting and combining financial information from the individual financial statements of a parent undertaking and its subsidiary undertaking(s) to prepare consolidated financial statements that present the financial information for a group as a single economic activity
Control	The ability of an undertaking to direct the financial and operating policies of another undertaking with a view to gaining economic benefits from its activities
Dominant influence	Influence that can be exercised to achieve the operating and financial policies desired by the holder of the influence, notwithstanding the rights or influence of any other party
Equity method	A method of accounting whereby the investment is initially recorded at cost and then adjusted thereafter for the post-acquisition change in the investor's share of the investee's net assets
Group	A parent undertaking and its subsidiary undertakings
Interest held on a long-term basis	An interest that is held other than exclusively with a view to resale
Interest in another entity	An interest in another entity refers to contractual and non-contractual involvement that exposes an entity to variability of returns from the performance of the entity
Parent	An entity that controls one or more entities
Power	Existing rights that give the current ability to direct the relevant activities
Protective rights	Rights designed to protect the interest of the party holding those rights without giving that party power over the entity to which those rights relate
Separate financial statements	Financial statements presented by a parent or an investor with joint control of, or significant influence over, an investee, in which the investments are accounted for at cost or in accordance with Section 11 *Basic Financial Instruments* or Section 12 *Other Financial Instruments Issues*
Subsidiary	An entity that is controlled by another entity (the parent)

IDENTIFYING A GROUP

In order to establish whether a parent company must prepare consolidated financial statements, it will be necessary to identify whether there is a group structure in place. For the purposes of this chapter, the term 'group structure' relates only to a parent that has control over a subsidiary and is therefore required to prepare consolidated financial statements.

The term 'control' is vital in the identification of a group. A parent obtains control over a subsidiary if the parent has the power to govern the financial and operating policies of the subsidiary so as to obtain economic benefits from the subsidiary's activities. A key point to note here is that control is based on substantive rights. However, an investor that only holds protective rights does not have the power to direct the activities of the entity. The substantive rights need to be exercisable when the decision regarding the direction of the relevant activities needs to be made.

Control will normally be obtained in two specific situations:

- Where the parent company holds more than half of the voting rights in the subsidiary or
- Where the parent company has the ability to direct the financial and operating policies of the subsidiary.

Example – Control obtained through ownership interest

The following is the illustration of the P Group:

P

owns
80% of the
voting rights

S

In this example, P owns 80% of the voting rights in S. If a parent holds more than half of the voting rights in another entity that situation will give rise to control (note FRS 102 requires the parent to hold more than half of the 'voting' rights). In this context, a parent–subsidiary relationship exists and the P Group is required to prepare consolidated financial statements.

Example – Control obtained through other means

In the above example, P had obtained control of S through ownership interest (i.e. because P owned more than half of the voting rights in S). Consider if P only owned, say, 40% of the ownership interest in S – on the face of it, from a numerical perspective, it would seem that P does not control S and therefore no parent–subsidiary relationship exists and hence no consolidated financial statements need to be prepared.

However, if P had the power to appoint or remove a majority of S's board of directors, despite only holding a 40% ownership stake in S, then P would have control over S and regardless of the fact that ownership interest is only 40%, control would still be obtained through P's ability to appoint or remove the majority of the board and therefore in this instance consolidated financial statements would need to be prepared.

Groups often do not merely consist of a parent company holding an ownership interest in a subsidiary. There are many instances where the group structure may be complex. Larger groups, particularly those with overseas entities, can be extremely complicated and in some cases the establishment of various companies in a group and whether they qualify as subsidiary companies or not can be a fairly complex and long-winded exercise to complete. However, the key concept to keep in mind is that control is always based on substantive rights.

Example – Vertical group structure

Consider this group structure:

In this group structure, X owns 60% of Y and hence Y is a subsidiary of X due to that control. Y owns 75% of Z and therefore Z is a subsidiary of Y. The question arises as to whether X controls Z. In such structures, Z will be a subsidiary of X on the grounds that X controls Z through its control of Y and therefore Z is a subsidiary of X. X's effective ownership in Z is calculated as 60% × 75% = 45% of Z. This calculation is a useful tool to bring when it comes to the consolidation exercise, but it is irrelevant in determining the status of the investment. Status is always based on control.

Example – 'D-shaped' group

Consider the following group structure:

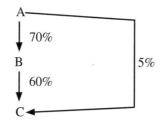

In this particular type of group structure (often referred to as a 'D-shaped' group), A's *indirect* and *direct* ownership interest will need to be established. Clearly as A owns 70% of B, B becomes a subsidiary of A. As B owns 60% of C, C becomes a subsidiary of B. The question arises as to the ownership interest of A and C. This can be calculated as follows:

Indirect ownership	
70% × 60%	42%
Direct ownership	
Per group structure	5%
A ownership interest	47%
Non-controlling interest	53%

The key to identifying subsidiaries in a complex group structure is based on establishing control. To establish control, the holdings of the parent and of other companies within the group need to be considered in aggregate. In addition, the date of acquisition should be considered to be the date the parent establishes control over that subsidiary. The parent will obtain control over a subsubsidiary at the *later* of the following dates:

- The date the parent acquired the subsidiary and
- The date the subsidiary acquired the subsubsidiary.

Example – Date control is obtained

---

1. P acquired 80% of S on 31 March 2014. S bought 70% of T on 31 July 2016.

   The date of the acquisition of T is 31 July 2016.

2. P bought 80% of S on 31 March 2014. S already owned T.

   The date of the acquisition of T is 30 March 2014.

SMALL GROUPS

Under the Companies Act 2006, there is no requirement to prepare group accounts for a group that qualifies as small. The following table outlines the size criteria for groups (note that the size criteria are set for changes in 2015, see below).

Group size	Turnover	Balance sheet (gross assets)
Small	£6.5m net	£3.26m net
	£7.8m gross	£3.9m gross
Medium	£25.9m net	£12.9m gross
	£31.1m gross	£15.5m gross

Small groups will not have an average employee head count of more than 50 and a medium-sized group will not have an average employee head count of more than 250.

Where references to 'net' and 'gross' are made, this is in relation to intra-group trading. Gross means that intra-group trading has not been eliminated, whilst net means that intra-group trading and the effects thereof have been eliminated.

Whilst group accounts are not required for small groups in the UK, there are additional disclosures required in the notes to the financial statements for the parent company (see the 'Disclosure Requirements' section later).

Planned changes for groups

In August 2014, BIS announced its consultation on increasing the size limits for companies and groups to be classified as micro, small, medium-sized and large following the introduction of the EU Accounting Directive. At the time of writing these proposals had not been finalised, but the proposed changes were as follows:

	Balance sheet £	Net turnover £	Average no. of employees
For group/consolidated accounts			
Medium-sized group	≤ 18,000,000 net	≤36,000,000 net	≤250
	≤21,600,000 gross	≤43,200,000 gross	
Large group	≥18,000,000 net	≥36,000,000 net	≥250
	≥21,600,000 gross	≥43,200,000 gross	

The table below outlines the minimum and maximum thresholds permitted under the proposed small companies regime.

	Balance sheet £	Net turnover £	Average no. of employees
For group/consolidated accounts			
Small group (using minimum mandatory threshold values)	≤3,500,000 net	≤7,000,000 net	≤50
	≤4,200,000 gross	≤8,400,000 gross	
Small group (using maximum threshold values permitted)	≤5,100,000 net	≤10,200,000 net	≤50
	≤6,100,000 gross	≤12,200,000 gross	

Readers are advised to keep abreast of developments in this area by regularly reviewing the BIS's website.

EXEMPTIONS FROM PREPARING GROUP ACCOUNTS

There are certain exemptions from the requirements to prepare group accounts, which are contained in paragraph 9.3 to FRS 102. This particular paragraph exempts parent companies from preparing consolidated financial statements if any one of the following applies:

(a) If the parent company is itself a wholly owned subsidiary and its parent company is established under the law of a European Economic Area (EEA) State. There are further conditions that have to be complied with under section 400(2) of the Companies Act 2006.

(b) If the parent company is a majority owned subsidiary that also meets all the conditions required for exemption as a wholly owned subsidiary, which are prescribed in section 400(2) of the Companies Act 2006 together with the additional requirements in section 400(1) (b) of the Companies Act 2006.

(c) Where the parent company is not a wholly owned subsidiary of another company and that other company is not established under the law of an EEA State. Further conditions, which are outlined in section 401(2) of the Companies Act 2006, will also need to be complied with.

(d) Where the parent company is a majority owned subsidiary and it meets all the criteria for exemption as a wholly owned subsidiary, which are outlined in section 401(2) of the Companies Act 2006 together with the additional criteria set out in section 401(1) (b) of the Companies Act 2006.

(e) Where the parent and the group of which it heads up qualifies as a small group in accordance with section 383 of the Companies Act 2006. The group must also not be an ineligible group, which is set out in section 384 of the Companies Act 2006.

(f) Where the provisions in paragraph 9.9 of FRS 102 apply, which says that a subsidiary can be excluded from consolidation where:

- Severe long-term restrictions will essentially prohibit the exercise of the rights of the parent company over the assets or management of the subsidiary or
- The interest in the subsidiary is held exclusively with a view to subsequent resale and the subsidiary company has not previously been consolidated in the consolidated accounts prepared under FRS 102.

(g) If the parent company does not prepare accounts under the Companies Act 2006 and the legislation that the parent is reporting under also does not require group financial statements to be prepared.

An important point to emphasise is that a parent will not be exempt from consolidation under (a) to (d) above if any of its securities are traded on a regulated market of any EEA State.

EXCLUSIONS FROM CONSOLIDATION

There are two conditions noted above whereby a subsidiary company can be excluded from consolidation. These conditions are where there are severe long-term restrictions that will not allow the parent company to exercise its rights over the subsidiary's assets or management of the subsidiary. In addition, there may be occasions where the parent will acquire a subsidiary exclusively with a view to subsequent resale and therefore the results of the subsidiary will not be consolidated with those of the parent company.

When a subsidiary company meets the conditions for exclusion, the parent company must measure its interest in a subsidiary using:

- Cost less amounts recognised in respect of impairment or
- Fair value through other comprehensive income or
- Fair value through profit or loss.

All investments within a single class must be subjected to the same accounting policy choice; however, the parent may select different accounting policies for different classes of investment.

Having a choice regarding subsidiaries held with a view to resale is a new feature in FRS 102. Under previous UK GAAP, they would be measured at the lower of cost and net realisable value.

However, where a subsidiary is excluded from consolidation on the basis that it is held exclusively with a view to subsequent resale but it is held as part of an investment portfolio, it *must* be measured at fair value with changes in fair value being recognised in profit or loss. If it is not held as part of an investment portfolio, the parent will then choose one of the above methods for measuring the investment.

PRINCIPLES OF CONSOLIDATION

Once it has been established that there is a parent–subsidiary relationship and there are no grounds for exemption or exclusion from consolidation, the parent company must prepare consolidated financial statements showing the results of the group in line with its economic substance, which is that of a single trading entity.

Consolidation should start from the date of acquisition. The effective date of acquisition of a subsidiary is the date that control is obtained by the parent.

Accounting policies

Amounts included within the consolidation should be based on uniform accounting policies. If a subsidiary uses policies that differ to those of the parent in its individual financial statements, adjustments will need to be made on consolidation to ensure that uniform accounting policies are adopted.

Non-coterminous accounting periods

Subsidiaries should, wherever practicable, use the same accounting reference date and accounting period as the parent.

If a subsidiary uses a different date, interim financial statements should be prepared to the parent's accounting date for use in the consolidation. If this is not practicable, the subsidiary's financial statements for the previous financial year should be used, provided that the year-end did not end more than three months from the parent's year-end. In this case, any changes that have taken place in the intervening period that materially affect the view given by the group's financial statements should be taken into account by adjustments in the preparation of the consolidated financial statements.

Adjustments at acquisition

Adjustments should be made at the date of acquisition to reflect:

1. Fair values,
2. Accounting policy alignments and
3. Deferred tax considerations.

These adjustments will alter the net assets at the date of acquisition and will also affect:

- Net assets at the balance sheet date and
- Post-acquisition reserves of the subsidiary (for example, increased depreciation, release of provisions, increase in inventories, etc.).

Consolidated income statement (profit and loss account)

Each entity within the group will prepare its own set of financial statements (the 'separate' financial statements). The parent will then consolidate the separate financial statements with those of its own (subject to consolidation adjustments) to arrive at a set of consolidated (group) financial statements.

The preparation of the consolidated profit and loss account does not pose any real complexities *per se*. To prepare a consolidated profit and loss account, it is merely consolidating, line-by-line, up to the levels of profit after tax. After profit after tax, the amounts attributable to the parent and the non-controlling (minority) interests are shown, hence:

Up to profit after taxation:	amalgamate on a line-by-line basis
Non-controlling interests:	is the non-controlling interest share of the subsidiary's post-tax profit.

Intra-group sales

All intra-group sales are eliminated from both turnover (revenue) and cost of sales/other costs of the group. If there are any provisions for unrealised profit, then charge the change in the provision in the year to the cost of sales of the company making the intra-group sale.

Intra-group dividends and interest

Eliminate dividends from the subsidiary from the group's investment income and full amount of interest from investment income and interest payable.

Consolidated statement of financial position (balance sheet)

The preparation of the consolidated balance sheet is inherently more complicated than the consolidated profit and loss account. The assets and liabilities section of the balance sheet reflects the net assets that are under the control of the parent, whereas the capital and reserves section (i.e. equity) reflects the split of ownership between the parent and the non-controlling interest.

The basic method of preparing the consolidated balance sheet is as follows.

Area	*Method*
Assets	Amalgamate on a line-by-line basis
Liabilities	Amalgamate on a line-by-line basis
Share capital	Parent company only
Reserves	Group reserves comprise:
	Parent's reserves and
	Share of subsidiary's post-acquisition profit/loss
Goodwill	Capitalise and amortise
Non-controlling interests	Non-controlling interest's share of net assets at the balance sheet date

Intra-group balances

Intra-group trading balances (debtors and creditors) should cancel each other out. If they do not contra, it is more than likely due to cash or stock in transit. In-transit items should be adjusted for by adding them into stock/cash and amending the intra-group balance in the accounts of the receiving company prior to consolidation.

Intra-group dividends

Once each company has recognised dividends payable and receivable, intra-group amounts should be cancelled, which will then leave a balance for the consolidated balance sheet representing the amounts payable to the non-controlling interests.

Provision for unrealised profit

Provision should be made by eliminating the unrealised profit element of year-end stock from the consolidated balance sheet stock value and from the reserves of the company making the intra-group sale. Full charge is therefore made, where appropriate, against the non-controlling interests.

THE PURCHASE METHOD

In a business combination, the purchase method works in much the same way as the acquisition method of accounting worked in previous UK GAAP. Under the purchase method, the fair value of the costs that have been incurred to acquire the entity are measured. The costs that are directly attributable to the acquisition (for example, legal fees and due diligence fees) are added to the cost of the acquisition rather than immediately expensing them to profit or loss. This is a notable difference between FRS 102 and the same treatment under IFRS (IFRS 3 *Business Combinations* requires such costs to be written off to profit or loss). There are generally three steps in applying the purchase method, which are outlined in Section 19 *Business Combinations and Goodwill*:

(a) The identity of the acquirer is established.
(b) The cost of the business combination is measured.
(c) Allocate the cost of the business combination to the assets acquired and liabilities assumed as well as provisions for any contingent liabilities assumed. The cost is allocated at the date of acquisition.

Identifying the acquirer

The acquirer is the entity that is purchasing the subsidiary and that will be able to exercise control over the target entity.

Measuring the cost of the business combination

The cost of the business combination is the aggregate of:

• The fair values of assets to be acquired, liabilities to be assumed or incurred and equity instruments that are issued by the acquirer in exchange for control over the target entity and
• Costs that are directly attributable to the business combination.

Allocating the cost of the combination to assets and liabilities

At the date of acquisition, the acquirer will recognise the target's identifiable assets and liabilities and provisions for contingent liabilities that satisfy the recognition criteria that are laid down in paragraph 19.20 of FRS 102 at their fair values. The difference between the consideration paid and the assets acquired and liabilities incurred or assumed will generally be goodwill.

Where any elements of the consideration value are variable (for example, contingent consideration), any adjustment to the actual consideration paid is taken to be an amendment to the purchase consideration.

At the date of acquisition, the fair value of the target's assets and liabilities are determined. In reality, arriving at fair values long after a particular date is not always easy and hence, on transition to FRS 102, there is the exemption available not to restate earlier acquisitions.

Deferred tax is also recognised on fair value adjustments made to the assets and liabilities and goodwill will arise (see the next section 'Goodwill in a Business Combination').

GOODWILL IN A BUSINESS COMBINATION

Goodwill is the excess of the purchase consideration paid and the net assets that the parent has acquired in a subsidiary. Goodwill is dealt with in Section 19 of FRS 102 *Business Combinations and Goodwill*.

Example – Calculation of goodwill

On 1 January 2015 P acquired an 80% holding in S for a purchase consideration of £30,000. The entries in the books of P were:

DR investments (non-current assets)		£30,000
CR cash at bank	£30,000	

In the consolidated financial statements, the £30,000 investment in non-current assets will be removed and replaced with the goodwill arising on acquisition. If it is assumed that at the date of acquisition, S's net assets were £20,000, consisting of £10,000 issued ordinary share capital and £10,000 profit and loss account reserves, the goodwill arising on acquisition is as follows:

Cost of investment		£30,000
Less net assets acquired:		
Share capital	£10,000	
Reserves	£10,000	
		(£20,000)
Goodwill at acquisition		£10,000

Positive goodwill will appear as an asset in the consolidated financial statements and will be amortised over its expected useful life. An important point to consider is that where management cannot reliably assess the useful economic life of the goodwill, paragraph 19.23(a) presumes a maximum life of five years. This is a considerable reduction from previous UK GAAP, which contained a rebuttable presumption that goodwill has a useful economic life of up to 20 years. The five-year life is to be reviewed in future by the Department for Business Innovation and Skills.

FRS 102 does not consider goodwill to have an indefinite life – as a consequence, reporting entities must assess the useful economic life of goodwill and amortise goodwill over that estimated life.

In situations where there is a bargain purchase (for example, the acquisition of a financially distressed company), the fair value of the assets and liabilities will be more than the consideration paid. As a result, negative goodwill will arise and care needs to be taken to ensure that the amount of negative goodwill is appropriate. When such situations present themselves, the acquirer must:

- Review how the target's assets, liabilities and provisions for contingent liabilities have been calculated as well as reviewing the accuracy of the measurement of the cost of the combination.
- If the above results in no changes to the figures and negative goodwill still arises, then the negative goodwill is recognised on the balance sheet directly below positive goodwill and a subtotal is then struck.
- After initial recognition, the parent will recognise the excess up to the fair value of the non-monetary assets acquired in profit or loss when those non-monetary assets are recovered. Further excesses will be recognised in profit or loss in the period the parent company is expected to benefit from such assets.

Example – Consolidation schedule

Parent Co. (P) has owned 80% of Subsidiary Co. (S) for several years. P's year-end is 31 December 2015 and it is preparing consolidated financial statements for the year then ended. The draft financial statements of both companies for the year ended 31 December 2015 are as follows:

Balance sheets		*P*	*S*
Fixed assets		**£'000**	**£'000**
Tangible fixed assets		1,920	200
Investment in S		80	—
		2,000	200
Current assets			
Stock	Note 1	500	120
Trade debtors		650	40
Cash at bank		390	35
		1,540	195
Current liabilities			
Trade creditors		910	30
Dividend payable		100	40
Corporation tax		130	25
		1,140	95
Net current assets		400	100
NET ASSETS		2,400	300
Capital and reserves			
Share capital		2,000	100
Profit and loss account		400	200
		2,400	300
Profit and loss accounts		£'000	£'000
Turnover		5,000	1,000
Cost of sales	Note 1	2,900	600
Gross profit		2,100	400

Administrative expenses	1,700	320
Profit before taxation	400	80
Tax	130	25
Profit after tax	270	55

NOTE 1

P sold goods that cost £80,000 to S on 31 December 2015 for £100,000. These goods reached S on 4 January 2016 at which point the subsidiary recorded the transaction.

The consolidation schedule that will be used to produce the consolidated financial statements of the group can be drawn up as follows:

P Group Ltd
Consolidation schedule
For the year ended 31 December 2015

	P Limited		S Limited		Cons. adj.		Group	
	Dr	Cr	Dr	Cr	Dr	Cr	Dr	Cr
Turnover		5,000		1,000	100			5,900
Cost of sales	2,900		600			80	3,420	
Admin expenses	1,700		320				2,020	
Taxation	130		25				155	
NCI*						11	11	
Dividend (P only)	130						130	
Retained profit	140		55		(31)		164	
ASSETS								
Fixed assets	1,920		200				2,120	
Investments	–						–	
Stocks	500		120			80	700	
Trade debtors	650		40			(100)	590	
Cash at bank	390		35				425	
Total assets	3,460		395		(20)		3,835	
LIABILITIES								
Trade creditors		910		30				940
Dividend payable:								
P Limited		100						100
NCI				8				8
Corporation tax		130		25				155
Total liabilities		1,140		63				1,203

Net assets, group	**2,632**
Capital and reserves	
Share capital (P)	2,000
Reserves**	572
NCI***	60
	2,632

*NON-CONTROLLING INTERESTS

20% × £55,000 (profit after tax of subsidiary) = £11,000

**PROFIT AND LOSS RESERVES

	P Ltd
	£'000
P's reserves	400
Stock in transit (at cost)	80
Intra-group sale	(100)
Dividend receivable (40% × £40,000)	32
Share of S reserves	160 (80% × £200,000)
	572

***NON-CONTROLLING INTERESTS

20% × £300,000 = £60,000

STEP ACQUISITIONS

There may be occasions where a parent acquires a subsidiary in stages rather than in one outright transaction. A business combination undertaken in stages (step acquisition) is accounted for from the date of acquisition, which is the date on which the acquirer obtains control of the acquiree. The acquirer has control when it has the power to govern the financial and operating policies of an entity or business in order to obtain benefits from the acquiree's business.

As the business grows, the investor may decide to increase its investment. Alternatively, larger stakes could give rise to significant influence or joint control, which are accounted for under Section 14 *Investments in Associates* or Section 15 *Investments in Joint Ventures* respectively. Step acquisitions are often referred to as 'bought on the step' or 'piecemeal acquisitions'. Investments may be carried at cost and this cost is replaced by a share of net assets and goodwill when the investor has an ownership interest that gives it control. Therefore consolidated financial statements are prepared if the group is not exempt under Section 9 of FRS 102 or the Companies Act 2006. Many investments in subsidiaries start their life as a simple investment and therefore are accounted for under Section 11 *Basic Financial Instruments* and then grow to become an associate and eventually a subsidiary.

Example – Goodwill in a step acquisition

Several years ago, Company A acquired a 15% holding in Company B for £10,000. In 2015, Company A acquired a further 60% for £90,000 when the net assets of Company B were £85,000. On the date of acquisition, the fair value of the 15% holding was calculated at £12,000.

As Company A has acquired a further 60% shareholding, this means that Company B becomes a subsidiary of Company A (A now owns 75%). Goodwill is calculated as follows:

	£
Cost of additional investment	90,000
Fair value of the previous 15% holding	12,000
Fair value of net assets at date of acquisition	(85,000)
Goodwill	17,000

Example – Two-stage acquisition

Company A acquires 75% of Company B in two stages. Company A acquired 40% of Company B several years ago for £45,000 when the fair value of the net assets were £85,000. Since the date of acquiring its 40%, Company A has recognised its share of Company B's post-acquisition profits amounting to £5,500, resulting in a carrying amount of £50,500. During the year, Company A acquired a further 35% in Company B for a further £90,000 and the net assets in Company B at the date the additional shares were bought were £115,000. At the acquisition date, the fair value of the previous 40% holding was valued at £55,000.

The first step is to determine the effect on profit or loss and the second step is to determine the effect on goodwill.

On the date of acquiring the additional 35% in Company B, Company A needs to recognise a gain of £4,500 in profit or loss. This is the difference between the previously held 40% stake of £50,500 and the fair value of the initial 40% holding, which has been valued at £55,000.

The goodwill on acquisition is calculated as follows:

	£
Cost of additional investment	90,000
Fair value of the previous 40% holding	55,000
Fair value of B's net assets at acquisition	(115,000)
Goodwill on acquisition	30,000

DISPOSAL OF A SUBSIDIARY

The main consideration where disposals of interests are concerned is that a subsidiary should be consolidated up to the date that the parent loses control. Typically, an undertaking ceases to be a subsidiary of another when the group sells it or reduces its percentage interest in the undertaking such that it loses subsidiary status. Equally, a parent may lose control over the undertaking because of changes in the rights it holds or in those held by another party in that undertaking. Alternatively, it may be the case that there is a change in some other arrangement that gave the parent its control.

A reduction in percentage interest may arise from a direct disposal or from a deemed disposal and a gain or loss will normally arise on both a disposal and a deemed disposal.

The most common transaction that results in an undertaking ceasing to be a subsidiary is an outright disposal. The consolidated profit and loss account should include the trading results of the undertaking up to the date of it ceasing to be a subsidiary and appropriately disclosed as a discontinued operation. Any gain or loss arising on disposal would be included in the profit and loss account.

The profit or loss on disposal of all, or part, of a subsidiary will be the difference at the date of sale between:

1. The proceeds of the sale and
2. The group's share of the subsidiary undertaking's net assets disposed of.

Partial disposals – subsidiary to subsidiary

Where a partial disposal occurs and the parent still retains control (hence the subsidiary remains a subsidiary), albeit with reduced ownership by the parent, the non-controlling interests in that subsidiary should be increased by the carrying amount of the net identifiable assets that are now attributable to the non-controlling interests. However, no amount for goodwill that arose on the initial acquisition of the group's interest in that subsidiary should be attributed to the non-controlling interests.

Example – Reduction in ownership – parent retains control

P holds a 90% interest in S Limited. S has net assets of £4,000. P sells a 10% stake in S for £500 to the non-controlling interests.

In this example, P still holds control of S after the partial disposal to the non-controlling interests. The entries in the equity section of the balance sheet for P will be:

DR cash at bank	£500
CR non-controlling interests	£50
CR equity	£450

Partial disposal – subsidiary to associate

Where a partial disposal occurs and the parent loses control but retains significant influence, the disposal is accounted for and the undertaking is no longer treated as a subsidiary but is reclassified as an associate and therefore equity accounted in accordance with Section 14 *Investments in Associates*.

Example – Subsidiary reclassified to associate

P held a 100% ownership interest in S until 31 December 2015 when it sold a 60% stake to an unconnected party. The sale proceeds amounted to £675,000 and the cost of the investment in the subsidiary amounted to £600,000. Goodwill has been fully amortised.

At the date of sale the fair value of the net assets in S amounted to £800,000. The parent's profit and loss account will show a gain on the sale of the investment as follows:

	£
Sale proceeds	675,000
Less cost of investment in subsidiary	(600,000)
Gain	75,000

The consolidated financial statements will show a gain on sale of £195,000 calculated as follows:

Net assets and proceeds after disposal:	£
Share of net assets (£800,000 × 40%)	320,000
Sale proceeds	675,000
	995,000
Less net assets prior to disposal	(800,000)
Gain on sale to the group	195,000

In this scenario, after the sale has completed, S will no longer be a subsidiary to P, but instead as an associate and equity accounted in accordance with Section 14 of FRS 102. It will be included in the consolidated balance sheet as an investment in an associated undertaking at a value of £320,000 (40% × £800,000).

Partial disposal – subsidiary to investment

When a parent disposes of ownership interest in a subsidiary to such an extent that it owns less than 20% of the net assets, and therefore has neither control nor significant influence, the undertaking is accounted for as a simple investment in accordance with Section 11 *Basic Financial Instruments*.

Example – Subsidiary to investment

On 20 December 2015, P owned 100% of S. On 31 December 2015, P completed the sale of an 85% ownership interest in S to an unconnected third party for a purchase consideration of £750,000. Prior to the disposal the net assets of S were £500,000 and there was also a revaluation reserve account balance in respect of an owned item of property amounting to £20,000. At the date of disposal, the fair value of P's 15% investment was £130,000.

The gain on disposal is calculated as follows:

Disposal account	£'000	£'000
Net assets in S disposed of	500	
Sale proceeds		750
Interest retained		130
Revaluation reserve		20
Gain on disposal	400	___
	900	900

The gain of £400,000 is the difference between the gain on the 85% interest disposed of and the gain on the interest P has retained in S of 15% and can be proved as follows:

Disposal proceeds	750
Investment disposed (85% × £500,000)	(425)
Revaluation reserve balance	20
	345
Fair value of 15% of S	130
Less revised net assets (15% × £500,000)	(75)
Gain on disposal	400

DEEMED DISPOSALS

An undertaking may cease to be a subsidiary of a parent or the group may reduce its ownership interest as a result of a deemed disposal. A deemed disposal may arise where:

- The group does not take up its full allocation of rights in a rights issue.
- The group does not take up its full share of a scrip dividend.
- Another party exercises its options or warrants.
- The subsidiary issues shares to other non-group parties.

Deemed disposals have the same effect as changes in ownership by disposal and should be accounted for in the same way.

However, if a parent still retains control of a subsidiary following a deemed disposal, the transaction is accounted for as a transaction between shareholders. No gain or loss is recognised in the consolidated profit and loss account.

Example – Deemed disposal – parent loses control

P owns 600,000 of the 1 million shares in S, giving P a 60% holding in S. S's net assets in the consolidated financial statements of P are £100 million. When P acquired S, goodwill arose amounting to £12 million, which has not suffered any impairment. S issues a further 500,000 shares to a third party investor for £90 million, resulting in P's share falling from 60% to 40% (600,000 shares/1.5 million shares). As P's ownership falls from 60% to 40%, S is no longer a subsidiary of P. P will recognise S as an associate as it has significant influence over S at its fair value at the date S becomes an associate.

Example – Deemed disposal – parent retains control

Using the same facts as in the example above, P owns 600,000 of the 1 million shares issued in S, resulting in a 60% ownership interest. S then issues a further 90,909 shares to a third party for £17 million. In this example, P's interest in S is diluted from 60% to 55% (600,000/1,090,909). P still controls S because the holding is more than 50% and therefore S is still a subsidiary of P.

This deemed disposal is accounted for as a transaction between shareholders. P does not recognise any gain or loss and does not adjust any goodwill that was previously recognised on the acquisition of S. All P does in the consolidated financial statements is:

DR cash at bank	£17 million
CR non-controlling interests	£12.65 million*
CR equity	£4.35 million

*Previously, the non-controlling interests were 40% and the net assets of S are £100 million and hence 40% × £100 million equals £40 million. Non-controlling interests are now 45% and therefore 45% × £117 million (£100 million net assets plus £17 million proceeds from share issue) = £52.65 million. Therefore, £52.65 million less £40 million is an increase of £12.65 million.

The treatment of a disposal with no loss of control in FRS 102 does not have any impact on profit or loss and is significantly different than under the previous UK GAAP.

MERGER ACCOUNTING

Merger accounting was reintroduced into FRS 102 despite not being in the previous Exposure Drafts. The concept of merger accounting was introduced in the UK to recognise that two entities may come together to form a new entity. A key feature of merger accounting is that no one party controls another party – the combining entities are merged to form a new business. Where group reconstructions are concerned, merger accounting is an accounting policy choice and FRS 102 at paragraph 19.33(b) requires disclosure of whether a business combination has taken place using merger accounting or the purchase method.

Example – Mid-year merger

Breary Ltd. and Byrne Ltd. both have a year-end of 31 December. On 30 June 2015 the two entities were merged to form a new company, B & B Industries.

When a merger takes place part-way through an accounting year, the full year results of both combining entities are included in the consolidated financial statements (both the current year and the previous year). No fair value adjustments are made and there is no goodwill recognised.

As a merger is not the acquisition of a subsidiary by the parent, the carrying values of assets and liabilities of the combining parties are not required to be adjusted to fair value and the results and cash flows of the combining entities are brought into the financial statements as at the beginning of the financial year that the merger occurred. The comparative figures are then restated by combining the following for each individual entity that has been merged:

- The total of each entity's other comprehensive income for the previous reporting period and
- Each entity's statement of financial position (balance sheet) at the previous reporting date.

Adjustments will more than likely have to be made so as to align accounting policies in respect of carrying values and the overall results of the entities being merged.

If there is any difference between the nominal value of the issued shares *plus* the fair value of any consideration given and the nominal value of the shares received in exchange, the difference is shown as a movement on 'other reserves' in the consolidated financial statements. Any balances that are held in the share premium account or capital redemption reserve of the new subsidiary should be included by being shown as a movement on other reserves and then reported in the statement of changes in equity.

Costs that are incidental to the merger are excluded from any adjustments required above. Such expenses are charged to profit or loss as part of the combined profit and loss account of the combined entity at the date of the group reconstruction.

SEPARATE FINANCIAL STATEMENTS

Separate financial statements are those financial statements prepared by a parent entity whereby the investments in subsidiaries, associates or jointly controlled entities are accounted for under the cost or fair value model as opposed to being accounted for on the basis of the reported results and net assets of each investee. Separate financial statements are prepared in accordance with the Companies Act 2006 and GAAP.

Example – An entity that is not a parent

A company has a number of investments in associates and jointly controlled entities as part of its business model. The company, however, is not the parent of these investees.

Where a reporting entity is not a parent, FRS 102 requires such entities to account for any investments in associates using:

- The cost model less any accumulated impairment losses,
- The fair value model with fluctuations in fair value going through other comprehensive income or
- The fair value model with changes in fair value going through profit or loss.

For its jointly controlled entities, an entity that is not a parent is required to account for such using paragraph 15.9, which gives the entity the above choices to account for such jointly controlled operations.

DISCLOSURE REQUIREMENTS

The disclosure requirements in relation to consolidated financial statements are as follows:

- The fact that the financial statements are consolidated financial statements.

- How the conclusion has been drawn that the parent has obtained control when the parent does not own (either directly or indirectly) via the subsidiaries more than half of the voting rights.
- Differences between the reporting date of the parent and any subsidiaries that have been used in preparing the consolidated financial statements.
- Any significant restrictions on the ability of the subsidiary to transfer funds to the parent in the form of dividends or to repay loans.
- The name of any subsidiary that has been excluded from consolidation together with the reasons for the exclusion.

Small groups

For groups that are classed as 'small' and are therefore exempt from the requirement to prepare group financial statements, the following disclosures should be made in the individual financial statements relating to investments:

- The name of the subsidiary, associate or jointly controlled entity,
- The nature of the business,
- The country of incorporation,
- Class of shares and percentage of shares held,
- Aggregate capital and reserves (current and previous year) and
- Profit/(loss) for the year (current and previous year).

If the year- or period-end is not the same as the parent, the subsidiary's year- or period-end will also need disclosure.

Separate financial statements

A parent company preparing separate financial statements should disclose:

(a) The fact that the statements are separate financial statements and
(b) A description of the methods used to account for investments in subsidiaries, jointly controlled entities and associates.

For business combinations taking place during the period

In respect of business combinations that have taken place during the reporting period, the following disclosures should be made in accordance with paragraphs 19.25 and 19.25A to FRS 102:

- The names and descriptions of the combining entities or businesses,
- The date of acquisition,
- The percentage of any voting equity instruments acquired,
- The cost of the business combination,
- A description of the components of cost (for example, cash, shares or debt instruments),
- The amounts that have been recognised at the date of acquisition for each class of the target's assets, liabilities and contingent liabilities, including goodwill,
- The useful economic life of the goodwill,

- If the useful economic life of the goodwill exceeds five years, supporting reasons should be disclosed and
- The periods in which the excess exceeding the fair value of non-monetary assets in respect of negative goodwill will be recognised in profit or loss.

For each material business combination that has taken place during the accounting period, the acquiring company must also disclose the amounts of revenue and profit or loss of the acquiree since the date of acquisition that have been included within the group statement of comprehensive income for the accounting period. For individual, immaterial business combinations, such disclosures can be aggregated.

For all business combinations

In respect of all business combinations, the acquirer must disclose a reconciliation of the carrying amount in respect of goodwill at the beginning and the end of the accounting period. This reconciliation will disclose:

- Changes that have arisen due to new business combinations,
- Amortisation,
- Impairment losses,
- Previously acquired businesses that have been disposed of and
- Other changes.

In respect of the excess exceeding the fair value of non-monetary assets acquired that are to be recognised in subsequent accounting periods (in respect of negative goodwill), disclosure should be made of:

- Changes that have arisen due to new business combinations,
- Amounts that have been recognised in profit or loss,
- Previously acquired businesses that have been disposed of and
- Other changes.

The disclosures above need not be made for prior periods reported in the financial statements.

Group reconstructions

For all group reconstructions that have taken place during the accounting period, the combined business should disclose:

- The names of the combining entities (but not the reporting entity),
- Details of whether the combination has been accounted for as a merger or an acquisition and
- The date that the combination took place.

7 ACCOUNTING POLICIES, ESTIMATES AND ERRORS

INTRODUCTION

The importance of appropriate accounting policies in the preparation of financial statements is essential. This is because they form the 'backbone' of financial statements and can heavily influence reported profits/losses and net assets. As a result, accounting policies have to be applicable to the entity's circumstances – particularly where FRS 102 offers a choice in accounting policy in certain areas (for example, the revaluation model or cost model for fixed assets). On transition to FRS 102, new estimates may be necessary and preparers should consider such issues as early as possible.

Section 10 *Accounting Policies, Estimates and Errors* gives the guidance reporting entities will need in order to appropriately select and apply accounting policies that will be used in the preparation of the financial statements. Section 10 also deals with aspects concerning a change in an accounting policy as well as outlining the requirements that need to be applied in the event that an error is discovered.

Changes in accounting policy are usually only undertaken when the change will result in the financial statements giving a clearer picture as to the state of the entity's affairs (in other words, the change will result in a more true and fair view being portrayed by the financial statements). In addition, a change in accounting policy can arise, for example, where the standard-setters change a section in FRS 102 that will result in a different accounting practice being undertaken when applying the change.

ADOPTING ACCOUNTING POLICIES

When an entity is choosing its accounting policies it must do so with the objective in mind that the financial statements have to give a true and fair view in accordance with statutory requirements. Financial statements will give a true and fair view when the requirements of UK GAAP are applied correctly and consistently. The accounting policies that a reporting entity adopts must:

- Have relevance to aid the decision-making of users of the financial statements and
- Be reliable.

Accounting policies are deemed to be 'reliable' when they result in financial statements which:

- Faithfully represent the financial position, financial performance and cash flows of the entity,
- Reflect the commercial substance of transactions, other events and conditions,
- Are neutral,
- Are prudent and
- Are complete within the bounds of materiality.

Paragraph 10.5 to FRS 102 goes on to offer a hierarchy that management should adopt in achieving accounting policies that are both relevant and reliable. Management must have regard to the following (in descending order) when selecting an accounting policy:

- The specific requirements that are contained in a Financial Reporting Standard (FRS) or guidance issued by the FRC in the form of Abstracts that deal with similar and related issues (although paragraph 10.3 of FRS 102 does not require an entity to follow such requirements if the effect of doing so would not be material).
- The provisions contained in Statements of Recommended Practice (SORPs).
- The requirements in Section 2 *Concepts and Pervasive Principles* – specifically the definitions, recognition and measurement criteria in respect of assets, liabilities, income and expenses.

Management can also have regard to EU-endorsed IFRS – particularly in relation to aspects such as the disclosure of earnings per share (IAS 33 *Earnings per Share*) and operating segments (IFRS 8 *Operating Segments*).

An important point to emphasise where accounting policies are concerned is that, whatever an entity deems to be appropriate, the consistency in the application of an entity's accounting policies is critical. The only exception to this rule would be where an FRS or Abstract would require different policies for similar transactions, other events and conditions (which in reality is fairly uncommon).

Reporting entities are required to select accounting policies that are appropriate to their specific circumstances. An example of an accounting policy that may involve different practices is the treatment of borrowing costs – some entities may capitalise the borrowing costs whilst others may write them off immediately to profit or loss as and when they are incurred.

Measurement bases are the methods used to measure monetary amounts in the financial statements, such as at depreciated historic cost or at revaluation, lower of cost and estimated selling price less costs to complete and sell or at recoverable amount. Some typical examples of accounting policies that may involve different measurement bases are:

- Measuring the entity's fixed assets at cost or at revaluation.
- Measuring inventories (stock) using first-in first-out (FIFO) or weighted average cost.

Different entities will also present items within the financial statements in different places, for example some entities may disclose depreciation charges within cost of sales, whilst others may disclose depreciation charges within administrative expenses.

CHANGING ACCOUNTING POLICIES

Whilst it is not explicitly mentioned in Section 10, it is recommended that an entity reviews its accounting policies regularly to ensure that they remain appropriate in the company's circumstances. It follows, therefore, that an accounting policy should not be changed unless the new policy is considered to be more appropriate in the company's circumstances than the previous accounting policy. This is accentuated by paragraph 10.8(b) in FRS 102, which requires an accounting policy to be changed if the revised accounting policy will provide reliable and more relevant information concerning the entity's transactions, events or conditions and the effect of those transactions, events or conditions on the entity's financial position, financial performance or cash flows.

It would be inappropriate to change accounting policies on a very frequent basis as users would find it more difficult to compare the financial statements from one year to another, regardless of the fact that a change in accounting policy is applied retrospectively. However, if there is a change to FRS 102 or another FRC Abstract that requires an entity to change an accounting policy then it should do so in order to comply with paragraph 10.8(a).

In a group situation, the Companies Act 2006 and paragraph 9.17 to FRS 102 requires uniformity in group accounting policies – that is, all members of the group should have the same accounting policies. Appropriate consolidation adjustments should be made to the financial statements of subsidiaries that do not have aligned accounting policies so that uniformity is achieved. However, SI 2008/410 6 Schedule 3(2) acknowledges that there may be situations arising which mean that a subsidiary company, for whatever reason, may be mandated to adopt a different accounting policy than the parent (for example, if the subsidiary is in a jurisdiction that requires a certain accounting policy to be adopted). In such cases, the Companies Act 2006 does require disclosures concerning the departure, the reasons for it and its effect on the financial statements in the notes to the consolidated financial statements.

Paragraph 10.9 to FRS 102 acknowledges certain situations that may arise but that are not changes in accounting policy, such as:

- Where transactions, events or conditions occur that have not previously occurred (or that were immaterial) for which an accounting policy is applied.
- Where transactions, events or conditions differ in substance from previously occurring transactions and for which an accounting policy is applied.
- Switching from the fair value model to the cost model when a reliable measure of fair value is unavailable (or vice versa).

Example – Change in accounting policy

Company A is a provider of social housing and has always built its own houses and used loan finance to develop the land to build the houses. It then employs the services of a contractor to build the houses on the developed land. The company has always had an accounting policy that borrowing costs incurred on building its houses should be written off to the profit and loss account as and when they are incurred as opposed to capitalising the borrowing costs as part of the cost of the houses. This is an accounting policy choice that is permissible in Section 25 *Borrowing Costs*.

After careful consideration, the directors have agreed to change the accounting policy and capitalise the borrowing costs as part of the costs of the houses. This is to ensure that there is consistency and comparability with other social housing providers as it was found during research that the vast majority of social housing providers do capitalise the borrowing costs as part of the cost of the houses.

The switching from expensing the borrowing costs to capitalising them represents a change in accounting policy. This change must be applied retrospectively to the comparative period. The effect of retrospective application is to enable the financial statements to portray a view that would have been the case had the revised accounting policy always been in existence.

Example – Change in stock valuation

Company B has always valued its stock using the weighted average cost method and as at 31 December 2015, the stock value was £100,000. During the year to 31 December 2016, the directors decided to change the valuation from weighted average cost to first-in first-out on the basis that research concluded that this would enable the financial statements to provide reliable and more relevant information about the effect stock has on the company's financial affairs.

The company must revalue its prior year stock balance under the revised policy (FIFO) and if it is assumed that the stock valuation would have been £120,000 as opposed to £100,000 at 31 December 2015, the entries in the books in the prior year (i.e. a prior-year adjustment) would be:

DR retained earnings	£20,000
CR stock	£20,000

Retrospective application is used to ensure that the revised accounting policy is applied to the earliest period reported in the financial statements to ensure that the financial statements are both consistent and comparable.

To determine whether, or not, a change in accounting policy has occurred, the following three questions should be asked:

1. Has there been a change in the way the entity recognises amounts in the financial statements?
2. Has there been a change in the way that the entity measures amounts in the financial statements?
3. Has there been a change in the way the entity presents amounts in the financial statements?

If the answer to any of the above three questions is 'yes' then there has been a change in accounting policy.

A company has decided that the payroll costs in respect of the maintenance department of a chemical factory should be reclassified from administration expenses to cost of sales on the grounds that presenting such costs within administration expenses is distorting gross profit margins.

The reclassification of costs from one area of the profit and loss account (income statement) to another would give rise to a change in presentation, which is a change in accounting policy. As a result, the change should also be applied retrospectively to the prior year to achieve consistency and comparability.

Changes to a recognition policy could occur if:

- The reporting entity decides to capitalise development costs rather than writing them off to profit or loss as and when they are incurred.
- Changing revenue recognition practices relating to the sale of goods or rendering of services.

Changes to a measurement policy could occur if the reporting entity decides to carry buildings in the balance sheet (statement of financial position) at fair value as opposed to depreciated historic cost.

A change to a presentation policy could be where the reporting entity decides to present depreciation charges within administration expenses as opposed to cost of sales (or vice versa). The only effect of this change is to restate the comparative amounts on a comparable basis.

An important point to emphasise where accounting policies are concerned is the interaction with Section 35 *Transition to this FRS*. Transitional issues are discussed in Chapter 31 and a transition from previous UK GAAP to FRS 102 is not considered to be a change in accounting policy. The transitional process may look familiar to a change in accounting policy because of the retrospective application, but Section 35 is markedly different to Section 10 in that Section 35 contains various exemptions and exceptions from full retrospective application of various accounting policies. Therefore, on transition to FRS 102, whilst it is imperative that accounting policies are considered, any transitional adjustments arising as a result of the transition process must be dealt with under the provisions in Section 35 and not Section 10.

DEVELOPMENT OF AN ACCOUNTING POLICY IN THE ABSENCE OF SPECIFIC DIRECTION IN FRS 102

In rare situations, there may be occasion when a transaction or event occurs that is not specifically covered in FRS 102. In such situations, it is down to the management to devise an accounting policy. Care must be taken in such situations because management cannot follow an accounting treatment for a transaction or event that is inappropriate to the company's circumstances, as this would give rise to misleading information being presented in the financial statements. There may also be taxation implications for an inappropriate accounting treatment, as in many cases the taxation treatment of a transaction would follow the accounting treatment.

Management must develop an accounting policy, having regard to the *Concepts and Pervasive Principles* outlined in Section 2 to FRS 102. In developing a policy, the policy must be both *relevant* and *reliable*. This will involve the exercising of judgement on the part of management and advice should be sought if the subject is contentious to ensure that the right outcome is achieved.

ACCOUNTING ESTIMATES

The importance of accounting estimates is as equivalent to the importance of appropriate accounting policies because estimations can be very subjective and ultimately must enable the financial statements to give a true and fair view as well as being consistent with GAAP. There may be occasions when a number of estimation techniques are available and in such cases the entity must adopt the estimation technique(s) that are judged to be most appropriate in the entity's circumstances.

Essentially, estimation techniques are employed as a means for making best estimates where the value of items being measured is relatively unknown and can be used to measure:

- Depreciation methods for fixed assets (for example, reducing balance or straight-line methods).
- Fair values.
- General bad debt provisions.
- Provisions for sales returns.
- Impairment of fixed assets and goodwill.
- Revenue recognition for finance leases.
- Costs of stock and work-in-progress.
- Construction contract accounting.

CHANGES IN ACCOUNTING ESTIMATES

Changes to accounting estimates are not the same as accounting policy changes and it is important that this distinction is clearly understood because the accounting treatment between an accounting policy change and an estimation technique change is notably different. Changes to accounting estimates are not applied retrospectively – instead they are applied prospectively (i.e. to the current and subsequent accounting periods). This is because there is no change to recognition criteria, measurement bases or methods of presentation.

An important point to note about the nature of accounting estimate changes is that they are *not* correction of errors. Financial statements inherently contain a degree of estimations (such as accruals, tax provisions or general bad debt provisions). Paragraph 10.15 acknowledges that changes in accounting estimates that result from new information or developments are not to be classified as a correction of errors.

Example – Change of depreciation rate

A company has a policy of depreciating their motor vehicles on a five-year straight-line basis and the financial statements for the year ended 31 October 2016 are in the process of being completed. Management of the company have decided to change the method of depreciating their motor vehicles to a 25% reducing balance method on the grounds that this better reflects the consumption of the assets.

The company will apply the change in the 31 October 2016 financial statements and subsequently go forward with their new policy. The 2015 financial statements will not need to be adjusted as the change is not a change in accounting policy. The motor vehicles are still carried at cost less accumulated depreciation and the depreciation is still allocated to individual accounting periods that reflect the consumption of the economic benefits of the vehicles.

If a change in estimate will have the effect of changing assets and liabilities, or if the estimate relates to an item of equity, then the carrying amount of the related asset, liability or component of equity is changed accordingly in the period that the estimate is changed.

Under FRS 102, some entities will need to carefully consider their estimates; for example, if the entity carried goodwill and intangible assets under previous GAAP using an indefinite life, this will change under FRS 102 as the standard requires goodwill and intangible assets to be amortised on a systematic basis over the useful economic lives. Hence a reporting entity previously carrying intangible assets using an indefinite life will have to change the accounting practice on transition to FRS 102.

CORRECTION OF ERRORS

Under Section 10, errors are corrected by way of a prior-year adjustment if the error(s) is/are a *material* error(s). This is a notable difference between Section 10 of FRS 102 and FRS 3 *Reporting Financial Performance*. Under the provisions in previous FRS 3, an error would be corrected by way of a prior-year adjustment if the error was *fundamental*. The term 'fundamental' was taken to mean that the error essentially destroys the truth and fairness of the financial statements. Because of the significance that a fundamental error would have on the financial statements, it was inappropriate under FRS 3 to correct the error in the current year as the financial statements would still be misleading – in other words they would not be comparable. The same principle is contained within Section 10, although it is to be expected that there will be more errors corrected by way of a prior-year adjustment under FRS 102 than was the case under FRS 3.

Materiality is a matter of judgement, but is generally taken to mean that an item (for example, an error) is taken to be material if it could influence the decision-making of the users of the financial statements on the basis of the financial statements taken as a whole.

Section 10 refers to 'errors' as being the effects of:

- Mathematical error,
- Mistakes in applying the company's declared accounting policies,
- Oversights,
- Misinterpreting facts and
- Fraud.

Example – Immaterial error

Bart Baling Equipment Limited is preparing its financial statements for the year ended 30 November 2016. Extracts from the previous year's financial statements are as follows:

	30.11.2015
	£
Turnover	4,325,012
Pre-tax profit	274,201
Net assets	2,774,231

During the preparation of the 2016 financial statements, the accountant discovered an electricity bill that had been received on 6 January 2016 amounting to £4,000 (excluding value added tax), which related to the period from 1 October 2015 to 31 December 2015.

The materiality of the transaction has to be deciphered and such a bill is clearly immaterial to the financial statements as a whole. Certainly at 0.09% of revenue (£4,000/4,325,012 × 100) and 1.5% of pre-tax profit, the fact that a £4,000 electricity bill has been overlooked is not going to have a significant impact on the financial statements; hence it can simply be corrected in the current year.

In addition to over- or underestimations of tax provisions, other examples of errors that would be classified as immaterial would be amounts relating to:

- Accruals,
- Prepayments,
- Stock provisions and
- Bad debt provisions.

Such immaterial errors can be corrected in the current accounting period as opposed to a prior-year adjustment.

Material errors, on the other hand, must be corrected by way of a prior-year adjustment in order that the financial statements can achieve comparability. A prior-year adjustment is undertaken by correcting the error retrospectively by amending the prior-year financial statements.

Example – Error occurring in years not presented in the financial statements

Kai Construction Co. Limited presents financial statements to 31 October each year. The current year's financial statements are being prepared to 31 October 2015 by the newly appointed firm of accountants.

During the preparation of the 31 October 2015 financial statements, an error came to light and upon further investigation the accountant found that the error originally occurred in the 31 October 2013 financial year. The error has been judged to be material by the partner in charge.

The financial statements for the year ended 31 October 2015 will only show the results of the current year and the 2014 comparatives. As the error has occurred before the earliest prior period presented, the opening balances of relevant assets, liabilities and equity would have to be restated for the earliest prior period presented.

Example – Correction of a material error

The financial statements of Scanlon Enterprises Limited for the year ended 31 December 2015 are in the process of being completed. These financial statements are shown below:

Scanlon Enterprises Limited
Profit and Loss Account
for the year ended 31 December 2015

	2015	2014
	£'000	**£'000**
Turnover	4,000	3,500
Cost of sales	950	820
Gross profit	3,050	2,680
Administrative expenses	1,200	800
Profit on ordinary activities before taxation	1,850	1,880
Tax on profit on ordinary activities	700	600
Profit for the financial year	1,150	1,280

Scanlon Enterprises Limited
Balance Sheet
as at 31 December 2015

	2015	2014
	£'000	**£'000**
Tangible fixed assets	5,325	4,000
Current assets		
Stock	400	300
Trade debtors	175	100
Cash at bank	250	200
	825	600
Creditors: amounts falling due within one year	750	350
NET CURRENT ASSETS	75	250
TOTAL ASSETS LESS CURRENT LIABILITIES	5,400	4,250
Capital and reserves		
Called up share capital	100	100
Profit and loss account	5,300	4,150
	5,400	4,250

During the preparation of the financial statements for the year ended 31 December 2015, it was noticed that a large item of plant and machinery that had been purchased on

20 December 2014 had been allocated to repairs and renewals within the profit and loss account (shown within administrative expenses) amounting to £325,000. The financial statements do not contain any amendments in respect of this error, which the partner in charge of the assignment has judged to be material. This error will need to be corrected by way of a prior-year adjustment.

The administrative expenses in the 2014 financial statements will need to be reduced by £325,000 and the tangible fixed assets will also increase by this amount. However, the depreciation element will also have to be considered, so for the purposes of this illustration assume that the client writes off the value of all its plant and machinery over five years on a straight-line basis and they charge a full year depreciation in the year of acquisition but none in the year of disposal. Therefore £65,000 worth of depreciation (£325,000/5 years) will need to be accounted for. Note that the tax implications of this error have been ignored for the purposes of this illustration.

Scanlon Enterprises Limited

Profit and Loss Account

for the year ended 31 December 2015

	2015	2014
		(as restated)
	£'000	£'000
Turnover	4,000	3,500
Cost of sales	950	820
Gross profit	3,050	2,680
Administrative expenses	1,265	540
Profit on ordinary activities before taxation	1,785	2,140
Tax on profit on ordinary activities	700	600
Profit for the financial year	1,085	1,540

Scanlon Enterprises Limited

Balance Sheet

as at 31 December 2015

	2015	2014
		(as restated)
	£'000	£'000
Tangible fixed assets	5,520	4,260
Current assets		
Stock	400	300
Trade debtors	175	100
Cash at bank	250	200
	825	600
Creditors: amounts falling due within one year	750	350
NET CURRENT ASSETS	75	250

TOTAL ASSETS LESS CURRENT LIABILITIES	<u>5,595</u>	<u>4,510</u>
Capital and reserves		
Called up share capital	100	100
Profit and loss account	<u>5,495</u>	<u>4,410</u>
	<u>5,595</u>	<u>4,510</u>

The error will also need to be reported through the statement of changes in equity for the year ended 31 December 2015 as follows:

Scanlon Enterprises Limited

Statement of changes in equity

for the year ended 31 December 2015

	Share capital	Profit and loss reserves	Total
	£'000	*£'000*	*£'000*
Balance at 1 January 2014	100	2,870	2,970
Profit for the year (as previously stated)	—	<u>1,280</u>	<u>1,280</u>
Balance at 31 December 2014 (as previously stated)	100	4,150	4,250
Prior-year adjustment*	—	<u>260</u>	<u>260</u>
Balance at 31 December 2014 (as restated)	100	4,410	4,510
Balance at 1 January 2015 (as restated)	100	4,410	4,510
Profit for the year	—	<u>1,085</u>	<u>1,085</u>
Balance at 31 December 2015	<u>100</u>	<u>5,495</u>	<u>5,595</u>

*The prior-year adjustment has been calculated as:

Cost of asset capitalised	£325,000
Depreciation (five years)	<u>(£65,000)</u>
Prior-year adjustment	£260,000

DISCLOSURE REQUIREMENTS

In respect of changes in accounting policy, the disclosure requirements in Section 10 are split between those that relate to a change in accounting policy due to changes in FRS 102 and those that relate to voluntary changes because management deem the change will result in providing reliable and more relevant information for users.

Disclosure requirements for accounting policy changes due to changes in FRS 102

Entities should disclose:

1. The nature of the accounting policy change.
2. The amount of the adjustment for each line item in the financial statements affected for both the current and the previous period presented (to the extent that this is practicable).

3. The amount of any adjustments made that relate to periods before those that are presented in the financial statements (to the extent that this is practicable).

4. Where it is impracticable to disclose the amounts required in (2) and (3) above, an explanation of why this is the case.

Disclosure requirements for voluntary accounting policy changes

For accounting policy changes that have been effected due to management's conclusion that such changes will provide reliable and more relevant information for users, entities should disclose:

(a) The nature of the accounting policy change.

(b) Supporting reasons as to why the change in accounting policy provides reliable and more relevant information.

(c) The amounts of the adjustments to each financial statement line item affected (to the extent that this is practicable), showing separately:

   i. Adjustments for the current year,

   ii. Adjustments for each prior period presented and

   iii. In aggregate for periods prior to those presented.

(d) Where it is considered impracticable to disclose the amounts required in (c) above, an explanation as to the reasons why it is considered impracticable.

Changes in accounting estimate

Reporting entities applying changes to accounting estimates are required to disclose the nature of any change in an accounting estimate, together with the effect that the change has on assets, liabilities, income and expense for the current period. Paragraph 10.18 to FRS 102 outlines the necessary disclosures.

Where it is practicable to estimate the effect of the change in accounting estimates in one or more future periods, the entity should make disclosure of those estimates.

Correction of prior-period errors

Where errors are corrected by way of a prior-period adjustment, an entity should disclose the nature of the prior-period error together with the amount of the correction for each financial statement line item that is affected for each prior period presented (to the extent that this is practicable).

There should also be disclosures that show the amount of the correction at the beginning of the earliest period presented and where the entity considers that it is not practicable to determine either the amount of each correction for each financial statement line item affected for each prior period presented or the amount of the correction at the beginning of the earliest period presented, then an explanation should be disclosed as to the reasons why it is impracticable.

8 REVENUE RECOGNITION

INTRODUCTION

The issue concerning revenue recognition has been somewhat controversial over the years. Revenue is the headline figure in a company's financial statements and the controversy has largely surrounded some entities attempting to delay revenue recognition, or conversely accelerate revenue recognition, purely to engineer the financial statements to achieve a desired outcome (usually, though not exclusively, to manipulate profit for the purposes of taxation). Clearly such acts fail to achieve both relevance and reliability, which are notable characteristics that financial statements must contain according to the *Concepts and Pervasive Principles*. Manipulation of the revenue figure can also lead to enquiries by HM Revenue and Customs (HMRC) who may choose to impose penalties and interest on companies where it can be proved that deliberate manipulation of the revenue figure has taken place.

Regardless of any deliberate attempts to falsify, revenue itself has become more complex in recent years with arrangements such as service contracts tied in with purchase price. Clear guidance from accounting standards must therefore be assimilated and followed.

Revenue recognition is dealt with in Section 23 *Revenue* of FRS 102. This particular section is a very comprehensive section with appendices attached to it, which aim to help users apply the section correctly. It is possible, in the future, that the section may be amended in order to reflect the new requirements based on the standard issued by the International Accounting Standards Board (IASB) in collaboration with the US standard-setters (the Financial Accounting Standards Board (FASB)) in the form of IFRS 15 *Revenue from Contracts with Customers*. Whilst alignment of Section 23 with IFRS 15 is possible in the future, at the time of writing the Financial Reporting Council (FRC) had not intimated its intention to do so – although as IFRS 15 is a significant development for the IASB and the FASB, it is the author's opinion that the FRC may well align Section 23 in the future.

Section 23 deals primarily with four types of transactions and events:

- The sale of goods by a reporting entity (this applies whether the entity has produced the goods for sale or purchased the goods for resale),
- Rendering of services,

- Construction contracts in which the business is the contractor and
- Assets that yield revenue in the form of interest, royalties and dividends.

Income can arise in many situations in a business and therefore Section 23 has been limited in its scope because the Section recognises that a business can receive income from a variety of sources and hence some types of income are dealt with by other standards, which can be seen in the following table.

Type of income not dealt with in Section 23:	*Relevant Section of FRS 102:*
Lease agreements	Section 20 *Leases*
Dividends/other income from investments that are accounted for under the equity method	Section 14 *Investments in Associates* and Section 15 *Investments in Joint Ventures*
The change in fair value of financial assets and financial liabilities (or their subsequent disposal)	Section 11 *Basic Financial Instruments* and Section 12 *Other Financial Instruments Issues*
Fair value fluctuations in investment property	Section 16 *Investment Property*
The initial recognition of, and subsequent changes in, the fair value of biological assets related to agricultural activity	Section 34 *Specialised Activities*
Initial recognition of agricultural produce	Section 34 *Specialised Activities*

If a reporting entity is involved with insurance contracts, these are the subject of a separate FRS – namely FRS 103 *Insurance Contracts* – and therefore revenue and other income that arise from such transactions or events should be accounted for in accordance with the provisions in FRS 103.

In terms of measurement principles, the underlying principle in Section 23 is that a reporting entity must recognise revenue at the *fair value* of the consideration received or receivable. For financial reporting purposes, the term 'fair value' is taken to mean the amount for which an asset could be exchanged, or a liability settled, or an equity instrument granted between both knowledgeable and willing persons in an arm's length transaction (i.e. on normal commercial terms). The Glossary to FRS 102 points users to the relevant guidance in paragraphs 11.27 to 11.32 in the absence of any specific guidance in determining fair value.

In measuring revenue, the reporting entity must only include the gross inflows of economic benefits received and receivable within its financial statements from its own principal activities. This principle will affect those entities that act as an agent on behalf of a principal. In such an arrangement, the agent may collect amounts on behalf of the principal and then pay those amounts over to the principal less an element of the agent's commission. The issue here concerns how much revenue the agent recognises in its financial statements, as can be seen in the following example.

Example – Agent/principal relationship

Heaton Holidays Limited (Heaton) acts as an agent on behalf of Tom's Tours Limited (Tom), which operates in the travel and tourism industry. Heaton sells tailor-made holidays to the general public and the tours are booked through Tom. Heaton collects the monies from the customer and if any tours have been booked via Tom, those funds are paid over to Tom less commission for Heaton.

In this scenario, Heaton is acting as an agent to Tom. Paragraph 23.4 will be relevant to Heaton in this respect as it deals with the issue of the agent/principal relationship. This paragraph requires the agent to include in its revenue only the commission amount and not the amounts that have been collected on behalf of the principal. In respect of the tours booked by the customer, Heaton will only include its commission in the revenue figure – the amounts paid over to Tom will be recognised as a current liability in the balance sheet (statement of financial position) until such time as the principal amounts are paid over to Tom.

DEFERRED PAYMENT

There may be occasions when an entity may agree with its customer to defer payment beyond normal credit terms. In substance such an agreement will effectively be a financing arrangement and in such cases the fair value of the consideration will be the present value of all future receipts, which is determined using an imputed rate of interest. The most common example of such an arrangement is in respect of a supplier providing interest-free credit to its customer. Paragraph 23.5 to FRS 102 says that the imputed rate of interest is the more clearly determinable of either:

- The rate that is prevailing for a similar instrument of an issuer with a similar credit rating or
- The rate that, when applied to the nominal amount of the instrument, discounts it to the current cash sales price of the goods or services supplied by the seller.

Because deferred payment arrangements are, in substance, financing arrangements, this will give rise to the recognition of interest income. Interest income must be accounted for under the provisions in paragraph 23.29(a), which says that a business recognises interest revenue by applying the *effective interest method* as per the provisions in paragraphs 11.15 to 11.20. The calculation of the effective interest method must include any related fees, finance charges paid or received, transaction costs and other premiums or discounts. The effective interest method is a means of calculating the amortised cost of a financial instrument and then allocating the interest expense or income over the life of the instrument.

Example – Calculation of interest income

On 1 January 2014, Don's Domestic Appliances Ltd sells a batch of electrical equipment amounting to £3,000 to a customer, giving them a three-year interest-free credit period. The rate of interest that discounts the nominal amount of the instrument to the current cash sales price is 8%. Don's Domestic Appliances has a year-end date of 31 December each year.

For the year ended 31 December 2014, revenue will be calculated as ($£3,000 \times 1/1.08^3$) = £2,381. The interest element will be calculated as ($£2,381 \times 8\%$) = £190.

For the year ended 31 December 2015, interest income will be ($(£2,381 + 190) \times 8\%$) = £206 and in 2016 the remaining interest will be £223.

This treatment is to enable the full £3,000 transaction to be recognised in Don's Domestic Appliances financial statements over the full three-year period.

SPECIFIC CONSIDERATIONS

The principles of revenue recognition contained in Section 23 are applied separately to each transaction in order to reflect the substance of each transaction. This principle is broadly similar to the revised requirements in IFRS 15, which requires revenue to be recognised when a 'performance obligation' has been met.

Because certain criteria have to be met in respect of the sales of goods, rendering of services and recognition of revenue from income-bearing assets, it is important that the principles contained in Section 23 are applied correctly. It follows, therefore, that the timing of revenue recognition is critical in order that the financial statements give a true and fair view. Disproportionate delaying of revenue recognition can cause untold amounts of issues for a reporting entity, including the possibility of an enquiry by HMRC. Conversely, if a company were to accelerate revenue recognition (for example, to show more positive results than would otherwise be the case), there could also be taxation implications for the company (i.e. paying too much corporation tax) as the tax treatment would follow the accounting treatment where revenue recognition is concerned and hence revenue would be taxed in the year (or period) in which it is recognised in the financial statements.

Revenue recognition policies can, in many cases, be extremely subjective and it may be the case that a company is required to recognise revenue in an accounting period, despite the fact that the company has not even invoiced the customer. This usually occurs when a 'milestone' or a 'critical event' is passed and was evident in previous UK GAAP in Application Note G to FRS 5 *Reporting the Substance of Transactions*, which required revenue to be recognised in such instances (usually this occurs in service organisations). The principles of this have, however, been carried over into Section 23, albeit not with the exact wording as contained in the previous UK GAAP.

Whatever the accounting policy of the entity in respect of its revenue recognition, Section 23 is very specific in the timing of revenue, but does recognise that in many cases professional judgement will have to be applied to recognise the correct amount of revenue. Where judgements are applied, it is often beneficial to have these judgements adequately documented for the purposes of external audit (where the entity is subjected to statutory audit), for taxation purposes (in the event of any enquiries into the revenue recognition policies of the entity by HMRC) and for internal control purposes (in order that management can assess whether their revenue recognition policies are being correctly applied in the financial statements).

EXCHANGES AND SALES OF GOODS

Section 23 deals with two types of situations that an entity may encounter – the exchanges of goods (or services) and the selling of goods.

Exchange of goods

An entity can only recognise revenue in respect of transactions that possess *commercial substance*. The term 'commercial substance' is taken to mean that the cash flows of the business are likely to change as a result of the transaction. A transaction will lack commercial substance where the cash flows of the entity are unlikely to change. In this respect, paragraph 23.6 recognises two instances when a reporting entity should not recognise revenue:

- When goods or services are exchanged for similar goods or services or
- When goods or services are exchanged for dissimilar goods or services but the transaction lacks commercial substance.

In such instances, a company cannot recognise revenue in its financial statements.

Example – Exchange of dissimilar goods where commercial substance is present

Sharman Software (Sharman) is a company that operates in the software industry producing bespoke software for accountants and taxation advisers. It has been in operation for five years and has been relatively successful, although sales have seen a slow decline over the last couple of years because the market leaders have introduced more advanced technology, which has had a detrimental effect on the company's sales and market share. The software company is looking into the possibility of adding further products to its portfolio, including disclosure checklists, bookkeeping software and training sessions in an attempt to diversify and increase sales. It has entered into discussions with the Hughes Partnership (Hughes), who have become established in the line of business that Sharman wishes to diversify into, and they have agreed to work together to achieve the company's objectives.

During the negotiations, Sharman agreed to exchange some of its software to the same value as the value of the goods that Hughes will supply; hence no additional assets (for example, cash) will need to be transferred to/from either party in the transaction.

Paragraph 23.7 to FRS 102 says that when goods are sold or services are exchanged for dissimilar goods or services in a transaction that possesses commercial substance, revenue is recognised and measured:

1. At fair value of the goods or services that have been received, fair value being adjusted for the amount of any cash or cash equivalents that have been transferred,
2. If the amount in 1 above cannot be reliably measured, the transaction is measured at the fair value of the goods or services that have been given up and subsequently adjusted for the amount of any cash or cash equivalents that have been transferred or
3. Should the fair value of neither the goods nor services received or given not have the ability to be reliably measured, they are measured at the carrying amount of the goods or services given up and this amount is then adjusted for any cash or cash equivalents transferred.

In the example above, fair values can be obtained and therefore the transactions will be measured under point 1.

Sales of goods

Where the sales of goods are concerned (and this applies to both companies that manufacture and sell goods and those that purchase goods for resale), Section 23 outlines five specific criteria which have to be met before revenue can be recognised. The criterion are:

- All significant risks and rewards of ownership of the goods have to have passed from the seller (i.e. the reporting entity) to the buyer,
- There is no continuing managerial involvement usually associated with both ownership and control over the goods sold,
- The related revenue can be estimated reliably,
- It is probable that economic benefits directly attributable to the transaction will flow to the entity and
- The costs (to be) incurred in respect of the transaction can be reliably measured.

All of the above criteria have to be met before revenue can be recognised. If any of the above conditions cannot be met then revenue cannot be recognised.

The inherent difficulty will often be in establishing the point at which the risks and rewards of ownership have passed to the buyer. The concept of 'substance over form' must prevail here and such risks and rewards may not necessarily pass to the buyer when legal title to the goods is transferred (although this can be the case in lots of transactions – for example, in the retail sector). Risks and rewards of ownership of the goods are usually passed to the buyer (and hence the ability to recognise revenue) when the entity can satisfy all five criteria above.

Example – Revenue recognition and ongoing performance obligations

Company A Limited enters into a contract to sell 20 items of machinery to Company B. Company B is located in Italy and the terms of the contract specify that Company A will ship the machines to Company B, install the machinery and ensure that the machines are in full working capacity prior to Company B signing off the order as complete. At the point of signing off the order, Company B is confirming their satisfaction that the goods are in working order and that Company A Limited has performed all its obligations within the contract. The question arises as to whether Company A can recognise revenue on the sale on immediate despatch of the machinery?

The answer to this question is 'no'. This is because at the point of despatch of the machines, Company A Limited has an ongoing obligation to install the machinery and ensure that the machines are at full working capacity, at which point Company B will then sign off to say they are happy that the machinery is in full working order. Company A Limited can only recognise revenue on those machines when Company B signs off the order as complete, thus acknowledging that all contractual obligations owed to Company B have been fulfilled by Company A.

The example highlighted above illustrates the provisions contained in paragraph 23.12 to FRS 102. This paragraph notes that an entity cannot recognise revenue when it retains significant risks and rewards of ownership. This particular paragraph then goes on to outline four additional situations when an entity may retain significant risks and rewards of ownership:

- When the business still has obligations for unsatisfactory performance that is not covered by normal warranties,
- When revenue is dependent on the buyer subsequently selling the goods on to their customer,

- When the goods are shipped and then the selling entity has to install the machinery (where installation is a significant part of the contract, as in the example above) and
- In situations when the buyer has the right to cancel the purchase for a reason that is outlined in the sales contract, or at the buyer's sole discretion without giving any reason, and the seller is uncertain as to the probability of return.

Example – Sales returns

Alex's Appliances Ltd (Alex) buys and sells domestic appliances for sale to the general public and has been established for over 20 years. It has a good reputation and all the products that it sells are sold with a three-year warranty, which covers the appliance for manufacturer faults. Company policy is also to offer a 28-day money-back guarantee if a non-faulty item is returned within the 28-day window and this policy is well known.

In situations where the entity can make a 'best estimate' of the returns reliably, then revenue in respect of the sale of the goods can be recognised. However, in respect of provisions for sales returns, the requirements in Section 21 *Provisions and Contingencies* will be triggered and a provision for such returns must also be made as the returns policy creates a constructive obligation. Such provisions are usually based on past experiences of the entity and professional judgement will be applied in making such provisions.

There may also be conditions imposed in a contract, which means that the seller retains legal title to the goods sold until such time that the buyer pays. This is often the case with sales made on credit and such clauses would allow the selling company to take back the goods in the event of non-payment. Revenue can be recognised at the time of the sale in such situations because these circumstances would only mean that the selling company retains an *insignificant* risk of ownership of the goods.

Key point

Whilst in many situations it might be obvious when a sale of goods is eligible for revenue recognition, the key point to ensure is that all the five criteria laid down in paragraph 23.10 to FRS 102 are met. Reporting entities must take care to ensure that all risks and rewards of ownership are passed to the buyer before recognising a sale and if any risks are retained, these risks should only be insignificant to comply with paragraph 23.13.

RENDERING OF SERVICES

The preceding section of this chapter examined the principles involved in recognising revenue for the sale of goods (or exchanges of goods and services). In the vast majority of cases it is fairly obvious when revenue can be recognised for the sale of goods (although there are occasions when this can be fairly subjective and the criteria for revenue recognition may have to be carefully considered). Revenue recognition in respect of the rendering of services is inherently more subjective and the use of estimates will often be required, which can pose difficulties on the part of the accountant preparing the financial statements and the auditor who may challenge the estimate(s). The first step in recognising revenue in respect of services is to assess whether the outcome of the transaction can be measured reliably. This will often involve looking carefully at the contractual terms and then establishing whether the following conditions can be satisfied:

- The revenue associated with the transaction can be reliably measured,
- It is probable that economic benefits associated with the transaction will flow to the entity,
- The stage of completion can be reliably measured and
- The costs incurred to date and the costs required to complete the transaction can be measured reliably.

With regards to the rendering of services and the interaction of paragraph 23.3, it is the author's opinion that reporting entities need to exercise caution in correctly interpreting the wording. This is because there are some slight variations in the wording relating to the measurement of revenue. For example, paragraph 23.3 in FRS 102 refers to revenue being the fair value of the consideration 'received or receivable'. Under the previous UK GAAP, Application Note G to FRS 5 *Reporting the Substance of Transactions* at paragraph G4 said that a seller recognised revenue under an exchange transaction with a customer when, and to the extent that, it obtains the 'right to consideration' in exchange for its performance.

This subtle difference in wording might potentially allow for later recognition of profit, which would then have a consequential effect on the tax position of the company because the tax treatment would generally follow the accounting treatment. If the Financial Reporting Council become aware of any abuse of the wording in this section it would be likely that they would issue an Abstract to clarify the issue.

In addition, paragraph 23.15 to FRS 102 refers to a 'specific act' and a 'significant act'. The paragraph says that when a specific act is much more significant than any other act, the entity postpones revenue recognition until the significant act is executed. The previous Abstract (UITF 40/Application Note G to FRS 5) was more prescriptive in that it required revenue to be recognised in line with performance (for example, 'passing a milestone' or the occurrence of a 'critical event'), thus earning the 'right to consideration'. Hence there is the potential for the possibility of delaying the recognition of profit because of the relaxed wording than would otherwise have been the case under the previous UK GAAP, so care must be taken to ensure correct and appropriate amounts of revenue are recognised to avoid any contentious issues with HMRC or management.

Revenue recognition principles in respect of the rendering of services follow the same stance as those for the selling of goods in that obligations should have been discharged by the selling entity prior to revenue being recognised.

Example – Deferred income

A company sells computer hardware and software to commercial organisations and has a year-end of 31 March each year. It is currently preparing its financial statements for the year ended 31 March 2016. Certain customers take out support services in respect of the software supplied by the company and these customers are invoiced for a calendar year for the support costs (i.e. 1 January 2016 to 31 December 2016).

In this example, the company's year-end falls one-third of the way into the calendar year for which support services have been invoiced. The company has not fulfilled its obligations to its customers for 9/12 of the year and therefore revenue is not recognised for this 9/12, but revenue can be recognised for the previous 3/12 as obligations have been fulfilled. The remaining 9/12 will be recognised as deferred income within current liabilities in the company's balance sheet (statement of financial position).

Stage of completion

The amount of revenue associated with a transaction and the probability of economic benefits flowing to the entity can be fairly easy to ascertain in many instances. What often causes the difficulty is establishing the stage of completion. The 'stage of completion' is also referred to as the 'percentage of completion' and is a method used in recognising revenue in respect of service contracts and construction contracts. The method is very much based on professional judgement and in some cases is inherently difficult to apply and where the judgements used are significant (or material to the financial statements) it is often advisable to have documentation available that supports the use of such a method in the event of queries by management or HMRC.

The underlying principle where the stage of completion method is concerned is that the method employed must be the one that gives a 'best estimate' of the work performed (i.e. the most reliable method). Paragraph 23.22 to FRS 102 outlines possible methods that a reporting entity may wish to consider – although the methods are only 'possible' methods and an entity may have their own method for arriving at a stage of completion and provided that this gives the most reliable estimate, then its use should be continued. The possible methods outlined in paragraph 23.22 are:

- Looking at the proportion of costs that have been incurred to date for the work performed in relation to the total costs. This is often referred to as the 'cost method' and can be calculated as total costs incurred to date divided by total contract costs.
- Having surveys of work undertaken to arrive at an estimated stage of completion.
- The completion of a physical proportion of the contract work.
- The completion of a proportion of the service contract.

Example – Progress payment received

Cory Construction Limited has entered into a contract with its customer, Breary Builders, to construct a retail park. The terms of the contract make provision for a progress payment to be received by Cory Construction after the first 10% of the retail park has been constructed. The progress payment was received during the year to 31 October 2014 and the accountant has recognised this payment as revenue.

The accountant is incorrect to recognise the progress payment as revenue. This is on the basis that progress payments (and advances) from customers do not often reflect the work performed. The progress payment should have been credited to the contract account rather than to revenue. Revenue can only be recognised by reference to the stage of completion.

The principles of the percentage of completion method focus on three outcomes of a contract:

1. The contract will yield a profit,
2. The contract will yield a loss or
3. The outcome is uncertain.

Profit-yielding contracts

For contracts where the outcome is that the contract will generate a profit, revenue is recognised by reference to the stage of completion.

Example – Profit-generating contract

Cory Construction Limited (Cory) is preparing its financial statements for the year ended 31 March 2016. On 1 October 2015, Cory commenced work on a contract. The price agreed for the contract was a fixed price of £50 million. Cory purchased machinery at a cost of £15 million exclusively for use on the contract. The directors of Cory have estimated that the machinery will have no residual value at the end of the contract, which is due to finish on 30 September 2016. Costs incurred on the contract plus estimated costs to complete are as follows:

	Costs to date	*Estimate of costs to complete*
	£	£
Materials purchased	9,000	5,000
Labour and other overheads	7,000	8,000

All the costs that have been incurred to date have been debited to the contract account in the nominal ledger. Cory has appointed a valuation agent who has confirmed that at the reporting date the contract was 40% complete, at which point the customer made a progress payment amounting to £15 million. The finance department have credited this progress payment to the contract account in the nominal ledger. There have been no other entries made in respect of this contract.

The first step is to identify whether the contract is going to make a profit. The costs of the contract are as follows:

	£'000
Purchase of machine	15,000
Materials purchased	9,000
Labour and overheads	7,000
Estimate of costs to complete	13,000
Total costs	44,000
Fixed price contract	50,000
Profit on the contract	6,000

As the contract is profit-making the stage of completion method will be used for revenue recognition. The valuation agent has confirmed that the contract was 40% complete at the year-end, so Cory should take 40% of the total costs to cost of sales and 40% of the contract price to revenue; hence financial statement extracts will show:

	£'000
Revenue (40% × £50 million)	20,000
Cost of sales (40% × £44 million)	17,600
Gross profit	2,400 (or 40% × £6,000 profit)

The next step is to then work out the 'gross amount due from customer' for the balance sheet, which will be shown as an 'other current asset'. This is calculated as follows:

	£'000
Purchase of materials	9,000
Labour and other overheads	7,000
Plant depreciation (£15,000 × 6/12)	7,500
Total costs to date	23,500
Contract profit	2,400
	25,900
Less progress payment received	(15,000)
Gross amount due from customer	10,900

Loss-making contracts

Where contracts are loss-making, revenue is recognised by reference to the stage of completion and cost of sales is essentially a 'balancing figure' that will generate the required loss.

Example – Loss-making contract

Cory Construction has a contract that is expected to make a loss of £1,000. The finance director has calculated that the amount of the contract revenue to be recognised is £800.

The profit and loss account (income statement) will include £800 worth of contract revenue. The loss is estimated to be £1,000 and so the cost of sales will be £1,800 to generate the required loss (i.e. the cost of sales is the balancing figure).

This method is used because paragraph 23.26 says that expected losses are recognised immediately with a corresponding provision for an onerous contract.

Uncertain outcomes

Where the outcome of a contract cannot be estimated reliably, contract costs and revenues should also be recognised by reference to the stage of completion. Revenue is recognised only to the extent of contract costs incurred that are probable of being recovered, so therefore revenue will equal costs and hence no profit is recognised.

Example – Uncertain contract outcome

Cory Construction enters into a two-year contract. The project manager is unsure as to whether the contract will be profit- or loss-generating. Costs incurred to date amount to £10,000.

As the outcome of the contract cannot be estimated, the amount of revenue to be recognised in Cory Construction's financial statements is the same as costs incurred, resulting in no profit being taken. Therefore:

DR debtors	£10,000
CR revenue	£10,000

In the event that amounts that have been recognised as revenue are deemed to be uncollectible, the entity must recognise the uncollectible element as an expense within profit or loss as opposed to a reduction in revenue.

INTEREST, ROYALTIES AND DIVIDENDS

There are situations where a company will use another company's assets for use in their business. The use of assets by others will generate income for the owner of those assets in the form of interest, royalties or dividends and these issues are dealt with in Section 23 at paragraph 23.28. There are two conditions in paragraph 23.28 that have to be met before revenue can be recognised in respect of the use of such assets that yield interest, royalties and dividends, which are:

- It must be probable (i.e. more likely than not) that economic benefits (i.e. cash or other assets) associated with the transaction will flow to the entity and
- The amount of such economic benefits (i.e. revenue) can be reliably measured.

Once it has been established that the above criterion have been met, interest, royalties and dividends are measured on the following bases.

Interest

Interest revenue is recognised using the effective interest method. When using the effective interest method, the entity will include any related finance charges paid or received as well as other premiums or discounts. The effective interest method essentially discounts the expected future cash inflows and outflows expected over the life of an underlying asset.

Example – Calculation of interest using the effective interest method

Irene's Instruments Limited (Irene) sells a financial instrument to Bart Baling Equipment Limited (Bart) that has a nominal value of £1,000 for a discount of £900. Interest is paid to Irene at the end of each year of the life of the instrument, which amounts to 5%. Based on the nominal value of the instrument, the value of interest paid to Irene is £50 (£1,000 × 5%) per annum and the principal amount of £1,000 when the instrument matures in three years' time. The effective interest rate is 8.95% and the value of the interest shown using an amortisation table is as follows.

Year	Opening amortised cost	Interest and principal payments	Interest income (A × 8.95%)	Debt discount amortisation (C – B) excluding the principal payment in year 3	Closing amortised cost (A + D)
	A	B	C	D	
1	900	50	81	31	931
2	931	50	83	33	964
3	964	1,050	86	36	1,000

Royalty revenue

Royalty revenue is recognised in the entity's financial statements on an accruals basis (i.e. a receivables basis) and in accordance with the relevant agreement.

Example – Royalty revenue

The holder of a patent grants the rights to a customer to use it for a period of three years at a total amount of £12,000 over the life of the agreement.

Paragraph 23.29(b) requires royalties to be recognised on an accruals basis (i.e. when the right to receive a royalty payment has been obtained) and in accordance with the substance of the relevant agreement. In this example, the patent owner will recognise revenue of £4,000 per annum (£12,000/3 years) in years one, two and three of the agreement.

Dividend revenue

Dividends are recognised as income in the financial statements when the right to receive payment is established. This can often be different from the actual payment date and dividends are therefore recognised when it is receivable rather than when it is received. Generally this is the date on which the dividend is approved by the members of a company passing a written resolution to pay a dividend.

Example – Payment of a dividend

Byrne Enterprises Limited (Byrne) is a subsidiary of the parent company Williams Holdings Limited (Williams). Williams owns 60% of the net assets of Byrne and both companies have a 31 December 2014 year-end. On 30 November 2014, the board of Byrne declared a dividend to shareholders, which is due to be paid on 31 January 2015. The financial controller of Williams has included the dividend in the 2015 financial year as this is the year in which the company will actually receive the dividend in the bank account.

Paragraph 23.29(c) to FRS 102 says that dividends are recognised in the shareholder's financial statements when the right to receive payment is established. Often payment of the dividend might be made at a later date than when the resolution was passed to pay the dividend. The financial controller of Williams should, therefore, recognise the dividend in the 31 December 2014 financial statements and recognise a corresponding debtor even though the dividend will not actually be paid until the subsequent financial year. Byrne will also recognise a dividend creditor in its separate financial statements as a liability was created by the balance sheet date. On consolidation, the group financial statements will eliminate the intra-group dividend and only show dividends payable to the non-controlling interest (i.e. the remaining 40% shareholders).

HM REVENUE AND CUSTOMS REQUIREMENTS

HM Revenue and Customs (HMRC) are keen to ensure that reporting entities report the correct levels of profits on which corporation taxes are to be based. In particular, where revenue recognition policies are concerned these will often be subjected to close scrutiny to ensure that they are appropriate and result in the right amounts of revenue at the right time. This is because the tax treatment will generally follow the accounting treatment.

Where revenue is subjected to a large degree of estimation it is often advisable for entities to have some form of documentation that will allow the estimations to stand up to scrutiny. Care must also be taken to correctly interpret the requirements in Section 23 where revenue in respect of the rendering of services is concerned.

When a company receives the right to receive consideration, this will generally trigger the requirement to recognise revenue despite the fact that the entity may not invoice the customer until such time as the works are complete in their entirety (which may be in a different accounting period than when the right to consideration arose). In the event that revenue is delayed disproportionately, HMRC may levy penalties for misstated profits and hence misstated taxes if it can be proven that the entity was negligent in computing profits chargeable to corporation taxes.

DISCLOSURE REQUIREMENTS

The disclosure requirements for revenue recognition are contained in paragraphs 23.30 to 23.32 in FRS 102 and are fairly comprehensive. Disclosures should enable the entity's revenue recognition policies to be both clear and transparent and, therefore, Section 23 requires disclosure of:

- The entity's accounting policies in respect of revenue recognition. This should also include the methods that the entity has adopted to establish the stage of completion of transactions that involve the rendering of services.
- The amount of each category of revenue that the entity has recognised during the accounting period, showing separately (at a minimum), revenue arising from:
  - Sales of goods,
  - Rendering of services,
  - Interest revenue,
  - Royalty revenue,
  - Dividend revenue,
  - Commissions,
  - Grants and
  - Any other significant revenue streams.

Where the entity has undertaken (or is undertaking) construction contracts, the entity should disclose:

- The amount of contract revenue that the entity has recognised in the accounting period,
- The methods that the entity has employed to determine contract revenue recognised in the accounting period and
- The methods that the entity has employed to determine the stage of completion of contracts that are still in progress at the end of the accounting period.

In the balance sheet (statement of financial position), the entity should present:

- Gross amounts due from customers in respect of contract work as an asset and
- Gross amounts due to customers in respect of contract work as a liability.

9 ASSETS HELD FOR SALE AND DISCONTINUED OPERATIONS

INTRODUCTION

Companies will often make the decision to sell assets that they have on their balance sheets (statements of financial position). In addition, they may also make the decision to dispose of part of their business that constitutes a separate operation. For example, a supermarket may well have different trading arms, such as groceries, domestic appliances, credit cards and banking, and mobile telephones. The supermarket may decide to close, say, the domestic appliances division because of poor performance, which may give rise to a discontinued operation for the entity.

When the company makes the decision to sell an asset it may choose to sell one single asset in its entirety or sell a group of assets, which are often referred to as a 'disposal group'.

This chapter examines the issue of assets held for sale and discontinued operations. It closely interrelates with Section 17 *Property, Plant and Equipment* (covered in Chapter 13) and Section 27 *Impairment of Assets* (covered in Chapter 15). Section 5 *Statement of Comprehensive Income and Income Statement* is also particularly relevant in the context of discontinued operations, particularly the Appendix to Section 5, which gives an example showing the presentation of discontinued operations in the statement of comprehensive income/income statement.

MAJOR DISPOSALS OF ASSETS

When an entity decides to sell a group of assets these are referred to collectively as a *disposal group*. A disposal group is a group of assets that are to be disposed of either by way of sale or otherwise, together in a group in a single transaction. Any liabilities that are associated with those assets in the disposal group will also be transferred to the buyer in the transaction. This will also include goodwill that has been acquired in a business combination should the group be a cash-generating unit in which goodwill has been allocated (paragraphs 27.24 to 27.27).

When a reporting entity has a binding sales agreement for a major disposal of assets, or a disposal group, at the reporting date, certain disclosures are required to be made as follows:

- The facts and circumstances surrounding the sale,
- A description of the asset(s) or the disposal group and
- The carry amount of the assets or, for a disposal group, the carrying amounts of the underlying assets and liabilities.

Example – Illustrative disclosure concerning major disposal of assets

In September 2016, the group entered into a binding agreement with an unconnected third party to sell its manufacturing division on the basis that it no longer had a strategic fit with the group's future plans. The sales agreement provides for disposal proceeds of £120,000 and the expected completion date for the sale is expected to be in January 2017.

As at 30 November 2016 the carrying amount of the disposal group amounted to £152,000.

ASSET IMPAIRMENT

Section 27 *Impairment of Assets* requires an entity to undertake an impairment review to establish whether there are any indicators of impairment and this particular section outlines some potential indicators that the reporting entity must consider 'as a minimum'. Asset impairment is considered further in Chapter 15. However, for the purposes of this chapter, when an entity makes plans to dispose of an asset (or a group of assets) before the previously expected date, this gives rise to an indicator of impairment. When this occurs, the recoverable amount of the asset/disposal group must be calculated in order to ascertain whether the asset/disposal group is impaired. Should the asset/disposal group be impaired then a write-down to recoverable amount must be undertaken.

Specific examples of an asset becoming impaired are:

- The asset becoming idle,
- Plans to discontinue or restructure the operation to which the asset belongs,
- Plans to dispose of an asset before the previously expected date and
- The reassessment of the useful life of an asset as finite rather than indefinite.

Example – Indicator of impairment

A company is a manufacturer of domestic and commercial electrical appliances and has a year-end of 31 December each year. The financial statements for the year-end of 31 December 2015 are currently being prepared. Five years ago it won a ten-year contract with one of its customers to manufacture gas central heating boilers for installation in domestic properties. Whilst the company did not primarily undertake the manufacture of such equipment it did have the funds to invest in machinery to manufacture the boilers as well as available staff who had experience in assembling such equipment.

The company spent £2.5 million on this equipment, which was used solely for the manufacture of the gas central heating boilers and are depreciating this equipment on a straight-line basis over the life of the contract (i.e. over ten years). The company's accounting policy in respect of depreciation is to charge a full year in the year of acquisition but no depreciation in the year of disposal. The company purchased the equipment on 31 March 2010 and charged a full year's depreciation of £250,000 (£2.5 million/10 years) as the expected residual value at the end of this ten-year life is expected to be £nil. On 30 September 2015 the customer announced that due to adverse press reports relating to carbon monoxide leakages, they were withdrawing these boilers with immediate effect with no plans to continue the manufacture and sale of these boilers in the future. In October 2015, it was found that a manufacturing fault resulted in the carbon monoxide leakages and the company was in breach of contract and so the contract was immediately withdrawn and hence the equipment is now idle.

At 31 December 2015 the carrying amount of the equipment was £1 million (£2.5 million less six years depreciation at £250,000 per year).

The equipment has become idle because of the withdrawal of the contract following the investigation into carbon monoxide leakages. Clearly this is an indicator of impairment and hence the recoverable amount should be calculated and compared to the carrying value to assess the value of any necessary write-down of the equipment to recoverable amount.

DISCONTINUED OPERATIONS

A discontinued operation is part of an entity that has been disposed of and that:

- Represents a separate and major line of business or geographical area of the operations,
- Is part of a single and coordinated plan to dispose of a separate major line of business or geographical area of operations or
- Is a subsidiary that a parent company has acquired exclusively with a view to resale.

In order to qualify as a discontinued operation, the operation must have been disposed of by the reporting date. An entity will dispose of a discontinued operation either by way of sale or closure. It is not enough for management to have merely started the process of closing the operation and hence it follows that not all disposal groups will necessarily meet the criteria to be classified as a discontinued operation.

Paragraph 5.7D of FRS 102 requires an amount comprising the total of post-tax profit or loss of discontinued operations and the post-tax gain or loss attributable to the impairment or on the disposal of the net assets constituting discontinued operations to be disclosed either on the face of the statement of comprehensive income (or income statement, if presented) or within the notes to the financial statements.

In addition to the disclosures above, paragraph 5.7D requires a columnar layout showing an analysis between continuing and discontinued operations for each of the line items shown on the face of the statement of comprehensive income, up to and including post-tax profit or loss for the period. This layout is significantly different than was the case in previous UK GAAP. The standard does not require an analysis of items of other comprehensive income to be analysed between continuing and discontinued operations.

RESTATEMENT OF COMPARATIVES

Financial statements have to be consistent and comparable and, in recognition of this requirement, when an entity presents an operation as discontinued in the current year, it must revisit the previous year comparatives and re-present those financial statements to reflect the discontinued operation.

Example – Operation discontinued in the current accounting period

An entity decides to close one of its divisions that met the definition of a discontinued operation and the division was sold by the reporting date and the entity has a year-end of 31 December 2015. The current year's statement of comprehensive income shows an analysis of continuing and discontinued operations but the comparative period has not been analysed on the grounds that the financial director suggests that, as the operation was not sold until the current year, no additional analysis in the current year is required.

Paragraph 5.7E of FRS 102 says that when an entity presents an operation as a discontinued operation in the current year, it must present that operation as discontinued in the comparative year and hence, if the operation was continuing in the previous period, the comparative year would be re-presented as discontinued in the comparative period for the current year's financial statements.

An illustration showing the presentation of discontinued operations is shown below.

Statement of comprehensive income for the year ended 31 December 2015	Continuing operations	Discontinued operations	Total	Continuing operations	Discontinued operations	Total
	2015 £	2015 £	2015 £	2014 £	2014 £	2014 £
Turnover	X	X	X	X	X	X
Cost of sales	(X)	(X)	(X)	(X)	(X)	(X)
Gross profit	X	X	X	X	X	X
Administrative expenses	(X)	(X)	(X)	(X)	(X)	(X)
Profit on disposal of operations	—	X	X	—	—	—
Operating profit	X	X	X	X	X	X
Interest receivable and similar income	X		X	X		X
Interest payable and similar charges	(X)		(X)	(X)		(X)
Profit on ordinary activities before tax	X	X	X	X	X	X
Taxation	(X)	(X)	(X)	(X)	(X)	(X)

Profit on ordinary activities after tax	X	X	X	X	X	X
Other comprehensive income:						
			Total			Total
			2015			2014
Actual loss on defined benefit pension plan			(X)			(X)
Deferred tax movement relating to actuarial loss			X			X
Total comprehensive income for the year			X			X

The requirements to go back and retrospectively re-present comparatives only relate to the statement of comprehensive income – they should not be restated for the balance sheet (statement of financial position).

As far as the statement of cash flows (cash flow statement) is concerned, FRS 102 is silent on the treatment of discontinued operations and the presentation of such in the cash flow statement. It may be more beneficial (and straightforward) for reporting entities to carry on in the normal way without distinguishing cash flows between those that relate to continuing and those that relate to discontinued operations.

The presentation requirements in FRS 102 for discontinued operations are inherently more onerous than was the case under the previous GAAP at FRS 3 *Reporting Financial Performance*. However, the definition of a 'discontinued operation' in FRS 102 is less stringent than was the case under FRS 3 and therefore it is likely that more operations will be reportable as discontinued operations than was the case under previous FRS 3.

A point worth noting relates to the transition to FRS 102. Paragraph 35.9 of FRS 102 does not require a first-time adopter to retrospectively change the accounting that it followed for discontinued operations (paragraph 35.9(d)).

10 EMPLOYEE BENEFITS

INTRODUCTION

All companies provide employee benefits of some description to their employees, whether it be wages or salaries, holiday entitlement, company vehicles, medical care, provision of housing or a pension plan towards retirement. Regardless of the types of benefits the entity provides to its employees, the entity is required to account for them in some way within the financial statements and Section 28 *Employee Benefits* recognises that some employee benefits are fairly simple to account for, whilst other forms of benefits can be very complicated and often require specialist assistance to provide the necessary information for the accounting input and related disclosures to be made within the financial statements.

Section 28 refers to employee benefits as being all forms of consideration that are given to employees by an entity in exchange for the related service. The term 'employees' in the context of Section 28 also relates to directors and the management of an entity – in other words all individuals that are in the employment of the entity regardless of seniority. However, Section 28 does not apply to share-based payment arrangements that an entity may have in place as these are dealt with in Section 26 *Share-based Payment*.

The scope of Section 28, therefore, is primarily concerned with four types of employee benefits:

- Short-term employee benefits (i.e. those that the entity expects to pay within a 12-month period), such as:
  - Payroll costs,
  - Holiday entitlement,
  - Statutory payments such as statutory sick and maternity pay,
  - Profit-sharing and bonus arrangements and
  - Other benefits such as company cars or subsidised goods.
- Post-employment benefits that are payable to employees when they finish their employment with the entity (note that this type of benefit does not relate to termination benefits and nor does it relate to short-term employee benefits).

- Other long-term employee benefits, which are those types of benefits that are not short-term employee benefits, post-employment benefits or termination benefits. Examples of such benefits could include:
  - Long-term paid absences (for example, sabbatical leave),
  - Long-term disability benefits,
  - Profit-sharing and bonus arrangements,
  - Deferred remuneration and
  - Other benefits that are expected to be paid after more than 12 months from the reporting date.
- Termination benefits, which are those benefits provided to employees when their employment with the entity reaches completion. An employee's employment can be terminated by an employer either by way of:
  - A company's decision to terminate an employee's employment before the usual retirement date or
  - A decision by the employee to accept voluntary redundancy in exchange for termination benefits.

The previous UK GAAP at FRS 17 *Retirement Benefits* dealt with the issues relating to post-employment benefits, whereas Section 28 is much broader and the requirements given there can be expected to impact most entities.

RECOGNITION OF SHORT-TERM EMPLOYEE BENEFITS

The overarching principle within Section 28 is that an entity will recognise the cost of all short-term employee benefits when the employees concerned have become entitled to receive such benefits (in other words, recognition is on a receivables basis rather than a paid basis). Ordinarily such costs will be recognised as an expense within the entity's profit and loss account (income statement) – however, there may be occasions when such costs are to be recognised as the cost of an asset (for example, when the entity is required to comply with the provision in paragraph 13.8 of FRS 102 and recognise the cost of labour in the costs of conversion of inventories). There may also be occasions when the entity is required to recognise the cost of short-term employee benefits within property, plant and equipment (for example, when the entity is self-constructing an asset).

Example – Deductions in respect of a court order

A company has received an order from the courts to deduct set amounts of money from an employee's salary on a monthly basis in respect of childcare costs. These amounts are to be deducted from the employee's pay and then subsequently paid over by the employer to the relevant authority each month.

In this respect the company is not actually bearing the costs of the employee's childcare costs because it is deducting these costs from the employee's monthly salary. However, the company has an obligation by way of a court order to pay these amounts (on behalf of the employee) to the relevant authority. Any amounts that have not been paid to the relevant authority at the reporting date will be recognised as a liability in the entity's balance sheet (statement of financial position).

Section 28 at paragraph 28.5 says that an entity should recognise amounts in respect of services rendered by employees at the *undiscounted* amount that is expected to be paid in exchange for that service. Under the previous UK GAAP, it was extremely rare (in fact unheard of) for entities to discount amounts to present day values in respect of short-term employee benefits. In reality, such amounts would usually relate to amounts that have been worked by employees, but not paid until, say, the employee leaves the employment of the company.

Example – Accrued services

A company operates in the building industry and pays its employees on a weekly basis. The company's policy is that all employees must work a 'week in hand' – in other words, work completed in week one of a new employment will be paid at the end of week two.

In this example, the company will recognise a liability owed to the employee (the liability being the week in hand that the employee has worked, but not yet been paid for). When the employee leaves the employment of the company, the employee will receive payment in his/her final pay packet for the week that had been worked in hand. The amount recognised in the entity's balance sheet (statement of financial position) will be the undiscounted amount.

Holiday entitlement

Under the previous UK GAAP, there was no specific requirement for entities to make provisions for holiday entitlement that had been accrued by employees but not paid until the subsequent accounting period. Whilst no specific standard required these accruals, paragraph 11(b) to FRS 12 *Provisions, Contingent Liabilities and Contingent Assets* did cite amounts relating to accrued holiday pay that met the definition of a liability and hence, technically, should have been accrued for.

Holiday pay accruals under Section 28 may prove problematic for some companies – particularly larger companies that do not maintain a central record of such information. Adequate records will need to be maintained. In addition, as FRS 102 itself is retrospective (i.e. it is applied to earlier periods up to the date of transition to FRS 102), the previous year's financial statements should also include an accrual for holiday pay accrued by employees but not paid until the subsequent accounting period, and evidence will need to be obtained for that period as well. The amount to be accrued is the expected cost of accumulating compensated absences and the amounts recognised will be the undiscounted amounts; these are recognised in the balance sheet (statement of financial position) as a creditor falling due within one year.

Example – Recognition of future absences

Company A Limited employs in excess of 1,000 employees and operates in the manufacturing industry, which produces goods 24 hours a day, seven days a week. Historically the company has always had some staff members off on holiday or on sick leave and the financial director has calculated the amount of short-term absences that have accumulated at the year-end and made an accrual for these in accordance with Section 28.

The financial director has also made a provision for the expected absences due to illness in the future year in order to be 'prudent' as he feels that a provision should be made as this will inevitably fall due for payment in the succeeding financial year.

The financial director should *not* make a provision for future absences. This is because paragraph 28.7 says that a reporting entity must recognise the cost of other compensated absences, which are not accumulating compensated absences, only when the absences occur.

Profit-sharing and bonuses

Many companies nowadays enter into profit-sharing arrangements with their employees or offer bonus incentives. This is to give the employees an incentive to help to drive the company forward and make it more profitable so that everyone within the company benefits in some way. Such arrangements have become more common over the last decade as the way in which companies do business has become more diverse and, as a direct result, competition has increased.

Section 28 deals with profit-sharing and bonuses at paragraph 28.8. There are conditions that have to be met before a provision for profit-share payments or bonus payments are made in the financial statements and an entity can only make such a provision when:

- There is a present legal or constructive obligation to make such payments as a result of past events and
- A reliable estimate of the obligation can be made.

The two criteria above may seem familiar with many preparers of financial statements as they relate to the provisions and contingencies section of FRS 102. Essentially amounts in respect of profit-sharing and bonus arrangements should only be provided if the entity has an obligation at the reporting date to make such payments and these payments are made in the subsequent accounting period.

The term 'constructive obligation' can prove to be very subjective and such an obligation arises on the part of the entity when the entity's past practices or published policies create an expectation in the mind-sets of those affected (for example, stating to employees before the year-end that the directors will pay a bonus after the year-end that is to be based on pre-tax profit, which will create an expectation by the employees that they will receive a bonus and hence create an obligating event on the part of the company).

Example – Bonus provision

Zedcolour Co. Ltd has been established for many years and has always paid annual bonuses to its employees and directors based on a predetermined formula.

The company's year-end is 31 March 2015 and on this date it recognised a provision for a bonus payable to its staff and management amounting to £50,000 plus £6,900 representing 13.8% employer's national insurance contributions. This amount was included in the financial statements on 12 May 2015. On 6 June 2015, HM Revenue and Customs opened an aspect inquiry into the company's corporation tax return, disputing the inclusion of the bonuses and associated employer's national insurance on the grounds that it was paid in the succeeding financial year and therefore should be included in the 31 March 2016 financial statements and associated corporation tax computation. The inspector disputing the deduction claimed that there was no legal obligation on the part of the company to pay the bonus to its staff and management.

This is an example of where two sections of FRS 102 will interact. Section 21 *Provisions and Contingencies* can also apply in this situation. Whilst a *legal* obligation has not arisen to pay the staff and management a bonus, a *constructive* obligation has arisen because of the bonus scheme in place. It is the expectation of a bonus in the mindsets of the employees and management that has created an obligating event and therefore a provision in respect of the bonus can be made. Had Zedcolour Co. Ltd been, say, a newly incorporated business then it may well have been inappropriate to recognise such a provision if the resolution to pay a bonus had been made AFTER the year-end date. A newly incorporated entity would have to have some form of resolution in place before the year-end date and have communicated the resolution to those affected in order to meet the definition of a provision.

DEFINED CONTRIBUTION PENSION PLANS

Section 28 of FRS 102 deals with two specific examples, which relate to post-employment benefits (those benefits provided to employees when their employment ends due to retirement):

- Retirement benefits such as pensions and
- Other post-employment benefits (for example, post-employment life assurance and post-employment medical care).

A 'defined contribution pension plan' is one of two specific pension plans that are dealt with in Section 28 – the other one being a 'defined benefit pension plan'. Both pension plans are considerably different both in substance and how they are accounted for.

A defined contribution pension plan is the simplest form of pension plan to account for. In a defined contribution plan, the employer pays a fixed amount of contributions into a pension fund (usually on a monthly basis). In addition, the employee may also pay into the fund via their wage or salary. In terms of the employer, their only obligation is to pay their share of the contributions into the fund. Once this obligation has been fulfilled, the employer has no further obligation to pay into the fund, even if the fund has insufficient assets available to pay all employee benefits that relate to employee services that have been rendered in the current and previous periods.

The term 'defined contribution' derives its name based on the amount of contributions that the employee (and, where applicable, the employer) has paid into the fund. The amount of post-retirement benefit is defined by the amount of contributions that have been received by the employee and, where applicable, the employer.

To account for the defined contribution pension plan, an accrual or prepayment must be identified as appropriate.

Example – Accounting for a defined contribution plan

The Bury Corporation has a defined contribution pension plan in place for its employees. In the month of December 2015, it deducts an amount of £2,000 from its employees in respect of their share of the contributions. The employer also pays into the contribution an amount of £5,000 for each of its employees.

The deductions from the employees will be credited to current liabilities when the payroll figures are being posted into the accounting system. When these are subsequently paid over to the pension provider, the entries will be credit bank and debit pension fund liability to clear the liability. The employer's portion of the pension contributions will be debited to the employer's pension contributions in the profit and loss account.

In the above example, all contributions in respect of the employer are debited to profit or loss in the month the contributions arise. Because actuarial risk and investment risk in relation to the pension plan do not fall, in substance, on the employer there are no further entries to be made in the accounting records for the defined contribution pension plan.

If a company makes contributions into a defined contribution pension plan that are not expected to be settled within 12 months after the end of the company's accounting period in which the related employees have rendered the service, the company should recognise the present value of the contributions payable. In arriving at the present value of the contributions payable, the company must have reference to market yields, at the reporting date, on high-quality corporate bonds. The finance cost (i.e. interest charge) that will be taken to profit or loss will be the unwinding of the discount.

DEFINED BENEFIT PENSION PLANS

Defined benefit pension plans are inherently difficult plans to account for. In the UK such plans are often referred to as 'final salary pension schemes'. Defined benefit pension plans have proven to be fairly controversial over recent years due to the deficits that have been reported on such schemes (often running into tens of millions of pounds worth of deficits). The inherent problem with defined benefit pension plans, from the employer's perspective, is that actuarial risk and investment risk do, in substance, fall on the employer and as such the employer does have an obligation to pay further contributions into the defined benefit pension plan if the plan has insufficient assets available in order to pay employee benefits relating to service rendered in the current and previous years.

Example – Increased pension contributions in a defined benefit pension plan

Cahill Chemicals Limited operates a defined benefit pension plan for its employees and has a year-end of 31 October each year. On 31 October 2014, the company obtained a triennial valuation, which showed the value of the defined benefit fund to be in a deficit amounting to £8 million. The actuary included a recommendation that the company increases its monthly pension contributions by 30% in order to attempt to reduce the deficit. The directors of the company have refused to increase the contributions by 30% and have only increased them by 10%.

Investment risk and actuarial risk are borne, in substance, by the employer and as a consequence Cahill Chemicals Limited should increase its contributions to the suggested amount by the actuary. If the company refuses to accord with the actuary's instructions, The Pensions Regulator in the UK has the power to mandate the company to increase its contributions so as to meet its obligations in law to pay post-employment benefits to its employees following retirement.

There are many defined benefit pension plans in existence in the UK and Republic of Ireland, although these are proving to be very burdensome for companies – particularly in times of economic recession when the value of the pension plans themselves falls into deficit. The company is also required to report deficits in relation to defined benefit pension plans on its balance sheet (statement of financial position) because of the fact that investment and actuarial risk fall, in substance, on the company and hence the company has an obligation to meet any deficit that exists on the pension plan. The impact of this on a company's balance sheet can be significant and can result in huge fluctuations from one year to the next in net assets (or liabilities) depending on the results of the actuarial valuations. External factors can influence the actuarial valuations (such as the yield on market investments and the levels of quantitative easing) and so in times of economic recession, deficits and the impact of the accounting input to arrive at that deficit can be alarming. Conversely, in times of economic recovery, deficits can turn into considerable surpluses and, for accountants and preparers of financial statements, it can be very difficult to understand why these polarised fluctuations occur.

Accounting for a defined benefit pension plan

When accounting for a defined benefit pension plan, invariably the entity will need actuarial information. Paragraph 28.20 does not make it mandatory for an entity to engage the services of a professionally-qualified actuary to calculate the obligation in a defined benefit pension plan. In addition, the same paragraph does not mandate an entity to obtain comprehensive valuations undertaken by an actuary on an annual basis (although if the principal actuarial assumptions have changed significantly then such valuations should be obtained). This is markedly different than under the previous GAAP at FRS 17, which did mandate the use of a professionally-qualified actuary and the requirement for annual comprehensive valuations.

The reality is that many companies will have to engage the services of an actuary in order to be able to make the accounting input and associated disclosures within the financial statements because of the complexity involved in arriving at these calculations. In the absence of actuarial information (or the numbers to undertake the accounting input and make the associated disclosures), the defined benefit pension plan will be impossible to account for correctly and this will inevitably result in the financial statements failing to give a true and fair view, a characteristic that all financial statements prepared for general purposes must possess under the Companies Act 2006.

The calculation in respect of the net defined benefit liability is as follows:

1. The present value of the entity's obligations under the defined benefit plan at the reporting date *minus*
2. The fair value of the plan assets (if any) at the reporting date out of which the plan's obligations are to be settled.

Fair value in 2 above is determined as outlined in paragraphs 11.27 to 11.32 of FRS 102. However, if the asset is an insurance policy that exactly matches the amount and timing of some or all of the benefits payable under the plan, then fair value is deemed to be the present obligation of the related obligation.

When determining the present value of the entity's obligations in 1 above, paragraph 28.17 requires the entity to discount the future payments into the defined benefit pension plan having reference to market yields at the reporting date on high-quality corporate bonds. In addition, an entity must also ensure that the currency and the term of the corporate bonds (or government bonds) are consistent with the currency and estimated period of the future payments.

The defined benefit obligation (and the related expense) is measured using the *Projected Unit Credit Method*. The Projected Unit Credit Method is an actuarial valuation method that recognises each period of service rendered by an employee as giving rise to an additional unit of benefit entitlement. It works by measuring each unit separately in order to build up to the final obligation that the employee will be entitled to when they reach normal retirement. The related expense associated with the defined benefit obligation is based on the revisions to IAS 19 *Employee Benefits*, which occurred in 2011. Paragraph 28.23(a) to (d) says that the cost that should be recognised in profit or loss should be made up of:

- The change occurring in the net defined benefit liability that has arisen due to the employee service that has been rendered during the reporting period in profit or loss,
- Net interest on the defined benefit obligation during the reporting period in profit or loss,
- The costs incurred in relation to introductions, changes in benefits, curtailments and settlements recognised in profit or loss and
- The re-measurement of the net defined benefit liability in other comprehensive income.

Re-measurement of the net defined benefit liability will comprise:

- Actuarial gains and losses and
- Return on plan assets (excluding amounts included in net interest on the net defined benefit liability).

It is to be noted that any remeasurement of a plan's net defined benefit liability that is recognised within other comprehensive income cannot be reclassified to profit or loss in a subsequent accounting period.

Paragraph 28.24 says that the net interest on the net defined benefit liability is calculated by multiplying the net defined benefit liability by the discount rate as determined at the start of the accounting period. In performing this calculation, the entity must consider any changes in the net defined benefit liability during the period as a result of contribution and benefit payments. This revised treatment, which replaces the finance charge and expected return on plan assets (where income is credited with the expected long-term yield on the assets in the fund), may increase the annual benefit expense and, in turn, have a potential impact on earnings.

Example – Accounting for a defined benefit pension plan

A company operates a defined benefit pension plan, which it has done for several years, and the company has an accounting year-end date of 30 November each year. It is currently preparing financial statements for the 30 November 2014 year-end and the actuarial information relating to the defined benefit pension plan has been obtained, which shows the following information:

	30 November 2014 *£'000*	*30 November 2013* *£'000*
Plan assets		
Opening plan assets	4,197	4,021
Expected return on plan assets	218	216
Actuarial gain (loss)	230	(321)
Employer contributions	310	458
Employee contributions	31	33
Benefits paid	(141)	(210)
Closing plan assets	4,845	4,197
Plan liabilities		
Opening plan liabilities	5,208	4,597
Current service cost	69	67
Past service cost	–	–
Interest on scheme liabilities	248	259
Actuarial (gain) loss	318	462
Employee contributions	31	33
Benefits paid	(141)	(210)
Closing plan liabilities	5,733	5,208

A summary of the entries within the financial statements relating to the above accounting input is shown in the following table:

Profit and loss account	*Profit and loss account (finance costs)*	*Other comprehensive income*
Current service cost	Interest cost *less* expected return on plan assets	Differences between actual and expected return on plan assets
Past service cost		Changes that affect the plan's liabilities
Gains and losses on curtailments and settlements		Changes in the actuarial assumptions

In the above example, the amounts charged to profit and loss will be:

	30 November 2014 £'000	30 November 2013 £'000
Current service cost	69	67
Past service cost	Nil	Nil
Total operating charge	69	67

Amounts recognised in respect of the finance costs in the profit and loss account will be:

	30 November 2014 £'000	30 November 2013 £'000
Expected return on plan assets	218	216
Interest on scheme liabilities	(248)	(259)
Net finance cost	(30)	(43)

Amounts in other comprehensive will be as follows:

	30 November 2014 £'000	30 November 2013 £'000
Actuarial gain (loss)	(88)	(783)

Once the accounting input has been undertaken, the balance sheet (statement of financial position) will be as follows:

	30 November 2014 £'000	30 November 2013 £'000
Value of plan obligations	5,733	5,208
Value of plan assets	4,845	4,197
Deficit at reporting date	(888)	(1,011)

Multi-employer plans

When an entity has a multi-employer plan or a state plan, these are classified as a defined contribution or a defined benefit plan depending on the terms of the plan. There are occasions when a multi-employer plan (or state plan) contains insufficient information in order for it to be accounted for as a defined benefit pension plan and hence they are then classified as a defined contribution plan. This can be the case where the entity is unable to identify its share of the assets and liabilities associated with the pension plan.

Example – Defined benefit plan accounted for as a defined contribution plan

A school under local authority control converted to academy status in 2015 and has two forms of pension plans: the Teachers' Pension Scheme (TPS) and the Local Government Pension Scheme (LGPS). The LGPS is a defined benefit pension plan and the academy receives actuarial valuations each year in order that the accounting input and relevant disclosures can be made in the financial statements for the year ending 31 August each year.

The TPS is a multi-employer scheme and the academy is not able to identify its share of the underlying assets and liabilities of the scheme.

Under paragraph 28.11 of FRS 102, multi-employer plans and state plans are classified as defined contribution plans or defined benefit plans on the basis of the terms of the plan. In this case, however, there is insufficient information available for the academy to identify its share of assets and liabilities in the TPS and therefore the academy must account for the TPS as if it were a defined contribution plan and make the disclosures required under paragraphs 28.40 and 28.40A.

A point worth noting where such plans are concerned is in relation to agreements that the company has entered into to determine how the company will fund a deficit. Under FRS 17, reporting entities were previously not required to make provision for a liability where there is an agreement in place between the company and the multi-employer plan stipulating how the company will fund a deficit arising on the pension plan. Section 28 of FRS 102 was amended immediately before its final publication and that amendment results in a reporting entity having to recognise a liability on the balance sheet (statement of financial position), which represents the contributions payable that arise from an agreement determining how the business will fund a deficit to the extent that the liability relates to the deficit.

Group benefit plans are separate from multi-employer plans and the accounting treatment for such plans is considered below.

Introductions and changes to the plan: curtailments and settlements

Section 28 deals with issues concerning introductions of a defined benefit pension plan (i.e. when an entity introduces a new defined benefit pension plan) and changes that have occurred within the current period. Paragraph 28.21 of FRS 102 requires an entity to increase (or decrease) its defined benefit obligation in respect of introductions or changes and to reflect the corresponding debit or credit in profit or loss as either an expense or an income, depending on the situation involved.

Curtailments and settlements are also dealt with in Section 28. The terms 'curtailments' and 'settlements' are not defined in the Glossary contained within FRS 102; however, they are events that significantly change the liabilities relating to a defined benefit pension plan that are not covered by normal actuarial assumptions. A curtailment could arise by way of changes to the plan's rules.

Under previous UK GAAP, a curtailment was defined in FRS 17 *Retirement Benefits* as 'an event that reduces the expected years of future service of present employees or reduces for a number of employees the actual of defined benefits for some or all of their future service'. This definition was taken to mean that curtailments will essentially reduce the obligations that relate to future service and will ordinarily arise because of a significant reduction in employee numbers that can arise through redundancy.

Example – Changes to a defined benefit pension plan

On 31 July 2014, a company's defined benefit plan was valued as having a deficit amounting to £4 million. On 31 July 2015, the terms of the scheme were changed such that the changes had an effect on the benefits in the current financial year and the valuation as at 31 July 2015 was £4.5 million following the changes, but had the changes not taken place the valuation of the pension plan would have been £4.75 million. The financial statements recognise the defined benefit pension plan at an amount of £4.75 million.

The provisions in paragraph 28.21 say that when a defined benefit plan has its terms changed, the company must recognise any increase, or decrease, in the net defined pension liability to reflect the change with the corresponding entry being within profit or loss as an expense (or income as the case may be). In this example, the company should recognise the defined benefit pension plan at the amount following the change (i.e. £4.5 million) and hence should recognise the difference of £250,000 in profit or loss.

Many defined benefit pension plans have reported deficits over recent years; however, that is not to say that defined benefit pension plans can never be in surplus (i.e. the plan's assets are in excess of the plan's obligations to its members). Paragraph 28.22 says that an entity should only recognise an asset (i.e. a surplus in a defined benefit pension plan) when that surplus is able to be recovered. Recoverability can be through reduced contributions or by way of refunds.

Example – Defined benefit pension plan asset

During the year to 31 October 2014, an entity incurred expenses in relation to its defined benefit pension plan, which its insurers have agreed to reimburse. The entity is proposing to recognise the value of the reimbursement as an asset.

Paragraph 28.28 to FRS 102 says that it must be 'virtually certain' that a reimbursement will be received by the entity. This principle accords with the same principle as a contingent asset in Section 21 *Provisions and Contingencies* in that a contingent asset should only be recognised on the balance sheet (statement of financial position) when it is virtually certain. The term 'virtually certain' is not defined in the Glossary to FRS 102 but the term itself implies it must be more than probable (i.e. more likely than not) that reimbursement will be received.

Other long-term employee benefits

In financial reporting, 'long term' is taken to mean anything that is not settled within 12 months from the reporting date. For the purposes of Section 28, some long-term benefits may not be settled within 12 months of the reporting date and hence are long term. Some examples of long-term employee benefits might include:

- Long-term paid staff absences,
- Long-term disability benefits,
- Profit-sharing and bonus arrangements,
- Remuneration that is deferred longer than 12 months and
- Other general employee benefits that are to be settled after more than 12 months.

For long-term employee benefits, an entity must recognise such items as the net of:

1. The present value of the plan's obligation at the reporting date and
2. The fair value at the reporting date of the plan's assets (if any) from which the pension plan will pay obligations.

Any changes in liabilities in respect of long-term employee benefits will be recognised within profit or loss provided another section of FRS 102 does not require such changes to be recognised elsewhere (for example, within the cost of an asset).

Termination benefits

Legislation protects employees from any disadvantage towards the employee in respect of termination of employment (unfair dismissal). However, there are occasions when termination of an employee's employment is required (for example, through redundancy) and often the contracts of employment will make provisions for such benefits to be paid to the employee on termination of their employment. It is acknowledged in Section 28 that termination benefits do not provide an entity with future economic benefits (as the employee(s) concerned will no longer be in the employment of the company) and hence such payments are recognised immediately in profit or loss.

In respect of the defined benefit pension plan, an employee whose employment has been terminated for whatever reason will mean that the entity will have to account for a curtailment of retirement benefits, or other employee benefits.

Termination benefits are recognised as a liability and as an expense in the financial statements in two situations:

1. The employer is demonstrably committed to terminating the employment of an employee, or a group of employees, before the normal retirement date or
2. When a programme of voluntary redundancy has been initiated and the employer is committed to provide termination benefits as a means of encouraging voluntary redundancy.

The term 'demonstrably committed' means that the employer has initiated a formal plan (which is often communicated to employees) and there is no realistic possibility of any withdrawal from the plan.

Group plans

Where group plans are concerned, it is important that any contractual terms relating to the defined benefit pension plan are carefully scrutinised. This is because the risks of the defined benefit plan may be shared among group members.

If there is an agreement in place relating to the defined benefit pension plan, the agreement may provide for a method of charging the net defined benefit cost in relation to each individual subsidiary within the group. Where this is the case then each individual subsidiary will recognise – in its own financial statements – the net defined benefit cost of a defined benefit plan in accordance with the contractual provisions.

However, where there are no agreements in place, paragraph 28.38 says that the net defined benefit cost is recognised in the individual financial statements of the group member that is legally responsible for the plan. Other group members will recognise a cost that is equal to their contributions payable for the period.

DEFERRED TAX ISSUES ON PENSIONS

UK tax legislation says that a company is given corporation tax relief on pension contributions that are actually paid, as opposed to those pension contributions that are recognised within profit or loss. Therefore, as there may be a difference between the pension contributions that are to be accounted for under the provisions in Section 28 and the requirements of tax legislation, this will give rise to a timing difference, which will trigger deferred tax considerations.

The components of cost that make up the defined benefit pension plan charge in the profit and loss account are made up of various items, including:

- Current service cost,
- Past service cost,
- Gains or losses on curtailments and settlements,
- Interest cost and
- Expected return on the plan's assets.

Any actuarial gains and losses are reported through other comprehensive income and not as a direct expense within profit or loss.

Deferred tax issues will arise because of this accounting input and the tax relief that is given by HM Revenue and Customs on the contributions actually paid by the employer. Care should also be taken to ensure that the deferred tax is split between the element that is to be reported in profit or loss and the element that is to be taken through other comprehensive income.

Example – Deferred tax in a defined benefit pension plan

The Adams Group Ltd has obtained actuarial information to enable them to complete the accounting input and associated disclosures relating to their defined benefit pension plan. The plan is currently in deficit and is made up as follows:

Opening scheme liability	(200,000)
Contributions paid into the scheme	80,000
Past service cost	(20,000)
Interest cost	(70,000)
Expected return on plan assets	20,000
Actuarial loss	(20,000)
Closing scheme liability	(210,000)

The Adams Group pays corporation tax at the rate of 20% and deferred tax is calculated as follows:

	Deficit £	Tax relief £	Deferred tax asset £
Opening deficit	(200,000)		40,000
Contributions paid	80,000	(16,000)	
Profit and loss account	(70,000)	14,000	
Actuarial loss (OCI)	(20,000)	2,000	2,000
Balance carried forward	(210,000)	Nil	42,000

The profit and loss account charge consists of the past service cost of £20,000, the interest cost of £70,000 and deducted from these is the expected return on plan assets (which represents finance income) of £20,000.

Tax relief is granted by HM Revenue and Customs on the actual contributions that have been paid by the company and this is first allocated to the profit and loss account charge of £70,000. The difference between the contributions paid and the profit and loss account charge of £10,000 is allocated against the actuarial loss, which is reported through other comprehensive income.

DISCLOSURE REQUIREMENTS

Whilst there are no specific disclosures in respect of short-term employee benefits, the required disclosures are split between:

- Defined contribution pension plans,
- Defined benefit pension plans,
- Long-term benefits and
- Termination benefits.

Defined contribution pension plans

A company is required to disclose the amount it has recognised in profit or loss for its defined contribution pension plan.

Where an entity treats a defined benefit multi-employer plan as a defined contribution pension plan (due to insufficient information being available to use defined benefit pension plan accounting), disclosure is required of:

- The fact that the pension plan is a defined benefit pension plan together with the reason why it is being treated as a defined contribution pension plan, along with any other additional information about the plan's surplus or deficit and the implications (if any) for the company,
- The extent to which the entity can be liable to the plan for other entities' obligations under the terms and conditions of the multi-employer plan and
- How the entity has established the liability recognised in the financial statements.

Defined benefit pension plans

The following disclosures should be made in respect of a company's defined benefit pension plan:

- A general description of the type of the plan including funding policy.
- The date that the most comprehensive actuarial valuation was carried out and, if it was not as at the reporting date, a description of the adjustments made to measure the defined benefit pension obligation at the reporting date.
- A reconciliation of opening and closing balances for each of the following:
  - The defined benefit obligation,
  - The fair value of plan assets and
  - Any reimbursement recognised as an asset.
- The reconciliations above should show (where applicable):
  - The change in the defined benefit pension obligation arising from employee service rendered during the accounting period in profit or loss,
  - Interest income or expense,
  - Remeasurement of the defined benefit liability and showing separately actuarial gains and actuarial losses and the return on plan assets less amounts included in interest income or interest expense and
  - Plan introductions, changes, curtailments and settlements.
- The total cost relating to defined benefit pension plans for the period, showing separately:
  - Amounts recognised in profit or loss as an expense and
  - Amounts included in the cost of an asset.
- For each major class of plan asset, including (but not limited to) equity instruments, debt instruments, property and all other assets, the percentage or amount

that each major class constitutes of the fair value of the total plan assets at the reporting date.

- The amounts included in the fair value of plan assets for:
  - Each class of the entity's own financial instruments and
  - Any property occupied by, or other assets used by, the entity.
- The return on plan assets.
- The principal actuarial assumptions used, including (where applicable):
  - The discount rates,
  - The expected rates of salary increases,
  - Medical cost trend rates and
  - Any other material actuarial assumptions used.

Group disclosures

If the entity is involved in a defined benefit pension plan that shares risks between entities that are under common control, disclosure should be made of:

- The contractual agreement or stated policy for charging the cost of a defined benefit pension plan (or where there is no policy, disclosure of that fact).
- The policy for determining the contributions to be paid by the entity.
- When the entity accounts for an allocation of the net defined benefit cost, all the information required in the disclosure requirements above for the defined benefit pension plan are required to be made.
- If the entity accounts for the contributions payable for the period, the following should be disclosed:
  - A general description of the type of plan, including funding policy,
  - The date that the most recent comprehensive actuarial valuation was carried out; where this was not carried out at the reporting date, a description of the adjustments made to measure the defined benefit obligation at the reporting date should be made,
  - For each major class of plan assets, including, but not limited to, equity instruments, debt instruments, property and all other assets, the percentage or amount that each major class of asset constitutes of the fair value of the total plan assets at the reporting date and
  - The amounts included in the fair value of plan assets for each class of the entity's own financial instruments and any property occupied by, or other assets used by, the entity.

It may be that the reporting entity can cross-reference to the above disclosures in another group entity's financial statements, but only if:

- The group entity's financial statements separately identify and disclose the information required about the plan and
- That group entity's financial statements are available to users of the financial statements on the same terms as the financial statements of the entity and at the same time, or earlier than, the financial statements of the entity.

Long-term benefits

For each category of other long-term benefits that an entity provides to its employees, disclosure is required of:

- The nature of the benefit,
- The amount of the obligation and
- The extent of funding at the reporting date.

Termination benefits

For each category of termination benefits, the entity should disclose:

- The nature of the benefit,
- The accounting policy* and
- The amount of the obligation and the extent of funding at the reporting date.

*Note that no accounting policy choices are available for the other three categories of employee benefits.

For cases where there is uncertainty concerning the number of employees that will accept the offer of termination benefits (for example, in a redundancy programme), a contingent liability will arise. The disclosure requirements in Section 21 *Provisions and Contingencies* requires a company to disclose information concerning contingent liabilities unless the possibility of an outflow of economic benefits in settlement is remote.

11 INCOME TAX

INTRODUCTION

It is a common known fact that the amount of tax expense shown in a company's financial statements is not necessarily just merely the amount of corporation tax that the company will pay to HM Revenue and Customs (HMRC), as to base the tax expense merely on what falls due to HMRC during an accounting period would deviate from the accruals basis of preparing the financial statements. The profit (or loss) that a company generates in an accounting period is computed through the application of the UK Generally Accepted Accounting Practice (GAAP) and companies legislation. Because of the way in which accounting profit/loss and taxable profit/loss is subjected to differing legislation, there will be items making up accounting profit/loss that are not recognised for the purposes of tax legislation, whilst other items may fall to be subjected to tax in later accounting periods.

In the light of the inherent differences between UK GAAP, the Companies Act 2006 and tax legislation there has to be a mechanism whereby the tax implications that will occur in future accounting periods, but which relate to items in the current year's financial statements, are recognised in the current year's financial statements. This mechanism is known as *deferred tax* and is recognised in the income statement (profit and loss account) in addition to the amounts of corporation tax that are due to HMRC. Deferred tax arises as a result of 'timing differences', which occur because of the differences between tax rules and accounting rules and the recognition of deferred tax in the current year's financial statements, which will mean that the correct tax expense is recognised in the financial statements within the same accounting period as the income and expenditure to which the timing differences relate.

Section 29 *Income Tax* deals with the concept of taxation. Section 29 is a relatively small section in FRS 102 but is quite wide in its scope and also deals with all domestic and foreign taxes, which are based on taxable profit as well as withholding taxes that are payable by a subsidiary, associate or joint venture on their distributions to the reporting entity.

Health warning!

This chapter is not aimed at providing readers with in-depth tax knowledge – it is primarily concerned with the accounting for taxation aspects. As a result, the tax rates that are used in the worked examples are only illustrative to demonstrate the accounting aspects of current and deferred taxation. Value added tax is a particularly complicated tax to administer in practice but is generally fairly easy to account for from a technical accountancy perspective and this chapter does not go into a huge amount of detail where VAT is concerned. Should readers need further guidance on any aspects of taxation, they are recommended to seek guidance from a reputable taxation manual or from a taxation specialist.

VALUE ADDED TAX (VAT)

Companies that are registered for VAT with HMRC are required to charge VAT (output tax) on their taxable sales. Conversely, they are also eligible to reclaim VAT (input tax) on their taxable supplies. There are a number of VAT rates that companies can use depending on the nature of their supplies (for example, zero, reduced and standard rates of VAT) as well as the situation where their supplies are exempt, or partially exempt. There is also the *Flat Rate Scheme*, which can be applied where the entity's turnover is below a certain level and works by allowing an entity to calculate the VAT amount due to HMRC by simply applying a percentage rate to the entity's VAT-inclusive turnover, although when using the VAT Flat Rate Scheme, input VAT cannot be claimed on purchases, but is taken into account in calculating the flat rate percentage.

Paragraph 29.20 to FRS 102 requires an entity's turnover figure, which is shown as a headline figure in the income statement (profit and loss account), to be stated net of VAT and other similar taxes both on taxable outputs and VAT that is charged under the VAT Flat Rate Scheme. Conversely, all expenses must not include recoverable input VAT and other similar recoverable sales taxes.

Example – Irrecoverable VAT on a fixed asset

A company operates in the property management sector administering a government contract in which the company acts as an intermediary between the government and the owner of the property (the landlord). The company's activities are exempt from the requirements of VAT registration. On 31 October 2015, the company purchases 20 desktop computers and the supplier has invoiced the company for £10,000 plus VAT at the rate of 20%, giving a total due to the supplier of £12,000 (VAT is £2,000).

Paragraph 29.20 says that any irrecoverable VAT that is allocated to fixed assets (or to other items that are disclosed separately) in the financial statements must be included in the cost price of the fixed asset. Hence, the computer equipment additions should be included in the statement of financial position (balance sheet) at a cost of £12,000.

INCOME TAX

The term 'income tax' is somewhat ambiguous because it tends to be associated with the amount of tax an individual, rather than a corporate entity, pays. In recognition of this the term 'income tax' will be referred to from hereon in as 'corporation tax' and is the tax that is assessed on a company's profits at the end of each accounting period.

It is calculated by applying the appropriate percentage of tax to the company's *taxable* not *accounting* profit. As discussed at the introduction to this chapter, certain transactions are recognised in the financial statements to comply with accounting rules, which are ignored for the purposes of taxation. As a consequence, in almost all cases, a company's taxable profit will not be the same amount as the company's pre-tax accounting profit. Differences between these two profits form the basis of deferred taxation, which is discussed later in this chapter. A typical example of an item of expense that is included in the accounting profit/loss but is not recognised for taxation purposes is that of depreciation. The charge for depreciation is added back to accounting profit and HMRC's version of depreciation (capital allowances) is then given to the company (provided the related assets are eligible for such allowances); hence the corporation tax computation will look as follows:

TRADE COMPUTATION	**£**
Profit per the financial statements	X
Add:	
Depreciation expense	X
Less:	
Capital allowances	(X)
Profit chargeable to corporation tax (taxable profit)	X

The corporation tax year runs for the 'financial year' from 1 April to 31 March each year. In some cases this is inconsequential to companies, but for those companies whose accounting period/year straddles the corporation tax year it can be relevant – particularly where there is a change in corporation tax rate.

Example – Company's accounting year straddling two corporation tax years

Company A Limited has a year-end of 31 December 2013 and the financial statements have now been completed to final draft stage. The company's rate of corporation tax in financial year 2012 was 24% and in financial year 2013 was 23%. Assume, for the purposes of this example, that taxable profit is £400,000.

The corporation tax year runs from 1 April to 31 March, but the company's financial year ends on 31 December. Therefore, the taxable profit will have to be apportioned between two corporation tax financial years and the apportionment will be in days. Therefore:

1 January 2013 to 31 March 2013 = 90 days out of 365 days
£400,000 × 90/365   £98,630

1 April 2013 to 31 December 2013 = 275 days out of 365 days
£400,000 × 275/365   £301,370

£400,000

£98,630 will be charged to corporation tax at a rate of 24%, hence £23,671.
£301,370 will be charged to corporation tax at a rate of 23%, hence £69,315.
Ignoring the effects of marginal rate relief, this will give a tax liability of £92,986.

The above example illustrates how a change in corporate tax rates can affect a company's tax liability. If the rate of corporation tax stays constant from one financial year to the next, then the impact of a change in financial year for tax purposes is irrelevant.

Recognition and measurement of corporation tax

A company reporting under FRS 102 is required to recognise a liability for amounts due to HMRC in respect of corporation tax due on taxable profit for both current and past accounting periods. Where the amount of corporation tax paid exceeds the amount of corporation tax due, then the entity can recognise a current tax asset. This does not relate, however, to deferred tax assets, which are subjected to stringent criteria being met (see later in the chapter).

In measuring corporate (and deferred) taxes, the entity must use the rates of tax that have been enacted or substantively enacted by the balance sheet date. In practice it is likely that the accountancy firm preparing the tax computation will do so using an automated business tax software system and so such a system is likely to apply the appropriate rates of tax to the company's profits.

Withholding taxes

Withholding taxes also fall under the scope of Section 29. Withholding taxes are taxes on dividends or other income that are deducted at source from the payer of the dividends or other income and are then subsequently paid to the taxation authority by the payer. Withholding tax does not arise on dividends paid in the UK; however, it may become relevant for a company based in the UK that has investments that are located overseas.

There is often a significant difference in the way that dividend and other income that are subject to withholding tax are treated for the purposes of tax as opposed to dividend and other income that have been received by an entity with an imputed tax credit. Section 29 splits the treatment between those of outgoing dividends and similar amounts payable and those of incoming dividends and similar income receivable.

Outgoing dividends and similar amounts payable

Outgoing dividends and similar amounts payable must be recognised in the financial statements at an amount that includes withholding taxes but excludes other taxes (for example, attributable tax credits). This is because the imputed tax credit does not form part of the cost of the dividend as it is more concerned with the taxes paid by the payer of the dividend as opposed to those paid by (or on behalf of) the recipient of the dividend.

In practice, the above is fairly uncommon in the UK but it is the author's opinion that if a company based in the UK is required to deduct UK income tax on interest payable to a third party and pay this over to HMRC on behalf of the recipient, this is, in substance, similar to withholding taxes and therefore the author believes that interest payable should be shown gross in the profit and loss account (in other words, inclusive of the income tax deducted).

Example – Loan note interest paid

Several years ago, Company B Limited undertook a management buyout. The outgoing shareholders agreed to half-yearly payments in instalments over a five-year period by the raising of loan notes that were registered in a parent company. These loan notes attract interest at 2% above the Bank of England base rate every six months. During the year to 31 December 2015, the rate of income tax was 20% and the company is required to deduct this amount from the amount of interest due to the respective loan note holder and pay this over to HMRC.

The amounts of income tax that have been paid to HMRC should be shown within interest payable and similar charges in the profit and loss account. In the author's opinion, the net amount of interest actually paid to the loan note holder will not be a true reflection of the interest the company is to pay as it will be net of income tax. As a result, the tax due on the interest should be expensed to the profit and loss account in order that the interest charge in the profit and loss account is a true reflection of the actual interest charge the company is obliged to pay.

Incoming dividends and similar amounts receivable

Similarly, paragraph 29.19 says that incoming dividends and similar amounts receivable should be shown within the financial statements at an amount that includes withholding taxes but excludes other taxes (for example, attributable tax credits). Withholding taxes that have been suffered should be shown as part of the tax expense in the profit and loss account.

The requirement in paragraph 29.19 for the withholding tax to be shown as part of the tax expense is representative of the fact that tax has actually been suffered by the company (it has been withheld by the payer and so the company has received the payment NET of income tax). Withholding taxes will normally be applied to dividends and other income that a UK-based company receives from investments that are located overseas.

> **Example – Dividend received net of withholding tax**
>
> A UK-based company receives a dividend of £14,400 net of 20% withholding tax from an investment that is based in Farland. The accountant has debited the bank account and credited dividend income in the nominal ledger.
>
> The accountant should also make a provision for the withholding tax that has been suffered. The dividend has been received net of withholding tax and therefore the gross amount of the dividend is £18,000. Therefore, dividend income should be uplifted by an amount of £3,600 with a corresponding debit to the corporation tax charge in the profit and loss account. Hence:
>
> | | |
> |---|---|
> | DR corporation tax charge (profit and loss account) | £3,600 |
> | CR dividend income | £3,600 |
>
> *Being the withholding tax suffered on the dividend from the Farland investment.*

Presentation of current tax

Section 29 requires corporation tax to be recognised in the profit and loss account (income statement) for the period. The exception to this is where tax is attributable to a gain or loss that has been recognised in other comprehensive income and is reported in the statement of changes in equity. Where a gain or loss is recognised in other comprehensive income, then the tax associated with that gain or loss should also be recognised in other comprehensive income.

Example – Allocation of tax to other comprehensive income and profit or loss

The Grainger Group Limited is a parent company that is based in the UK and has a subsidiary company located in an overseas country known as Farland. The parent company's trading profit for the year is £900,000 and it has a foreign currency loan that suffered an exchange loss of £300,000. Corporation tax relief is available to the parent company on the exchange loss and the company pays tax at a rate of 20%. The company's taxable profit in this instance is £600,000 (trading profit £900,000 less £300,000 exchange loss).

The parent's tax liability for the year amounts to £120,000 (£600,000 × 20%). In the consolidated financial statements the loan will be treated as hedging the net assets of its foreign subsidiary and therefore the exchange loss is reported in other comprehensive income. The total tax charge that should be allocated between the profit and loss account and other comprehensive income is calculated as:

	£'000
Tax payable on trading profit (£900,000 × 20%)	180
Tax relief on exchange loss (£300,000 × 20%)	(60)
Total tax charge	120

Therefore, the £180,000 portion would be taken directly to the income statement (profit and loss account) with the tax relief obtained on the exchange loss being reported in other comprehensive income.

Reporting entities will not be able to offset current tax assets against current tax liabilities. The only exception to this rule is where the entity has a legally enforceable right to set off the amounts and it intends to either settle on a net basis or to realise the tax asset and settle the tax liability at the same time. This is to enable compliance with paragraph 29.24 to FRS 102.

DEFERRED TAXATION

As mentioned in the introduction, the vast majority of transactions that are recorded in the financial statements will have some form of tax consequence, whether the tax consequences arise in the current period or in the future period. The issue about future tax consequences is that, in reality, they cannot be avoided – the company will still pay more or less tax in the future due to transactions that have taken place in the current financial year. This can be highlighted with a simple illustration relating to fixed assets. A lot of fixed assets purchased by entities can be deductible for tax purposes in both the current and subsequent accounting periods.

In order to achieve the accruals concept of accounting, it is therefore necessary to account for the future tax consequences of transactions recorded in the current accounting period by a mechanism known as deferred tax. Deferred tax itself can either be an asset or a liability (see the two sections, 'Deferred tax assets' and 'Deferred tax liabilities', below). The objectives of deferred tax are essentially twofold:

- To ensure that the future tax consequences of past transactions and events are recognised as assets or liabilities within a reporting entity's financial statements and
- To disclose any additional special circumstances that may have an effect on future tax charges.

Under previous UK GAAP, aspects concerning taxation were found in FRS 16 *Current Tax* and FRS 19 *Deferred Tax*. Taxation issues were also considered in FRS 17 *Retirement Benefits*, which dealt with tax relief on a company's pension contributions and the attribution of the tax effects to the profit and loss account and the statement of total recognised gains and losses. Unlike FRS 16 and FRS 19, Section 29 combines the requirements of both current and deferred taxes.

In the previous exposure drafts issued by the (now defunct) Accounting Standards Board, the matter of deferred tax was based on the method of computation under *IFRS for SMEs*, which in turn is based on mainstream IAS 12 *Income Taxes*. The Exposure Draft required the calculation of deferred tax to be under the *temporary difference* approach, whereas in the UK accountants have always been used to dealing with deferred tax from a *timing difference* approach. The two approaches are fundamentally different: the temporary difference approach focuses on the balance sheet (statement of financial position), so, for example, a deferred tax liability would arise if the carrying value of an asset was greater than its tax base or if the carrying value of a liability is less than its tax base. Timing differences, on the other hand, focus on the profit and loss account (income statement) and are differences between a company's taxable profits and its results as stated in the financial statements that arise from the inclusion of gains and losses in tax assessments in periods different from those in which they are recognised in the financial statements.

For the purposes of Section 29, a timing difference will arise when an item is included in the tax computation in the current accounting period but the same transaction has been recognised in a different accounting period. The actual definition of a timing difference is found in paragraph 29.6 to FRS 102.

Deferred tax has always been a somewhat controversial issue within the profession, with some practitioners questioning its relevance. However, it is a concept that has been brought into FRS 102 and, to a certain extent, will require further consideration, which is discussed later. There are some points that preparers of financial statements will need an awareness of where Section 29 is concerned:

- Paragraph 29.8 says that deferred tax will be recognised in a company's financial statements in respect of tax allowances for the cost of a fixed asset when these are received before or after the depreciation of the fixed asset is recognised in profit or loss. If, and when, the client has met all the conditions imposed by HM Revenue and Customs for retaining the relevant capital allowances, deferred tax is then reversed.
- When a client has a subsidiary, associate, branch or an interest in a joint venture, it must recognise deferred tax when income or expenses from these sources have

been recognised in the financial statements but will subsequently be included in the tax computation in a future period. There are two exceptions to this rule:

- Where the reporting entity has control over the reversal of the timing difference and
- There is probability that reversal of the timing difference will not take place in the foreseeable future.

Timing difference 'plus'

As mentioned earlier, the previous Exposure Draft, FRED 44, required deferred tax to be calculated using the temporary difference approach. On publication of this Exposure Draft, there was a certain element of outcry in the profession about the complexities inherent in the temporary difference approach (it would have essentially meant more deferred tax balances being recognised and was quite a deviation from what UK GAAP accountants were used to). The previous Accounting Standards Board (ASB) took on board the criticisms and decided to redraft this particular area of the Exposure Draft. However, the proviso was that the method of computing deferred tax must be such that the final outcome is as near as possible to the same answer that would be arrived at under the international equivalent – IAS 12. This proviso resulted in the timing difference *plus* approach being born.

The 'plus' part builds on the timing difference approach that was contained in previous FRS 19 and that many UK accountants are familiar with. However, the intention by the former ASB was to ensure that the calculation of deferred tax in a company's financial statements is the same in many (but not all) cases as that calculated under IAS 12. The ASB achieved this by removing the fewer exceptions that were contained in FRS 19.

One notable example of this is in respect of fixed assets that are subjected to the revaluation model (as permitted in Section 17 *Property, Plant and Equipment*). Under the previous FRS 19, paragraph 14 did not require deferred tax to be recognised on a revaluation gain in respect of a non-monetary asset that is subjected to the revaluation model unless the entity has:

- Entered into a binding agreement to sell the revalued asset(s) and
- Recognised the gains and losses expected to arise on the sale.

This exception is now outlawed by paragraph 29.15 of FRS 102, which now requires deferred tax in respect of a non-depreciable property whose value is measured using the revaluation model to be measured using the tax rates and allowances that apply to the sale of the asset.

Likewise with assets carried under the revaluation model, where a business has an investment property that is measured using fair value in accordance with Section 16 *Investment Property*, deferred tax is recognised using the tax rates and allowances that apply to the sale of the investment property. There is an exception to this rule in paragraph 29.16, which relates to investment property that has a limited useful life and where the business is going to consume the economic benefits associated with the investment property over time.

FRS 102 also introduces a couple of further instances where deferred tax consideration will be triggered and one of these is in relation to a business combination (previously referred to in the UK GAAP as an 'acquisition'). Paragraph 29.11 says that when the tax base of an asset acquired in a business combination (not goodwill) is less than the value at which it is recognised in the acquirer's financial statements, then a deferred tax liability is recognised to represent the additional tax that will be paid in the future. Conversely, when the tax base of an asset is more than the amount recognised for the asset in the financial statements, a deferred tax asset is recognised to represent the additional tax that will be avoided in respect of that difference. A deferred tax asset or liability is recognised for the additional tax that the business will either avoid or pay due to the difference in value at which a liability is recognised and the amount that is assessed to be owed to HMRC. Any amounts that are attributable to goodwill are to be adjusted by the amount of deferred tax recognised.

Examples of timing differences that may trigger deferred tax considerations are:

- Accelerated capital allowances in respect of a company's acquisition of a fixed asset(s),
- Pension liabilities that have been accrued in the financial statements, which are then granted tax relief by HMRC when they are subsequently paid and
- Intra-group profits held in stock, which are unrealised at group level and reversed on consolidation.

Permanent differences

A permanent difference is not a timing difference. A permanent difference will arise because certain items of income and expenditure are not recognised by HMRC. For example, depreciation expense is required to be accounted for according to UK GAAP and the Companies Act 2006; however, HMRC does not recognise depreciation as an expense and will require it to be 'added back' in the computation of taxable profit/loss. Depreciation is therefore a permanent, as opposed to a timing, difference.

MEASUREMENT OF DEFERRED TAX

There are no differences to the measurement of deferred tax in Section 29 as there was in the previous FRS 19. An entity will measure a deferred tax asset or liability using the tax rates and laws that have been enacted, or substantively enacted, at the reporting date and that are expected to apply to the reversal of the timing differences. There are some other issues that should be considered in addition to this requirement:

- Where different tax rates apply to different levels of taxable profit, deferred tax is to be measured using an average rate(s) that has been enacted or substantively enacted at the reporting date and that will apply to the taxable profit or loss of the periods in which the company expects the deferred tax asset or liability to be realised or settled.

- Paragraph 29.14 of FRS 102 recognises that in some jurisdictions taxes are payable at higher or lower rates depending on whether all or part of the profit or profit and loss account reserves are paid out as dividends to shareholders. Paragraph 29.14 also goes on to say that in other jurisdictions, taxes may be refundable or payable if all, or part, of the profit or profit and loss account reserves are paid out as a dividend to shareholders. This paragraph requires an entity to measure current and deferred taxes using the rates that are applicable to profits that are eligible to be distributed as a dividend until such time that the entity recognises a liability to pay a dividend. At the time a liability is recognised in the financial statements, the entity recognises a current or deferred tax liability/asset as well as the associated tax expense/income.

DISCOUNTING DEFERRED TAX BALANCES

An issue that, in practice, is largely going to go unnoticed is that it is no longer permissible to discount deferred tax balances to present day values. The reality is that hardly anyone discounts deferred tax balances for the time value of money, so this prohibition in FRS 102 is not going to be of major consequence to the vast majority of entities.

Deferred tax assets

There are occasions when a timing difference will give rise to a deferred tax asset. The most common example in the UK that will be familiar with most accountants is unused tax losses that are carried forward to be offset against future profits. Another example of a timing difference that may give rise to a deferred tax asset are provisions made for retirement benefits where tax relief is only granted by HMRC when actual contributions are paid as opposed to when the pension expense is recognised in the financial statements.

One of the main principles in financial reporting is that an asset cannot be stated at any more than its recoverable amount. To accord with this principle, a deferred tax asset should only be recognised to the extent that it is regarded as recoverable on the basis of all evidence available to the entity. In other words, an entity can recognise a deferred tax asset when it is more likely than not that there will be suitable taxable profits from which the future reversal of the underlying timing differences can be deducted. This requirement goes somewhat further than merely saying that there must be evidence that the company will yield a profit in the future – it would have to yield *sufficient* taxable profit in order to utilise the deferred tax asset. FRS 102 uses the term 'probable' (in other words it must be 'probable' that the deferred tax asset will be recovered), which is taken to mean 'more likely than not' in the Glossary to FRS 102.

Tax losses that are carried forward to the next accounting period will give rise to a deferred tax asset and therefore must only be recognised to the extent that it is probable that they will be recovered against the reversal of deferred tax liabilities. Like its predecessor, FRS 19, the default presumption is that the mere existence of tax losses should be taken as strong evidence that there may not be other future taxable profits against which the unutilised tax losses can be relieved. There should be evidence to the contrary that the company will be able to utilise deferred tax assets.

Example – Evidence that deferred tax assets can be utilised

Cory Construction Co. Ltd has reported a significant loss in its financial statements to 31 December 2015, amounting to £100,000. The taxable loss amounts to £80,000 and the company pays corporation tax at a rate of 20%. The financial statements are due to be approved and authorised for issue on 7 March 2016. On 1 March 2016, the company received confirmation that it had been awarded a five-year contract to assist in the construction of 30 private houses and a sports complex for a large, multi-national construction company. The contract is very profitable and is due to commence on 1 June 2016.

The awarding of the lucrative contract is strong evidence that there will be suitable taxable profits available in order to utilise a deferred tax asset as at 31 December 2015. The company is therefore permitted to recognise a deferred tax asset of £16,000 (£80,000 × 20%). This is in recognition of the fact that the company's corporation tax liability for the year ended 31 December 2016 will be lower due to the offsetting of the taxable loss against taxable profits for the year then ended.

The term 'suitable taxable profit' means the taxable profit from which HMRC would permit the underlying timing differences in respect of the deferred tax asset to be offset.

Deferred tax liabilities

Deferred tax liabilities are often more common than deferred tax assets and arise because of timing differences. Timing differences are said to arise in one period and are capable of reversal in the next, or subsequent, accounting periods. Deferred tax is never recognised on permanent differences (apart from those that arise on the initial recognition of a business combination).

Because of timing differences, the impact on the tax expense reported in the financial statements will be higher or lower than it would have been had the corporation tax liability been solely based on reportable profit or loss with no timing differences. Increases or future decreases of corporation tax liabilities are recognised in an entity's balance sheet (statement of financial position) as either a deferred tax asset or a deferred tax liability.

Example – Timing difference on an item of fixed asset

Cahill Concrete Limited purchases an item of machinery to make concrete for £10,000 in the year to 31 December 2015. This item of machinery qualifies for HMRC *Annual Investment Allowance* (AIA). Under AIA a company can write off the entire cost of a qualifying asset, for taxation purposes, by way of accelerated capital allowances. The company's declared accounting policy in respect of this machinery is to charge a full year's depreciation in the year of acquisition with no depreciation charge in the year of disposal. The directors have assessed the item of machinery to have a useful economic life of ten years with zero residual value at the end of this assessed useful economic life.

Financial statement extracts for the year-end of 31 December 2015 will show the following in relation to the new machine:

	£
Cost	10,000
Depreciation charge (£10,000/10 years)	(1,000)
Net book value	9,000

The directors have taken advantage of HMRC AIA and therefore the same machine will have a value for taxation purposes of zero. As a result, a difference arises between the net book value per Cahill Concrete financial statements and the tax written-down value of the same machine amounting to £9,000. This difference is a timing difference, which will give rise to a deferred tax liability. If it is to be assumed that Cahill Concrete Limited pays tax at 20% then the deferred tax liability will be £1,800 (£9,000 × 20%).

This deferred tax liability arises because Cahill Concrete Limited has made a cash flow saving in the year it acquired the machine by taking advantage of accelerated capital allowances (the AIA). This allowance will not be available in the next accounting period for the same machine and therefore the tax liability will essentially be higher.

The timing difference plus approach uses the income statement liability method in order to recognise the tax effects of timing differences as either liabilities for tax payable in the future or as assets that are recoverable in the future.

Example – Deferred tax calculation

The Bury Corporation (Bury) prepares financial statements to 31 March each year. There are two matters relevant to the financial statements for the year ended 31 March 2016 as follows:

MATTER 1

On 1 April 2015 Bury purchased a new machine at a cost of £80,000. This machine does not qualify for any accelerated capital allowances from HMRC. The directors have assessed that the machine will have a zero residual value at the end of its useful economic life of eight years. Bury's accounting policy in respect of this machine is to depreciate such machinery on a straight-line basis over its estimated useful life.

MATTER 2

Demand for Bury's products has risen substantially and so on 1 April 2017 the company purchased an additional machine at a cost of £150,000 to help meet the demand from its customers. This new machine also does not qualify for any accelerated capital allowances. The directors have assessed that at the end of this machine's useful economic life of seven years, the residual value will be approximately £10,000. The company's accounting policy in respect of this machine is to depreciate it on a straight-line basis over its useful economic life.

HMRC grant Bury capital allowances at a rate of 18% on such assets and these are granted on a reducing balance basis. Bury pays tax at a rate of 20%.

The deferred tax calculation is worked out as follows:

	2015	2016	2017	2018	2019
Per financial statements					
Carrying value b/fwd	–	70,000	60,000	180,000	150,000
Additions	80,000	–	150,000	–	–
Depreciation	(10,000)	(10,000)	(30,000)	(30,000)	(30,000)
Carrying value c/fwd	70,000	60,000	180,000	150,000	120,000
Per tax computation					
Pool b/fwd	–	65,600	53,792	167,109	137,029
Additions	80,000	–	150,000	–	–
Capital allowances	(14,400)	(11,808)	(36,683)	(30,080)	(24,665)
Pool c/fwd	65,600	53,792	167,109	137,029	112,364
Timing differences					
Capital allowances	14,400	11,808	36,683	30,080	24,665
Depreciation	(10,000)	(10,000)	(10,000)	(10,000)	(10,000)
Originating (reversing)	4,400	1,808	6,683	80	(5,335)
Cumulative timing differences	4,400	6,208	12,891	12,971	7,636
Deferred tax balances					
Tax on opening cumulative difference	–	880	1,242	2,578	2,594
Tax on closing cumulative difference	880	1,242	2,578	2,594	1,527
Tax provided (released)	880	362	1,336	16	(1,067)

Deferred taxation in business combinations

One of the additional situations that will give rise to deferred tax considerations under the timing difference plus approach is the area of business combinations. For clarity, the term 'business combinations' has traditionally been known as an 'acquisition'.

In a business combination, assets and liabilities of the target are measured at fair value. Often these fair values will differ from the amounts that the same assets and liabilities are carried at in the financial statements. In situations when the amount that can be deducted for tax purposes in relation to assets (not goodwill) in a business combination is less than the value it is recognised in the financial statements, a deferred tax liability is recognised – if the amount that can be deducted for tax is more than the carrying value, a deferred tax asset is recognised.

Conversely, deferred tax assets will arise where tax will be avoided because of a difference between the amount at which a liability is recognised and the amount that will be assessed for the purposes of tax, although deferred tax liabilities will arise where future tax will be paid in respect of such liabilities.

When it comes to the issue of consolidated financial statements, all members of a group should follow the same accounting policies for the purposes of consolidated financial statements. The conformity to uniform accounting policies is more than likely going to trigger consolidation adjustments (for example, if a parent has a subsidiary that is located overseas that has not followed group accounting policies due to local legislation or local GAAP requirements). In such situations, this will result in additional timing differences arising in the consolidated financial statements for which deferred tax should be recognised.

Example – Deferred tax in a business combination

North Limited acquires 100% of the net assets of South Limited for a purchase consideration of £1.1 million out of cash. South Limited has a valuable customer list that failed to meet the recognition criteria as an intangible asset on South's balance sheet (statement of financial position) as it has been internally generated. Tax relief has been obtained by South Limited for the expenditure it incurred in creating the customer list.

At the date of acquisition, the customer list was valued at £150,000 and the fair value of the other assets in the acquisition amount to £600,000. North Limited pays corporation tax at the rate of 20%.

The difference between the tax base of the asset (which is £nil as HMRC have granted tax relief already in respect of this expenditure) and the fair value of the intangible asset of £150,000 gives rise to a deferred tax liability of £30,000 (£150,000 × 20%). The amount attributed to goodwill is adjusted by this deferred balance, which is calculated as follows:

	£
Cost of business combination	1,100,000
Fair value of customer list	(150,000)
Fair value of other net assets in the combination	(600,000)
Deferred taxation	30,000
Goodwill	380,000

Assume for the purposes of this illustration that the customer list has a useful economic life of five years; then in the consolidated financial statements it will be amortised at an annual rate of £30,000 (£150,000/5 years). The deferred tax liability will be released to the consolidated profit and loss account over a five-year period; hence £6,000 (£30,000/5 years).

The issue of tax in a group context poses certain difficulties because they are not as straightforward as the separate financial statements. In a group situation, some members might be profitable whilst others may be loss-making and therefore there is the issue of transferring losses from a loss-making entity to a profit-making entity. Other group members may also operate in different countries with other members of the group operating in the same country as the parent. As consolidated financial statements are prepared in line with the economic substance of the group – that is, as a single reporting entity – it follows that the group's tax position should be viewed as a whole.

When it comes to the consolidation itself, some consolidation adjustments can give rise to tax consequences. For example, if income and expenses are included in total comprehensive income in different periods than they are reported on the individual company's tax return, then timing differences will arise. In addition to timing differences, some consolidation adjustments can also give rise to permanent differences.

> **Example – Consolidation adjustment giving rise to deferred tax asset**

East Limited has a wholly owned subsidiary, West Limited, and the group's year-end is 31 October 2016. On 30 October 2016, West Limited sold goods to East Limited for £70,000, which cost £60,000. These goods are still held in East's warehouse at the year-end. For group financial statement purposes, a consolidation adjustment is required to be made in order to eliminate the £10,000 unrealised profit of £10,000 from the consolidated profit and loss account. Both group companies pay corporation tax at the rate of 20% and, in respect of this transaction alone, East Limited has recorded a current tax charge amounting to £2,000 (£10,000 × 20%).

The subsidiary's current tax charge will be eliminated on consolidation by way of a deferred tax credit in the profit and loss account and a deferred tax asset. This is because the consolidation adjustment required to eliminate the unrealised profit results in a timing difference on consolidation on the grounds that West Limited has declared the profit on the sale of stock to the parent (East Limited) on its corporation tax return in a different period from when it is recognised in total comprehensive income in the group; hence a deferred tax asset is recognised. This deferred tax asset will be recognised in the 31 October 2016 consolidated financial statements and will be released at the tax rate of the selling entity when it was included in the corporation tax return. There will not be any adjustments made in respect of changes in corporate tax rates.

Fixed assets subjected to grants

Grants are the subject of Section 24 *Government Grants* in FRS 102 and it might be the case that a reporting entity receives a grant towards the cost of all, or part, of a qualifying fixed asset. In these situations, Section 24 requires an entity to recognise the grant as deferred income and release it to profit or loss over the life of the asset to which the grant relates (in other words to match the grant income with the depreciation charges of the asset concerned). There are certain types of grant that are not subjected to corporation tax (hence non-taxable) although, in some situations, tax legislation may require the cost of the asset to be reduced for the purposes of capital allowances.

Grants in relation to fixed assets are referred to herein as 'capital-based' grants. When a capital-based grant is not subject to corporation tax, there will not be any deferred tax consequences. This does not, however, preclude the requirement to subject the grant to any capital allowances that may be available in respect of the asset, such as the AIA.

Taxable capital-based grants will, however, give rise to a timing difference between the profit for accounting purposes and the profit for tax purposes. Section 24 and the Companies Act 2006 prohibit capital-based grants from being offset against the cost of the asset. Because of this prohibition the deferred tax calculation will be twofold:

1. A debit balance on the deferred tax account will arise in respect of the unamortised balance of the grant.
2. A credit balance on the deferred tax account will arise in respect of the accelerated capital allowances (for example, the AIA).

Both of the above can be offset against each other.

Leasing

Leases are dealt with in Section 20 *Leases*. This particular section recognises two types of lease: an operating lease and a finance lease. When a lease is an operating lease, there will be no deferred tax issues to consider. This is because the amount that has been debited to the profit and loss account in respect of the operating lease payment is the same amount that has been charged in arriving at taxable profit; hence no timing difference arises. The only exception that would normally give rise to deferred tax considerations for operating leases is where there are accrued rentals that could give rise to a potential timing difference. It is also to be noted that leasing costs of cars with high emissions are subject to a disallowance for taxation purposes.

Leasing is a common mechanism of obtaining an asset in the UK under a leasing arrangement with a lessor. Such arrangements generally give rise to timing differences between the amounts that are recorded in an entity's profit and loss account (income statement) and the amounts that are recorded in the corporation tax computation. Ordinarily, timing differences will arise when a lessee enters into a finance lease (where the risks and rewards of ownership generally pass to the lessee) and tax legislation requires the capital allowances associated with the leased asset to be claimed by the lessor and not the lessee. Generally, HMRC usually accepts the accounting treatment under Section 20 of FRS 102 and therefore there may not necessarily be any deferred tax issues to consider. However, in principle, there are timing differences that may exist and this can be illustrated using an example where the finance lessee cannot claim capital allowances from HMRC but can, instead, claim tax relief on the total rents that have been paid to the lessor.

Example – Deferred tax considerations in a lease transaction

Spring Limited enters into a finance lease with Summer Limited for a fixed asset that does not qualify for capital allowances under UK taxation legislation. The term of the lease is for five years and Summer Limited will make payments amounting to £12,000 for Spring Limited on an annual basis.

Summer Limited will record a fixed asset at an amount of £48,000, which is the present value of the minimum lease payments amounting to £60,000 (£12,500 × 5 years). If it is to be assumed that Summer's depreciation policy is to depreciate the fixed asset over its estimated useful life of five years and that the fixed asset will have zero residual value at the end of its life then depreciation can be calculated at £9,600 (£48,000/5 years).

The deferred tax calculation is as follows:

	Year 1	Year 2	Year 3	Year 4	Year 5
Rental paid	12,000	12,000	12,000	12,000	12,000
Interest (7.93%)	(3,806)	(3,158)	(2,455)	(1,699)	(882)
Capital amount	8,194	8,842	9,545	10,301	11,118
Timing differences					
Interest	3,806	3,158	2,455	1,699	882
Depreciation	9,600	9,600	9,600	9,600	9,600
	13,406	12,758	12,055	11,299	10,482
Tax relief on rentals	12,000	12,000	12,000	12,000	12,000
Timing difference	(1,406)	(758)	(55)	701	1,518
Net book value	38,400	28,800	19,200	9,600	=
Outstanding capital	39,806	30,964	21,419	11,118	=
Cumulative timing difference	(1,406)	(2,164)	(2,219)	(1,518)	=

Defined benefit pension schemes

Tax legislation in the UK states that a company is granted tax relief on pension contributions usually in the period in which the contributions are paid, as opposed to when contributions are recognised in profit or loss. Therefore, when there is a difference between the pension contributions recognised in profit or loss and the contributions that have actually been paid, this will give rise to a timing difference for the purposes of deferred taxation.

Under a defined benefit pension scheme, there are various components of the scheme that are reported in profit or loss, such as:

- Current service cost,
- Past service cost,
- Gains or losses on curtailments and settlements,
- Interest cost and
- Return on scheme assets.

Certain items in a defined benefit pension scheme are also reported in other comprehensive income such as actuarial gains and losses. Because of the nature of these schemes, the way such costs are accounted for will often result in tax relief being granted by HMRC for the actual contributions *paid* by the company, but also consideration has to be given to the deferred tax on the timing differences that arise between the contributions paid and the costs that have been recognised in profit or loss. A further complication arises in deferred tax because some of the deferred tax attributable to the timing differences may have to be split between the portion recognised in profit or loss and the portion that is to be recognised in other comprehensive income.

Example – Deferred tax in a defined benefit pension scheme

A company based in the UK operates a defined benefit pension scheme for its staff and has done so for several years. Actuarial information has been obtained from the professionally qualified actuaries, which show the following information:

	£
Opening scheme liability	(200,000)
Contributions paid into the scheme	80,000
Past service cost	(20,000)
Interest cost	(70,000)
Expected return on scheme assets	20,000
Actuarial loss	(20,000)
Closing scheme liability	(210,000)

The company pays tax at the rate of 20%. When there is a deficit on the defined benefit pension scheme, this will give rise to a deferred tax asset because essentially the deficit will require more payments to be made if the members of the scheme required to be paid out all at once and hence tax relief would be granted on the deficit – hence a deferred tax asset. The deferred tax asset is calculated as follows:

	Deficit £	*Tax relief £*	*Deferred tax asset £*
Opening deficit	(200,000)		40,000
Contributions paid	80,000	(16,000)	
Charges to P&L	(70,000)	14,000	
Actuarial loss (OCI)	(20,000)	2,000	2,000
Balance c/fwd	(210,000)	–	42,000

The profit and loss account charge is made up of the past service cost of £20,000, the interest cost of £70,000 less the expected return on plan assets of £20,000. Tax relief will be granted by HMRC on the contributions paid and this is allocated to the profit and loss account charge. The difference between the contributions paid and the profit and loss account charge of £10,000 (£80,000 less £70,000) is allocated against the actuarial loss, which is reported in other comprehensive income.

Share-based payment

Share-based payment transactions are dealt with in Chapter 19 and in Section 26 *Share-based Payment* in FRS 102. Under the provisions in Section 26, a reporting entity that has entered into a share-based payment arrangement with its employees is required to recognise the cost of equity-settled share-based payment transactions on the basis of the fair value of the award at the grant date and this is then spread over the vesting period. Under UK tax law, the amount of tax relief that is granted to an entity by HMRC will often not be the equivalent amount that has been charged in profit or loss. This is because under UK tax legislation, HMRC will grant tax relief on the share options at the date the share options are exercised and the amount of tax relief granted will be measured at the share option's intrinsic value at that date. The 'intrinsic' value of a share option is the difference between the share's fair value (market price) at the date of the exercise and the option's exercise price.

For the purposes of deferred tax, a timing difference will arise when the entity recognises the share-based payment charge in the profit and loss account (income statement). The timing difference represents the difference between the cumulative amount of the charge and the related amount of the purposes of taxation that will be received by HMRC in the future. This is, of course, provided that the deferred tax asset meets the recognition criteria in Section 29, which is that there will be suitable taxable profits yielded by the entity from which the deferred tax asset can be utilised.

When the share option's intrinsic value falls below fair value at the date of the grant, this might suggest that the deferred tax asset is not recoverable. In such instances, management would have to consider the need to write this deferred tax asset down to its recoverable amount.

Example – Deferred tax on a share-based payment arrangement

On 1 April 2016, Westhead Trading Limited (Westhead) issues 100,000 share options with a fair value of £300,000, all of which are expected to vest in three years' time. It is expected that on this date all shares will be exercised and all share options will be exercised in year 4. Westhead pays corporation tax at the rate of 20% and the intrinsic value of all the share options at the end of each year is as follows:

Year	Intrinsic value
	£
1	290,000
2	260,000
3	340,000
4	360,000

In each year, Westhead will recognise £100,000 (£300,000/3 years) in profit and loss as an expense in relation to the share-based payment arrangement. UK tax legislation says that tax relief is not granted on share options until they are exercised. As a result, a timing difference arises that triggers deferred tax considerations.

There are two accounting policy choices available to Westhead on which deferred tax can be based:

Option 1: deferred tax based on the cumulative share-based payment charge in profit and loss

Option 2: deferred tax based on the intrinsic value at the reporting date

Option 1: Deferred tax based on the cumulative share-based payment charge

In year 1, Westhead will charge £100,000 to the profit and loss account in respect of the share-based payment arrangement. As the intrinsic value in year 1 is £290,000, this covers the tax relief that will be granted. Under this option, deferred tax is based on the cumulative share-based payment charge but only to the extent of the intrinsic value of the option. The deferred tax asset is £20,000 (£100,000 × 20%).

In year 2, the cumulative share-based payment charge is £200,000 and this is also covered by the intrinsic value of £260,000. Hence, the deferred tax asset is £40,000 (£200,000 × 20%).

In year 3, the cumulative share-based payment charge is £300,000 and this is covered by the intrinsic value of £340,000. Hence the deferred tax asset is £60,000 (£300,000 × 20%).

The financial statement extracts of Westhead for years 1 to 3 will show the following:

| Year | Profit and loss account | | Balance sheet |
	Charge	Deferred tax	deferred tax asset
	£	£	£
1	100,000	(20,000)	20,000
2	100,000	(20,000)	40,000
3	100,000	(20,000)	60,000
	300,000	(60,000)	

Option 2: Deferred tax based on the intrinsic value at the reporting date

If Westhead were to base deferred tax on the intrinsic value of the options at the reporting date, the tax deductions in respect of the cumulative share-based payment charge is pro rata of the total intrinsic value of the share options at the reporting date. This is capped at the cumulative payment charge.

Year 1
In year 1, the timing difference is £96,667 (£290,000 × 1/3) and the deferred tax asset is therefore £19,333 (£96,667 × 20%).

Year 2
In year 2, the timing difference is £173,333 (£260,000 × 2/3) and the deferred tax asset is therefore £34,667 (£173,333 × 20%).

Year 3
In year 3, the deferred tax asset is £60,000 (£300,000 × 20%). A deferred tax asset is not recognised in respect of the options' intrinsic value of £340,000 over the cumulative share-based payment charge of £300,000.

The financial statement extracts of Westhead will show the following:

| Year | Profit and loss account | | Balance sheet |
	Charge	Deferred tax	deferred tax asset
	£	£	£
1	100,000	(19,333)	19,333
2	100,000	(15,334)	34,667
3	100,000	(25,333)	60,000
	300,000	(60,000)	

In year 4, the share options are exercised and tax relief is granted on those share options based on the intrinsic value. In year 4, the intrinsic value of the shares is £360,000 and therefore tax relief of £72,000 (£360,000 × 20%) is granted by HMRC in this year. In year 4, the deferred tax asset is reversed through the profit and loss account. The profit and loss account will then be credited with £12,000, being the difference between the tax relief granted by HMRC (£72,000) and the reversal of the deferred tax asset of £60,000. Extracts of the movement in the financial statements of Westhead are as follows:

		Profit and loss account		*Balance sheet*	
	Charge	*Corporation tax*	*Deferred tax*	*Tax debtor*	*Deferred tax*
End of year 3	£300,000		£60,000		£60,000
Year 4 movement	Nil	(£72,000)	(£60,000)	£72,000	(£60,000)
	£300,000	(£72,000)	–	£72,000	–

DISCLOSURE REQUIREMENTS

The disclosure requirements in relation to income tax are set out in paragraphs 29.25 to 29.27 of FRS 102, which are as follows:

- Information should be disclosed that will enable the users of the financial statements to understand the nature and financial effect of the current and deferred tax consequences for recognised transactions and events.
- The major components of tax expense (or income), which may include:
  - Current tax charge (credit),
  - Adjustments to the tax charge in the current period, which relates to tax in respect of prior years,
  - The amount of deferred tax expense (or income) in respect of timing differences that have originated and/or reversed,
  - The amount of deferred tax expense (or income) in respect of tax rate changes or the introduction of new taxes,
  - Adjustments made to the deferred tax charge (credit), which have arisen as a result of the tax status of the company, or its shareholders, changing, and
  - The amount of the tax charge (credit), which has arisen due to a change in accounting policies or the correction of a material error.

Reporting entities should also separately disclose:

- The total amount of current and deferred taxation, which relates to items that have been recognised as items of other comprehensive income or equity,
- A reconciliation between:
  - The tax charge (credit) included in the profit and loss account and
  - The profit or loss on ordinary activities before taxation multiplied by the appropriate tax rate,
- The amount of the net reversal of deferred tax assets and liabilities that is expected to occur during the next financial year together with a brief explanation for the expected reversal,
- An explanation as to any changes in the applicable tax rate(s) compared with the previous period,

- The amount of deferred tax assets and liabilities that the entity has at the end of the accounting period for each type of timing difference as well as the amount of any unused tax losses and tax credits,
- Where applicable, the expiry date of timing differences, unutilised tax losses and tax credits and
- Where paragraph 29.14 applies to a reporting entity, there should be an explanation of the nature of the potential tax consequences that would arise if the entity paid a dividend to its shareholders.

12 INTANGIBLE ASSETS

INTRODUCTION

Intangible assets are dealt with in Section 18 *Intangible Assets other than Goodwill* in FRS 102. Whilst goodwill is clearly an intangible asset, FRS 102 deals with the issue of goodwill in Section 19 *Business Combinations and Goodwill*. Impairment issues relating to intangible assets are covered in Section 27 *Impairment of Assets*. Section 18 also does not cover:

- Deferred acquisition costs and intangible assets that have arisen from contracts that fall under the scope of FRS 103 *Insurance Contracts* (although the disclosure requirements in Section 18 do apply to such assets),
- Intangible assets that are held for sale in the ordinary course of business,
- Financial assets,
- Mineral rights and mineral reserves (for example, oil, gas and similar non-regenerative resources) and
- Heritage assets.

An intangible asset is an asset that does not have a physical substance – in other words, you cannot see or touch the intangible asset. In quite a lot of cases, the accounting for intangible assets can be a fairly complicated exercise in terms of how the asset is identified. For the purposes of financial reporting, an intangible asset is identifiable when it is capable of being separated or divided from the entity and then sold, transferred, licensed, rented or exchanged. An intangible asset is also identifiable when it arises from contractual or other legal rights irrespective of whether (or not) the rights to the intangible asset are transferable or separable from the entity.

Example – Classification as inventory

A company's principal activity is the granting of licences to third parties to undertake various activities.

Whilst licences do tend to meet the definition of an intangible asset, these licences will be classified as inventory because they are held for the business's principal activity.

> **Example – Taxi licence**
>
> In the UK, a taxi driver is legally obliged to obtain a taxi licence in order to operate a vehicle as a taxi.
>
> The licence would meet the recognition criteria as an intangible asset because the intangible asset arises from legal rights regardless of the fact that the licence may not be separable from the underlying business as it can only be transferred to other taxi operators.

> **Example – Computer software**
>
> A laptop computer is required to have various software installed in order to operate (for example, an operating system).
>
> The software would essentially be the non-physical component of the computer equipment and the specific software is therefore regarded as an integral part of the computer in order for it to operate. As the software is treated as an integral part of the related hardware, it is not treated as an intangible asset but is instead accounted for under the provisions in Section 17 *Property, Plant and Equipment*.

In some cases judgement will need to be exercised in order to determine whether an integral part of an asset is to be classified as intangible or tangible and it may be the case that certain elements of an asset are treated separately for accounting purposes. For example, a database may be contained on a computer. The computer equipment that contains the database may well have a different useful economic life to the database and therefore it would be appropriate in this instance to account for the computer equipment and the database separately.

CATEGORIES OF INTANGIBLE ASSETS

There are many different types of intangible assets, which are often classified into various categories, including:

- Intangible assets that arise through contract-related activities, such as franchises, licensing agreements and service or supply contracts,
- Goodwill in a business combination (which is accounted for in accordance with Section 19),
- Intangible assets arising through technological activities such as computer software,
- Artistic-related intangible assets such as motion pictures or works of art and
- Customer lists and relationships.

This list is not exhaustive and other intangible assets could contain the characteristics of an intangible asset. Whatever the category of intangible assets, it is important that care is taken to ensure that an intangible asset has the appropriate characteristics present, which are:

- Identifiability: the asset is separable, that is, capable of being separated or divided from the entity and sold, transferred, licensed, rented or exchanged, either separately or together with a related contract, asset or liability, or it arises from contractual or other legal rights,
- It is a non-monetary asset and
- Does not possess a physical substance.

In light of the above characteristics, this may result in the recognition of more intangible assets than was the case under the previous UK GAAP at FRS 10 *Goodwill and Intangible Assets* (where assets were previously only recognised when separable **and** controlled through custody or legal rights).

RECOGNITION AND MEASUREMENT

In order to qualify for recognition on the balance sheet (statement of financial position), there are two criteria that have to be considered:

1. Is it probable that expected future benefits will flow to the entity from the intangible asset?
2. Can a reliable cost or value be measured?

If the answer to the above questions is 'yes', then the intangible asset will qualify for recognition on the balance sheet (statement of financial position). In determining whether it is probable that expected future benefits will flow to the entity, Section 18 requires reporting entities to use their judgement in assessing the future economic benefits. This will require management using reasonable and supportable assumptions, which will then be used as a basis for estimating the intangible asset's useful economic life.

The concept of control is extremely pivotal in the determination of an intangible asset. Essentially control exists when the business has the power to obtain economic benefits from the asset and the entity has the power to restrict access of the asset to others. Generally in such contexts, control is obtained through legal rights (for example, the granting of a copyright). Where legal rights cannot be obtained it will be inherently more difficult to prove control is present.

Example – Specialised staff

A business is involved in the development of clinical drugs and employs a team of highly skilled and specialist staff to undertake both the research into new drugs and the development of those (and existing) drugs.

It is not appropriate to recognise such staff as an intangible asset on the balance sheet (statement of financial position) on the grounds that management will be unable to evidence control over those staff. This is because the staff could leave their employment with the company at any time.

Example – Customer relationships

A company has a number of customers for which it undertakes fixed-term contracts.

Where the business can demonstrate that the contracts contain legally enforceable provisions that give rise to a revenue stream for the business, the recognition criteria for an intangible asset will be met. Conversely, where there are no legal rights to protect or control the relationship of customers this will give rise to no control over the customer relationships and hence the recognition criteria will not be met.

In assessing the recognition criteria, Section 18 says that it must be 'probable' that future economics will flow to the entity. The Glossary to FRS 102 defines 'probable' as 'more likely than not'. As a result, where management determine that it will be more likely than not that future economic benefits will flow to the entity from the intangible asset, the criteria will be satisfied.

On initial recognition, an intangible asset is measured at its cost. The composition of cost can be made up of several different elements and will include:

- Purchase cost
- Import duties
- Non-refundable purchase taxes
- Directly attributable costs in preparing the asset for its intended use

The total cost recognised on the balance sheet (statement of financial position) should be net of any trade discounts or rebates granted to the entity.

Example – Deferred payment

A business acquires an intangible asset on deferred credit terms.

In such a situation, the entity will recognise the asset at its cash price equivalent, which will be the discounted amount. The difference between the discounted amount and the total payment is regarded as interest, which is payable over the period of the credit granted.

Cost can comprise various elements and one element are those costs that are 'directly attributable' in preparing the asset for its intended use. Such costs can include:

- Legal fees,
- Employee costs that are directly attributable in bringing the asset to its working condition,
- Costs involved in testing to ensure the asset is working correctly and
- Other professional fees that are directly attributable in bringing the asset to its working condition (for example, fees to register a legal right).

Example – Other costs incurred

A company is launching a new service and has recognised an intangible asset on its balance sheet (statement of financial position) that meets the recognition criteria. Included in the cost of the intangible asset is an amount in respect of advertising the new service.

The cost of advertising new products or services does not form the cost of the intangible asset and this cost should be written off to profit or loss in the period in which it is incurred.

Advertising expenditure (as in the example above) is considered not to be an expense that can form the cost of an intangible asset. In addition, general administration expenses and costs incurred in conducting business in a new location or with a new class of customer are considered not to be expenses that can be capitalised as part of the cost of an intangible asset.

After initial recognition at cost, a business has two choices to measure the asset:

- Cost model or
- Revaluation model.

Under the cost model, the business will measure an intangible asset at cost less accumulated amortisation and accumulated impairment losses.

Under the revaluation model, the intangible asset is carried at its revalued amount, which is its fair value at each reporting date less any subsequent accumulated amortisation and impairment losses. In reality few intangible assets will be carried under the revaluation model because in order to carry assets under the revaluation model there has to be an *active market*. An active market is one whereby similar assets are traded and thus provides a reliable measure of value.

Care also needs to be taken with the revaluation model because it does not permit the revaluation of intangible assets that have not previously been recognised as assets and nor does it permit intangible assets to be initially recognised at amounts other than cost. In all instances, intangible assets are always recognised on the balance sheet (statement of financial position) at cost and then the revaluation model is applied (where this model is chosen as a subsequent measurement).

Example – Intangible asset carried under the revaluation model

An entity has decided to apply the revaluation model to its intangible assets. On 1 January 2016 the intangible asset was carried in the balance sheet (statement of financial position) at a fair value of £10,000. On 31 December 2016, the fair value of the intangible asset had increased to £15,000.

Where the fair value of an intangible asset increases as a result of revaluation, the increase is recognised in other comprehensive income and accumulated in equity (usually under the heading of 'Revaluation surplus').

The entries in the books on 31 December 2016 will be:

DR intangible asset   £5,000
CR revaluation surplus (equity)   £5,000

Being revaluation to fair value at 31 December 2016.

Example – Active market no longer exists

On 1 January 2016, a company's intangible asset had a fair value of £10,000. However, in the year to 31 December 2016 an active market was no longer available from which to derive a fair value at the year-end.

Where the fair value of an intangible asset cannot be determined by reference to an active market, the carrying amount of the asset will be its revalued amount at the date of the last valuation by reference to an active market that was available less any subsequent amortisation and impairment.

When an intangible asset is acquired in a business combination, Section 18 at paragraph 18.11 says that the cost of the intangible asset is its fair value at the date of acquisition. A key point to emphasise where intangible assets are acquired in a business combination is that they are recognised separately to that of goodwill on the grounds that an intangible asset's value has been measured with sufficient reliability and it is irrelevant whether, or not, the same intangible asset was recognised on the acquiree's balance sheet (statement of financial position).

In reality it is often difficult to identify certain types of intangible asset and then assign a reliable value to them. In such cases entities will only record identifiable intangible assets that they can reliably measure the value.

Intangible asset obtained by way of grant

There may be occasions when an intangible asset is obtained by way of a grant and in such cases the provisions laid down in Section 24 *Government Grants* will apply. However, where an intangible asset is obtained by way of a grant there is no exchange transaction and therefore the cost of the intangible asset will be the fair value at the date the grant is received or receivable. Examples of such assets would be airport landing rights, fishing quotas, import licences and TV and radio station operating licences.

Example – Fishing quota

A company obtains a licence that grants them the right to obtain up to 70,000 tonnes of fish from certain waters in a year. The licence is for five years at a cost of £80,000.

The licence is essentially a grant because it grants the entity the right to obtain up to 70,000 tonnes of fish per year and will therefore be recognised on the balance sheet (statement of financial position) at its fair value of £80,000 and amortised over a five-year period.

Exchange of assets

An entity may acquire an intangible asset in exchange for a non-monetary asset(s) or a combination of monetary and non-monetary asset(s). The probability recognition criteria in respect of an intangible asset acquired separately in an exchange transaction are deemed to be satisfied.

When an entity is involved in an exchange transaction, the intangible asset acquired in the exchange is measured at fair value. There are two exceptions to this:

1. Where the exchange transaction lacks commercial substance or
2. The fair value of the asset received and the asset given up cannot be measured reliably. Where this is the case, the asset's cost is measured at the carrying amount of the asset that has been given up.

In instances where the fair value of either the asset given up or the asset received can be reliably measured, then an entity would account for the exchange transaction on the basis of the fair value of the asset given up (unless the fair value of the asset received is more clearly evident). As a consequence, entities would immediately recognise any gain or loss on the exchange on the grounds that most transactions entered into have commercial substance and hence the recognition of gains and losses would normally take place.

An exchange transaction will not possess commercial substance if the financial positions of both parties do not change – in other words they are still in the same economic position after the exchange transaction as they were before.

Example – Transaction lacking commercial substance

Company A has a database that has a fair value of some £4,000. Company B has a database with a fair value of some £3,900. The two companies both decide to exchange databases for the fair values attributed to each database at the same time.

This transaction lacks commercial substance because the two companies' economic positions do not change. This is evident because the configuration of the cash flows of the asset received does not differ from the configuration of the cash flows of the asset given up. The term 'configuration of cash flows' means the risk, amount and timing of the cash flows.

Example – Exchange of patents

Company C owns the rights and obligations to a patent that has a carrying value of £6,000. It has agreed to exchange this patent with Company D and both parties have agreed that the fair value of Company C's patent at the time of exchange is £8,000. Company D's patent cannot be reliably measured and the terms of the agreement provide for no additional monetary or non-monetary consideration.

The patent acquired by Company C will be recognised at an amount of £8,000 as this is the patent's value that can be reliably measured and is used by both parties in the transaction as a value of the consideration if the other patent cannot be reliably measured. Company C will recognise a gain of £2,000, which is the difference between the carrying amount of Company C's original patent (£6,000) and the fair value of the patent given up (£8,000).

As patents are both generally considered to be unique, the exchange has commercial substance.

Intangible assets acquired in business combinations

When a business combination takes place, an intangible asset that is acquired as part of this business combination satisfies the recognition criteria as an intangible asset because its fair value at the date of acquisition can normally be measured with sufficient reliability and the probability of future economic benefits is assumed. Care must be taken for intangible assets such as trademarks, internet domain names, licensing and royalty agreements and franchise agreements because these are restricted as they arise from legal or other contractual rights. In such instances it would be necessary to consider whether there is a history or evidence of the same or similar assets. Where no such history exists, the intangible assets would not be separately recognised in the balance sheet (statement of financial position), but would be included as part of goodwill.

Example – Intangible asset acquired in a business combination

Company A acquires 100% of the net assets of Company B (i.e. Company B becomes a wholly owned subsidiary of Company A). Company B has a valuable customer list that has not arisen through contractual or legal rights.

Provided the fair value of the customer list can be measured reliably at the date of acquisition, the customer list would be recognised as a separate asset (i.e. not within goodwill).

RESEARCH AND DEVELOPMENT

Many companies will carry out research and development; for example, a pharmaceutical company that is looking to bring out a new drug will carry out lots of research and development activities. The issue of research and development can be quite problematic in practice because of the extremely different accounting treatments between expenditure that falls to be classified as 'research' and expenditure that falls to be classified as 'development'.

An intangible asset that is in the process of being created and that essentially falls under the scope of Section 18 must be divided into the research phase and the development phase. In situations whereby it is not possible to distinguish the two phases, all of the expenditure should be classified as research expenditure.

Research activities can include:

- Activities whose objective is to obtain new knowledge such as market research,
- Undertaking a search for suitable applications for the findings of research and
- Searching for alternatives for materials, products and processes.

Development activities can include:

- The design of tools and other equipment used in new technology,
- Constructing prototypes and models,
- Testing prototypes and models,
- Constructing a pilot plant that is not of a scale that would give rise to commercial production and
- Designing a selected alternative for new or improved outputs (such as materials, processes or products).

The basic distinction between the 'research' phase and the 'development' phase is that the development phase is essentially further advanced than the research phase.

Accounting for expenditure in the research phase

All expenditure incurred during the research phase (both pure and applied research) should be written off to profit or loss as incurred. FRS 102 prohibits any intangible asset being recognised on the balance sheet (statement of financial position) that arises from research expenditure or from the research phase of an internal project. The primary reason for this prohibition is because the entity is unable to demonstrate that future economic benefits will flow to the entity from the asset and hence does not meet the definition of an intangible asset, nor the criteria for recognition.

Example – Intangible assets acquired during the research phase

A company is involved in the design of a new drug and is undertaking research in order to hopefully progress on to the development stage. It has incurred expenditure on patents that will be required during the research and development phase of the project.

When a company purchases patents it essentially purchases 'rights' and these rights would qualify for recognition as separate intangible assets in their own right, regardless of the fact that they are being used for the research phase of a project. The reason is that the 'future economic benefits' criteria are assumed to be automatically satisfied where a company separately acquires an intangible asset. Some may argue that the purchase of a patent in a research project may not necessarily give rise to future economic benefits (it may be that the project becomes unfeasible and is abandoned). However, a counter-argument would be the fact that the patent has been acquired for value and therefore it is likely that it can be sold again for value.

There are certain expenses that Section 18 specifically requires to be written off to profit or loss and not recognise them as intangible assets:

- Brands, logos, publishing titles, customer lists and items that are similar in substance that have been internally generated,
- Costs in relation to start-up activities (for example, company secretarial costs for the formation of a new company or expenditure incurred in opening a new business/branch/office or the expenditure incurred in starting operations in a new business/branch/office),
- Costs of staff training or training activities,
- Advertising expenditure or other forms of promotional expenditure (an exception would be where the expenditure meets the definition of 'inventories held for distribution at no or nominal consideration'),
- Relocation and reorganisation expenditure and
- Goodwill that has been internally generated.

Development expenditure

Section 18 gives entities an accounting policy choice where development expenditure is concerned. An entity can choose to recognise an internally generated intangible asset that has arisen as a direct result of the development phase of a project or alternatively the expenditure can be written off to profit or loss. Whichever accounting policy is adopted by the reporting entity it must be applied consistently to all development expenditure.

Where the entity chooses to recognise development expenditure as an intangible asset on the balance sheet (statement of financial position), it can only do so if, and only if, the expenditure meets the strict criterion laid out in paragraph 18.8H to FRS 102. This criterion requires the reporting entity to be able to demonstrate all of the following:

- It is technically feasible that the intangible asset will be completed so it can either be used or sold,
- The entity intends to complete the intangible asset and use it or subsequently sell it,
- The entity has the ability to use or sell the intangible asset,
- How the intangible asset will generate economic benefits for the entity as well as demonstrating that there is a market in existence for the output of the intangible asset or, where the plan is to use the intangible asset internally, the usefulness of the intangible asset,
- The entity has adequate technical, financial and other resources at its disposal in order to complete the development of the intangible asset and then to use or sell it and
- The entity can reliably measure the expenditure attributable to the intangible asset during the development phase.

If any expenditure does not meet the conditions in the above bullet points, it must be expensed as incurred.

Example – Development of a new drug

A UK-based pharmaceutical company is considering the development of a new drug to combat a new air-borne illness that has recently begun to mutate in the Far East. The project director has structured the project as follows:

1. Identify the need for a new drug.
2. Commission research for any existing drugs in that part of the world.
3. Commission research for any existing drugs in other parts of the world that may be effective in the prevention of the illness.
4. Undertake research for any other competitors' use of equivalent drugs that may combat this illness.
5. Commission the design of the new drug and the ingredients.
6. Prepare a shortlist from step 5 above.
7. Obtain a budget from finance for the new drug and compare this budget to the shortlist prepared in step 6.
8. Prepare a further shortlist of three possible alternatives based on feedback from managers.
9. Send the final three to the board of directors for their approval.
10. Develop the new drug.
11. Undertake testing on the new drug.
12. Roll out the new drug.

The recognition criteria at each stage should be considered to determine when the capitalisation criteria have been met. Once the recognition criteria have been met, the entity can start to capitalise the directly attributable costs.

At stage 5, the technical feasibility of completing the intangible asset for use and the entity's ability to use the asset have been confirmed.

At the end of stage 7, it has been deciphered how the intangible asset will generate future economic benefits as well as an existence for the output of the project (the new drug). A budget has also been prepared that confirms the availability of adequate technical, financial and other resources to complete the development and to use/sell the asset.

At stage 10 all the recognition criteria have been met and the board of directors have approved the project, which gives rise to evidence of an intention to complete the project and the budgeted information will provide evidence of the entity's ability to measure the expenditure reliably.

AMORTISATION

FRS 102 says that all intangible assets have a finite life. This is markedly different to the previous UK GAAP at FRS 10 *Goodwill and Intangible Assets*, which acknowledged that it may be the case that some intangible assets have an indefinite life. This is no longer the case under Section 18 and the useful life of an intangible asset cannot exceed the period of the contractual or (other) legal rights. FRS 102 does acknowledge that it might not necessarily be the case that an intangible asset is written off over the period of the asset's contractual or (other) legal rights, but recognises that an entity may write the intangible asset off over a shorter period if the entity deems this appropriate (i.e. in situations where the entity may not use the asset over the full period of the contractual or (other) legal rights).

Assigning a useful life to an intangible asset can be somewhat problematic in certain situations. Where an entity is unable to make a reliable estimate of the useful life of the intangible asset, paragraph 18.20 says that the useful life shall not exceed five years. This is a substantial reduction from previous UK GAAP; FRS 10 permitted a life of up to 20 years, so on transition there could well be some accelerated write-downs of intangible assets where the useful life is not able to be determined reliably.

The depreciable amount of an intangible asset should be written off (amortised) on a systematic basis over the asset's useful life, with the amortisation charge being recognised in profit or loss. An exception to recognising the amortisation charge in profit or loss would be where another section of FRS 102 requires the charge to be recognised in the cost of inventory or property, plant and equipment.

Amortisation must commence when the intangible asset is available for use. This means when the asset is in the location and condition necessary for it to be used in the manner intended by management. Conversely, amortisation will cease once the intangible asset is derecognised.

Section 18 permits entities to choose an amortisation that best reflects the entity's pattern of consumption of the intangible asset. However, where this pattern cannot be reliably determined, paragraph 18.22 requires the entity to adopt the use of the straight-line method of amortisation. In reality, this is the most preferred method due to its simplicity.

The depreciable amount of a fixed asset is calculated as cost less residual value. The balance is then written off over its expected useful life using appropriate rates of depreciation/amortisation. Where intangible assets are concerned it is automatically assumed that the residual value of an intangible asset will be zero. There are two exceptions to this presumption:

- Where there is a commitment by a third party to acquire the asset at the end of its useful economic life or
- An active market exists for the asset and:
  - Residual values can be obtained by reference to this market and
  - It is more likely than not that this active market will exist at the end of the asset's useful life.

In reality, few active markets exist for intangible assets and so in the vast majority of cases the residual value of an intangible asset will be zero.

Entities must make regular reviews of amortisation methods and amortisation periods. This is because situations may arise that change how the intangible is used, market prices may change, technological advances may affect the valuation of the asset or other changes might take place within the entity that alter the residual value or the useful life of the intangible asset. When such circumstances arise, the entity must review its previous estimates and where current expectations differ then the residual value, amortisation method or useful life should be amended accordingly. Such changes will be treated as a change in estimation technique in accordance with Section 10 *Accounting Policies, Estimates and Errors* and will be applied prospectively (in other words, no prior year adjustment needs to be made).

DERECOGNITION

An entity must derecognise an intangible asset when the entity either:

- Disposes of the intangible asset or
- Where it is concluded that no future economic benefits are expected from either its use or disposal.

On derecognition, the entity must recognise a gain or loss on disposal within profit or loss.

DISCLOSURE REQUIREMENTS

Paragraphs 18.27 to 18.29A deal with the disclosure requirements for intangible assets. These paragraphs require the following disclosures for each class of intangible assets:

(a) Useful lives or amortisation rates used by the entity together with the reasons for choosing those periods,
(b) Amortisation methods adopted by the entity,
(c) Gross carrying amount and any accumulated amortisation (which is combined with accumulated impairment losses) at the start and end of the reporting period,

(d) Cross-references to the line items in the statement of comprehensive income (income statement, where presented) where amortisation of intangible assets is included and

(e) A reconciliation of the opening carrying amount to the closing carrying amount showing separately:
   i. Additions (distinguishing between those from internal development and those acquired separately),
   ii. Disposals,
   iii. Acquisitions by way of business combinations,
   iv. Revaluations,
   v. Amortisation,
   vi. Impairment losses and
   vii. Other changes.

Paragraph 18.27 does not require this reconciliation to be presented for prior periods.

Reporting entities must also disclose:

(a) A description, carrying value and remaining amortisation period of any intangible asset that is considered to be material to the financial statements,

(b) For those intangible assets that have been acquired by way of a grant and initially recognised at fair value disclose:
   i. The fair value initially recognised for such intangible assets and
   ii. The carrying amounts,

(c) The existence and carrying values of any intangible assets in which the entity has restricted title or which are pledged as security for liabilities and

(d) Any amounts in respect of contractual commitments for the acquisition of intangible assets.

For research and development expenditure, reporting entities must disclose the total amount of research and development expenditure that has been recognised as an expense in the period.

For intangible assets that are accounted for under the revaluation model, the following must be disclosed:

(a) The effective date of the revaluation,

(b) Whether an independent valuer was involved in the valuation,

(c) The methods and significant assumptions that were applied in estimating the fair value of the asset and

(d) The carrying amount that would have been recognised in respect of revalued assets had they been carried under the cost model.

13 PROPERTY, PLANT AND EQUIPMENT AND INVESTMENT PROPERTIES

INTRODUCTION

This chapter deals with two issues relating to tangible fixed assets: that of investment property and property, plant and equipment. FRS 102 *The Financial Reporting Standard applicable in the UK and Republic of Ireland* deals with these two issues in separate sections, namely Section 16 *Investment Property* and Section 17 *Property, Plant and Equipment*. The two Sections have been combined in this chapter to reflect the fact that in practice these issues are dealt with interchangeably but are found within the same area of the balance sheet (statement of financial position). The first part of the chapter will deal with property, plant and equipment whilst the latter part of the chapter looks at the accounting treatment and disclosure issues surrounding investment property.

Property, plant and equipment are commonly referred to in the UK as 'fixed assets' or 'tangible fixed assets' (the word 'tangible' meaning that they have a physical form). Property, plant and equipment are assets that:

- Are held by the entity for use in the production or supply of goods or rendering of services services, for rental to others, or for administrative purposes and
- Are expected to be used by the reporting entity for more than one accounting period.

Whilst the above paragraphs acknowledge what FRS 102 classes to be an item of property, plant and equipment, preparers of financial statements must also keep in mind the definition of an asset that is laid down in Section 2 *Concepts and Pervasive*

Principles (dealt with in Chapter 2). Section 2 essentially says that an asset is a resource that is controlled by the entity; the resource has arisen because of past events (i.e. the purchase or transfer of the asset) and from which the entity will derive future economic benefits (i.e. sales or other forms of revenue/income).

Many in the profession say that an asset is simply something that an entity owns, which was the case back in the 1980s. However, as time passed and modern accounting practices became more established, the definition of an asset as something that an entity owns has become more complex. The definition of an asset in the *Concepts and Pervasive Principles* in Section 2 of FRS 102 does not include the words 'own' or 'owns' anywhere but does include the word 'controlled', which is pivotal to the definition of an asset.

Accounting principles work on the basis of control and from which future economic benefits are expected to flow to the entity. 'Future economic benefits' stem from items of property, items expected to be converted into cash in the near future (such as debtors), or cash itself – in other words, that an asset will generate another asset for the entity. If the entity is unable to control the asset, it should not recognise such an asset on the balance sheet (statement of financial position). This becomes more of a problem in areas such as leasing where the concept of substance over form must be reported. For assets that are subjected to leases, one has to look to the substance of the transaction (the term 'substance' refers to the commercial reality of the transaction). Essentially, where the risks and rewards of ownership of the asset subjected to the lease are transferred to the lessee (the party entering into the lease), this means that the asset must appear on the lessee's balance sheet. If the risks and rewards of ownership of the asset have not passed to the lessee, this means the asset will not appear on the balance sheet of the lessee, but the rentals will be charged to the profit and loss account as and when they are incurred. This is because the lessee does not have the ability to control the asset (nor the risks and rewards associated with the asset). Leases are examined more closely in Chapter 20.

There are generally two types of fixed (non-current) asset that are reported on an entity's balance sheet, tangible and intangible, and this chapter deals with tangible assets (Chapter 12 deals with the issues of intangible assets). However, it is to be noted that Section 17 of FRS 102 does not deal with the following types of property, plant and equipment:

- Biological assets related to agricultural activity (this is dealt with in Section 34 of FRS 102 *Specialised Activities*, which are looked at in Chapter 30) or
- Heritage assets (again these are dealt with in Section 34 of FRS 102) or
- Mineral rights and mineral reserves (oil, natural gas and similar non-regenerative resources). These are also dealt with in Section 34.

RECOGNITION OF AN ITEM OF PROPERTY, PLANT AND EQUIPMENT

Reporting entities must take care in how they recognise items of property, plant and equipment (PPE) because this can lend itself to a wide scope for error and may cause problems during, say, the audit of the financial statements. Preparers must therefore consider the requirements in paragraph 2.27 to FRS 102, which outlines specific criteria that must be met before recognition of an item of PPE can take place. The criteria say that an entity can recognise a transaction as PPE on the balance sheet if, and only if:

- It is more likely than not that the entity will receive future economic benefits associated with the item and
- The cost of the item can be reliably measured.

If these criteria cannot be met in full, the transaction will not be recognised as an item of PPE.

Many reporting entities have an accounting policy in respect of PPE whereby a set benchmark will be in place for recognising items of PPE and any items that are below this benchmark will be written off to profit or loss as and when the transaction is incurred (this usually happens with items that will be used in the entity for more than one year but where such items have a negligible value). This is generally to reduce the sheer number of items that will appear within an entity's fixed asset register; however, again care must be taken where such policies are in place, as can be illustrated as follows.

Example – Items used for more than one accounting period with a negligible value

A garage uses lots of ancillary tools to undertake work on customers' cars, including spanners, wheel braces and hammers, and has an accounting policy which says that only items over £500 will be capitalised as items of PPE. During the year, the garage purchased a spanner for £15 and wrote this amount off to the profit and loss account as repairs and renewals expenditure.

As the spanner only cost £15, it is clearly below the capitalisation threshold and therefore it would be deemed acceptable to write this amount off to profit or loss as repairs and renewals expenditure.

Example – Individual assets below the capitalisation threshold but collectively go over the threshold

An academy school has a policy of writing off items of expenditure relating to assets to profit or loss where the transaction is less than £1,000. During the academic year to 31 August 2014, the academy purchased 50 laptop computers at a cost of £300 each (i.e. a total of £15,000 excluding value added tax) and it is expected that the laptops will be used by the academy for the next three years. This amount has been written off to the academy's statement of financial activities on the basis that the business manager considers each laptop computer to be below the capitalisation threshold of £1,000.

In this instance, it is the author's opinion that such a transaction would fall to be classified as items of fixed assets. This is because each laptop is similar in nature and will be used by the academy for a period of more than 12 months. Whilst each laptop individually is below the capitalisation threshold of £1,000, the transaction should be looked at in aggregate (which would clearly result in the £15,000 meeting the academy's capitalisation policy) and therefore the £15,000 should be included on the academy's balance sheet and the laptops depreciated over their expected useful life of three years.

The above two examples illustrate the need for preparers to carefully consider whether items purchased for an entity that will be used by the entity over more than one accounting period meet a capitalisation threshold if there are more than one of similar items (as in the laptop example above). It may be deemed acceptable to write off an item of PPE to profit or loss on the grounds that the expenditure is deemed negligible, but consideration must be given to bulk purchases and whether these fall to be classed as 'spare parts and servicing equipment'.

In recognition of the above, FRS 102 at paragraph 17.5 does acknowledge that past practice for spare parts and servicing equipment used in an entity have, in the past, been treated as an entity's inventory and written off to profit or loss (as cost of sales) when the entity consumes them. Paragraph 17.5 then goes on to refer to 'major' spare parts and standby equipment. The paragraph requires major spare parts and standby equipment that are going to be used by a reporting entity for more than one accounting period to be treated as property, plant and equipment. This equally applies to spare parts and servicing equipment, which can only be used for an item of property, plant and equipment. On transition to FRS 102, some entities will potentially need to reclassify some items of major spare parts and standby equipment as well as spare parts to property, plant and equipment so as to comply with the requirements of paragraph 17.5.

In many cases it is always clear-cut when an item of an expenditure falls to be classed as an item of PPE, but in some cases this issue may become a 'grey' area and therefore preparers of financial statements must carefully consider the requirements in Section 2 of FRS 102 and consider whether future economic benefits will flow to the entity as a result of the transaction, if the item will be used for more than one accounting period and whether it meets the capitalisation threshold imposed by the entity. Considering those three issues will often lead to the appropriate accounting treatment.

Example – Purchase of a building

An entity purchases a new building to house its operations during the year to 31 December 2016. Both the land and the building were purchased by freehold mortgage by the entity for a sum of £250,000. The surveyor has valued the land the building is housed on at a value of £80,000.

Paragraph 17.8 says that land and buildings are separable assets. Because of this, both land and buildings must be accounted for separately regardless of the fact that they were both acquired together. The land element will not be depreciated as the land has an indefinite life, but the building will be depreciated over its expected useful economic life.

Example – Replacement roof on a building

During a severe storm that hit parts of the UK, the roof on a commercial building was damaged. The roofing contractor has deemed the existing roof to be beyond repair and the directors have therefore agreed to have a replacement roof put on the building at a cost of £8,000.

This transaction will be treated as an item of repairs and renewals expense and will be written off to profit or loss when the transaction takes place. The replacement roof will not be capitalised as part of the cost of the building because it will not provide incremental future economic benefits to the entity – it is merely a replacement.

Paragraph 17.6 says that if the replacement part of an item of PPE is expected to provide incremental future economic benefits to the entity then it can add the replacement part to the carrying amount of an item of PPE. In this example, however, the roof is not deemed to add any future economic benefit, but if the new roof were, say, to be housed on an additional storey that the entity had built, then it would fall to be classified as part of the cost of the building.

Reporting entities will initially measure the cost of property, plant and equipment at cost. The components of cost include the purchase price (including import duties) and any non-refundable VAT (for example, if the company is not VAT registered). All trade discounts and rebates are deducted from the cost price.

In addition to the components of cost in the above paragraph, all costs that are *directly attributable* (incremental) in bringing the asset to its location and working condition are also included in the carrying amount, for example:

- Cost of employees' wages that arise directly from construction or acquisition of the asset,
- Cost of site preparation,
- Initial delivery and handling costs,
- Installation and assembly costs,
- Costs of testing the asset functions correctly,
- Professional fees (such as engineers),
- An initial estimate of dismantling and removal costs (sometimes referred to as 'decommissioning costs') of the asset and restoring the site on which the asset is located and
- Borrowing costs that relate to a qualifying asset (see Section 25 *Borrowing Costs* and Chapter 14 *Borrowing Costs*).

Paragraph 17.11 outlines certain costs that it considers NOT to be an item of property, plant and equipment and as such the reporting entity must write the following costs to profit or loss as and when they are incurred:

- Costs incurred by the entity in opening a new facility,
- Costs incurred in relation to the introduction of a new product or service (including costs of advertising and promotional activities),
- Costs of conducting business in a new location or with a new class of customer (including the costs of staff training) and
- Administration and general overheads.

An issue that was not specifically covered in the previous GAAP relates to payments that are deferred beyond normal credit terms. Paragraph 17.13 says that where payment for an item of property, plant and equipment is deferred beyond normal credit terms, the cost must be the present value of all future payments.

Exchange of assets

In some instances, an entity may choose to exchange one type of asset for another type of asset. The cost of the acquired asset is measured at its fair value unless:

- The exchange transaction lacks commercial substance or
- The fair value of neither the asset received nor the asset given up is reliably measurable. In that case, the asset's cost is measured at the carrying amount of the asset given up.

Because reporting entities will normally account for the exchange of non-monetary assets on the basis of the fair value given up or the fair value of the asset received, entities will immediately recognise any gains or losses on the transaction. However, where the fair value of the asset given up or the asset received can be measured reliably, the asset acquired is measured at the carrying amount of the asset given up (which also applies where the transaction lacks commercial substance). Section 17 does not give any indications as to when a transaction does or does not lack commercial substance and this will require judgement on the part of the accountant. The general principle that should be considered when determining whether a transaction lacks commercial substance is to look at the entity's future cash flows. If the transaction does not result in the entity's future cash flows changing in any way, and thus the entity will still be in more or less the same position as it was prior to the transaction taking place, the transaction will lack commercial substance.

Example – Transaction lacking commercial substance

Company A Limited has an item of plant used in its production process that has a carrying value at 31 December 2015 of £10,000 and a fair value of £10,350. It exchanges this item on 31 December 2015 for an identical item of plant with a fair value of £10,200 and cash of £150.

This transaction lacks commercial substance because other than the outflow of cash of £150, the entity's cash flows are not expected to change because of the transaction – it is still in more or less the same position it was in prior to the transaction being undertaken.

In this example, Company A recognises the asset as the cash paid out of £150 and the second machine as property, plant and equipment with a carrying value of £9,850.

SUBSEQUENT MEASUREMENT OF PROPERTY, PLANT AND EQUIPMENT

Items of property, plant and equipment that meet the recognition criteria are initially recorded at their cost price (cost includes various components described above). After initial recognition, an entity may choose to carry this asset using depreciated historic cost (the cost model) or the revaluation model (see the next section). When an entity elects to carry an asset under the revaluation model it must subject all the assets in that particular asset class to that model – in other words it cannot value certain items within a class of asset under the revaluation model and others using depreciated historic cost.

Under the depreciated historic cost model property, plant and equipment are carried at cost less accumulated depreciation and less any amounts recognised in respect of impairment.

Example – Depreciated historic cost

An entity purchased an item of machinery on 1 January 2015 for £10,000. The directors have assessed the useful economic life of this asset to be ten years with no residual value at the end of this ten-year life. The depreciation policy is to depreciate the asset on a straight-line basis over its estimated useful life with a full year's charge in the year of acquisition and no depreciation in the year of disposal.

Under the depreciated historic cost model, the asset will be carried as follows:

	£
YEAR 1	
Cost	10,000
Depreciation	(1,000)
Net book value year 1	9,000
YEAR 2	9,000
Depreciation	(1,000)
Net book value year 2	8,000

and so on either until the entity disposes of the machine prior to the end of year 10 or until the carrying value falls to zero.

It is very difficult for an entity to measure an item of property, plant and equipment using the revaluation model and then elect to change to the depreciated historic cost model (unless the election is made to do so at the date of transition to FRS 102; see the 'Transitional Issues' section in the later part of this chapter). This is because to do so would be an accounting policy change and a change in accounting policy is only deemed to be appropriate if required by FRS 102 or if the change would result in more relevant and reliable financial information. It is difficult to see how switching from the revaluation model back to the depreciated historic cost model would result in more relevant and reliable information being produced because inherently fair value is more reliable than depreciated historic cost, so entities must be prepared to justify any switch from the revaluation model to the depreciated historic cost model.

REVALUATION OF PROPERTY, PLANT AND EQUIPMENT

An alternative to the depreciated historic cost model is to apply the revaluation model to items of property, plant and equipment. As mentioned in an earlier section, where an entity chooses to adopt the use of the revaluation model for an asset, it must subject all the assets in that asset class to the revaluation model.

Example – Revaluation model for buildings

> Company A Limited is a plant hire company that operates from a head office in the North West of the United Kingdom and has five other branches across the country. Each of the buildings that houses the head office and the branches are owned by Company A Limited. The directors have elected to use the revaluation model to carry land and buildings in the statement of financial position (balance sheet).
>
> As the directors have elected to use the revaluation model for land and buildings, the directors must subject all buildings, and the land they are housed on, to the revaluation model. They will not be able to select certain properties to be subjected to revaluation with the balance being carried under the depreciated historic cost model because to do so would not be consistent.

When an entity subjects an item of property, plant and equipment (not an investment property) to the revaluation model, it does so in accordance with the alternative accounting rules set out in SI 2008/410 and therefore must value each asset separately to comply with the separate valuation principle outlined in paragraph 15 to Schedule 1. The principle of subjecting all assets in the same class to the revaluation model is set out in Section 17 to FRS 102 (specifically paragraph 17.15) and this is deliberately the case so as to avoid reporting entities from subjecting certain assets for revaluation merely because they have increased in value.

The concept of the revaluation model for property, plant and equipment means that reporting entities will carry a revaluation reserve account in their statement of financial position (balance sheet) under the equity section. It is important to note that such a revaluation reserve account can only relate to *owned* items of property, plant and equipment and *not* to *investment property* (see later in the chapter). Gains on revaluation are credited to the revaluation reserve account in the equity section of the statement of financial position (balance sheet) and then reported in other comprehensive income. There is an exception to this treatment, which relates to the reversal of a revaluation decrease of the same asset that was previously recognised as an expense – in such cases the revaluation gain will be reported through profit or loss to achieve the matching concept but only to the extent that the gain reverses a previously recognised loss reported in profit or loss.

Where a property (or any other type of non-monetary asset) is subject to the revaluation model, deferred tax considerations will also come into the equation to accord with the requirements in Section 29 *Income Tax*. Such issues are examined in detail in Chapter 11.

Section 17 does not specifically address the subsequent treatment for revaluation surpluses accumulated in equity. However, such revaluation surpluses should not sit within equity into perpetuity – they should instead be transferred from the revaluation reserve account into retained earnings (profit and loss account reserves) over the gradual life of the asset or when the asset is retired from use or disposed of. The amount to be transferred from revaluation reserve into retained earnings is the difference between the depreciation based on the asset's revalued carrying amount and the depreciation based on the asset's original cost.

Revaluation losses are taken to the revaluation reserve account in the equity section of the statement of financial position (balance sheet) and then reported in other comprehensive income. Losses are taken to the revaluation reserve account only to the extent that a credit balance exists on the revaluation reserve account (in other words, a loss cannot create a debit balance on the revaluation reserve account). Should a loss exceed the balance on the revaluation reserve, any remaining loss once the revaluation reserve account has been used up completely is reported within profit or loss as an expense.

Example – Accounting treatment – revaluation of a building

Westhead Trading Limited purchases a building on 1 January 2015 for £100,000. The directors have elected to carry this building in the financial statements under the revaluation model and the company's declared accounting policy in respect of depreciation is to write it off on a straight-line basis over its estimated useful economic life of 50 years (equivalent to 2% straight-line on an annual basis). The financial statements for the year ended 31 December 2017 are being prepared and the company has appointed an independent, well-established firm of chartered surveyors to undertake a valuation of the building. The latest valuation shows that the building has a market value as at 31 December 2017 of £105,000.

The net book value as at 31 December 2015 would have been:

	£
Cost at 1 January 2015	100,000
Depreciation charge to 31 December 2015	(2,000)
Depreciation charge to 31 December 2016	(2,000)
Net book value as at 31 December 2016	96,000

The chartered surveyors have confirmed that the building is worth £105,000 on 31 December 2017, so Westhead Trading's balance sheet must show the value of this building at that carrying amount as it is being carried under the revaluation model. The entries in the books of Westhead Trading to deal with this revaluation are as follows:

Debit building – cost	5,000
Credit revaluation surplus (in the equity section of the balance sheet)	5,000
Being uplift of initial cost to valuation	
Debit accumulated depreciation (balance sheet)	4,000
Credit revaluation surplus	4,000
Being reversal of accumulated depreciation charge to date	
Debit depreciation expense (profit and loss account)	2,234
Credit depreciation charge (balance sheet)	2,234

Being depreciation charge for the year ended 31 December 2017 (based on revalued amount over 47 years)

The depreciation charge going forward will be based on the building's revalued amount. However, the clock does not start again in relation to the building's useful economic life. At the end of 31 December 2017, it will still only have 47 years left to run.

Section 17 of FRS 102 does not specifically require valuations of property, plant and equipment subjected to the revaluation model to be valued every year. Instead, Section 17 says that valuations should remain up to date and therefore should be undertaken with sufficient regularity so that the carrying amount of the asset does not differ materially from its market value at the end of the reporting period. The overarching principle here is that the frequency of the valuation is determined by the fluctuation in market value.

Some assets will inherently contain more volatility in their fair value than others (for example, it is likely that land and buildings would be more volatile than other items of property, plant and equipment) and therefore regular valuations of land and buildings will be needed to ensure that carrying values are not materially different than market values. Conversely, where other items of property, plant and equipment are less volatile, then the frequency of revaluations will also be less frequent.

Where the term 'material' is concerned, this is of course subject to individual judgement. The overarching principle concerning materiality is that an item is material if a transaction's omission or misstatement could reasonably influence the decisions of the user of the financial statements and this is a responsibility of management of an entity.

In practice, the reality is that the main item of property, plant and equipment that is subjected to the revaluation model is that of land and buildings. FRS 102 at paragraph 17.15C requires a valuation of land and buildings to be undertaken by 'professionally qualified valuers'. A professionally qualified valuer would normally be an individual that:

- Holds a recognised and relevant qualification,
- Has relevant expertise and experience in valuing such assets and
- Has sufficient knowledge relating to the state of the market in the location and category of the asset being subjected to valuation.

Where land and buildings are concerned, reporting entities would commission a member of the Royal Institution of Chartered Surveyors to undertake such valuations.

DEPRECIATION OF PROPERTY, PLANT AND EQUIPMENT

Depreciation is the systematic allocation of the depreciable amount of an asset over its useful economic life. The depreciable amount of an asset is calculated as cost (or other amount substituted for cost) less residual (scrap) value.

Example – Calculation of depreciable amount

Byrne Enterprises Limited manufactures baling equipment for use in farming. It purchases an item of machinery to manufacture certain parts of the baling equipment for £35,000. The directors of Byrne Enterprises have assessed the useful economic life of this equipment to be ten years and at the end of this useful economic life estimate that the residual value of the machine will be £10,000.

The depreciable amount can be calculated as follows:

	£
Cost	35,000
Less estimated residual value	(10,000)
Depreciable amount	25,000

Assume the accounting policy of Byrne Enterprises Limited is to depreciate this machine on a straight-line basis over its estimated useful life; the annual depreciation expense will be £2,500. At the end of year 10, the net book value of the machine will be £10,000 (£35,000 less (£2,500 × 10)), which will represent the residual value anticipated by the directors at the end of the machine's useful economic life.

A company's annual depreciation charge should be recognised in profit or loss. However, paragraph 17.17 recognises that there may be other sections of FRS 102 that require the depreciation charge to be recognised as part of the cost of an asset. Paragraph 17.17 cites an example of the depreciation of manufacturing property, plant and equipment and acknowledges that depreciation charges in respect of these should be recognised in the cost of inventories.

Section 17 requires land and buildings to be accounted for separately regardless of the fact that they may be acquired together. Land has an indefinite useful life (although there are some circumstances when this may not be the case). However, buildings do not have an indefinite life and must be depreciated. Also, it is worth noting that any increases in the value of land on which a building sits does not affect the depreciable amount of a building nor does it give rise to the need for non-depreciation of buildings.

There is more emphasis in FRS 102 on component depreciation than was the case in the previous FRS 15. Therefore, when an entity purchases an item of property, plant and equipment the initial cost of such is allocated to its major components, which are considered to have a significantly different pattern of consumption within the entity. Each major component of an asset is depreciated separately over its estimated useful economic life. Where it is not considered that an asset has major components, then such assets are depreciated over their estimated useful lives as single assets.

Example – Use of component depreciation

A company purchases a machine for £1,000 and can identify the major components as the shell of the machine, which costs £600, and a major component, which operates the machine and has a cost attributed to it of £400. The shell of the machine is considered to have a useful economic life of ten years, whilst the directors estimate that the major component will need to be replaced after a period of five years.

In this example, the company will depreciate the major component over its expected useful economic life of five years, whilst the remainder of the machine will be depreciated over its useful economic life of ten years.

An asset's useful life is either:

- The period over which an asset is expected to be available for use by an entity or
- The number of production or similar units expected to be obtained from the asset by the entity.

In practice, companies will usually estimate useful lives of assets over the period in which the asset is expected to be available for use by the entity. For example, many companies generally depreciate computer equipment over a three-year period. Some items of plant may produce a certain number of items of output until it wears out and therefore it might be that the entity could set a useful life at the maximum units of output expected before the machine eventually wears out. There are a number of variables that could be used to assess useful economic life, but the point to keep in mind is that the useful life of an item of property, plant and equipment will (in many cases) be less than its physical life. Indeed, a computer may be deemed by an entity to have a useful life of three years, but could well be expected to continue to work for a much longer time period. Whatever method is used by an entity to estimate useful lives, it is important that it is relevant to the asset in question. Factors that entities may consider are:

- Expiry dates of leases associated with the asset,
- Levels of expected usage of the asset,
- Technical or commercial obsolescence and
- Levels of repairs and maintenance that might be expected.

Depreciation charges must commence when the asset is available for use. The term 'available for use' is taken to mean that the asset is in the location and condition deemed necessary for it to be capable of operating in the manner in which management intended. This is the point at which the asset's useful economic life begins. Depreciation will cease when the asset is derecognised. However, if the entity decides to adopt the 'usage method of depreciation' then no depreciation may be charged when the asset is idle (this tends to be the case with manufacturing equipment where a company manufactures products, for example, that are seasonal). Care must be applied, however, when the usage method of depreciation is adopted because any instances when a machine becomes idle could give rise to an indicator of impairment and therefore trigger the provisions in Section 27 *Impairment of Assets* (see Chapter 15).

Section 17 does not prescribe methods of depreciation that an entity should use. Instead, it merely refers to the most commonly established methods of depreciation that preparers of financial statements will not be unfamiliar with, which include:

- The reducing balance method (often referred to as the 'diminishing balance' method),
- The straight-line method and
- The units of production method.

The *reducing balance method* works by charging a fixed percentage on the remaining carrying value each year; therefore an asset costing £10,000 that is depreciated at a rate of 25% each year depreciates by £2,500 in year 1. Depreciation in year 2 is £1,875 (£10,000 – £2,500) × 25% and so on. The idea behind the reducing balance method is that it charges more depreciation in earlier years and less in later years to reflect the fact that more repairs and maintenance expenditure costs will be incurred in later years as the asset gets older and requires more maintenance. It is not uncommon to see the reducing balance method applied to motor vehicles as motor vehicles require fewer repairs and maintenance in the earlier years, but do require a higher level of maintenance in later years.

The *straight-line* method of depreciation is the most commonly used method in practice (mainly because of its simplicity). This method is appropriate for assets where the level of consumption is expected to be reasonably consistent over the years or cannot be readily ascertained. For example, an item of machinery costs an entity £10,000; the entity expects it to have a residual value at the end of this ten-year life of £1,000 and the company's declared accounting policy is to depreciate it on a straight-line basis over its estimated useful life. Depreciation charges will be (£10,000 – £1,000)/10 years = £900 per annum. Charging £900 per annum in depreciation will reduce the asset's cost to its residual value at the end of its useful economic life.

In terms of residual values, FRS 102 contains more emphasis in such values potentially requiring to be adjusted upwards or downwards, as estimates of such values are based on current prices. In contrast, FRS 15 only permitted an upwards adjustment in limited circumstances.

The *units of production* method is different in that it assumes that depreciation is a function of use of an asset as opposed to the passage of time. There are various factors that an entity can consider when it uses the units of production method (such as how many expected hours the machine is to work or the total number of units the machine will be expected to produce). An entity will ordinarily use this method of depreciation when an asset's usage is varied from one period to the next because this method will match cost against revenue in a more orderly manner rather than being 'top heavy' on cost by way of straight-line or reducing balance methods of depreciation.

Example – Unit of production method

Bury Corporation Limited purchases an item of machinery for £200,000 with an expected residual value at the end of its expected life assumed to be £20,000. The directors expect the machine to be in production for 600,000 hours and therefore the depreciation rate per hour usage can be calculated as £0.30 (£200,000 – £20,000/600,000). If Bury Corporation was to use the machine for 90,000 hours in year 1, the depreciation charge would be £27,000 (£0.30 × 90,000).

Changes in depreciation method

A change in depreciation method is a change in the estimation technique and is therefore not applied retrospectively (it is not a change in accounting policy because the entity is still consuming the asset at its original cost, albeit at a slower or faster rate than originally anticipated). A company would ordinarily change a depreciation method when there is expected to be a change in the pattern of consumption of the asset.

Example – Change in depreciation method

A company has depreciated its motor vehicles on a five-year straight-line basis. During the year to 31 December 2015, the company has decided that, based on past occurrences, it would be more realistic to depreciate its fleet of motor vehicles at a rate of 25% on a reducing balance basis. This is because the company has seen an increase in maintenance costs, usually from year 2 of ownership.

The change in depreciation rate is a change in estimation technique and therefore the revised change will apply for the year ended 31 December 2015 and going forwards. The company would not restate prior years' financial statements to reflect the decision to change to the reducing balance method as this is not a change in accounting policy.

Property, plant and equipment subjected to revaluation

Property, plant and equipment which are subjected to the revaluation model (not investment properties) must have their valuations kept up to date (in other words the fair value should not be materially different than the carrying amount). The basis for the carrying amount and depreciable amount of an item of property, plant and equipment subject to revaluation is the revalued amount. The question arises as to what happens to accumulated depreciation when an asset is revalued. There are two potential methods that an entity can adopt – the entity can:

- Eliminate the accumulated depreciation against the gross carrying value and restate the net amount so that it is equivalent to the revalued amount or
- Restate accumulated depreciation proportionately to the change in the gross carrying amount of the asset so that the net book value of the asset after the revaluation is equal to the revalued amount.

Example – A school building revalued using the depreciated replacement cost method

A school is subjected to a revaluation using the depreciated replacement cost method. Details of the value of the building (excluding land value) before the revaluation are as follows:

	£
Cost	1,000,000
Accumulated depreciation (2% straight line)	(60,000)
Net book value	940,000

The building is revalued to £1 million on a depreciated replacement cost consisting of £1.2 million cost and £200,000 depreciation and the values after the revaluation are shown below:

	£
Cost	1,000,000
Increase in revaluation	200,000
Building at revalued gross replacement cost	1,200,000
Accumulated depreciation	60,000
Additional depreciation on revaluation	140,000
Accumulated depreciation after revaluation	1,200,000

The overall increase in value of the building is £60,000 (£1 million less £940,000) and can be proved by taking the increase in revaluation of £200,000 and deducting the additional depreciation on revaluation of £140,000 with the resulting figure of £60,000 being the overall increase in value.

ASSET CONSTRUCTION

It might well be the case that an entity decides to construct its own asset as opposed to purchasing the asset outright or by way of lease arrangement. This is usually common when a company decides to construct a building.

Whilst FRS 102 is silent on the way to account for an asset under construction, the established practice is to accumulate relevant costs under the category 'asset under construction' within the statement of financial position (balance sheet). It is important that such costs incurred during the construction phase still meet the recognition criteria for an asset. Costs such as finance costs incurred on the construction of an asset are dealt with in Chapter 14 *Borrowing Costs* (which is also dealt with in Section 25 *Borrowing Costs*).

Where assets under construction take place, the question arises as to whether these should be subjected to depreciation or amortisation in the same way as other assets. This can be illustrated by way of an example as follows.

> **Example – Asset under construction**

A property management company is in the process of having a bespoke property management software system designed and installed by a software company. This software system will handle all aspects of the company's property management from agreeing contracts with tenants and landlords, dealing with property repair requests, payment of landlord rents and the associated incoming of rent receipts. The software developers have given an expected lead time to have the system written, installed and running two years from 1 February 2015.

On 30 April 2015, the company had incurred costs that met the recognition criteria for an intangible asset amounting to £20,000. The company accountant has charged amortisation at a rate of 10% on a straight-line basis on this amount in the belief that the entity must charge amortisation and depreciation on all assets.

The software system is still in the process of construction and is therefore not being consumed by the entity as at 30 April 2015 – indeed the software developer's lead time would suggest that no amortisation would be appropriate in the 2016 financial year also.

As the company is not 'consuming' the asset, it is not appropriate to charge amortisation on this system. Depreciation or amortisation of an asset begins when it is available for use. The term 'available for use' is taken to mean that the asset is in the location and condition necessary for it to be capable of operating in the manner intended by management and is at the same point when the asset's useful life begins.

In light of this, the accountant should not charge amortisation on the asset under construction.

SUBSEQUENT EXPENDITURE ON PROPERTY, PLANT AND EQUIPMENT

Section 17 does not go into a significant amount of detail where the issue of subsequent expenditure on an existing asset is concerned. In contrast, FRS 15 *Tangible Fixed Assets* went into much greater detail and examined the issues that had to be met before capitalisation of subsequent expenditure took place. The overarching principle where subsequent expenditure is concerned is that such expenditure can only be capitalised as part of the carrying amount of an asset if it enhances the asset in any way from its previously assessed state.

Example – Increased output per hour of a machine

A company incurs expenditure amounting to £10,000 to improve the output of one of its machines so that instead of producing 100 units of output per hour, it products 200 units of output per hour.

As this expenditure enhances the performance of the machine from its previously assessed state, it can qualify for capitalisation as part of the carrying amount of the asset.

Example – Replacement engine on an aircraft

An airline is required under legislation to replace the engines of its aircraft on a five-year cycle. The engines themselves will have a much shorter useful economic life than the rest of the aircraft and therefore it would be appropriate to account for the engines using 'component accounting'. Hence the aircraft's engines would be identified as assets with a separate life from the rest of the aircraft and written off to zero over five years. After the five years have elapsed the engines will then be replaced and the cost of the new replacement engines will be added to the cost of the aircraft and this cost will then be depreciated over a five-year cycle.

In situations when preparers of FRS 102 financial statements are unsure as to whether an item of subsequent expenditure meets the recognition criteria for an asset, they are directed to the *Concepts and Pervasive Principles* in Section 2 to decipher the most appropriate accounting treatment. However, users are encouraged to keep in mind the fact that costs incurred on a replacement part for an item of property, plant and equipment should only be capitalised if the expenditure does meet the recognition criteria. If the expenditure does not meet the recognition criteria, it should be recognised in profit or loss as repairs and maintenance expense.

Example – Replacement part for an asset

A company purchases an item of machinery for £75,000 and concludes that the entire sum is eligible for recognition on the balance sheet (statement of financial position) as an item of property, plant and equipment (i.e. the machine is not broken down into its individual components and each component depreciated separately). The directors assess that the machine has a useful economic life of ten years with zero residual value. At the end of year 5 the machine breaks down completely and a replacement component is purchased for £30,000. The maintenance engineer confirms that other than the component that has broken down and been replaced, the rest of the machine is in good working order and therefore the entity expects to use the rest of the machine over the remainder of its estimated useful life of five years.

The cost of the replacement component meets the definition of an asset because future economic benefits will be expected to flow to the entity as a result of the expenditure. Whilst the original purchase price did not explicitly state the cost of the component, the new component's cost can be used as an indicator of the likely cost of the component on the date the machine was originally purchased, which can be discounted using an appropriate discount rate. If the discount rate is assumed to be 5%, the discounted value of the cost of the new component is £23,506 (£30,000/1.05^5). After five years' worth of depreciation, the current carrying value of the new component would be £11,753 (£23,506 × 5/10), which would then be derecognised from the unamortised carrying value of the asset of £37,500 at the end of year 5 and the cost of the new component amounting to £30,000 would then be added to the asset. The revised carrying value of £55,747 (£37,500 + £30,000 – £11,753) would then be depreciated over its remaining useful life of five years.

Paragraph 17.7 refers to the concept of 'major inspections', which relate to inspections for faults regardless of whether parts of the item are replaced. Where a major inspection is undertaken, the cost of such an inspection is capitalised as part of the carrying amount of the asset as a replacement if the recognition criteria are satisfied and any remaining carrying amount of the cost of the previous major inspection is derecognised. Paragraph 17.7 is clear where this issue is concerned in that derecognition of previous major inspections takes place regardless of whether the cost of the previous major inspection was identified in the transaction in which the item was acquired or constructed.

QUALIFYING CRITERIA FOR INVESTMENT PROPERTY

Careful thought needs to be applied where investment property is concerned to ensure that inappropriate classification as property, plant and equipment does not occur. FRS 102 at Section 16 *Investment Property* deals with the issues concerning investment property including its recognition and measurement and disclosure issues. Paragraph 16.2 also outlines what FRS 102 considers to be investment property and says that such property is held by the owner (or by a lessee under a finance lease) so as to earn rentals from such property or for the capital appreciation of the property (or both). Investment property is not property that is used to supply goods or services (or for administrative purposes) within the business; nor is it property that is for sale in the ordinary course of business.

Therefore, when a company owns a building for which its intention is to hold it for its capital appreciation, or to earn rentals from the building from a third party, it falls not to be classed as owned property, plant and equipment, but instead as investment property.

Example – Investment property held under an operating lease

During the year to 31 December 2015, Cahill Corporation Limited decided to take out an operating lease on two properties that it will rent out to an unconnected third party for a period of ten years. The company accountant has classified these properties as investment property.

Paragraph 16.3 to FRS 102 says that a property interest that is held under an operating lease can be classified and accounted for as investment property (and hence Section 16 will apply going forwards) if, and only if, the property meets the definition of an investment property. In this example, Cahill Corporation is going to rent the property out to an unconnected third party and therefore will fall to be classed as an investment property. However, paragraph 16.3 also says that the lessee (in this example, Cahill Corporation) must also be able to measure the fair value of the property interest without undue cost or effort on an ongoing basis.

Example – Mixed use property

During the year to 31 January 2016, Whatmough Windows Limited purchased a new building, which consists of a very large manufacturing division, two office blocks and storage facilities. The directors of the company have assessed that one of the office blocks is surplus to the company's requirements and could be rented out to third parties with a view to selling the office block in the future.

This property could fall to be classed as a mixed use property and the office block that is going to be used for investment purposes would need to be separated from the owned property and accounted for in accordance with Section 16. However, in situations where the investment property component cannot be measured reliably without undue cost or effort, then the entire property must be accounted for as property, plant and equipment in accordance with Section 17.

ACCOUNTING TREATMENT FOR INVESTMENT PROPERTY

Upon initial recognition, a reporting entity will recognise investment property at cost. Cost is broken down into various categories and is not necessarily simply the purchase price of the property, but can also include items that are directly attributable to acquiring the investment property, such as:

- Legal fees,
- Brokerage fees,
- Property transfer taxes and
- Other costs that are directly attributable to the purchase of the property.

Should payment for the acquisition of an investment property be deferred, for whatever reason, the cost to be recognised in respect of the property must be the present value of all future payments.

After initial recognition at cost, the entity should apply the fair value model to subsequent measurement. This involves ascertaining the fair value of the investment property at each reporting date and accounting for any fair value gains or losses through profit or loss for the year/period. This concept is markedly different from the old UK GAAP at SSAP 19 *Accounting for Investment Properties*, which required all fair value fluctuations to generally be recognised within the investment property revaluation reserve reported in the equity section of the statement of financial position (balance sheet) and included within the statement of recognised gains and losses.

Example – Revaluation gain

Byrne Enterprises Limited has owned an investment property for several years. On 31 December 2015 the property had a fair value of £110,000. The company is preparing financial statements for the year ended 31 December 2016 and on this date commissioned a valuation from a firm of chartered surveyors to value the investment property. The valuation confirms that the market value of the property as at 31 December 2016 has risen to £120,000.

The uplift of £10,000 as at 31 December 2016 will be reported through profit or loss for the accounting period (within operating profit), so the entries will be:

Debit investment property	£10,000
Credit profit or loss	£10,000

Being fair value gain on investment property for the year

An important point to emphasise is that the £10,000 fair value gain reported in profit or loss is NOT distributable to shareholders as a dividend. This is because the gain is not a realised gain for the purposes of a dividend. Many commentators are advising reporting entities to have a separate 'undistributable reserve' account within the equity section of the statement of financial position (balance sheet). Whilst there is nothing in company law that requires this, if this practice is adopted, it is important that the balance on this account passes through profit or loss for the year and is not merely sent directly to the undistributable reserve account. In addition, Section 29 *Income Tax* would also require deferred tax to be recognised on the revaluation gain as the investment property would be classed as a non-monetary asset that has been subject to the revaluation model (for which deferred tax under FRS 102 would apply) – see the later section 'Deferred Tax Issues Relating to Investment Property'.

In situations where the directors confirm that obtaining fair values would result in undue cost or effort, they should then account for the properties in accordance with Section 17 *Property, Plant and Equipment* using the cost model. However, it is unlikely that obtaining fair values for investment property would result in undue cost or effort, because the entity merely has to commission a valuation by a qualified valuation agency and therefore entities that do consider obtaining fair values that result in undue cost or effort must have justifiable reasons for so doing.

INVESTMENT PROPERTY SUBJECT TO LEASING ARRANGEMENTS

Leased property that is classified as an investment property is accounted for in accordance with paragraphs 20.9 and 20.10 to FRS 102. This treatment applies equally to property that would otherwise be classified as property held under an operating lease. Therefore, the property is recognised at the *lower* of the fair value of the property and the present value of the minimum lease payments. There will also be a corresponding entry in the company's statement of financial position (balance sheet) representing a finance lease obligation for the property (however, the finance lease obligation must NOT include any lease premiums paid, which are treated as part of the minimum lease payments for the purposes of ascertaining cost).

Under the previous SSAP 19, the standard excluded investment property that had been let to, and occupied by, another group member. FRS 102 does not include such an exemption.

DEFERRED TAX ISSUES RELATING TO INVESTMENT PROPERTY

Deferred tax issues are dealt with in Section 29 of FRS 102 *Income Tax*, which is covered in Chapter 11. One of the main changes relating to the concept of deferred tax in FRS 102 is that it covers a wider scope than the previous FRS 19 *Deferred Tax* and this can be illustrated where investment property is concerned.

FRS 102 now requires deferred tax to be considered in respect of non-monetary assets that have been subjected to the revaluation model. This would therefore include investment properties as these will be carried in the statement of financial position (balance sheet) at their fair value at each reporting date. In contrast to FRS 102, FRS 19 previously did not require deferred tax to be considered on assets that had been subjected to the revaluation model unless the company has:

- Entered into a binding agreement to sell the revalued assets and
- Recognised the gains and losses expected to arise on the sale.

As a result, FRS 102 does require an entity to measure deferred tax on revalued assets using the tax rates and allowances that apply to the sale of the investment property. There is an exception to this rule in paragraph 29.16 to FRS 102, which relates to investment property that has a limited useful life and where the company is going to use the economic benefits associated with the investment property over time. The question arises, however, as to the tax rates and allowances that apply to the sale of the investment property. Clearly many reporting entities will hold investment property on their statement of financial position (balance sheet) for many years with no intention of selling and therefore the rates of tax that would apply to the sale would not yet be available. In this instance, a company would use the latest tax rates and allowances that have been announced by the Chancellor for the future (in other words, the latest tax rates that the government have intimated may be in place).

Example – Deferred tax on a revalued investment property

A company has a year-end of 31 December 2015 and on this date it had an investment property with a carrying value of £100,000. The company commissioned an independent firm of chartered surveyors to carry out a valuation of the property for financial reporting purposes and the independent valuer confirmed that the property had an open market value of £110,000 on 31 December 2015.

The entries in the books of the company to comply with paragraph 16.7 of FRS 102 will be:

DR investment property	£10,000
CR profit or loss	£10,000

Being revaluation uplift on investment property

Deferred tax on this revaluation would then be recognised as the adjustment to fair value affects profit. Assuming the company pays tax at 22% in that financial year, the deferred tax that will be recognised is £2,200 (£10,000 × 22%). The entries in the books will be:

DR deferred tax expense	£2,200
CR deferred tax liability	£2,200

Being deferred tax on investment property

RECLASSIFICATION OF INVESTMENT PROPERTY TO PROPERTY, PLANT AND EQUIPMENT

Generally an investment property will be transferred to property, plant and equipment and accounted for under the provision of Section 17 *Property, Plant and Equipment* when the property first meets, or ceases to meet, the definition of investment property. However, where the entity has recognised property as investment property but circumstances arise whereby a reliable measure of fair value is no longer available without undue cost or effort being applied by the company, the investment property is then transferred to property, plant and equipment until a reliable measure of fair value becomes available. The value at which the property is transferred to property, plant and equipment is its carrying value on the date of the transfer from investment property. In reality, this is not going to be likely due to the fact that fair values for investment property are likely to be available by commissioning an independent valuation agency.

TRANSITIONAL ISSUES

On transition to FRS 102, a first-time adopter can use:

- Fair value as deemed cost or
- Revaluation as deemed cost.

Fair value as deemed cost is obtained at the date of transition to FRS 102 and then that fair value can be used for property, plant and equipment, investment property or intangible assets meeting the recognition and revaluation criteria in Section 18 *Intangible Assets other than Goodwill* as deemed cost as at that date. It is worth emphasising where fair values are concerned that, from a purely practical point of view, they are easier to obtain at, or close to, the date of transition to FRS 102.

In terms of an entity using revaluation as deemed cost for property, plant and equipment, investment property or intangible assets, a revalued amount can be used as deemed cost that has been obtained at, or before, the date of transition to FRS 102. However, if a revalued amount is used and the revaluation was carried out before the date of transition to FRS 102 then the entity should depreciate/amortise the intervening period between the date of the revaluation and the date of transition to FRS 102 to arrive at a deemed cost as at the date of transition.

DISCLOSURE ISSUES

For property, plant and equipment, FRS 102 requires the following to be disclosed for each class of property, plant and equipment:

(a) The measurement bases the entity has used to determining the gross carrying amount,

(b) The methods of depreciation,

(c) The useful lives of property, plant and equipment or the depreciation rates used,

(d) The gross carrying value and the accumulated depreciation (aggregated with accumulated impairment losses) at the start and end of the reporting period,

(e) A reconciliation of the carrying amount at the beginning and end of the reporting period showing separately:
   i. Additions,
   ii. Disposals,
   iii. Acquisitions arising because of business combinations,
   iv. Revaluations,
   v. Transfers to or from investment property if a reliable measure of fair value becomes available or unavailable,
   vi. Impairment losses that the entity has recognised or reversed in profit or loss to comply with Section 27 *Impairment of Assets*,
   vii. Depreciation and
   viii. Other changes.

In addition, the entity must also make disclosure of the following:

(f) The existence and carrying values of property, plant and equipment to which the entity has restricted title or which the entity has pledged as security for its debts/liabilities and

(g) The amount of contractual commitments for the acquisition of property, plant and equipment.

For items of property, plant and equipment that have been subjected to the revaluation model, the following must be disclosed:

(h) The date the revaluation took place,
(i) Whether the entity used an independent valuer,
(j) The methods and significant assumptions applied in estimating the fair value of the asset(s) and
(k) For each class of property, plant and equipment carried at revaluation, the carrying amount that would have been recognised had the assets been carried under the cost model.

For investment property, paragraph 16.10 requires the following to be disclosed for all investment property carried at fair value through profit or loss:

(l) The methods and significant assumptions that have been applied in determining the fair value of the investment property,
(m) The extent to which the fair value of the investment property is based on a valuation undertaken by an independent valuer who holds a recognised and relevant professional qualification and has recent experience in the location and class of the investment property being valued; if there has been no such valuation, that fact shall be disclosed,
(n) The existence and amounts of restrictions on the realisability of the investment property or the remittance of income and proceeds of disposal,
(o) The entity's contractual obligations to purchase, construct or develop investment property or for repairs, maintenance or enhancements and
(p) A reconciliation between the carrying amounts of investment property at the start and end of the period, showing separately:
    i. Additions, disclosing separately those additions that have arisen because of business combinations,
    ii. Net gains or losses arising from fair value adjustments,
    iii. Transfers to property, plant and equipment because a reliable measure of fair value is no longer available without undue cost or effort being applied,
    iv. Transfers to and from inventories and owner-occupied property and
    v. Other changes.

In addition, paragraph 16.11 also requires an entity to provide all relevant disclosures required in Section 20 *Leases* concerning leases into which the entity has entered.

In respect of investment properties, the Companies Act 2006 requires all properties to be depreciated. Under FRS 102 and the small companies regime, investment properties carried at revaluation are not subjected to depreciation because they are carried at fair value at each reporting date. This is known as a departure from the Companies Act (i.e. invoking the true and fair override) and whenever a departure of the Companies Act takes place, disclosure should be made of such departures within the financial statements. For investment properties, an example of such a disclosure within the accounting policies section of the notes to the financial statements is as follows.

Example – Disclosure of departure from the Companies Act 2006

No depreciation is provided for in respect of investment properties in accordance with the Financial Reporting Standard applicable in the UK and Republic of Ireland [state alternative financial reporting framework]. Such properties are held for their investment potential and not for consumption within the business. This is a departure from the Companies Act 2006, which requires all properties to be depreciated and the directors to consider that to depreciate them would not enable the financial statements to give a true and fair value. Investment properties are stated at their market value at the reporting date.

14 BORROWING COSTS

INTRODUCTION

There is a specific section in FRS 102 that deals with the concept of borrowing costs, which is that of Section 25 *Borrowing Costs*. In the previous UK GAAP, such issues were dealt with in FRS 15 *Tangible Fixed Assets* but it has become more widely prevalent that entities often construct their own assets and the issue concerning borrowing costs had to be addressed.

Borrowing costs had been the subject of lots of debate with the previous Accounting Standards Board (ASB) (now the Financial Reporting Council) who had previously issued a discussion paper entitled *Measurement of Tangible Fixed Assets* that discussed the issue. The discussion paper outlined that the capitalisation of borrowing costs should either be mandatory or prohibited, but not optional. However, the consensus was that different entities have valid reasons for either writing borrowing costs off to profit or loss or capitalising them and thus the argument was finely balanced. On this basis, the ASB permitted borrowing costs to either be capitalised or written off to profit or loss provided the accounting treatment was consistent from one period to the next.

In the previous Exposure Draft of UK GAAP, FRED 44 prohibited the capitalisation of borrowing costs and followed the same stance as the *IFRS for SMEs* and required such costs to be expensed to profit or loss as and when they arise. Housing associations were unhappy with this proposal because they incur a significant amount of borrowing costs in the construction of social housing and, based on feedback during the commentary period, the ASB decided to allow the option to capitalise or write off to profit or loss.

In reality this is an area of FRS 102 that is unlikely to have a major effect on most entities.

DEFINITION AND RECOGNITION OF BORROWING COSTS

Borrowing costs are costs that are incurred by an entity when it borrows funds. Typical costs will be loan interest.

For the purposes of Section 25, borrowing costs include:

(a) Interest expense that the reporting entity calculates using the effective interest method as described in Section 11 *Basic Financial Instruments*,

(b) Finance charges in respect of finance leases accounted for in accordance with Section 20 *Leases* and

(c) Exchange differences arising from foreign currency borrowing costs to the extent that they are regarded as an adjustment to interest costs.

A reporting entity may capitalise borrowing costs that are directly attributable to the acquisition, construction or production of a *qualifying asset*. Conversely, the entity may choose to write such costs off to profit or loss; however, whichever policy is chosen by the entity, it is important that it is applied consistently. Where an entity has chosen a policy of writing borrowing costs off to profit or loss but then subsequently chooses to capitalise such costs, this will trigger a change in accounting policy and the provisions in Section 10 *Accounting Policies, Estimates and Errors* will become applicable. For the purposes of this Section, it is important that the asset is regarded as a qualifying asset. The term 'qualifying asset' is taken to mean an asset that takes a substantial amount of time to get ready for its intended use or sale. A 'substantial amount of time' is taken to mean more than 12 months. The FRS outlines various types of qualifying assets, which include:

- Power generation facilities,
- Inventories,
- Intangible assets,
- Investment property and
- Manufacturing plants.

Assets such as financial instruments and inventories that are produced over a short period of time will not fall to be classified as qualifying assets for the purposes of Section 25. Also, Section 25 does not recognise assets that are ready for their intended use or sale when the entity acquires such assets as qualifying assets.

Example – Qualifying asset

Kai Construction Ltd has seen rapid expansion over the last few years and has outgrown their current office and warehousing facilities. They have been actively looking for alternative premises to house their operations and store all their plant and equipment, but without success. The directors of Kai Construction have therefore decided to construct their own head office and warehousing facilities as the major advantage of them doing this is that they can ensure the building is tailored specifically to their exact requirements. It is anticipated that the construction will take approximately two years to complete and the company has taken out a long-term loan to finance part of the construction.

The head office and warehousing facilities will fall to be classed as a qualifying asset for the purposes of capitalising the borrowing costs because the construction is expected to take a substantial period of time to get ready. A 'substantial period of time' to get ready is taken to mean more than 12 months.

In terms of borrowing costs themselves, an entity may source funding for the acquisition, construction or production of a qualifying asset. The funding in this respect would have been avoided if the entity had not incurred expenditure on the qualifying asset. Alternatively, an entity may use its general borrowings to fund (or part-fund) the acquisition, construction or production of a qualifying asset (see the next section).

Where the entity borrows funds specifically for the purposes of obtaining qualifying assets and chooses to capitalise the borrowing costs as part of the cost of the qualifying asset, the entity must determine the amount of borrowing costs that are eligible for capitalisation net of any investment income that it receives on the temporary investment of those borrowings.

CAPITALISATION RATE

Some entities may choose to take out separate borrowing to fund the acquisition, construction or production of a qualifying asset. However, this is not always the case and it may be the case that an entity chooses to use existing borrowings to fund (or part-fund) some of the acquisition, construction or production. Where existing borrowings are used, the use of a capitalisation rate must be adopted.

If the entity chooses to use its general borrowings to fund (or part-fund) a qualifying asset, the borrowing costs that are eligible for capitalisation are determined by applying a capitalisation rate to the expenditure on that asset. Expenditure on the asset is the average carrying amount of the asset during the accounting period, which must also include previously capitalised borrowing costs. The capitalisation rate that is to be used in the accounting period is the weighted average of rates that apply to the entity's general borrowings that are outstanding during the period and must exclude any borrowings that are specifically for the purpose of obtaining other qualifying assets.

Example – Capitalisation rate

Irene Interiors Limited is constructing a new building to house its showroom, which is likely to take three years to complete and hence qualifies as a qualifying asset. The entity has three sources of borrowings during an accounting period:

	Outstanding liability £'000	*Interest charge £'000*
Seven-year loan	9,000	1,500
35-year long-term loan	14,000	2,000
Repayable bank overdraft	6,000	750

Should all of the above borrowings be used to finance the construction of a qualifying asset, the capitalisation rate will be calculated as follows:

$$\frac{1,500,000 + 2,000,000 + 750,000}{9,000,000 + 14,000,000 + 6,000,000} \times 100 = 14.66\%$$

If the seven-year loan is used to finance another specific qualifying asset, the capitalisation rate that should be used on the other qualifying assets will be:

$$\frac{2,000,000 + 750,000}{14,000,000 + 6,000,000} \times 100 = 13.75\%$$

SUSPENSION OF ASSET CONSTRUCTION

Paragraph 25.2D (a) says that an entity should capitalise borrowing costs as part of the cost of a qualifying asset from the point at which it first incurs both the expenditure on the asset and the borrowing costs as well as the point in time when it commences activities to prepare the asset for its intended use or sale. However, when active development of the asset is temporarily suspended, capitalisation of borrowing costs must also be temporarily suspended. Capitalisation of borrowing costs must also cease completely when substantially all the activities that are required to be completed to prepare the qualifying asset for its intended use or sale are finished.

> **Example – Suspension of capitalisation of borrowing costs**
>
> Weavers Windows Limited is in the process of constructing a new purpose-built building to house its headquarters. The company has a year-end date of 31 December 2015 and work commenced on 1 January 2015. However, due to a dispute with a supplier, construction was suspended on 1 March 2015 and did not resume until 31 October 2015.
>
> Paragraph 25.2D (b) says that the capitalisation of borrowing costs must be suspended during extended periods where active development of the asset has paused. Therefore during the period between 1 March 2015 and 31 October 2015, no capitalisation of borrowing costs should take place.

TRANSITIONAL ISSUES

On transition to FRS 102, a reporting entity has a choice of whether to capitalise borrowing costs as part of the cost of a qualifying asset, or write such costs off to profit or loss. Section 35 *Transition to this FRS* says that where a reporting entity chooses to capitalise borrowing costs as part of the cost of a qualifying asset, then the date of transition to FRS 102 can also be the date on which capitalisation commences.

DISCLOSURE ISSUES

Where an entity has chosen to capitalise borrowing costs as part of the cost of a qualifying asset, the financial statements must disclose:

(a) The amount of borrowing costs capitalised in the period and
(b) The capitalisation rate used.

15 IMPAIRMENT OF ASSETS

INTRODUCTION

The underlying theme in financial reporting is that a company's assets should not be carried in the balance sheet (statement of financial position) at any more than recoverable amount. The idea behind this concept is to prevent a company from misleading users of the financial statements into thinking that a company's assets are higher than they are realistically worth.

Companies have been criticised in the past for including assets in the balance sheet that should not either be classified as an asset (i.e. expenditure that should have gone to profit or loss has been put on the balance sheet) or ignoring the need to revisit the carrying values of assets at each reporting date and consider whether, or not, the carrying values are appropriate in the light of all available facts to the management at the reporting date.

Section 27 *Impairment of Assets* places a specific requirement on companies under its scope to carry out impairment tests on assets when the carrying value of the asset (i.e. the value at which it is stated in the balance sheet) may be more than its recoverable amount. Section 27 does not, however, apply to the following types of assets:

- Assets that arise through construction contracts (Section 23 *Revenue* and Chapter 8 in this book apply),
- Deferred tax assets (Section 29 *Income Tax* and Chapter 11 in this book apply),
- Assets that arise through employee benefits (Section 28 *Employee Benefits* and Chapter 10 in this book apply),
- Financial assets that fall under the scope of Section 11 *Basic Financial Instruments* and Section 12 *Other Financial Instruments Issues* (Chapter 17 in this book apply),
- Investment property that is measured at fair value (Section 16 *Investment Property* and Chapter 13 in this book apply),
- Biological assets and agricultural activity measured at fair value less estimated costs to sell (Section 34 *Specialised Activities* and Chapter 25 apply) and
- Deferred acquisition costs and intangible assets that have arisen from contracts that fall under the scope of FRS 103 *Insurance Contracts*.

The vast majority of entities will more than likely encounter the issue of trade debtors that have suffered impairment (i.e. bad debts). There is a Staff Education

Note available from the FRC website (www.frc.org.uk) named Staff Education Note 3 *Impairment of Trade Debtors* that gives practical guidance in this area.

Impairment tests can prove to be extremely problematic for reporting entities; however, notwithstanding the inherent complexities, directors of companies reporting under FRS 102 have a legal duty to ensure that the financial statements the entity prepares for statutory purposes give a true and fair view. The need for adequate impairment testing has risen in the ranks over recent years since the global economic crisis because during such times the values of assets can diminish quite considerably. Company auditors should also have an appreciation of the need for entities not to carry assets in the balance sheet at any more than a recoverable amount because, in so doing, audit risk (the risk that the auditor forms an incorrect opinion on the financial statements) is increased.

For the purposes of Section 27, the term 'recoverable amount' is the *higher* of an asset's (or cash-generating unit's) fair value less costs to sell and its value in use. If the carrying value of the asset is above its recoverable amount then this means the asset is impaired and a write-down, by way of the recognition of an impairment loss, is needed.

INDICATORS THAT AN ASSET IS IMPAIRED

An asset is impaired when its carrying value in the financial statements is higher than its recoverable amount. As mentioned above, recoverable amount is the higher of an asset's fair value less costs to sell and its value in use. If there is no indicator of impairment then there is no need to calculate the asset's recoverable amount.

Entities are required to assess assets for indicators of impairment at each reporting date. The term 'reporting date' is not merely restricted to the year-end date, but should also include interim reporting dates, and thus it follows that a reporting entity may undertake an impairment test on the same asset (or group of assets or cash-generating units) more than once a year.

If an asset does not generate cash flows, which are largely independent of other assets (or groups of assets), then the starting point for the determination of the recoverable amount in an impairment test will be at the level of individual assets. Where no independent cash flows are generated then recoverable amount is determined for the *cash-generating unit* (CGU) to which the asset belongs (a 'cash-generating unit' was referred to as an 'income-generating unit' in the previous UK GAAP). Paragraph 27.8 of FRS 102 says that a CGU is the smallest group of assets that generate cash inflows, which are largely independent of the cash inflows from other assets (or groups of assets). It is also worth mentioning at this point that a CGU can also be a single asset.

A problem that can sometimes arise is that it may not be possible to estimate the recoverable amount of an individual asset for two reasons:

- The asset's value in use cannot be estimated to be close to its fair value less costs of disposal and
- It does not generate cash inflows, which are largely independent of those from other assets.

When these situations present themselves, the recoverable amount of the CGU to which the asset belongs (i.e. the asset's CGU) must be determined.

Example – Identification of a CGU

A company operates 250 hotels, which are spread across the country. The head office comprises central sales, marketing, finance and HR functions. Each hotel generates their own income, which is remitted to head office and which is largely independent of other hotels in the chain. Management set each hotel a target every quarter and each hotel is monitored closely by management.

In this scenario it is likely that each hotel will form an individual CGU.

Example – Identification of a CGU

A manufacturing company operates a group of machinery. Each machine produces goods for which there is an active market. Most of the goods produced by the machines are used internally in the manufacturing company.

When an active market exists for the output produced by an asset (or a group of assets), this asset/group of assets should be identified as a CGU regardless of the fact that some (or all) of the output is used internally.

FRS 102 identifies two sources of information that must be taken into account when determining whether an asset might be showing indicators of impairment:

1. Internal sources and
2. External sources.

INTERNAL SOURCES

Sources of information from the internal activities of the entity, which can indicate that an asset is impaired, are as follows.

Obsolescence or damage that affects the asset

For example, a company may purchase a batch of assets from a supplier for £2 million and shortly afterwards they may be superseded by a better product, resulting in the manufacturer dropping their selling price. It may also be the case that an asset (or a group of assets) might become damaged and hence their recoverable amount may be lower than their carrying value in the company's balance sheet. In these cases assets would be showing signs of impairment and thus would need to be written down to a recoverable amount.

Adverse changes within the entity

The entity may have undergone some changes of an adverse nature (for example, the discontinuation of an operating segment) that may affect the way in which assets are used in the business. The affected assets may well become idle or redundant or may result in a previously finite useful life now being determined as indefinite. Such occurrences would render the asset/group of assets impaired.

Deterioration in the asset's performance

As an asset is used continuously within the business its performance may become less efficient as it becomes older. This deterioration in performance may render the recoverable amount of the asset/group of assets to be less than the carrying value and hence a write-down to recoverable amount would be needed.

Previous budgeted/forecasted information being superseded

Management may prepare their own budgets/forecasts and such recent budgets and forecasts may reveal a declining net cash inflow or profitability than originally forecast.

Example – Increased competition in the marketplace

Cory's Computers has held a large market share of the home computing industry for several years. It has always sourced high-quality materials to be used in the manufacture of its products and because it buys a large amount of its materials overseas and in bulk it has managed to secure relatively high levels of discounts, which it has passed on to its consumers in the selling price. The year-end of Cory's Computers is 31 December each year and the company is currently half-way through the financial year to end on 31 December 2016. Production levels and sales targets are currently ahead of budgets.

Management of Cory's Computers had been made aware (unofficially) that their major competitor, Marks Microcomputers, had developed a new product that is going to revolutionise the home computing market. The product developed by Marks Microcomputers is much faster, uses the latest Bluetooth technology that is still currently emerging in the market and has double the memory capacity compared to Cory's Computers. The board of Cory's Computers are significantly concerned about the impact that this new product will have on their market share as they have acknowledged that they will experience significant difficulty and a high level of costs in keeping pace with Marks Microcomputers. However, the finance director has said that they do not need to undertake an impairment review of their plant and machinery (which is carried in the balance sheet at a significant amount) on the basis that their production levels and sales are currently ahead of budget.

The finance director is incorrect in his assertion that Cory's Computers should not undertake an impairment review on its plant and machinery. This is because changes in the market and demands for Cory's Computers' products can have a substantial impact on the plant and machinery's value, which is based on the economic benefit to be obtained from its continued use.

The fact that production levels and sales targets are above budgeted forecasts is not sufficient to render the need to carry out an impairment review as unnecessary. This is because management are required to assess the impact of the competing new product on demand for its existing product as well as on future expected cash flows. Management have already acknowledged that they will experience significant difficulty and a high level of costs in trying to keep up with its competitor and thus this will invariably mean that the plant and machinery in Cory's Computers will need to be written down to a recoverable amount.

The internal sources above are not exhaustive and there may be other sources of internal evidence that may give rise to an asset or a group of assets suffering from impairment.

External sources of information

As well as internal sources of information that an entity should consider when assessing whether an asset, or a group of assets, is showing indicators of impairment, an entity should also consider sources external to the entity in assessing impairment. Such external sources can include the following:

Decline in market values for the asset

A decline in market values for an asset, or a group of assets, may occur when the decline in value is significantly greater than would otherwise be the case due to the passage of time or normal use. This can occur, for example, due to technological obsolescence or a change in demand for the products that the asset(s) produces. When such instances occur, management must consider whether such situations render the asset or group of assets impaired.

Significant adverse changes arising in the marketplace

There may well be events that occur (or that may potentially occur) within the marketplace that could render an asset, or group of assets, impaired. For example, a change in the technological, market, economic or legal environment may be so significant that it causes the value of assets to fall below recoverable amount.

Example – Introduction of legislation

Company A's principal activity is the manufacture of pesticides. It has a licence to manufacture a certain pesticide that can only be used in controlled circumstances because it is highly dangerous and could cause severe health issues and even death if used incorrectly. Because of the product's highly dangerous nature the company has a group of plant and machinery that constitutes a cash-generating unit that is used solely for the manufacture of this pesticide. No other products are manufactured using this group of machinery.

During the year to 31 December 2015, the government announced plans to eventually phase out the use of this pesticide because it was found to be harming wildlife for which it was not originally intended. In addition, there have been an increasing number of accidents – some quite serious – as a result of the use of this pesticide. Legislation is expected to be brought in during 2017 that will eventually ban the use of this pesticide.

As the government is planning to bring in legislation that will effectively ban the pesticide from use and hence render the plant and machinery used in its development at Company A redundant, the plant and machinery should be written down to recoverable amount. The introduction of legislation to ban the pesticide is an example of an external source of information that may render the machinery's carrying value to be in excess of a recoverable amount because the future cash flows brought into the entity from the plant and machinery are likely to be less than originally planned had the government not announced its plans to bring in legislation to ban the pesticide.

Increased interest rates or market rates of return

Increases in interest rates or market rates of return are an issue that reporting entities are required to consider when it comes to assessing whether an asset, or a group of assets, are impaired. This is because any long-term increases in interest rates might affect the discount rate which is used to calculate the asset's recoverable amount. However, a marginal increase in short-term interest rates is unlikely to lead to an impairment charge where there has been significant headroom in a previous test. In addition, increases in short-term interest rates are not necessarily going to result in an impairment review having to be carried out.

Carrying amounts exceed estimated fair value

Carrying amounts of assets may exceed fair value when the company might, for example, consider selling and it commissions a valuation of the company including all its assets. The market values of the assets might be less than the carrying value and in such cases this would be a clear indicator that the carrying value of the assets should be written down to a recoverable amount.

IMPAIRMENT OF INVENTORIES

The concern with inventories is that the inventory figure can be manipulated so as to achieve a desired profit (or loss) figure or balance sheet position because the closing inventories valuation has an impact on both the income statement (profit and loss account) and the balance sheet (statement of financial position). This scope for manipulation is somewhat reduced where the entity is independently audited but it is a risk that is present in all entities, both large and small.

The problem with inventories is that in some entities there is a high degree of estimation technique employed by management in arriving at the closing inventories figure (especially if the client also has large amounts of work-in-progress). Extreme care should be taken when it comes to inventory valuations – particularly where estimations are concerned and where the entity has slow-moving items of inventory or where inventory quickly becomes obsolete.

Section 27 deals with the impairment of assets other than inventories (such as tangible and intangible fixed assets and the like). However, the section also deals with inventories because entities are expected to give consideration as to whether inventories are showing indicators of impairment and hence require writing down accordingly.

The FRS uses the term *'selling price less costs to complete and sell'*. In the context of 'tradition', this term is essentially the same as 'lower of cost or net realisable value'. Essentially if the selling price less costs to complete and sell is lower than the carrying value, the inventory is impaired and must be written down to its selling price less costs to complete and sell (the new term in FRS 102 for 'net realisable value'). Such write-downs are recognised immediately in profit or loss.

Example – Impracticable to determine selling price less costs to complete and sell

Company A has a batch of inventories that it has been struggling to sell throughout the year. On 31 December 2015, after exhausting all attempts, management conclude that it is unable to determine the selling price less costs to complete and sell.

Paragraph 27.3 of FRS 102 says that if it is impracticable (i.e. after making every reasonable effort to do so) to determine the selling prices less costs to complete and sell for inventories on an item-by-item basis, the entity may then group items of inventory relating to the same product line that have similar purposes or end uses and are produced and marketed in the same geographical area so as to assess impairment.

Reversals of impairments

At each reporting date (note that the term 'reporting date' does not necessarily mean just the year-end date; it can also mean interim dates) an entity must make a new assessment of selling price less costs to complete and sell. There may be occasions when previous circumstances that caused inventories to be impaired no longer exist and hence there is clear evidence of an increase in selling price less costs to complete and sell due to the change in the circumstances.

In such cases, the reporting entity can reverse the previous impairment but care should be taken because the reversal is limited to the amount of the original impairment loss.

Example – Reversal of a previously recognised impairment

Diane's Domestics sells domestic appliances to members of the general public and has a year-end date of 30 September each year but has quarterly interim reporting periods. On 6 July 2015 the manufacturer of the EcoWash brand of washing machines announced a problem with its washing machines that may cause the machine to break down suddenly. The value of these washing machines in Diane's Domestics inventory at 30 September 2015 prior to any impairment was £45,000. Management were able to determine that the selling price less costs to complete and sell these items of machinery for parts as at 30 September 2015 was £25,000 and hence wrote down the value of the inventory by £20,000, with the corresponding debit being charged to cost of sales in the financial statements.

The manufacturer performed an inspection on the batch of washing machines held in Diane's Domestics warehouse on 3 January 2016 but found no evidence of the problem in the batch of machines and the manufacturer said that these machines could now go back on sale at their original prices.

In this example there is clear evidence that the circumstances surrounding the original impairment have ceased to apply and therefore the original impairment of £20,000 can be reversed.

Had the manufacturer also increased their cost price as a result of the problem now no longer applying, Diane's Domestics would still only be able to reverse the original £20,000 impairment; in other words it would not be able to reverse £20,000 plus the rise in cost price of the machinery.

IMPAIRMENT OF OTHER ASSETS

The overarching principle in Section 27 is that if, and only if, the recoverable amount of an asset is less than its carrying amount then the entity should reduce the carrying amount of that asset to its recoverable amount by the recognition of an impairment loss. When the entity recognises an impairment loss, the loss is recognised immediately in profit or loss. The exception to this accounting treatment is when the asset is carried at a revalued amount (for example, property accounted for under Section 17 *Property, Plant and Equipment*) and therefore any impairment loss in respect of the revalued asset is recognised in the revaluation reserve to the extent of the revaluation surplus in the revaluation reserve.

Indicators of impairment have been discussed in the section above 'Indicators that an Asset is Impaired'. When circumstances indicate that an asset is, in fact, impaired, then in addition to carrying out an impairment test, the entity should also review the remaining useful life of the asset together with the depreciation/amortisation method or residual value for the associated asset and adjust it in accordance with the relevant section of FRS 102 (e.g. Section 17 or Section 18 *Intangible Assets other than Goodwill*). This principle applies even if no impairment loss is actually recognised in the financial statements.

Determining recoverable amount

For the purposes of impairment testing, recoverable amount is the higher of fair value less costs to sell and value in use. The term 'fair value less costs to sell' is the amount that could be obtained from the sale of an asset in an arm's length transaction and between willing and knowledgeable parties less the costs of the associated disposal. In other words, it is the value of an asset in the market when the sale is undertaken on normal commercial terms.

FRS 102 acknowledges that the best evidence of a fair value less costs to sell figure is in a binding sale agreement whereby the price will be predetermined by the parties to the sale in the agreement. Another viable alternative way of obtaining a fair value less costs to sell figure would be a market value in an active market. The term 'active market' means a market in which such transactions are regularly traded and prices can be obtained reliably.

Example – Fair value less costs to sell unavailable

In assessing an asset for impairment, a company is trying to arrive at figures for fair value less costs to sell and value in use. It has managed to arrive at an estimate for value in use that is in excess of the asset's carrying value but the entity is having difficulty in arriving at fair value less costs to sell.

In such a case it would not be necessary to obtain a figure for fair value less costs to sell. This is because if either value in use or fair value less costs to sell is in excess of the asset's carrying value then the asset is not impaired and hence there is no need to try to estimate the other amount.

In the above example the entity was having difficulty in arriving at a fair value less costs to sell figure. It might be the case that an entity has no reason to believe that an asset's value in use figure materially exceeds its fair value less costs to sell. In these instances it is possible to use the asset's fair value less costs to sell figure as recoverable amount and this example might well apply to an asset that is held for disposal.

Determining value in use

Arriving at a value in use figure is more complicated because it involves the calculation of the present value of future cash flows that are expected to be received from the asset (or group of assets) being subjected to the impairment test. There are two steps involved in arriving at a value in use figure:

- First, estimate the future cash flows (both inflows and outflows) that are expected to occur from continuing use of the asset as well as from the asset's ultimate disposal and
- Second, apply the appropriate discount rate to those future cash flows to arrive at a present value of those cash flows.

Whilst the above might seem fairly straightforward, there are certain factors that must be included in the calculation of an asset's value in use, including:

- A reliable estimation of the future cash flows that the entity expects to receive from the asset,
- Any expected variations in the amount or timing of those future cash flows (such as seasonal variations),
- Time values of money (represented by the current market risk-free interest rate),
- The cost of bearing the inherent uncertainty in the asset and
- Other related factors such as illiquidity and other issues that market participants would take into account when pricing the future cash flows that the entity would derive from the asset.

From the above it is clear that value in use calculations are not an 'exact science' and in real life there are significant amounts of judgement that must be applied when arriving at a value in use figure.

When the entity is estimating the future cash flows the entity would expect to receive from the asset, it must include:

- The projected estimated cash inflows that the entity would expect to receive from continuing use of the asset,
- Associated cash outflows that would need to be incurred to generate the cash inflows from continuing use of the asset (note that such cash outflows would also include the outflows directly attributable in preparing the asset for use) and
- Estimated cash flows that are expected to be received or paid on disposal of the asset.

Where available, a reporting entity might wish to utilise any budgets or forecasts to estimate the cash flows as this might prove helpful. However, an important point is that when estimating future cash flows, the entity must do so based on the asset in its *current* condition. For example, future estimated cash flows should *not* include amounts that are expected as a result of restructuring costs to which the entity is not yet committed or cash flows that might have to be incurred in order to improve the asset's performance.

When estimating cash flows, any cash inflows or outflows that arise from financing activities or tax receipts or payments should *not* be included.

Because cash flows for the value in use calculation have to be discounted to present day values (to take into account the time value of money), the entity needs to exercise caution in its choice of discount rate(s). It must use a pre-tax rate(s) that reflects current market assessments of:

(a) The time value of money and
(b) Any risks that are directly related to the asset for which the estimated future cash flows have not yet been adjusted.

Another point to note when an entity is deciding on the discount rate(s) to be used to discount the future cash flows is that they should not reflect the risks for which the future cash flows have already been adjusted because otherwise the risks will be double-counted, resulting in distorted discounted cash flows.

All investment decisions take into consideration the effects of the time value of money together with the risks associated with expected future cash flows and hence these are taken into account in the measurement of an asset's value in use. FRS 102 requires cash flows to be discounted at a pre-tax rate that reflects both current market assessments of the time value of money together with the risks that are specific to the asset for which future cash flow estimates have not yet been adjusted.

Future cash flows being discounted at a pre-tax discount rate (as per FRS 102) is not the same as discounting cash flows at a post-tax discount rate.

Example – Calculating a pre-tax rate from a post-tax rate

An entity invests in an asset that costs £100 and requires a rate of return of 14% from the asset. The company pays corporation tax at a rate of 30% and the asset qualifies for 100% capital allowances from HM Revenue and Customs. All cash flows from the asset arise at the end of the first year in which the asset is acquired.

The post-tax cash flows required by the entity amount to £114. As a result, pre-tax cash flows must amount to £120. Pre-tax cash flows amounting to £120 will result in an overall corporation tax charge of £6, which is made up of the profit before depreciation of £36 (£120 × 30%) less the tax relief obtained on the cost of the asset of £30 (£100 × 30%). Hence the required pre-tax rate is 20%.

The above example is quite a simple method of arriving at a pre-tax rate from a post-tax rate but in reality there will be added complications.

Once fair value less costs to sell and value in use have been obtained, the recoverable amount can be calculated and then compared to carrying value to determine if the asset (or group of assets) is impaired.

Example – Calculation of recoverable amount

An entity has a manufacturing division that manufactures roller-shutter doors and associated components, which are sold on to contractors. The manufacturing division operates a large group of heavy industrial machines that manufacture the curtains, bottom-rails, guides, angles, barrels and canopies. The reporting date of the entity is 31 December

2015 and as at that date these machines have a book value of £140,000. The directors consider that this group of machines constitute a cash-generating unit under Section 27.

The directors have undertaken an exercise relating to the expected cash inflows and outflows, which have all been based on reduced productivity levels due to the age and condition of the machinery. The analysis is shown below:

Year	Revenues £	Costs £
2016	70,000	27,000
2017	75,000	45,000
2018	85,000	65,000
2019	30,000	20,000

The original manufacturer of the plant has been approached to give a reliable estimate of the estimated fair value of the machinery in the cash-generating unit. The manufacturer has informed the directors that the fair value that an informed, unconnected third party should expect to pay for the equipment is £82,150.

The directors have based their value in use calculations having reference to the above cash flows and have discounted them at a rate of 5%, which is the entity's cost of capital. Using this discount rate produces a present value of £93,656, which is calculated as follows:

Year	Cash flows £	PV factor	Present value £
2016	43,000	0.952	40,936
2017	30,000	0.907	27,210
2018	20,000	0.864	17,280
2019	10,000	0.823	8,230
Value in use			**93,656**

As value in use exceeds the manufacturer's net selling price, then value in use is selected to represent the recoverable amount. This is lower than the carrying value of the group of assets as at 31 December 2015 and therefore an impairment loss of £46,344 (£140,000 less £93,656) is recognised.

The impairment loss is recognised as an operating expense as either depreciation or a separate heading in the profit and loss account.

IMPAIRMENT OF CASH-GENERATING UNITS

The term 'cash-generating units' is a similar concept to an 'income-generating unit' in the old UK GAAP. When it comes to an impairment in respect of a cash-generating unit (CGU) issues can get somewhat complicated. Similar principles still apply in that if the recoverable amount of the CGU is less than its carrying amount then an impairment loss is recognised, but Section 27 requires the loss to be allocated in a specific order:

1. First, reduce any goodwill allocated to the asset or CGU; then
2. Any remaining impairment loss is allocated against other assets in the CGU on a pro rata basis based on the carrying value of each asset in the CGU.

Example – Allocation of an impairment loss in a CGU

A subsidiary that has been classified as a CGU has the following assets in its balance sheet (statement of financial position) as at 31 December 2015:

Balance sheet (extract)

Fixed assets:	£
Property	60
Plant and machinery	90
Goodwill	30
	180

In the board meeting, the directors have assessed that the recoverable amount of the above net assets is £135.

The impairment loss amounts to £45 (£180 – £135) and must be allocated to goodwill and then to the rest of the assets in the CGU on a pro rata basis.

£30 of the impairment loss will be allocated to goodwill, reducing the carrying amount of the goodwill down to £nil. £6 is allocated to the property with the remaining £9 being allocated to the plant and machinery.

The balance sheet extracts will now be as follows:

Balance sheet (extract)

Fixed assets:	£
Property	54
Plant and machinery	81
Goodwill	–
	135

In contrast, under the previous UK GAAP at FRS 11 *Impairment of Fixed Assets and Goodwill* the goodwill impairment charge would have been allocated first to goodwill and then subsequently to any capitalised intangible asset in the CGU and finally to the tangible assets in the unit on a pro rata basis. Under the provisions in Section 27 of FRS 102, impairment losses are simply allocated first to goodwill and then to all other assets in the CGU on the basis of their carrying amount in the CGU.

When allocating an impairment loss in a CGU it is important to point out that neither goodwill nor any other asset in a CGU can be reduced below the *highest* of:

- Fair value less costs to sell (if determinable),
- Value in use (if determinable) and
- Zero.

Example – Allocation of an impairment loss

The management of Company A have carried out an impairment test on one of its group of assets, which is considered to be a CGU. Financial statement extracts for the year ended 31 December 2015 are shown below:

Goodwill	£140,000
Property, plant and equipment	£210,000

The CGU has suffered an impairment loss of £160,000 during the year due to stiff competition in the marketplace and the setting up of a business within the area by a large competitor.

The finance director has calculated fair value less costs to sell for goodwill of £70,000 and value in use is £60,000. The directors have not been able to arrive at a figure for fair value less costs to sell or value in use for the property, plant and equipment.

The impairment loss of £160,000 will first be allocated to goodwill with the remainder being applied to the property, plant and equipment. However, under Section 27 neither the goodwill nor any asset in the CGU can be reduced below the highest of fair value less costs to sell, value in use and zero.

As fair value less costs to sell is higher than value in use, the goodwill will be carried in the balance sheet at £70,000, so of the £160,000 impairment £70,000 (£140,000 less £70,000) will be allocated to goodwill with the remaining £90,000 being allocated to the property, plant and equipment, resulting in the balance sheet extracts showing the following:

Goodwill	£70,000
Property, plant and equipment	£120,000

GOODWILL IMPAIRMENT

Goodwill has long since been a controversial issue within the world of accountancy. This is largely because of its subjective nature, which was tested in the case of *Commissioners of Inland Revenue v Muller & Co Margarine* [1901] AC 217. Lord MacNaghten, the presiding judge, said:

'What is goodwill? It is a thing very easy to describe, very difficult to define. It is the benefit and advantage of the good name, reputation and connection of the business. It is the attractive force which brings in custom. It is the one thing which distinguishes an old established business from a new business at its first start. Goodwill is composed as a variety of elements. It differs in its composition in different trades and in different businesses in the same trade. One element may preponderate here, and another there.'

FRS 102 acknowledges that goodwill, in isolation, cannot be sold and nor can it generate cash flows that are independent of the cash flows of other assets and so it follows that goodwill cannot be measured directly. The fair value of goodwill, therefore, is derived from the measurement of fair value of the CGU(s) from which it belongs.

Goodwill arises when a business combination takes place and (in the case of positive goodwill) is the excess of the purchase consideration over the fair value of the net assets obtained in the combination. Goodwill that arises in a business combination must be allocated to each of the acquirer's CGUs, which are expected to benefit from the synergies of the combination. This concept applies regardless of whether other assets or liabilities of the acquiree are assigned to those units.

When a parent acquires a subsidiary, it may not acquire the entire subsidiary – in other words part of the net assets may be owned by third parties known as the 'non-controlling interest' (or 'minority interest', which some accountants may be more familiar with). When determining recoverable amount for the purpose of impairment testing, part of that recoverable amount of a CGU will be attributable to the non-controlling interest in the subsidiary and therefore the carrying value of the CGU must be notionally adjusted before being compared to the recoverable amount. This is achieved by 'grossing up' the carrying amount of goodwill that has been allocated to the CGU so that it includes the goodwill attributable to the non-controlling interest. Once the goodwill has been grossed up it can then be compared to the recoverable amount to determine if the CGU is impaired.

Example – Impairment loss in a CGU that is not wholly owned

Breary Breeze Blocks (Breary) acquires 80% of the net assets in Cory Concrete (Cory) on 1 January 2015 (the date of acquisition) for a consideration of £340 million. At the date of acquisition, the fair value of Cory's net assets and contingent liabilities is £300 million. Group policy is to recognise goodwill to the extent of the parent's own and hence the Breary Group recognises:

1. Fair value of net assets and contingent liabilities	£300m
2. Goodwill (*)	£100m
3. Non-controlling interest (£300m × 20%)	£60m

*Goodwill

Cost of investment	£340m
Less net assets acquired (£300m × 80%)	(£240m)
Goodwill	£100m

On 31 December 2015 the Breary Group carries out an impairment test and assesses the recoverable amount to be £200 million. Cory's assets of £300 million are being depreciated over their useful economic lives of ten years and there is no residual value expected at the end of this estimated useful economic life. As management have been unable to reliably estimate the useful economic life of goodwill, this is being amortised over a five-year period in accordance with Section 19 *Business Combinations and Goodwill.*

Part of the £200 million recoverable amount will belong to the non-controlling interest's share of goodwill that has not been recognised. Paragraph 27.26 of FRS 102 requires the carrying value of Cory to be notionally increased by the goodwill attributable to the non-controlling interest. Once this has been done, the grossed up value is then compared to the recoverable amount of £200 million to establish if it is impaired. This can be illustrated as follows:

	£m	£m
Goodwill (£100m × 4/5)		80
Unrecognised non-controlling interest in goodwill (W1)		20
Gross carrying value of identifiable net assets	300	
Accumulated depreciation	(30)	
		270
Notionally adjusted carrying value		370
Recoverable amount		(200)
Impairment loss		170

<u>W1</u>

Goodwill attributable to Breary's interest of 80% was £100 million, therefore goodwill attributable to the non-controlling interest is 1/4 (of the 80%), thus £25 million, and so at the end of 2015 it is £20 million (£25m × 4/5).

The impairment loss then needs to be allocated. It is first allocated to goodwill of £80 million (above) as the remaining £20 million belongs to the non-controlling interest.

	Carrying value of CGU		Impairment	Post-impairment
	£m	*£m*	*£m*	*£m*
Goodwill attributable to parent		80	(80)	
Gross carrying amount of identifiable assets	300			
Accumulated depreciation	(30)			
Carrying amount of identifiable net assets		270	(70)	200
Carrying value		350		
Recoverable amount		200		
Impairment loss in the parent		150	(150)	

The impairment loss in the parent can be proved by saying total impairment loss for notional purposes of £170 million less the unrecognised goodwill belonging to the non-controlling interest of £20 million equals the parent's impairment loss of £150 million.

Goodwill unable to be allocated to CGUs

In the instance that management is unable to allocate goodwill to an individual CGU (or groups thereof) on a non-arbitrary basis, then for the purposes of Section 27 the entity must test whether goodwill is impaired by determining the recoverable amount of either:

(a) The acquired business in its entirety when the goodwill relates to a business that has not been integrated (i.e. restructured or dissolved into the reporting entity or other subsidiaries) or

(b) The entire group of businesses and excluding any businesses that have not been integrated where the goodwill relates to a business that has been integrated.

To comply with this principle, the reporting entity will need to separate goodwill into two components:

• Goodwill that relates to businesses that have been integrated and
• Goodwill that relates to businesses that have not been integrated.

REVERSAL OF IMPAIRMENTS

It is possible for impairment losses that have been charged to profit or loss in one accounting period to be reversed in subsequent accounting periods. The only way that a reversal of a previously recognised impairment loss can occur is when the reasons for the original impairment loss cease to apply. The consequence of this is twofold: not only do entities need to test assets for impairment at each reporting date, but they should also determine whether previous impairment losses may no longer apply or have decreased.

When there are indicators that an impairment loss previously recognised no longer exists, or has decreased, the entity then considers whether all, or part, of the impairment loss should be reversed. Care must be taken here because it is not as straightforward as simply reversing all, or part, of the previous impairment. Regard has to be given as to whether the previous impairment loss on the asset was based on:

(a) The recoverable amount of that individual asset or
(b) The recoverable amount of the CGU to which the asset belongs.

Recoverable amount based on an individual asset

There are four requirements that apply when a recoverable amount was based on an individual asset:

- At the current reporting date, the entity must estimate the recoverable amount of the asset.
- Where the estimated recoverable amount exceeds the carrying amount, the entity increases the carrying amount in the financial statements to recoverable amount subject to the next bullet point. This results in a reversal of an impairment loss and is recognised in profit or loss unless the related asset is carried under the revaluation model and therefore all (or some) of the impairment reversal may have to be recognised in equity and reported in other comprehensive income if the previous impairment loss was also recognised in equity.
- Reversals of impairment losses cannot increase the carrying value of an asset over and above the carrying value that it would have been reported at in the entity's financial statements (net of depreciation or amortisation) had no impairment loss been recognised in prior years.
- Once the reversal has been accounted for in the financial statements, the reporting entity must then adjust the related depreciation/amortisation charge for the asset in future periods so as to allocate the asset's revised carrying value less residual value (if any) on a systematic basis over the remaining useful life of the asset.

Example – Prior period impairment loss based on an individual asset

Aidan Co. Limited (Aidan) has a year-end of 31 December each year. On 31 December 2015 it had an asset with a net book value of £90,000 but because of indicators that a competitor was about to enter the marketplace and introduce a brand new machine that would be much more powerful than the machine owned by Aidan its recoverable amount was calculated at £30,000 and so in the 2015 financial statements an impairment loss of £60,000 (£90,000 less £30,000) was recognised in the financial statements. Had the asset not suffered impairment it would have been recognised in the financial statements as at 31 December 2015 as £75,000, as depreciation is being charged on this asset over a ten-year period on a straight-line basis.

The directors have now obtained evidence that their competitor is no longer introducing a new machine into the marketplace due to extreme levels of cost that would have to be incurred and therefore consider that the original circumstances giving rise to the impairment no longer exist. The finance director is proposing to reverse the entire impairment loss of £60,000.

If the asset had not suffered any impairment in 2015 the carrying value would have been £90,000 and in 2016 would have been £75,000. Assuming that the carrying value of the machine is still at its post-impairment value of £30,000 the maximum amount of the reversal that the finance director could reverse in 2016 is £45,000 (i.e. £75,000 less £30,000). This is because paragraph 27.30(c) of FRS 102 says that the reversal of a previously recognised impairment loss cannot increase the carrying value of an asset above the carrying amount that would have been determined (net of depreciation or amortisation) had no impairment loss been recognised for the asset in previous years.

The finance director should therefore debit the carrying value of the asset in the balance sheet with £45,000 to bring the carrying amount up from £30,000 to £75,000 and credit impairment in the profit and loss account. The finance director should then adjust the depreciation charge for the asset in future periods to allocate the asset's depreciable amount over its estimated useful life (in this example it will be over a remaining five-year period).

Recoverable amount estimated for a cash-generating unit

There are five requirements that apply when the reversal relates to recoverable amount that was estimated for a cash-generating unit (CGU), which are as follows:

- The reporting entity must arrive at an estimate of recoverable amount of the CGU at the current reporting date.
- When the estimated recoverable amount exceeds the carrying value of the CGU the excess is regarded as a reversal of an impairment loss. The reversal is allocated first to the assets (excluding goodwill) of the unit pro rata on the basis of the carrying value of each asset in the CGU and then to goodwill allocated to each CGU. If the asset has been subjected to revaluation then the impairment reversal will follow the original impairment that would ordinarily be posted to a revaluation reserve.
- An impairment reversal cannot increase the carrying amount of an asset above the lower of:
  - The asset's recoverable amount and
  - The carrying amount that would have been recognised (net of depreciation or amortisation) had no impairment loss originally been recognised.
- Excess amounts of impairment losses that arise because of the above restrictions are allocated to assets pro rata based on the other assets in the CGU.
- When the impairment has been reversed, the entity should then adjust the depreciation/amortisation charge for each asset in the CGU in future periods to allocate the asset's revised carrying value less residual value (if any) on a systematic basis over the asset's remaining useful economic life.

> **Example – Reversal of an impairment loss based on the amount of a CGU to which the asset belongs**

Entity A Ltd has a year-end of 31 December each year. On 31 December 2014 the company accounted for an impairment loss of £360,000 on a separate division, which it classed as a CGU. Extracts from the financial statements of the CGU are shown below:

| | 31 December 2014 | | |
	Post impairment £'000		Pre impairment £'000
Goodwill	nil	(Note 1)	220
Plant	480	(Note 2)	500
Machinery	1,380	(Note 2)	1,500
	1,860		2,220

Note 1

The impairment loss is £360,000 and to comply with the requirements in Section 27, £220,000 of this loss is allocated first to goodwill to write goodwill off to zero.

Note 2

Before the impairment, the plant is in the ratio of 500:1,500, which means that the plant represents 25% of the remaining assets. Allocating 25% of the impairment loss would reduce the plant to £465,000 (£500,000 less (25% × £140,000)), which takes the value below its recoverable amount and hence is not permitted under Section 27. Therefore, the maximum impairment permitted is £20,000 and therefore the remaining £15,000 would be allocated against the machinery.

The impairment that is allocated to the machinery is calculated as follows:

$$(75\% \times £140,000) = £105,000 + £15,000 = £120,000$$

On 31 December 2015, extracts from the financial statements of the company are as follows:

	31.12.15 £'000	31.12.14 £'000
Goodwill	nil	nil
Plant	384	480
Machinery	1,104	1,380
	1,488	1,860

Circumstances indicate that the reasons for the impairment in 2014 no longer apply to the entity and the directors have corroboratory evidence that an amount of £310,000 can be reversed from the original impairment. The order in which this has to be reversed is:

- First, to the assets (excluding goodwill) of the unit pro rata on the basis of the carrying value of each asset and
- Finally, to any goodwill that has been allocated to the CGU.

Had no impairment loss been recognised in 2014, the carrying value of the assets (based on depreciation being charged at 20% on a reducing balance basis) would be as follows:

	£'000
Goodwill	220
Plant	400
Machinery	1,200
	1,820

The plant currently represents 26% (£384/(£384 + £1,104) × 100) of the total assets in the CGU. If the company were to allocate 26% of the £310,000 reversal to the plant, this would result in the net book value of the plant being higher than the carrying value of £400,000 had no impairment been made and, to comply with paragraph 27.31 of FRS 102, only £16,000 of the reversal can be allocated to the plant.

The machinery has a carrying value of £1,104,000 and if the remaining 74% of the impairment reversal was to be allocated to machinery this, too, would result in the carrying value exceeding the value that would have been reported had no impairment been recognised in 2014. Therefore only £96,000 (£1,200,000 less £1,104,000) of the remaining £294,000 impairment reversal can be allocated to the machinery.

The remaining balance of the reversal is taken to goodwill and the extracts of the financial statements will be as follows after allocating the reversal of impairment:

	31.12.15	*31.12.14*
	£'000	*£'000*
Goodwill	198	nil
Plant	400	480
Machinery	1,200	1,380
	1,798	1,860

FRS 102 is notably different from the previous UK GAAP at FRS 11 *Impairment of Fixed Assets and Goodwill* in that FRS 102 allows impairments of intangible assets to be reversed more often than FRS 11 and therefore there is a different treatment as to how the reversal must be accounted for when the impairment relates to a cash-generating unit.

DISCLOSURES

For each class of assets, a reporting entity should disclose:

- The amount of impairment losses that have been recognised in profit or loss during the period and the line item(s) in the statement of comprehensive income (or income statement if this is presented) in which the impairment losses have been recognised and
- The amount of any reversals of previously recognised impairment losses that have been recognised in profit or loss during the period, together with the line items in the statement of comprehensive income (or income statement if this is presented) that contains those impairment loss reversals.

The above disclosures are required for each of the following classes of asset:

- Inventories,
- Property, plant and equipment (this class includes investment property accounted for under the cost model),
- Goodwill,
- Intangible assets excluding goodwill,
- Investments in associated undertakings and
- Investments in joint ventures.

For impairment losses, a reporting entity is required to disclose a description of the circumstances and events that have led to the recognition or reversal of an impairment loss.

16 GOVERNMENT GRANTS

INTRODUCTION

There are situations when a company may receive grants to help them set up their operations (for example, in a deprived area to encourage employment opportunities) or to receive grants to help them with day-to-day expenditure (such as new start-up grants) or help with the cost of assets.

Section 24 *Government Grants* of FRS 102 deals with the accounting and disclosure requirements for grants and whilst some of the concepts are largely the same as the previous UK GAAP in SSAP 4 *Accounting for Government Grants*, FRS 102 introduces a new 'performance model', which was not previously seen in the old SSAP 4.

Section 24 itself is a fairly short section and, for the purposes of this section, a government grant is assistance provided by the government in the form of resources (for example, cash) and in return for which the entity has to comply with certain, past or future, conditions that relate to the entity's operative activities.

Section 24 does not deal with government assistance provided to an entity in the form of benefits that are available in determining taxable profit (or loss) or are determined or limited on the basis of income tax liability. For the purposes of Section 24, government assistance is action that is provided by the government and is designed to provide an economic benefit to an entity (or entities) qualifying under specified criteria.

Paragraph 24.7 goes on to state some useful examples of government assistance including tax holidays, investment tax credits, accelerated depreciation allowances and reduced income tax rates.

THE PERFORMANCE MODEL

Under the previous SSAP 4, only the 'accrual model' was permitted for the recognition of grants. However, Section 24 introduces the new concept of the 'performance model', which was not previously recognised in the UK GAAP (or even in the international equivalent in IAS 20 *Accounting for Government Grants and Disclosure of Government Assistance*).

The adoption of the performance model is an accounting policy choice (which must be applied consistently on a class-by-class basis). Where a reporting entity adopts the performance model, the recognition criteria for the grant are as follows:

- A grant is recognised in income when the grant proceeds are received (or receivable) provided that the terms of the grant do not impose future performance-related conditions.
- If the terms of a grant do impose performance-related conditions on the recipient, the grant is only recognised in income when those performance-related conditions are met.
- Any grants that are received before the revenue recognition criteria are met are recognised in the entity's financial statements as a liability (usually as 'deferred income' within creditors).

The term 'performance-related conditions' means any conditions that require the entity to perform a certain level of service or provide a certain level of goods. Once the entity has rendered those services or delivered those goods, the entity becomes entitled to the resources that were conditional on the entity's performance. For example, a grant may be conditional on the entity employing a set number of employees from a certain area of the community; once the entity reaches that benchmark, the entity will receive the grant.

THE ACCRUAL MODEL

This model is probably the most familiar model to accountants and FRS 102 requires that grants that are accounted for under the accrual model be distinguished between grants relating to revenue (a revenue-based grant) or grants relating to assets (a capital-based grant). There are four methods of accounting for grants under the accrual model, depending on whether they are revenue- or capital-based grants:

- Grants relating to revenue are recognised in profit or loss on a systematic basis over the periods in which the entity recognises the related costs for which the grant is intended to compensate.
- Grants that are received in respect of expenses or losses already incurred by the entity are recognised in profit or loss in the period when the grant becomes receivable.
- Capital-based grants are recognised in profit or loss on a systematic basis over the useful life of the asset (usually to match the associated depreciation charge).
- Grants relating to an asset that is deferred are recognised as a liability (usually as 'deferred income' within creditors) and are not deducted from the carrying value of an asset.

SMALL COMPANIES

Government grants are dealt with in the FRSSE (effective January 2015) in paragraphs 6.54 to 6.57. The key difference here relates to the interaction with the prohibition in the Companies Act 2006 to offset the grant against the cost of an asset. Paragraph 6.54 to the FRSSE (effective January 2015) says that to the extent that the grant is made towards the expenditure in relation to a fixed asset, in principle it may be deducted from the purchase price or production cost of that asset. There is no explicit prohibition to ALL entities that apply the FRSSE in the preparation of their financial statements. However, paragraph 6.54 does say that companies that are governed by the accounting and reporting requirements of UK companies legislation must not offset the grant against the cost of an asset, but instead recognise any unamortised grant as deferred income.

At the time of writing, the Financial Reporting Council (FRC) had tentatively decided to withdraw the FRSSE (see Chapter 4) and bring all small companies reporting under the FRSSE under the scope of FRS 102 by the inclusion of Section 1A *Small Entities* in FRS 102. Readers affected by the FRSSE are advised to keep abreast of developments in this area by regularly reviewing the FRC website at www.frc.org.uk.

Grants can only be recognised in profit or loss under the FRSSE (effective January 2015) when the conditions for the grant's receipt have been complied with and there is reasonable assurance that the grant will be received by the entity. However, if any of the grant is repayable (either wholly or in part), any repayment is first set off against any unamortised balance in deferred income, with the remainder being recognised in profit or loss. It is worth noting that if there is no unamortised balance left in deferred income, the entire repayment is recognised in profit or loss.

INTERACTION WITH THE COMPANIES ACT 2006

Paragraph 24.5G of FRS 102 addresses an issue that was not explicitly dealt with under the previous SSAP 4. SSAP 4 offered a choice of accounting for a capital-based grant (as does its international equivalent, IAS 20). Under SSAP 4 an entity could either recognise the deferred portion of the grant within liabilities as deferred income or it could choose to offset the grant against the cost of the related asset. Where the reporting entity chose the latter method, the grant would be recognised within profit or loss by way of reduced depreciation charges as the cost base used to calculate depreciable amount would be lower. However, the issue here was with the requirements of the Companies Act 2006 and the fact that the Companies Act prohibits grants from being offset against the cost or production price of an asset because the statutory definitions of 'purchase price' or 'production cost' make no provision for any deduction from such amounts in respect of a grant (the references are to paragraphs 17 and 27 of Schedule 1 to SI 2008/410 respectively).

This prohibition in the Companies Act 2006 seemingly only applies to entities that apply the Companies Act in the preparation of their financial statements (i.e. incorporated entities). The option in SSAP 4 to offset the grant against the cost of an asset would have been, on the face of it, eligible for non-incorporated entities (such as sole traders, partnerships and some entities in the public benefit sector). The overall impact on profit or loss due to this prohibition is, in fact, nil, as can be illustrated as follows.

Example – Capital-based grant: calculation of depreciation charges

A company purchases a new item of machinery for £100,000 funded out of cash and the directors have assessed the useful economic life of this machine to be five years with zero residual value at the end of this life. The company's accounting policy in respect of depreciation is to charge a full year in the year of acquisition and no depreciation in the year of disposal. The company received a government grant in respect of this machine for £30,000. The grant has initially been recorded in the books as follows:

Debit cash at bank	£30,000
Credit plant and machinery	£30,000

Being receipt of capital-based government grant

Under this accounting treatment, the annual depreciation charge in respect of this machine would be calculated as follows:

Cost	£100,000
Less government grant	£30,000
Depreciable amount	£70,000

The depreciation charge would therefore be £70,000 ÷ 5 years = £14,000 per annum.

However, the provisions in FRS 102 at paragraph 24.5G prohibit the above treatment (not simply for incorporated entities, but for all entities that apply FRS 102 in the preparation of their financial statements). As a consequence of this prohibition, the following would be required:

New machine	
Cost	£100,000
Depreciation charge	£100,000 ÷ 5 years = £20,000 per annum

Government grant	
£30,000 released over five years	£6,000 per annum

Net effect on profit and loss	
Depreciation charge	£20,000
Government grant released	£6,000)
Overall net charge to profit and loss	£14,000

Net effect on balance sheet	
Deferred income within one year	£6,000
Deferred income more than one year	£18,000

In the example above, there is no overall difference to the charges taken to the profit and loss account (income statement). It is still taking an overall charge of £14,000 – under FRS 102 (and the Companies Act 2006), all amounts are to be shown gross and no netting-off is to take place.

DISCLOSURE REQUIREMENTS

The disclosure requirements in respect of government grants are outlined in paragraph 24.6 of FRS 102 and are as follows.

An entity shall disclose the following:

(a) The accounting policy that the entity has adopted for grants in accordance with paragraph 24.4,
(b) The nature and amounts of grants that the entity has recognised in its financial statements,
(c) Any unfulfilled conditions and other contingencies attaching to grants that the entity recognised in income during the period and
(d) Any other forms of government assistance from which the entity has directly benefited.

For companies applying the FRSSE (effective January 2015), paragraph 6.57 requires the following information to be disclosed in the financial statements:

(a) The effects of government grants on the results for the period and/or the financial position of the entity and
(b) Where the results of the period are materially affected by the receipt of forms of government assistance (other than grants), the entity must disclose the nature of that assistance and, to the extent that the effects on the financial statements can be measured, an estimate of those effects.

Point to Note

The Financial Reporting Council (FRC) have intimated that there will be future changes to the way in which grants are accounted for. At the time of writing there was no indication as to when these changes were to be consulted upon, or when they may take effect, so users are advised to keep an eye on the FRC website to keep abreast of developments in this area.

17 FINANCIAL INSTRUMENTS

INTRODUCTION

FRS 102 *The Financial Reporting Standard applicable in the UK and Republic of Ireland* splits the accounting for basic financial instruments into two sections: Section 11 *Basic Financial Instruments* and Section 12 *Other Financial Instruments Issues*. This chapter combines both sections but the first section will deal with basic financial instruments, whilst the latter section of the chapter looks at more complex financial instruments.

Accounting for financial instruments has become increasingly complex over the years, due in large part to the complicated nature of certain instruments (for example, derivatives) and the diversity in which businesses operate and raise finance. An increase in emphasis on fair value accounting has also given rise to accounting for financial instruments becoming inherently more complex.

Whilst Section 11 deals with 'basic' financial instruments, the contents of the section are not easy to read or digest as the wording is quite complex in many areas. For the purposes of Section 11, the term 'basic' refers to those financial instruments that satisfy the conditions outlined in paragraph 11.8; 'other' financial instruments are those that are remaining.

In the broadest terms, a financial instrument is a contract that results in a financial asset arising in one entity and a financial liability arising in another. In other words, when one party wishes to raise finance for whatever reason, another party is the provider of that finance.

BASIC FINANCIAL INSTRUMENTS

Choice in accounting policy

FRS 102 offers entities a choice on how it should account for all its financial instruments, which are as follows:

- Under the provisions of Section 11 and Section 12 (if applicable) in full or
- Using the recognition and measurement provisions in EU-endorsed IAS 39 *Financial Instruments: Recognition and Measurement*/IFRS 9 *Financial Instruments* together with the disclosure requirements of Sections 11 and 12.

It is to be noted that as the use of IFRS 9 is via FRS 102, the UK's Financial Reporting Council has noted that EU endorsement is not relevant (EU endorsement had not taken place at the time of going to press). Several parts of Sections 11 and 12 are consistent with IFRS 9 (for example, the treatment of accounting for investments).

Whichever accounting policy an entity chooses in dealing with its financial instruments, it must ensure that the policy choice is consistent and is applied to all financial instruments that the entity is a party to.

Types of basic financial instrument

Section 11 gives examples of financial instruments that it considers would normally fall to be accounted for under the Section 11 provisions. In general practice, straightforward trade debtors, trade creditors and regular bank loans would be treated as basic financial instruments. Questions often arise in the context of Section 11 FRS 102 as to the accounting for current assets and current liabilities. These will be recorded in terms of the cash obligation due and hence there is no requirement for preparers to get involved with discounting. The examples that Section 11 gives as financial instruments, which would normally satisfy the criteria for recognition as basic financial instruments, include:

- Cash,
- Demand and fixed-term deposits in which the entity is the depositor,
- Commercial paper and commercial bills held,
- Accounts, notes and loans receivable and payable,
- Bonds and similar debt instruments,
- Investments in non-convertible preference shares and non-puttable ordinary and preference shares and
- Commitments to receive a loan and commitments to make a loan to another entity that meet the conditions outlined in paragraph 11.8(c) of FRS 102.

The following types of financial instruments would not normally fall to be classed as basic and therefore would normally be accounted for under the provisions in Section 12:

- Asset-backed securities, for example collateralised mortgage obligations, repurchase agreements and securitised packages of receivables,
- Options, rights, warrants, futures contracts, forward contracts and interest rate swaps that can be settled in cash or by exchanging another financial instrument,
- Financial instruments that qualify and are designated as hedging instruments in accordance with the requirements in Section 12 and
- Commitments to make a loan to another entity and commitments to receive a loan, if the commitment can be settled net in cash.

In order to determine whether a financial instrument is 'basic' and hence falls under the scope of Section 11, it is necessary to look to the conditions outlined in paragraph 11.8 of FRS 102. This paragraph says that an entity shall account for the following types of financial instruments as basic financial instruments in accordance with Section 11:

(a) Cash,
(b) A debt instrument (such as an account, note or loan receivable or payable) that meets the conditions outlined in paragraph 11.9 and that is not a financial instrument described in paragraph 11.6(b) (i.e. options, warrants, rights, futures contracts, forward contracts and interest rate swaps that can be settled in cash or by exchanging another financial instrument),
(c) Commitments to receive, or make, a loan to another entity, which:
    i. Cannot be settled net in cash and
    ii. When the commitment is executed, are expected to meet the conditions in paragraph 11.9 and
(d) An investment in non-convertible preference shares and non-puttable ordinary or preference shares.

The problems begin to emerge when it comes to (b) above, although the reality is that the conditions might only need to be consulted in complex situations because in practice it would be fairly obvious whether a debt instrument is 'basic' or 'complex'. However, the following conditions must be met in order for a debt instrument to fall to be classed as 'basic'.

Condition (a) Return to the holder (the lender)

The return that the holder (i.e. the lender) receives must be:

  i A fixed amount,
 ii A positive fixed rate of return or a positive variable rate of return or
iii A combination of a positive, or negative, fixed rate and a positive variable rate.

In respect of (iii) above, paragraph 11.9 cites an example of LIBOR plus 200 basis points or LIBOR less 50 basis points, but not 500 basis points less LIBOR. In other words, if the terms of the loan specified that the interest rate on the capital amount is calculated as 12-month LIBOR *less* 5% then this would not meet the definition of a basic financial instrument because both the fixed and the variable rates are not positive. As a consequence, the instrument would not be classed as a basic financial instrument accounted for at amortised cost but would fall to be classed as complex financial instruments and accounted for at fair value through profit or loss in accordance with Section 12.

Example – Bond paying a variable rate of return

A company issues a bond that pays a variable rate of return and is based on the profitability of the company.

This bond has a return that is not based on quoted, or observable, interest rates. As a result the bond is not a basic debt instrument and cannot be accounted for under Section 11. It would be accounted for under the provisions in Section 12.

1. Contractual provisions

The contract may contain provisions for repayments of the capital amount or the return the lender receives (but not both) to be linked to a single relevant observable index of general price inflation of the currency in which the debt instrument is denominated, provided such links are not leveraged.

2. Determinable variation of the return to the holder

The contract may contain provisions for a determinable variation of the return to the lender during the life of the instrument, provided that:

(a) The new rate satisfies condition (a) (i.e. the return to the lender above) and the variation is not contingent on future events other than:
  i. A change of a contractual variable rate,
  ii. To protect the lender against credit deterioration of the borrower,
  iii. Changes in levies applied by a central bank or arising from changes in relevant taxation or law or
(b) The new rate is a market rate of interest and satisfies condition (a) (i.e. the return to the lender above).

If the contract enables the lender a unilateral option to change the terms of the contract then these are not determinable for this purpose.

Example – Fixed-rate loan

Entity A enters into a fixed interest rate loan with its bank that has an initial tie-in period of three years. After this period, the interest rate reverts to the bank's standard variable interest rate.

The initial fixed rate is a return to the lender, which is permitted by paragraph 11.9(a) (ii). A bank's standard variable interest rate is an observable interest rate and, in accordance with the definition of a variable interest rate, is a permissible link. To comply with paragraph 11.9(a) (ii) of FRS 102, the variable rate should be a positive rate.

The variation of the interest rate after the tie-in period is not contingent on future events and since the new rate (i.e. the bank's standard variable rate) meets the condition of paragraph 11.9(a), paragraph 11.9(aB) (i) is met.

Example – Loan interest higher than the bank's standard variable rate

Entity B enters into a loan in which the interest is referenced to 2.5 times the bank's standard variable rate.

In accordance with the definition of a variable rate, the contractual interest rate payable can be linked to a single observable interest rate. A bank's standard variable rate is an observable rate and meets the definition of a variable rate; however, Entity B is paying interest at 2.5 times the bank's standard variable rate and the link to the observable interest rate is leveraged. Therefore, the rate in this example is not a variable rate as described in paragraph 11.9(a). The instrument is measured at fair value in accordance with Section 12.

Condition (b) Contract contains no detrimental provisions

The contract must not make any provisions that would result in the lender losing out on any amount of capital or interest attributable to the current or prior periods. If any class of debt is subordinate to other classes then this would not be an example of such a provision because the subordinate class would still be treated as a debt instrument.

Example – Interest in a debt instrument

A financial institution acquires the interest-only element of a loan that has been issued by one of its associates. The cash flows attributable to the capital element of the loan remain with the associate. Conditions in the transfer allow cash flows to be paid in advance of the predetermined date of maturity in the loan.

Paragraph 11.9(b) says that there should be no contractual provisions within the agreement that, by its terms, results in the holder of the instrument losing the principal amount. In this example the principal amount would be the amount that the entity paid to buy the interest-only element of the loan from the associate. If the borrower chooses to settle the loan earlier than the date of maturity, the financial institution may not recover its investment because it will not receive all the interest receipts that it has paid for on taking over the interest-only element of the loan. Because the financial institution could lose some, or all, of its original investment, the interest-only debt instrument cannot be accounted for under Section 11 and hence cannot use the amortised cost model. Instead, the financial institution must account for it as a complex financial instrument via Section 12 at fair value through profit or loss.

Condition (c) Contractual provisions that are beneficial to the lender

Where a contract allows the borrower to prepay a debt instrument, or the contract allows the lender to put it back to the borrower before maturity, then these conditions should not be contingent on future events. This can be overridden in certain situations, for example to protect:

(1) The lender against credit deterioration of the borrower (such as defaults, reduction in credit rating or violations in loan covenants) or a change in control of the borrower or
(2) The lender or borrower against changes in levies that are applied by a central bank or that arise due to changes in legislation (including tax legislation).

Example – Early repayment

Company A enters into a contract with Company B to borrow funds from Company A over a ten-year period. The contract makes provision that in the event of early termination, Company B will compensate Company A for the early termination.

Where a contract makes provisions for early termination, this will not result in a breach of this condition.

Condition (d) Extension of contractual terms

Provisions may exist within a contract that allow the term of the debt instrument to be extended. When this happens, any return to the lender and any other contractual provisions that apply during the extended term must satisfy the conditions in (a) to (c) above.

As can be seen from the above conditions, whilst Section 11 concerns *basic* financial instruments, the conditions that have to be met are not the easiest to comprehend. Fortunately only in complex cases will these provisions need to be consulted, but this is an area that accountants need to be aware of in the new UK GAAP.

Generally most debt instruments will have a fixed redemption date, although in some circumstances they can be repayable on demand (for example, a short-term loan) and such provisions will be determined by reference to the agreement between the parties. In addition, cash flows in relation to a debt instrument might not necessarily be fixed, as they could vary depending on circumstances (for example, variable interest rates).

FRS 102 was amended to open up the possibility of the 'basic' classification further so as not to require fair value measurement when the risk profit does not suggest it necessary. These amendments were included in FRS 102 published on 22 August 2014.

Recognition and measurement for basic financial instruments

An entity should only recognise a financial asset or a financial liability when the entity becomes a party to the contractual terms of the instrument.

Example – Planned transaction

An entity is planning on raising finance in the next six months by way of a mixture of share issues and a working capital loan. The finance director is proposing to recognise these transactions within the current period's financial statements as the future transactions are considered likely to occur in the opinion of the board of directors.

Planned future transactions, regardless of the likelihood of them occurring, cannot be recognised in the financial statements as assets or liabilities on the basis that the entity has not become a party to the transaction. Such transactions will give rise to assets or liabilities when the entity becomes a party to the transaction when contractual rights or acquired obligations have been incurred.

When the entity does become a party to the contractual terms and the instrument satisfies the criteria to be accounted for under Section 11 as a basic financial instrument, then the instrument is initially recognised at its transaction price. 'Transaction price' should also include transaction costs; transaction costs are those costs that are directly attributable to the acquisition of the debt instrument. The exception to this accounting is where the debt instrument is measured at fair value through profit or loss. In such cases transaction costs are not included in the initial measurement of the financial instrument, which can be illustrated using the following examples.

Example – Investment in a listed company

Company A acquires some equity shares in Company B. Company B is a listed company on a recognised stock market.

Company A should measure the investment in Company B at the cost of the investment *excluding* transaction costs, which should be recognised in profit or loss. After initial recognition, Company A should account for its investment in Company B at fair value through profit or loss.

The Companies Act 2006 allows investments in listed shares to be measured at either cost or fair value and so the impact of the above is that reporting entities will start to have movements in profit or loss.

Example – Investment in an unlisted company

Company C acquires some equity in Company D. Company D is a privately owned company and is not listed on a recognised stock market.

Company C should measure the investment in Company D at the cost of the investment *including* the incremental transaction costs. This is because (unlike in Company B's situation above) it will not be possible for Company C to obtain a reliable fair value of its investment in Company D at subsequent reporting dates.

Transaction costs that are expected to be incurred on the transfer or disposal of a financial instrument are not included in the initial or subsequent measure of the financial instrument.

Paragraph 11.13 then goes on to deal with financing transactions. A financing transaction might occur in relation to a sale of goods or services when it has been agreed that payment is to be deferred beyond normal business terms or is financed at a rate of interest that is not considered to be a market rate of interest. When these situations present themselves, the company must measure the financial asset or financial liability at the present value of the future payments discounted at a market rate of interest for a similar debt instrument.

Example – Loan to another entity

Fred is the sole director of Company E. He is very good friends with Bill who is the sole director of Company F. Bill's company is having a few cash flow difficulties due to a downturn in the market, so Fred agrees to make a long-term loan to Bill.

This represents a financing transaction and the financial statements of Company E will show a receivable (a debtor) in its financial statements that represents the present value, inclusive of interest payments and repayment of capital, of the amount receivable from Company F.

Example – Bank loan

In order to finance their working capital requirements before implementation of their expansion programme, Company G approaches their bank for a loan. The bank agrees to the loan at a market rate of interest and the proceeds are duly credited to Company G's bank account the day after the loan agreement is signed.

When an entity takes out a bank loan (or indeed any other form of loan), a payable (a creditor) is recognised in the balance sheet (statement of financial position). Under Section 11, this will be the present value of the cash payable to the bank (i.e. including interest payments and repayment of principal).

Example – Goods purchased from a supplier

Company H buys goods on normal credit terms from Company I. The terms of credit are 30 days from the date of the invoice.

For goods that are purchased from a supplier on normal (i.e. short-term) credit terms, a trade payable (trade creditor) is recognised at the undiscounted amount due to the supplier – in other words, at the invoice price. FRS 102 does not require any discounting to be applied in these respects (and this would also apply to normal trade debtors).

Amortised cost

After initial recognition, debt instruments that meet the conditions in paragraph 11.8(b) of FRS 102 are recognised at *amortised cost*. The term 'amortised cost' is the amount at which a financial asset or a financial liability is measured on initial recognition. Deducted from this amount are the principal repayments, plus or minus the cumulative amortisation using the *effective interest method* of any difference between the initial amount recognised and the amount at redemption. Deducted from this are any amounts in respect of uncollectibility or impairment losses.

When recognising financial instruments at amortised cost, the 'effective interest method' is used. This is a method of calculating the amortised cost of a financial instrument (or a group of financial instruments) and then allocating the interest income/expense over the life of the instrument(s). This method uses the *effective interest rate*, which is a rate that exactly discounts estimated future cash payments or receipts through the expected life of the instrument to the carrying value of the financial asset or financial liability. The method can be illustrated using the following example.

Example – Calculating amortised cost using the effective interest method

A company borrows £1 million on 1 January 2015 for a ten-year period by issuing loan notes. The lender charges an arrangement fee of £12,500. Interest is payable at a rate of 7% and this is payable annually starting at the inception of the loan. The redemption amount of the loan is at par at the end of year 10. The company has chosen not to prepay any of the loan amounts and the discount rate that would be necessary so as to be equivalent to 10 annual payments of £70,000 (i.e. £1 million × 7% per annum) plus the redemption amount at maturity of £1 million to the initial carrying value of £987,500 is 7.179%. The opening value is calculated as:

Primary amount of loan	£1,000,000
Less arrangement fee	(£12,500)
Carrying value at start of loan	£987,500

Using the amortised cost and effective interest method, the loan interest will be allocated to profit or loss over the life of the loan and will amount to £712,500, which is the total of the interest coupon plus the fee, as follows:

Date	Carrying amount at beginning of period £	Interest charge at 7.179% £	Cash out-flow £	Carrying amount at end of period £
1 Jan 2015	987,500	70,893	70,000	988,393
31 Dec 2015	988,393	70,957	70,000	989,350
31 Dec 2016	989,350	71,025	70,000	990,375
31 Dec 2017	990,375	71,099	70,000	991,474
31 Dec 2018	991,474	71,178	70,000	992,652
31 Dec 2019	992,652	71,262	70,000	993,914
31 Dec 2020	993,914	71,353	70,000	995,267
31 Dec 2021	995,267	71,450	70,000	996,717
31 Dec 2022	996,717	71,554	70,000	998,271
31 Dec 2023	998,271	71,729*	70,000	1,000,000
		712,500	700,000	
31 December 2024 = Repayment of principal amount of loan				(1,000,000)
Carrying value of the loan as at 31 December 2024				£nil

*Adjusted for rounding difference.

Financial instruments measured at cost

An entity can measure a financial instrument at cost as opposed to amortised cost. Such instruments can include unlisted investments where the fair value of such investments cannot be reliably estimated.

Fair value through profit or loss

An entity may choose, upon initial recognition, to designate debt instruments that satisfy the conditions in paragraph 11.8(b) and commitments to make and receive a loan that satisfies the conditions in paragraph 11.8(c) to designate such instruments at fair value through profit or loss. When this choice is applied the entity should have regard to paragraphs 11.27 and 11.32, which provide guidance on fair value. FRS 102 does impose conditions on designating basic financial instruments at fair value through profit or loss and in the light of such conditions an entity should only designate financial instruments at fair value through profit or loss because so doing:

- Eliminates, or significantly reduces, a measurement or recognition inconsistency (which is often referred to as an 'accounting mismatch') that would otherwise arise through measuring assets, debt instruments or recognising the gains on losses on which assets or debt instruments occur on a different basis or
- A group of debt instruments or a combination of financial assets and debt instruments is managed, and its performance evaluated, on a fair value basis as per the entity's documented risk management or investment strategy and information about the group is provided to the entity's key management personnel ('key management personnel' being defined in Section 33 *Related Party Disclosures*).

Example – Amortised cost or fair value designation

Gabriella Enterprises holds a bond that is traded in an active market. The bond has a fixed rate of interest and a fixed redemption date. On the redemption date the bond is to be repayable at par value.

The bond in this example is quoted in an active market; however, this does not prohibit the entity from classifying the bond as a basic financial instrument and hence accounting for it under the provisions of Section 11 at amortised cost. Conversely, Gabriella Enterprises may choose to designate the debt instrument at fair value through profit or loss on initial recognition, providing that so doing results in more relevant information being provided within the financial statements.

Investments in shares

The only financial instruments that fall within the scope of Section 11 and are measured at fair value are investments in non-convertible preference shares and non-puttable ordinary or preference shares where the shares are publicly traded and their fair value can otherwise be measured reliably. However, financial instruments that also fall within the scope of Section 12 should have regard to the fair value hierarchy contained in Section 11 (at paragraphs 11.27 to 11.32). This fair value hierarchy works as follows:

First priority	Obtain the best evidence of fair value from a quoted price for an identical asset in an active market. The quoted price is usually the bid price.
Second priority	If quoted prices are unavailable, the price of a recent transaction for an identical asset should be able to provide evidence of fair value provided there has not been a significant change in economic circumstances or a significant lapse of time since the transaction took place. The price is adjusted accordingly if the entity has evidence that the price is not a good estimate of fair value (for example, if it reflects the price paid in a distressed sale).
Third priority	Where there is no active market for the asset in question and recent transactions of an identical nature are not a good estimate of fair value, the entity should estimate fair value using a valuation technique.

Investments where the fair value cannot be measured reliably are carried at cost less impairment.

Valuation techniques

A market is considered to be active when transactions occur within it with sufficient frequency so as to provide reliable information on prices on a continuous basis. Where there is no active market on which to base the fair value of an asset, then the fair value hierarchy suggests the use of a valuation technique in order to arrive at a fair value. Such valuation techniques include the following:

- Recent arm's length market transactions,
- Reference to the current fair value of another asset that is substantially the same as the asset being measured,
- Discounted cash flow analysis or
- The use of option pricing models.

The objective of a valuation technique is to estimate what the transaction price would have been at the date of measurement in an arm's length transaction between knowledgeable and willing persons (i.e. in a transaction undertaken on normal commercial terms).

The transaction price that the valuation technique will arrive at must be a reasonable estimate of the instrument's fair value at the measurement date and it follows, therefore, that the valuation process must reflect how the market could be expected to price the instrument. To achieve this objective, the valuation process must use, as far as is practicable, market inputs and rely less on entity-specific inputs. In the broadest terms, the valuation process must consider all factors that market participants would consider in arriving at a price and be consistent with accepted methodologies for pricing financial instruments.

In reality, the valuation process is complex and the starting point for any valuation process is to consider the data that the entity itself has available that may help in the process. This data can be adjusted if it indicates that other market participants may use different data. In this respect, the entity does not have to go into significant depth to gather information regarding market participants' assumptions, but conversely the entity cannot ignore their assumptions when it is reasonably available.

Examples of valuation techniques include:

- Price/earning models,
- Discounted cash flows and
- Option pricing models.

In cases where there is a common valuation technique used by market participants to price the asset, and that technique has been demonstrated to provide reliable estimates of prices obtained in actual market transactions, then the entity should adopt the use of that technique.

In arriving at a fair value using a valuation technique, the entity would usually incorporate their own credit risk and hence the value should include the impact of own credit risk to the extent that credit risk affects the price for which the liability could be exchanged in an arm's length transaction.

Where derivatives are concerned (which are accounted for under Section 12), the entity would need to incorporate their own credit risk when the derivative instrument is in a liability position at the reporting date.

Impairment

Where the entity has financial assets in its statement of financial position (balance sheet) it should carry out an assessment at the end of each reporting period as to whether there is objective evidence of any impairment of those assets that are measured at cost or amortised cost. When the entity concludes that there is objective evidence that a financial asset is impaired then it should recognise an impairment loss within profit or loss immediately.

The following examples are indicators that a financial asset may be suffering from impairment at the reporting date (this list is not exhaustive or conclusive):

- The borrower is suffering from financial difficulties.
- There are arrears in repayments or capital and/or interest.
- The terms of the instrument have been renegotiated in situations that would not otherwise apply to other borrowers.
- It is likely that the borrower is going to file for bankruptcy or enter into other arrangements with its creditors.
- There is observable data that suggest there is a measurable decrease in the estimated future cash flows from the financial asset (or group of financial assets) since the initial recognition of that/those asset(s), even though the decrease cannot yet be identified with the individual financial asset(s) (in the group).
- Significant technological, market, economic or legal changes that have an adverse effect in the market in which the lender operates.

When undertaking an assessment of impairment, the entity must assess the following individually:

- All equity instruments, regardless of their significance and
- Other financial assets that are individually significant.

Measurement of an impairment loss

When a financial asset is measured at cost or amortised cost, the impairment is equivalent to the difference between the asset's carrying amount and the present value of estimated cash flows, which are discounted at the asset's original effective interest rate.

Example – Variable interest rate

A financial asset has a variable interest rate attached to it and the directors have concluded that the asset has suffered impairment during the year.

Where a financial instrument has a variable interest rate, the discount rate that the entity uses for measuring any impairment loss is the current effective interest rate determined under the contract.

When the financial asset is measured at cost less impairment the impairment loss is the difference between the carrying amount of the financial asset and the best esti- ' mate of the amount that the entity would receive for the financial asset if it were to be sold at the reporting date. The best estimate itself is an approximation and the amount the entity could receive at the reporting date may be zero.

Example – Impairment of a financial asset

A company purchases a debt instrument for £10,000, which is to be settled on maturity at a premium of £2,500 (i.e. £12,500) over a five-year period. The coupon rate of interest is 4.7% with interest of £590 being payable annually. The amortisation table in respect of the debt instrument is as follows:

Year	Opening amortised cost £	Finance cost £	Cash flow £	Closing amortised cost £
1	10,000	1,000	590	10,410
2	10,410	1,040	590	10,860
3	10,860	1,090	590	11,360
4	11,360	1,130	590	11,900
5	11,900	1,190	13,090*	–

*£12,500 + £590.

At the end of year 2, the amortised cost of the instrument is £10,860 and on this date the company concludes that the debt instrument has become impaired and no further interest payments will be received on this debt. The capital elements of the payments will continue to be paid.

The company calculates that the present value of the principal repayment in three years' time is £9,391 (£12,500/1.1^3).

The company will recognise an impairment loss of £1,469 (£10,860 less £9,391).

Reversal of an impairment

Reversals of previously recognised impairment losses can be recognised if the reduction in the previous impairment loss can be related objectively to an event occurring after the impairment loss was recognised. Paragraph 11.26 of FRS 102 gives an example of an improvement in the debtor's credit rating. However, care must be taken when dealing with a reversal of an impairment loss because the reversal of the previous impairment loss must not result in a carrying amount of the financial asset (net of any allowances) that exceeds what the carrying amount would have been had the impairment not been recognised.

Example – Reversal of an impairment loss

In the previous year's financial statements, Entity A had written down a financial asset to the recoverable amount for the purposes of impairment due to a reduction in the debtor's credit rating. Prior to the write-down, the financial asset was carried in the balance sheet (statement of financial position) at an amount of £11,000 and was written down to recoverable amount of £8,000. In the current financial year the debtor's credit rating was significantly upgraded and Entity A is proposing to reverse the whole impairment loss of £3,000 on the basis of the improved credit rating. Had the instrument not been written down at the end of the previous year, it would have been carried in the balance sheet at an amount of £10,000.

The maximum amount of the impairment reversal that the entity can recognise is £2,000. This is because paragraph 11.26 says that any reversal shall not result in a carrying amount of the financial asset (net of any allowance account) that exceeds what the carrying amount would have been had no impairment previously been recognised. Had no impairment been recognised, the instrument would have been carried in the balance sheet at £10,000 but was written down to £8,000. To reverse the entire £3,000 would result in the instrument being carried at £11,000, which is £1,000 more than it would have otherwise been carried at had no impairment loss been recognised.

DERECOGNITION OF BASIC FINANCIAL INSTRUMENTS

Derecognition of financial assets

There are strict derecognition criteria laid down in Section 11 that essentially focus on the risks and rewards of ownership of financial assets. Paragraph 11.33 says that a financial asset should be derecognised in an entity's financial statements if any of the following situations apply:

- The contractual rights to the cash flows have expired or are settled (e.g. a receipt of cash in settlement of the amount owing on a trade debtor) or
- The entity transfers to another party substantially all of the risks and rewards of ownership of the financial asset or
- The entity has retained some of the significant risks and rewards of ownership but has transferred control of the asset to another party which:
  - Has the practical ability to sell the asset in its entirety to another third party and
  - Is able to exercise that ability unilaterally, and without imposing additional restrictions on the transfer.

When the above conditions are met the entity is to derecognise the asset and separately recognise any rights and obligations retained or created in the transfer.

Example – Sales ledger sold to a finance house

A company sells its sales ledger on to a finance house. The terms of the sale say that the company has no responsibility for slow or non-payment of debts by its customers and that on collection the company must remit all monies collected promptly to the finance house. The sale proceeds are less than the par value of the debtors and the finance house pays a market rate for the collection/statement service provided by the company.

The company has rescinded all risks and rewards of ownership of the sales ledger to the finance house and therefore must derecognise the value of the trade debtors. No liability is recognised to the finance house in respect of the sales proceeds, but a liability is recognised to the finance house in respect of cash collected from debtors yet to be paid over by the reporting date.

As the proceeds from the sale of the sales ledger are less than the face value of the debtors, a loss is recognised in the income statement (profit and loss account), which represents the difference between the carrying amount of the trade debtors at the time of the sale and the proceeds received from the sale.

Section 11 only permits an entity to derecognise a financial asset when, essentially, the risks and rewards associated with the financial asset have been transferred. There may be situations when an entity receives consideration for a financial asset, but still retains significant risks and rewards associated with the asset. In such cases the financial asset will NOT qualify for derecognition.

Example – Risks and rewards retained

A company sells its sales ledger to a finance house for less than the par value of the trade debtors. The company collects monies from is debtors and then remits these funds to the finance house on a prompt basis. The terms of the sale make provision for the company to buy back any debtors that fall in arrears for more than 120 days.

In this example, the company has retained the significant risk of slow or non-payment. The company will not remove the trade debtors from its balance sheet because of this retention of risk and the proceeds from the finance house will be treated as a liability (i.e. as a loan).

Derecognition of financial liabilities

Paragraph 11.36 of FRS 102 requires a reporting entity to derecognise a financial liability (or part thereof) only when it is extinguished. This means that the obligation specific in the financial liability is discharged, cancelled or expires. Any difference that arises between the carrying value of the financial liability and the consideration paid (which also includes any non-cash assets transferred as part of the consideration or liabilities assumed) is recognised in profit or loss.

The offsetting of financial assets against financial liabilities can only take place in two specified situations, which are when the entity:

- Has a legally enforceable right to set off the recognised amounts and
- Intends either to settle on a net basis or to realise the asset and settle the liability simultaneously.

OTHER FINANCIAL INSTRUMENT ISSUES

This section of Chapter 17 takes a look at more complex financial instruments that do not fall to be accounted for under Section 11 and therefore fall under the scope of Section 12 *Other Financial Instruments Issues*. FRS 102 recognises that many companies nowadays tend to have more complicated financial instruments in their portfolio (for example, derivative financial instruments), which will need to be accounted for separately from those that are considered basic, and hence FRS 102 deals with complex financial instruments in a separate standard.

Notwithstanding the approach by FRS 102 to deal with certain instruments separately, the scope section of Section 12 does acknowledge that even if a company only has *basic* financial instruments, it must still consider the requirements in Section 12 to ensure that they are exempt from its scope.

Scope of Section 12

The scope of Section 12 does NOT cover the following:

1. Financial instruments that are covered by Section 11 *Basic Financial Instruments*.
2. Investments in subsidiaries (dealt with in Section 9 *Consolidated and Separate Financial Statements)*, investments in associates (dealt with in Section 14 *Investments in Associates*) and joint ventures (dealt with in Section 15 *Investments in Joint Ventures*).
3. Employers' rights and obligations under employee benefit plans (dealt with in Section 28 *Employee Benefits*).
4. Insurance contracts (including reinsurance contracts) that the entity issues and reinsurance contracts that the entity holds (dealt with in FRS 103 *Insurance Contracts*).
5. Financial instruments that meet the definition of an entity's own equity and the equity component of compound financial instruments issued by the reporting entity that contain both a liability and an equity component (dealt with in Section 22 *Liabilities and Equity*).
6. Leases, unless the lease could (as a result of non-typical contractual terms) result in a loss to the lessor or the lessee (otherwise they are dealt with in Section 20 *Leases*).
7. Contracts for contingent consideration in a business combination (dealt with in Section 19 *Business Combinations and Goodwill*). Although this exemption only applies to the acquirer.
8. Any forward contract between an acquirer and a selling shareholder to buy or sell an acquiree that will result in a business combination at a future acquisition date. The term of the forward contract should not exceed a reasonable period normally necessary to obtain any required approvals and to complete the transaction.
9. Financial instruments, contracts and obligations to which Section 26 *Share-based Payment* applies, except for contracts within the scope of paragraph 12.5.
10. Financial instruments issued by an entity with discretionary participation features (see FRS 103 *Insurance Contracts*).
11. Reimbursement assets accounted for in accordance with Section 21 *Provisions and Contingencies*.
12. Financial guarantee contracts (see Section 21).

Entities that have financial instruments in 4 or 10 above or hold the financial instruments in 4 above should apply FRS 103 to those insurance contracts.

The vast majority of contracts to purchase or sell a non-financial item such as a commodity, inventory or property, plant and equipment are excluded from the scope of Section 12 as they are not financial instruments. However, Section 12 does apply to all contracts to buy or sell non-financial items and hence would apply to contracts that (due to contractual terms) could result in a loss to the buyer or seller that is unrelated to changes in the price of the non-financial item, changes in foreign exchange rates or a default by one of the counterparties.

In addition to the above, Section 12 applies to contracts to buy or sell non-financial items if the contract can be settled net in cash or another financial instrument, or by exchanging financial instruments as if the contracts were financial instruments, with the exception of contracts that were entered into, and continue to be held, for the purpose of the receipt or delivery of a non-financial item in accordance with the entity's expected purchase, sale or usage requirements.

Section 12 itself is a relatively short section (spanning to just over six pages long) – however, the issues that are dealt with in this short section are complicated and in many places lack guidance. As a result of this lack of guidance, it is important that preparers of financial statements read it in conjunction with Section 11 (as the two essentially go hand in hand) together with the relevant parts of the Companies Act 2006.

Section 11 and Section 12 are closely related and whilst Section 12 only deals with financial instruments that are NOT basic, Section 11 gives examples of financial instruments that it considers to be within the scope of Section 12 – i.e. complex financial instruments – and includes:

- Asset-backed securities, such as collateralised mortgage obligations, repurchase agreements and securitised packages of receivables,
- Options, rights, warrants, futures contracts, forward contracts and interest rate swaps that can be settled in cash or by exchanging another financial instrument,
- Financial instruments that qualify and are designated as hedging instruments in accordance with the requirements of Section 12 and
- Commitments to make a loan to another entity and commitments to receive a loan if the commitment can be settled in cash.

In addition, paragraph 11.11 also requires the following to be accounted for in accordance with Section 12:

- An investment in another entity's equity instruments, other than non-convertible preference shares and non-puttable ordinary and preference shares and
- Investments in convertible debt, because the return to the holder can vary with the price of the issuer's equity shares rather than just with market interest rates.

Accounting policy choice

In respect of financial instruments that fall under the scope of Section 12, an entity can choose to apply one of the following accounting policy options:

1. The provisions of both Section 11 and Section 12 in full or
2. The recognition and measurement provisions of EU-endorsed IAS 39 *Financial Instruments: Recognition and Measurement* and the disclosure requirements of Section 11 and Section 12 or
3. The recognition and measurement provisions of IFRS 9 *Financial Instruments* and/or IAS 39 (as amended following the publication of IFRS 9) and the disclosure requirements of Sections 11 and 12.

When the entity chooses options 2 or 3 above, it applies the scope of the relevant standard to all its financial instruments. The choice of 1, 2 or 3 above is an entity's accounting policy choice and hence the provisions within Section 10 *Accounting Policies, Estimates and Errors* is relevant in this respect (notably paragraphs 10.8 to 10.14), which contain requirements for determining when a change in accounting policy is appropriate, how such a change should be dealt with in the financial statements and what information the entity should disclose in its financial statements relating to the change in accounting policy.

An important point to emphasise is that whatever choice the entity makes, that accounting policy must be applied to *all* of the entity's financial instruments. IAS 39 (and IFRS 9) are very complicated standards (notwithstanding IAS 39's eventual transition to IFRS 9, which is intended to be a simpler standard to apply) and in the rare circumstance that an entity is contemplating making the IAS 39/IFRS 9 choice it must undertake a thorough and comprehensive review of its financial instruments before committing to such a choice. This can be illustrated using the following example.

Example – Entity considering the IAS 39 option

An entity has a combination of both basic and complex financial instruments and is considering the accounting policy to adopt for the measurement of its financial instruments. The finance director understands that one of the options available in FRS 102 is to apply the provisions in EU-adapted IAS 39.

If the entity were to choose the IAS 39 option, then it would have to account for all of its financial instruments (which includes both basic and complex) using this option. Taking this example one step further, if the entity has (for example) some publicly traded fixed asset equity investments where the fair value can be measured reliably (by reference to the stock market), then changes in this fair value under EU-endorsed IAS 39 would be recognised in other comprehensive income because the investment would fall to be classified as 'available for sale'. If the entity were to opt for the accounting policy choice in paragraph 12.2(a) and hence apply the provisions in Section 11 and Section 12, then the fair value changes in the investment would be taken through profit or loss.

The example above highlights the importance of an entity giving careful and thorough thought to its chosen accounting policy for financial instruments and to make sure that the policy chosen is appropriate and relevant in the entity's circumstances.

Recognition and measurement of more complex financial instruments

Likewise with Section 11, only when the entity becomes a party to the contractual provisions of a financial instrument can it recognise a financial asset or a financial liability.

Under the provisions in Section 12, when a financial asset or financial liability is initially recognised, it is measured at its fair value, which is normally the transaction price including transaction costs (transaction costs being the incremental costs that are directly attributable to the acquisition, issue or disposal of a financial asset or financial liability, or the issue or reacquisition of an entity's own equity instruments).

Example – Deferred transaction cost

> Entity A becomes a party to a financial instrument (a financial asset) with Entity B. The terms of the contract allow for a maturity date in three years' time, which is considered to be beyond normal business terms for an instrument of this nature.
>
> If payment for an asset is deferred beyond normal business terms, Entity A must measure the asset at the present value of future payments. These are discounted at a market rate of interest for a similar debt instrument.

Example – Transaction costs EXCLUDED

> A financial instrument qualifies as being measured at fair value as the instrument is publicly traded on a recognised stock market and hence subsequent changes in this fair value are taken through profit or loss.
>
> To comply with the requirements of paragraph 12.7, the financial accountant dealing with this transaction has included the transaction costs on initial recognition of the financial instrument.
>
> Whilst paragraph 12.7 does require transaction costs to be included in the transaction price, the initial measurement of financial assets and liabilities, which are measured at fair value through profit or loss, should not include the transaction costs. These should be expensed to profit or loss.

Subsequent measurement

After initial recognition, all financial instruments that fall under the scope of Section 12 are measured at fair value through profit or loss. There are, however, two exceptions to this rule:

- Equity instruments that are not publicly traded and whose fair value cannot otherwise be reliably measured. This also includes contracts that are linked to such instruments, which, if exercised, will result in the delivery of such instruments. These types of instruments are to be measured at cost less impairment.
- Hedging instruments (for example, forward foreign currency contracts and interest rate swaps) that are in a designated hedging relationship where hedge accounting is adopted.

Example – Fair value no longer available

> A financial instrument was publicly traded until half-way through the financial year. At the year-end, the entity was unable to obtain a reliable measure of fair value as no active market existed at the year-end.

In this example, where a reliable measure of fair value is no longer available, its fair value at the last date the instrument was reliably measurable is treated as the cost of the instrument. The entity should, therefore, measure the instrument at this cost less impairment until a reliable measure of fair value becomes available (if at all).

In the example above, the fair value of the financial instrument was not available at the year-end and so was measured at its last reliable fair value. This can also apply to an instrument (or a contract linked to such an instrument) that is not publicly traded.

Determination of fair value

As discussed earlier in the chapter, fair value is determined by reference to Section 11 using the fair value hierarchy outlined in paragraph 11.27 of FRS 102, which is illustrated as follows for the purposes of this section:

First priority	Obtain the best evidence of fair value from a quoted price for an identical asset in an active market. The quoted price is usually the bid price.
Second priority	If quoted prices are unavailable, the price of a recent transaction for an identical asset should be able to provide evidence of fair value provided there has not been a significant change in economic circumstances or a significant lapse of time since the transaction took place. The price is adjusted accordingly if the entity has evidence that the price is not a good estimate of fair value (for example, if it reflects the price paid in a distressed sale).
Third priority	Where there is no active market for the asset in question and recent transactions of an identical nature are not a good estimate of fair value, the entity should estimate fair value using a valuation technique.

Derivative financial instruments

As discussed at the start of this chapter, FRS 102 splits financial instruments into two portions: 'basic' and 'other'. The 'other' category will include instruments such as foreign exchange forward contracts and loans with complicated terms as well as derivative financial instruments. Under the previous UK GAAP, many of these instruments were not recognised on the balance sheets (statements of financial position) of reporting entities but were instead disclosed. Under FRS 102, such instruments are required to be brought on to the balance sheets of reporting entities and measured at fair value, with fluctuations in fair value going through profit or loss. Hence the balance sheet position and reported profits (or losses) of entities that previously did not apply FRS 26 *Financial Instruments: Recognition and Measurement* will change and the changes may be significant in some cases.

In respect of derivative financial instruments, assuming FRS 26 was not adopted, derivative financial instruments were previously accounted for on settlement, but under FRS 102 they will be recognised earlier. In some cases, an entity may not be aware that they are, in fact, carrying derivative financial instruments in the form of interest rate swaps, options, foreign exchange contracts or hedges that the banks may have incorporated into their financing agreements. In some cases this may not apply to companies falling under the scope of Section 12, but finance agreements must be carefully scrutinised to check if they do, in fact, involve derivative financial instruments, because this will complicate matters further and involve the use of Section 12 provisions.

A derivative financial instrument is a contract that possesses all three of the following characteristics:

(a) The value of the instrument changes in response to changes in an interest rate, financial instrument price, commodity price, foreign exchange rate, price index, price rate, credit rating, credit index or some other variable, provided in the case of a non-financial variable where the variable is not specific to a party to the contract.

(b) There is no initial net investment needed, or the initial net investment is smaller than would otherwise be the case for other types of contracts that would be expected to have a similar response to changes in market factors.

(c) The instrument is to be settled at a future date.

The following table highlights examples of financial instruments that would meet the definition of a derivative financial instrument, together with the underlying variable:

Type of contract	Underlying variable
Interest rate swap	Interest rates
Foreign exchange swap	Currency rates
Commodity swap	Commodity prices
Share swap	Share prices
Credit swap	Credit rating or credit price
Treasury bond option (call or put)	Interest rates
Currency option (call or put)	Currency rates
Commodity option (call or put)	Commodity prices
Interest rate futures linked to government debt (treasury futures)	Interest rates
Currency futures	Currency rates
Commodity futures	Commodity prices
Currency forward	Currency rates

Example – Derivative financial instrument

Company A enters into a contract that requires it to pay Company B £20,000 if the share price of Company C rises by £5 per share or more during a six-month period. Conversely, Company A will receive £20,000 if the share price of Company C declines by £5 per share during that same six-month period. If price changes are within the ± range, no payments will be made or received by either party.

This arrangement would qualify as a derivative financial instrument – the underlying variable being the share price of Company C.

Example – Accounting for a derivative financial instrument (call option)

Company A purchased a call option on 2 January 2016 when the shares in Company B were trading at £100 per share. The contract gives Company A the option to purchase 1,000 shares in Company B at an option price of £100 per share and the option expires on 30 April 2016. The call option is purchased by Company A for a sum of £400.

On acquisition of the call option, Company A will record the transaction as:

DR call option   £400
CR cash   £400

This payment is generally known as the 'option premium' and is usually much less than the cost of purchasing the shares directly. The option premium consists of the 'intrinsic value' and the 'time value'. The intrinsic value is the difference between the market price and the strike price at any point in time. It represents the amount realised by the holder of the call option if exercising the option immediately. When Company A purchases the option, the intrinsic value will be zero because the market price equals the strike price.

The time value refers to the option's value over and above its intrinsic value. The time value reflects the possibility that the option has a fair value greater than zero. This is because there is some expectation that the price of B's shares will increase above the strike price during the term of the option and therefore the time value for the option is £400 as there is no intrinsic value.

On 31 March 2016, the price of B's shares increases to £120 per share. The intrinsic value of the call option is now £20,000. This is because Company A can exercise the call option and purchase 1,000 shares from Company B for £100 per share and it can then subsequently sell those shares in the market for £120 per share. This results in a gain for Company A of £20,000 (£120,000 less £100,000) on the option contract. The increase in the intrinsic value is as follows:

DR call option   £20,000
CR profit and loss   £20,000

A market appraisal indicates that the time value of the option as at 31 March 2016 is £100. Company A records this change in value of the option as follows:

DR profit and loss   £300
CR call option   £300 (£400 less £100)

The settlement of the call option contract is recorded as follows:

DR cash   £20,000
DR loss on settlement   £100
CR call option   £20,100

Example – Directors' personal guarantees

The directors of Company A have entered into personal guarantees with the company's bank for the company's liabilities, which require the directors to pay the bank an amount of £50,000 each if the company is to cease trading whilst its loans are in subsistence.

The question arises as to whether these personal guarantees for the company's borrowings given by the directors would be viewed as a financial instrument valued at fair value?

The personal guarantee would not be a financial instrument from the company's perspective because the guarantee is between the directors and the bank, but the personal guarantees would clearly be a disclosable transaction under the provisions in Section 33 *Related Party Disclosures*.

Example – Forward foreign currency contract

Daniels' Disposable Clothing buys and sells disposable clothing throughout the world. It has sourced a new supplier in Spain that can supply the disposable clothing cheaper than its existing supplier. The directors have agreed to the company purchasing a one-off order from this supplier to corroborate the quality of the supplier's products. The order was placed on 30 December 2015 at which point Daniels' Disposable Clothing entered into a forward contract with the bank to purchase €500 on the delivery date of 30 June 2016 at a rate of €1.5 to £1. Daniels' Disposable Clothing has a year-end date of 31 December 2015. Delivery of the goods has been agreed to take place on 30 April 2016.

The company does not apply hedge accounting and the company will account for the derivative financial instrument (the forward foreign currency contract) therefore at fair value through profit or loss. The company's bank has provided fair values for the derivate contract as follows:

At 31 December 2015   £3
At 30 June 2016   £37

The historical cost of the derivative on inception of the forward foreign currency contract is assumed to be £nil.

Spot rates of exchange on delivery and on settlement of the supplier are assumed.
The derivative financial instrument will be accounted for as follows:

		DR	CR
30.12.15	Derivative	0	
	Cash		0
	Historical cost of the forward foreign currency contract (the derivative instrument)		
31.12.15	Derivative	3	
	Profit and loss		3
	Increase in fair value of the derivative instrument		
30.04.16	Property, plant and equipment	350	
	Trade creditors		350
	Cost price of goods at spot rate of 1.43 (€500/1.43)		

30.06.16	Trade creditors	350	
	Profit and loss	20	
	Cash		370

Settlement of supplier at spot rate of 1.35 (€500/1.35)

| 30.06.16 | Derivative | 34 | |
| | Profit and loss account | | 34 |

Increase in fair value of derivative between 01.01.16 and 30.06.16*

| 30.06.16 | Cash | 37 | |
| | Derivative | | 37 |

Settlement under the forward contract**

*Fair value of derivative at 30.06.16 = £37 (£3 + £34).
**Difference between €500 at spot rate 1.35 and contract rate of 1.5.

Derecognition of financial instruments

The derecognition provisions of financial statements accounted for under Section 12 are the same as those outlined in paragraphs 11.33 to 11.38 and so these paragraphs apply when derecognising a financial instrument accounted for under Section 12.

HEDGE ACCOUNTING

On 23 July 2014, the Financial Reporting Council issued amendments to FRS 102, which amended the criteria that determined the classification of whether a financial instrument would fall to be classed as 'basic'. Under the revised FRS 102, derivatives such as interest rate swaps, forward contracts and option contracts would not be considered 'basic' financial instruments and would therefore be measured at fair value through profit or loss. These amendments essentially replaced the restrictive hedge accounting requirements of FRS 102 with a revised set of hedge accounting principles that were based on the hedge accounting model in IFRS 9 *Financial Instruments*. The amendments allow more opportunities for entities applying FRS 102 in their financial statements to apply hedge accounting.

The amendments also replaced the requirement that an entity must expect the hedging instrument to be 'highly effective' in offsetting the hedged risk in order to be able to apply hedge accounting. The revisions instead require there to be an 'economic relationship between the hedged item and the hedging instrument'.

The requirement to apply hedge accounting is an accounting policy option – it is not mandatory to use hedge accounting. In the broadest terms, a company might decide to opt for hedge accounting to mitigate its exposure to risk (for example, foreign currency risk). A point worth emphasising at the outset where hedge accounting is concerned is that FRS 102 (and EU-endorsed IFRSs) contain strict criteria for the use of hedge accounting and in some cases an entity might not be able to adopt hedge accounting simply because it cannot meet the demanding criteria. A hedging relationship will qualify for hedge accounting only if all of the following conditions are met:

- Within the hedging relationship are a hedged instrument and a hedged item described in paragraphs 12.16 to 12.17C of FRS 102,
- The hedging relationship is consistent with the risk management objectives of the entity for undertaking hedges,
- An economic relationship exists between the hedged item and the hedging instrument,
- The hedging relationship has been documented so that the risk being hedged, the hedged item and the hedging instrument are clearly identified and
- The entity has determined and documented causes of hedge ineffectiveness.

The hedging documentation referred to above should be prepared at the inception of the hedge because hedge accounting will only apply from the date on which all the conditions above are met.

Essentially hedge accounting recognises the offsetting effects on profit or loss of fair value fluctuations of the hedging instrument and the hedged item so that both the hedged item and the hedging instrument are recognised in the same accounting period. The idea behind this concept is to reduce volatility of earnings between accounting periods.

Example – Forward foreign exchange contract

The Happy Holiday Company enters into a forward foreign currency contract so as to hedge against foreign exchange risk in respect of committed foreign purchases, which are expected to take place in the subsequent financial year.

If the holiday company did not apply hedge accounting, then the gain on loss on the derivative instrument would be recognised in profit or loss in the current period, whilst the foreign exchange gain or loss on the purchases would be recognised in the subsequent accounting period.

A 'hedged item' can be a recognised asset or liability, an unrecognised firm commitment, a highly probable forecast transaction or a net investment in a foreign operation. Alternatively, a hedged item might also be a component of such items. A key provision where these items are concerned is that the hedged item must be reliably measurable.

There are four conditions outlined in paragraph 12.16B that have to be met before a group of items, including components of items, can be eligible to be classed as a hedged item:

- It consists of items that are individually eligible hedged items,
- The items within the group share the same risks,
- The items within the group are managed together on a group basis for the purposes of risk management and
- It does not include items with offsetting risk positions.

Types of hedging relationship

FRS 102 identifies three types of hedging relationship.

Fair value hedge

A fair value hedge is a hedge of the exposure to the changes in the fair value of a recognised asset or recognised liability. A fair value hedge can also be a hedge of the exposure in the fair value of an unrecognised firm commitment, or a component of any such item, that is attributable to a particular risk that could affect reported profit or loss of an entity.

From the date on which the four conditions above are met, an entity will account for a fair value hedge as follows:

1. Gains or losses arising on the hedging instrument are to be recognised in profit or loss and
2. The hedging gain or loss on the hedged item will adjust the carrying value of the hedged item (where applicable) and this will also be recognised in profit or loss. In respect of a hedged item of an unrecognised firm commitment, the cumulative hedging gain or loss on the hedged item is recognised as an asset or a liability and the corresponding gain or loss is recognised in profit or loss.

If the unrecognised firm commitment referred to in 2 above is the hedged item, then the initial carrying value of the asset or liability that results from the entity meeting the firm commitment is adjusted so as include the cumulative hedging gain or loss of the hedged item that was recognised in the balance sheet (statement of financial position).

In addition, where an adjustment referred to in 2 above takes place and the hedged item is a financial instrument that is measured at amortised cost, then the adjustment is amortised to profit or loss. Paragraph 12.22 requires such amortisation to take place as soon as the adjustment exists and amortisation is to begin no later than when the hedged item ceases to be adjusted for hedging gains and losses and is based on a recalculated effective interest rate at the date amortisation commences.

Cash flow hedge

A cash flow hedge is a hedge of the exposure to variability in cash flows that is attributable to a particular risk associated with all, or a component of a, recognised asset or liability or a highly probable forecast transaction that could affect reported profit or loss. An example of a cash flow hedge is a hedge against exposure to variability of some future interest payments on a variable-rate debt.

Accounting for cash flow hedges is quite in-depth and in respect of such hedges once the conditions outlined in the four bullets above are met, a cash flow hedge is accounted for as follows:

(a) The separate component of equity (i.e. the cash flow hedge reserve) is adjusted to the *lower* of the following in absolute amounts:

    i. The cumulative gain or loss on the hedging instrument from the date the conditions in paragraph 12.18 of FRS 102 are met and

    ii. The cumulative change in fair value on the hedged item, which is the present value of the cumulative change of expected future cash flows from the date on which the conditions in paragraph 12.18 are met,

(b) That portion of the gain or loss on the hedging instrument that is effective is recognised in other comprehensive income,

(c) Any remaining gain or loss on the hedging instrument or any gain or loss that is required to balance the change in the cash flow hedge reserve calculated in accordance with (a) above is considered to be hedge ineffectiveness and is recognised in profit or loss and

(d) The amount accumulated in the cash flow hedge reserve is accounted for as follows:

    i If a hedged forecast transaction results in the recognition of a non-financial asset or non-financial liability or a hedged forecast transaction for a non-financial asset/liability subsequently becomes a firm commitment for which fair value hedge accounting is applied, the entity must remove that amount from the cash flow hedge reserve and include it directly in the initial cost or other carrying value of the asset or liability,

    ii. For other cash flow hedges (i.e. those not covered in (i) above), that amount is reclassified from the cash flow hedge reserve to profit or loss in the same period(s) during which the hedged expected cash flows affect profit or loss and

    iii. Where the amount is a loss that is not expected to be recovered, the amount of the loss not expected to be recovered is reclassified to profit or loss immediately.

Hedge of a net investment in a foreign operation

An example of a hedge of a net investment in a foreign operation would be where an entity issues debt in a foreign currency or enters into a forward exchange contract so as to hedge the risk of foreign currency exchange gains and losses on the net investment.

Accounting for hedges of a net investment in a foreign operation are accounted for similarly to cash flow hedges from the date on which the conditions in paragraph 12.18 are met:

- The portion of the gain or loss that is considered effective is recognised in other comprehensive income and
- Any ineffective portion is recognised in profit or loss.

Cumulative gains or losses on the hedging instrument that relate to the effective portion in equity are not reclassified to profit or loss on disposal, or partial disposal, of the foreign operation.

Example – Hedge of a foreign exchange risk

Entity A Limited wishes to purchase a machine from its supplier based in Austria at a cost of €500. Entity A has arranged for delivery to take place on 30 April 2016 with payment to be made on 30 June 2016.

Entity A enters into a forward foreign currency contract on 1 December 2015 for the purchase of €500 on 30 June 2016. The rate in the forward contract is €1.50:£1 and Entity A has a year-end of 31 December 2015.

The forecast transaction is considered to be highly probable and the relationship meets the criteria for hedge accounting to be applied.

Fair values for the derivative are as follows:

31 December 2015	£3
30 June 2016	£37

Under hedge accounting, Entity A will record the transaction as follows:

		DR £	CR £
1.12.15	Derivative (forward foreign currency contract)	0	
	Cash		0
	Fair value of the derivative at inception of the contract		
31.12.15	Derivative	3	
	Other comprehensive income		3
	Increase in fair value of the derivative at year-end		
30.04.16	Property, plant and equipment	350	
	Trade payables		350
	Fixed asset addition €500 @ 1.43		
30.06.16	Trade payables	350	
	Profit or loss	20	
	Cash		370
	Settlement of supplier invoice €500 @ 1.35		
30.06.16	Derivative	34	
	Other comprehensive income		34
	Increase in fair value of derivative at settlement		
30.06.16	Cash	37	
	Derivative		37
	Settlement under forward foreign currency contract		

The gain above is recycled into profit or loss in the same period(s) that the asset affects profit or loss (i.e. through the charging of depreciation on the acquired asset).

Discontinuation of hedge accounting

An entity must cease the application of hedge accounting when:

(a) The hedging instrument has expired, is sold, terminated or exercised or
(b) The conditions in paragraph 12.18 of FRS 102 can no longer be met.

When an entity ceases to apply hedge accounting, it does so prospectively.

Where the entity ceases to apply fair value hedges, the cessation is accounted for under the provisions in paragraph 12.22 (i.e. adjustments are amortised to profit or loss if the hedged item is a financial instrument measured at amortised cost). Amortisation is based on a recalculated effective interest rate at the date amortisation commences.

Where cash flow hedges are discontinued, the amount accumulated in the cash flow hedge reserve within equity are reclassified to profit or loss immediately. However, if the future hedged items are still expected to occur then the cumulative gain or loss in the cash flow hedge reserve is dealt with in accordance with paragraph 12.23(d).

For a net investment hedge the portion of the gain or loss on the hedging instrument that is determined to be effective is recognised in other comprehensive income with any ineffective portions being recognised in profit or loss. The amount accumulated in equity is not reclassified to profit or loss.

DISCLOSURE REQUIREMENTS: FINANCIAL INSTRUMENTS

The disclosures below are effectively the same for both basic financial instruments and other financial instruments (unless hedge accounting is used and hence there will be additional disclosures required).

Accounting policies

The entity must disclose its accounting policies in respect of the measurement basis (bases) used for its financial instruments together with other accounting policies used for financial instruments so as to enable a better understanding of the financial statements.

Items recognised in the statement of financial position (balance sheet)

The carrying amounts of the following categories of financial assets and financial liabilities in total should be disclosed either on the face of the balance sheet (statement of financial position) or in the notes to the financial statements:

(a) Financial assets measured at fair value through profit or loss,
(b) Financial assets classed as debt instruments measured at amortised cost,
(c) Financial assets classed as equity instruments measured at cost less impairment,
(d) Financial liabilities measured at fair value through profit or loss (showing separately any financial liabilities not held as part of a trading portfolio, which are also not derivatives),

(e) Financial liabilities measured at amortised cost and

(f) Loan commitments measured at cost less impairment.

Information should also be disclosed that will enable the users to evaluate the significance of financial instruments on the entity's financial position and performance.

For financial assets and financial liabilities measured at fair value, the entity must disclose the basis for determining fair value, whether this be in an active market or through the use of a valuation technique.

Where a valuation technique has been used, the entity must disclose the assumptions applied in determining fair value for each class of financial assets or financial liabilities.

Where a reliable measure of fair value is no longer available for ordinary or preference shares, which are measured at fair value through profit or loss, the entity must disclose this fact.

If the entity is within a group and the disclosures above are included in the consolidated financial statements, then provided the entity is not a financial institution, the group member will be exempt from disclosing information in its own financial statements for most financial instruments.

Derecognition

Where the entity has transferred financial assets to a third party and the criteria for derecognition are not met, the entity must disclose the following information for each class of such assets:

(a) The nature of the assets,

(b) The nature of the risks and rewards of ownership to which the entity remains exposed and

(c) The carrying amount of the assets and of any associated liabilities that the entity continues to recognise.

Collateral

If the entity has pledged any financial assets as collateral for liabilities (including contingent liabilities), the entity must disclose:

(a) The carrying amount of the financial assets that have been pledged as collateral and

(b) The terms and conditions that relate to that pledge.

Defaults

Where there has been a breach in the terms for loans payable or a default in the payment of capital, interest, sinking fund or redemption terms that have not been remedied by the reporting date, the entity must make the following disclosures:

(a) Details of the breach or default,

(b) The carrying amount of the related loan creditor at the reporting date and

(c) Whether the breach or default was remedied or the terms of the loans payable were renegotiated before the financial statements were authorised for issue.

Income, expense gains or losses

An entity must make the following disclosures in respect of items of income, expense, gains or losses:

(a) Income, expense, net gains or net losses, including changes in fair value that have been recognised on:
    i. Financial asses measured at fair value through profit or loss,
    ii. Financial liabilities measured at fair value through profit or loss (separate disclosure is needed of movements on those financial liabilities that are not held as part of a trading portfolio and are not classified as derivative instruments),
    iii. Financial assets measured at amortised cost and
    iv. Financial liabilities measured at amortised cost.

(b) Total interest income and interest expense calculated using the effective interest method for both financial assets and financial liabilities that are not measured at fair value through profit or loss and

(c) The amount of any impairment loss recognised for each class of financial asset.

Financial instruments at fair value through profit or loss

For financial instruments at fair value through profit or loss that are not held as part of a trading portfolio and are not derivative financial instruments, the entity should disclose:

(a) The amount of the change in fair value during the period that is due to changes in credit risk of the instrument, determined either:
    i. As the amount of change in fair value not attributable to changes in market conditions that give rise to market risk or
    ii. Using an alternative method that the reporting entity believes to more faithfully represent the amount of change in the instrument's fair value from changes in the credit risk of the instrument.

(b) The method that the entity has used to establish the amount of change related to changes in own credit risk or, if the change cannot be reliably measured or is not material, that fact.

(c) The difference between the financial liability carrying value and the amount that the entity would be contractually required to pay at the redemption date to the holder of the liability.

(d) If the liability is a compound financial instrument (i.e. contains a mix of debt and equity) and has multiple features that substantially modify the cash flows and the values of those features are interdependent, then the entity must disclose the existence of those features.

(e) Any difference between the fair value on initial recognition and the amount that would be determined at that date using a valuation technique together with the amount that has been recognised in profit or loss.

(f) Other information that will enable the users of the financial statements to evaluate the effect of relevant risks that arise from financial instruments that the entity is exposed to at the reporting date. This can include, but is not limited to, credit risk, market risk and liquidity risk. The disclosures made by the entity should include how the entity manages those risks and the entity's exposure to those risks.

Financial institutions

If the reporting entity is a financial institution (which is not a retirement plan) additional disclosures contained in paragraph 34.17 of FRS 102 will also have to be made.

For retirement benefit plans, additional disclosures contained in paragraphs 34.39 to 34.48 are needed.

DISCLOSURE REQUIREMENTS: HEDGE ACCOUNTING

For each type of hedging relationship, a reporting entity should disclose:

(a) A description of the hedge,
(b) A description of the financial instruments that have been designated as hedging instruments and their fair values at the reporting date and
(c) The nature of the risks that are being hedged together with a description of the hedged item.

Fair value hedge

Where the entity uses a fair value hedge, it should disclose:

(a) The amount of change in fair value of the hedging instrument recognised in profit or loss for the period.
(b) The amount of the change in fair value of the hedged item that has been recognised in profit or loss for the period.

Cash flow hedge

Where the entity uses a cash flow hedge, it should disclose:

(a) The periods when the cash flows are expected to occur as well as when they are expected to affect profit or loss.
(b) A description of any forecast transaction for which hedge accounting had previously been applied but which is no longer expected to occur.
(c) The amount of the change in fair value of the hedging instrument that has been recognised in other comprehensive income during the reporting period.
(d) The amount, if any, that has been reclassified from equity to profit or loss for the period.
(e) The amount, if any, of any excess of the fair value of the hedging instrument over the change in the fair value of the expected cash flows that have been recognised in profit or loss for the period.

Net investment in a foreign operation

Where the reporting entity uses hedge accounting for a net investment in a foreign operation, it should separately disclose the amounts that have been recognised in other comprehensive income and the amounts recognised in profit or loss.

18 INVENTORIES AND WORK-IN-PROGRESS

INTRODUCTION

Many companies in the UK and Republic of Ireland have inventories (stocks) and work-in-progress (WIP) in their balance sheet (statement of financial position) at the year-/period-end. Accounting for such assets can cause significant complexities and, as is usually the case for WIP, involves a large degree of estimation on the part of management. Auditors are particularly concerned with material amounts of inventory and WIP largely because of the impact that such valuations can have on both the profit and loss account and balance sheet of the entity. Manipulation of such figures can have dramatic effects on a company's reported results and whilst such practices are relatively rare they have been proven to exist and cause severe distortions in a company's gross profit margins and balance sheet position.

Inventories are dealt with in Section 13 *Inventories* of FRS 102. Whilst this is a relatively short chapter it covers some vital principles that accountants need to be aware of, as well as additional disclosure requirements over and above those of the previous UK GAAP. The scope section of Section 13 confirms that inventories are assets that:

(a) Are held for sale in the ordinary course of business (in other words they are not being used in the business),
(b) Are in the process of production for such a sale (i.e. WIP) or
(c) Are in the form of materials or supplies that are to be consumed in the company's production process or by way of the rendering of services.

Example – A fleet of vehicles

A company's principal activity is the renting of cars to the general public. It has a fleet of 20 motor cars and 15 vans that are rented each day. Once the vehicles have reached a mileage of 7,000 miles or more they are then put up for sale to the general public.

In this example the fleet of cars and vans would not be treated as inventory whilst they are being rented to the general public; they would instead be classed as tangible fixed

---

assets and accounted for under the provisions in Section 17 *Property, Plant and Equipment*. This is because prior to being put up for sale they are not held for sale in the ordinary course of business; they generate income for the company by way of rentals and thus meet the recognition criteria for property, plant and equipment.

There are certain items for which Section 13 does not apply, which are as follows:

(a) Any WIP that arises in a construction contract that also includes any directly related service contracts. Section 23 *Revenue* would apply in this instance.
(b) Financial instruments. Section 11 *Basic Financial Instruments* and Section 12 *Other Financial Instruments Issues* would apply.
(c) Biological assets that relate to agricultural activity. In this respect Section 34 *Specialised Activities* would apply.
(d) Inventories that are measured at fair value through profit or loss at each reporting date.

MEASUREMENT OF INVENTORIES

Traditionally many accountants (and trainee accountants) have been very familiar with the terminology 'lower of cost and net realisable value'. To all intents and purposes this principle still exists in FRS 102, but the terminology has been replaced with *'lower of cost and estimated selling price less costs to complete and sell'*. Whilst the principle is still the same, accountants should recognise that the term 'net realisable value' is not used in FRS 102.

In addition, it should be noted that the term 'estimated selling price less costs to complete and sell' is not the same as 'fair value less costs to sell'. This is because fair value is the amount that could be obtained from knowledgeable and willing third parties in an arm's length transaction. The cost of inventories is largely constant and it follows, therefore, that 'estimated selling price' is usually the price that a third party would pay in exchange for the goods or services, and hence is company-specific. Fair values are not necessarily company-specific as they might be obtained by reference to an active market that is external to the reporting entity.

> **Example – Lower of cost and estimated selling price less costs to complete and sell**
>
> Lockland Chemical Company Limited manufactures chemicals for use in detergents and other household cleaning products and has a year-end date of 31 December 2015. On 30 September 2015 it shipped a batch of chemicals overseas to its customer. These had a cost price of £25,000 and the company raised an invoice for £45,000 plus value added tax.
>
> On receipt of the chemicals they were rejected by the customer because of defects proven by their laboratory staff. The chemicals were immediately shipped back to Lockland Chemical Company who performed their own laboratory tests and confirmed that the chemicals were indeed defective. A credit note was raised for the full value of the invoice and the chemicals were re-mixed and shipped again.
>
> The batch of chemicals that were defective were still included in the company's inventory at a cost of £25,000 at the year-end. On 10 January 2016 a third party confirmed

that they would take the batch of chemicals for a price of £10,000 as they could use them in their products (which are unrelated to the chemicals produced by Lockland Chemical Company). Management agreed to this proposal and duly shipped the chemicals over to the third party who paid £10,000 plus value added tax upfront for them.

The treatment of the inventories at the year-end above would fall to be classed as an adjusting event under the provisions in Section 32 *Events after the End of the Reporting Period*. This is because the estimated selling price less costs to complete and sell becomes apparent after the year-end. As a consequence, management should write down the cost of the inventory from £25,000 to £10,000 and recognise the £15,000 write-down in profit or loss.

Example – Inventory held as free samples

A company holds a stock of inventories and other items of promotional material for distribution to customers and potential customers free of charge so they can sample their goods. The cost of these goods are minimal to the company and they have valued the samples held at the year-end at nil value.

Paragraph 13.4A of FRS 102 says that a company that holds inventory for distribution at no, or nominal, consideration should measure such inventories at cost. This cost, when applicable, should be adjusted for any loss of service potential. To comply with this paragraph, the company should restate the inventory to cost adjusted for any loss of service potential rather than simply measuring them at nil value.

COST OF INVENTORIES AND WORK-IN-PROGRESS

To comply with the provisions in Section 13, an entity should value its inventories and WIP at the lower of cost and estimated selling price less costs to complete and sell. The components of 'cost' often include items over and above simply the purchase price of a good. They can include:

- The purchase price,
- Conversion costs and
- Other costs directly attributable in bringing the inventories to their present location and condition.

Purchase price

There are several elements to the purchase price of inventories. In addition to the purchase price itself, the components of purchase price can also include:

- Import duties and other taxes that are irrecoverable (an example of an irrecoverable tax is value added tax when the entity is not registered for such a tax),
- Transport and handling costs and
- Miscellaneous costs that are directly attributable to the company acquiring finished goods, materials and services.

Deducted from the above are any trade discounts, rebates, volume discounts and other such items when establishing the cost of inventories.

Example – Volume discounts received after the year-end

A company buys and sells disposable clothing around the world. Several years ago the company entered into an agreement with its supplier for volume discounts. Such discounts are only made aware to the company after the year-end despite the discounts relating to purchases in the current financial year. The question arises as to whether the company should include the full discount in profit or loss without being allocated to specific items of inventory at the year-end or whether a proportion of the discount should be allocated to the items held in the company's inventory at the year-end.

The company should allocate a proportion of the discount to the items held in inventory at the year-end. For example, if the company purchased £10,000 worth of products in the year and it holds inventory with a cost of £1,000 at the year-end then 10% of the discount should be allocated to the inventory items held at the year-end. The remaining 90% should be taken through profit or loss as a deduction from cost of sales. This is because the company is not able to allocate the discount to specific items of inventory throughout the year and hence it follows that the company should spread the discount over all the items that have been purchased during the year. This concept applies whether the goods or sold or unsold.

Example – Deferred payment

Company A buys a batch of machinery from Company B. There is an agreement between the two companies that payment can be deferred for two years (normal credit terms being anything between 30 and 90 days credit). However, Company A has agreed to pay Company B half of the profit that it yields on the sale of the machinery at the end of the two-year period.

In these circumstances, payment has been deferred beyond normal credit terms and this is going to result in a difference between the purchase price that would ordinarily be paid under normal credit terms and the deferred settlement amount. The difference is to be recognised as interest expense in Company A's books over the period of the financing. It is NOT added to the cost of the machinery in the inventories and so Company A should record the inventory at the price the company would pay under normal credit terms, which assumes no financing element. The only exception to this rule would be where the inventory is a qualifying asset under Section 25 *Borrowing Costs* (a qualifying asset being an asset under construction that takes a substantially long period of time to complete) and where the entity has an accounting policy of capitalising such borrowing costs.

When a company enters into an arrangement under deferred payment terms, but there is no price available under normal credit terms, the cost price is arrived at by discounting the deferred settlement amount (which is representative of the future cash flows) using a market rate of interest. It is at this amount that the goods will be included in inventory.

Costs of conversion

In a manufacturing organisation, the costs of conversion would normally include costs that are directly related to the units of production (i.e. direct labour).

In addition, they should also include additional direct expenses and any amounts for subcontract work.

The costs of converting raw materials to finished goods must also be taken into consideration and such costs must be allocated on a systematic basis, which will include both fixed and variable production overheads. Examples of fixed production overheads include:

- Rent and rates,
- Taxes,
- Repairs and maintenance of factory buildings and machinery,
- Depreciation of factory machinery and
- Costs of factory management and administration.

Fixed production overheads remain relatively constant (hence the term 'fixed') and are indirect costs associated with the costs of production. Fixed production overheads do not change if the levels of production change; thus, for example, if the company produces more or less of a product, the fixed overheads will remain relatively constant.

When a company is allocating fixed overheads they do so on a systematic basis, which is ordinarily the normal levels of productive capacity. This is not an 'exact science' and consideration has to be given to issues such as planned maintenance and other situations that would result in production loss. A company's normal levels of productive capacity would be the average amount of production that could be expected to be achieved over a number of periods in normal circumstances, having taken account of situations that would give rise to a loss of production. If the company has not had abnormally high or low levels of production in a period, then actual production levels could be used if they approximate to normal capacity. Should a company experience abnormally high levels of production (for example, if they have an inordinately large order for goods) then the allocation of fixed production overheads is reduced in order that inventory is not measured above cost with any unallocated overheads being recognised as an expense in the period in which they arise. All variable overheads are allocated on the basis of actual use of the production facilities.

Variable overheads are, by definition, variable with the levels of production and can include indirect materials and indirect labour.

Example – Variable overhead

A company manufactures barbecues and produces 10,000 barbecues in the months of February and March, with a total variable overhead amounting to £20,000. The company increases its production of barbecues in the month of April to 15,000 barbecues and its variable overhead rises as a consequence to £30,000.

In the months of February and March the total variable overhead per unit amounted to £2.00 (£20,000/10,000 units). In the month of April the production increased to 15,000 units at a cost of £30,000 but the overhead per unit stayed constant at £2.00 per unit (£30,000/15,000 units).

Example – Allocation of overheads when production is higher than normal

Pete's Plastics Limited is a plastics manufacturer and is preparing its financial statements for the year-ended 31 December 2015. At full capacity the manufacturing and production line can undertake 9,000 labour hours per year but normal capacity is 7,500 hours per year. The cost accountant has produced the following data for the year ended 31 December 2015:

Actual labour hours for the year	8,500 hours
Fixed production overhead	£3,000
Opening inventory	1,000 units
Units produced in the year	8,500 units
Units sold in the year	7,700 units
Closing inventory at 31 December 2015	1,800 units
Cost formula for inventories	First-in first-out

As one unit takes one hour (i.e. 8,500 actual hours/8,500 units produced) it is now possible to work out the overhead absorption rate per hour based on the following calculation:

Production overhead/Labour hours for normal activity:
£3,000   / 7,500 hours   =   £0.40 per hour

Under normal circumstances, management would allocate overhead costs to the goods produced using the normal overhead absorption rate of £0.40 per unit. However, in this example production has been higher than normal and if the rate of £0.40 per hour is used the amount allocated to all units produced would be £3,400 (8,500 units × £0.40). This is higher than the actual overhead incurred in the year of £3,000 and if used would result in closing inventory being recorded above cost, in contravention of Section 13 requirements.

Therefore, in periods of high production like this (labour hours are 8,500 actual against 7,500 normal) the overhead absorption rate should be adjusted so as to reflect actual production and hence the calculation would be:

£3,000/8,500 units = £0.35

This rate would result in the production overhead being recognised as part of inventory at £630 (1,800 units at £0.35) as opposed to £720 (1,800 units at £0.40).

Other costs

Other costs that are directly attributable in bringing the inventory to its location and present condition can be included within the cost of the inventory. However, FRS 102 does outline some costs that cannot be recognised within the cost of inventory and should be recognised as expenses in the period that they are incurred:

- Abnormal amounts of wasted materials, labour or other production costs.
- Storage costs: the exception to this is where such costs are necessary during the production process before a further stage in the production process.
- Selling costs, which also include advertising costs.

In many cases a service provider may not have inventories but in the instance that they do, the service provider should measure them at the costs of their production. Ordinarily these costs would be made up of labour and other costs of personnel (including supervisory personnel and directly attributable overheads) that are directly engaged in providing the service. It follows, therefore, that expenses relating to sales and general administration are not included in the cost of inventories but are included in profit or loss as expenses in the period in which they are incurred.

In addition, a point worth emphasising where a service provider does have inventories is that the cost does not include any profit margins or other costs not directly attributable to the service as these are often built into the prices that are charged to the service provider's customer.

Agricultural produce

Section 34 *Specialised Activities* deals with agricultural produce harvested from biological assets. For example, milk is the agricultural produce from a cow and wool is the agricultural produce from sheep. When an entity is involved in such specialised activities, any inventories that comprise agricultural produce that has been harvested from its biological assets are measured at *either* fair value less estimated costs to sell *or* the lower of cost and estimated selling price less costs to complete and sell at the point of initial recognition. For the purposes of Section 13, the choice of measurement above becomes the cost of the inventories at that date.

By-products

It is often the case that a production process can result in more than one product being produced such as the main product and a by-product. Paragraph 13.10 of FRS 102 recognises that this may occur and says that if the costs of the raw materials, or conversion of each product, are not separately identifiable then the entity should allocate them on a rational and consistent basis between the products. The paragraph then goes on to acknowledge that generally most by-products are immaterial due to their nature and if this is the case the entity should measure them at selling price less costs to complete and sell and then deduct this amount from the cost of the main product. This will then ensure that the carrying value of the main product in inventory is not materially different from its cost.

COST METHODOLOGIES

There are various methodologies in existence for the measurement of the cost of inventories rather than using actual costs for every type of inventory. To use actual costs could prove to be disproportionately time-consuming and ineffective, although in some cases it might be appropriate to use such a method (for example, where the stock is relatively low).

Section 13 permits the use of standard costing (which is generally used in the manufacturing industry) for the allocation of both fixed and variable costs, and this method takes into consideration normal levels of materials and supplies, labour, efficiency and capacity utilisation. The retail method of inventory valuation is also permitted in FRS 102 and works by reducing the selling price of inventory by the appropriate percentage gross margin. The retail method can also work by converting the selling price of the retailer's stock to cost by using a ratio known as the 'cost-to-retail' ratio, which is calculated by dividing the cost of goods available for sale by the retail value of the goods available for sale. This will give a more relevant and reliable inventory valuation at the retailer's year-end.

A reporting entity may also use the most recent purchase price for valuing its inventories. However, there is a proviso in using this method, which is that it must result in a valuation that is a close approximation to cost. Care must be taken when using most recent purchase prices because if prices are rising it may result in an excessive price being used, which would not be a close approximation to cost and hence would result in the entity recognising profit that has not yet been earned through the sale of the goods.

FRS 102 requires the cost of inventories to be measured using either:

- First-in first-out (FIFO) or
- Weighted average cost.

Under no circumstances can the last-in first-out (LIFO) method of cost measurement be used under FRS 102. Previous SSAP 9 *Stocks and Long-Term Contracts* did permit the use of LIFO but the standard did not favour its application because it resulted in a valuation that did not bear much resemblance to actual cost and acknowledged this by stating that the directors of companies that used LIFO must have justified reasons for its use. This problem is overcome in FRS 102 because the use of LIFO is simply outlawed in paragraph 13.18.

Example – First-in first-out

The following information is extracted from the inventory system of Rob's Running Shoes Limited from 1 July 2015 to 31 December 2015 (no inventory was purchased in the month of December 2015):

Date of purchase	Number	Cost per unit £	Total cost £
1 July (opening inventory)	200	10	2,000
15 July	250	12	3,000
5 August	100	15	1,500
6 September	450	9	4,050
3 October	325	13	4,225
21 November	50	11	550
Total available for sale	1,375		15,325
Pairs sold	600		
Closing inventory 31.12.15	775		

Using FIFO the shoes in the opening inventory are sold first, followed by the shoes purchased on 15 July, those purchased on 5 August and 50 of the 450 purchased on 6 September. Cost of goods sold is calculated as follows:

Date of purchase	Number	Cost per unit £	Total cost £
1 July (opening inventory)	200	10	2,000
15 July	250	12	3,000
5 August	100	15	1,500
6 September	50	9	450
	600		6,950

As the cost of goods sold is £6,950 the closing inventory is £8,375 (£15,325 less £6,950).

Under the weighted average cost methodology the total cost of £15,325 is divided by the total number of running shoes available for sale (1,375), which equals £11.15 per unit. The shop sells 600 pairs of shoes in the second half of the year and hence results in the cost of goods sold of £6,690 (600 × £11.15). The closing inventory is therefore £8,635 (£15,325 less £6,690) under the weighted average cost.

CONSIGNMENT INVENTORIES

Consignment inventories (or consignment stock as it is most commonly known as in the UK) is stock that is legally owned by one party but is held by another. The issue in identifying whether consignment stock goes on the balance sheet of the dealer or the holder of the inventory is to look at the substance of the arrangement.

If the reporting entity (the dealer) has consignment stock that, in substance, belongs to the manufacturer then it is not recognised on the dealer's balance sheet as an asset until such time the transfer of title takes place. If the dealer does have consignment stock that is, in substance, an asset of the dealer then the stock is recognised as such on the dealer's balance sheet together with a corresponding liability to the manufacturer. If the dealer has paid a deposit to the manufacturer this is deducted from the liability. Such accounting treatments usually (but not exclusively) arise in motor dealerships.

DISCLOSURE REQUIREMENTS

Various disclosures are required by reporting entities, which are dealt with in paragraph 13.22 of FRS 102. The financial statements should disclose the following:

(a) The entity's accounting policies that it has adopted to measure inventories together with the cost formula used,
(b) The total carrying amount of inventories (carrying amount being in classifications that are appropriate to the entity),
(c) The amount of inventories that have been recognised as expenses during the accounting period,
(d) Any impairment losses that have been reversed or recognised in accordance with Section 27 *Impairment of Assets* and
(e) The total carrying amount of any inventories that have been pledged as security for the company's liabilities.

19 SHARE-BASED PAYMENT

INTRODUCTION

Share-based payment arrangements have become increasingly common over the last few years in order to remunerate directors and employees. Share-based payment transactions can also be used as consideration to third parties (for example, settling a liability in the form of shares or share options). Section 26 *Share-based Payment* of FRS 102 deals with the accounting and disclosure requirements relating to share-based payment transactions. The section covers the following share-based payment arrangements:

(a) Equity-settled share-based payment transactions. These are where the entity:
  i. Receives goods or services in exchange for its own equity instruments, which may also include share options, or
  ii. Receives goods or services but has no obligation to settle the transaction with the supplier.

(b) Cash-settled share-based payment transactions. These are where the company obtains goods or services and in so doing incurs a liability to the third party, which is settled by transferring cash or other assets. The amount of cash or other assets transferred to the third party is based on the price of the company's shares or other equity instruments of another group entity.

(c) Transactions whereby the company receives or acquires goods or services and the arrangement offers a choice of whether the company settles the transaction in cash or by issuing equity instruments (both parties in the transaction have this option).

In a group situation, a share-based payment transaction may be settled by another member of the group on behalf of the company. In this respect, the same conditions in the points above will still apply in respect of:

(a) One member of a group receiving goods or services (including shareholders of any group entity) and another member having the obligation to settle the share-based payment transaction or

(b) One member of a group having an obligation to settle a share-based payment transaction for which another member has received the goods or services.

The exception to the above is when the transaction is not in respect of goods or services supplied to the receiving group member.

Example – Share appreciation rights

An entity decides to offer share appreciation rights to employees as part of their remuneration package as an incentive for employees to help increase the company's profitability and financial position. The share appreciation rights allow employees to become entitled to a future cash payment based on the increase in the company's share price over a specific period of time. There is also the option, should the employees wish, to receive a right to shares that are redeemable at a certain point in time, on cessation of employment or at the employee's option.

This arrangement is to be accounted for by the company as a cash-settled share-based payment transaction.

The overarching principle in Section 26 is for a business that has entered into a share-based payment arrangement to be provided with guidance on how to recognise the share-based payment arrangement within the financial statements because there is no associated cash flow. Hence Section 26 provides the accounting treatment that a business that is undertaking such transactions should adopt in order to reflect the effect of share-based payment transactions in the profit and loss account (income statement or statement of comprehensive income).

The scope of Section 26 also applies to government-mandated arrangements in which equity instruments are acquired by investors without the investor providing any goods or services or where the goods or services that have been provided are of less value than the fair value of the equity instruments granted.

Example – Equity instruments not covered under the scope of Section 26

Entity A acquires 100% of the net assets of Entity B. The consideration comprised a mixture of cash and equity instruments of Entity A. At the same time Entity A also forms a joint venture with Entity C in which it also issues equity instruments.

Section 26 deals with transactions whereby the company acquires goods and/or services as consideration in exchange for equity instruments of the company (or group) or incurs a liability that is based on the value of the equity instruments of the entity (or group). As a consequence, only when a transfer of equity instruments is for another purpose other than payment for goods or services would the transaction fall outside the scope of Section 26.

However, in this example, if equity instruments were granted to the employees of the acquiree (Entity B) then these would fall under the scope of Section 26. The exception to this would be where the transaction is between the entity and the employees acting in their capacity as shareholders because then the transaction would not be consideration for employee services.

RECOGNITION OF A SHARE-BASED PAYMENT TRANSACTION

Generally, goods or services that are received by a company in a share-based payment transaction are recognised when the company obtains the goods or services. The debit is to profit and loss (or the debit may be taken to assets, such as fixed assets, if they qualify for recognition as such) with the credit side going either to equity or to liabilities.

Equity-settled share-based payment transactions are credited to equity, with cash-settled share-based payment transactions being credited to liabilities.

Vesting conditions and grant date

Vesting conditions are those conditions that a third party must satisfy in order to become entitled to receive cash, other assets or shares of the business in a share-based payment transaction by the *vesting date*. The 'vesting date' is the date on which the shares are able to be exercised.

If a share-based payment transaction involves goods, then the vesting date is relatively easy to establish because it is the date on which the goods are received. The difficulty arises when employee services are involved. If a company issues shares that vest immediately (i.e. the employee is not required to complete a specified period of service before the vesting date) then the presumption is that these shares are a form of employee consideration relating to past service and therefore the company immediately recognises an expense for the employee service with a corresponding increase in equity or in liabilities.

When the shares vest at some point in the future (i.e. the employee is required to complete a specified period of service before the vesting date) then the business must account for those employee services as they are rendered during the vesting period. The business will also recognise an increase in equity or liabilities.

The 'grant date' is the date on which the entity and another party (which includes employees) agree to a share-based payment arrangement and is also the date on which the entity and the counterparty have a shared understanding of the terms and conditions of the arrangement. At the grant date the business essentially confers on the party the right to cash, other assets, or equity instruments of the entity on the proviso that the specified vesting conditions (if any) are met. If the agreement is subject to an approval process (for example, by way of approval from the shareholders in a general meeting), then the grant date becomes the date on which approval is obtained, as can be seen in the following example.

Example – Establishing the grant date

In the annual general meeting held on 31 December 2015, the directors and shareholders voted unanimously in favour of offering employees share options in the company in order to entice employees to assist in boosting the profitability and financial position of the business. Letters were sent to employees on this date offering options to subscribe to 20,000 shares in the business at £8 per share.

On 11 January 2016, the awards were approved by the shareholders and during this time the share price of the company had increased to £11 per share. The chief executive has queried as to whether the shares are granted on the date the share options were resolved in the annual general meeting or the date on which the share options were approved by the shareholders.

Any allotment of shares or rights to shares in a company must be approved by the shareholders in a general meeting or alternatively by the entity's articles. As the award in this example was subjected to shareholder approval the grant date becomes 11 January 2016.

In some instances a company might issue share options with vesting conditions attached to them – for example, the employee may have to complete a certain speci-fied period of service before becoming entitled to the shares (this would represent a vesting condition that is conditional on service). Conditions might also be imposed in the share-based payment agreement that are conditional on the performance of the company – for example, the company might have to reach a certain benchmark profit target. Such examples are known as non-market conditions and are taken into consid-eration when estimating the number of equity instruments that are expected to vest. However, market conditions (such as specified increases in the entity's share price) are NOT taken into consideration when estimating the number of equity instruments expected to vest. This is because these conditions have already been taken into con-sideration when fair-valuing the shares.

At the vesting date the entity must revise the estimated number of equity instru-ments expected to vest so that they equal the number of equity instruments that have ultimately vested. In terms of estimating the fair value of the shares or share options at the measurement date, all market and non-vesting conditions must be taken into consideration with no subsequent adjustment, regardless of the outcome of the market or non-vesting conditions, but provided that all other vesting conditions have been satisfied.

Example – Simple share-based payment transaction

On 1 January 2015, Charlotte Champagne Co. Ltd grants 2,000 share options to each of its three directors. The terms of the share-based payment agreement includes a condi-tion that states that all the directors must still be in the employment of the company on 31 December 2017 when the share options vest. The fair value of each option as at 1 January 2015 is £11 and it is expected that all of the options will vest. A further condition in the agreement is that the options will only vest if the share price reaches £18 per share. On 31 December 2015 the share price was only £9 and, due to market conditions, it is not expected to rise in the next two years. Due to a downturn in business, it is only expected that two directors will be employed by the company on 31 December 2017.

Increases in the share price of an entity are ignored for the purposes of calculating the value of the share options as at 31 December 2015, as this is a market condition. However, the company must take into consideration the fact that only two directors will be in the employment of the company on 31 December 2017 and hence the calculation will be:

2,000 options × 2 directors × £11 × 1 year/3 years = £14,667

To account for this transaction the entries will be to debit the profit and loss account and credit equity. The company could credit the transaction directly to the profit and loss reserve account; it may also create an additional equity account such as a 'Share-based payment' account. What it must not do is to take the credit to a share premium account.

Equity-settled share-based payment transactions

In an equity-settled share-based payment arrangement, the entity must measure the goods or services received and the corresponding increase in equity at the fair value of the goods or services received unless fair value cannot be estimated reliably. If the company cannot estimate fair value reliably then it must measure the value having reference to the value of the equity instrument granted. However, generally it is not possible to reliably estimate the fair value of the services that the entity has received.

Where employee services are concerned, the entity must measure the fair value of the equity instruments at the grant date; for transactions with third parties (i.e. not employees), the measurement date becomes the date on which the entity obtains the goods or the third party renders the relevant service.

Example – Payment of fees through a share-based payment arrangement

Zedcolour Trading Limited is a newly formed company with a year-end of 31 December 2015. During the year it has received extensive advice from a technical consultant on its activities. The technical consultant has agreed to receive her fees in the form of shares of the company as the company is in its infancy.

The fair value of these shares has been independently valued at £15,000 when it was initially agreed that the consultant be paid by way of shares. The value of the services rendered by the consultant amounted to £13,500. The consultant has been informed that HMRC have decided, using relevant factors in determining employment status, that she is an employee in the eyes of tax legislation.

As the consultant is to be considered as an employee, management should recognise the service at the fair value of the granted equity instruments, which is £15,000.

Example – Shares given to an employee by the owners

Mr Breary owns 100% of Concrete Creations Limited. To reward his employee for his efforts, Mr Breary gives his employee one share in the company.

This transaction would fall under the scope of a share-based payment because the share is being settled by the sole shareholder. If it is assumed that the fair value of the company was £100,000 the accounting entry would be:

DR share-based payment expense	£1,000	
CR equity		£1,000

Government-mandated plans

Paragraph 26.17 of FRS 102 acknowledges that in some jurisdictions there are arrangements that are established in legislation under which equity investors may acquire equity in a business without having to perform any services or supply any goods in exchange for such equity or they could provide goods or services that are clearly less than the fair value of such goods or services.

When these arrangements occur, they are accounted for as equity-settled share-based payment transactions. The entity should measure the portion of the unidentifiable goods or services (to be) received as the difference between the fair value of the share-based payment and the fair value of any identifiable goods or services (to be) received measured at the grant date.

Shares

This section applies to shares, share options and equity-settled share appreciation rights.

In measuring the fair value of shares (including the related goods or services that the entity has received), there is a three-tier hierarchy, which must be referred to as follows.

Level:

1. Where an observable market price is available for the equity instrument granted, the entity should use that price.
2. If there is not an observable market price available, the fair value of the equity instruments granted is estimated using entity-specific observable market data. This can include (among other things) a recent transaction in the entity's shares or a recent independent valuation of the entity or its principal assets.
3. Where an observable market price is not available and obtaining a reliable measurement of fair value under 2 above is impracticable ('impracticable' is taken to mean after exhausting all attempts to obtain a reliable measurement) then the entity is to indirectly measure the fair value of the shares by way of a valuation method that uses market data to the greatest extent practicable so as to obtain an estimation of the price of the equity instruments that would be paid on the grant date in an arm's length transaction. In adopting the valuation methodology, the entity's directors must use their judgement and ensure that the valuation method is appropriate in the circumstances of the entity.

Cash-settled share-based payment transactions

In respect of cash-settled share-based payment transactions, the entity must measure the goods or services acquired, together with the associated liability, at the fair value of the liability. At each subsequent reporting date until the liability is settled, the entity must re-measure the fair value of the liability. Any changes in the fair value of the liability are then recognised in profit or loss for the period.

Example – Cash-settled share-based payment

On 31 December 2015, the managing director of Daniel's DIY (an owner-managed business) is awarded a share-based payment of 1,000 shares, which represents 10% of the company's share capital and on this date the company is valued at £750,000.

During discussions the managing director made reference to the unlisted status of the company and the owners confirmed that they do not want external investors being involved in the business. The managing director expressed concern that he may not be able to convert his shares into cash if he leaves the company or dies. The owners want to retain the managing director for as long as possible as the growth of the company has largely been down to him and therefore they incorporate a provision in the agreement that the company will buy back the shares on retirement, death or where the cessation of employment is not due to incompetence, acting in the detriment of the company or being convicted of a criminal offence. If such acts occur, the shares will be forfeited for nil consideration.

Because of the buyback clause, the share-based payment arrangement is to be classified as cash-settled because eventually the company will have to settle the transaction via a cash payment (if there had been no buyback clause it would be an equity-settled share-based payment arrangement). At each reporting date the outstanding liability will be re-measured at fair value, with changes in the fair value being recognised in profit or loss for the period.

Therefore, on 31 December 2015 the company should recognise the cash-settled share-based payment as:

DR share-based payment expense	£75,000	
CR liabilities		£75,000

If the share-based payment arrangement allows the entity to settle the transaction in cash/other assets or by issuing shares, the entity must account for the transaction as a cash-settled share-based payment unless:

(a) The entity has a past practice of settling by way of shares/equity instruments or

(b) There is no commercial substance to the option. This would arise when the cash settlement amount bears no relationship to the fair value (and is likely to be lower than the fair value) of the equity instrument.

Where the above two circumstances present themselves, the entity should account for the transaction as an equity-settled share-based payment arrangement.

AMENDMENTS TO A SHARE-BASED PAYMENT ARRANGEMENT

An entity may make amendments to existing share-based payment arrangements that are beneficial to the employee. This could arise when, for example, the entity reduces the exercise price of an option or reduces the vesting period by way of changing or eliminating a performance condition. Modifications to vesting conditions are to be taken into consideration when accounting for the share-based payment transaction, which is achieved as follows:

(a) Where the change increases the fair value of the equity instruments granted or increases the number of equity instruments granted, the entity should include the incremental fair value granted in the measurement of the amount recognised for services received as consideration for the equity instruments granted. This incremental fair value is the difference between the fair value of the modified equity instrument and the original equity instruments, which are both estimated as at the date of the modification.

(b) Where a modification occurs during the vesting period, the entity includes the incremental fair value granted in the measurement of the amount recognised for services received over the vesting period from the date of the modification to the date when the modified equity instruments vest. This is in addition to the amount based on the grant date fair value of the original equity instruments, which is recognised over the rest of the original vesting period.

(c) When the modification reduces the total fair value of the share-based payment arrangement or is not otherwise beneficial to the employee, the entity should continue to account for the services that it has received as consideration for the equity instruments granted as if the modification had never occurred.

Example – Modifications to a share-based payment agreement

In the year to 31 December 2015, Weavers Windows Limited operated a share option award with an option exercise price of £10, which is equivalent to the market value of the shares at the grant date. In the annual general meeting, the directors have agreed to a new award into which existing share options will be rolled. Due to the introduction of the new award scheme, the existing award scheme was cancelled and the company issued new share options to its employees under the new award. The new share options are granted at a price of £7 as the price of the old shares had fallen to £6 since the grant date of the old award.

This is an example of a modification (rather than a cancellation of one award scheme replaced with another). This is because Weavers Windows Limited has replaced a cancelled award with another and hence it is treated as if it had been modified. Weavers Windows Limited would account for the incremental fair value of the new award at the date the modification took place and then spread this over the vesting period of the new award. The company would continue to charge for the original award over the original vesting period.

CANCELLING A SHARE-BASED PAYMENT ARRANGEMENT

When an entity cancels a share-based payment arrangement (or, alternatively, settles an existing share-based payment arrangement), the entity should account for such as an acceleration of vesting and hence it would immediately recognise the amount that would otherwise have been recognised for services received over the remainder of the vesting period.

Example – Cancellation of a share-based payment arrangement

On 1 January 2014, Bart Baling Equipment (Bart) made an award of 100 shares to its sales manager. The terms of the agreement stated that the sales manager must remain in the employment of the company for a period of three years. At the grant date the fair value of the shares was £1,500 and it was expected that the employee would remain in the employment of the company for a three-year period; thus it was expected that the award was to vest.

Due to changes in the business one year later (1 January 2015), it was decided to cancel the award and the company settled the award in cash on a pro rata basis and the sales manager received £500 (£1,500 × 1/3); this amount was duly recognised in the financial statements.

Paragraph 26.13 of FRS 102 says that a cancellation should be accounted for as an acceleration of vesting and the entity should immediately recognise the amount that would otherwise have been recognised for services received over the remaining vesting period. As a result of this paragraph, Bart should recognise £1,000 (£1,500 less £500) and with the associated credit being taken to equity.

GROUP PLANS

Group companies may also enter into share-based payment agreements with employees or third parties and paragraph 26.16 of FRS 102 deals with these issues accordingly. This paragraph confirms that if a share-based payment award is granted to employees of one, or more, members in a group, the expense can be recognised and measured using a reasonable allocation of the expense for the group as a whole. The problem with this is that there is often uncertainty as to which member(s) of the group should reflect the share-based payment expense in its own separate financial statements. Factors that should be considered in these situations are:

- Whether a service company arrangement exists and staff have been seconded to another member entity. In such cases the principal employer will be the service company and should take the share-based payment charge in its own separate financial statements.
- The entity that bears the cost of the employment. Where staff undertake tasks for different member entities within a group, there will often be inter-company recharges taking place. In such instances the share-based payment charge will follow the costs of the employee (i.e. the member entity receiving the recharge).
- Determining which member entity receives the award associated with the employee. For example, if a director acts in the capacity of director of the parent company and the director of a subsidiary company within the group, consideration must be given as to whether the director receives the reward for the group as a whole or whether the director receives the reward merely in respect of his duties as director of the subsidiary. Where the director receives the reward in respect of his duties as director of the subsidiary, the subsidiary company will take the charge in its own separate financial statements as the subsidiary would be deemed the principal employer.
- The terms of the employee contract. This may make provisions for the employee being temporarily seconded to another entity within the group. Where the employee is seconded then the entity receiving the secondment would be deemed to be the principal employer for the period of the secondment and hence should take the charge in its own separate financial statements whilst the employee is on secondment.

- In addition to the bullet point above relating to the employee's contract, share-based payment charges would be included within the financial statements of a group entity that has overall responsibility in sanctioning overtime and bonuses for employees.

DISCLOSURE REQUIREMENTS

There are extensive disclosures that are required to be made in the financial statements of an entity undertaking a share-based payment arrangement. These disclosures are:

(a) A description of each type of share-based payment arrangement that was in existence at any time during the reporting period. The disclosures should also include the general terms and conditions of each arrangement (for example, vesting requirements, maximum option terms and the method of settlement (equity or cash)). Where an entity has multiple types of share-based payment arrangements that are similar in nature then paragraph 26.18 does allow this information to be aggregated.

(b) The number and weighted average exercise prices of the share options for each of the following groups of options are:
   i. Those outstanding at the beginning of the period,
   ii. Those granted during the period,
   iii. Those forfeited during the period,
   iv. Those that were exercised during the period,
   v. Those that have expired during the period,
   vi. Those that are outstanding at the end of the period and
   vii. Those that are exercisable at the end of the period.

Equity-settled share-based payment arrangements

For equity-settled share-based payment arrangements, the entity should disclose details of how it has measured the fair value of goods or services received or the value of the equity instruments granted. Where the entity adopts the use of a valuation methodology, the entity should disclose the method and its reasons for choosing the methodology.

Cash-settled share-based payment arrangements

For cash-settled share-based payment arrangements, the entity should disclose information about how it has measured the liability.

Modifications during the period

The entity should disclose information that explains modifications made to any share-based payment arrangements during the period.

Group plans

Where the entity is part of a group share-based payment arrangement and the entity recognises and measures its share-based payment charge based on a reasonable allocation of the expense recognised for the group, disclosure of this fact should be made as well as the basis for the allocation.

Other disclosures

In addition to the disclosures above, the entity should also disclose:

- The total expense that it has recognised in profit or loss for the period and
- The total carrying value at the end of the period for liabilities that have arisen due to share-based payment transactions.

The objective of the above disclosures is to show the effect on the entity's profit or loss and financial position for the reporting period.

20 LEASES

INTRODUCTION

Leases serve a commercial purpose for many businesses; however, they have proved to be somewhat problematic for the accountancy profession due to the subjective nature of how they can be financially represented and the ability to manipulate transactions to achieve a desired outcome (usually to achieve 'off-balance sheet finance'). There has been an ongoing project with the International Accounting Standards Board and the US Financial Accounting Standards Board to overhaul the ways in which leases are accounted for, which is covered later in the chapter.

Leasing is dealt with in Section 20 *Leases* of FRS 102. At the outset, this particular section confirms that Section 20 does not deal with the following types of leasing transactions:

- Leases granted to a lessee to enable them to explore for or use minerals, oil, natural gas and similar non-regenerative resources (Section 34 *Specialised Activities* deals with these issues).
- Licensing agreements for such items as motion picture films, video recordings, plays, manuscripts, patents and copyrights (Section 18 *Intangible Assets other than Goodwill* deals with these issues).
- Measurement of property, plant and equipment held by lessees, which are accounted for as investment property and measurement of investment property provided by lessors under operating leases (see Section 16 *Investment Property*).
- Measurement of biological assets held by lessees under finance leases and biological assets provided by lessors under operating leases (see Section 34 *Specialised Activities*).
- Leases that could lead to a loss to the lessor or the lessee as a result of non-typical contractual terms.

FRS 102 uses a 'risks and rewards' approach to lease classification. In other words, if the risks and rewards of ownership of the asset subjected to the lease remain with the lessor, the lease is deemed to be an operating lease, whereas if the risks and rewards pass from the lessor to the lessee, the lease is deemed to be a finance lease.

FINANCE LEASES

Section 20 still determines the classification of a lease in much the same way as SSAP 21 *Accounting for Leases and Hire Purchase Contracts* did. The overarching principle in the determination as to whether a lease is financing or operating is considered in the light of the substance of the arrangement – in other words looking at who bears the risks and rewards of ownership of the asset being subjected to the lease. If the risks and rewards of ownership have been passed to the lessee, the lease will be classified as a finance lease.

Identifying a finance lease

Old UK GAAP at SSAP 21 in the Guidance Notes provided a 90% benchmark test (often referred to as a 'bright line test') where if the present value of the minimum lease payments that the lessee is required to pay equated to 90% or more of the fair value of the leased asset, then this will give rise to a finance lease. The notable difference between old UK GAAP SSAP 21 and FRS 102 is that Section 20 does not contain any 90% benchmark that was contained in SSAP 21; instead it offers five examples of situations that, individually, or in combination, would normally lead to a lease being classified as a finance lease, and a further three indicators of situations that individually or in combination could also lead to a lease being classified as a finance lease. The first five indicators are as follows:

- At the end of the lease term, the lease transfers ownership of the asset to the lessee.
- There is an option to purchase the asset at a price that is expected to be sufficiently lower than the fair value of the asset at the date the option becomes exercisable. In addition, it is reasonably certain, at the commencement of the lease, that the option will be exercised.
- The lease term is for the major part of the economic life of the asset, even if legal title is not transferred to the lessee at the end of this term.
- At the commencement of the lease the present value of the minimum lease payments that the lessee is obliged to make amounts to at least substantially all of the fair value of the leased asset.
- The leased assets are of such a specialised nature that only the lessee can use them without major modifications having to be made to them.

The fourth point above refers to the term 'substantially all'. This is the term that has essentially replaced the 90% test that was contained in the old SSAP 21; hence more judgement will be needed on the part of the preparer of the financial statements.

There are three additional indicators of situations that could also lead to classification of a lease as a finance lease, which are as follows:

- Should the lessee cancel the lease before the agreed term, the lessor's losses associated with the cancellation are borne by the lessee.
- Gains or losses from the fluctuation in the residual value of the leased asset accrue to the lessee.

- At the end of the lease, the lessee has the ability to continue the lease for a secondary period at a rent that is much lower than market rent (often referred to as a 'peppercorn' rent).

It is important to understand that the situations above are not exhaustive and this is reflected in the wording in paragraph 20.7, which confirms that all of the above situations are not always conclusive. The key to determining the correct lease classification will all depend on whether the risks and rewards of ownership have transferred to the lessee or have remained with the lessor at the inception of the lease. Paragraph 20.8 says that lease classification is made at the start of the lease and the classification is not changed during the lease term (i.e. from operating to financing or vice versa) unless the lessee and the lessor agree to a change in the provisions of the lease (other than simply renewing the lease). Where such provisions are changed, the lease classification is then re-evaluated.

Accounting for a finance lease by the lessee

Once a lease has been determined as a finance lease, then on initial recognition, Section 20 would require a lessee to recognise its rights of use of that asset at an amount equivalent to the fair value of the leased asset or, if lower, the present value of the minimum lease payments, which are determined at the inception of the lease. When a company incurs costs that are directly attributable in negotiating and arranging a lease, these costs are added to the amount that has been recognised in the balance sheet (statement of financial position) as an asset.

Example – Present value of minimum lease payments

Company A Limited enters into a finance lease with Company B Limited. Company A is trying to work out whether the present value of the minimum lease payments at the commencement of the lease are higher or lower than the fair value of the leased asset but is unsure which rate to use to discount the minimum lease payments down to present day values.

Paragraph 20.10 to FRS 102 says that the present value of the minimum lease payments shall be calculated using the interest rate implicit in the lease. If this cannot be determined, the lessee's incremental borrowing rate will be used instead.

The term 'interest rate implicit in the lease' is the discount rate, which, if applied at the start of the lease, would cause the total present value of (a) the minimum lease payments the lessee is obliged to make to the lessor and (b) the unguaranteed residual value to be the same as the sum of (1) the fair value of the leased asset and (2) any initial directly attributable costs of the lessor.

Example – Incremental costs

Company C Limited enters into a finance lease with Company D Limited but also incurs legal fees in negotiating and arranging the lease. Company C Limited is unsure as to the accounting treatment in respect of the legal fees.

Paragraph 20.9 requires that costs that are incremental in arranging the lease (such as legal fees) be added to the amount recognised in respect of the leased asset and therefore the legal fees will be capitalised as part of the cost of the leased asset in the lessee's balance sheet.

After initial recognition, paragraph 20.11 to FRS 102 requires a lessee to split the minimum lease payments between the capital element of the lease and the interest cost (as was previously the case under SSAP 21). However, the reduction in the outstanding liability is calculated using the *effective interest method*. The effective interest method is a method of calculating the amortised cost of either a financial asset or a financial liability (or a group of financial assets and liabilities) and therefore allocating the interest component of the lease payments over the relevant lease term. Under the effective interest method:

- The amortised cost of the finance lease liability is the present value of future payments discounted at the effective interest rate.
- The interest expense in a period is equivalent to the carrying amount of the liability at the beginning of the period multiplied by the effective interest rate for the period.

Effective interest rate

The effective interest rate in a lease is the rate that exactly discounts the rental obligations, plus any unguaranteed residual amount at the end of the lease term to the fair value of the leased asset and is determined on the basis of the carrying amount of the asset on initial recognition. Section 11 *Basic Financial Instruments* at paragraphs 11.15 and 11.16 give more guidance on the effective interest method and the effective interest rate (see also Chapter 17 in this publication). Essentially paragraph 11.16 to FRS 102 says that under the effective interest method:

(a) The amortised cost of a financial asset (liability) is the present value of future cash receipts (payments) discounted at the effective interest rate and

(b) The interest expense (income) in a period equals the carrying amount of the financial liability (asset) at the beginning of a period multiplied by the effective interest rate for the period.

Example – Interest allocation

On 1 January 2015, Company D enters into a finance lease. The terms of the lease make provision for Company D to pay the lessor six annual payments of £200 in advance. The cash price of the asset being subjected to the lease amounts to £870 and the interest rate implicit in the lease (i.e. the rate that exactly discounts the six instalments of £200 to the fair value of the asset is 15%).

The finance cost will be allocated as follows:

Rental obligations	6 × £200	£1,200
Cash price of asset		(£870)
Interest by deduction		£330

Period	Opening obligation £	Rental paid £	Obligation during period £	Finance cost 15% £	Closing obligation £
1	870	(200)	670	101	771
2	771	(200)	571	86	657
3	657	(200)	457	69	526
4	526	(200)	326	49	375
5	375	(200)	175	25	200
6	200	(200)	–	330	

Example – Accounting for a finance lease by the lessee

For the purposes of this example:

- Assume that asset ownership is transferred to the lessee and fair market value of the leased asset is lower than the present value of minimum lease payments.
- A three-year lease is initiated on 1 January 2015 for equipment with an expected useful life of five years.
- Three annual lease payments of £52,000 are required beginning on 1 January 2015 (note that the payment at the beginning of the year changes the present value computation). The lessor pays £2,000 per year for insurance on the equipment.
- The lessee can exercise a bargain purchase option on 31 December 2017 for £10,000. The expected residual value at 31 December 2020 is £1,000.
- The lessee's incremental borrowing rate is 10% (implicit interest rate is unknown).
- The fair market value of the property leased is £140,000.

The lease is classified as a finance lease because it contains a bargain purchase option. Note that, in this case, the present value versus the fair market value test is also clearly fulfilled.

The present value of the lease obligation is calculated as follows:

Present value of bargain purchase option £10,000 × 0.7513*		£7,513
Present value of annual payments	(£52,000 – £2,000) × 2.7355**	£136,775
		£144,288

*The present value of an amount of £1 due in three periods at 10% = 0.7513.
**The present value of an annuity due of £1 for three periods at 10% = 2.7355.

Note that in the example above, the present value of the lease obligation is greater than the fair value of the asset. Also note that since the lessor pays £2,000 a year for insurance, this payment is treated as executory costs and hence is excluded from the calculation of the present value of the annual payments. Since the present value is greater than the fair value, the lease obligation (as well as the leased asset) is recorded at the fair value of the asset leased (being the lower of the two). The entry on 1 January 2015 is:

DR property, plant and equipment	£140,000	
CR finance lease obligation		£140,000

According to the principles in Section 20, the apportionment between interest and capital is to be such that interest recognised reflects the use of a constant periodic rate of interest applied to the remaining balance of this obligation. When the present value exceeds the fair value of the leased asset, a new, effective rate must be computed, which will be applied to the liability. (Note, however, that if an impairment were subsequently recognised on the asset as an expense in the period of the impairment, following the procedures set forth in Section 27 *Impairment of Assets*, this would not affect the recorded amount of the lease obligation (i.e. the liability) and thus would not alter the initially determined interest rate). In this example, the interest rate was determined to be 13.265%. The amortisation of the lease takes place as follows:

Year	Cash payment	Interest expense	Reduction in lease	Balance of lease obligation
Start				£140,000
1 Jan 2015	£50,000	£nil	£50,000	£90,000
1 Jan 2016	£50,000	£11,939	£38,061	£51,939
1 Jan 2017	£50,000	£6,890	£43,110	£8,829
31 Dec 2017	£10,000	£1,171	£8,829	£nil

Disclosure requirements – finance leases for lessees

Paragraphs 20.13 and 20.14 to FRS 102 of Section 20 requires the following disclosures to be made in the financial statements of lessees in respect of finance leases:

(a) The carrying amount at the end of the reporting period for each class of asset,
(b) The total of the entity's future minimum lease payments at the end of the reporting period, for each of the following periods:
  i. Not later than one year,
  ii. Later than one year and not later than five years and
  iii. Later than five years and
(c) A general description of the lessee's significant leasing arrangements. This could include disclosure on contingent rents or renewal or repurchase options.

In addition, paragraph 20.14 requires disclosure concerning assets accounted for under Section 17 *Property, Plant and Equipment* and Section 27 *Impairment of Assets*, which apply to lessees for assets leased under finance leases.

It is also worth mentioning that the balance sheet of the lessee must split finance lease obligations between creditors falling due within one year and creditors falling due after more than one year.

Accounting for a finance lease by the lessor

Lessors recognise assets that are subject to finance leases in their balance sheet (statement of financial position) as a receivable (a debtor) at an amount that is equal to the net investment in the lease. The net investment in the lease is the gross investment in the lease, but discounted at the interest rate implicit in the lease. For the purposes of this calculation, the gross investment is the total of:

- The minimum lease payments receivable by the lessor under the finance lease plus
- Any unguaranteed residual value accruing to the lessor.

A key point to understand where this accounting treatment is concerned is that – in substance – the lessor does not actually own the asset. The lessor has essentially made a loan to the lessee at an amount that is equivalent to the net investment in the lease. The lessor receives rentals that pay off both the capital element and provide the lessor with interest income. The finance income is recognised on a pattern that reflects a constant periodic rate of return on the lessor's net investment outstanding.

For a lessor, the term 'minimum lease payments' includes:

- The payments over the lease term that the lessee is, or can, be required to make (which excludes contingent rentals),
- Costs for services and taxes to be paid and reimbursed to the lessor and
- Any residual value guaranteed to the lessor by:
  - The lessee,
  - A party related to the lessee or
  - A third party unrelated to the lessor that is financially capable of discharging the obligations under the guarantee.

Example – Change in unguaranteed residual value

A lessor has recognised a finance lease as a receivable, which has been calculated using the gross investment in the lease and discounted at the interest rate implicit in the lease. A year later it is clear that the unguaranteed residual value that was used to calculate the gross investment in the lease has changed quite significantly due to technological advances in the marketplace.

Where there is an indication that the estimated unguaranteed residual value used in the calculation of the gross investment in the lease has changed significantly, paragraph 20.19 says that the income allocation over the lease term shall be revised and any reduction in respect of amounts accrued is recognised immediately in profit or loss.

Example – Accounting for a finance lease by the lessor

Heavy Haulage Leasing Company Limited supplies heavy-duty haulage equipment to the haulage and shipping industry. Lessees have the option of entering into either finance or operating leases depending on (a) their individual requirements and (b) their credit rating and financial stability. In recent years the company has seen a rise in demand for its equipment because haulage companies are becoming less financially stable due to the volatility in fuel prices as well as such equipment becoming inherently more expensive to repair and maintain as it gets older.

On 1 January 2015, Tasha Transport (Tasha) entered into a finance lease with Heavy Haulage Leasing for the lease of ten items of heavy-duty machinery and the terms of the lease are as follows:

- The term of the lease is for five years with an option for Tasha to renew the lease for a further three years. If Tasha renews for a further three years the rentals will still be the same as under the existing lease.
- The estimated life of each asset subjected to the lease is ten years.
- The lessee guarantees a residual value of £140,000 at the end of the five-year lease term. The terms of the lease say that this guarantee will be null and void if the lease is renewed for the three-year period after the end of the five-year lease term.
- Heavy Haulage must receive equal annual payments over the life of the lease and title to the equipment is assigned back to Heavy Haulage after the expiration of the lease term.
- Payments are due on 31 December each year.
- Heavy Haulage has paid £200,000 for the heavy duty machinery but for an outright purchase the value would be £250,000.
- At the end of the five-year lease, the equipment is expected to have a residual value of £30,000 and £25,000 at the end of eight years.
- Heavy Haulage requires a return on the investment of 12%, which is also the interest rate implicit in the lease.

MINIMUM LEASE PAYMENTS

The first issue to consider is the annual lease payments due to the lessor. The present value of the minimum lease payments is arrived at using the interest rate implicit in the lease (which is 12%) and the lease term (which is eight years, including the option to renew the lease after the non-cancellable period ends). Therefore:

Cost of machinery for an outright purchase *less* present value of residual value =
Present value of minimum lease payments

£250,000 – (0.40388* × £25,000) / 4.96764**
£239,903/4.96764 = the minimum lease payments
Therefore, the minimum lease payments = £48,293.15

*0.40388 is the present value of £1 due in eight periods at a 12% interest rate.
**4.96764 is the present value of an annuity of £1 for eight periods at a 12% interest rate.

CONSIDERATION OF THE LEASE CLASSIFICATION

In this example, the entire lease term is for eight years (including the option to renew at the end of the non-cancellable term). The estimated useful life of the asset is ten years and therefore as the lease term is for the major part of the economic life of the asset, the lease falls to be classed as a finance lease (as per paragraph 20.5(c)). In addition, the present value of the minimum lease payment of £239,903 equates to 96% of the fair value of the asset (which is £250,000) and therefore is considered to be 'substantially all' of the fair value of the leased asset (as per paragraph 20.5(d)).

GROSS INVESTMENT IN THE LEASE

The next issue for consideration is the amount that the lessor (Heavy Haulage) will record in its books. The gross investment in the lease is the total minimum lease payments *plus* the unguaranteed residual value. Therefore:

$$(£48,293.15 \times 8) + £25,000 = £411,345.20$$

COST OF SALES

The cost of sales in Heavy Haulage's financial statements will be the historical cost of the goods of £200,000. However, if the lessor had incurred any additional direct costs that were directly attributable to these goods (for example, legal fees) then these would be added to cost of sales; however, in this example, no such additional costs have been incurred. The unguaranteed residual value is deducted from the cost of sales of (£25,000 × 0.40388) and therefore the cost of sales in relation to this lease is:

	£	
Cost of goods	200,000	
Less present value of unguaranteed residual	(10,097)	(£25,000 × 0.40388)
	189,903	

SALES FIGURE

The sales price that Heavy Haulage will recognise in the books is adjusted so that it equals the present value of the minimum lease payments of £239,903.

UNEARNED FINANCE INCOME

The next step is to work out the unearned finance income; this is equal to the gross investment in the lease (i.e. the lease debtor) *less* the present value of the components that make up the gross investment. The components that make up the gross investment are the minimum lease payments of £48,293.15 and the unguaranteed residual value of £25,000. The present value of these components is £250,000 [(£48,293.15 × 4.96764) + (£25,000 × 0.40388)].

The unearned finance income is therefore £161,345 (£411,345 – £250,000).

ENTRIES REQUIRED IN HILL HAULAGE BOOKS TO RECORD THE LEASE

Hill Haulage will record the lease transaction as follows:

	DR £	CR £
Lease debtor	411,345.20	
Cost of sales	189,903.00	
Stock		200,000.00
Turnover/sales		239,903.00
Unearned finance income		161,345.20
	601,248.20	601,248.20

AMORTISATION OF FINANCE INCOME

The finance income must be based on a pattern that reflects a constant periodic rate of return on the lessor's net investment in the finance lease (paragraph 20.19). To achieve this, an amortisation table can be set up to allocate the finance income as follows:

Period	Rent received £	Interest £	Reduction in capital £	Closing investment £
1.1.2015				250,000.00
31.12.2016	48,293.15	30,000.00	18,293.15	231,706.85
31.12.2017	48,293.15	27,804.82	20,488.33	211,218.52
31.12.2018	48,293.15	25,346.22	22,946.93	188,271.59
31.12.2019	48,293.15	22,592.59	25,700.56	162,571.03
31.12.2020	48,293.15	19,508.52	28,784.63	133,786.40
31.12.2021	48,293.15	16,054.37	32,238.78	101,547.62
31.12.2022	48,293.15	12,185.71	36,107.44	65,440.18
31.12.2023	48,293.15	7,852.97	40,440.18	25,000.00
	386,345.20	161,345.20	225,000.00	

Disclosure requirements – lessor accounting

The disclosure requirements relating to lessor accounting are outlined in paragraph 20.23(a) to (f), which says that a lessor shall make the following disclosures for finance leases:

(a) Provide a reconciliation between the gross investment in the lease at the end of the accounting period and the present value of minimum lease payments receivable at the end of the reporting period. In addition, the lessor should also disclose the gross investment in the lease together with the present value of minimum lease payments receivable at the end of the reporting period, for each of the following periods:
    i. Not later than one year,
    ii. Later than one year and not later than five years, and
    iii. Later that five years,
(b) Any finance income that is unearned,
(c) The unguaranteed residual amounts accruing to the benefit of the lessor,
(d) The accumulated allowances minimum lease payments deemed uncollectible,
(e) Contingent rents recognised as income in the reporting period and
(f) A general description of the lessor's significant leasing arrangements. This could include information about contingent rent, renewal or purchase options and escalation clauses, subleases and restrictions imposed by lease arrangements.

OPERATING LEASES

Operating leases are inherently less complicated to account for than finance leases. Rental expense is recognised in the profit and loss account as the payments are made or incurred (i.e. payable). Section 20 requires that expenses in relation to operating leases are recognised on a systematic basis that is representative of the time pattern of the user's benefit even if payments are not made on that basis. Generally, lease payments in an operating lease are made on a straight-line basis and the associated recognition of income in the lessor's financial statements would be made on the same basis. This treatment is not conclusive and other systematic or rational bases may well be a better representation of the physical use of the leased property. Where such alternative bases to the straight-line basis are considered to be representative of the time pattern of the user's benefit and consumption of the asset, that alternative basis should be used.

Identifying an operating lease

An operating lease is a lease other than a finance lease and, as a direct consequence, if a lease does not essentially transfer all the risks and rewards of ownership of the asset to the lessee, the lease is classed as operating and accounted for as such.

Example – Identifying an operating lease

A company leases a fleet of five motor vehicles for use by its sales people under a contract hire agreement. The useful economic life of the vehicles is considered to be five years and each of the vehicles is leased for a period of two years. The terms of the lease restrict the annual mileage to 15,000 miles for each car and if the vehicles are returned with mileage in excess of the 30,000 miles included in the lease, the company must pay an additional 10 pence per mile. The company is not the registered keeper of the vehicle, nor the legal owner and no title passes to the company at any point during or after the lease term. The leasing company is responsible for the routine maintenance of the vehicles and the risks and rewards of vehicle ownership also remain with the leasing company.

In this example, the risks and rewards of ownership remain with the lessor and in substance the lessee is merely hiring the vehicles from the lessor. No asset will be recognised in the balance sheet.

Accounting for an operating lease by a lessee

The accounting for an operating lease by the lessee is much simpler than a finance lease. Essentially, all the payments will be written off to the profit and loss account as and when they are incurred or become payable. No assets are recognised on the balance sheet of a lessee in respect of an operating lease and generally the payments are made on a straight-line basis over the life of the lease.

Example – Operating lease rentals in the lessee's books

Emery Limited has an item of machinery that it uses in its manufacturing process under an operating lease (risks and rewards of ownership have been confirmed as remaining with the lessor). The lease term is for three years with payments being made at £100,000 per annum. The terms of the lease make provision for an increase in rentals at 3% per annum to reflect an average rate of inflation. The accounting for this lease will be as follows in the books of Emery Limited:

	DR £	CR £
Year 1:		
Lease expense – profit and loss	100,000	
Cash at bank		100,000
Year 2:		
Lease expense – profit and loss	103,000	
Cash at bank		103,000
Year 3:		
Lease expense – profit and loss	106,090	
Cash at bank		106,090

Disclosure requirements – lessee accounting for operating leases

The disclosure requirements for lessees in respect of operating leases are contained in paragraph 20.16 to FRS 102. This paragraph requires a lessee to make the following disclosures for operating leases:

(a) The total amount of future minimum lease payments under non-cancellable operating leases for each of the following periods:
  i.   Not later than one year,
  ii. Later than one year and not later than five years and
  iii. Later than five years and
(b) Lease payments recognised as an expense in profit or loss.

Accounting for an operating lease by the lessor

As with finance leases, the accounting for an operating lease in the books of the lessor is less complicated than a finance lease. Payments received by a lessor under an operating lease are recorded as rental income in the period in which they are received or receivable. Revenue is recognised by the lessor using a straight-line basis unless an alternative basis of systematic and rational allocation is a better reflection of the time pattern of the earnings received under the lease.

The lessor will carry the asset subjected to the operating lease as a fixed asset (property, plant and equipment) and will depreciate such asset(s) in accordance with Section 17 *Property, Plant and Equipment*. Depreciation should be allocated on the basis that is consistent with the lessor's similar assets.

Example – Rentals received under an operating lease

Heap Limited has an item of machinery that it leases out under an operating lease (risks and rewards of ownership have been confirmed as remaining with Heap). The lease term is for three years with payments being made at £100,000 per annum. The terms of the lease make provision for an increase in rentals at 3% per annum to reflect an average rate of inflation. The accounting for this lease will be as follows in the books of Heap Limited:

	DR	CR
	£	£
Year 1:		
Bank	100,000	
Lease income		100,000
Year 2:		
Bank	103,000	
Lease income		103,000
Year 3:		
Bank	106,090	
Lease income		106,090

Disclosure requirements – lessor accounting for operating lease

The disclosure requirements for lessors that have entered into operating leases to lease assets to lessees are contained in paragraph 20.30 to FRS 102. This paragraph says that a lessor should make the following disclosures for its operating leases:

(a) The future value of minimum lease payments under non-cancellable operating leases for each of the following periods:
   i. Not later than one year,
   ii. Later than one year and not later than five years and
   iii. Later than five years,
(b) Total contingent rents that the lessor has recognised as income and
(c) A general description of the lessor's significant leasing arrangements. These could include, for example, contingent rent information, renewal or purchase options and escalation clauses.

In addition to the above disclosures, paragraph 20.31 requires disclosures relating to assets to be made in accordance with Section 17 *Property, Plant and Equipment* and Section 27 *Impairment of Assets*.

MANUFACTURER/DEALER LESSORS

It is often the case that a manufacturer or a dealer offers its customer a choice of acquiring an asset either through an outright purchase or by way of leasing. If the customer opts for a lease, paragraph 20.20 recognises that there are two types of income that arise:

- A profit or loss that arises on the sale of the asset at a normal sales price less any volume or trade discounts and
- Finance income over the term of the lease.

Example – Revenue at the inception of a lease

A manufacturer enters into a lease with a lessee. The lease falls to be classed as a finance lease as the risks and rewards of ownership pass to the lessee at the start of the lease. The asset has a fair value of £100,000 and the present value of the minimum lease payments that accrue to the manufacturer have been calculated to be £96,500. The present value has been calculated using a market rate of interest. The question arises as to which amount should be recognised as revenue.

Paragraph 20.21 to FRS 102 says that the sales revenue, which is recognised at the inception of a lease by a manufacturer or dealer lessor, is the lower of:

- The fair value of the asset or
- The present value of the minimum lease payments accruing to the lessor, computed at a market rate of interest.

As a result, the lessor will recognise revenue of £96,500.

The cost of sales that is to be recognised in the manufacturer/dealer lessor's financial statements is the cost (or carrying amount, if different) of the leased asset *less* the present value of the unguaranteed residual value.

Example – Cost of sales

A manufacturer enters into a lease with a lessee. The cost of the asset is £75,000 and at the end of the lease, the unguaranteed residual value has been calculated to have a present value of £10,000. The cost of the sale is therefore £65,000 (£75,000 less £10,000).

The difference between the amount recognised as turnover in respect of a finance lease for a manufacturer/dealer lessor and the cost of the sale is the resulting selling profit. This is recognised according to the company's policy in respect of outright sales.

Example – Restriction of selling profit

A manufacturer enters into a finance lease with a lessee and to entice the customer to enter into the lease, agrees to charge an artificially low rate of interest in the lease.

When a manufacturer or dealer lessors enters into a finance lease with a lessee and charges an artificially low rate of interest, the selling profit must be restricted to the amount that would apply if a market rate of interest were charged. Any costs that have been incurred by a manufacturer or dealer lessor with regards to negotiating and arranging the lease are recognised as an expense when the selling profit is recognised.

SALE AND LEASEBACK TRANSACTIONS

In a sale and leaseback transaction, the owner of the property (the seller-lessee) sells an item of property (the asset) and then immediately leases all, or part, of it back from the buyer (the buyer-lessor). Such transactions are usually entered into when the seller-lessee is experiencing cash flow difficulties and needs access to a source of finance. Such transactions have become increasingly prevalent over the years with banks and finance houses entering into such transactions as opposed to entering into alternative loan finance.

The accounting for a sale and leaseback transaction is made up of two, very distinct, parts:

1. There is a sale of an asset and
2. There is a lease agreement for the same asset in which the seller is the lessee and the buyer is the lessor.

In a sale and leaseback arrangement, the structure of the agreement is usually such that the sales proceeds of the asset are greater than its fair value. Therefore, there is an immediate benefit to the seller-lessee because they will have the advantage of an increased gain on the sale of the asset and the buyer-lessor sees an advantage in higher rental payments and a larger depreciable basis.

A sale and leaseback transaction can result in either a finance or an operating lease and the accounting treatment depends on the classification of the type of lease.

If the sale and leaseback results in a finance lease, any gain on disposal of an asset is not recognised immediately in profit or loss (unlike if the asset was sold outright). Instead, any gain recognised is deferred and amortised over the lease term.

Example – Gain on disposal in a finance leaseback

Alex Co. Limited sells a building to a finance house and immediately leases it back under a finance lease. At the inception of the finance leaseback, the building had a net book value of £100,000 and the proceeds received were £150,000. Alex Co. Limited has recognised the £50,000 as a gain on disposal of property, plant and equipment in its financial statements.

The gain on disposal of £50,000 should NOT be recognised in profit or loss and should be deferred and released to profit or loss over the term of the lease. Assuming that the lease term is for five years, Alex Co. Limited should recognise £10,000 (£50,000/5 years) over the term of the lease. Any remaining deferred income is shown within creditors in the balance sheet and split between the amount falling due within one year and after more than one year (as would normally be the case for current and long-term creditors).

If a sale and leaseback transaction results in the lease falling to be classed as an operating lease, and there is evidence that the transaction is at fair value, the seller-lessee does recognise any profit or loss at the inception of the lease immediately.

Example – Sale price below fair value

Alicia Co. Limited sells a building to a finance house and immediately leases it back. However, the terms of the lease confirm that the risks and rewards of ownership remain with Alicia Co. Limited and therefore the lease falls to be classed as an operating sale and leaseback lease. The fair value of the building is £120,000 and the sales proceeds amounted to £100,000. The terms of the operating lease make no provision for compensation for the £20,000 loss by way of rentals that are below market price.

In this example, the £20,000 loss is recognised in profit or loss immediately. However, if the terms of the lease made provision that the loss is compensated for by way of future lease payments at below market price, Alicia Co. Limited would defer and amortise the loss in proportion to the lease payments over the term for which the expected asset is to be used.

Example – Sales price above fair value

Alicia Co. Limited sells a building to a finance house and immediately leases it back. However, the terms of the lease confirm that the risks and rewards of ownership remain with Alicia Co. Limited and therefore the lease falls to be classed as an operating sale and leaseback lease. The fair value of the building is £120,000 and the sales proceeds amounted to £150,000.

In this example, the proceeds are £30,000 higher than fair value and therefore Alicia Co. Limited must defer this excess over the period for which the asset is expected to be used.

When a sale and leaseback transaction is entered into, the disclosures required for both lessees and lessors apply equally. Paragraph 20.35 requires a description of the significant leasing arrangements to also include a description of any unique or unusual provisions within the lease or terms of the sale and leaseback transactions.

POTENTIAL CHANGES TO LEASE ACCOUNTING

The issue of leasing has been the subject of much debate around the globe over the last couple of years. The problem that has been identified with leasing arrangements surrounds the concept of 'off-balance sheet finance'. This is where leasing arrangements are, in substance, finance leases and therefore reportable on an entity's balance sheet, whereas, in fact, the leases are kept off the balance sheet and accounted for as an operating lease.

The International Accounting Standards Board (IASB) are responsible for issuing mainstream IFRSs. IFRS for SMEs is essentially based on IFRS (although extremely condensed to be appropriate for its target audience, being SME companies). FRS 102 is based on IFRS for SMEs and, therefore, whilst the Financial Reporting Council have not yet intimated it may change the standards on leasing, the issue surrounding leases is a topical issue that UK and Republic of Ireland practitioners and accountants should be aware of.

At a meeting in London on 13 June 2012, the IASB and the US standard-setters, the Financial Accounting Standards Board (FASB), both agreed on a revised method of accounting for leasing arrangements that would include two types of lease transactions based on the length of time a lease is taken out in comparison to the value of the leased asset. This meeting followed up from an exposure draft issued in 2010 '*2010 Leases*', which caused an element of outcry among those that report under IFRS. The proposals in 2010 introduced a 'right of use' model, which was considered to be a significant change to lease accounting. The exposure draft suggested that all leases, regardless of whether risks and rewards remain with the lessor or pass to the lessee, should be treated as a finance lease and therefore essentially eradicating the operating lease classification.

These proposals came in for a substantial amount of criticism from those entities that use genuine operating leases as a means of financing assets. Indeed, many professional accountants and analysts said that the model would seriously distort the financial statements, particularly EBITDA.

Had the proposals been given the go-ahead and been enshrined into IFRS, a company would have had to apply the 'effective interest method' on the liability owed to the lessor. This means that a company would have an interest charge based on its outstanding liability, so the financial statements would reflect a higher charge in earlier years, whilst a lower rate of interest would be recognised in later years, therefore giving rise to the expense profile being 'front-loaded' in the earlier years of a leasing arrangement.

Other entities were also concerned as to the effect the proposals would have on them because the revised accounting treatment would result in lower asset turnover ratios, lower return on capital employed and a detrimental impact on gearing ratios. For companies that have loan covenants in subsistence with their lenders, the proposals were quite worrying as it could mean that loan covenants may well be breached.

The IASB and FASB tentatively agreed that all leases should be recorded on the balance sheet, but acknowledged the need to consider the ways in which the classification and pattern of expense should be recognised within profit or loss.

On 13 June 2012, the IASB and FASB agreed on an approach for lease accounting in respect of the expense that would be recognised in profit or loss. This would affect companies that report under IFRS and US GAAP and the IASB and FASB are planning to issue a standard in the next couple of years.

Under the 'compromise', the two boards agreed that some lease contracts would be accounted for under a similar approach to the treatment outlined in the 2010 exposure drafts; hence all such leases will be reported on the balance sheet. This treatment would apply to the vast majority of lease transactions that are entered into for periods of more than one year.

There are some leases that would be accounted for in a similar way to an operating lease – in other words, by way of a straight-line expense into profit or loss – and this treatment would apply to those leases that represent a relatively small percentage of the life (or value) of the leased asset. Hence, if a lease transaction is not significant over the life of the asset, the treatment is the same as that under an operating lease.

Expensing leasing payments on a straight-line basis to profit or loss for those leases that represent a relatively small percentage of the life or value of the leased asset would eliminate an 'uneven spread' because otherwise if such short leases with a relatively small percentage of the life or value of the leased asset were placed on the balance sheet, this would result in depreciation charges and interest charges on the liability; hence there would be a higher expense reported in profit or loss in the early part of a lease transaction.

The proposals are extremely controversial at the time of writing and the IASB have intimated that they expect to issue a standard in 2015/2016, although there are many in the profession that are against the proposals, including professional bodies, and this timeline could potentially be extended further given the controversial nature of the proposals (although the IASB are keen to have the leasing standard finalised in 2015/16).

For the UK and Republic of Ireland, it is important that an awareness of the leasing proposals is borne in mind because if the proposals are enshrined into IFRS, it could well be that eventually the UK and Republic of Ireland also follow suit so as to ensure that FRS 102 is converged as far as possible to the international counterpart.

In May 2013, the IASB issued an Exposure Draft (ED), which contained a dual approach to the recognition of lease expense. The ED acknowledged that there are a wide variety of leasing transactions all with different economics and hence the ED proposed a dual approach to the recognition, measurement and presentation of expenses and cash flows that arise from a lease.

Under the proposals, an entity would determine which approach to apply based on the amount of consumption of the underlying asset. This principle identifies that there is a difference between a lease for which the lessee pays for the part of the underlying asset that it consumes during the term of the lease and a lease for which the lessee merely pays for use.

The ED splits assets into 'Type A' and 'Type B'. Type A leases are most equipment (plant, equipment and vehicles) where the income statement will recognise the amortisation and interest charges, with the cash flow statement recognising the principal and interest paid. Type B leases are most property leases where the income statement will recognise a single lease expense and the cash flow statement will recognise the total cash paid. The ED then goes on to acknowledge that when a lessee enters into a Type A lease, it effectively acquires the part of the underlying asset that it consumes and is paid for over time by the leasing payments. It follows, therefore, that the lessee will amortise its right-of-use in the same line item as other similar expenses (such as depreciation of property, plant and equipment) and interest on the lease liability in the same line as interest on other, similar financial liabilities.

Conversely, in a Type B lease, the lease payments represent amounts paid to provide the lessor with a return on its investment in the underlying asset (in other words, a charge for the use of that asset). The charge itself would be relatively constant over the term of the lease and hence such payments are presented as one amount in the income statement on a straight-line basis.

SMALL COMPANIES

There are no major differences between the way a finance and operating lease is accounted for under the FRSSE (effective January 2015) and lease accounting found in Section 7 *Leases* to the FRSSE (effective January 2015). The disclosure requirements under the FRSSE (effective January 2015) are found in paragraphs 7.16 to 7.18.

For lessees, disclosure is made of:

(a) Either:
    i. The gross amounts of assets that are held under finance leases plus the related accumulated depreciation in respect of (1) land and buildings and (2) other fixed assets in total or
    ii. As an alternative from separate disclosure from that in respect of owned fixed assets, the information in (i) above may be combined so that the totals of gross amount, accumulated depreciation, net amount and depreciation allocated for the period for (1) land and buildings and (2) other fixed assets in aggregate for those assets that the entity holds under finance leases are included with similar amounts for owned fixed assets. However, where this alternative treatment is used by the reporting entity, the net amount of assets that are held under finance leases and the amount of depreciation allocated for the period in respect of assets under finance leases that have been included in the overall total should be disclosed separately.
(b) The amounts of finance lease obligations (net of interest charges allocated to future periods). These are to be disclosed separately from other obligations and liabilities and can be disclosed either on the face of the balance sheet or in the notes to the accounts.
(c) The amount of any commitments existing at the balance sheet date in respect of finance leases that have been entered into but will commence after the year-end.

For operating leases, lessees are required to disclose the lease payments that the entity is committed to make during the next year, which are then analysed into those that:

- Expire within that year,
- Expire within the second to fifth years inclusive and
- Expire over five years from the balance sheet date.

For lessors, disclosure should be made up of:

(a) The gross amounts of assets that are held for use in operating leases together with the related accumulated depreciation charges,
(b) The cost of assets that have been acquired, whether by purchase or through a finance lease, for the purpose of letting under finance leases and
(c) The net investment in:
- Finance leases and
- Hire purchase contracts

at each balance sheet date.

With planned changes to the small companies regime (see Chapter 4), it is likely that the disclosure requirements may change, but the general accounting for leases (finance versus operating) will remain the same.

21 PROVISIONS AND CONTINGENCIES

INTRODUCTION

FRS 102 deals with provisions and contingencies in Section 21 *Provisions and Contingencies*. Section 21 also deals with financial guarantee contracts, unless:

1. An entity has opted to apply the provisions in IAS 39 *Financial Instruments: Recognition and Measurement* and/or IFRS 9 *Financial Instruments* to its financial instruments or
2. An entity has elected under FRS 103 *Insurance Contracts* to continue the application of insurance contract accounting.

Before the introduction of accounting standards governing the accounting requirements for provisions, companies were able to 'massage' the profits (or losses) and report figures that were 'desired' as opposed to 'true and fair'. This particular method of profit manipulation was coined 'big bath accounting' and was quite common before the introduction of SSAP 18 *Accounting for Contingencies*, which was superseded by FRS 12 (IAS 37) *Provisions, Contingent Liabilities and Contingent Assets*. A typical scenario using 'big bath accounting' entailed a company calculating 'actual' profits and then deciding these were too high (usually because if profit was too high in one year, shareholders would expect an even higher profit in the next year). Management would then create a provision for expenditure that had not actually occurred, or been committed to, at the balance sheet date and this would have the effect of reducing profit and (on the face of it) increasing liabilities. In the next year when profit was not quite as high as originally anticipated some (or all) of the provision recognised in the previous year was reversed and it was for this reason that FRS 12 (IAS 37) was issued; in other words, preventing management from looking 'bottom up' in the profit and loss account and using the profit figure as a driver for figures above profit.

The guidance that was previously contained in FRS 12 has largely been carried over into Section 21 and so there is little in the way of change that companies will encounter in their dealings with provisions and contingencies.

Section 21 does not deal with financial instruments, including loan commitments, which fall under the scope of Section 11 *Basic Financial Instruments* or Section 12 *Other Financial Instruments Issues*. Nor does Section 21 deal with insurance (or reinsurance) contracts that are issued by an entity and reinsurance contracts that the entity holds or financial instruments issued by an entity with a discretionary participation feature that falls under the scope of FRS 103 *Insurance Contracts*.

Section 21 also will not apply to executory contracts unless they are onerous contracts. The term 'onerous contracts' means a contract whereby the costs that the entity cannot avoid outweigh the benefits the entity will receive under the contract.

MEANING OF A PROVISION

A provision is a liability of an entity that is uncertain, in terms of both its timing and amount.

Care must be taken in ensuring that any amounts in respect of a provision meet the definition of such. To that end, Section 21 specifies three criteria that must be met before an amount qualifies for recognition of a provision. A provision can only be recognised when:

(a) There is a present obligation at the reporting date that has arisen because of a past event,
(b) It is probable (in other words, more likely than not) that the entity will have to transfer cash or other resources to settle the obligation and
(c) The amount of the obligation can be estimated reliably.

If the above criteria cannot be met, the entity must not recognise a provision but instead make disclosure of a contingency in the financial statements.

This criteria were introduced to counter the act of big bath accounting. The key driver in the recognition of a provision is (a) above – in other words, the entity must have an obligation at the reporting date. An obligation can be created in two ways:

* A 'constructive' obligation or
* A 'legal' obligation.

Constructive obligation

Paragraph 2.20(a) and (b) of Section 2 *Concepts and Pervasive Principles* says that a constructive obligation is an obligation that derives from an entity's actions when:

* Through an established pattern of past practice, published policies or a sufficiently specific current statement, the entity has indicated to other parties that it will accept certain responsibilities and
* Because of the above, the entity has created a valid expectation on the part of those other parties that it will discharge those responsibilities.

The meanings above are emphasising that it is essentially the *past practice* of the entity that puts valid expectations into the mindsets of others that will, in turn, create a constructive obligation.

Example – Bonus payment

A company has been in existence for over 20 years and has a long-established practice of paying bonuses to its management team using a predetermined formula on year-end profits if they exceed a certain benchmark. This benchmark has not been increased for the last ten years and the directors have intimated that they have no intention of increasing the benchmark.

Monthly management accounts are prepared with reasonable accuracy and at the year-end 31 December 2015 these showed a relatively high level of profitability. The company accountant has made an accrual for a bonus, together with the associated employer's national insurance contributions.

The company has created a constructive obligation by way of an established pattern of past practice by paying bonuses. It is this past practice that gives rise to the constructive obligation because it has created an expectation in the mindsets of management that they will receive a bonus. As the company has a constructive obligation, it would be permissible to recognise the bonus provision in the year-end 31 December 2015 financial statements.

The above example illustrates the situation whereby management have a valid expectation because of the entity's past practice. Care, however, must be taken to ensure that the obligation can be demonstrable as a constructive obligation. If the company's past practice was not to pay a bonus year on year, then it would be difficult to make such a provision unless there was adequate documentation prior to the year-end (for example, a board resolution declaring the bonus).

Paragraph 21.11C deals with the issue relating to the *restructuring* of a company. This paragraph says that a restructuring gives rise to a constructive obligation (and therefore recognition of a provision) only when an entity:

(a) Has a detailed and formal plan in place for the restructuring, which identifies at least:
    i. The business or part of a business that will be affected,
    ii. The principal locations affected,
    iii. The location, function and estimated number of employees who will be compensated for terminating their services,
    iv. The expenditures that will be undertaken and
    v. When the plan will be implemented and
(b) Raises a valid expectation in those that will be affected that the entity will carry out the restructuring by starting to implement that plan or by announcing its main features to those affected by it.

Examples of factors that may fall under the definition of restructuring include:

- A line of business being sold or terminated,
- Closure of business locations or the relocation of business activities,
- An entity's management structure being changed or
- Other fundamental reorganisations that have a material impact on the effect and nature of the company's operations.

Legal obligation

A legal obligation is an obligation that can be enforced by law. Normally it is obvious when the company has a legal obligation (for example, because of a court order). Provisions can also be made for normal day-to-day transactions, such as provisions for goods and/or services received by the balance sheet date but not invoiced.

Section 21.6 is strict on its approach to an entity's future actions (the future conduct of its business). This is because such actions do not meet the definition of a provision and the entity has not got an obligation at the balance sheet date for its future actions, regardless of how likely (or unlikely) they are to occur.

Example – Recognition of future costs

A company has an item of machinery that requires a major component to be overhauled every five years. The directors wish to provide for 1/5 of the cost of the future overhaul in the current year's financial statements.

The directors will not be able to provide for the future overhaul costs as a liability. These costs are merely an 'intention' at the balance sheet date as opposed to an 'obligation'. The directors could well decide to sell the item of machinery before the five years have expired.

Example – No obligating event at the balance sheet date

Breary Brick Company has an overseas depot that operates in a jurisdiction that has just introduced legislation that now mandates the use of air filters for all companies in the brick industry to be fitted to all buildings. The number of air filters to be fitted is determined by the size of each building. Breary Brick Company has calculated that it will need 250 air filters to be fitted at a cost of £15,000 to fit. Legislation was passed on 1 October 2015 and as at 31 December 2015 the company had not fitted the air filters. The finance director of Breary Brick Company has made a provision in the balance sheet for £15,000 on the basis that it is a legal requirement and that the company will, inevitably, have to fit the air filters.

This provision should not be recognised because at the balance sheet date no obligating event (the fitting of the air filters) had actually taken place.

On 31 December 2016 the company had still not fitted the air filters and the director commented that 'the company does not have the financial resources available to meet this expenditure and therefore whilst nobody from the authorities has been in to the company to inspect we have fitted them, we will not have them fitted'. The financial director remained sceptical about this comment and continued to recognise the provision.

Again, there is still no obligating event (despite a year passing) as no obligating event has occurred (the fitting of the air filters). There could well be a reason to make a provision for fines and penalties that may be levied under legislation because in this respect an obligating event has arisen (the non-compliance with legislation).

Example – Irrecoverable trade debtors and impaired brand

Smyth Sunbeds supplies sunbeds to beauty salons throughout the country. The company's year-end is 31 October 2016 and on this date the management undertook a review of the aged debtors listing. Management determined that there were a number of very overdue debts that they considered to be impaired. In addition, Smyth Sunbeds has its own outlets and utilises its own developed brand, FastTan Tanning. Recent adverse press reports in respect of FastTan Tanning have resulted in a significant decline in demand for this brand and management have therefore estimated that the recoverable amount of the FastTan Tanning brand is below its carrying amount in the balance sheet. The question arises as to whether provisions for impairment of the financial and non-financial assets within the balance sheet fall under the scope of Section 21.

The impairment loss on the trade debtors is not actually a provision insofar as Section 21 is concerned. Smyth Sunbeds would actually recognise a reduction in the trade debtors (a financial asset) by way of a provision for bad debts.

In respect of the impairment of the brand, the brand should be presented net of the impairment in the balance sheet in accordance with Section 27 *Impairment of Assets*. An impairment charge is not a probable outflow of economic resources, but instead it is a reduction in the cash flows expected from the brand. As a result, an impairment charge does not fall within the scope of Section 21.

RECOGNITION AND MEASUREMENT OF A PROVISION

FRS 102 says that where a provision qualifies for recognition, it should be recognised in the financial statements as the best estimate of the amount that will be required to settle the obligation. In many cases this will be obvious – especially where the monetary amounts are known. Estimates, however, may be required for items such as interest charges or penalties.

When a provision involves a large population of items, paragraph 21.7(a) of FRS 102 requires the estimate to reflect the weighting of all possible outcomes by their associated probabilities. Where there is a continuous range of potential outcomes and each outcome is as likely as another outcome, the mid-point range is used.

Example – Provision for defective goods

Scanlon Electricals sells electrical products such as dishwashers, washing machines, televisions and audio equipment. It sells goods to the general public with a warranty that covers customers for the costs of repairs that occur during the first six months from the date that the customer purchases the equipment. The company is preparing its financial statements for the year ended 31 December 2015 and it has calculated that if all the products sold contained minor defects, the costs of repair would be £1 million. If major defects occurred in all the products, the costs of repair would be £4 million.

The management of Scanlon Electricals has concluded that past experience, and future expectations, suggest that for the coming year, 75% of the goods sold will contain no defects, 20% will contain minor defects and 5% will have major defects.

The provision for the year ended 31 December 2015 can be calculated as follows:

75% × £nil	£nil
Plus	
20% × £1 million	£200,000
Plus	
5% × £4 million	£200,000
	£400,000

Where provisions are concerned, consideration must be given to the time value of money. This is because the time value of money may become a material issue to the reporting entity and paragraph 21.7 of FRS 102 requires the provision to be the expected value of the expenditure expected to be required in order to settle the obligation. Where the time value of money is material, the discount rate (or rates) used in discounting the obligation to present day values must be the pre-tax rate (or rates) that reflect market assessments of the time value of money and risks that are specific to the liability. In practice, it is likely to be fairly uncommon for the effects of the time value of money to be material and in many cases no discounting will be required because the cash flows associated with the provision will not be sufficiently far into the future for discounting to have a material impact.

There are some instances when a provision may be settled by a third party – for example, an insurance company. Before an entity can recognise a provision as an asset, the entity must consider whether reimbursement is virtually certain. In the opinion of the author, the term 'virtually certain' is more stringent than 'probable' and therefore an asset should only be recognised if the third party has confirmed that it will settle the provision.

Example – Settlement of a provision by a third party

A firm of accountants has been sued by one of its clients for the negligent preparation of a tax return. The firm has made a provision for a liability in its year-end financial statements that is equivalent to the levels of penalties and interest that are to be levied by HMRC and the firm's professional indemnity insurers have confirmed that they will reimburse the firm for these costs. This confirmation has been received by the professional indemnity insurers in writing and the reimbursement will take place after the firm's year-end has passed.

In this respect, the firm will be able to recognise a provision in respect of the reimbursement asset because it is virtually certain that the obligation will be settled by the insurers. However, the firm must make sure that, in order to comply with paragraph 21.9 to FRS 102, the amount of the reimbursement provided for within the financial statements does not exceed the amount of the provision. In addition, the firm will not be able to offset the asset against the provision – the two must be presented separately in the firm's statement of financial position (balance sheet). However, the expense within the firm's income statement can be presented net of the amount recognised for reimbursement.

At each reporting date, management must undertake a review of the provisions and make adjustments that reflect the current best estimate of the amount that would be required to settle the obligation at that reporting date. This is important because if a provision is long-standing, information may well come to light during the year that would result in a change to the estimate having to be made. When adjustments are made to provisions, they must be recognised in profit or loss. The only exception to recognising adjustments in profit or loss are if the provision was recognised as part of the cost of an asset.

When the time value of money is a material issue and therefore the entity recognises a provision at its present value of the amount required to settle the obligation, any unwinding of the discount must be recognised as a finance cost in profit or loss during the period in which it arises.

ONEROUS CONTRACTS

An onerous contract is a contract in which the unavoidable costs of the contract outweigh the economic benefits that the reporting entity will receive under it.

Paragraph 21.11A says that where an entity has a contract that has become onerous, the present obligation under the contract is recognised and measured as a provision. A typical example of an onerous contract is when a company has an operating lease for a building that it cannot sublet.

Example – Onerous contract

Company A Limited occupies two properties. One of the properties is owned by Company A and the other property is occupied under an operating lease and is owned by an unconnected third party. The provisions in the lease state that Company A Limited will pay the landlord monthly rentals amounting to £1,000 per month from 1 April 2015 to 31 March 2019. However, due to a reduction in trade, Company A has been forced to downsize and has abandoned the property it occupied under an operating lease from 1 April 2016.

Company A has vacated a property it held under an operating lease but the contract is onerous as Company A is still committed to pay the landlord future rents until 31 March 2019. Therefore the present obligation under the contract is recognised and measured as a provision in Company A's financial statements.

Example – Provision for future operating losses

Company B Limited has an operating lease on a café situated in a vibrant town centre location. The landlord has notified Company B that the property's central heating system has to be replaced, and because of health and safety legislation the café must close for a few weeks commencing on 1 July 2016. Company B's year-end is 30 April 2016 and the accountant is proposing to make a provision for the rent that will still be payable to the landlord during the week that the café is closed.

Section 21 to FRS 102 prohibits the recognition for providing for future losses (paragraph 21.6). A provision in respect of rent paid under the lease can also not be made unless the contract is onerous. The contract would only be onerous if the unavoidable costs of meeting the obligations under it exceed the economic benefits expected to be received under the contract. In this example, the operating lease cannot become onerous simply because the tenants expect to incur an operating loss for a small period of time. The facts in this example are that the rent payable over the full lease term is more than likely going to be recovered through future sales when the café is re-opened and so the contract is, therefore, not onerous.

Example – Termination of a contract

Company C Limited has a contract with a supplier and this contract is onerous. The provisions in the contract stipulate that Company C will enter into the contract on 1 January 2016 and it will run for three years until 1 January 2019. Company C wishes to terminate the contract in 2017 because a competing supplier has offered more favourable terms, but it will incur an early termination fee to terminate the contract by the existing supplier.

Company C wishes to make a provision in the 2016 financial statements for the costs of terminating the contract.

In this example, the contract has been determined as an onerous contract. It should, therefore, make provision for the net cost of terminating this contract. This is because the contract has automatically been deemed to be onerous. However, often consideration will need to be given as to whether the business in which the products are used is profitable. If it is profitable, the contract will not be onerous and the early termination fees should be charged when such fees are incurred (i.e. in 2017).

MEANING OF A CONTINGENT LIABILITY AND A CONTINGENT ASSET

Paragraph 21.12 to FRS 102 says that a contingent liability is either a possible, but uncertain, obligation or a present obligation, which is not recognised within the entity's financial statements because it fails to meet the recognition criteria for a provision. Contingent liabilities are not recognised in an entity's financial statements although the exception to this rule relates to contingent liabilities that have been assumed by the acquirer of an acquiree in a business combination and for which the provisions in paragraphs 19.20 and 19.21 to FRS 102 will apply.

Contingent liabilities must be disclosed as such within the entity's financial statements, unless the possibility of an outflow of economic resources is considered to be remote.

Example – Contingent liability

A company has made a provision for damages amounting to £10,000 in its financial statements for the year ended 31 December 2015 in respect of a legal claim brought against the company by one of its customers. The legal advisers have advised that at the reporting date they are uncertain as to the potential outcome of the case.

The company should not recognise a provision for damages of £10,000 because it is not 'probable' that an outflow of resources will be required to settle the case. The legal advisers are unsure as to the outcome of the case. In such scenarios, disclosure of a contingent liability in the notes to the financial statements should be made.

A contingent asset is directly the opposite of a contingent liability and, again, is not reflected within the financial statements of an entity. Contingent assets should only ever be recognised if it is 'virtually certain' that an entity will realise the contingent asset (for example, an insurance company agreeing to pay out a claim to the company).

Summary – provisions and contingencies

	Contingent liabilities	
There is a present obligation that probably requires a transfer of economic benefits to settle.	There is a possible obligation or a present obligation that may, but may not, require a transfer of economic benefits to settle.	There is a possible obligation or a present obligation where the likelihood of a transfer of economic benefits is remote.

| A provision is required and disclosures are required relating to the provision. | No provision is recognised but disclosure as a contingent liability is required. | No provision is recognised and no disclosure is required. |

Contingent assets

| **Inflow of economic benefits is virtually certain.** | **Inflow of economic benefits is probable but not virtually certain.** | **Inflow is not probable.** |
| The asset is not contingent, thus provision should be made. | No asset is recognised but disclosures are made in the notes to the financial statements. | No asset is recognised and no disclosure is made. |

EVENTS AFTER THE REPORTING PERIOD RELATING TO CONTINGENCIES

Where contingencies are concerned, management should undertake a review of events after the reporting period (often referred to as a 'post balance sheet events review') to determine whether a contingent liability exists. This is because a liability is only contingent if there is uncertainty surrounding the outcome at the time the financial statements are approved. Because of the time period that lapses between the reporting date and the date on which the financial statements are approved, it may well be the case that once a post balance sheet events review is undertaken, there may not be a contingent liability that requires disclosure but a requirement to recognise a provision or neither.

DISCLOSURE ISSUES

Disclosure issues relating to provisions and contingencies are dealt with in paragraphs 21.14 to 21.17A. They are split according to their nature as follows:
Disclosure requirements relating to:

- Provisions,
- Contingent liabilities,
- Contingent assets,
- Prejudicial disclosures and
- Disclosure about financial guarantee contracts.

Provisions

In respect of each class of provision, an entity is required to disclose:

(a) A reconciliation that shows:
   i. The carrying value of provisions at the beginning and end of the period,
   ii. Additional provisions during the period, including adjustments that result from changes in measuring the discounted amount,
   iii. Amounts charged against the provision during the period and
   iv. Any unused amounts reversed during the period.

(b) A brief description concerning the nature of the obligation together with the expected amount and timing of any resulting payments.

(c) An indication as to any uncertainties over the amount or timing of those outflows.

(d) The amount of any expected reimbursement, together with the amount of any asset that has been recognised in relation to that expected reimbursement.

It is to be noted that comparative information is not required in respect of the above disclosures.

Contingent liabilities

Paragraph 21.15 to FRS 102 says that unless the possibility of any outflow of resources in settlement is remote, an entity shall disclose, for each class of contingent liability at the reporting date, a brief description of the nature of the contingent liability and, when practicable:

(a) An estimate of the contingency's financial effect, which is measured in accordance with paragraphs 21.7 to 21.11,

(b) Indications relating to the uncertainties concerning the amount or timing of any outflow and

(c) The possibility of any reimbursement.

If it is not possible (i.e. impracticable) to make one or more of these disclosures, the entity shall disclose that fact.

Contingent assets

Where an inflow of resources (i.e. economic benefit) is probable (more likely than not) but not virtually certain, an entity shall disclose a description of the nature of the contingent assets at the end of the reporting period and, where it is practicable, an estimate of the contingency's financial effect, measured using the principles set out in paragraphs 21.7 to 21.11. If it is impracticable to make this disclosure, that fact shall be stated.

Prejudicial disclosures

The section recognises that only in extremely rare cases might disclosure of some, or all, of the information required in paragraphs 21.14 to 21.16 of FRS 102 seriously prejudice the position of an entity in a dispute with third parties on the subject matter of a provision or contingency.

When management conclude that the disclosures required in paragraphs 21.14 to 21.16 would seriously prejudice the entity, then paragraph 21.17 permits the entity not to make such disclosures but must disclose, instead, the general nature of the dispute, together with that fact and the reason why the information has not been disclosed.

Disclosure about financial guarantee contracts

If the reporting entity has issued any financial guarantee contracts, then it must disclose the nature and business purpose of such contracts. Also, paragraph 21.17A requires an entity to provide the disclosures required by paragraphs 21.14 and 21.15.

22 STATEMENT OF CASH FLOWS

INTRODUCTION

The statement of cash flows is one of the primary financial statements and forms part of a complete set of general purpose financial statements. Therefore, the statement of cash flows is given the same levels of prominence as that of the statement of comprehensive income/income statement (profit and loss account), the statement of financial position (balance sheet) and the statement of changes in equity.

Section 7 *Statement of Cash Flows* deals with the issues relating to the statement of cash flows and whilst companies adopting the small companies regime in the UK have a choice as to whether to present a statement of cash flows or not (small company financial reporting encourages but does not mandate small companies from presenting a statement of cash flows), there is no option in FRS 102 for companies to present a statement of cash flows. The exception is where an entity adopts the provisions in FRS 101 *Reduced Disclosure Framework*. The result of this is that many smaller entities that do not choose to report under the small companies regime will be preparing a cash flow statement for the first time under FRS 102.

The following entities are not covered under the scope of Section 7:

- Mutual life assurance companies.
- Retirement benefit plans.
- Investment funds that meet all of the following conditions:
    - Substantially all of the fund's investments are highly liquid,
    - Substantially all of the fund's investments are carried at market value and
    - The fund provides a statement of changes in net assets.

OBJECTIVE OF THE STATEMENT OF CASH FLOWS

The vast majority of companies in the United Kingdom and Republic of Ireland have a profit motive in mind and there are large variations of external stakeholders that take an interest in the financial affairs of a company. Profit is merely one element of the financial statements in which stakeholders take an interest; there are other areas such as the financial position of a company (for example, the level of net assets) that interest some users and the ability of the company to generate cash. Cash generation is a crucial aspect in business because whilst profit is understandably desirable in many companies, unless this profit is cash-backed the company will not survive in the long term.

Example – Corporation tax arrears

A reporting entity has suffered from a decline in sales during the year to 31 December 2015 due to the economy being in recession and cash flow has been extremely tight. The company had to enter into a payment arrangement with HM Revenue and Customs (HMRC) to pay its corporation tax liability over a period of time and, as at 31 December 2015, the company was still paying this liability off. Despite a difficult year, the reporting entity made a small profit on which corporation tax is payable.

The income statement (profit and loss account) will include the tax charge on the profit for the year, the statement of financial position (balance sheet) will show the total liability due to HMRC (the cumulative liability) and the statement of cash flows (cash flow statement) will show the total amount of corporation tax paid in the accounting period. From this information, the user can establish that the company has arrears in respect of its corporation tax. Without the statement of cash flows, it could be inherently difficult for a user to gain a clear understanding of the entity's financial position at the year-end.

The statement of cash flows therefore shows users the cash effects of transactions with parties that are external to the business and the impact that these cash flows have on the entity's cash position. Unlike the income statement/statement of comprehensive income and the statement of financial position, the statement of cash flows is prepared on a cash basis because, as its name defines, only those transactions that involve the flow of cash are reported in the statement itself.

FORMAT OF THE STATEMENT OF CASH FLOWS

Section 7 of FRS 102 brings about a significant presentational change to the way in which preparers of financial statements will prepare the statement of cash flows. FRS 1 *Cash Flow Statements* required reporting entities preparing a cash flow statement to prepare the statement under several cash flow classifications as follows:

- Operating activities
- Dividends from joint ventures and associates
- Returns on investments and servicing of finance
- Taxation
- Capital expenditure and financial investments
- Acquisitions and disposals
- Equity dividends paid
- Management of liquid resources
- Financing

Section 7 of FRS 102 requires the cash flow statement to be prepared using only three types of cash flow classification:

- Operating activities
- Investing activities
- Financing activities

Operating activities

A company's *operating activities* are the day-to-day revenue-producing activities that are not investing or financing activities. This category is essentially a 'default' category that encompasses all cash flows that do not fall within investing or financing classifications. Section 7.4 to FRS 102 gives various examples of cash flows arising from operating activities as follows:

(a) Receipts of cash from the sale of goods and rendering of services,
(b) Receipts of cash from royalties, fees, commissions and other revenues,
(c) Payments of cash to suppliers for goods and services,
(d) Payments of cash to and on behalf of employees,
(e) Payments or refunds of income tax, unless they can be specifically identified with financing and investing activities,
(f) Cash receipts and payments from investments, loans and other contracts held for dealing or trading purposes, which are similar to inventory acquired specifically for resale and
(g) Cash advances and loans made to other parties by financial institutions.

A notable difference here is in relation to corporation tax paid by the reporting entity. Corporation tax paid during a year would have been included in the 'taxation' cash flow classification under FRS 1. However, under Section 7 it is included within operating activities provided that corporation tax is not attributable to any investing or financing activities.

Investing activities

Investing activities are those activities that involve the acquisition and disposal of long-term assets – for example, monies used for the purchase of non-current (fixed) assets and cash receipts from the disposal of such assets. In addition to cash payments to acquire and cash receipts in respect of the disposal of fixed assets, paragraph 7.5 to FRS 102 gives further examples of activities that would typically fall under investing activities:

- Cash payments to acquire equity or debt instruments of other entities and interests in joint ventures (other than payments for those instruments classified as cash equivalents or held for dealing or trading),
- Cash receipts from sales of debt or equity instruments of other entities and interests in joint ventures (other than receipts for those instruments classified as cash equivalents or held for dealing or trading),
- Cash advances and loans made to other parties (except those whose principal activity is that of a financial institution),
- Cash receipts from the repayment of advances and loans made to other parties,

- Cash payments for futures contracts, forward contracts, option contracts and swap contracts, except when the contracts are held for dealing or trading, or the payments are classified as financing activities and
- Cash receipts from futures contracts, forward contracts, option contracts and swap contracts, except when the contracts are held for dealing or trading, or the receipts are classified as financing activities.

Financing activities

Financing activities are those activities that change the equity and borrowing composition of the company. This can include the cash proceeds received by the company for issuing additional shares of the proceeds received from the raising of a loan. In addition to funds received for issuing shares and raising loans, paragraph 7.6 to FRS 102 includes examples of cash flows that would appear under financing activities as follows:

- Cash payments to owners to acquire or redeem the entity's shares,
- Cash proceeds from issuing debentures, notes, bonds, mortgages and other short-term or long-term borrowings,
- Cash repayments of amounts borrowed and
- Cash payments by a lessee for the reduction of the outstanding liability relating to a finance lease.

Cash equivalents

The term 'cash equivalents' relates to investments that are both short term and highly liquid. They are investments that can be converted into known amounts of cash and are not subject to significant changes in value.

Example – Cash equivalents

Company A Limited has an accounting year-end of 31 December 2015 and is reporting under FRS 102. The company has a bank overdraft that it has used at the end of the accounting period due to a large customer requiring additional extensions to its credit limit. At the year-end the overdraft amounted to £120,000 net of outstanding cheques and lodgements. The directors consider that this overdraft forms an integral part of the company's cash management. The agreed overdraft facility is £200,000 and this facility has just been renewed by the company's bankers who are satisfied with the performance of the company over the accounting period. The terms of the overdraft are that it is repayable on demand and will be reviewed on 2 January 2016. The finance director has included the bank overdraft within the financing activities section of the statement of cash flows as he considers the overdraft to be similar to the entity's existing borrowings.

Paragraph 7.2 considers a bank overdraft to normally be considered as financing activities (similar to borrowings). However, where the overdraft is repayable on demand and also forms an integral part of the business's cash management function then they should be classed as a component of cash and cash equivalents.

Indirect and direct methods

Section 7 offers a choice for reporting entities to prepare their statement of cash flows using either the 'direct' or the 'indirect' method of preparation. Whilst FRS 102 does not prescribe a set method for entities, it is implicitly preferred by UK GAAP for entities to use the direct method because this uses the major classes of gross cash receipts and payments and thus is considered to be more informative. However, the reality is that reporting entities tend to favour the use of the indirect method merely because it is inherently less complex than the direct method. In any event, both methods of preparation are acceptable.

As mentioned above, the direct method uses the major classes of gross cash receipts and gross cash payments and can be illustrated as follows.

Example – The direct method

	2016	2015
	£'000	*£'000*
Cash flows from operating activities		
Cash receipts from customers	X	X
Cash payments to suppliers	(X)	(X)
Cash paid to employees	(X)	(X)
Interest paid	(X)	(X)
Corporation tax paid	(X)	(X)
Net cash from operating activities	X	X

The indirect method adjusts profit or loss for the effects of non-cash items that make up a company's profit, such as depreciation, accruals and prepayments, as well as adjusting profit for the changes in working capital. This can be illustrated as follows.

Example – The indirect method

	2016	2015
	£'000	*£'000*
Cash flows from operating activities		
Profit for the year	X	X
Adjustments for:		
Depreciation	X	X
Amortisation	X	X
Profit on disposal of property, plant and equipment	(X)	(X)
Equity-settled share-based payment		
Transaction	X	X
(Increase) decrease in inventories	(X)	X
(Increase) decrease in trade receivables	(X)	X
Increase (decrease) in trade payables	X	(X)
Interest paid	(X)	(X)
Corporation tax paid	(X)	(X)
Net cash from operating activities	X	X

Presentation of cash and cash equivalents

Ordinarily the amount of cash and cash equivalents presented at the foot of the statement of cash flows will be in agreement with the amounts of cash and cash equivalents reported in the company's statement of financial position (balance sheet) at the end of the accounting period. Therefore, if this is the case, then reporting entities will not be required to present a reconciliation of amounts reported in the statement of cash flows to the equivalent items that are reported in the company's statement of financial position under paragraph 7.20.

However, where the totals for cash and cash equivalents are not readily identifiable (for example, because they may relate to different balance sheet amounts), sufficient information should be disclosed to enable the movements to be understood by the users. This is required by FRS 102 on the basis that cash and cash equivalents per the statement of cash flows are not necessarily the same as the single figure per the balance sheet.

DIVIDENDS AND INTEREST

Under previous UK GAAP at FRS 1, dividends paid were disclosed in the cash flow statement under the cash flow classification of 'equity dividends paid'. However, Section 7 to FRS 102 considers both dividends and interest as either operating or financing cash flows. In general, paragraph 7.4 requires a company to present cash flows from interest and dividends both paid and received separately and consistently from one period to the next as either operating, investing or financing cash flows.

Interest paid and interest and dividends received could be classified by a company as operating cash flows because they are included in profit or loss for the accounting period. Alternatively, they may be classified as financing cash flows if they are costs of obtaining financial resources or are returns on investments.

Dividends paid to shareholders may be classified as financing activities because they are a cost of obtaining financial resources. However, FRS 102 does permit an entity to classify dividends paid as a component of cash flows from operating activities on the grounds that they are paid out of operating cash flows.

Example – Illustrative statement of cash flows under FRS 102			

	Note	2016	2015
		£'000	*£'000*
Operating activities			
Profit before tax		X	X
Adjustments	1	X	(X)
Net changes in working capital	2	X	X
Taxation paid		(X)	(X)
Cash flows from operating activities		X	X
Investing activities			
Purchase of fixed assets		(X)	(X)
Proceeds from disposal of fixed assets		X	X

Acquisition of subsidiary (net of cash)	(X)	(X)
Interest received	X	X
Cash flows from investing activities	(X)	(X)
Financing activities		
Proceeds from issue of share capital	X	X
New loan raised	X	X
Capital repayments	(X)	(X)
Interest paid	(X)	(X)
Dividends paid	(X)	(X)
Cash flow from financing activities	(X)	(X)
Net changes in cash and cash equivalents	X	X
Cash and cash equivalents at start of year	X	X
Cash and cash equivalents at end of year 3*	X	X

*A note reconciling the cash and cash equivalents reported in the statement of cash flows to the cash and cash equivalents reported in the balance sheet will not be required if these amounts are identical to the amount similarly described in the balance sheet.

MATERIAL NON-CASH TRANSACTIONS

By definition, the statement of cash flows excludes all non-cash transactions because its objective is to report how an entity has generated cash during an accounting period and how that cash has been used in the business. However, where material non-cash transactions are concerned, paragraph 7.18 does require an entity to disclose such transactions elsewhere in the financial statements in such a way that the information disclosed provides all the relevant information about an entity's investing and financing activities.

Paragraph 7.19 gives some examples of non-cash transactions, which are:

(a) The acquisition of assets either by assuming directly related liabilities or by means of a finance lease,
(b) The acquisition of an entity by means of an equity issue and
(c) The conversion of debt to equity.

In practice, such issues can be disclosed at the foot of the statement of cash flows or alternatively cross-referenced to a detailed disclosure note in the notes to the financial statements. Whatever preference is adopted by the company, it is important that such material non-cash transactions are disclosed with sufficient detail to enable users to gain an understanding of the impact that such material non-cash transactions have on the entity.

SMALL COMPANIES

Smaller companies that choose to report under the small companies regime (for example, the FRSSE) are encouraged, but not mandated, to report cash flow information. However, where an entity chooses to report cash flow information, they can do so by using the indirect method. The FRSSE (effective January 2015) gives an example of a cash flow statement on page 86 using the following format (please note at the time of writing the FRC were consulting on withdrawing the FRSSE):

	£	£
Cash generated from operations		
Operating profit/(loss)	(X)	
Reconciliation to cash generated from operations:		
Depreciation	X	
Increase in stocks	(X)	
Decrease in trade debtors	X	
Decrease in trade creditors	(X)	
Increase in other creditors	X	
		X
Cash from other sources		
Interest received	X	
Issues of shares for cash	X	
New long-term bank borrowings	X	
Proceeds from sale of tangible fixed assets	X	
		X
Application of cash		
Interest paid	(X)	
Tax paid	(X)	
Dividends paid	(X)	
Purchase of fixed assets	(X)	
Repayments of amounts borrowed	(X)	
		(X)
Net increase in cash		X
Cash at bank and in hand less overdrafts at beginning of year		(X)
Cash at bank and in hand less overdrafts at end of year		X
Consisting of:		(X)
Cash at bank and in hand	X	
Overdrafts included in bank loans and overdrafts falling due within one year	(X)	
	X	

Major non-cash transactions: finance lease

During the year the company entered into finance lease arrangements in respect of assets with a total capital value at the inception of the lease of £X.

CONSOLIDATED FINANCIAL STATEMENTS

Parent companies should prepare a consolidated statement of cash flows that reflects the cash flows of the group entity. Adjustments will need to be made to eliminate intra-group cash flows (in other words eliminating those cash flows to and from the group as a whole). The principle behind the consolidated statement of cash flows is to show the results of the group in line with its economic substance – that of a *single* reporting entity.

The group statement of cash flows is prepared from the consolidated financial statements and as such reflects the cash flows of the group as a whole. The principles underpinning the group statement of cash flows is essentially the same as preparing a statement of cash flows at the individual company level. However, there are some important issues that arise in the preparation of the group statement of cash flows, which relate to:

- Dividends paid out to non-controlling interests,
- Dividends received from equity accounted investees, such as associates and
- Cash flows arising from the acquisition or disposal of subsidiary companies.

Dividends paid out to non-controlling interests

There are various transactions that affect non-controlling interests (usually referred to as 'minority interests' in the UK and Republic of Ireland). Non-controlling interests (NCI) are those additional investors in the company who hold the remainder of the shares. Such transactions include:

- Proposed dividends to NCI,
- NCI share of foreign exchange losses,
- NCI share of after-tax profit and
- NCI share of any revaluation gains/losses.

The dividends paid to NCI can be calculated as a balancing figure by way of a control account (or a 'T' account if preferred) as follows:

	Debit	Credit
Opening NCI b/fwd		X
Dividend proposed		X
Share of after-tax profit		X
Share of revaluation gain		X
Share of foreign exchange loss	X	
Dividends paid in the year*	X	
Closing NCI c/fwd	Y	
	X	X
Closing balance c/fwd (proof):		
NCI	X	
Proposed dividend to NCI	X	
	Y	

*= balancing figure

Dividends received from equity accounted investees, such as associates

The calculation of dividends received from associates and joint ventures can be calculated using a control account (or a 'T' account if preferred):

	Debit	Credit
Fixed asset investment b/fwd	X	
New shares	X	
After-tax profit	X	
Dividends from associate		X*
Closing balance c/fwd		Y
	X	X
Closing balance c/fwd (proof):		
Fixed asset investment c/fwd	X	
Dividends due from associate	X	
	Y	

*= balancing figure

Example – Dividends to parent and NCI

Extracts from the financial statements of Alicia Interiors Limited for the year ended 31 December 2015 are as follows:

	2015	*2014*
	£'000	*£'000*
Net assets in associate	300	280
Proposed dividend to parent company	60	65
Proposed dividend to NCI	4	8
Non-controlling interests	54	34

Income statement

Income from associate	24
NCI	(45)

Statement of changes in equity

Dividend on ordinary shares	(95)

*= balancing figure

The above will be dealt with as follows in the statement of cash flows for Alicia Interiors Limited for the year ended 31 December 2015:

		£'000
Dividend from associate	(W1)	4
Dividend paid to NCI	(W2)	(29)
Equity dividend paid	(W3)	(100)

W1

Net assets in associate b/fwd	280
Share of profit	24
Dividends received (balancing figure)	(4)
Balance c/fwd	300

W2

Opening balance (dividend)	8
NCI	34
To income statement	45
Dividends paid to NCI (balancing figure)	(29)
Balance c/fwd (dividend)	(4)
NCI	(54)

W3

Balance b/fwd	65
Per SoCIE	95
Dividends paid to group (balancing figure)	(100)
Balance c/fwd	60

Cash flows arising from the acquisition or disposal of subsidiary companies

The group statement of cash flows should deal with the acquisition and disposal of subsidiary companies separately.

If a parent company acquires a subsidiary during the accounting period then, when calculating the operating cash flows, subtract the inventory, receivables and payables, etc., at the acquisition date from the movement on these items.

If a parent company disposes of a subsidiary in the period, then when calculating the operating cash flows, remember to add the inventory, receivables and payables, etc., at the date of acquisition from the movement on these items.

When comparing the group statements of financial position, each of the individual net assets of a subsidiary that has been acquired or disposed of in the accounting period must be excluded. This is because the overall net cash effect has already been dealt with as a purchase of the subsidiary and net cash (or overdraft) acquired.

Example – Acquisition of a subsidiary in the accounting period

---

Lucas Limited acquired Gabriella Limited for £22 million during the year to 31 December 2015. The terms of the acquisition included consideration of £3 million 25p shares with a market value of £4 each. The balance was paid in cash.

On the date of acquisition, the net assets of Gabriella were as follows:

	£'000
Tangible non-current assets	13,000
Inventory	8,995
Trade and other receivables	14,280
Cash at bank	2,830
Trade and other payables	(23,224)
Bank overdraft	(5,182)
Non-controlling interests	(5)
	10,694

The group statement of cash flows for the Lucas Group will be as follows:

	£'000
Investing activities	
Purchase of subsidiary	(10,000)
Overdraft acquired on acquisition (£5,182 – £2,830)	(2,352)

Notes to the group statement of cash flows (extract)

	£'000
Net assets acquired	
Tangible non-current assets	13,000
Inventories	8,995
Trade and other receivables	14,280
Cash at bank	2,830
Trade and other payables	(23,224)
Bank overdraft	(5,182)
Non-controlling interests	(5)
	10,694
Goodwill (balancing figure)	11,306
	22,000
Satisfied by:	
Shares allotted (3,000 × £4)	12,000
Cash (balancing figure)	10,000
	22,000

If it is assumed that pre-tax profit of the Lucas Group for the year was £20 million. Included in the pre-tax profit are depreciation charges of £3.2 million and in the year the Lucas Group sold an item of machinery with a net book value of £1.1 million for £1 million. The balance sheet extracts are as follows:

	2015	2014
	£'000	£'000
Tangible non-current assets	165,110	143,228
Inventories	92,113	60,142
Trade and other receivables	45,687	23,164
Trade and other payables	75,897	41,231

The impact on the statement of cash flows is as follows:

	£'000	£'000
Profit before tax		20,000
Loss on disposal of non-current assets		100
Depreciation		3,200
Increase in inventory (92,113 – (60,142 + 8,995))		(22,976)
Increase in receivables (45,687 – (23,164 + 14,280))		(8,243)
Increase in payables (75,897 – (41,231 + 23,224))		11,442
Net cash flow from operating activities		3,523
Investing activities:		
Purchase of tangible non-current assets (W1)	(13,182)	
Sale of non-current assets	1,000	
		(12,182)
Purchase of subsidiary (see previous example)	(10,000)	
Overdraft acquired with subsidiary	(2,352)	
		(12,352)

W1

Opening balance b/fwd	143,228
Subsidiary acquired (see previous example)	13,000
Depreciation charge	(3,200)
Disposals	(1,100)
Balance c/fwd	(165,110)
Additions = balancing figure	13,182

The above examples for subsidiary companies concentrated on the acquisition of a subsidiary during the accounting period. However, it is not uncommon for parent companies to dispose of a subsidiary and the cash effects of such disposals will affect the group statement of cash flows, as can be illustrated as follows.

Example – Disposal of a subsidiary

Alex Limited has held a 75% investment in James Limited for several years. On 31 December 2015, Alex Limited disposed of the investment in its entirety for £1.5 million in cash. Extracts from the financial statements of James Limited are as follows:

Statement of Financial Position (Extract)

	£'000
Inventory	489
Receivables	525
Cash at bank	110

Consolidated Statement of Financial Position (Extract) of Alex Group as at 31 December 2015

	2015	2014
	£'000	£'000
Inventory	1,645	1,983
Receivables	4,385	4,662
Cash at bank	410	165

The impact of the disposal on the Alex Group statement of cash flows for the year ended 31 December 2015 can be illustrated as follows:

	£'000
Profit before tax	X
Increase in inventory (1,645 + 489 – 1,983)	(151)
Increase in receivables (4,385 + 525 – 4,662)	(248)
Net cash disposed of in subsidiary	X
Acquisitions and disposals:	
Disposal of subsidiary	1,500
Net cash disposed of in subsidiary	(110)

NOTES TO THE GROUP STATEMENT OF CASH FLOWS (EXTRACT)

Net assets disposed of:	*£'000*
Inventories	489
Receivables	525
Cash	110
Non-controlling interests	(X)
	X
Profit/(loss) on disposal	X
	1,500
Satisfied by:	
Cash	1,500

DISCLOSURE ISSUES

Paragraph 7.21 to FRS 102 requires an entity to disclose, together with commentary from management, the amount of significant cash and cash equivalent balances held by the entity that are not available for use by the entity. Cash and cash equivalents that are held by an entity may not be available for use by the entity because of, among other reasons, foreign exchange controls or legal restrictions.

23 INVESTMENTS IN ASSOCIATES AND JOINT VENTURES

INTRODUCTION

The issue relating to associates and joint ventures is twofold. First, FRS 102 deals with the issue of accounting for investments in associates at both separate and consolidated financial statements levels in Section 14 *Investments in Associates*. Second, joint ventures are also dealt with separately in Section 15 *Investments in Joint Ventures* and this Section also covers the issue of accounting for an entity's investments in joint ventures at both separate and consolidated financial statements levels. This chapter combines the two for ease of reference and looks at the accounting for investments in associates in the first half of the chapter with the latter half of the chapter dealing with joint ventures.

The scope of Section 14 is fairly short and deals with the accounting for investments in associates in both the consolidated financial statements and how an entity should account for its investments in associated undertakings in its own individual financial statements when the reporting entity is *not* a parent (i.e. when the entity does not have any subsidiaries). With regards to investments in associates in the individual financial statements of a parent company, such issues are dealt with in paragraphs 9.24 and 9.26 of FRS 102.

The scope of Section 15 is again fairly short and deals with the accounting for joint ventures in the consolidated financial statements and the accounting for investments in joint ventures in the individual financial statements of a venturer that is *not* a parent (i.e. when the venturer does not have any subsidiaries). In addition, Section 15 also deals with the accounting for investments in jointly controlled operations and jointly controlled assets in the separate financial statements of a venturer that *is* a parent. With regards to investments in jointly controlled entities in the individual financial statements of a venturer that is a parent company, such issues are also dealt with in paragraphs 9.24 and 9.26 to FRS 102.

IDENTIFYING AN INVESTMENT IN AN ASSOCIATE

To be able to identify when an entity has an investment in an associated undertaking, it is important to understand what gives rise to an entity having an investment in an associate.

Firstly, an associate does not necessarily have to be a company (i.e. an incorporated entity). An associate can also be an unincorporated entity, such as a partnership. The key to identifying an investment in an associate is to establish whether the reporting entity has *significant influence* over the investment. For the purposes of financial reporting, the term 'significant influence' is NOT control because if the investor has control over the investee, this would give rise to a parent–subsidiary relationship. It follows therefore that an associate is not a subsidiary and nor is it an interest in a joint venture.

SIGNIFICANT INFLUENCE

The term 'significant influence' means that the investor has the power to participate in the financial and operating policy decisions of the investee (the associate). As stated above, significant influence is not control or joint control over those policies. Significant influence usually arises when the investor holds between 20 and 50% of the net assets (or voting rights) in an undertaking (unless it can be clearly demonstrated otherwise). As there is no control relationship, the investor is not required to prepare consolidated financial statements in respect of the associate. The concept of control versus significant influence is vital because the lack of control sets associates apart from subsidiaries and joint ventures.

Reference is made above to the investor holding between 20 and 50% of the net assets (or voting rights) in an undertaking to achieve significant influence. As is always the case with such numeric benchmarks, care must be exercised because significant influence (like control) can be obtained in a variety of ways; for example, significant influence might be achieved through:

- Interchange of managerial personnel,
- Material transactions between the investor and the investee,
- Participation in the policy-making process,
- Provision of essential technical information or
- Representation on the board of directors or equivalent governing body.

Situations could arise (although such situations are fairly uncommon) where the investor might hold, directly or indirectly (for example, through subsidiary undertakings), between 20 and 50% of the voting power in the associate. However, unless it can be clearly demonstrated that this is not the case, it follows that significant influence will be obtained by such a holding.

Conversely, the investor might hold, directly or indirectly (for example, through subsidiary undertakings), less than 20% of the voting power of the associate. In such cases it is generally the default presumption that the investor does not have significant influence, unless it can be clearly demonstrated that such influence does, in fact, exist.

The emphasis is, therefore, on the substance of the arrangement and Section 14 does acknowledge that a substantial (or majority) ownership interest by another investor does not preclude an investor from having significant influence.

INITIAL MEASUREMENT AND EQUITY ACCOUNTING

There are two scenarios that need to be considered where investments in associates are concerned under FRS 102:

1. The investor is *not* a parent entity and
2. The investor *is* a parent entity.

This distinction is important because there are essentially two methods of accounting for investments in associates under FRS 102 depending on whether the investor is a parent company and hence prepares consolidated financial statements.

Investor is *not* a parent entity

When the investor is *not* a parent entity (i.e. it does not have any subsidiary companies and therefore does not prepare consolidated financial statements), investments in associates can be accounted for in the separate financial statements using one of three accounting policy choices as follows:

- Under the cost model,
- At fair value through other comprehensive income or
- At fair value through profit or loss.

When the investor is not a parent entity and the entity chooses to adopt the cost model, it measures the investment in the associate at cost price, but must also take into consideration any impairment losses that have been accumulated and accounted for in accordance with Section 27 *Impairment of Assets*. The objective of this requirement is to ensure that the investment is not carried in the investor's balance sheet (statement of financial position) at any more than its recoverable amount.

Under the cost model, any dividends (and other distributions) that are received from the associate are recognised in the financial statements of the investor as income. There is no consideration given as to whether the dividends (or other distributions) are made out of profits from the associate that have arisen before or after the investor acquired the associate. This is the same treatment as the previous UK GAAP, although not previously specifically stated.

Under the 'fair value through other comprehensive income model', the investment in the associated undertaking is recognised in the investor's financial statements initially at the transaction price. At each reporting date any changes in the investment's fair value are recognised in other comprehensive income having reference to paragraphs 17.15E and 17.15F and the fair value guidance, which is in paragraphs 11.27 to 11.32 of FRS 102. If it is impracticable to measure fair value reliably without incurring undue cost or effort, the investor shall use the cost model.

> **Example – Fair value through other comprehensive income**
>
> In 2014 an investor acquired significant influence over an associated undertaking and recognised the investment at its transaction price of £20,000. In 2015, the investment was subjected to a revaluation exercise which resulted in its carrying amount in the investor's balance sheet increasing to £25,000. The accountant has recognised the increase in profit or loss as 'other income'.
>
> Where an investment is increased as a result of a revaluation exercise, the increase is recognised in other comprehensive income and accumulated in equity (usually as a revaluation surplus). The only time such a revaluation can be recognised in profit or loss is to the extent that a revaluation gain reverses a revaluation decrease of the same investment that had been previously recognised in profit or loss.

Investor *is* a parent entity

When the investor *is* a parent entity and therefore produces consolidated financial statements then it must account for all investments in associated undertakings using the *equity method* of accounting. The equity method of accounting recognises investments in associates at the transaction price, which will also include associated transaction costs. This price is then subsequently adjusted to reflect the investor's share of the profit or loss, other comprehensive income and equity of the associate. This method of accounting is looked at in detail in the next section. However, there are different requirements for an investment in an associate that is held as part of an investment portfolio.

> **Example – Investment in associate held as part of an investment portfolio**
>
> An entity is the parent of a group of companies, some of which are wholly owned and the rest are not wholly owned but the parent owns the majority of the voting rights and are hence subsidiary companies. In addition, the parent has a number of associated undertakings that are held as part of an investment portfolio.
>
> Where an associated undertaking is held as part of an investment portfolio, it must be carried in the consolidated financial statements at fair value with changes in that fair value going through profit or loss.

Equity accounting

The equity method of accounting is a method whereby an equity investment is initially recognised at its transaction price, which should also include *transaction costs*. Transaction costs are those costs that would otherwise have been avoided had the investment in the associate not been undertaken – in other words, they are costs that are directly attributable to the investment (for example, legal fees in connection with the investment).

After initial recognition at the transaction price (inclusive of transaction costs), the carrying amount of the investment is then adjusted to reflect the investor's share of the associate's profit or loss, other comprehensive income or equity. Where equity accounting is concerned, there are some important points that should be noted and are discussed below.

Distributions and other adjustments to the carrying amount

Dividends received from the associated undertaking will reduce the carrying value of the investment. This is because dividends are a form of return on the investment in the associated undertaking and hence do not go into profit or loss.

In addition, the carrying value of the associated undertaking may also need to be adjusted as a consequence of changes in the associate's equity that have arisen from items of other comprehensive income.

Example – Dividends from an associate

North Co. (North) owns a 35% ownership interest in South Co. (South), which cost North £80,000 on 31 December 2015. On 31 December 2016, the profit of South was £70,000 and it had proposed a dividend (prior to the year-end) of £10,000.

The dividend is the return on the investors' investment in South. The investment of £80,000 is increased for North's share of the profit of £24,500 (£70,000 × 35%). The investment is then reduced by the value of the dividend of £3,500 (£10,000 × 35%) because the dividend is a return on this investment; hence it decreases the investment's carrying amount. Therefore, the carrying amount of the investment in North's books as at 31 December 2016 is as follows:

	£
Initial cost	80,000
Share of profit	24,500 (this is reflected in the profit and loss of North)
Dividend from associate	(3,500)
Carrying value at 31 December 2016	101,000

Potential voting rights

Potential voting rights are taken into consideration by the investor in establishing whether significant influence exists and hence accounting for the investment as an associated undertaking. These rights will not affect the measurement of the investor's interest in the associate; rather these should be based on present ownership interests.

Implicit goodwill and fair value adjustments

When an investor undertakes an investment in an associate, the difference between the cost of the acquisition and the fair values of the net identifiable assets of the associate are accounted for as goodwill and the rules contained in Section 19 *Business Combinations and Goodwill* will be applied. Any goodwill recognised in the transaction will, therefore, be amortised over its estimated useful life. Note that under FRS 102 goodwill cannot have an indefinite useful life.

Because fair values will be used, there will often be a difference between the fair values of the assets and the book values of those assets, which will give rise to additional depreciation/amortisation on the part of the investor. Where this occurs, the investor is required to account for any additional depreciation or amortisation of the associate's depreciable/amortisable assets, which will also include goodwill, on the basis of the excess of their fair values over their carrying values at the date of acquisition.

Impairment

When there are indicators that an investment in an associate is, or could be, impaired, the investor must test the entire carrying amount of the investment for impairment by applying the provisions in Section 27 *Impairment of Assets* as if the investment were a single asset. An important point to emphasise here is that if any goodwill has been included as part of the carrying amount of the investment in the associate, the goodwill element is *not* tested separately for impairment, but is instead tested for impairment as part of the investment as a whole.

Investor's transactions with associates

There are two types of potential trading between investors and associates: 'upstream' transactions are where the associate sells goods/services to the investor; 'downstream' transactions are where the investor will sell goods/services to the associates. Regardless of the direction of the sale, the investor must eliminate any unrealised profits and losses, but only to the extent of the investor's interest in the associate. There may also be indicators of impairment when unrealised losses exist on such transactions and hence the provisions in Section 27 might be triggered.

Date of associate's financial statements

When the investor uses the equity method, the investor must use the financial statements of the associate as of the same date as the financial statements of the investor unless it is impracticable to do so. Such impracticalities may arise due to legislation that may dictate the associate's year-end and thus may not be coterminous with the investor's year-end. When it is impracticable for the associate to have the same year-end as the investor, the investor must use the most recent available financial statements of the associate and make adjustments for any significant transactions or events that occur between the intervening year-end dates.

Associate's accounting policies

There may well be differences between the accounting policies of the associate and the accounting policies of the investor. Where this is the case, the investor should make adjustments to the associate's financial statements to reflect the investor's accounting policies so that the equity method of accounting can be applied. The only exception to this is when it is impracticable to do so.

Losses in excess of the carrying amount of the investment

The investor will discontinue recognising its share of further losses when the investor's share of the losses of the associate equals or exceeds the carrying value of the investment. Additional losses should be recognised as a provision, but only to the extent that the investor has a legal or constructive obligation (as per Section 21 *Provisions and Contingencies*) or the investor has made payments on behalf of the associate.

Example – Loss-making associate

On 1 April 2015, East Co. (East) invests £5 million in exchange for a 30% share of the equity of West Co. (West). In addition, East also makes a loan to West of £9 million, which is unsecured and East has not committed itself to any further funding. The financial statements of West as at 31 March 2016 show a loss of £20 million. The question arises as to how East should account for this loss.

East's share of the £20 million loss is £6 million (£20 million × 30%). If the loan to West is considered to be part of the investment in West, then the carrying amount of the associate is reduced by £6 million from £14 million (£5 million investment + £9 million loan) to £8 million (the ownership interest is reduced to £nil and the loan is reduced to £8 million). However, if the loan is not part of the investment in West, East accounts for the loss as follows:

1. The interest in West is reduced from £5 million to £nil.
2. A loss of £1 million (£5 million investment less £6 million loss) remains unrecognised because East has not provided any commitments to further funding.
3. As the associate is loss-making, this loss is an indicator of impairment and East should test the loan for impairment in accordance with Section 27 *Impairment of Assets*.

Discontinuing the equity method

An investor should cease using the equity method from the date that significant influence ceases. Provided that the investment has not become a subsidiary (as per Section 19 *Business Combinations and Goodwill*) or a joint venture (as per Section 15 *Investments in Joint Ventures*), the accounting for the investment depends on the circumstances of the loss of significant influence.

If the investor loses significant influence over the associate because of a full, or partial, disposal, the investor will derecognise the associate. The difference between the disposal proceeds and the carrying value of the investment in the associate relating to the proportion disposed of or lost will be recognised in profit or loss at the date that significant influence is lost. Following this disposal, any remaining interest in the undertaking will be accounted for using Section 11 *Basic Financial Instruments* or Section 12 *Other Financial Instruments Issues* as appropriate. The cost that will be used (and hence the value it will be initially recognised as a financial asset) in applying Section 11 or Section 12 will be the amount of the investment at the date that significant influence was lost.

However, if the investor loses significant influence for reasons other than a partial disposal, the investor will regard the carrying amount of the investment at the date that significant influence is lost as a new cost basis and will account for the investment under Section 11 or Section 12 as appropriate.

JOINT VENTURES: DEFINITIONS AND CLASSIFICATIONS

Joint ventures are dealt with in Section 15 *Investments in Joint Ventures*. Section 15 is a fairly short section and deals with the accounting treatment for joint ventures in consolidated financial statements as well as investments in joint ventures in the separate financial statements of a venturer that is not a parent. Finally it deals with the accounting for a joint venture for investments in jointly controlled operations and jointly controlled assets in the separate financial statements of a venturer that is a parent. For venturers that are parents and have investments in joint ventures, in their separate financial statements such investments will be accounted for in accordance with paragraphs 9.26 and 9.26A of FRS 102 as appropriate.

Defining a joint venture

The important point to emphasise at the outset is that a joint venture is a *contractually agreed* sharing of control over an economic entity. One party cannot have overall control over the entity because otherwise this would fail to meet the definition of a joint venture and may fall, instead, to be classified as a parent–subsidiary relationship. Joint control only exists when there is a contract in place in which the strategic financial and operating decisions of the activity require the unanimous consent of all parties in the venture. Such decisions cannot be made unilaterally or without the consent of ALL parties in the venture because otherwise this will not result in the venture meeting the definition of a joint venture.

Classifying a joint venture

A joint venture is the contractual sharing of joint control over an economic entity. In a joint venture the venturers have joint control for their mutual benefit and each party will conduct its part of the contractual arrangement with a view to its own benefit. All the venturers have the ability to plan an active role in setting the strategic operating and financial policies of the joint venture, which means that their interests do not necessarily only occur at the outset of the arrangement; all the venturers have an ongoing say in all strategic decisions.

Section 15 acknowledges that a joint venture can take various forms and it makes three distinct classifications of joint venture:

- Jointly controlled operations
- Jointly controlled assets
- Jointly controlled entities

Jointly controlled operations

In a jointly controlled operation, each venturer:

- Uses its own resources (for example, its own property, plant and equipment and carries its own inventories),
- Carries out its own part of a joint operation separately from the activities of the other venturer(s),
- Owns and controls its own resources, which it uses in the joint operation,

- Incurs its own expenses and liabilities and
- Raises its own finance.

The agreement that is put in place over the joint venture will outline how the venturers share the goods or service outputs of the joint operation (together with any revenue from their sale and any common expenses) in order that the venturer can recognise these in its own separate financial statements. In the venturer's own separate financial statements it will also recognise the assets that it controls and the liabilities that it incurs.

Example – A jointly controlled operation

A and B both agree to develop and manufacture a new brand of high-speed aeroplane. A agrees to develop and manufacture the engines and B agrees to develop and manufacture the body of the aeroplane. Each venturer pays the costs and takes a share of the revenue from the sale of the aeroplanes as per the agreement between them both.

In its individual financial statements, each venturer shows the assets that it controls and the liabilities that it has incurred, together with the expenses that it incurs and its share of the income from the sale of the aeroplanes.

From the above example it can be seen that Section 15 treats a jointly controlled operation as if the venturers conducted their tasks independently. This is why a venturer will account for the assets it controls and the liabilities and expenses that it incurs independently in its own books. However, the accounting entries in the books of the venturer's own financial statements will flow into the consolidated financial statements if the venturer prepares them with no further adjustments or consolidation procedures are required.

Jointly controlled assets

When an asset is jointly controlled, each venturer should recognise:

- Its share of the jointly controlled assets;
- Any liabilities that it has incurred on behalf of the joint venture;
- Its share of any joint liabilities incurred by the joint venture;
- Its share of income and expenses incurred by the joint venture; and
- Any expenses it has incurred in respect of its interest in the joint venture in its own financial statements.

Example – A jointly controlled asset

Pete and Jenny jointly own a property. Each party takes a share of the rents and bears a share of the running costs of the property.

The shared items are the property itself, revenue from rents received, maintenance costs of the property, depreciation of the property and a share of the liabilities incurred jointly with the other venturers.

The separate costs that Pete and Jenny incur are loan interest to finance their share of the property.

Section 15 apportions to each venturer its share of revenues, expenses, assets and liabilities in its own financial statements and in its accounting records. This treatment is the same sort as that for a jointly controlled operation and hence the accounting entries flow through to the consolidated financial statements if they are prepared. No further adjustments, or consolidation procedures, are required.

Jointly controlled entities

A jointly controlled entity is one that involves the creation of a company (i.e. an incorporated entity) or an unincorporated setup (such as a partnership) that is jointly controlled by the venturers.

Example – A jointly controlled entity

Les and Lisa set up a housing development company, L&L Properties Ltd, and each transfers assets and liabilities to combine their activities. The contractual arrangement is that both Les and Lisa have joint control and decisions relating to the financial and operating policies of the venture have to be unanimous.

Because the decisions relating to the financial and operating policies of the venture have to be unanimous, this means that this is a jointly controlled entity under the provisions in Section 15.

In terms of accounting treatment of a jointly controlled entity, this is where issues become slightly more complex. This is because whilst the jointly controlled entity operates in the same way as other types of joint arrangements, the exception where a jointly controlled entity is concerned is that the contractual arrangement establishes joint control over the economic activity of the entity.

Jointly controlled entities are inherently more complex to account for than any other type of joint arrangement. As with associates discussed earlier in this chapter, there are two issues that need to be considered:

- Venturers that are parents and
- Venturers that are not parents.

Venturers that are parents

Venturers that are parents and hence prepare consolidated financial statements should account for their investments in jointly controlled entities by using the equity method of accounting. This is the same equity method as that used in Section 14 *Investments in Associates* at paragraph 14.8. Where the equity method of accounting applies to a parent with investments in jointly controlled entities, the parent should substitute 'significant influence' for 'joint control' where paragraph 14.8 refers to significant influence. Additionally, the parent should also substitute 'associate' for 'jointly controlled entity'. However, the exception to this applies when a venturer that is a parent holds investments in jointly controlled entities as part of an investment portfolio that is carried at fair value. In this instance any changes in fair value are recognised in profit or loss in the parent's consolidated financial statements.

Venturers that are not parents

A venturer that is not a parent, but has one or more interests in jointly controlled entities, accounts for interests in jointly controlled entities using either:

- The cost model,
- The fair value model through other comprehensive income or
- The fair value model through profit or loss.

The cost model

Under the cost model, venturers that are not parents measure their investments in jointly controlled entities at cost less accumulated impairment losses that have been recognised in accordance with Section 27 *Impairment of Assets.*

Any dividends or distributions that have been received from the investment are recognised in income. This applies regardless of whether the dividend or distribution has been received from accumulated profits of the jointly controlled entity before or after the date of acquisition.

Fair value model

Venturers that are not parents recognise an investment in a jointly controlled entity at its transaction price. After initial recognition at the transaction price, the venturer will then measure investments in jointly controlled entities at fair value and refer to the fair value guidance outlined in paragraphs 11.27 to 11.32 of FRS 102. Any changes in the fair value are recognised in accordance with paragraphs 17.15E and 17.15F of FRS 102, which says that if an asset's carrying value is increased as a result of a revaluation, the increase is recognised in other comprehensive income and accumulated in equity. An exception to this would be where the increase reverses a revaluation decrease of the same asset previously recognised in profit or loss.

Decreases in an asset's carrying amount as a result of a revaluation are recognised in other comprehensive income to the extent of any previously recognised revaluation increases accumulated in equity in respect of that asset. Any excess of the decrease over the revaluation surplus is recognised in profit or loss.

In cases when it is impracticable to measure fair value reliably without undue cost or effort, a venturer should use the cost model.

As with the cost model, any dividends or distributions that have been received from the investment are recognised in income and this rule applies regardless of whether the dividend or distribution has been received from accumulated profits of the jointly controlled entity before or after the date of acquisition.

Fair value through profit or loss

When an entity designates an investment in a jointly controlled entity to be carried at fair value with changes in fair value going through profit or loss, the entity should have regard to paragraphs 11.27 to 11.32 of FRS 102 on how to determine fair value.

JOINT VENTURES: OTHER ISSUES

There are a couple of other issues that reporting entities need to be aware of when they have investments in joint ventures under FRS 102 and these relate to:

- Transactions between a venturer and a joint venture and
- When the investor does not have joint control.

Transactions between a venturer and a joint venture

If a venturer contributes, or sells, assets to a joint venture any recognition of a gain or loss from the transaction must reflect the substance of the transaction. Whilst the assets are retained by the joint venture and the risks and rewards of ownership of those assets have been passed to the joint venture, the venturer should only recognise that portion of the gain or loss that is attributable to the interests of the other venturers. The full amount of any loss is recognised in the venturer's financial statements when the contribution, or sales proceeds, provides evidence of an impairment loss.

If a venturer purchases assets from the joint venture, no profits are recognised until the venturer resells the assets to an unconnected party. The venturer will recognise its share of the losses resulting from such transactions in the same way as profits. The only exception to this rule is in respect of impairment losses, which are recognised immediately.

When the investor does not have joint control

As stated earlier in this chapter, in order for a joint venture to be classified as such, there has to be a contractually agreed sharing of control over an economic entity. As a consequence, no one party can have control or significant influence because joint control must be present to be able to classify an investment as a joint venture.

When joint control is not present, paragraph 15.18 requires the investment to be accounted for in accordance with Section 11 *Basic Financial Instruments* or Section 12 *Other Financial Instruments Issues*. Where significant influence can be demonstrated, then the investment is accounted for in accordance with Section 14 *Investments in Associates*.

DISCLOSURE REQUIREMENTS

This section will look at the disclosure requirements in respect of investments in associates and investments in joint ventures as follows.

Investments in associates

Unless the Regulations require otherwise, investments in associates are classified in both the individual and consolidated financial statements as fixed assets.

In addition, both the individual and consolidated financial statements should disclose:

- The accounting policy in respect of investments in associates,
- The carrying value of investments in associates and
- Fair values of investments in associates that have been accounted for under the equity method and for which published prices are available.

Investments in associates accounted for under the cost model

When investments in associates have been accounted for under the cost model, any dividends or other distributions that have been recognised as income are to be disclosed.

Investments in associates accounted for under the equity method of accounting

For investments in associates that have been accounted for using the equity method, the investor should disclose its share of the profit or loss of such associates together with its share of any discontinued operations of such associates.

Investments in associates accounted for using the fair value model

For investments in associates that the investor has accounted for using the fair value model, the entity should disclose the basis for determining fair value. If a valuation technique is used, the entity must disclose the assumptions applied in determining fair value.

When a reliable measure of fair value is no longer available for the investments in associates, this fact is to be disclosed.

Investors that are not parents

For investors that are not parents, the individual financial statements should disclose summarised financial information about the investments in associates as well as the effect of including those investments as if they had been accounted for under the equity method of accounting.

However, investing entities that are exempt from preparing consolidated financial statements (or which would be exempt if they had subsidiaries) do not have to comply with this disclosure requirement.

Investments in joint ventures

The following information should be disclosed in both the individual and consolidated financial statements:

(a) The reporting entity's accounting policy for recognising investments in jointly controlled entities,

(b) The carrying value of investments in jointly controlled entities,

(c) The fair value of investments in jointly controlled entities that have been accounted for under the equity method, but for which published price quotations are available and

(d) The total amount of the entity's commitments relating to joint ventures that should also include its share in the capital commitments that have been incurred jointly with other venturers in addition to its share of the capital commitments of the joint ventures themselves.

Joint ventures accounted for under the equity method of accounting

For joint ventures that have been accounted for using the equity method of accounting, separate disclosure of the venturer's share of the profit or loss of such investments together with its share of any discontinued operations of such jointly controlled entities should be made.

Joint ventures accounted for in accordance with the fair value model

In respect of joint ventures accounted for in accordance with the fair value model, the venturer should disclose the basis for determining fair value. If a valuation technique is used, the entity must disclose the assumptions applied in determining fair value.

When a reliable measure of fair value is no longer available for the joint venture, this fact is to be disclosed.

Venturers that are not parents

The individual financial statements of venturers that are not parents should disclose summarised financial information concerning the investments in jointly controlled entities, together with the effect of including those investments as if they had been accounted for under the equity method of accounting.

However, if investing entities are exempt from preparing consolidated financial statements (or would be if they had subsidiaries), this disclosure requirement is not required.

24 RELATED PARTIES

INTRODUCTION

The concept of related parties can be very complicated for some companies – particularly much larger, more complex entities that have a wide range of activities. Section 33 *Related Party Disclosures* deals with the disclosures that are needed where related party transactions are entered into during a reporting period. The overarching objective of Section 33 is to ensure that the financial statements contain sufficient narrative to ensure that users' are aware of the possibility that the reported financial position and performance has been affected by the existence of related parties and transactions with those related parties. Section 33 is a wholly disclosure standard.

Related party issues are also covered in the Companies Act 2006 – for example, where transactions with directors are concerned. As a result, directors' transactions that fall under the scope of the Companies Act 2006 must also be disclosed in the abbreviated financial statements of companies that are submitted to Companies House and included on the public record.

Related party transactions have proved to be problematic for both companies and auditors over the years. This is mainly due to their subjective nature and, in some rarer cases, the reluctance of directors to make the relevant disclosures as required under the standards. Over the years, the standard-setters have attempted to make the issues concerning related parties more understandable – however, the standard itself has become more complex over the years as business developments have both evolved and at the same time become more complex.

ISSUES RELATING TO DIRECTORS

The directors of a company may enter into transactions with the company itself – for example, by receiving remuneration, dividends, loans or be involved in other companies that transact with the company. In financial reporting, transactions with directors are deemed to be material by nature and therefore fall under the scope of related party transactions. However, there are complexities that are addressed within this chapter that may also need consideration and where the transaction may not, necessarily, require disclosure within the financial statements.

It is extremely commonplace within the UK and Republic of Ireland for directors of companies (particularly companies at the smaller end of the scale) to also be the shareholder(s). In their capacity as shareholders, the directors may receive dividends from the company. The question of dividends and their disclosure has ignited much debate over the years following the repealing of the need to disclose directors' shareholdings in the shares of the company within the directors' report.

Prior to April 2007, the directors' report disclosed the number of shares (or percentage holding) that the directors held in the company. Post April 2007, this disclosure was repealed. The issue then arose as to how the related party issues were satisfied. Prior to the repealing of directors' shareholdings in the directors' report, it was generally felt that the user of the financial statements could decipher the amount of dividend that a director had received from the company in their capacity as shareholder and hence the related party issues were satisfied. Following the repealing of the disclosure of shareholdings, it was felt that the related party issues were no longer satisfied and so the question arose as to whether, or not, dividends paid to directors in their capacity as shareholders should be disclosed within the financial statements.

The previous UK GAAP and, indeed, Section 33 do not specifically refer to 'dividends' as being disclosable. However, Section 33 at paragraph 33.8(a) does say that transactions that are entered into between the reporting entity and its principal owner(s) (in this context being the shareholders) are disclosable as related party transactions.

This confusion in the wording led many entities to fail to adequately disclose the value of the dividends paid to directors in their capacity as shareholders. Professional bodies clarified that dividends paid to director-shareholders should be disclosed within the financial statements in order to fulfil the related party issues. However, the requirement to satisfy the related party issues was purely from a financial reporting perspective and not a Companies Act 2006 perspective. As such, disclosure should only be made within the full financial statements and not the abbreviated financial statements as filed at Companies House. Care needs to be taken where this is concerned because only 'transactions with directors' require disclosure within the abbreviated financial statements as these are a Companies Act requirement – related party issues are a financial reporting requirement covered by GAAP and are therefore related to the full financial statements in order that the full financial statements give a true and fair view.

DEFINITION AND IDENTIFICATION OF A RELATED PARTY

The definition of a related party can be found in paragraph 33.2 to FRS 102. The term 'control' is used in this definition and for the purposes of related party relationships, 'control' is the power to govern the financial and operating policies of the entity. This is usually (but not always) achieved through a holding in the voting rights of an entity of more than 50%. However, control can be obtained through other means, such as the power to appoint the majority of the board of directors. The term 'significant influence' is also used in the definition of a related party. Significant influence is usually achieved through a holding in the voting rights of between 20 and 50%; again, an entity can demonstrate it has significant influence through other means – not merely a holding in voting rights of between 20 and 50%.

A related party relationship arises when a person or entity is related to the reporting entity preparing financial statements.

(a) A person or close member of that person's family is related to a reporting entity if that person:

  (i)   Controls or has joint control over the reporting entity,
  (ii) Has significant influence over the reporting entity or
  (iii) Is a member of the key management personnel of the entity or holds a position in key management of the parent company.

As well as individuals, entities can also be related parties of another entity and paragraph 33.2(b) outlines the conditions that could apply and trigger a related party relationship:

  (i)   Where the entity and the reporting entity are both members of the same group – i.e. the parent, subsidiary and fellow subsidiary are all related to each other,
  (ii)   Where one entity is a joint venture or an associate of the other entity,
  (iii) Where both entities are joint ventures of the same third party,
  (iv)   Where one entity is a joint venture and the other entity is an associate of the third party,
  (v)   Where the entity is a post-employment benefit plan for the benefit of the employees of either the reporting entity or of an entity that is related to the reporting entity; in situations where the reporting entity is itself a post-employment benefit plan, the sponsoring employees are also related parties,
  (vi)   If the reporting entity is controlled by any individuals in (a) above and
  (vii) Where an individual has significant influence over the entity or holds a position in the key management personnel of the entity (or the parent of the entity).

A key point to note when determining whether a related party relationship exists is to consider the substance, and not the legal form, of the relationship, and in this context Section 33.4 acknowledges that the following are not considered to be related parties:

  • Two entities that have a director or other member of key management personnel in common or where the member of key management personnel in one entity holds significant influence over another entity,
  • Two venturers that share joint control in a joint venture,
  • Providers of finance, trade unions, public utilities and government departments and agencies (for example, HM Revenue and Customs) that conduct transactions in the ordinary course of business and
  • Customers, suppliers, franchisors, distributors or general agents with whom a company enters into a significant volume of transactions.

Example – Related party relationships

Company A Limited has an associated company (Company B Limited). Company B Limited has a wholly owned subsidiary (Company C Limited) that provides management charges to Company A Limited. The question arises as to whether Company C is related to Company A for related party disclosure purposes.

Paragraph 33.4A says that, for the purposes of defining a related party, an associate will include the subsidiary (subsidiaries) of the associate. The paragraph goes on to say that a joint venture will also include subsidiaries of the joint venture. In this example, therefore, Company C is related to Company A for the purposes of related parties.

TRANSACTIONS WITH RELATED PARTIES

The overarching objective of Section 33 is to ensure that the user can gain an understanding as to the effect that related party transactions have on the financial statements. Transactions with related parties may be undertaken on an 'arm's length' basis, which means that commercial prices are charged or market rates of interest are charged on loans but they can also be undertaken on a non-arm's length basis and it is because of these situations that transactions with related parties must be disclosed.

Material related party transactions should be disclosed within the financial statements. The question arises, therefore, as to what is construed as 'material' in the context of Section 33. Materiality is defined in the Glossary to FRS 102 and the definition essentially says that if an item is omitted or misstated within the financial statements and this omission or misstatement could influence the decisions of users taken on the basis of the financial statements as a whole, then the item is material. The definition also acknowledges that there is no 'one-size-fits-all' where materiality is concerned – it all depends on the size and nature of the omission or misstatement. In addition, what may be considered material in one company (for example, a small, owner-managed business) may not be considered material in another company (for example, a large 'blue-chip' PLC). Where materiality is concerned, care must be taken to consider both the size and nature of the omission or misstatement both in isolation and in combination.

Example – Immaterial transactions

A company provides canteen facilities to its staff (which includes management and directors). The finance director purchased a sandwich from the canteen. The question arises as to whether this transaction would fall to be classified within the financial statements as a related party transaction.

The definition of 'material' in the Glossary to FRS 102 states that transactions are only material when their disclosure might reasonably be expected to influence the decisions of users. The purchase of such a trivial item from the company by the director would not be in the interests of the users. On the other hand, if the director were to purchase a property from the company at a price that is substantially less than fair value, this transaction would be considered material and would require disclosure.

Judging materiality can be somewhat problematic for practitioners. In the example above it is fairly clear what is, and what is not, considered to be material in the context of related party transactions and the needs of users. However, there are many occasions in real life when transactions are not as 'clear-cut' and become borderline. Section 33 does not provide prescriptive benchmarks for materiality and the facts of each case need to be considered in isolation. In some instances, key management personnel could well enter into several small transactions and these transactions will all need to be aggregated to see if they do become material for the purposes of related party disclosures.

When considering materiality, preparers of financial statements do so with regards to the needs of users. Users can include a variety of third parties including investors, employees, banks and financiers, trade creditors and such like. In financial reporting this tends to be a balancing act because each user will have varying needs and in some cases financial statements cannot meet the information needs of all types of users – although it is generally accepted that there are needs that are common to all users. As a result, when considering whether disclosure of a particular related party is material, the needs of the users should be a factor that is considered.

In terms of disclosure requirements, the following related party issues should be disclosed in accordance with Section 33:

- Disclosure of parent–subsidiary relationships,
- Compensation paid to key management personnel and
- Related party transactions.

Disclosure of parent–subsidiary relationships

The financial statements of a reporting entity should disclose the relationship between a parent and its subsidiaries. This requirement applies regardless of whether, or not, there have been any related party transactions. Disclosure should also be made in the financial statements of the name of the entity's parent and, where different, the name of the ultimate controlling party. When an entity or the ultimate controlling party do not prepare financial statements, which will be made publicly available, the name of the next most senior parent that does prepare financial statements that are publicly available should be disclosed (if such a next most senior parent exists).

Compensation paid to key management personnel

The term 'key management personnel' applies to those individuals within the company that have the responsibility of overseeing the stewardship of the entity. In other words, key management personnel manage, control, direct and run the company in the best interests of the shareholders. The term 'compensation' includes all employee benefits covered in Section 28 *Employee Benefits* as well as share-based payment awards, which are accounted for under the provisions in Section 26 *Share-based Payment*.

Section 33 requires all compensation, in totality, paid to key management personnel to be disclosed within the financial statements.

Example – Classification of key management personnel

A plant hire company has two divisions – one in the north of the UK and one in the south. Each division has a branch manager who is not a director.

The branch managers would be considered to be key management personnel because they are responsible for directing and controlling half of the company's principal activities.

Related party transactions

This is where the bulk of the related party disclosure requirements are concerned. A related party transaction occurs when one related party enters into a transaction to provide goods, services or obligations to another related party. A transaction can be entered into for related party purposes for nil consideration.

Example – Dividends paid to director-shareholders

A company reporting under FRS 102 pays a dividend to its shareholders, who also act in the capacity of directors, at the year-end.

Dividends paid to directors who are also the shareholders of the company are considered to be a related party transaction and should be disclosed as such in the financial statements.

When a related party transaction occurs, the requirements in paragraph 33.9 will apply. This paragraph requires an entity to disclose the nature of the related party relationship and additional information concerning transactions, balances that are outstanding at the reporting date and any commitments necessary so that the user has an understanding as to the potential effect of the related party relationship on the financial statements. This requirement is over and above the requirement to disclose key management personnel compensation. The paragraph specifies minimum disclosures that must be made where related party transactions are concerned, including:

- The amount of the related party transactions,
- Amounts outstanding at the reporting date and:
  - Terms and conditions relating to outstanding balances and details of whether such balances are secured,
  - The nature of the consideration that will be provided to settle the outstanding balance(s) and
  - Details relating to any guarantees that have been given or received,
- Details of any amounts that have been provided for in respect of uncollectible amounts that are still outstanding and
- The amount recognised in profit or loss related to amounts recognised for bad or doubtful debts.

Paragraph 33.10 requires the above disclosures to be made separately for each of the following categories:

- Companies that have control, joint control or significant influence over the reporting entity,
- Companies over which the reporting entity has control, joint control or significant influence,
- Key management personnel of the reporting entity or its parent (in totality) and
- Other parties that are related.

There are a wide range of transactions and events that could be construed as a related party transaction that falls under the scope of Section 33, and paragraph 33.12

offers some examples of such transactions. However, the list in Section 33 should not be taken to be exhaustive and, as mentioned earlier in the chapter, transactions should be considered in the light of their substance and not just their legal form.

Examples of transactions that would fall to be classified as a related party transaction include:

- Purchases and sales of goods and/or services,
- The sale or purchase of property or other assets,
- Leasing transactions,
- Transfers that occur under the terms of a licence,
- Guarantees,
- The settlement of loans or other liabilities by the reporting entity or on behalf of another party and
- Defined benefit pension plans where risks among the group members are shared.

EXEMPTION FROM DISCLOSURE OF RELATED PARTY TRANSACTIONS

There are instances when an entity may enter into a related party transaction but may not have to make disclosure of those transactions. Such instances are fairly rare, but do occur in practice.

The main exemption relates to group companies. Where members of a group enter into transactions then paragraph 33.1A allows companies an exemption of making such disclosures. However, there is a condition where the subsidiary that is a party to the transaction must be a wholly owned subsidiary. Therefore, if the parent owns, say, 80% of the voting rights in the subsidiary (with the remaining 20% owned by external shareholders) any transactions between the subsidiary and the parent will still fall to be disclosed as a related party transaction because the subsidiary is not wholly owned.

The other exemption relates to national, regional or local governments. Where a state (a national, regional or local government) has control, joint control or significant influence over a reporting entity then the entity is exempt from disclosure of transactions with such states. This also applies to transactions that may be entered into with another entity that is also controlled, jointly controlled or significantly influenced by a state. The exemptions in these cases, however, do not apply to the requirement to disclose parent–subsidiary relationships in accordance with paragraph 33.5.

CONTROLLING PARTIES

The term 'control' in the context of financial reporting is when one party can direct the financial and operating policies of the other parties. Control can be achieved through ownership of more than 50% of the voting rights in an entity; alternatively, control can be achieved through other (non-numerical) attributes, such as the power to appoint the majority of the board of directors. The controlling party will have a view to gaining economic benefit from such control.

A typical example would be where a director holds 75% of the shares in a company. By virtue of this shareholding (i.e. more than 50%) the director has control of the company.

Companies are invariably controlled by another party and this controlling party can either be the shareholders or another company. Where the company is controlled by another party, disclosure should be made of:

- The name of the controlling party and
- The name of the ultimate controlling party, if different.

These disclosures are required regardless of whether, or not, transactions have been entered into between the parties. In situations when the controlling party of the reporting entity is unknown, disclosure of this fact should be made. A point to note where control is concerned is that disclosure need only be made when there is control; disclosure need not be made where there is merely significant influence.

Example – Joint control

Company A Limited is an owner-managed business with an issued share capital of 100 £1 ordinary shares, which are split equally between Mr and Mrs Leavitt. Both Mr and Mrs Leavitt have hands-on day-to-day running of the company, are both involved in the decision-making and have control over the company's operational and financial policies.

In this case, both Mr and Mrs Leavitt are the controlling parties because they are considered to be acting 'in concert' in respect of the financial and operational affairs of the company and therefore disclosure can be made as follows:

The directors are considered to be the ultimate controlling party by virtue of their ability to act in concert in respect of the operational and financial policies of the company.

It is also worth pointing out that this could also be the case when, for example, a company has four shareholders who own (say) 25% of the voting rights. Numerically, no one director will have control, but as they all act in concert in respect of the financial and operational affairs of the business, they will collectively be considered to be the ultimate controlling party.

Example – One controlling party

Company B Limited is, again, an owner-managed business with an issued share capital of 100 £1 ordinary shares. The split of the shareholding is as follows:

- Mr Leavitt   51%
- Mrs Leavitt   49%

In this instance, Mr Leavitt has control over the company because he owns the majority of the shares. Disclosure in this respect can be as follows:

The company is under the ultimate control of Mr Leavitt by virtue of his controlling shareholding in the company.

Example – Identifying the controlling party in a group structure

A group is structured as follows:

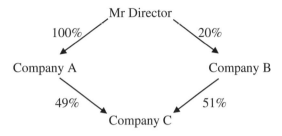

The question arises as to who the ultimate controlling party/parties is/are in the above group.

Mr Director indirectly owns ((100% × 49%) + (20% × 51%)) = 59.2% of Company C. However, it is Company B that has ultimate control of Company C. Mr Director is also not the ultimate controlling party of Company C because he cannot exercise control over that company and nor does he control Company B (as he only owns 20%), which controls Company C.

Mr Director does control Company A, but Company A cannot exercise control over Company C. Despite this, Mr Director is still a related party of Company C because his 100% ownership of the voting rights in Company A gives him significant influence over Company C. He also has significant influence over Company B, which controls Company C. As a result, if transactions have occurred between Mr Director and Company C, these transactions should be disclosed as related party transactions in Company C's financial statements.

A point worth noting is that Section 33 of FRS 102 does not require the names of related parties to be disclosed.

COMPANIES ACT 2006

There are many disclosures that are required under the small companies regime and within Section 33 that are not specifically required under the Companies Act 2006 and can be ignored for the purposes of the abbreviated financial statements.

A summary of the main disclosure requirements under Companies Act 2006 is shown within the following table:

Disclosure in	Disclosure required	Section of Companies Act 2006
Directors' report	Names of the directors	S416
Notes	Details of directors' remuneration	S412
Notes	Directors' benefits, pensions and compensation	SI 2008/410 Schedule 5 Part I
Notes	Highest paid directors' remuneration	SI 2008/410 Schedule 5 Part II
Notes	Advances, credits and guarantees by the company to the director(s)	S413

| Notes | Details of guarantees entered into by the company or subsidiary by the director(s) | S413 |
| Notes | Ultimate parent company for subsidiaries | SI 2008/410 Schedule 9 |

For group companies, the disclosure requirements in the notes under Companies Act 2006 are as follows:

Disclosure	**Section of Companies Act 2006**
Information about related undertakings	S409
Disclosure by parent of the name and financial information for each subsidiary	SI 2008/410 Schedule 1–3, 15–17
Names of, and information about, joint ventures	SI 2008/410 Schedule 18
Names of, and information on, significant holdings of company or group in investees	SI 2008/410 Schedule 4–6, 20–23
Alternative disclosure if compliance with S409 (above) would result in information of excessive length	S410
Disclosure by subsidiary of ultimate parent company	SI 2008/410 Schedule 9
Disclosure of details of investments of consolidated undertakings in, and names of, associated undertakings (i.e. between 20 and 50% of voting rights)	SI 2008/410 4 Schedule 19

Dividends to director-shareholders

Dividends paid to directors in their capacity as shareholders have been addressed in the paragraph above 'Issues Relating to Directors'. Dividends paid to directors in their capacity as shareholders are considered to be a related party issue, rather than as a 'transaction with directors'. Transactions with directors are required to be disclosed under the Companies Act 2006 (and hence will appear within the abbreviated financial statements) whereas dividends paid to directors in their capacity as shareholders should only be disclosed within the full financial statements to comply with the related parties disclosure standard.

DIRECTORS' REMUNERATION AND OTHER BENEFITS

Directors' remuneration and other benefits would fall to be classed as 'key management personnel compensation', which includes all employee benefits as defined in Section 28 *Employee Benefits*. Ordinarily directors' remuneration and other benefits are shown separately within the financial statements (usually underneath the 'operating profit' disclosure). It is the author's opinion that this practice of separate disclosure is likely to continue under the FRS 102 reporting regime.

The components of remuneration can be made up of several items, including:

- Wages and salaries,
- Golden hellos,
- Benefits in kind,
- Bonuses and
- Other economic benefits that are received by directors during employment.

Disclosure is needed relating to directors' remuneration and other benefits to accord with the provisions laid down in the Companies Act 2006: Schedule 5 to SI 2007/410. Part 1 to Schedule 5 applies to quoted and unquoted companies, whereas Part 2 applies only to unquoted companies.

Schedule 5 SI 2008/410 – Part 1[1]

Part 1 of Schedule 5 SI 2008/410 requires the following to be disclosed in respect of directors' remuneration:

(a) The aggregate amount of remuneration paid to, or receivable by, directors in respect of qualifying services,

(b) The aggregate amount of gains made by directors on the exercise of share options,

(c) The aggregate of the amount of money paid to, or receivable by, directors and the net value of assets (other than money and share options) received or receivable by directors under long-term incentive schemes in respect of qualifying services and

(d) The aggregate value of any company contributions:
   (i) Paid, or treated as paid, to a pension scheme in respect of directors' qualifying services and
   (ii) By reference to which the rate or amount of any money purchase benefits that may become payable will be calculated.

Further disclosures are required under Schedule 5 relating to pension contributions. The number of directors for whom retirement benefits are accruing under money purchase schemes and defined benefit schemes must be disclosed (with a comparative figure also).

Schedule 5 SI 2008/410 – Part 2[2]

Extensive disclosures are required under Part 2, which only apply to unquoted companies. Disclosures need to be made in respect of the following.

Details of the highest paid director

Part 2

1. Where the aggregate remuneration and other benefits total £200,000 or more, there must be shown:
   (a) So much of the total of those aggregates as is attributable to the highest paid director and
   (b) So much of the aggregate mentioned in (d) (i) and (ii) in Part 1 above that is so attributable.
2. Where subparagraph (1) applies and the highest paid director has performed qualifying services during the financial year by reference to which the rate or

---

[1]Companies Act 2006 Schedule 5 2008/410 Part 1.
[2]Companies Act 2006 Schedule 5 2008/410 Part 2.

amount of any defined benefits that may become payable will be calculated, there must also be shown:

    (a) The amount at the end of the year of his accrued pension and

    (b) Where applicable, the amount at the end of the year of his accrued lump sum.

3. Subject to (4), where subparagraph (1) applies in the case of a company that is not a listed company, there must also be shown:

    (a) Whether the highest paid director exercised any share options and

    (b) Whether any shares were received or receivable by that director in respect of qualifying services under a long-term incentive scheme.

4. Where the highest paid director has not been involved in any of the transactions specified in (3) above, that fact need not be stated.

Excess retirement benefits of directors and past directors

Part 3

1. Subject to subparagraph (2), there must be shown the aggregate amount of:

    (a) So much of the retirement benefits paid to or receivable by directors under pension schemes and

    (b) So much of retirement benefits paid to or receivable by past directors under such schemes.

This (in each case) is where the benefits are in excess of the retirement benefits to which they were respectively entitled on the date on which the benefits first became payable or 31 March 1997, whichever is the later.

2. Amounts paid or receivable under a pension scheme need not be included in the aggregate amount if:

    (a) The funding of the scheme was such that the amounts were or, as the case may be, could have been paid without recourse to additional contributions and

    (b) Amounts were paid to or receivable by all pensioner members of the scheme on the same basis.

3. In subparagraph (2), 'pensioner member', in relation to a pension scheme, means any person who is entitled to the present payment of retirement benefits under the scheme.

4. In this paragraph:

    (a) References to retirement benefits include benefits otherwise than in cash and

    (b) In relation to so much of retirement benefits as consist otherwise than in cash, references to their amount are to the estimated money value of the benefit.

The nature of any such benefit must also be disclosed.

Compensation to directors for loss of office

Part 4

1. There must be shown the aggregate amount of any compensation to directors or past directors in respect of loss of office.
2. This includes compensation received or receivable by a director or past director:
   (a) For loss of office as director of the company or
   (b) For loss, while director of the company or on or in connection with his ceasing to be a director of it, of:
      (i) Any other office in connection with the management of the company's affairs or
      (ii) Any office as director or otherwise in connection with the management of the affairs of any subsidiary undertakings of the company.
3. In this paragraph references to compensation for loss of office include:
   (a) Compensation as consideration for, or in connection with, a person's retirement from office and
   (b) Where such a retirement is occasioned by a breach of the person's contract with the company or with a subsidiary undertaking of the company:
      (i) Payments made by way of damages for the breach or
      (ii) Payments made by way of settlement or compromise of any claim in respect of the breach.
4. In this paragraph:
   (a) References to compensation include benefits otherwise than in cash and
   (b) In relation to such compensation references to its amount are to the estimated monetary value of the benefit.

The nature of any such compensation must be disclosed.

Sums paid to third parties in respect of directors' services

Part 5

1. There must be shown the aggregate amount of any consideration paid to or receivable by third parties for making available the services of any person:
   (a) As a director of the company or
   (b) While director of the company:
      (i) As director of any of its subsidiary undertakings or
      (ii) Otherwise in connection with the management of the affairs of the company or any of its subsidiary undertakings.
2. In subparagraph (1):
   (a) The reference to consideration includes benefits otherwise than in cash and
   (b) In relation to such consideration the reference to its amount is to the estimated money value of the benefit.

The nature of any consideration must be disclosed.
3. For the purposes of this paragraph a 'third party' means a person other than:
   (a) The director himself or a person connected with him or a body corporate controlled by him or
   (b) The company or any of its subsidiary undertakings.

DIRECTORS' ADVANCES, CREDITS AND GUARANTEES

Statutory instruments (SIs) 2008/409 and 2008/410 brought about significant changes in the way that directors' advances, credits and guarantees are reported in the financial statements. In reality, the disclosure that caused the most problems was in relation to advances to a director. Where advances to a director take place, the disclosures required under the Companies Act 2006 are:

1. The amount of the advance(s),
2. Indication of the interest rate,
3. Main terms and conditions of the advance and
4. Any amounts repaid.

The term 'advance' is essentially an amount that has been loaned to the director by the company, which then results in a debtor in the company's financial statements (or the increase of an existing debtor). The requirements in the Companies Act 2006 require each amount advanced to the director to be shown separately. This caused an element of outcry within the profession because the wording of the Act was such that the disclosure could be too voluminous and, as a result, it is generally accepted that the aggregation of smaller and similar items could be deemed acceptable to reduce the burden of over-disclosure. What is expected to be disclosed, however, are *material* advances and *material* repayments. The term 'material' is a judgemental concept on the part of the preparer of the financial statements – there is no quantitative amount specified in the Act for what would be considered material.

The introduction of the new requirements in the Companies Act 2006 repealed the requirement to disclose the maximum amounts that directors' current accounts became overdrawn within the accounting period and there is also no requirement to disclose transactions in which a director has a material interest.

The true and fair concept in the companies legislation is complied with by applying the requirements in the UK GAAP (FRS 102/small companies regime) and hence disclosure requirements for accounting standards purposes and Companies Act purposes can be illustrated in the following example.

Example – Disclosure of a director's current account for related party purposes

Leyla Westhead is the director of a company with a year-end of 31 December 2015. On 1 January 2015, the opening balance on the director's current account is a credit balance of £5,000 (i.e. in favour of Leyla Westhead). Each month the director's private car loan is paid out of the company bank account amounting to £1,000 per month and on 1 December 2015, Leyla received a dividend of £16,000 (this was also the date of declaration of the dividend). The director's current account working paper will be as follows:

	£
Opening balance 1 January 2015	5,000
Dividend	16,000
Payments on behalf of director	(18,000)
Balance due from company at year-end	3,000

Debit balances arise from June 2015 until November 2015 because the dividend was not declared until 1 December 2015. The debit balances arising from June to November will be disclosed as advances to the director as follows:

Advances to director

Six monthly payments of £1,000 on the director's behalf, interest-free and repayable on demand	£6,000
Repayment	£6,000

Directors' guarantees

In respect of guarantees, Section 413 (4) requires the financial statements of a company to disclose:

- The main terms,
- The maximum liability incurred by the company and
- Any amounts paid and any liability incurred for fulfilling the guarantee.

In addition, the aggregate maximum liability and aggregate amounts paid and incurred should also be disclosed.

25 SPECIALISED ACTIVITIES

INTRODUCTION

Section 34 *Specialised Activities* is a fairly vast standard as it covers a wide variety of specialist activities that certain entities reporting under FRS 102 may be involved with. The section covers the following types of activities:

- Agriculture
- Extractive Activities
- Service Concession Arrangements
- Financial Institutions
- Retirement Benefit Plans: Financial Statements
- Heritage Assets
- Funding Commitments
- Incoming Resources from Non-Exchange Transactions
- Public Benefit Entity Combinations and Public Benefit Entity Concessionary Loans

Each of the above types of activity are considered in each of the following sections of this chapter. Within Section 34 in FRS 102 are two appendices offering guidance on funding commitments (Appendix A) and guidance on incoming resources from non-exchange transactions (Appendix B). These two appendices are considered to be integral parts of FRS 102 and should be used by reporting entities that are affected by such activities.

AGRICULTURE

Section 34 of FRS 102 outlines the accounting treatment, measurement and disclosures relating to agricultural activity and agricultural produce. The term 'agricultural activity' is taken to mean the entity's management of the biological transformation of biological assets for sale into agricultural produce or into additional biological assets. A 'biological asset' is a living animal or plant with the associated agricultural produce being the harvested product from the entity's biological asset. The way that these two issues closely interact with each other can be illustrated in the following table:

Biological asset	Agricultural produce	Harvested product
Cattle	Milk	Cheese
Bushes	Leaf	Tea, tobacco
Vines	Grape	Wine
Plants	Cotton	Thread, clothing
Sheep	Wool	Yarn

Section 34 applies to biological assets and agricultural products at the point of harvest only where they relate to agricultural activity. Section 34 does not apply to:

- Land that is related to agricultural activity,
- Land owned by the entity that is used for agricultural activity,
- Land owned by a third party and rented to the entity for agricultural activity,
- Intangible assets used for agricultural activity,
- Leased biological assets held by a lessee under an operating lease and
- Agricultural produce after the point of harvest (such produce will likely be inventory and hence Section 13 *Inventories* will apply).

Recognition and measurement: agriculture

A biological asset or an item of agricultural produce can only be recognised in the entity's financial statements as an asset when, and only when, the following three criteria are met:

1. The entity controls the asset as a result of past events,
2. It is probable that future economic benefits will flow to the entity and
3. The fair value of the cost of the asset can be reliably measured.

In terms of measurement, there is an accounting policy choice open for reporting entities applying Section 34. For each class of biological asset, together with its related agricultural produce, an entity must choose between the following accounting policies:

- The fair value model or
- The cost model.

Example – Adoption of the fair value model

An entity operating in the agricultural industry has decided to apply the fair value model as its accounting policy choice for biological assets and related agricultural produce.

Two years after applying the fair value model, the finance director has requested that this accounting policy be changed to the cost model as he finds this method much easier to apply and is considering changing the policy by instigating the requirements in Section 10 *Accounting Policies, Estimates and Errors* and applying the change retrospectively.

Paragraph 34.3B says that where the entity chooses the fair value model for a class of biological assets and related agricultural produce, it must not subsequently change its accounting policy to the cost model. Therefore, the finance director will be unable to apply this change and must continue with the use of the fair value model.

Fair value model

On initial recognition, a biological asset is to be recognised at fair value less costs to sell. After initial recognition, the entity must continue recognising the biological asset at fair value less costs to sell. All changes in fair value less costs to sell are recognised within profit or loss.

The term 'costs to sell' are directly attributable costs (i.e. incremental costs) that the entity will incur in selling the asset. Such incremental costs can include commissions to brokers and dealers, levies by regulatory agencies and commodity exchanges as well as transfer taxes and duties.

Agricultural produce that is harvested from the entity's biological assets are measured at the point of harvest and also at fair value less costs to sell. This measurement is also the cost at that date in the application of Section 13 *Inventories*.

When considering fair value, a number of factors must be taken into consideration by the reporting entity and there is a hierarchy contained within paragraph 34.6 of FRS 102, which is summarised as follows:

1. Active market	Where an active market exists for the biological asset or agricultural produce for such assets in their present location and condition, then that quoted price is the appropriate basis for determining the fair value of that asset.
2. Recent transaction price	Where no active market exists the most recent market transaction price can be used provided there has not been a significant change in economic circumstances in the intervening period between the date of the transaction and the reporting date.
3. Market prices for similar assets	These should be adjusted for the points of differences.
4. Sector benchmarks	This could be, for example, the value of cattle expressed per kilo of meat or the value of an orchard expressed per hectare.
5. Present value of future cash flows	These can be used where fair value may be readily determinable despite market determined prices or values not being available for a biological asset in its present condition. In this case the entity must decipher whether the present value of expected net cash flows (discounted to a current market determined rate) results in a fair value that is a reliable measure.

In the above, the term 'active market' is taken to mean a market in which the items traded within the market are homogeneous; willing buyers can be found at any time and prices are available to the public.

Example – Fair value cannot be measured reliably

An entity is trying to establish the fair value of a biological asset. There is no active market and all attempts to arrive at a reliable measure of fair value have been unsuccessful.

Where the entity cannot reliably measure fair value of a biological asset, then the entity must apply the cost model to that biological asset until such time that a reliable measure of fair value can be determined.

Cost model

When the reporting entity adopts the cost model in measuring biological assets it measures those assets at cost less accumulated depreciation and less any accumulated impairment losses.

Agricultural produce that is harvested from the entity's biological assets is measured (at the point of harvest) at either:

- The *lower* of cost and estimated selling price less costs to complete and sell or
- Its fair value less costs to sell.

Where the entity measures such assets at fair value less costs to sell, then any gain or loss that arises on initial recognition of agricultural produce at fair value is included in profit or loss.

When applying the provisions in Section 13, or another section of FRS 102, this cost then becomes the cost for the purposes of Section 13 or another relevant section of FRS 102.

Disclosures – fair value model

The following disclosures should be made within the financial statements for each class of biological asset using the fair value model:

(a) A description of each class of biological asset.
(b) The methods and significant assumptions that the entity has applied in determining the fair value of each class of biological asset.
(c) A reconciliation of changes in the carrying amount of each class of biological asset between the beginning and end of the current reporting period. The reconciliation itself should include:
    i. The gain or loss that has arisen from changes in fair value less costs to sell,
    ii. Increases that have arisen due to purchases,
    iii. Decreases arising due to sales,
    iv. Decreases arising from harvest,
    v. Increases that have arisen from business combinations and
    vi. Other changes.

There is no requirement to produce the above reconciliation in (c) for the comparative period presented.

Where the entity measures any individual biological asset at cost then it must disclose the reasons why fair value cannot be reliably measured. In situations when the fair value becomes reliably measurable during the period, disclosure must be made as to why fair value has become reliably measurable together with the effect of the change.

When the entity uses the fair value model, it must also disclose the methods and significant assumptions that the entity has applied in establishing the fair value at the point of harvest of each class of agricultural produce.

Disclosures – cost model

For those entities applying the cost model for biological assets, disclosures should be made as follows:

(a) A description of each class of biological asset.
(b) The depreciation methods adopted by the entity.
(c) The useful lives or the depreciation rates used.
(d) A reconciliation of changes in the carrying amount of each class of biological asset between the beginning and end of the reporting period to include:
   i. Increases that have arisen due to purchases,
   ii. Decreases arising due to sales,
   iii. Decreases arising from harvest,
   iv. Increases that have arisen from business combinations,
   v. Impairment losses that have been recognised or reversed in profit and loss and
   vi. Other changes.

For agricultural produce that has been measured at fair value less costs to sell, disclosure should be made of the methods and significant assumptions that the entity has applied in establishing fair value at the point of harvest in relation to each class of agricultural produce. There was no specific coverage regarding biological assets under the previous UK GAAP.

EXTRACTIVE INDUSTRIES

This particular section of the chapter should be read in conjunction with IFRS 6 *Exploration for and Evaluation of Mineral Resources* because Section 34 specifically requires entities whose activities fall under the scope of an extractive industry to apply the provisions in IFRS 6.

IFRS 6 also makes reference to other IFRSs and Section 34 requires that those references be taken to be references to the relevant section or paragraph with FRS 102.

When applying IFRS 6 (specifically paragraph 21 in IFRS 6), a cash-generating unit (or group of cash-generating units) cannot be larger than an operating segment and paragraph 34.11B of FRS 102 requires the reference in IFRS 6 to IFRS 8 *Operating Segments* to be ignored.

Transitional issues

On transition to FRS 102, it may not be practical for an entity to apply a particular requirement of paragraph 18 to IFRS 6 to previous comparative amounts. When this is the case, the reporting entity must disclose that fact.

Under the previous UK GAAP, a reporting entity may have accounted for exploration and development costs relating to oil and gas properties in the development or production phases in cost centres that included all properties in a large geographical area. If this was the case, then on transition to FRS 102, a reporting entity can elect to measure those oil and gas assets on the following basis:

- For exploration and evaluation assets: at the amount that has been derived under the previous GAAP.
- For assets in the development or production phase: at the amount determined for the cost centre under the previous GAAP. This amount is allocated on a pro rata basis to the cost centre's underlying assets using reserve volumes or reserve values that were in existence at the date of transition to FRS 102.

In respect of the second bullet point above, the entity would need to test the exploration and evaluation assets, together with assets in the development and production phase, for impairment.

SERVICE CONCESSION ARRANGEMENTS

In a service concession arrangement, there are generally two parties: 'the grantor' and 'the operator'. The 'grantor' is usually a government department or public sector body and the 'operator' is usually a private sector entity and FRS 102 gives guidance for both parties.

A 'service concession arrangement' is an arrangement whereby a public body, or public benefit entity, enters into a contract with the operator to construct, upgrade, operate and maintain infrastructure assets for a specified period of time. This 'specified period of time' is referred to in FRS 102 as the 'concession period' and the operator is paid for its services over the concession period. A service concession arrangement is usually in place when the following two conditions apply:

1. The grantor controls, or regulates, the types of services that the operator must provide using the infrastructure assets as well as to whom the service is provided and at what price the service is provided and
2. Through ownership or beneficial entitlement, the grantor controls any significant residual interest in the assets at the end of the service concession arrangement.

> **Example – Infrastructure assets having no residual value at the end of the arrangement**
>
> A grantor enters into a contract with an operator to provide services using its infrastructure assets. At the end of the arrangement the infrastructure assets will have no significant residual value.
>
> Provided the grantor controls, or regulates, the types of services that the operator must provide using the infrastructure assets, as well as specifying to whom the services are to be provided and at what price, then the arrangement should be accounted for as a service concession arrangement, regardless of the fact that the infrastructure assets will have no residual value at the end of the arrangement.

In respect of the infrastructure assets, the grantor's control over any significant residual interest in those assets should restrict the operator having the ability to sell, or pledge as security, the infrastructure assets and give the grantor a continuing right of use of those infrastructure assets over the concession period.

In reality, there may be some infrastructure assets that are partly controlled by the grantor and partly controlled by another (unregulated) party. When this is the case there could, in substance, be a lease from the grantor to the operator of those assets that are either separable or used for the additional services.

Example – Infrastructure assets with partial control

A city hospital consists of the main hospital that treats NHS patients and also has a private wing that treats patients for specialist dental operations. The private wing is owned by a consortium of investors and not by the NHS.

The private wing that treats patients for specialist dental operations is physically separable and is capable of being operated independently. If this part of the infrastructure is to be used for unregulated purposes then it should be analysed separately.

In more complex cases, there could be arrangements in place that contain a group of contracts and sub-arrangements as elements of the service concession arrangement as a whole. Where this applies, the arrangement must be treated as a whole when the group of contracts and sub-arrangements are linked in such a way that the commercial substance of the arrangement cannot be understood without reference to them as a whole. In such cases the situation might be further complicated because the contractual terms or arrangements effectively meet the scope requirements of both Section 20 *Leases* and Section 34. However, in such cases the requirements of Section 34 will prevail and the arrangement will be accounted for as a service concession arrangement.

Where an arrangement does not meet the criteria for a service concession arrangement, then the arrangement is accounted for under different sections of FRS 102, namely:

- Section 17 *Property, Plant and Equipment* or
- Section 18 *Intangible Assets other than Goodwill* or
- Section 20 *Leases* or
- Section 23 *Revenue*.

Whichever section of FRS 102 the arrangement is accounted under will all depend on the nature of the arrangement.

Grantor accounting under a finance lease liability model

Where infrastructure assets are concerned, the accounting for a grantor for such assets (tangible property, plant and equipment or intangible assets as appropriate) under a finance lease liability model will be the same as assets in a normal finance lease. The grantor must recognise the infrastructure assets as assets in its balance sheet (statement of financial position) together with a liability that represents the obligations under the service concession arrangement. Assets recognised should be accounted for subsequently in accordance with the provisions in Section 17 *Property, Plant and Equipment* or Section 18 *Intangible Assets other than Goodwill*. The associated liability should be recognised as a finance lease liability and hence the provisions in paragraph 20.11 of FRS 102 will apply.

The grantor should not recognise the infrastructure assets if no liability to make payments to the operator is recognised.

Operator accounting – financial assets and/or intangible assets

An important concept to address at the outset is that the operator has *access* to operate the infrastructure assets in order to provide the public service on behalf of the grantor. The operator does not have a *right to control* the use of the public service assets and hence cannot recognise the infrastructure assets as property, plant and equipment in its statement of financial position (balance sheet).

Notwithstanding the fact that the operator cannot recognise the infrastructure assets in its own financial statements, it does recognise an asset in the form of the consideration that it receives from the grantor. The consideration the operator receives can take a variety of forms, but is usually:

- A financial asset such as an unconditional right to receive a specified or determinable sum of cash or another financial asset and/or
- An intangible asset that is the right to charge users for use of the infrastructure asset that the operator constructs or upgrades.

Where the second bullet applies (i.e. the operator has a right to charge users for use of the asset) then it is important to address that a 'right to charge users' is not the same as an unconditional right to receive cash. This is because there is no unconditional right to receive cash in such an arrangement; the amounts received by the operator are essentially contingent on the extent to which the general public uses the asset.

Where the operator receives a financial asset (for example, cash or other forms of assets), such assets are recognised at fair value of the consideration received or receivable. This amount is to be based on the fair value of the construction (or upgrade) services provided. Subsequently such assets should be accounted for under Section 11 *Basic Financial Instruments* and Section 12 *Other Financial Instruments Issues* as appropriate.

Where the operator receives an intangible asset, such assets are to be recognised at fair value of the consideration received or receivable. Subsequently such assets should be accounted for under Section 18 *Intangible Assets other than Goodwill*.

Example – Mixture of consideration

The consideration received by an operator from a grantor in respect of infrastructure assets is comprised of both cash and a right to charge users for the use of the asset.

In cases where the operator receives a mixture of consideration then to the extent that grantor gives a financial asset (for example, cash) the operator recognises a financial asset. The financial asset should be recognised initially at fair value of the consideration received or receivable (based on the fair value of the construction (or upgrade) services provided). After initial recognition at fair value, the operator accounts for the financial asset under Section 11 and Section 12 as appropriate.

To the extent that the operator has a right to charge members of the public to use the asset, it should recognise an intangible asset in the statement of financial position (balance sheet).

The intangible asset is to be initially recognised at fair value for the consideration received or receivable (based on the fair value of the construction (or upgrade) services provided). After initial recognition at fair value, the operator accounts for the intangible asset in accordance with Section 18 *Intangible Assets other than Goodwill*.

Operator accounting – revenue and borrowing costs

Revenue that the operator receives in respect of the operating services it performs using the infrastructure assets should be accounted for under the provisions in Section 23 *Revenue*.

Where borrowing costs are concerned, any such costs attributable to a service concession arrangement are expensed to profit or loss in the period in which the costs are incurred. The exception to this treatment is where the operator has an intangible asset. Where the operator has an intangible asset, the borrowing costs that are attributable to the service concession arrangement can be capitalised if the operator has a policy of capitalising borrowing costs. The entity will account for any capitalised borrowing costs in accordance with Section 25 *Borrowing Costs*.

Transitional issues for operators

In respect of service concession arrangements that have been entered into prior to the date of transition to FRS 102, a first-time adopter of FRS 102 is not required to apply the provisions in paragraphs 34.12E to 34.16A. Arrangements entered into prior to the date of transition should continue to be accounted for using the same accounting policies, which are applied at the date of transition.

Transitional issues for grantors

Due to advice received by the Financial Reporting Council by the Accounting Council, grantors should give retrospective effect to paragraphs 34.12E to 34.12H of FRS 102. This is because grantors are not able to apply the transitional exemptions that are available to operators.

FINANCIAL INSTITUTIONS

Section 34 deals with the disclosure requirements of financial institutions; in the context of Section 34, a financial institution is one that is not a retirement benefit plan. These disclosures are required in addition to those required in Section 11 and Section 12. The disclosures commanded by Section 34 are required to be made in both:

- The individual financial statements of the financial institution that is not a retirement benefit plan and
- The consolidated financial statements of the group, which contain a financial institution that is not a retirement benefit plan and when the financial instruments that are held by the financial institution are material to the group.

A point worth emphasising where the second bullet point above is concerned is that where the financial instruments held by the financial institution are material to the group the disclosures apply regardless of whether the principal activity of the group is that of a financial institution or not, but only need to be given in respect of financial instruments held by entities within the group that are financial institutions.

Section 34 requires the following disclosures to be made for financial institutions.

The significance of financial instruments for financial position and performance

Information should be disclosed in the financial institution's financial statements, which will enable the users to evaluate the significance of financial instruments on the financial position and financial performance of the financial institution.

Paragraph 34.20 requires a disaggregation of the statement of financial position line item by class of financial instrument.

Impairment

Where the financial institution uses a separate allowance account to take impairments, the financial institution must disclose a reconciliation of the changes that have taken place during the period for each class of financial asset.

Fair value

For those financial instruments that are carried at fair value in the financial institution's statement of financial position (balance sheet), there should be disclosure for each class of financial instrument of the level in the fair value hierarchy (as outlined in paragraph 11.27 of FRS 102) into which the fair value measurements are classified.

Risks

The nature and extent of risks that arise from financial instruments should be disclosed. The disclosures must enable the users to understand the nature and extent of:

- Credit risk,
- Liquidity risk and
- Market risk

arising from financial instruments to which the financial institution is exposed at the end of the reporting period.

In particular, the financial institution should disclose:

(a) The exposure to risks and how they have arisen,
(b) The objectives, policies and processes of the financial institution in managing the risk and the methods that have been applied to measure the risk and
(c) Any changes in (a) or (b) from the previous reporting period.

Credit risk

For each class of financial instrument, the financial institution should disclose:

(a) The amount that best represents the institution's maximum exposure to credit risk at the end of the reporting period. An exception to this requirement is in respect of financial instruments whose carrying value best represents the maximum exposure to credit risk.

(b) A description of the collateral that is held as security and of other credit enhancements together with details of the extent to which these mitigate credit risk.

(c) The amount by which any related credit derivatives (or similar instruments) mitigate the financial institution's maximum exposure to credit risk.

(d) Information concerning the credit quality of financial assets for which payments are not overdue nor are the financial assets impaired.

Section 34 requires financial institutions to make disclosure in the financial statements, by class of financial asset, including an analysis of:

(a) The age of financial assets whose payments are overdue but that are not impaired and

(b) The financial assets that are individually determined to be impaired at the reporting date together with factors that the financial institution has considered in establishing that the financial assets are impaired.

In instances when a financial institution obtains financial or non-financial assets during the reporting period by obtaining possession of collateral or 'calling on' other credit enhancements such as guarantees, and those assets meet the recognition criteria in other sections of FRS 102, the financial institution should disclose:

(a) The nature and carrying amount of the assets that have been obtained and

(b) When the assets are not readily convertible into cash, the financial institution's policies for the disposal of those assets or for using them in its operations.

Liquidity risk

A maturity analysis is to be disclosed by financial institutions in respect of financial liabilities that disclose the remaining contractual maturities of financial liabilities at undiscounted amounts. These should be separated between derivative and non-derivative financial liabilities.

Market risk

For each type of market risk, a financial institution is required to provide a sensitivity analysis that it is exposed to, showing the impact on profit or loss and equity. Disclosure should also be made as to the methods and assumptions used.

Some financial institutions might prepare a sensitivity analysis that reflects the interdependencies between risk variables. If the financial institution uses that sensitivity analysis to manage financial risks then it may use that analysis instead.

Capital

Disclosure should be made in the financial institution's financial statements that enables the users to evaluate the institution's objectives, policies and processes for managing capital. Disclosure should be made as follows:

(a) Qualitative information concerning the institution's objectives, policies and processes for managing capital, including:

    i. A description of what it manages as capital,

    ii. When externally imposed capital requirements occur, the nature of those requirements together with details of how those requirements are included into the management of capital and

    iii. How it is meeting its objectives for managing capital.

(b) Summary quantitative data concerning what it manages as capital. The section recognises that some financial institutions consider some financial liabilities as being part of capital, whilst others regard capital as excluding some components of equity.

(c) Changes in (a) and (b) from the previous period.

(d) Whether the financial institution has complied with any externally imposed capital requirements during the period to which it has been subjected.

(e) Where the financial institution has not complied with such externally imposed capital requirements during the period, the consequences of non-compliance should be disclosed.

The disclosures above should be based on the information that the financial institution has provided internally to key management personnel.

Some financial institutions manage their capital in several ways, as well as being subjected to differing capital requirements. Care must be taken here to achieve the objectives of the disclosure requirements so as not to provide useful information or distort a financial statements user's understanding. If an aggregate disclosure of capital requirements and how capital is managed would fail to provide useful information or would otherwise distort the user's understanding then the financial institution should disclose separate information for each capital requirement to which the entity is subject.

Cash flows reported on a net basis

Paragraph 34.33 allows a financial institution that prepares a statement of cash flows in accordance with Section 7 *Statement of Cash Flows* to report the following activities on a net basis:

(a) Cash receipts and cash payments in relation to the acceptance and repayment of deposits that have a fixed maturity date,

(b) The placement of deposits with, and withdrawal of deposits from, other financial institutions and

(c) Cash advances and loans that have been made to customers together with the repayment of those cash advances and loans.

The above requirements do not mandate the entity to prepare a statement of cash flows.

RETIREMENT BENEFIT PLANS: FINANCIAL STATEMENTS

Retirement benefit plans can be 'defined benefit plans' and 'defined contribution plans'. Both types of plan are discussed in more detail in Chapter 10 *Employee Benefits*.

In addition to them both being distinct in their accounting, both plans may have combined elements. Where defined benefit and defined contribution elements are material, the financial statements should distinguish between the two.

FRS 102 covers retirement benefit plans because their financial statements are also intended to give a true and fair view.

The financial statements of a retirement benefit must include:

- A statement of change in net assets available for benefits (this is more commonly known as a 'fund account'),
- A statement of net assets available for benefits and
- Notes that comprise the plan's significant accounting policies and other explanatory information.

The net assets of the plan that are available for benefits should be measured at fair value. Changes in fair value should be recognised in the statements of changes in net assets available for benefits.

The format of the statement of changes in net assets available for benefits (fund account) is set out in paragraph 34.37 of FRS 102 and a retirement benefit plan shall present the following:

(a) Employer contributions,
(b) Employee contributions,
(c) Investment income (for example, interest and dividend income),
(d) Other income,
(e) Benefits paid or payable,
(f) Administrative expenses,
(g) Other expenses,
(h) Taxes on income,
(i) Profits and losses on disposal of investments and changes in the value of investments and
(j) Transfers to and from other plans.

The statement of net assets should present the following information:

(a) The plan's assets at the end of the period, suitably classified and
(b) The plan's liabilities except the actuarial present value of promised retirement benefits.

In terms of the valuation of assets, this should be presented in the notes to the financial statements.

Disclosure requirements

There are extensive disclosure requirements that a retirement benefit plan must make in its financial statements, which are outlined as follows.

Assets (other than financial instruments at fair value)

Assets held by the retirement benefit plan, with the exception of financial instruments held at fair value, should be disclosed in accordance with the relevant section of FRS 102. For example, if the retirement benefit plan holds investment property then the disclosure requirements in Section 16 *Investment Property* (at paragraph 16.10) should be made.

Significance of financial instruments on the financial position and financial performance

Information should be disclosed within the financial statements that enables the users to evaluate the significance that financial instruments have on the plan's financial position and financial performance.

In addition, the retirement benefit plan should also disclose a disaggregation of the statement of net assets that are available for benefits by class of financial instrument. For the purposes of Section 34, a 'class' is a grouping of financial instruments that is appropriate to the nature of the information that has been disclosed and that also takes into consideration the characteristics of those financial instruments.

Fair value

Where the retirement benefit plan has financial instruments that are valued at fair value in the statement of net assets available for benefits, disclosure should be made in relation to each class of financial instrument of where in the fair value hierarchy (as per paragraph 11.27) each of the fair value measurements is categorised.

Nature and extent of risks

Information should be disclosed in the financial statements of a retirement benefit plan that enables users of the financial statements to understand the nature and significance of both credit risk and market risk arising from financial instruments that the retirement benefit plan is exposed to at the end of the reporting period. In particular, the retirement benefit plan should disclose:

(a) The exposures to risk and how they have arisen,
(b) The plan's objectives, policies and processes for managing the risks and the methods that it has adopted to measure the risk and
(c) Any changes in (a) or (b) from the previous period.

The following information should also be disclosed for a retirement benefit plan in relation to credit risk.

Credit risk

The disclosures in respect of credit risk essentially follow on from the above disclosures relating to the nature and extent of risks and the following disclosures should be made by each class of financial instrument:

(a) The amount that is a best representation of the plan's maximum exposure to credit risk at the end of the reporting period. (There is an exemption available from this disclosure, which is where the carrying amount of the plan's financial instruments best represents the plan's maximum exposure to credit risk.)
(b) A description of the collateral held as security and of other credit enhancements together with details of how these mitigate credit risk.

(c) The amount by which any related credit derivatives (or similar instruments) mitigate that maximum exposure to credit risk.

(d) Information concerning the credit quality of financial assets whose payments are not overdue and have not suffered impairment.

There may be occasions when the retirement benefit plan obtains financial or non-financial assets during the reporting period by way of taking possession of collateral that it holds or 'calling on' other credit enhancements. Where such assets meet the recognition criteria in other sections of FRS 102, the following information should be disclosed:

(a) The nature and carrying value of the assets obtained and

(b) If the assets are not readily convertible into cash, the plan's policies for the disposal of such assets or for retaining them.

Actuarial liabilities for defined benefit plans

There is no requirement for a defined benefit plan to recognise a liability representing the promised retirement benefits. However, there is a requirement for the plan to prepare a report alongside the financial statements, which contains disclosure of information relating to the actuarial present value of promised retirement benefits, including:

(a) A statement of the actuarial present value of promised retirement benefits, which is to be based on the most recent valuation of the scheme,

(b) The date that the most recent valuation of the scheme was undertaken and

(c) The significant actuarial assumptions that have been made together with the methods that have been adopted to calculate the actuarial present value of promised retirement benefits.

Example – Defined contribution plan statement of net assets available for benefits

ABC Limited Defined Contribution Plan
Statement of Net Assets Available for Benefits
31 December 2014

Assets	£
Investments at fair value	
Government securities	X
Municipal bonds	X
Local equity securities	X
Foreign equity securities	X
Local debt securities	X
Foreign corporate bonds	X
Total investments	X
Receivables	
Amounts due from stockbrokers on sale of securities	X
Accrued interest	X

Dividends receivable	X
Total receivables	X
Cash	X
Total assets	**X**

Liabilities

Amounts payable

Amounts due to stockbrokers on purchase of securities	X
Benefits payable to participants	X
Total amounts payable	X
Accrued expenses	X
Total liabilities	**X**
Net assets available for benefits	**X**

Example – Defined benefit plan statement of net assets available for retirement benefits

---

XYZ Defined Benefit Plan
Statement of Net Assets Available for Benefits, Actuarial Present Value of
Accumulated Retirement Benefits and Plan Excess or Deficit
31 December 2014

1. Statement of net assets available for benefits

Assets

Investments at fair value	£
Government securities	X
Municipal bonds	X
Local equity securities	X
Foreign equity securities	X
Local debt securities	X
Foreign corporate bonds	X
Total investments	X

Receivables

Amounts due from stockbrokers on sale of securities	X
Accrued interest	X
Dividends receivable	X
	X
Total receivables	
Cash	X
Total assets	**X**

Liabilities
Amounts payable
Amounts due to stockbrokers on purchase of securities X
Benefits payable to participants X
Total amounts payable X

Net assets available for benefits X

2. Actuarial present value of accumulated plan benefits

Vested benefits X
Non-vested benefits X
Total X

**Excess of net assets available for benefits over actuarial
present value of accumulated plan benefits** X

XYZ Defined Benefit Plan
Statement of Changes in Net Assets Available for Benefits
31 December 2014
£

Investment income
Interest income X
Dividend income X
Gain on fair value in investments X
Total investment income X

Plan contributions
Employer contributions X
Employee contributions X
Total plan contributions X

Total additions to net asset value X

Plan benefit payments
Pensions X
Lump sum payments on retirement X
Severance pay X
Commutation of superannuation benefits X
Total plan benefit payments X

Total deductions from net asset value X

Net increase in asset value X
Net assets available for benefits at start of year X
Net assets available for benefits at end of year X

HERITAGE ASSETS

A heritage asset is a tangible or intangible asset with historic, artistic, scientific, technological, geophysical or environment qualities that contributes to the nation's society, knowledge and/or culture. Paragraphs 34.49 to 34.56 of FRS 102 deal with the accounting for heritage assets but those particular paragraphs of FRS 102 do not deal with the following:

- Investment property (Section 16 *Investment Property* applies),
- Property, plant and equipment (Section 17 *Property, Plant and Equipment* applies) or
- Intangible assets (Section 18 *Intangible Assets other than Goodwill* applies).

When an entity owns, for example, a work of art that is not principally maintained for its contribution to knowledge and culture, the entity cannot apply Section 34, but must instead account for the work of art in accordance with Section 17 principles.

It might also be the case that the entity operates from a heritage asset (a historical building, for example) and in this case Section 34 will also not apply to the entity but rather it must apply the provisions in Section 17 to account for the building. The key theme underlying the application of Section 34 is that the asset must be maintained principally for its contribution to knowledge and culture, although entities owning such assets may wish to consider the appropriateness of applying the disclosure requirements contained in paragraphs 34.55 and 34.56.

Recognition and measurement

An asset that meets the classification of a heritage asset must be shown separately in the entity's statement of financial position (balance sheet) from other assets. The entity must account for such assets using either the cost or revaluation model set out in Section 17 of FRS 102.

The cost or value of a recently acquired heritage asset will be known. However, if the cost is unavailable and this information cannot be obtained using means that are commensurate with the benefits to the users of the financial statements then the entity does not recognise the heritage asset on the statement of financial position (balance sheet) but instead makes a disclosure (see disclosure requirements below).

The provisions in Section 27 *Impairment of Assets* will also apply to a heritage asset and at each reporting date the entity must consider whether there are any indicators of asset impairment. If there are, then the entity is required to write the heritage asset down to a recoverable amount by way of an impairment loss. A heritage asset might be impaired, for example, if it suffers breakage.

Disclosure requirements

In respect of all the heritage assets that an entity holds, disclosure should be made as follows:

(a) The nature and scale of heritage assets held by the entity.

(b) The entity's policy for acquiring, preserving, managing and disposing of heritage assets. This should also include a description of the records that the entity has maintained concerning its collection of heritage assets and information on which access to heritage assets is permitted.

(c) The accounting policies adopted for heritage assets. This should also include details of the entity's measurement bases.

(d) Where heritage assets have not been recognised in the entity's statement of financial position (balance sheet), disclosure should be made in the notes which:
  i. Explain the reasons why,
  ii. Describe the significance and nature of those assets and
  iii. Disclose information that is useful in assessing the value of those heritage assets.

(e) For heritage assets that have been recognised on the entity's statement of financial position (balance sheet) the following should be disclosed:
  i. The carrying value of heritage assets at the start of the accounting period and at the end of the reporting period. There should also be an analysis between classes or groups of heritage assets recognised at cost and those that are recognised at valuation and
  ii. For heritage assets stated at valuation, there should be sufficient information disclosed to understand the valuation (such as the date of the valuation, the methods used, whether the valuation was carried out by an external valuer and, if so, their qualifications and any limitations on the valuation).

(f) There should be a summary of transactions that relate to heritage assets for the reporting period and each of the previous FOUR reporting periods, which disclose:
  i. The cost of acquisitions of heritage assets,
  ii. The value of heritage assets acquired by way of donations,
  iii. The carrying value of heritage assets that have been disposed of in the reporting period together with the proceeds received and
  vi. Any impairment that has been recognised.

(g) In exceptional circumstances where it has been impracticable for the entity to obtain a valuation of heritage assets acquired by donation, the reasons why should be disclosed.

The standard does allow this disclosure information to be grouped together provided that in so doing it does not obscure significant information.

If it is impracticable to make the disclosures in (f) above then they do not need to be given for any accounting period that is earlier than the previous comparable period; however, a statement to the effect that it is impracticable to make the disclosures should be made.

		2014	2013
		£'000	*£'000*
Non-current assets			
Property, plant and equipment		100,000	800,000
Heritage assets		700	700
Financial assets		<u>25,000</u>	<u>20,000</u>
		125,700	820,700

Example – Presentation of heritage assets

FUNDING COMMITMENTS

When an entity undertakes to provide resources to other entities, the provisions in paragraphs 34.57 to 34.63 are triggered. These particular sections of FRS 102 are more likely to be used by charities and public benefit entities that often commit to provide funding to other parties for a specified period of time (usually over several years). Because of the variety of entities that may make funding commitments, the Accounting Council of the Financial Reporting Council decided not to make this area specific to public benefit entities (PBEs) despite the fact that, in reality, PBEs are really the only types of entity that are likely to apply this particular section.

The issue for funding commitments is concerned with the recognition of a liability that represents the funding commitment by the entity. The definition of a liability specifically requires there to be a present obligation rather than an expectation that there will be an outflow of economic resources.

The requirements of paragraphs 34.57 to 34.63 in FRS 102 do not apply to commitments to make a loan because such commitments are covered in Section 11 *Basic Financial Instruments* or Section 12 *Other Financial Instruments Issues*. In applying paragraphs 34.57 to 34.63, the reporting entity must also have regard to the substance of the commitments and hence reference is made in paragraph 34.58 to Section 2 *Concepts and Pervasive Principles* and Section 21 *Provisions and Contingencies* for which the standard specifically requires the entity to have regard to.

Recognition and measurement

The entity must recognise a liability and, usually, a corresponding expense when a commitment is made to provide resources to another party. However, the following conditions must be met:

(a) The definition and recognition criteria for a liability have been met,
(b) The obligation (which might also be a constructive obligation) is such that the entity making the commitment cannot realistically withdraw from it and
(c) The entitlement of the other party to the resources being committed does not depend on the satisfaction of performance-related conditions.

The term 'performance-related conditions' are conditions imposed in a contract that must be met before the entity performing the conditions becomes entitled to payment or a transfer of other assets (in other words the good or service must be provided).

For commitments that are performance-related, these are recognised when the performance-related conditions have been met.

In recognising a liability, the entity measures it at the present value of the resources that have been committed.

Example – Charity providing funding

A charity has agreed to provide funding to a local enterprise whose objective is to provide training in the use of information technology for a deprived area of a community so that they stand a better chance of gaining employment. The charity has agreed funding for a four-year period commencing on 1 January 2015.

The terms of the commitment are that the local enterprise must provide evidence each year that the funds have been used for the purposes intended and until such evidence is provided the charity will not release the subsequent year's funds.

In this example, the charity will not recognise the full four-year commitment to provide funding because of the performance conditions that have been imposed in the agreement (the performance condition being that the local enterprise has to provide evidence that the funds have been used for the purposes intended).

If, on the other hand, the charity had not imposed such performance-related conditions in the agreement, and hence the local enterprise was free to use the funds at its own discretion (often referred to as 'unrestricted funds'), then the charity would normally recognise the full four-year commitment as a liability.

Disclosure requirements

Where the reporting entity has made a commitment, disclosure should be made in the financial statements as follows:

(a) The commitment that has been made,
(b) The timeframe of that commitment,
(c) Any performance-related conditions that have been attached to the commitment and
(d) Details of how the commitment is going to be funded.

The disclosures specified above can be aggregated, but care must be taken when aggregating disclosures so as not to obscure significant information. Separate disclosures do, however, need to be made for recognised and unrecognised commitments.

INCOMING RESOURCES FROM NON-EXCHANGE TRANSACTIONS

Paragraphs PBE34.64 to PBE34.74 deal with incoming resources from non-exchange transactions. In addition, there is also accompanying guidance to this Section in Appendix B of Section 34 in FRS 102.

A 'non-exchange transaction' is a transaction in which one party (the donee) receives value from another entity (the donor) without the donee giving the donor value that is equal in exchange (or approximately equal in exchange). A typical example of such a transaction would be a donation or a legacy.

> **Example – Incoming resource from a non-exchange transaction**
>
> The Briary School for Girls has decided to convert to academy status in which it will be free from local authority control. On conversion to the academy the local authority donates the school building to the academy for nil consideration.
>
> This would be an example of an incoming resource from a non-exchange transaction. The academy has not transferred economic resources (or other assets) to the local authority in exchange for the school building.

Recognition and measurement

There are three possible recognition methods available to an entity that has a receipt of resources from non-exchange transactions as follows:

1. If the transaction does not impose specified future performance-related conditions on the recipient then it is recognised as income when the resources are received or receivable,
2. If the transaction does impose specified future performance-related conditions on the recipient, then the transaction is only recognised in income when the performance-related conditions are met and
3. Where resources are received before the criteria for recognising revenue are met the transaction is recognised as a liability.

Funds may be restricted for certain purposes (referred to as 'restricted funds'). Any restrictions imposed on funds does not stop the resource from being recognised in income when it is receivable.

When considering the above three recognition criteria, the entity must also have regard as to whether the resource can be reliably measured as well as considering whether recognising the resource outweighs the costs. If it is not practicable to place an estimate on the value of the resource with sufficient reliability, then the resource is included in the accounting period in which the resource is sold.

Incoming resources from non-exchange transactions are measured as follows:

(a) In respect of donated services and facilities that would otherwise have been purchased, these are to be measured at the value to the entity.
(b) Any other incoming resources from non-exchange transactions are to be measured at the fair value of the resources received or receivable.

Disclosure requirements

In respect of incoming resources from non-exchange transactions, the entity must disclose:

(a) The nature and amounts of resources receivable from non-exchange transactions that have been recognised in the financial statements.
(b) Any unfulfilled conditions or other forms of contingencies that are attached to resources from non-exchange transactions that have not been recognised in income and
(c) An indication of other forms of resources from non-exchange transactions from which the entity has derived benefit.

PUBLIC BENEFIT ENTITY ISSUES

A 'public benefit entity' is an entity whose principal activity is to provide goods or services to members of the general public, community or social benefit.

There are two issues relating to public benefit entities:

1. Public benefit entity combinations and
2. Public benefit entity concessionary loans.

Public benefit entity combinations

Paragraphs PBE34.75 to PBE34.86 only apply to public benefit entities (PBEs) in relation to the following categories of combinations that involve an entity in its entirety or only part of an entity:

(a) Combinations that take place at nil or nominal consideration and are, in substance, a gift and
(b) Combinations that are able to meet the definition of a merger.

Combinations that are, in substance, a gift

When a combination is, in substance, a gift the provisions in Section 19 *Business Combinations and Goodwill* apply; however, the following issues need to be taken into consideration as well.

Where there is an excess of the fair value of assets received over the fair value of liabilities assumed, the excess is recognised as a gain in income and expenditure and this value represents the gift of the value of one entity to another; hence it is recognised as income.

Conversely, where there is an excess of the fair value of liabilities assumed over the fair value of assets received, this loss is also recognised in income and expenditure and this value represents the net obligations that the entity has assumed and for which the entity has not received a financial reward; hence it is recognised as an expense.

Combinations that are a merger

When a combination meets the criteria to be accounted for as a merger, the entity will apply the merger accounting method. This method uses the book values (not fair values) of the assets and liabilities of the parties involved in the combination. The only adjustments to these values will be to ensure that accounting policies are the same for both combining entities, as the standard requires uniform accounting policies to be used in merger accounting.

Comparative amounts are restated by including the results for the combining entities for the previous reporting period and their statements of financial position (balance sheets) for the previous reporting date. All comparative figures should be marked as 'combined' figures.

Incremental costs that are directly attributable to the merger are to be expensed in the period in which they are incurred.

If a combination is not a merger nor in substance a gift, then the provisions in Section 19 must be applied.

Disclosure requirements

For combinations where merger accounting has been applied, disclosure in the newly combined entity's financial statements should be made as follows:

(a) The names and description of the combining entities or businesses,
(b) The date that the merger took place,
(c) An analysis of the principal components of the current year's total comprehensive income, which should indicate:
   i. The amounts that relate to the newly formed merged entity for the period after the date of the merger and
   ii. Amounts that relate to each party to the merger up to the date of the merger,
(d) An analysis of the previous year's total comprehensive income of each party to the merger as at the date of the merger,
(e) The total carrying value of the net assets of each party to the merger as at the date of the merger and
(f) In relation to significant adjustments needed to align accounting policies, details of the nature and amount together with details of any further adjustments that have been made to net assets as a result of the merger.

Public benefit entity concessionary loans

Public benefit entity concessionary loans are loans that are made between public benefit entities or between entities that are within a public benefit entity group and another party. The loans are below market rates of interest, are not repayable on demand and are for the purposes of furthering the objectives of the public benefit entity or the public benefit entity parent.

Recognition and measurement – public benefit entity concessionary loans

An entity that makes or receives a public benefit entity concessionary loan has a choice in accounting treatment. It can use either:

- The recognition, measurement and disclosure requirements of Section 11 *Basic Financial Instruments* or Section 12 *Other Financial Instruments Issues* or
- The accounting treatment that is set out in paragraphs PBE34.90 to PBE34.97 of FRS 102 (which are discussed below).

A public benefit entity that makes or receives a concessionary loan should initially measure the arrangement at the amount received or paid and recognise them within the statement of financial position (balance sheet).

After initial recognition in the statement of financial position (balance sheet), the carrying value of the concessionary loan is adjusted to take account of any interest that is payable or receivable. Impairment losses are recognised each reporting period to the extent to which a loan is deemed irrecoverable.

Presentation and disclosure

In respect of concessionary loans made and received, these are presented in the statement of financial position (balance sheet) as either separate line items on the face of the statement of financial position (balance sheet) or in the notes to the financial statements. Concessionary loans should also be presented separately between those that are repayable and those that are receivable both within and after more than one year.

Within the entity's accounting policies should be an explanation of the measurement basis (or bases) that the entity has used for concessionary loans together with any additional accounting policies that will enable the user to fully understand these transactions within the financial statements.

Disclosure within the financial statements should be made as follows:

(a) The terms and conditions of the concessionary loan arrangements and
(b) The value of concessionary loans that have been committed at the reporting date but have not yet been taken up.

The standard requires separate disclosure of concessionary loans made or received but does allow multiple loans made or received to be disclosed in aggregate, provided that the aggregation does not obscure significant information.

26 LIABILITIES AND EQUITY

INTRODUCTION

There are certain transactions that occur in the business world that often lend themselves to some element of deciphering as to whether they should fall to be classed as debt (i.e. as a liability) or as an equity instrument. In some cases a transaction may have to be 'split accounted' so as to correctly allocate the transaction between the liability portion and the equity portion. Section 22 *Liabilities and Equity* gives guidance to preparers of FRS 102 financial statements for classifying financial instruments between liabilities and equity. Section 22 also deals with the issue of when a financial instrument contains a mixture of both debt and equity (referred to in the section as a 'compound' financial instrument).

Share transactions can become complicated and Section 22 deals with the issue relating to distributions to owners (shareholders) and how a company deals with accounting for purchases of its own equity. The scope of Section 22 also extends to non-controlling interests (often referred to as 'minority interests' in the UK) and how they are to be accounted for in a company's consolidated financial statements.

For share-based payment transactions, the accounting for such transactions is dealt with in Section 26 *Share-based Payment*, which is examined in Chapter 19 of this book. In addition, Section 22 does not deal with the following types of financial instruments:

- Investments in subsidiaries, associates and joint ventures, which fall under the scope of Section 9 *Consolidated and Separate Financial Statements*, Section 14 *Investments in Associates* and Section 15 *Investments in Joint Ventures*.
- The rights and obligations associated with employers under employee benefit plans accounted for under the provisions in Section 28 *Employee Benefits*.
- Contracts in relation to contingent consideration in a business combination – such issues are dealt with in Section 19 *Business Combinations and Goodwill* (although this exemption only applies to the acquirer in a business combination).

- Financial instruments, contracts and obligations that exist under share-based payment transactions, which are covered in Section 26 (although paragraphs 22.3 to 22.6 in Section 22 will apply to treasury shares which are issued, purchased, sold, transferred or cancelled in employee share option plans, employee share purchase plans and other share-based payment arrangements).
- Insurance (and re-insurance) contracts, which are issued and held and accounted for in accordance with the provisions in FRS 103 *Insurance Contracts*.
- Financial instruments that have discretionary participation features (these are also accounted for under the provisions in FRS 103).
- Financial guarantee contracts – these are dealt with in Section 21 *Provisions and Contingencies*.

This particular chapter will deal with complex issues concerning share capital. However, it is to be emphasised that cases which affect the equity structure of a company's or a shareholder's ownership interest in a company, professional advice should be sought to ensure that the maximum benefits are obtained by both the company and the shareholder(s) concerned.

INTERACTION OF FINANCIAL LIABILITIES AND EQUITY

When an entity receives finance from a third party the finance can either represent a financial liability (for example, a loan, which is debt) or it can represent an introduction of funds from an investor that contains no requirement to pay the investor cash (i.e. interest) or other types of redemption features (so is treated as equity). However, there are situations when an entity receives finance from a third party that contains a mixture of the two (i.e. debt *and* equity). This is particularly relevant for compound financial instruments, which contain redemption features or entitle the holder of the instrument to receive cash (for example, periodic dividend payments).

'Split accounting' is used in cases where compound financial instruments are concerned, which effectively splits the financial instrument into its debt and equity components. Some critics of the international equivalent of the financial instruments (presentation) standard, IAS 32 *Financial Instruments: Presentation*, are calling for the debt/equity split to be abandoned on the grounds that the method has been in existence for over a century and has been left behind by the creation of more complex financial instruments. Other critics argue that the debt/equity split is, in real life, so overly complicated that it is simply no longer appropriate in the modern business world. One of the inherent difficulties that can be highlighted in IAS 32 is the fact that the standard itself takes the stance that a financial instrument is only equity when there is no guaranteed payment to the holder of the financial instrument from the issuing company. In this particular case, the owners of the equity instrument cannot sell their shares other than back to the issuer, which is then obligated to buy them. Effectively, the angle from which IAS 32 works would mean that these shares are liabilities and where their value increases, the fair value in the liability increases and is hence charged to profit and loss.

Notwithstanding the arguments for and against the split between equity and debt, Section 22 works on the basis that equity is the residual interest in the assets of an entity after all liabilities have been deducted. The scope of equity covers all investments by an entity's owners (i.e. the shareholders) and additions to those investments that have been earned through the entity's ordinary course of business (i.e. retained profits). Deducted from this equity are both dividends (referred to as 'distributions' in Section 22) and any losses that the company generates in an accounting period.

The definition of a financial instrument has become extremely complex over the last couple of decades – largely due to the increased use of financial instruments as a means of funding a business, but also due to the increasingly complex nature of some of the more common financial instruments that are used in the modern business world. In financial reporting, a financial liability is defined as:

(a) A contractual obligation:
    i. To deliver cash or another financial asset to another entity or
    ii. To exchange financial assets or financial liabilities with another entity under conditions that are potentially unfavourable to the entity or
(b) A contract that will, or may, be settled in the entity's own equity instruments and:
    i. Under which the entity is, or may be, obliged to deliver a variable number of the entity's own equity instruments or
    ii. Which will, or may, be settled other than by the exchange of a fixed amount of cash or another financial asset for a fixed number of the entity's own equity instruments. For this purpose the entity's own equity instruments do not include instruments that are themselves contracts for the future receipt or delivery of the entity's own equity instruments.

Paragraph 22.5 of FRS 102 gives some useful examples of financial instruments that can fall to be classified as *either* liabilities or equity:

- An instrument (or components of instruments) subordinate to all other classes of instruments classified as equity if they make provision to deliver to another party a pro rata share of the entity's net assets on liquidation. Such instruments are classed as liabilities if the distribution of net assets on liquidation is subject to a maximum amount.
- Puttable instruments are equity where the holder receives a right to a pro rata share of the net assets of the entity when the put option is exercised, which is determined by:
  - Taking the entity's net assets on liquidation and dividing these into units of equal amount and
  - Multiplying the above by the number of units held by the instrument holder.
- Financial instruments are classed as liabilities if they entitle the holder of the instruments to receive fixed amounts of cash (for example, dividends).
- Puttable instruments that are classified as equity in a subsidiary's financial statements will be classified as a liability in the group (consolidated) financial statements.

- Preference shares where the terms of the shares make provision for the holder of the preference shares to receive periodic payments of cash or contain a redemption feature.

Some financial instruments that meet the definition above can also be accounted for as an equity transaction because, in substance, they represent the residual interest in the net assets of the entity. This is the case with a puttable instrument, which is classified as an equity instrument if the instrument has all of the following features:

- The holder of the instrument is entitled to a pro rata share of the entity's net assets in the event of a liquidation.
- The instrument is in a class of instruments that is subordinate to all other classes.
- The financial instruments that are held in a class of instruments subordinate to other classes of instruments all have similar features.
- Apart from the contractual provision for the issuer to repurchase or redeem the instrument in exchange for cash or other assets, the instrument does not contain any other rights to deliver cash or other financial assets to another entity or to partake in an exchange of financial assets or financial liabilities with another entity under conditions that are potentially unfavourable to the entity. In addition, the contract is not one that will, or may, be settled in the entity's own equity instruments.
- The total expected cash flows associated with the instrument are based, substantially, on the profit or loss, change in recognised net assets or the changes in fair value of the recognised and unrecognised net assets of the entity over the life of the instruments.

Example – Shares in co-operative entities

Aidan has subscribed to shares in a recently formed credit union in his home town (a credit union is a financial institution that is owned and controlled by its members). The terms of the subscription make reference to the credit union having an unconditional right to refuse redemption of the members' shares.

Paragraph 22.6 deals with the issue of members' shares in a co-operative entity and says that such shares fall to be classed as equity if:

- The entity has an unconditional right to refuse redemption of the members' shares or
- Redemption is unconditionally prohibited by law, regulation or the entity's governing charter.

As a result, the shares to which Aidan has subscribed will fall to be classified as equity in the credit union's balance sheet (statement of financial position).

The overarching principle, therefore, is that a financial liability is classified as debt when the contract provides the holder of the financial instrument with the right to receive cash or other assets from the entity.

Example – Financial liability

An entity enters into a contract with an unconnected third party to raise finance. The terms of the loan make provisions for the finance provider to receive annual amounts of interest at a rate of 6%. The loan matures in five years at a premium of 10%.

The financial instrument is the loan note. The terms of this instrument make provisions for the holder of the loan note (the finance provider) to receive periodic interest payments as well as redemption after the five-year period has elapsed. This loan note is a financial liability and will be recognised as such in the entity's balance sheet (statement of financial position), split at the balance sheet date between the current portion (the portion falling due within one year) of the liability and the non-current portion (the amount falling due after more than one year).

Had the loan in the above example contained provisions that give the holder of the instrument the option to convert the capital element to shares at the date of maturity of the loan, then this would fall to be classified as 'convertible debt' and the liability would be split between its debt portion and its equity portion (the equity portion representing the holder's option to convert to shares at maturity). This issue is considered in the later section, 'Convertible Debt'.

Transaction costs

Transaction costs in relation to the issue of equity instruments are treated as a deduction from equity and are stated net of any related income tax benefit.

Transaction costs are costs that directly relate to the purchase, issue or disposal of a financial asset or a financial liability or the issue or reacquisition of an entity's own equity instruments. The term 'incremental costs' is used in the standard and is taken to be one that would not have been incurred by the entity had the entity not purchased, issued or disposed of the financial asset or financial liability or had not issued or reacquired its own equity instrument(s).

ORDINARY SHARE CAPITAL

Most, if not all, companies will have ordinary share capital in issue and the amount of issued ordinary share capital can range from 1p to hundreds of thousands of pounds (if not more in some cases). The Glossary to FRS 102 defines an ordinary share as an equity instrument that is subordinate to all other classes of equity instrument. In other words, an ordinary share is any share that is not a preference share; nor does it have any related predetermined dividend amounts (dividends on ordinary shares are essentially at the discretion of the entity).

Ownership of an ordinary share in an entity represents equity ownership in the company and entitles the holder of the ordinary share to vote in matters put before the shareholders in general meetings in proportion to their percentage ownership in the company. Ordinary shares entitle the holder to receive dividends (provided any dividend is available following dividends paid on preference shares) and they also entitle the holder to receive their share of the residual economic value of the company should the business be wound up. As ordinary shares are subordinate to other classes of shares, ordinary shareholders rank bottom when it comes to dividends (bondholders and preference shareholders rank above ordinary shareholders). Another inherent disadvantage in owning ordinary shares is that they are also considered unsecured creditors in the event that the company ceases to trade.

'Potential ordinary shares' are financial instruments (or other contracts) that entitle their holders to ordinary shares within the business. Typically potential ordinary shares can be found in convertible debt (provided that the conversion of loan capital is into an equity instrument at the redemption date). Other potential ordinary shares can be found within:

- Preference shares,
- Warrants for ordinary shares,
- Rights granted under employee share plans entitling employees to receive ordinary shares and
- Rights to ordinary shares subject to contingencies (i.e. the (non-)occurrence of future events).

For the purposes of accounting, ordinary shares are invariably classified as equity shares (and referred to as such) because the issuer (the company) usually has discretion over any dividend payments that may be received on the shares. In contrast to preference shares, which mandate the company to make periodic dividend payments on them as well as invariably containing redemption features, ordinary shares do not contain such requirements to transfer cash to the holder of the ordinary shares.

The classification of shares into ordinary shares must, therefore, be carefully considered in light of relevant facts. HM Revenue and Customs guidance at ESSUM43230 *Shares to be used: Ordinary share capital* says that:

'It does not matter whether or not the class of shares in question is called "ordinary". For example, shares described as "preference shares" can be ordinary share capital if the rights they confer satisfy the definition in Section 989. Each case should be examined carefully on its own facts.'[1]

In some cases, preference shares can be classified as ordinary shares if they do not contain any redemption features nor entitle the holder to receive cash (although in the vast majority of cases it is relatively uncommon for such preference shares to contain such provisions).

PREFERENCE SHARE CAPITAL

Invariably preference share capital – whilst being a form of shares – is generally treated as a liability. This is because of the definition of a financial liability and the fact that a preference share more often than not entitles the holder of the share to receive cash in the form of dividend payments (which are treated as a finance cost in the entity's financial statements). For listed companies that have to calculate earnings per share in accordance with EU-endorsed IAS 33 *Earnings per Share*, basic earnings

---

[1]HMRC ESSUM43230.

are always calculated after taking into consideration the dividends attributable to preference shareholders, as this amount is not available for distribution to the ordinary shareholders. Preference shares are essentially a hybrid of ordinary shares and corporate bonds. They are attractive to investors who wish to seek inflation-beating income with little risk of missed payments or default as they offer the holder of the preference shares solid income returns and are relatively safe.

In a dividend payout, a preference shareholder will rank higher than an ordinary shareholder. In addition, should the company cease trading or be put into liquidation, preference shareholders will have a right to be paid company assets first. In respect of voting in a general meeting, preference shareholders usually do not have voting rights. There can be potentially four classifications of preference share:

1. Cumulative preference shares: where dividends must be paid including those dividends declared but not yet paid (for example, due to cash flow restraints),
2. Non-cumulative preference shares: where dividends declared but not yet paid are not included,
3. Participating preference shares: these give the holder of these shares dividends *plus* shares of extra profit based on certain conditions and
4. Convertible preference shares: these are preference shares that can be exchanged for a specified number of ordinary shares.

Issuing preference shares and increasing rates of dividend

Preference shares may be issued with an increasing rate of dividend. For example, a company may issue further preference shares at a premium with compensation provided by the payment of dividends by the company at rates above the market rate in later periods. When a company issues such preference shares, the discount or premium on the initial issue of the preference shares must be amortised to profit and loss account reserves using the effective interest method.

Repurchase of preference shares

In situations when a repurchase of preference shares takes place by the company and the fair value of the consideration received for the preference shares exceeds the carrying value of the preference shares, the difference (the excess) is charged to profit and loss reserves. If the fair value of the consideration received for the preference shares is less than the carrying value of the preference shares, the difference is added to profit or loss attributable to ordinary shareholders.

Conversion of preference shares into ordinary shares

Companies may try to encourage preference shareholders to convert their shares into ordinary shares; to entice the preference shareholders to convert to ordinary shares, the terms of the conversion may incorporate favourable terms. In such circumstances, the excess of the fair value of the ordinary shares over the fair value of the ordinary shares that are issuable on conversion under the original terms is to be treated as a return to shareholders and is deducted when calculating profit or loss attributable to ordinary shareholders.

The treatment of preference shares can be summarised in the table as follows:

Redemption of shares	Payment of dividends	Recognition as
Non-redeemable	Discretionary	Equity
Non-redeemable	Non-discretionary	Liability
Redeemable at issuer's option at some future point in time	Discretionary	Equity*
Redeemable at issuer's option at some future point in time	Non-discretionary	Liability plus an embedded call option derivative**
Contractually redeemable at a fixed/ determinable amount at a fixed/ determinable date	Discretionary	Compound financial instrument***
Redeemable at holder's option at some future point in time	Discretionary	Compound financial instrument
Redeemable at holder's option at some future point in time	Non-discretionary	Liability plus an embedded put option derivative

*In this case there is no contractual obligation to pay the holders of the shares cash. Options to redeem the shares for cash do not actually meet the definition of a financial liability. As a result, any dividends paid on these preference shares would be recognised in equity.

**The entire proceeds would be classified as a liability because the dividends will be set at market rates and as such the proceeds will be equivalent to their fair value, at the date of issue, of the dividends payable to perpetuity. In respect of the issuer call option to redeem the shares for cash, this would be classed as an embedded derivative.

***The liability portion of the compound instrument is equal to the present value of the redemption amount. The equity amount is equal to the proceeds *less* the liability portion. The dividends related to the equity portion are recognised in equity.

REVALUATION RESERVE

The provisions in Schedule 1 to SI 2008/410 incorporate rules relating to the transfer of amounts to and from a revaluation reserve account. In particular, Schedule 35(1) to SI 2008/410 1 says that where a company has valued an item in accordance with one of the alternative accounting rules, the revaluation surplus or deficit must be credited or debited to a revaluation reserve account.

The revaluation reserve account is found within the equity section of the balance sheet (statement of financial position) and is used to take fair value gains and losses for assets that are subjected to the revaluation model, which is permitted in Section 17 *Property, Plant and Equipment*. It has to be disclosed on the face of a company's balance sheet (statement of financial position) and it is generally preferred to describe the account as a revaluation reserve account (although some companies choose to describe the account using alternative names – for example, 'revaluation surplus'). A key point to emphasise with the revaluation reserve is that such reserves are not distributable as dividends as they are not realised profits for the purposes of a dividend.

In addition the treatment of fair value gains for investment property is markedly different under Section 16 *Investment Property* than under previous SSAP 19 *Accounting for Investment Properties* in that fair value gains and losses are taken directly to profit or loss rather than accumulated in equity in a revaluation surplus account.

A company may transfer an amount from the revaluation reserve account to profit and loss reserves provided the amount that was previously charged represents a realised profit. The Companies Act 2006 also allows a company to apply the whole, or a part, of the revaluation reserve in wholly, or partly, paying up unissued shares in the company to be allotted to the members as fully or partly paid shares.

Any amounts of the revaluation reserve that are not considered necessary going forward in respect of the valuation method that the company has adopted will be reduced.

DIVIDENDS

Dividends (commonly referred to in financial reporting as 'distributions') are payments to equity holders by the company as a return on their investment. Dividends are paid to shareholders to give them their share of the company's profit for the year and are non-reciprocal transfers. The Companies Act 2006 defines a 'distribution' as any distribution of a company's assets to its shareholders (whether or not it is made in cash), other than a distribution that is made by way of any of the following:

- The issue of either fully paid or partly paid bonus shares,
- The redemption or the purchase of any of the company's own shares, either out of capital, out of the proceeds of a fresh issue of shares or out of unrealised profits in accordance with Chapters 3, 4 or 5 of Part 18 of the 2006 Act,
- The reduction of share capital by either of the following means:
  - Extinguishing or reducing the liability in respect of share capital that is not paid up or
  - Repaying paid-up share capital and
- The distribution of assets to shareholders on a winding-up.[2]

Dividends paid to equity holders are not reported in profit or loss – they are treated as a debit against equity. As a consequence, dividends are no longer reported on the face of the profit and loss account after profit after tax. They are instead reported as a movement on reserves within the notes to the financial statements. However, some companies do have a policy of showing dividends on the face of the profit and loss account and, if this is the case, it is important that the dividends are shown as a debit against equity and not as a debit against profits for the period. This can be achieved as follows:

Profit after tax	X
Opening reserves brought forward	X
Dividends	(X)
Closing reserves carried forward	X

---

[2]Companies Act 2006 Section 829(1)(2).

If the dividend is shown immediately after profit after tax it will not be regarded as a debit against reserves, but instead as a charge against profit for the year and because of the substance of the transaction (an equity transaction), this would be incorrect.

Dividends declared after the reporting date

Dividends that are declared (the term 'declared' meaning appropriately authorised and no longer at the discretion of the entity) after the reporting date, but before financial statements are authorised for issue, are not recognised as a liability at the reporting date on the basis that the entity did not have an obligation to pay the dividends at the reporting date. Disclosure of such dividends should be made if these dividends are material.

Dividends to preference shareholders and compound financial instrument holders

Preference shareholders rank higher than ordinary shareholders in terms of the order in which the dividends are paid out. In the company's financial statements, dividends paid on preference shares are not accounted for in the same way as dividends paid to ordinary shareholders; this is because preference shares that contain a redemption feature or entitle the holder of the preference shares to receive cash are classed as a financial liability. As a consequence of this treatment, dividends paid to preference shareholders are treated as an interest expense in the paying company's financial statements.

In respect of compound financial instruments (financial instruments with both debt and equity features), there will be a consequential effect on the amounts recognised as interest expense and dividends. In allocating the sums to be recognised as a liability and as equity, the present value of the redemption amount is treated as a financial liability, with the balance of the proceeds being recognised within equity. The unwinding of the discount is recognised in the financial statements as interest expense and the discretionary dividends on the shares relate to the equity portion and are recognised as a dividend accordingly.

CONVERTIBLE DEBT

Convertible debt is debt by which the terms of the financial instrument provides the holder of the loan to convert the capital amount to shares at a later date (usually at redemption). The characteristics of such debt is similar to compound financial instruments in that it contains both debt and equity (the equity portion being the option to convert the loan into shares at a later date). In respect of such debt, the instrument will need to be 'split accounted' so the instrument can be recognised as debt and equity in the financial statements.

Example – Convertible loan with debt and equity features

On 1 April 2013 an 8% convertible loan with a nominal value of £600,000 was issued at par to Company A Limited. It is redeemable on 31 March 2016 at par. Alternatively, it can be converted into equity shares on the basis of 100 new shares for each 200 worth of loan note.

An equivalent loan note without the conversion option would carry interest at 10%. Interest amounting to £48,000 (£600,000 × 8%) has already been paid to the note holders and included as a finance cost in profit and loss.

Present value rates are as follows:

		8%	10%
End of year	1	0.93	0.91
	2	0.86	0.83
	3	0.79	0.75
	4	0.73	0.68

In this example there is the option to convert the shares into equity, but there is also the obligation to pay cash to the loan note holders (the 8% interest). There is also the issue that an equivalent loan note *without* the conversion option would have carried interest at a rate of 10%. The loan notes attract interest at a rate of 8% but as it is only an option, in order to calculate the correct amounts to be recognised in debt and equity the entire cash flows have to be discounted at a rate of 10%. Using this information the debt and equity instruments can be calculated as follows:

	8% interest (£600k × 8%)	Factor at a rate of 10%	Present value (rounded down)
Year 1 – 2013	48,000	0.91	43,600
Year 2 – 2014	48,000	0.83	39,800
Year 3 – 2015	48,000	0.75	36,000
			119,400
Year 4 – 2016	648,000	0.68	440,600
Amount to be recognised as a financial liability			560,000
Initial proceeds received			(600,000)
Amount to be recognised as equity			40,000

Convertible debt is becoming more widespread as it preserves cash at redemption and is also helpful in times of economic difficulty. However, the disadvantage to existing shareholders is that their ownership interest in the company becomes diluted once the loan note holders exercise their option to convert loan capital into equity.

Example – Conversion of loan into equity

Company B Limited receives a loan from Company C Limited amounting to £100,000 in 2011, the terms of which require redemption in 2014. Given the global economic crisis, it was clear from the cash flow position of Company B that it would be unable to repay the loan at the agreed redemption date. Company C Limited accepted 100,000 ordinary £1 equity shares in full and final settlement.

No gain or loss will arise on this transaction as the debt is simply transferred to equity (assuming no premium on the issues of shares) by the following entries:

DR loan	£100,000
CR equity	£100,000

If a premium had existed on this transaction, it would be transferred to a share premium account.

Example – Gain arising on settlement of a loan

Use the same facts as in the example above, but in this example consider that the fair value of the equity shares issued in exchange were £75,000. In this case there would be a gain arising on the settlement of the debt and the entries in the books of Company B Ltd would be:

DR loans   £100,000
CR equity   £75,000
CR profit and loss   £25,000 (gain on elimination of debt)

SHARE SPLITS

When a company undertakes a share split (sometimes referred to as a 'stock split') it divides its existing shares into multiple shares. This has the effect that whilst the number of issued shares increases by a specific multiple, the total value of the shares remains the same because no real value has been added to the shares as a result of the split.

Example – Share split

Tony's Tablets Limited operates in the computer hardware sector and over the last five years has experienced significant success due to the launch of three new tablet computers. As a direct result of this success, the share price of the company has risen and the company is keen to attract new investors to raise finance to launch three further products within the next five years. The shares have been valued in round lots of £500 each and the finance director has concerns that this price will be too costly for investors and has suggested a share split.

The share split has been agreed in the general meeting and is to be a two-for-one split. Therefore, each shareholder will receive an additional share for each share that he or she already owns. Doing a share split in this manner has the advantage of attracting further investors because an investor would need to invest £50,000 to purchase 100 shares. However, in this scenario if each share was worth only £250 then investors would only need to pay £2,500 to own 100 shares as opposed to £5,000.

BONUS SHARE ISSUES

A 'bonus issue' (often referred to as a 'scrip issue' or 'capitalisation issue') is when a company will issue further shares to shareholders in proportion to their existing holding. The amount of shares issued in proportion to existing holdings will vary across each company, but are often done in the proportion of one share for every five shares held.

Bonus issues are very advantageous for the company and for the shareholder. From the company's perspective, a bonus issue could be undertaken as opposed to paying dividends to existing shareholders and in this case cash is preserved – in addition, if the company is undercapitalised then the levels of dividends paid by the company are likely to be higher than they would be if a bonus issue was undertaken, because then the levels of dividends will be lower as they are based on a higher number of shares.

From the shareholders' perspective, a bonus issue is advantageous because they receive additional shares in the business at no extra cost to them.

Any change in capital structure will not affect the profit and loss account as the change is merely a change in the company's capital structure. In addition, where a company issues new shares by way of a bonus issue, the only effect is to increase the number of shares that are outstanding after the issue; the issue itself has no impact on earnings because no flow of funds has taken place.

Example – Accounting for a bonus issue of shares

During the year to 31 October 2014, a company makes a bonus issue of shares to its shareholders of one share for every six shares held. All shareholders take up the offer of the bonus issue and the value of the issue is £20,000.

The bonus issue will be treated as a transaction within equity and the journals to account for the issue will be:

DR profit and loss reserves	£20,000
CR issued share capital	£20,000

RIGHTS ISSUES

A 'rights issue' is a way in which a company can raise finance by selling additional shares to existing shareholders in proportion to their current shareholding. Rights issues are a common means of raising finance in particularly difficult trading times (such as in economic difficulties). As an incentive to the existing shareholders, a company will offer the shares at a discounted price to the current share price – although there is no 'hard and fast' rule that says that this is always the case – a company may well offer a rights issue at market value of the shares if the company so chooses. If the shareholder(s) choose not to take up a rights issue, then their shareholding in the company will become diluted as additional shareholders take up the rights issue.

In terms of the share price, the 'actual cumulative rights price' is the value of the share with rights attached immediately before the rights issue. Conversely, the 'theoretical ex-rights price' is the expected share price immediately after the rights issue.

When considering whether (or not) to take up the offer of a rights issue, investors should carefully consider the financial stability of the company. If the company has a lot of other borrowings then this can be a warning sign. Little can be achieved for companies undertaking a rights issue that is already highly geared unless the company can show signs of improvement.

When a company undertakes a rights issue, it is often the case that the price of the shares is set below that of the market price (i.e. the company offers a 'discount'). This discount element is essentially a bonus issue of shares because existing shareholders are receiving additional shares for free. Clearly this will have an impact on earnings (and earnings per share).

Example – Rights issue

On 1 January 2015, Clowes Limited had 500,000 ordinary £1 shares in issue. In an attempt to raise finance to expand its operations, it offered existing shareholders a rights issue of one share for every five shares held. This rights issue was offered on 1 April 2014.

The rights issue in this example is one share for every five held; therefore 500,000 shares have already previously been issued and thus the additional shares in the rights issue will be 500,000 × 1/5 = 100,000.

SHARE PREMIUM ACCOUNT

One of the ways in which a company can raise finance is through the issuing of additional shares. The issuing of shares can be undertaken at a price that exceeds the fair value of the shares on the market. In today's modern business world, banks and financiers often require the shareholders to subscribe to additional shares (often at a premium) to demonstrate their confidence in the company. If shareholders do not wish to subscribe to further shares in the business (at a premium or otherwise) this can indicate that the shareholders do not have confidence in the business.

Companies that issue shares for more than their par (face) value do so at a premium and the Companies Act 2006 requires the premium received on these shares to be accounted for separately within the financial statements (i.e. through a 'share premium account').

Example – Issuance of shares at a premium

On 1 October 2014, the issued share capital of Weavers Windows Limited was 10,000 ordinary £1 shares. The economic recovery that has started has seen the company's order book increase significantly and the directors are keen to take advantage of this recovery and increase its competitive advantage. They are seeking to expand operations in the north of the country where demand for their products is experiencing continued growth. In an attempt to raise finance, the company has undertaken a share issue and issued a further 5,000 shares at £2 each and the cash for these shares was received on 1 March 2015.

On 1 March 2015, the company will account for the share issue as follows:

	£
DR cash at bank	10,000
CR ordinary share capital	5,000
CR share premium	5,000

The excess of par value to issue price is taken to the share premium account. The ordinary share capital of the business in the balance sheet (statement of financial position) will only represent the par value of the share issue.

SHARE BUYBACKS

It is not uncommon to hear of companies purchasing their own shares from shareholders. Typical scenarios include shareholders who wish to sell their shares in a company where other shareholders may not wish to buy them or where the shareholders are unable to raise the cash to purchase them.

The accounting for such buybacks can be tricky and there is a whole host of legalities to consider, some of which are obvious whereas others are not so.

The Companies Act 2006

The Companies Act 2006 (CA06) deals with the acquisition by a company of its own shares in Part 18 in sections 658 to 737. Section 658 places a restriction on companies acquiring their own shares (whether by purchase, subscription or otherwise) unless the exceptions in section 659 apply. The exceptions are summarised as follows:

1. A limited company may acquire any of its own fully paid shares otherwise than for valuable consideration.
2. Section 658 does not prohibit:
   - The acquisition of shares in a reduction of capital duly made,
   - The purchase of shares in pursuance of an order of the court under:
     - section 98 (application to court to cancel resolution for re-registration as a private company),
     - section 721(6) (powers of court on objection to redemption or purchase of shares out of capital),
     - section 759 (remedial order in case of breach of prohibition of public offers by private company) or
     - part 30 (protection of members against unfair prejudice),
   - The forfeiture of shares, or the acceptance of shares surrendered in lieu, in pursuance of the company's articles, for failure to pay any sum payable in respect of the shares.

Accounting issues

Section 686(1) of the Companies Act 2006 only allows redeemable shares to be redeemed if they are fully paid. A similar principle is contained in section 691(1), which prohibits companies from purchasing their own shares if the shares are not fully paid. Section 691(2) also requires companies that purchase their own shares to pay for those shares on purchase.

Section 733 under Chapter 7 of the Companies Act 2006 *Supplementary Provisions* makes reference to the 'capital redemption reserve'. Section 733(2) requires a company whose shares are redeemed or purchased wholly out of the company's profits to transfer a sum equivalent to the amount by which the company's share capital is diminished on cancellation of the shares. This transfer is required to maintain the company's capital and also to protect creditors.

In addition, section 733 also requires:

- A transfer to the capital redemption reserve where shares are redeemed or purchased wholly or partly out of the proceeds of a fresh issue and
- The aggregate amount of the proceeds is less than the aggregate nominal value of the shares redeemed or purchased (section 733(3)(a) and (b)).

- The amount by which a company's share capital is diminished in accordance with section 729(4) (on the cancellation of shares held as treasury shares) must be transferred to the capital redemption reserve.

The company can only then use the capital redemption reserve to make a bonus issue of shares.

Example – Repurchase of shares

The balance sheet of Company A Limited is as follows:

	£
Cash at bank	40,000
Ordinary share capital (£1 shares)	18,000
Profit and loss account	22,000
	40,000

A resolution was passed for the company to repurchase 4,000 shares at par value. The accounting for such would be as follows:

DR ordinary share capital	4,000
CR cash at bank	4,000

Redemption of share capital

DR profit and *loss* account	4,000
CR capital *redemption* reserve	4,000

Share capital redeemed – maintain share capital

Company A's *balance* sheet will now look like this:

	£
Cash at bank	36,000
Ordinary share capital (£1 shares)	14,000
Capital redemption reserve	4,000
Profit and loss account	18,000
	36,000

Share buyback at a premium

There may be occasions when a company may decide to repurchase some shares at a premium. Using the same example as the one above, if we assume that the company repurchased the shares at a 50p premium, the journals would be:

DR ordinary share capital	4,000
DR profit and loss reserves (4,000 shares × 0.50p)	2,000
CR cash at bank	6,000

Redemption of share capital at a premium of £2,000

A further journal would then be required in order that the capital of the company is maintained as follows:

DR profit and loss account	4,000
CR capital redemption reserve	4,000

To maintain the capital of the company
Company A's balance sheet would now look like this:

	£
Cash at bank	34,000
Ordinary share capital (£1 shares)	14,000
Capital redemption reserve	4,000
Profit and loss account	16,000
	34,000

The above is the step-by-step process, whereas the Companies Act 2006 expresses the accounting treatment as follows (which ends up with the same result):

CR cash at bank	6,000
DR profit and loss reserves	6,000
DR ordinary share capital	4,000
CR capital redemption reserve	4,000

The company has still maintained capital at £18,000 and the company has made the purchase out of distributable profits (because the total debited to profit and loss account reserves is the £6,000, which is equivalent to the consideration for the share buyback).

Shares purchased out of a fresh issue of shares

The general rule is that any premium that is paid on the shares that a company acquires must be made out of distributable profits. However, section 687(4) in the Companies Act 2006 says that if the redeemable shares were issued at a premium, any premium payable on their redemption may be funded from the proceeds of the new share issue. The amount of the premium that can be funded in this way is equal to the lower of:

1. The aggregate of the premiums the company received on issuance of the shares that it is now redeeming or
2. The amount of the company's share premium account after crediting the premium (if any) on the new issue of shares it makes to fund the purchase or redemption.

Example – Shares purchased out of a fresh issue

On 1 January 2015, Company B Limited issued 100,000 ordinary £1 shares. Included in this share issue are Fred's 10,000 ordinary shares, which were issued to him at a premium of 0.10p per share. Following this issue the balance on Company B's share premium account was £3,500. On 1 January 2017, Company B made a bonus issue of shares to its shareholders and used the entire balance on the share premium account on the issuance of the bonus shares.

In 2017, Fred announced that he would like to retire and has asked the company to purchase his shares. The company has agreed to purchase his shares for £2.50 per share (hence at a premium of £1.50 per share) and in order to do this has made a further issue of 10,000 ordinary shares with a par value of £1 at a premium of 0.75p (hence issued at £1.75). The balance to purchase Fred's shares of £7,500 has been made out of the bank account.

The premium on the purchase is the lower of the initial premiums the company received on the original issuance of the shares and the balance on the share premium account after the issue as follows:

	£	£
Par value of shares purchased		10,000
Lower of:		
– Initial premium on share issue	1,000	
(10,000 shares at 10p premium)		
– Balance on share premium account including premium on new issue of shares	7,500	1,000
Total (which cannot exceed proceeds of new issue)		11,000
Balance funded from distributable profit		14,000
Cost of purchase of Fred's shares		25,000

To record the above in the accounts, the journals will be:

DR cash at bank	17,500
CR share capital	17,500

Being new share issue of 10,000 £1 shares at £0.75 premium

DR share capital	10,000
DR share premium	1,000*
DR profit and loss account	14,000**
CR cash at bank	25,000

Being purchase of 10,000 ordinary £1 shares at a premium of £1.50

*Section 692(4) of the Companies Act 2006 allows the share premium account to be reduced by part of the premium payable on the purchase/redemption that is allowed to be funded out of the proceeds of the new share issue rather than it being made out of profit and loss account reserves.

**See reconciliation above.

You will note that in this scenario there have been no amounts credited to the capital redemption reserve. This is because the par value of the shares purchased (£10,000) is less than the total proceeds of the new issue of £17,500 (10,000 shares @ £1.75) and therefore the company's capital has been maintained, so there is no need for a transfer to the capital redemption reserve.

Permissible capital payments

Section 710 of the Companies Act 2006 deals with the concept of the *permissible capital payment* (PCP). The PCP is the amount by which the purchase or redemption costs exceed the amount of profits available for distribution plus the proceeds of any new share issue; hence it is calculated as the purchase price of shares less (distributable profit + proceeds from new share issue) = PCP.

The objective of the PCP is to make sure that a company makes use of its available profits and any proceeds arising from new share issues before it makes any payments out of capital.

Section 734(2) says that where the PCP is less than the nominal value of the shares redeemed or purchased, the difference is transferred to the capital redemption reserve. Conversely, where the PCP is greater than the nominal value of the shares redeemed/purchased, section 734(3) says the excess can be used to reduce any of the following:

- Capital redemption reserve
- Share premium
- Fully paid up share capital
- Revaluation reserve

Example – Permissible capital payment

The balance sheet of Company C Limited is as follows:

	£
Cash at bank	20,000
Ordinary share capital (£1 shares)	16,000
Profit and loss account	4,000
	20,000

One of the shareholders has expressed his disagreement with the way the company is being run and it has been agreed that the company should purchase 6,000 shares at par from the shareholder on the grounds that the relationship has become irretrievable. Clearly the company has insufficient reserves available to make the purchase and therefore a payment out of capital will be required. Company C Limited is required to follow the rules in the Companies Act 2006 (sections 709 to 723) and once these procedures have been carried out, the journals will be as follows:

DR ordinary share capital	6,000
CR cash	6,000

Payment to redeem shares

DR profit and loss account	4,000
CR capital redemption reserve	4,000

Maintenance of capital and protection of creditors

Company A's balance sheet will now look like this:

	£
Cash at bank	14,000
Ordinary share capital (£1 shares)	10,000
Capital redemption reserve	4,000
	14,000

In this example the PCP would be 6,000 £1 shares requiring redemption less profit and loss reserves of £4,000 equals £2,000 (or the shortfall on the profit and loss account reserves balance immediately before the purchase).

In the example above, the scenario indicated that the company would just be making an outright purchase of shares at par with no additional shares being issued. This is not always the case and it might be that the company issues new shares but still needs a PCP.

Example – Issuance of new shares and the need for a PCP

Company D Limited has the following balance sheet:

	£
Cash at bank	14,000
Ordinary share capital (£1 shares)	10,000
Share premium account	2,500
Profit and loss account	1,500
	14,000

Company D wishes to buy 4,000 shares, which were originally issued at par value to a shareholder that is retiring. The company has agreed to buy these shares back at a premium of 0.30p. The company has also agreed to issue a further 1,000 ordinary £1 shares at a premium of £2.00.

	£
Purchase cost (4,000 × £1.30)	5,200
Profit and loss account reserves	(1,500)
Proceeds from new share issue (1,000 × £3)	(3,000)
Permissible capital payment	700
Value of purchase at par value	4,000
Proceeds from new share issue	(3,000)
Permissible capital payment	(700)
Transfer to capital redemption reserve	300

In order to get the above transaction into the accounts, the company will make the following journal entries:

DR cash at bank	3,000
CR ordinary share capital	1,000
CR share premium account	2,000

Being issue of new shares at £2 premium

DR ordinary share capital	4,000
DR profit and loss account	1,200
CR cash at bank	5,200

Effect of buyback of 4,000 shares at a 30p premium

DR profit and loss account	300
CR capital redemption reserve	300

To maintain the company's capital

Company D's balance sheet will now look like this:

	£
Cash at bank and in hand	11,800
Ordinary share capital (£1 shares)	7,000
Share premium	4,500
Capital redemption reserve	300
Profit and loss account	Nil
	11,800

TREASURY SHARES

Treasury shares are shares in a company that have been issued and then subsequently reacquired by the business. Monies received for treasury shares are deducted from equity and hence no gain or loss in profit or loss on the purchase, sale, transfer or cancellation of the treasury shares is recognised.

Under companies legislation, shares can only be transferred into and classed as treasury shares when they have been purchased by a company from a shareholder out of distributable profit or by cash.

The Companies Act 2006 deals with the rules governing treasury shares in sections 724 to 732 of the Act. Buyback Regulations came into force on 30 April 2013 that essentially relaxed certain statutory requirements that would otherwise apply when a company undertakes a share buyback. A notable change in the Regulations is that private companies can now hold shares in treasury, regardless of whether they have been bought back in relation to an employee share scheme (prior to the Buyback Regulations, only qualifying shares could be held in treasury – i.e. those in a listed company or traded on the Alternative Investment Market or a regulated market).

DISTRIBUTABLE PROFIT

The term 'distribution' is not merely just dividends paid to shareholders, but is taken to be a distribution of all company assets to its members. Section 829 of the Companies Act 2006 defines a 'distribution' as 'every description of distribution of a company's assets to its members, whether in cash or otherwise, subject to the following exceptions:

(a) An issue of shares as fully or partly paid bonus shares;
(b) The reduction of share capital:
   i. By extinguishing or reducing the liability of any of the members on any of the company's shares in respect of share capital not paid up; or
   ii. By repaying paid up share capital;
(c) The redemption or purchase of any of the company's own shares out of capital (including the proceeds of any fresh issue of shares) or out of unrealised profits in accordance with Chapters 3, 4 or 5 of Part 18; and
(d) A distribution of assets to members of the company on its winding-up.[3]

---

[3]Companies Act 2006 S829.

Section 830(1) says that a company can only make a distribution out of profits available for that purpose. Essentially, a company's distributable profit is its accumulated, realised profits (so far as not previously distributed or capitalised) less its accumulated, realised losses (so far as not previously written off in a reduction or reorganisation of its share capital). As a consequence of this definition, realised losses cannot be offset against realised profits. The term 'realised profit' is generally accepted as meaning profits that are realised in the form of cash or other assets that are readily convertible into cash. In determining whether a profit is realised the directors of a company must look to the overall commercial effect on the company and not merely to the transactions and arrangements in isolation.

More information in relation to profits available for distribution can be found in the Institute of Chartered Accountants in England and Wales's (ICAEW) Technical Release *Tech 02/10* available from www.icaew.com.

DISTRIBUTIONS

In respect of distributions to the entity's owners (i.e. the shareholders), the entity should reduce equity for the value of these distributions. In addition, disclosure should be made as to the value of any non-cash assets that have been distributed to the entity's owners during the reporting period. The exception to this requirement is where the non-cash assets are ultimately controlled by the same parties both before, and after, the distribution has taken place.

27 EVENTS AFTER THE REPORTING PERIOD

INTRODUCTION

It is a generally accepted concept that financial statements for a specific period-/year-end are prepared and authorised for issue some time after the reporting date has elapsed. Certainly for private companies in the UK, Companies House allows a period of nine months from the company's year-end to file their financial statements. One of the main issues that arises due to this time period is what happens in relation to transactions or events that take place between the reporting period (the period- or year-end) and the date that the financial statements are authorised for issue, which may have a direct (or indirect) impact on the financial statements in question.

Section 32 *Events after the Reporting Period* deals with such transactions and events and there is also a degree of interaction between Section 32 and that of Section 21 *Provisions and Contingencies*. This particular chapter will deal with the issues contained in Section 32.

Section 32 is aptly named 'Events after the Reporting Period' and this particular Section takes its name from *IFRS for SMEs*, which is based on IAS 10 *Events after the Reporting Period*. Accountants and practitioners in the UK and Republic of Ireland will be more familiar with terminology such as 'post balance sheet events' and 'subsequent events', which amount to the same thing.

The provisions in Section 32 are no different than in the previous UK GAAP at FRS 21 *Events after the Balance Sheet Date*.

Section 32 covers all events (both favourable and unfavourable) that lead up to the date that the financial statements are authorised for issue. Favourable and unfavourable events are subdivided into two component parts between those events that require the financial statements to be amended and those that do not require the financial statements to be amended, but may require additional disclosure notes to be made within the notes to the financial statements to allow the user to gain a greater understanding of transactions and events that have taken place in the intervening period. This is accentuated by the date of signing an auditor's report because the date of an auditor's report is taken to be the date at which the auditor has been satisfied that the financial statements take into consideration all transactions and events that require either adjustment or disclosure up to and including the date of the auditor's report.

Such transactions and events are classified into 'adjusting' and 'non-adjusting' events and the classification as adjusting or non-adjusting will depend on whether the transaction or event presents information relating to conditions that existed at the reporting date or that have arisen after the reporting date.

ADJUSTING EVENTS

An adjusting event is an event that requires changes to the amounts that have been included in the financial statements. Such events are classified as adjusting events because their conditions existed at the balance sheet date and hence require reflection in the amounts presented in the financial statements.

Example – Bankruptcy of a customer

Byrne Enterprises Limited is preparing its financial statements for the year ended 31 January 2016. Included within the trade debtors figure is an amount of £125,000 due to Byrne Enterprises by its customer, Humphries Co. Limited. The financial statements of Byrne Enterprises are due to be authorised for issue on 31 March 2016; on 28 February 2016, Byrne Enterprises received notification from the insolvency practitioner that Humphries Co. Limited had gone into liquidation. The correspondence received from the insolvency practitioner indicated that after liquidation there would be no proceeds available to pay off unsecured creditors.

The bankruptcy of a customer so soon after the reporting date is evidence that the debt will not be recovered at the reporting date. The general principle in financial reporting is that assets should not be carried in the balance sheet (statement of financial position) at any more than their recoverable amount and therefore the bad debt should be provided against in the financial statements for the year ended 31 January 2016.

Other examples that assets may be impaired and thus require writing down include:

- The settlement of a court case after the reporting date, which confirms that the reporting entity had a liability at the reporting date.
- Receipt of information after the reporting date, which confirms an asset has suffered impairment.
- The sale of inventory after the reporting date, which may give evidence concerning their net realisable value.
- The cost of assets purchased after the reporting date or proceeds received from the sale of an asset sold prior to the reporting date.
- Determination of profit-sharing bonus payments after the reporting date.
- Discovery of fraud and/or errors in the financial statements.

The above would be adjusting events if their conditions existed at the reporting date.

Settlement of a court case

The settlement of a court case after the reporting date is an example of an adjusting event because this confirms that the reporting entity had an obligating event at that date. The settlement can either be by way of an 'out of court' settlement or by way of judgement.

In either case, the financial statements of the reporting entity should be adjusted to take account of the settlement and to recognise the liability that had, in substance, arisen at the reporting date.

The settlement of a court case after the reporting date also confirms whether the provisions in Section 21 *Provisions and Contingencies* have been adequately applied in either the current or previous accounting periods. If the reporting entity had not created a provision at the year-end, then clearly the settlement of a court case would necessitate a provision being recognised because the recognition criteria have been met (by virtue of the fact that the entity has an obligating event at the reporting date). Conversely, it may well be that the reporting entity is the claimant in a court case and hence the recognition of an asset would be appropriate in these situations because Section 21 says that it must be 'virtually certain' that the asset will be realised and hence these 'virtually certain' criteria would be met if judgement is awarded in favour of the reporting entity. Care, however, must be taken by entities that are claimants in court cases because the mere fact that a court case is ongoing at the year-end, and indeed subsequent to the year-end, would not be just cause for the recognition of an asset – the 'virtually certain' criteria would only be met by judgement being awarded to the claimant entity.

Confirmation of asset impairment

The intervening period between the reporting date and the date that the financial statements are authorised for issue can give rise to an indication that an asset is impaired. The classic illustration of this situation is the bankruptcy of a customer who owes money at the reporting date but who ceases trading and goes into liquidation in the period between the balance sheet date and the date that the financial statements are authorised for issue. Where this is the case, the bankruptcy of a customer will be an adjusting event and hence the debt will need writing down to recoverable amount (which will more than likely be nil).

Conversely, where an entity's asset(s) are destroyed after the reporting date but before the financial statements are authorised for issue, this would give rise to a non-adjusting event and if it is a material event, then disclosure should be made in the financial statements of the event, together with its financial effects.

Sale of inventory and net realisable value

During the period between the reporting date and the date the financial statements are authorised for issue, the net realisable value of inventory held at the reporting date may become known. This can occur where (for example) slow-moving or obsolete inventory is sold on to a third party. Estimates of net realisable value are based on the most reliable evidence available at the time the estimates are being made (often at the year- or period-end). In cases where a third party purchases inventory for amounts less than the original estimation, the inventory should be written down in the financial statements to actual net realisable value.

Cost and sales proceeds of assets

This particular aspect can be illustrated with an example.

Example – Sale of a property

A construction company has entered into negotiations with its customer to sell a property to its customer and then adapt that property to be bespoke to the customer's requirements. The construction company has a year-end of 31 October 2016 and the commercial conveyancing transaction commenced on 1 July 2016. Planning permission had to be obtained from the local authority before any work can begin on the construction of the building and this was granted by the local authority on 1 November 2016. Completion took place on 30 November 2016 and the financial controller is planning to recognise the sale proceeds in the financial statements to 31 October 2016 on the grounds that he believes this to be an adjusting event as planning permission was granted immediately after the year-end.

The financial controller is incorrect in recognising sales proceeds at the year-end date. This is because the receipt of the planning permission does not give rise to a condition that existed at the reporting date for which the granting of planning permission would give additional evidence. This is because no sale had taken place by the year-end and the sale was conditional on the basis of the customer being granted planning permission. The granting of the planning permission will determine whether, or not, there is an eventual sale; there is a new event that causes the sale.

Profit-sharing and bonus payments

The issue concerning profit-sharing and bonus payments needs to be carefully considered by entities because this can also have potential taxation implications on the company if the timing of the obligating event is not correct.

Many entities will offer profit-sharing and bonus payments to its employees based on year-end results. In the vast majority of cases, the actual year-end results may not be known until some time after the year-end because financial statements are often completed and authorised for issue some months after the year-end. Where an entity has an obligation at the year-end to make such payments (for example, by way of a board resolution and subsequent announcements to those who will receive the profit-share or bonus payment before the year-end) then this will give rise to an adjusting event and the financial statements should be adjusted to take account of the profit-share and bonus payments to be made.

The timing is critical because the entity must have a present legal or constructive obligation in order to make the payments and hence adjust the financial statements at the year-end. If the timing of this is incorrect and the financial statements are incorrectly adjusted then there could well be problems with any tax relief obtained from HM Revenue and Customs.

Example – Reduction of bonus payments and interaction with Section 21 *Provisions and Contingencies*

Company B Limited has always paid bonuses to its two directors based on 5% of pre-tax profit. The draft management accounts as at 31 March 2016 include a gross bonus, plus employer's national insurance amounting to £11,500 each following the resolution by the board to pay a bonus based on the draft figures as at 20 March 2016. This bonus is not paid until such time as the financial statements are approved because of various adjustments that are often incorporated into the finalised financial statements. The financial statements are approved four months after the year-end and because of a large stock write-off due to damaged products, the profits have reduced to an extent that the gross bonus plus the employers' national insurance should only be £4,500 each.

This is clearly an adjusting event and the bonuses will need to be reduced because the conditions to pay the bonus existed at the reporting date. In addition, the company had an 'obligating event' due to the resolution to pay the bonus to the directors and hence created an expectation in the mind-sets of the directors that they would receive a bonus. This is an example of how Section 32 interacts with Section 21 *Provisions and Contingencies.*

The above example relating to employment bonuses also ties in to the provisions in Section 28 *Employee Benefits*, which is dealt with in Chapter 10.

Discovery of fraud/error

Where the discovery of fraud or error occurs after the reporting date but the event itself took place prior to the year- or period-end, these are adjusting events. This issue should also be carefully considered because it is not uncommon for frauds to have taken place over more than one accounting period and this, therefore, could give rise to further prior-year adjustments having to be undertaken. In more serious cases, frauds can also bring into doubt the ability of the entity to continue as a going concern.

Example – External fraud

Company C Limited makes an investment in various marketable securities in an overseas entity. The auditors are completing the work on these investments and it transpires that these securities have suffered a diminution in value (an impairment) due to fraud. The year-end is 31 December 2015 and the fraud was discovered on 4 April 2016. The question arises as to whether this gives rise to an adjusting event.

It has to be established whether, or not, the marketable securities actually existed at the reporting date. If the investment did exist then any post year-end loss would not be adjusted for on the grounds that Company C could have sold their investment in the marketable securities at the reporting date.

Conversely, if the marketable securities never existed then Company C would not have been able to sell the investment at the balance sheet date, which would give rise to the loss becoming an adjusting event because the conditions existed at the reporting date (the conditions being the non-existence of the investment).

NON-ADJUSTING EVENTS

By definition, 'non-adjusting' events do not get adjusted within the financial statements. This is due to the fact that their conditions did not exist at the reporting date. Instead, disclosure of material non-adjusting events should be made within the financial statements to enable users to understand the effect that transactions and/or events that have taken place between the date of the financial statements and the date they are authorised for issue have on the financial effect of the company. No guidance is provided in Section 32 relating to what is meant by the term 'financial effect' – for example, the effect non-adjusting events have on an entity's profit or loss or financial position or cash flows. However, the overarching principle in Section 32 is for users to appreciate the impact that non-adjusting events have on the financial statements taken as a whole.

Example – Discontinued division

A supermarket operates four different classes of business division: groceries, mobile telephone providers, internet service providers and domestic appliances. Each division is considered to be material to the financial statements of the company. The financial year-end is 31 July 2016 and the financial statements have not yet been approved. On 30 September 2016, the company's directors decided that because of extremely difficult trading conditions, and a heavy loss, it would discontinue the domestic appliances division. This announcement was made on 1 October 2016.

This is a non-adjusting event because the decision to discontinue the division took place after the reporting date. However, because the division is considered to be material to the financial statements, the entity would need to make disclosure within the financial statements concerning the closure of this division.

Example – Bonus issue of shares

Lucas Lighting Limited has a year-end of 31 July 2016. On 4 August 2016 it offers a bonus issue to its shareholders of one share for every five shares held. The decision to issue this bonus issue was taken because the company has recently been experiencing a few cash flow difficulties and the issue of bonus shares would be undertaken rather than paying a dividend to its existing shareholders and thus enabling the company to preserve cash. The shareholders have agreed on the basis that the company has just recently secured a lucrative six-year contract to supply services, which is likely to be very profitable, and hence shareholder confidence in the company has not diminished. The question arises as to whether the bonus issue should be disclosed as a non-adjusting event in Lucas Lighting's 31 July 2016 financial statements.

Section 32 outlines the disclosure requirements concerning non-adjusting events at paragraph 32.11. Paragraph 32.11 at point (f) does require the issue or repurchase of an entity's debt or equity instruments to be disclosed and hence the bonus issue of shares would fall to be disclosed within the financial statements as at 31 July 2016 as a non-adjusting event.

Some examples of additional non-adjusting events are:

- A significant business combination or the disposal of a major subsidiary after the period-/year-end.
- Management's announcement of a plan to discontinue an operation of the business or the announcement of a major restructuring of an entity.
- Major purchases of assets.
- The destruction of a major production facility by fire after the reporting date.
- Major ordinary and potential ordinary share transactions after the reporting date.
- Unusually large changes in asset prices or foreign exchange rates after the reporting date.

- A change in tax rates or tax laws that are enacted, or announced, after the reporting date and that have a significant effect on both current and deferred tax assets and liabilities.
- Entering into significant commitments or contingent liabilities.
- The commencement of litigation that arises out of events that occur after the reporting date.

Significant business combination/disposal of a major subsidiary

When an entity undertakes a business combination (as defined in Section 19 *Business Combinations and Goodwill*) after the reporting date but before the financial statements are authorised for issue this will be a non-adjusting event that would need disclosure within the financial statements. If, for whatever reason, this disclosure is deemed by management to be impracticable, then that fact should be disclosed together with the reasons why management consider disclosure to be impracticable. Ordinarily, the disclosures will involve describing:

- The names and descriptions of the combining entities,
- The date of acquisition,
- The percentage of net assets acquired,
- Any areas of the acquiree's operations that the acquirer has disposed of as a result of the combination,
- The cost of the business combination,
- Details of the identifiable assets, liabilities and contingent liabilities,
- Positive goodwill and negative goodwill arising as a result of a bargain purchase and
- Post-acquisition activities.

Management plans to discontinue an operation

This issue interacts with major restructuring of an organisation and the issue here is twofold. First, the restructuring may give rise to evidence of impairment at the reporting date, which would be an adjusting event. However, entities should not make any provisions for future restructuring costs because Section 21 *Provisions and Contingencies* at paragraph 21.11D says that an entity should only recognise a provision for restructuring costs when the entity has a legal or constructive obligation.

The key to determining whether an entity has an obligation at the reporting date, and hence should adjust the financial statements, would be to determine if the entity has announced the restructuring plans before the year-end and hence if the restructuring plan did exist at the year-end. In cases where such plans did not exist at the year-end but were announced subsequent to the year-end and before the financial statements are authorised for issue, this would be a non-adjusting event.

Major asset purchases

Major assets that are purchased after the year-end and before the reporting date would fall to be classed as a non-adjusting event. Capital commitments that exist at the reporting date are also usually disclosed within the notes to the financial statements and recognised as and when the transaction takes place.

There is no distinct section within FRS 102 that deals specifically with assets that are 'held for sale', unlike in IFRS 5 *Non-Current Assets Held for Sale and Discontinued Operations*, which outlines the criteria that should be met before an asset can be held for sale. However, paragraph 17.27 says that the entity derecognises items of property, plant and equipment when the entity disposes of the asset or when the entity does not expect any further economic benefits to be derived from the asset (including its disposal), and the same criteria apply to intangible assets accounted for under Section 18 *Intangible Assets other than Goodwill*.

Destruction of assets

The classic example in financial reporting is the destruction of a manufacturing plant by fire after the reporting date. This would fall to be classed as a non-adjusting event on the basis that the plant was still in existence at the reporting date and the destruction by fire took place during the intervening period. In this context, disclosure of the event and its financial effects should be made.

Major potential ordinary share transactions after the reporting date

An example of this situation would arise where the entity has convertible loans that are about to expire. These would be classified as a non-adjusting event and disclosure should be made to bring to users' attention the effect that the loan note holders' conversion of capital to ordinary shares would have on the entity (and the dilutive effect for existing shareholders).

Other situations that would give rise to a non-adjusting event would be the issuance of ordinary shares after the reporting date, bonus issues and rights issues of shares.

Unusually large changes in asset prices or foreign exchange transactions

Changes that arise in asset prices or foreign exchange rates that take place after the reporting date are not normally indicative of conditions that were in existence at the reporting date. Where an inordinate change in asset prices or foreign exchange rates takes place during the intervening period and are considered to be material (either in nature or monetary amount) that knowledge of them could influence the decisions of users taken on the basis of the financial statements as a whole, they should be quantified and disclosed as a non-adjusting event.

Such unusually large changes in asset prices or foreign exchange transactions are not considered to be adjusting events because recoverable amounts are often driven by the market and do not normally reflect the conditions that existed at the reporting date.

Changes in tax rates

The Chancellor will normally announce tax rates in the Budget and therefore proposed changes in tax legislation and tax rates will not normally be recognised in the financial statements unless they have been enacted, or substantively enacted, by the reporting date. However, in the event that changes in tax laws and rates may have a significant impact on either current or deferred tax and that are announced or enacted after the reporting date, but before the financial statements are authorised for issue, then disclosure should be made to enable users to understand the financial effect that such changes in tax rates will have on the entity's financial statements.

Entering into significant commitments or contingent liabilities

Commitments that are entered into after the reporting date but before the financial statements are authorised for issue are non-adjusting events because the commitment did not exist at the reporting date. Therefore where the entity enters into commitments with a third party, for which the effect is likely to be material, disclosures adequate for the purposes of users' understanding of the financial effect of the commitments should be made in the year-end accounts. The commitments will not be adjusted as there was no liability in existence at the reporting date.

Contingent liabilities are not recognised in the financial statements regardless of whether they occur after or before the year-/period-end on the basis that they fail to meet the recognition criteria in Section 21 *Provisions and Contingencies*. However, where the entity enters into material contingent liabilities between the date of the balance sheet and the date the financial statements are authorised for issue, disclosure should be made together with their estimated financial effect.

Litigation after the reporting date

Where a reporting entity is involved in litigation that commences after the year-/period-end, but before the financial statements are authorised for issue, disclosure should be made. There is no liability recognised because the litigation did not exist at the reporting date and therefore any amounts likely to be paid or received to settle the claim are not recognised in the year-/period-end financial statements.

The provisions in Section 21 concerning disclosures that are likely to seriously prejudice the outcome of a case may also need to be considered when dealing with litigation after the reporting date in the context of post balance sheet events.

PAYMENT OF DIVIDENDS

Dividends that are proposed after the reporting date cannot be recognised retrospectively in the financial statements at the reporting date. This requirement also applies where the financial statements have not yet been authorised for issue.

The reason for such a prohibition is down to the fact that at the reporting date no obligation existed. However, dividends proposed will be disclosed within the financial statements.

Dividends are recognised when they are declared and a dividend is declared when they are authorised by the directors and are therefore no longer at the discretion of the entity.

Example – Interim dividend

An entity has a year-end of 31 October 2016 and on 30 September 2016 declared an interim dividend to shareholders. Due to a restriction on the company's cash flow on 30 September 2016, the shareholders unanimously agreed to receive only half of the dividend on 30 September 2016 with the remaining half being paid at a time when the company's cash flow would permit. The directors do not have the ability to cancel dividends to shareholders.

In this scenario, the remaining half of the dividend due to the shareholders would be recognised as a liability because the directors do not have the ability to cancel them and hence the company has a legal obligation to the shareholders to pay the remaining half of the dividend when the cash flow permits.

Final dividends are recognised as a liability in the period in which they are declared. A dividend is declared when it is appropriately authorised and no longer at the discretion of the reporting entity and will remain a liability until such time as the dividend is actually paid. This principle also applies to dividends that are receivable – in other words, the receiving party will recognise a dividend debtor at the same time that the paying company recognises a dividend creditor, provided that the recognition criteria have been met.

Example – Approval of a dividend after the year-end date

A company has a year-end of 31 December 2015 and is in the process of preparing its financial statements for the year then ended. On 4 April 2016, the draft figures have been completed to the final draft stage and the annual general meeting is about to take place. In that meeting, the directors have decided to declare a dividend for the year ended 31 December 2015, amounting to £4 per share, and the finance director is proposing to include this dividend in the financial statements for the year then ended.

The directors have approved the paying of a dividend after the year-end. The issue the company has is that there was no constructive obligation at the year-end to pay the dividend (a constructive obligation would arise where the board resolved to pay the dividend before the year-end and this dividend is appropriately authorised). Therefore, in this example, as no constructive obligation arises, the company is not permitted to retrospectively recognise the dividend in the 31 December 2015 year-end financial statements. The dividend must be recognised in the 2015/16 financial statements.

Example – Approval of a dividend prior to the year-end date

A company has a year-end of 31 December 2015 and produces monthly management accounts, which are presented to the board and which are discussed in monthly meetings of the directors. The November 2015 management accounts show a healthy profit and on 10 December 2015, the directors decide that a dividend should be proposed in the year-end financial statements amounting to £5 per share because there would be more than sufficient profit available to meet the payment of this dividend to the shareholders.

In this scenario, the company has foreseen that profitability is more than sufficient in order to pay a dividend and they have passed the proposal in the board meeting on 10 December 2015 (which is well before the year-end of 31 December 2015). A constructive obligation arises because the passing of this resolution in the general meeting gives rise to a liability to the shareholders. As a result, the company is able to include the dividend in the financial statements as at 31 December 2015.

The key issue to establish in order to include dividends in the financial statements at, or after, the year-end will depend on whether a constructive obligation has been met. In other words, dividends declared after the reporting date (in the eyes of Section 32) are, in fact, non-adjusting events and are therefore disclosed, not adjusted for, in the financial statements.

GOING CONCERN

Going concern is a vital concept in the preparation of financial statements and Section 3 *Financial Statement Presentation* deals with such issues at paragraphs 3.8 and 3.9. It is usually the default presumption that a reporting entity will prepare financial statements on the going concern basis; that is, that the directors consider the business to be in operation for the foreseeable future. In order for the directors to be able to make a conclusion as to whether, or not, the business will be in operation for the foreseeable future, FRS 102 requires management to consider all available information available relating to the future for a period of at least 12 months from the date at which the financial statements are authorised for issue.

A company will not be able to prepare financial statements on a going concern basis if management are planning to put the company into liquidation or cease trading or they consider that they have no realistic alternative but to cease trading and instigate liquidation proceedings. In such cases, management will usually prepare the financial statements on a 'break-up' basis, where assets are restated at the amount that could be realistically obtained in a sale and will reclassify all long-term liabilities to current liabilities.

Management must also take into consideration any material uncertainties that may give rise to the going concern basis being inappropriate. In this context, 'material uncertainties' are significant events that may occur in the future and may result in the company being forced into liquidation or having to cease trading. This could occur, for example, where the organisation is dependent on a large contract being renewed and the renewal date is some months after the financial statements are approved. When this is the case, the notes to the financial statements must include adequate disclosures relating to these material uncertainties.

The going concern presumption is an assertion made by management that the company is to continue in business for the foreseeable future. In assessing the company's ability to continue as a going concern, management must take into consideration:

- The economic conditions the organisation is operating in,
- The state of the company's cash flow,
- Whether borrowing facilities are going to be renewed and
- Whether external factors such as interest rates or customers' abilities to pay are likely to affect the company as a going concern.

If the directors consider that the company is NOT a going concern, then they must disclose:

- The fact that the company's financial statements have not been prepared on the going concern basis,
- Details of the basis that the directors have adopted in preparing the financial statements (for example, the 'break-up' basis) and
- The reason why the company is not considered to be a going concern.

There are various conditions that may indicate that a company is not a going concern and the following gives some examples of these conditions (note, however, that this list is NOT exhaustive and there may be additional reasons why the going concern ability of a business may be called into question):

- A net liability or net current liability position on the balance sheet,
- Adverse key financial ratios,
- Arrears or discontinued dividends,
- A deteriorating relationship with suppliers,
- An inability to comply with the terms of loan/finance agreements,
- A loss of major market share, franchise, licence or principal supplier,
- Major debt repayments falling due where refinancing is necessary to the organisation's continued existence,
- Major restructuring of debt,
- Significant operating losses or significant deterioration in the value of assets used to generate cash flows and
- Financiers/banks refusing to renew borrowing facilities or 'calling in' debts (such as overdrafts) on demand.

Example – Going concern presumption not appropriate

Cahill Caravans has been in business for over 40 years; however, over the last few years demand for caravans has fallen because of the economic climate. The financial statements for the year ended 30 April 2016 are about to be prepared. On 4 April 2016, Cahill Caravans received notification from its major customer that it had ceased trading because of severe cash flow difficulties and the receivers had been called in. The receiver has confirmed that even after selling off assets, the company will not be in a position to pay off any of its debts to unsecured creditors. Cahill Caravans is one of those unsecured creditors. The customer owes £175,000 and the directors have therefore concluded that they have no realistic alternative but to close down.

In this example, the financial statements must not be prepared on the going concern basis on the grounds that the company will not be in business for the foreseeable future. An alternative basis must be used, which may be the 'break-up' basis (or realisable value basis). All fixed assets would be reclassified as current as they will be sold off to generate some cash. All creditors falling due after more than one year will be reclassified as current liabilities and the financial statements will also contain disclosure that the going concern basis of preparing the financial statements is not appropriate as well as disclosing the basis on which the financial statements have been prepared.

AUTHORISING THE FINANCIAL STATEMENTS FOR ISSUE

In the UK, the financial statements of a company are not formally approved by the shareholders but they are instead 'laid' before the members. FRS 102 requires an organisation to disclose the date on which the financial statements were authorised for issue together with details as to who gave that authorisation. Where the owners of a company have the powers to amend the financial statements after they have been issued, that fact must also be disclosed.

In practice, the financial statements will normally be approved by the board of directors and once they are approved by the board, they will be authorised for issue. Therefore, it follows that it will be the board of directors who authorised the financial statements for issue and, ordinarily, the entity's owners or any other third party do not have the power to amend the financial statements once they have been issued, so this part of paragraph 32.9 will be unlikely to apply.

The reason why these disclosures need to be made is so that users of the financial statements can understand that the financial statements will not reflect events after the date of authorisation.

Example – Executive and non-executive directors

A company has a unitary board that comprises both executive and non-executive directors. The audit committee is also involved in the oversight of the financial statements.

Where a company's board comprises both executive and non-executive directors, the non-executive directors will be heavily involved in reviewing and monitoring financial information, which will more than likely be achieved through an audit committee. In addition, both executive and non-executive directors have equal responsibility for the financial statements. Therefore, financial statements will not be authorised for issue unless they have been seen by the non-executive directors.

DISCLOSURE REQUIREMENTS

The disclosure requirements where events after the reporting period are concerned are dealt with in paragraphs 32.9 to 32.11. Paragraph 32.11 outlines various examples of non-adjusting events, which would normally give rise to disclosures within the financial statements.

In relation to each non-adjusting event, a reporting entity should disclose:

(a) An outline of the non-adjusting event and

(b) An approximation of the event's financial effect. Where the entity is unable to arrive at an approximate estimate of the event's financial effect, disclosure should be made that such an estimate cannot be made.

28 FOREIGN CURRENCY TRANSLATION

INTRODUCTION

In today's modern business environment, entities undertake business around the world. The advantage of cheaper prices, better quality products and wider access to customers means that companies are not just confined to doing business in their domestic base. This is where foreign currency issues will become relevant to the entity. A company might purchase goods and/or services from a supplier that is based overseas; conversely, the company might sell goods and/or services to one of its customers that is located in an overseas jurisdiction. In more complex situations, a company might undertake overseas transactions through subsidiaries and associates as well as branches of their operations.

Section 30 *Foreign Currency Translation* deals with the issues concerning foreign currency. The section acknowledges that reporting entities may have transactions denoted in foreign currency or alternatively the entity itself may have foreign operations (i.e. a subsidiary or subsidiaries based overseas). The reporting entity may also present its financial statements in a foreign currency (for example, in US dollars).

When a company undertakes transactions that are denoted in a foreign currency, the transactions must be translated into the currency of the company undertaking the purchase. For example, if an entity based in the UK purchases goods from its supplier in Spain, the invoice will be denoted in euros and will need to be translated into sterling at the date of the transaction.

In the broadest terms, accounting for foreign currency involves the translation of information from one currency into another currency and then dealing with any exchange differences on translation. The characteristics of assets and liabilities in the translation process do not change, they are merely restated from one currency into another.

There are three types of exchange rate that are used depending on the entity's circumstances:

- **Historical rate of exchange**: this is the exchange rate that prevails as at the date of the transaction or the date of revaluation.
- **Average rate of exchange**: this is only generally applied to items that make up profit or loss.
- **The closing rate of exchange** (often referred to as the 'spot rate'): this is the exchange rate prevailing at the balance sheet date.

FUNCTIONAL CURRENCY

A pivotal theme in Section 30 is the need for the entity to identify its *functional currency*. Once the entity has identified its functional currency then any transactions that are not in this functional currency mean that the company has entered into a foreign currency transaction and hence the requirements in Section 30 become applicable.

The standard itself says that an entity's functional currency is the currency of the primary economic environment in which the entity operates. Put simply, this means the currency in which the entity normally undertakes its business and is a matter that is judged at entity level. For example, a company that is based in the UK would normally have a functional currency, which is that of the Great British Pound (GBP) because the UK would be the country in which the entity normally generates and spends cash; however, in some situations it may be a different currency. For many companies reporting in the UK and Republic of Ireland the functional currency will be a matter of fact – it is either GBP or euros. However, in some rarer situations it may not be as clear and hence judgement will need to be exercised so as to establish the entity's functional currency.

Paragraph 30.3 of FRS 102 acknowledges that there are certain factors that a company must consider when it comes to determining its functional currency, such as:

- The currency that would have an influence over sales prices for goods and services,
- The country whose competitive forces and regulations essentially determine the sales prices of those goods and services and
- The currency that would influence the price of labour, material and other such costs in the provision of goods and services.

These three bullet points are the *primary* indicators of an entity's functional currency. In addition, the standard also recognises some *secondary* indicators. The secondary indicators are the currency in which a company generates funds from financing activities and the currency in which receipts from operating activities are usually retained.

As Section 30 works on a 'primary' and 'secondary' approach to determine an entity's functional currency, the primary economic environment in which the entity operates is given more weight. Secondary indicators include currencies from financing and operating activities and whilst more weight is placed on primary indicators, all the indicators contained in paragraphs 30.3 and 30.4 need to be considered.

The reason that the section approaches the functional currency approach in a hierarchical manner is to avoid any practical difficulties in determining the functional currency. Therefore, if all the primary indicators identify a particular currency as the functional currency, there is no need to consider the secondary indicators (i.e. the currency in which funds from financing and operating activities are generated and retained). It follows, therefore, that the secondary indicators are intended to provide the entity with additional guidance when the primary indicators are not absolute in their conclusion.

Functional currency of foreign operations

When a subsidiary, branch, associate or joint venture of the reporting entity is located overseas and hence its activities are conducted in a currency that is not that of the UK or Republic of Ireland, paragraph 30.5 of FRS 102 outlines four additional factors that must be considered in order to determine the functional currency of the foreign operation in order to establish if it is the same as that of the reporting entity. These additional four factors are outlined as follows:

Level of autonomy

Consideration should be given as to whether the activities of the foreign operation are carried out with a significant degree of autonomy or if it is merely an extension of the reporting entity. An example of the former is where the entity accumulates cash, incurs its own expenses and arranges its own borrowings. An example of the latter is where it merely obtains goods or services from the reporting entity, sells those goods/ services on and then remits any proceeds back to the reporting entity.

If there is no significant level of autonomy then the activities of the foreign operation are an extension of the reporting entity and therefore the foreign operation will have the same currency as the reporting entity.

Frequency of the transactions with the reporting entity

When there are few transactions with the reporting entity this would indicate that the functional currency is different from that of the reporting entity. Conversely, where there are significant intercompany transactions with the reporting entity, this would indicate that the functional currency is the same as the reporting entity.

Cash flows

When the cash flows occur in the local currency of the foreign operation and do not affect the reporting entity's cash flows this would be an indicator that the functional currency is different from that of the reporting entity. However, where the cash flows of the foreign operation directly affect the cash flows of the reporting entity, and such cash flows are readily available for remittance to the reporting entity, this would be an indicator that the functional currency is the same as that of the reporting entity.

Financing

If the borrowing of the foreign operation is in the local currency and is serviced by operating activities of the foreign operation then this would indicate that the local currency is different from that of the reporting entity. Where there are significant funding levels, or reliance on funding, from the reporting entity to service existing debt obligations then this would indicate the functional currency is the same as that of the reporting entity.

The above factors are those that should be considered by management in assessing the functional currency of the foreign operation, but they are not conclusive nor exhaustive in all respects. This is because even after considering all of the above, it might still be unclear as to the functional currency of the foreign operation. In today's modern business environment the foreign operation could have a diverse range of activities with cash flows arising in many currencies and hence the judgement of management would be needed to determine the functional currency that most faithfully represents the economic effects of the underlying transactions, events and conditions. Where management's judgement is required, they should ensure that they consider the primary indicators laid down in Section 30 *before* considering the secondary indicators.

Change in functional currency

If an entity changes its functional currency – for example, if there is a change in the currency that mainly influences the sales prices of goods and services – then the change in functional currency is applied prospectively from the date of the change. A change in functional currency can only occur if there is a change to the underlying transactions, events and conditions. Because of the prospective nature of the change, the rate of exchange at the date of change is used and the resulting translated amounts for non-monetary assets will be treated as their historical cost.

PRESENTATION CURRENCY

An entity's 'presentation currency' is the currency in which it presents its financial statements. FRS 102 acknowledges that an entity may present its financial statements in any currency (or currencies). However, where the financial statements are presented in a currency that is not its functional currency, the entity must translate its income, expenses and financial position into the presentation currency.

Example – Group financial statements

The Heyes Group of companies contains several subsidiaries, some of which are located in overseas jurisdictions. The majority of the subsidiaries report their financial information in euros whilst others report in their domestic currencies.

In order to prepare the consolidated financial statements, each entity's income, expense and financial position must be translated into a common currency (i.e. the presentation currency of the parent) in order that the consolidated financial statements may be presented.

There is a specific method in FRS 102 to translate financial statements from a functional currency into a presentational currency, which is as follows:

(a) The assets and liabilities for each balance sheet (statement of financial position) presented, which also includes comparatives, is translated at the closing rate (spot rate) at the reporting date.

(b) Items of income and expenses for the profit and loss account (statement of comprehensive income), which also includes comparatives, are translated at the exchange rates prevailing at the date of the transactions.

(c) Any resulting exchange differences on translation are recognised in other comprehensive income.

Example – Purchase of goods from an overseas supplier

Entity A supplies kayaks and canoe equipment for sale to the general public and outdoor sports companies. Entity A has recently sourced a new supplier in Farland whose currency is the dinar (D). Entity A has a year-end of 31 December 2015. On 30 September 2015, Entity A placed an order with its new supplier for ten canoes. The goods were delivered on 15 October 2015 and the invoice was for D5,000, dated 23 October 2015. The exchange rate on 23 October 2015 for D1 into £1 was 1.187.

The invoice was entered into Entity A's purchase ledger at an amount of £4,212.30 (D5,000/1.187).

Entity A settled the invoice on 4 January 2016 when the exchange rate had moved from 1.187 to 1.180, which results in the liability to the supplier increasing to £4,237.29 (D5,000/1.180). A loss of £24.99 arises due to the translation of the amount at the rate of exchange, which is recognised in profit or loss for the accounting period.

In respect of (b) above relating to the translation of the profit and loss account, FRS 102 acknowledges that in reality it is going to be impractical to translate every transaction that makes up an entity's profit and loss account into its presentation currency using exchange rates at the date of each transaction. For reasons of practicality, the FRS allows an entity to use approximate exchange rates (for example, an average rate of exchange). However, care needs to be taken when using average exchange rates because if rates fluctuate significantly then it will be inappropriate for the entity to use an average rate.

The determination of an average rate of exchange by management will all depend on a number of factors, including the frequency and value of the transactions undertaken; the period over which the exchange rate applies and any seasonal variations that the entity may be subjected to and any weighting that the management may deem to be appropriate. Materiality should also be taken into consideration because exchange differences may become material throughout the accounting period. Management have a variety of means to arrive at an average exchange rate, some of which may be derived from simple formulas, such as monthly or quarterly averages, through to more sophisticated methods. It may be relatively easy to come up with an average exchange rate where the fluctuations in rates have been stable throughout the period; however, in periods where changes in exchange rates are volatile, then it would be more appropriate to base an average exchange rate on a shorter period of time (i.e. a week).

In cases where an entity's functional currency is subjected to hyperinflation (inflation that is out of control), then its financial statements are adjusted using the procedures outlined in Section 31 *Hyperinflation* prior to applying the requirements of paragraphs 30.17 to 30.21 of FRS 102.

MONETARY AND NON-MONETARY ITEMS

The procedure for translating assets and liabilities into the entity's functional currency will depend on whether the asset or liability in question is a monetary asset or liability or a non-monetary asset or liability.

Monetary items are those items that are to be received or paid in a fixed or determinable number of units of currency. Examples of such monetary items are:

- Cash and bank balances
- Trade debtors and trade creditors (trade receivables and trade payables)
- Loans and hire purchase contracts
- Provisions for liabilities that are to be settled in cash
- Forward exchange contracts
- Foreign currency swaps and options and other derivative financial instruments
- Pensions and other employee benefits expected to be paid in cash

When translating monetary items, FRS 102 requires the closing rate (spot rate) to be used.

Non-monetary items can include:

- Intangible assets and goodwill
- Property, plant and equipment
- Inventories
- Prepaid goods and services
- Equity investments
- Provisions that are to be settled by the entity by transferring a non-monetary asset

In terms of translating non-monetary items, this will all depend on whether the non-monetary item is measured at historical cost or at fair value. Where a non-monetary item has been measured at historical cost, then it is translated using the exchange rate at the date of the transaction. For a non-monetary item that is measured at fair value, it is translated using the exchange rate at the date when the fair value was determined.

Example – Non-monetary asset with impairment

The functional currency of Bury Enterprises Limited is sterling. At the start of the year to 31 December 2015 it purchased an asset amounting to CU228,000 from its overseas supplier amounting to £120,000. When the transaction was entered into the exchange rate was £1 = CU1.90. At the reporting date, the asset's recoverable amount in foreign currency is CU175,000 when £1 = CU1.4. Although there is an impairment loss in foreign currency amount there is no impairment loss recognised because the recoverable amount at the reporting date of £125,000 is higher than the carrying value.

In respect of non-monetary assets that are measured at fair value in a foreign currency, these are translated using the exchange rates that apply when the fair value was determined.

Example – Investment property

Whatmough Enterprises Limited has a portfolio of investment properties in its balance sheet. Two of these investment properties are located in Spain where the currency is the euro. Fair value gains and losses in respect of its investment properties are recognised in profit or loss so as to comply with Section 16 *Investment Property*.

On the balance sheet date, 31 December 2015 (the reporting date and the date the fair value was determined), the fair values of all investment properties had increased due to general rises in property values. At the balance sheet date £1 = 0.76 euros and the two investment properties had risen by €4,000 and €5,000 respectively.

The euro amounts are translated into sterling using the rate of exchange at the date the fair values were determined and hence the increase in fair values of £5,263 and £6,579 will also include exchange differences arising on the retranslation of the opening euro carrying value. This exchange difference is recognised as part of the change in fair value in profit or loss for the period.

Generally, exchange differences arising on translation are recognised in profit or loss with the exception of net investments in a foreign operation (see the next section). However, if another section of FRS 102 requires a gain or loss on a non-monetary item to be recognised in other comprehensive income, any exchange component of that gain or loss is also recognised in other comprehensive income. Conversely, when a gain or loss on a non-monetary asset is recognised within profit or loss, the exchange component of that gain or loss is also recognised in profit or loss.

Example – Revaluation of property

Finch Limited has a functional currency of sterling. It holds a property based in Farland that it acquired at a cost of CU900,000 when the exchange rate was £1 = CU1.6. The property's fair value increased to CU1,350,000 at the year ended 31 December 2015 when the exchange rate was £1 = CU1.8.

The property is not an investment property and thus is accounted for under Section 17 *Property, Plant and Equipment* and hence the fair value gain is taken to the revaluation reserve and reported in other comprehensive income. Ignoring depreciation, the amount that would be reported in equity is:

	£
Value at balance sheet date = CU1,350,000 @ 1.8 =	750,000
Value at acquisition date = CU900,000 @ 1.6 =	(562,500)
Revaluation surplus to other comprehensive income	187,500

The revaluation surplus is reconciled as follows:

Change in fair value = CU450,000 @ 1.8	250,000
Exchange component of change = CU900,000 @ 1.8 – CU900,000 @ 1.6	(62,500)
	187,500

The above example illustrates the treatment of a gain or loss on a non-monetary item that is recognised in other comprehensive income. In the example above, had the property been (for example) an investment property, then the revaluation gain would have been recognised in profit or loss and hence the exchange component of that gain or loss would have also been recognised in profit or loss.

NET INVESTMENT IN A FOREIGN OPERATION

The term 'net investment in a foreign operation' means the amount of the reporting entity's interest in the net assets of the foreign operation.

The reporting entity may have a monetary item that is receivable, or payable, from/to a foreign operation. Such items may be regarded as an extension of, or reduction in, the reporting entity's net investment in that foreign operation. When this is the case, it may not be appropriate to include the resulting exchange differences on translation of such monetary items included in the consolidated income statement. This is because any exchange differences that arise on equivalent financing with equity capital would be taken to other comprehensive income in the consolidated financial statements.

Any exchange differences that arise on monetary items that form part of a reporting entity's net investment in a foreign operation are recognised in profit and loss in the separate financial statements of the reporting entity or in the individual financial statements of the foreign operation, as appropriate. In the consolidated financial statements that contain the net investment in a foreign operation, such exchange differences are recognised in other comprehensive income and accumulated in equity. On disposal of the net investment in a foreign operation, the accumulated foreign exchange translations are not included in profit or loss on disposal.

When the reporting entity has a monetary item that is receivable from or payable to a foreign operation and this monetary item is not planned for settlement or settlement is not likely to occur in the foreseeable future, this is treated as a part of the entity's net investment in that foreign operation.

Example – Loan to a foreign operation

Entity A has a net investment in a foreign operation (Entity B). Four years ago Entity A made a loan to Entity B that is repayable on demand. There is demonstrably no intent by Entity A to expect repayment of the loan and hence the loan is rolled over each year despite Entity B having funds available to repay the debt.

In substance this loan would be considered to be a capital contribution and hence would be treated as forming part of the net investment in Entity B. The fact that the loan is repayable on demand might, in some respects, be viewed to be short term. However, in substance, there is demonstrably no intent by Entity A to require repayment and hence the loan would be accounted for in accordance with paragraph 30.13 of FRS 102.

In the example above, if Entity A had provided Entity B with a long-term loan with, say, a maturity date of 20 years from the date the loan is originally made, this would not necessarily be treated as part of the net investment in the foreign operation simply by virtue of the length of the maturity date from the date the loan was made. The exception to this would be where management of Entity A had expressed their intention to renew the loan at the maturity date. In the absence of such a resolution by management, the maturity date would imply that settlement is planned in the future and therefore would not form part of the net investment in the foreign operation. Management should carefully document their intentions to ensure the treatment applied is correct and appropriate in the circumstances to avoid any contentious issues with auditors.

It follows, therefore, that a long-term loan to a foreign operation would only form part of the net investment in the foreign operation (for the purposes of FRS 102) if the loan is neither planned, nor likely, to be settled in the foreseeable future and therefore any exchange differences on such loans are taken to other comprehensive income on consolidation.

Non-controlling interest

On consolidation of a subsidiary that is not wholly owned, the exchange differences that relate to the foreign operation that arise on translation are to be apportioned between those that belong to the parent and those that belong to the non-controlling interest (minority interest). Those exchange differences attributable to the non-controlling interest are allocated to, and recognised as part of, non-controlling interest in the consolidated balance sheet (consolidated statement of the financial position).

Translating a foreign operation into the presentation currency

Normal consolidation procedures should apply when incorporating assets, liabilities, income and expenses of a foreign operation with those of the reporting entity. In other words, all intra-group trading is eliminated and intra-group balances are removed on consolidation. The translation procedures set out in paragraphs 30.17 to 30.21 (i.e. those procedures to translate from foreign currency to the presentation currency) are applied.

An intra-group monetary asset or liability, regardless of whether the monetary asset or liability is long or short term, cannot be eliminated against the corresponding intra-group asset or liability without showing the results of the currency fluctuations in the consolidated financial statements, because the monetary item is essentially a commitment to convert one currency into another currency and will therefore give rise to a gain or loss through the currency fluctuation. Therefore, in the consolidated financial statements, the reporting entity will continue to recognise such exchange differences in profit or loss. The exception to this would be where any items form part of the net investment in the foreign operation and hence would be reported through other comprehensive income and accumulated in equity.

Where goodwill has arisen on the acquisition of a foreign operation, together with any changes in the fair value of assets and liabilities on the acquisition of the foreign operation, such assets and liabilities are treated as assets and liabilities of the foreign operation. As a consequence, such assets and liabilities are expressed in the functional currency of the foreign operation and are to be translated by the reporting entity into the presentation currency of the reporting entity using the closing rate at the reporting date.

DISCLOSURE REQUIREMENTS

In respect of its foreign currency translation, a reporting entity must disclose:

- The total value of exchange differences that it has recognised in profit or loss during the accounting period, with the exception of those exchange differences that have arisen on financial instruments measured at fair value through profit or loss in accordance with Section 11 *Basic Financial Instruments* and Section 12 *Other Financial Instruments Issues*.

- The total value of exchange differences that have arisen during the period and classified in equity at the end of the accounting period.
- The currency in which the financial statements are presented. In situations where the presentation currency differs from that of the functional currency, the reporting entity must state that fact and disclose the functional currency together with the reasons why the presentation currency is different from the functional currency.
- If there has been a change in the functional currency of either the reporting entity or a significant foreign operation, the entity must disclose that fact together with the reasons for the change in functional currency.

29 SMALL COMPANY ABBREVIATED FINANCIAL STATEMENTS

INTRODUCTION

Under the provisions of Section 444 of the Companies Act 2006, a company classed as small can file 'abbreviated financial statements' with the Registrar of Companies (Companies House). Medium-sized companies can also file such financial statements, although the abbreviated financial statements that medium-sized companies file are not significantly different from the full financial statements (generally only omitting an analysis of turnover and derivative gross profit or loss).

At the time of writing the small companies regime was undergoing a significant overhaul due to the new EU Accounting Directive, which the UK has until July 2015 to transpose into companies legislation (Chapter 4 examines this issue in more detail). At present the thresholds for small and medium-sized companies are as follows:

	Balance sheet total (gross assets)	Turnover	No. of employees
Small company	£3.26m	£6.5m	50
Small group	£3.26m net	£6.5m net	50
	£3.9m gross	£7.8m gross	
Medium-sized company	£12.9m	£25.9m	250
Medium-sized group	£12.9m net	£25.9m net	250
	£15.5m gross	£31.1m gross	

Where references to 'net' and 'gross' are made, this is in relation to intra-group trading. 'Gross' means that intra-group trading (and the effects of such) have not been eliminated; 'net' means that intra-group trading (and the effects of such) have been eliminated.

Under proposals issued on 29 August 2014, the small companies regime is to undergo significant change due to the implementation of the EU Accounting Directive into UK legislation to allow more companies the opportunity of taking advantage of the small companies regime and hence include less disclosure in their financial statements with a view to cutting costs. The proposals contain a revised summary of the small companies regime as follows:

	Balance sheet (gross assets) £	Turnover £	Average no. of employees
For individual company accounts			
Micro-entity	≤316,000	≤632,000	≤10
Medium-sized company	≤18,000,000	≤36,000,000	≤250
Large company	≥18,000,000	≥36,000,000	≥250
For group/consolidated accounts			
Medium-sized group	≤ 18,000,000 net	≤36,000,000 net	≤250
	≤21,600,000 gross	≤43,200,000 gross	
Large group	≥18,000,000 net	≥36,000,000 net	≥250
	≥21,600,000 gross	≥43,200,000 gross	

The Directive also sets out a mandatory minimum threshold for small companies and a company will qualify as small if it does not exceed the limits of at least two of the three criteria. There is an added concession for small companies only in the Directive, which allows Member States to increase the balance sheet total and net turnover values by up to 50% so as to allow more companies to access the less burdensome small companies regime if they so wish. At the time of writing the new plans were currently scheduled to apply for accounting periods commencing on or after 1 January 2016.

The table below outlines the minimum and maximum thresholds permitted under the proposed small companies regime.

	Balance sheet £	Net turnover £	Average no. of employees
For individual company accounts			
Small company	≤3,500,000	≤7,000,000	≤50
(using minimum mandatory threshold values)			
Small company	≤5,100,000	≤10,200,000	≤50
(using maximum threshold values permitted)			
For group/consolidated accounts			
Small group	≤3,500,000 net	≤7,000,000 net	≤50
(using minimum mandatory threshold values)	≤4,200,000 gross	≤8,400,000 gross	
Small group	≤5,100,000 net	≤10,200,000 net	≤50
(using maximum threshold values permitted)	≤6,100,000 gross	≤12,200,000 gross	

The proposals acknowledge that if BIS were to adopt the minimum thresholds that define a small company, this would only offer a small increase of around 7% over the current thresholds and hence just 1,000 medium-sized companies would then fall into the small companies regime. BIS therefore proposes to adopt the maximum small company thresholds so as to allow an additional 11,000 companies access to the small companies regime.

At the time of writing the above proposals were at the consultation stage. The Financial Reporting Council is expected to issue an Exposure Draft outlining their intentions when the comment period closes on 30 November 2014. Final standards are expected to be issued in the summer of 2015 outlining the small companies regime and therefore readers are advised to keep abreast of developments on the Financial Reporting Council website at www.frc.org.uk.

Under the current Companies Act 2006, abbreviated financial statements are prepared in accordance with the following provisions:

Small company
SI 2008 No. 409 Schedule 4 (Part 1) – abbreviated balance sheet
SI 2008 No. 409 Schedule 4 (Part 2) – limited disclosures

Medium-sized company
SI 2008 No. 410 Schedule 1 and Regulation 4 – minimal disclosure exemptions within medium-sized company profit and loss account

The EU Accounting Directive described above is set to replace the 4th and 7th Accounting Directives.

CONTENT OF ABBREVIATED FINANCIAL STATEMENTS

A concept that is important to address at the outset is that financial statements are not intended to give the full true and fair view, unlike the full financial statements. This is because accounting standards are not applied to the abbreviated financial statements and hence they contain fewer disclosures than the full financial statements and for a small company generally only comprise the abbreviated balance sheet with limited disclosure notes. Some critics of small company abbreviated financial statements argue that insufficient information is made available on the public record so as to gauge the financial performance of a company in order to reach decisions. In their consultation document, BIS are proposing to introduce a requirement for small companies to prepare both an abbreviated balance sheet and an abbreviated profit and loss account; this option has previously not been taken up in the UK as small companies generally only publish an abbreviated balance sheet if they wish. At the time of writing, BIS was seeking views on whether small companies should have the choice of preparing an abbreviated balance sheet and profit and loss account if they wish.

For medium-sized companies the contents of the abbreviated financial statements are much more vast and are generally the full statutory accounts but without an analysis of turnover and derivative gross profit or loss.

The following table summarises the current content requirements of a set of abbreviated financial statements. In the light of planned changes relating to the EU Accounting Directive these requirements may be changed in the future and hence readers are advised to ensure they keep abreast of developments on the Department for Business Innovation and Skills website at www.gov.uk/department-for-business-innovation-skills.

	Small company	*Medium-sized company*
Directors' report/business review (or strategic report)	No report	Full report
Profit and loss account (income statement)	No profit and loss account (income statement)	Profit and loss account (income statement) must disclose turnover but can combine items to disclose resulting gross profit or gross loss
Balance sheet	Abbreviated balance sheet following SI 2008/409 Schedule 4 format and showing debtors and creditors falling due after more than one year	Full balance sheet following SI 2008/410 Schedule 1 format
Cash flow statement (statement of cash flows) and other primary statements	Not required	Full primary statements required including the cash flow statement (statement of cash flows)
Notes	Only limited disclosure notes required and no requirement to disclose directors'/employees' remuneration and auditors' remuneration	Full notes excluding turnover analysis (although disclosure of turnover required)
Auditors' report	Special report	Special report

For small companies, the format and content of the abbreviated financial statements are set out in regulations under SI 2008/409 Schedule 4. The provisions in the regulations allow small companies to deliver to Companies House a copy of the balance sheet prepared under Format 1 or Format 2 in the following order and under the headings given in the relevant format adopted.

Format 1 balance sheet

 A. Called up share capital not paid
 B. Fixed assets
  I. Intangible assets
  II. Tangible assets
  III. Investments
 C. Current assets
  I. Stocks
  II. Debtors
  III. Investments
  IV. Cash at bank and in hand
 D. Prepayments and accrued income
 E. Creditors: amounts falling due within one year
 F. Net current assets (liabilities)
 G. Total assets less current liabilities
 H. Creditors: amounts falling due after more than one year

    I.   Provisions for liabilities
    J.   Accruals and deferred income
    K. Capital and reserves
        I. Called up share capital
        II. Share premium account
        III. Revaluation reserve
        IV. Other reserves
        V. Profit and loss account

Format 2 balance sheet

ASSETS

    A. Called up share capital not paid
    B. Fixed assets
        I. Intangible assets
        II. Tangible assets
        III. Investments
    C. Current assets
        I. Stocks
        II. Debtors
        III. Investments
        IV. Cash at bank and in hand
    D. Prepayments and accrued income

LIABILITIES

    A. Capital and reserves
        I. Called up share capital
        II. Share premium account
        III. Revaluation reserve
        IV. Other reserves
        V. Profit and loss account
    B. Provisions for liabilities
    C. Creditors*
    D. Accruals and deferred income

*Creditors under format 2 must be split between those that fall due within one year and those that fall due after more than one year.

Regardless of which format the company adopts, the abbreviated financial statements must include a statement in a prominent position on the balance sheet (above the signature of the director), which confirms that the financial statements have been prepared in accordance with the provisions applicable to companies subject to the small companies regime (SI 2008/409 Schedule 4.1(2)).

The abbreviated financial statements must be approved by the board of directors and signed on behalf of the board by a director(s) of the company. Approval by the director(s) must be on the balance sheet.

Special auditors' report

Where a company is not exempt from the statutory audit requirement but delivers abbreviated financial statements to the Registrar of Companies (or in situations where the company might otherwise be exempt from audit, but voluntarily chooses to have an audit), then the abbreviated financial statements must also contain a special auditor's report confirming that in the auditor's opinion:

- The company is entitled to deliver abbreviated financial statements in accordance with the relevant section 444(3) (small companies) or 445(3) (medium-sized companies) as appropriate and
- The abbreviated financial statements have been properly prepared in accordance with regulations under SI 2008/409 Schedule 4 (small companies) or regulations under SI 2008/410 Schedule 1 (medium-sized companies).

The special auditor's report does not have to include the full auditor's report reproduced for the abbreviated financial statements, except in the following situations:

(a) The full auditor's report was qualified or
(b) The full auditor's report contains a statement under section 498(2) (a) or (b) (adequate accounts, records or returns inadequate or accounts not agreeing with records or returns) or section 498(3) (failure to obtain necessary information and explanations).

Example – Auditor's report on a small company (APB Bulletin 2008/4)

Independent Auditor's Report to Smallco Limited under Section 449 of the Companies Act 2006

We have examined the abbreviated accounts set out on pages 2 to 6, together with the financial statements of Smallco Limited for the year ended 31 December 2015 prepared under section 396 of the Companies Act 2006.

This report is made solely to the company, in accordance with section 449 of the Companies Act 2006. Our work has been undertaken so that we might state to the company those matters we are required to state to it in a special auditor's report and for no other purpose. To the fullest extent permitted by law, we do not accept or assume responsibility to anyone other than the company, for our work, for this report, or for the opinions we have formed.*

Respective responsibilities of directors and auditors

The directors are responsible for preparing the abbreviated accounts in accordance with section 444 of the Companies Act 2006. It is our responsibility to form an independent opinion as to whether the company is entitled to deliver abbreviated accounts to the Registrar of Companies and whether the abbreviated accounts have been properly prepared in accordance with the regulations made under that section and to report our opinion to you.

We conducted our work in accordance with Bulletin 2008/4 issued by the Auditing Practices Board**. In accordance with that Bulletin we have carried out the procedures we consider necessary to confirm, by reference to the financial statements, that the company is entitled to deliver abbreviated accounts and that the abbreviated accounts are properly prepared.

Opinion

In our opinion the company is entitled to deliver abbreviated accounts prepared in accordance with section 444(3) of the Companies Act 2006 and the abbreviated accounts on pages 2 to 6 have been properly prepared in accordance with the regulations made under that section.

John Smith (senior statutory auditor)
For and on behalf of ABC LLP, Statutory Auditors
Address
Date

---

*This paragraph is known as the 'Bannerman paragraph' and is recommended by ICAEW (Audit 1/03 – *The Audit Report and Auditors' Duty of Care to Third Parties*).

**The Auditing Practices Board no longer exists but Bulletin 2008/4 was issued by them. The Auditing Practices Board was incorporated into the Financial Reporting Council in 2012.

The following example shows an illustrative auditor's report on the abbreviated accounts of a small company where there is material uncertainty regarding the company's ability to continue as a going concern and hence an emphasis of matter paragraph was used in the full report.

Example – Emphasis of matter paragraph used in the auditor's report

Independent Auditor's Report to ABC Limited under Section 449 of the Companies Act 2006

We have examined the abbreviated accounts set out on pages 2 to 6 together with the financial statements of ABC Limited for the year ended 31 December 2015 prepared under section 396 of the Companies Act 2006.

This report is made solely to the company, in accordance with section 449 of the Companies Act 2006. Our work has been undertaken so that we might state to the company those matters we are required to state to it in a special auditor's report and for no other purpose. To the fullest extent permitted by law, we do not accept or assume responsibility to anyone other than the company, for our work, for this report, or for the opinions we have formed.*

Respective responsibilities of directors and auditors

The directors are responsible for preparing the abbreviated accounts in accordance with section 444 of the Companies Act 2006. It is our responsibility to form an independent opinion as to whether the company is entitled to deliver abbreviated accounts to the Registrar of Companies and whether the abbreviated accounts have been properly prepared in accordance with the regulations made under that section and report our opinion to you.

We conducted our work in accordance with Bulletin 2008/4 issued by the Auditing Practices Board**. In accordance with that Bulletin we have carried out the procedures we consider necessary to confirm, by reference to the financial statements, that the company is entitled to deliver abbreviated accounts and that the abbreviated accounts are properly prepared.

Opinion

In our opinion the company is entitled to deliver abbreviated accounts prepared in accordance with section 444 of the Companies Act 2006, and the abbreviated accounts have been properly prepared in accordance with the regulations made under that section.

Other information

On 18 April 2016 we reported as auditor to the members of the company on the financial statements prepared under section 396 of the Companies Act 2006 and our report included the following paragraph:

Emphasis of matter – going concern

In forming our opinion on the financial statements, which is not qualified, we have considered the adequacy of the disclosure made in note 29 to the financial statements concerning the company's ability to continue as a going concern. The company incurred a net loss of £85,000 during the year ended 31 December 2015 and, at that date, the company's current liabilities exceeded its total assets by £45,000. These conditions, along with the other matters explained in note 29 to the financial statements, indicate the existence of a material uncertainty, which may cast significant doubt on the company's ability to continue as a going concern. The financial statements do not include the adjustments that would result if the company was unable to continue as a going concern.

John Jones (senior statutory auditor)
PQR LLP, Statutory Auditors
Address
Date

*This paragraph is known as the 'Bannerman paragraph' and is recommended by ICAEW (Audit 1/03 – *The Audit Report and Auditors' Duty of Care to Third Parties*).

**The Auditing Practices Board no longer exists but Bulletin 2008/4 was issued by them. The Auditing Practices Board was absolved into the Financial Reporting Council in 2012.

THE STRATEGIC REPORT

For financial years that end on or after 30 September 2013, the Companies Act 2006 (Strategic Report and Directors' Report) Regulations 2013 will apply. Companies that qualify as small or that would also qualify as small except for being, or having been, a member of an ineligible group are exempt from the requirements to prepare a strategic report. Parent companies that prepare consolidated financial statements must also prepare a 'group strategic report', which relates to all the undertakings that have been included in the consolidation.

For companies that are not small, the strategic report will be filed with the abbreviated financial statements.

The strategic report is a report in addition to that of the directors' report and this requirement has been introduced by new section 414A to 414D to the Companies Act 2006. At the same time of introducing those sections, section 417 of the Companies Act 2006 was repealed. The consequence for unquoted companies is that the strategic report will essentially mirror the requirements of the business review.

The main difference between the strategic report and the business review is that the strategic report must be presented separately in the financial statements from the directors' report. In addition, section 414D to the Companies Act 2006 requires the strategic report to be separately approved by the board of directors and signed on behalf of the board by a director or the company secretary.

Content of the strategic report

The overarching objective of the strategic report is to inform the shareholders and help them to assess how the directors have discharged their duty to promote the success of the company. To achieve this objective, the strategic report must:

- Contain a fair review of the company's business that is a balanced and comprehensive analysis of the development and performance of the company's business in the period and of its position at the end of it.
- Contain a description of the principal risks and uncertainties facing the company.
- To the extent necessary for an understanding of the development, performance or position of the company's business, include an analysis using key financial performance indicators and, where appropriate, include information relating to environment and employee matters. 'Key performance indicators' are factors by reference to which the development performance or position of the company's business can be measured effectively. A company qualifying as medium sized for a financial year does not need to include non-financial information.

- Where appropriate include references to, and additional explanations of, amounts included in the company's annual accounts.
- Contain matters otherwise required by the regulations, like the Large and Medium-Sized Companies and Group Accounting Regulations (SI 2008/410), to be disclosed in the directors' report that the directors consider to be of strategic importance to the company. However, when a company chooses to disclose in the strategic report information that is required to be included in the directors' report, it should state in the directors' report that it has done so and should also indicate which information has been disclosed elsewhere.

For quoted companies, the strategic report must contain additional information as follows:

- The main trends and factors likely to affect the future development, performance and position of the company's business and information about environmental matters (including the impact of the company's business on the environment), the company's employees, social, community and human rights issues, including information about any policies of the company in relation to those matters and the effectiveness of those policies. If the report does not contain the information on environmental matters, employees and social, community and human rights issues, it must state which of those kinds of information it does not contain.
- A description of the company's strategy and the company's business model.
- A breakdown showing at the end of the financial year the number of persons of each sex who were directors of the company, the number of persons of each sex who were senior managers of the company (other than those who were directors) and the number of each person of each sex who were employees of the company.
- A company is not required to disclose information in the strategic report about impending developments or matters in the course of negotiation if the disclosure would, in the opinion of the directors, be seriously prejudicial to the interests of the company.

The amendments to the Companies Act 2006 have resulted in some disclosures no longer being required in the directors' report, in particular:

- A description of the principal activities of the company during the year,
- Details of charitable donations,
- Policy and practice on payment of creditors and
- The acquisition of own shares by private companies.

MICRO-ENTITY ISSUES

On 1 December 2013, legislation came into force in the form of SI 2013/3008 *The Small Companies (Micro-Entities' Accounts) Regulations 2013* following a European initiative to reduce costs for small and medium-sized businesses.

The legislation applies to financial years ending on or after 30 September 2013 where the financial statements of the company are filed at Companies House on or after 1 December 2013. Certain entities such as charities and LLPs are not eligible to apply the micro-entities regime.

A micro-entity is a company that meets two of the three following conditions:

1. Turnover not more than £632,000
2. Balance sheet total not more than £316,000
3. Average number of employees not more than 10

The turnover figure is adjusted proportionately where the accounting period does not span more than one year.

For filing requirements with the Registrar of Companies, the concept of abbreviated accounts does not apply to micro-entities. Therefore, a micro-entity could file the 'full' micro-entity financial statements that have been supplied to the shareholders. Alternatively, there is an option not to file the directors' report and/or profit and loss account and hence simply file the balance sheet. The notes included at the foot of the balance sheet for the micro-entity should be filed also if the micro-entity takes advantage of the latter option.

APPENDIX – SMALL COMPANY ABBREVIATED FINANCIAL STATEMENTS

These illustrative abbreviated financial statements are intended to be a guide only as to the form and content. They are not designed to be prescriptive and impending changes to legislation at the time of writing may mean additional statements or disclosures may be required. In all cases preparers of financial statements are advised to consult a reputable disclosure checklist to ensure that the financial statements they are preparing, whether abbreviated or full financial statements, are complete and accord with legislation and Generally Accepted Accounting Practice.

Report of the Independent Auditors to ABC Limited Under Section 449 of the Companies Act 2006

We have examined the abbreviated accounts set out on pages 3 to 7, together with the full financial statements of ABC Limited for the year ended 31 December 2015 prepared under Section 396 of the Companies Act 2006.

This report is made solely to the company, in accordance with Section 449 of the Companies Act 2006. Our work has been undertaken so that we might state to the company those matters we are required to state in a special auditors' report and for no other purpose. To the fullest extent permitted by law, we do not accept or assume responsibility to anyone other than the company, for our work, for this report, or for the opinions we have formed.

Respective responsibilities of directors and auditors

The directors are responsible for preparing the abbreviated accounts in accordance with Section 444 of the Companies Act 2006. It is our responsibility to form an independent opinion as to whether the company is entitled to deliver abbreviated accounts to the Registrar of Companies and whether the abbreviated accounts have been properly prepared in accordance with the Regulations made under that section and to report our opinion to you.

Basis of opinion

We conducted our work in accordance with Bulletin 2008/4 issued by the Auditing Practices Board. In accordance with that Bulletin we have carried out the procedures we considered necessary to confirm, by reference to the financial statements, that the company is entitled to deliver abbreviated accounts and that the abbreviated accounts to be delivered are properly prepared.

Opinion

In our opinion the company is entitled to deliver abbreviated accounts prepared in accordance with Section 444(3) of the Companies Act 2006, and the abbreviated accounts have been properly prepared in accordance with the Regulations made under that section.

John Smith (senior statutory auditor)
For and on behalf of
XYZ LLP Statutory Auditors
Address
Date

ABC Limited
Abbreviated Balance Sheet
31 December 2015

	Notes	31.12.15		31.12.14	
		£	£	£	£
Fixed assets					
Tangible assets	2		37,521		45,244
Investments	3		121,177		121,177
			158,698		166,421
Current assets					
Stocks		532,841		524,917	
Debtors		1,522,667		1,331,604	
Cash at bank and in hand		20,577		353,020	
		2,076,085		2,209,541	
Creditors: amounts falling due within one year	4	1,055,260		1,216,752	
NET CURRENT ASSETS			1,020,825		992,789
TOTAL ASSETS LESS CURRENT LIABILITIES			1,179,523		1,159,210
PROVISIONS FOR LIABILITIES			(1,112)		(1,233)
PENSION ASSET/(LIABILITY)			7,200		(710,400)
NET ASSETS			1,185,611		447,577
CAPITAL AND RESERVES					
Called up share capital	5		194,000		194,000
Profit and loss account			991,611		253,577
SHAREHOLDERS' FUNDS			1,185,611		447,577

The abbreviated accounts have been prepared in accordance with the special provisions of Part 15 of the Companies Act 2006 relating to small companies.

The financial statements were approved by the Board of Directors on 27 March 2016 and were signed on its behalf by:

A Smith (Director)   B Jones (Director)

The notes form part of these abbreviated accounts.

ABC LIMITED
Notes to the Abbreviated Accounts
For the Year Ended 31 December 2015

1. ACCOUNTING POLICIES

Accounting convention

The financial statements have been prepared under the historical cost convention and in accordance with the [insert relevant small companies framework].

Preparation of consolidated financial statements

The financial statements contain information about ABC Limited as an individual company and do not contain consolidated financial information as the parent of a group. The company has taken the option under section 398 of the Companies Act 2006 not to prepare consolidated financial statements.

Turnover

Turnover represents sales of goods despatched net of VAT and trade discounts provided in the normal course of business. Revenue is recognised when the goods are despatched, which is the same day on which the goods are delivered and hence is the point at which the risks and rewards of ownership pass to the buyer.

Tangible fixed assets

Depreciation is provided at the following annual rates in order to write off each asset over its estimated useful life:

Plant and machinery	–	at varying rates on cost
Fixtures and fittings	–	at varying rates on cost
Motor vehicles	–	25% on cost

Tangible fixed assets are stated at cost, net of depreciation and any provision for impairment. Residual values of fixed assets are calculated on prices prevailing at the date of acquisition. Profits or losses on the disposal of fixed assets are included in the calculation of profit for the period.

Stocks

Stocks are stated at the lower of cost and estimated selling price less costs to complete and sell. Stocks are used on a first-in first-out (FIFO) basis. Net realisable value is based on estimated selling price, less further costs to complete and sell. Provision is made for obsolete, slow-moving or defective items where appropriate.

Taxation

Current tax is provided at amounts expected to be paid (or recovered) using the tax rates and laws that have been enacted or substantively enacted by the balance sheet date.

Deferred tax is recognised in respect of all timing differences that have originated but not reversed at the balance sheet date where transactions or events that result in an obligation to pay more tax in the future or a right to pay less tax in the future have occurred at the balance sheet date. Timing differences are differences between the company's taxable profits and its results as stated in the financial statements that arise from the inclusion of gains and losses in tax assessments in periods different from those in which they are recognised in the financial statements.

A net deferred tax asset is regarded as recoverable and therefore recognised only to the extent that, on the basis of all evidence, it can be regarded as more likely than not that there will be suitable taxable profits from which the future reversal of the underlying timing differences can be deducted.

Deferred tax is measured at the tax rates that are expected to apply in the periods in which the timing differences are expected to reverse, based on tax rates and laws that have been enacted or substantively enacted by the balance sheet.

Research and development

Expenditure on research and development is written off in the year in which it is incurred.

Foreign currencies

Assets and liabilities in foreign currencies are translated into sterling at the rates of exchange ruling at the balance sheet date. Transactions in foreign currencies are translated into sterling at the rate of exchange ruling at the date of the transaction. Exchange differences are taken into account in arriving at the operating result.

Hire purchase and leasing commitments

Where the company enters into a lease which entails taking substantially all the risks and rewards of ownership of an asset, the lease is treated as a finance lease. The asset is recorded in the balance sheet as a tangible fixed asset and is depreciated over its estimated useful life. Where there is no reasonable certainty that the company will obtain ownership by the end of the lease term, the asset is fully depreciated over the shorter of the lease term and its useful life. Future instalments under such leases are included in liabilities. Rentals payable are apportioned between the finance element which is charged to profit and loss using the effective interest method and the capital element which reduces the outstanding obligation for future instalments.

All other leases are accounted for as operating leases and the rentals are charged to profit or loss on a straight-line basis over the life of the lease.

Pension costs and other post-employment benefits

The company subscribes to a pension scheme, the benefits of which are based on final pensionable pay. The assets of the scheme are held separately from those of the company. Contributions to the scheme are charged to profit or loss so as to spread the cost of pensions over the employees' working lives with the company.

The company operates a defined contribution pension scheme. Contributions payable for the year are charged to profit or loss.

Financial instruments

Financial instruments are classified and accounted for according to the substance of the contractual arrangement, as either financial assets, financial liabilities or equity instruments. An equity instrument is any contract that evidences a residual interest in the assets of the company after deducting all its liabilities.

Investments

Fixed asset investments are shown at cost less provisions for impairment.

2. TANGIBLE FIXED ASSETS

	Total
	£
COST	
At 1 January 2015	1,308,646
Additions	8,699
Disposals	(12,716)
At 31 December 2015	1,304,629
DEPRECIATION	
At 1 January 2015	1,263,402
Charge for the year	16,422
Eliminated on disposal	(12,716)
At 31 December 2015	1,267,108
NET BOOK VALUE	
At 31 December 2015	37,521
At 31 December 2014	45,244

3. FIXED ASSET INVESTMENTS

	Investments
	£
COST	
At 1 January 2015	
and 31 December 2015	121,177
NET BOOK VALUE	
At 31 December 2015	121,177
At 31 December 2014	121,177

The company's investments at the balance sheet date in the share capital of companies include the following:

Subsidiary

DEF Limited
Nature of business: chemical processing

	% holding
Class of shares: ordinary	100

The aggregate capital and reserves for this company amount to £nil (2014: £nil). This company has not been consolidated as it was dormant throughout the period.

Associated company

GHI Limited
Country of incorporation: India
Nature of business: chemical processing

	% holding
Class of shares: ordinary	26

	31.12.15	*31.12.14*
	£	£
Aggregate capital and reserves	2,402,860	1,812,350
(Loss)/profit for the year	(185,479)	258,566

4. CREDITORS

Creditors include an amount of £13,226 for which security has been pledged.

5. CALLED UP SHARE CAPITAL

Allotted, issued and fully paid:

Number:	*Class:*	*Nominal value:*	*31.12.15*	*31.12.14*
			£	£
194,000	Ordinary	£1	194,000	194,000

6. ULTIMATE PARENT COMPANY

WXY Limited is regarded by the directors as being the company's ultimate parent company.

WXY Limited is a company located in the UK under company number 12345678.

7. DIRECTORS' ADVANCES, CREDITS AND GUARANTEES

The following advances and credits to a director subsisted during the years ended 31 December 2015 and 31 December 2014:

	31.12.15	*31.12.14*
	£	£
A Smith		
Balance outstanding at start of year	7,776	7,776
Amounts repaid	(7,776)	(9,004)
Balance outstanding at end of year	—	7,776

In 2013 the company made an advance to the director amounting to £27,000 for the purchase of a motor vehicle. The company charges interest on this loan at HM Revenue and Customs official rate of interest. The loan is repayable over a three-year period. During the year interest amounting to £140.34 (2014: £509.23) was charged on this advance.

8. ULTIMATE CONTROLLING PARTY

The company is controlled by WYX Limited, its parent undertaking, which is incorporated in England and Wales under company number 12345678. The ultimate controlling related party is Mr A Smith by virtue of his controlling shareholding in that company.

30 REDUCED DISCLOSURE FRAMEWORK

INTRODUCTION

FRS 101 *Reduced Disclosure Framework* brings a new reduced disclosure regime for the separate financial statements of subsidiaries, which also includes intermediate parents and ultimate parents. The effect of FRS 101 is to enable such entities to use the recognition and measurement principles contained in EU-adopted IFRS and at the same time provide the advantage of exemption from a number of disclosures that are required by EU-adopted IFRSs. The advantage of applying FRS 101 in a group situation is that the individual financial statements of a subsidiary, intermediate parent and ultimate parent can be vastly reduced in terms of disclosures because the IFRS disclosure requirements are quite exhaustive.

FRS 101 brings with it certain exemptions from disclosure requirements and hence less complexity within the financial statements themselves. Many companies will welcome such a regime as financial statements are often blamed for 'over-disclosure', which essentially results in the dilution of the meaningfulness of the financial statements.

The reduced disclosure framework has been incorporated within FRS 102 *The Financial Reporting Standard applicable in the UK and Republic of Ireland* for those companies that are reporting under FRS 102 rather than EU-adopted IFRS and the disclosure exemptions can be found in paragraph 1.12 of FRS 102.

Scope of FRS 101

The scope paragraph in FRS 101 says that FRS 101 can be applied to the separate financial statements of a *qualifying entity*. A 'qualifying entity' is a member of a group in which the parent heading up the group prepares consolidated financial statements that are made publicly available and are intended to give a true and fair view in respect of the assets, liabilities, financial position and profit or loss of the group. A qualifying entity must be included within that consolidation and must not be a charity.

The term above also includes qualifying subsidiaries (including those with overseas parent companies) and ultimate parent companies.

FRS 101 may also not be applied to the consolidated financial statements.

REDUCED DISCLOSURES FOR SUBSIDIARIES
AND ULTIMATE PARENTS

When it has been established that an entity is a qualifying entity for the purposes of FRS 101, there are certain disclosure exemptions that it can take advantage of in its own financial statements. Some of the concessions in FRS 101 may not apply to every company eligible to apply FRS 101 and, as is always the case in these matters, there are conditions that have to be met in order that FRS 101 can be used.

A qualifying entity for the purposes of FRS 102 (i.e. one that is required by section 399 of the Companies Act 2006 to prepare consolidated financial statements and is not eligible to apply any of the exemptions contained in sections 400 to 402 of the Companies Act 2006) or which voluntarily chooses to prepare consolidated financial statements cannot take advantage of the disclosure exemptions, which are outlined in paragraph 1.12 in the consolidated financial statements.

There are conditions which must be fulfilled before a reporting entity can apply the provisions of FRS 101 in its financial statements, which are outlined below.

Notifying the shareholders in writing

To be eligible to apply FRS 101 in its separate financial statements, the shareholders of the entity must have been notified in writing and do not object to the entity applying FRS 101 in its financial statements.

A shareholder may be entitled to object to the entity applying FRS 101 in its financial statements if they hold (in aggregate) 5% or more of the total allotted shares in the entity or more than half of the allotted shares in the entity that are not held by the immediate parent. There may be a timescale imposed by the entity as to when the shareholder(s) can serve their objections together with a specified format that the objection should take. A shareholder that is also the immediate parent of the entity also has the right to object to the entity applying FRS 101 in its financial statements.

Compliance with the relevant financial reporting framework for recognition, measurement and disclosure requirements

In respect of an entity reporting under EU-adopted IFRS, a qualifying entity can apply FRS 101 in its financial statements if it also applies, as its financial reporting framework, the recognition, measurement and disclosure requirements mandated by EU-endorsed IFRS that have been amended, where necessary, so as to comply with the Companies Act 2006 and the Regulations. This is because the entity applying FRS 101 in its financial statements must still prepare Companies Act financial statements (as defined in section 395(1) (a) of Companies Act 2006) and not IAS accounts as defined in section 395(1) (b) of the Act.

For entities applying FRS 101 that are using FRS 102, the entity must apply the recognition, measurement and disclosure requirements of FRS 102 in its financial statements.

Disclosures in the notes

A reporting entity applying FRS 101 in its financial statements must also disclose in the notes to the financial statements:

- A brief narrative summary of the disclosure exemptions that the entity has adopted in preparing its financial statements and
- The name of the parent of the group in whose consolidated financial statements the qualifying entity's financial statements have been included. In addition, the entity should also disclose where those consolidated financial statements can be obtained.

Qualifying entities which are not financial institutions reporting under FRS 102

This section outlines the disclosure exemptions for those qualifying entities that are applying the provisions in FRS 102 in their financial statements. The next section will be applicable to those qualifying entities that apply EU-adopted IFRS in their financial statements.

<u>Relevant section of FRS 102</u>	<u>Disclosure exemption</u>
Section 4 *Statement of Financial Position*	Reconciliation of the number of shares outstanding at the beginning and end of the period.
Section 7 *Statement of Cash Flows*	No requirement for a statement of cash flows for the period.
Section 11 *Basic Financial Instruments* (see below)	The disclosure requirements contained in paragraphs 11.39 to 11.48A. However, equivalent disclosures should be made in the consolidated financial statements of the group in which the entity is consolidated.
Section 12 *Other Financial Instruments Issues* (see below)	The disclosure requirements in paragraph 12.26 relating to the disclosures required in Section 11 and the disclosures required in respect of financial instruments that are not held as part of a trading portfolio and are not derivative instruments.
	Disclosure requirements in respect of hedging relationships in paragraphs 12.27 to 12.29.
	In respect of the above exemptions, the exemption is conditional on the equivalent disclosures being made in the consolidated financial statements of the group in which the entity is consolidated.
Section 26 *Share-based Payment*	The requirements in paragraphs 26.18(b), 26.19 to 26.21 and 26.23 provided that for a qualifying entity that is:
	• A subsidiary, the share-based payment arrangement concerns equity instruments of another group entity and
	• An ultimate parent, the share-based payment relates to its own equity instruments and its separate financial statements are presented alongside the consolidated financial statements
	In both cases above, the equivalent disclosures are made within the consolidated financial statements of the group in which the entity is consolidated.
Section 33 *Related Party Disclosures*	Paragraph 33.7 relating to key management personnel compensation.

Qualifying entities that are financial institutions reporting under FRS 102

For those qualifying entities that are financial institutions and are reporting under the provisions in FRS 102, the disclosure exemptions in the above table relating to Section 11 *Basic Financial Instruments* and Section 12 *Other Financial Instruments Issues* do not apply. In all other respects, the disclosure exemptions above can apply to a qualifying entity that is a financial institution.

In all cases qualifying entities reporting under FRS 102 must make reference to the Application Guidance in FRS 100 *Application of Financial Reporting Requirements* in establishing whether the consolidated financial statements of the parent provide the disclosures that are equivalent to the requirements of FRS 102 when not applying the disclosure exemptions from which relief is provided in paragraph 1.12 of FRS 102.

Qualifying entities that are not financial institutions reporting under EU-adopted IFRS

In respect of a qualifying entity that is not a financial institution and reports under EU-adopted IFRS, the following disclosure exemptions are available from when the relevant standard is applied:

Relevant IFRS	Disclosure exemption
IFRS 2 *Share-based Payment*	Paragraphs 45(b) and 46 to 52, provided that for a qualifying entity that is: • A subsidiary, the share-based payment arrangement concerns equity instruments of another group entity and • An ultimate parent, the share-based payment arrangement concerns its own equity instruments and its separate financial statements are presented alongside those of the consolidated financial statements of the group. In both cases above, the equivalent disclosures should be made in the consolidated financial statements of the group in which the entity is consolidated.
IFRS 3 *Business Combinations*	Disclosure requirements in respect of paragraphs 62, B64(d), B64(e), B64(g), B64(h), B64(j) to B64(m), B64(n) (ii), B64(o) (ii), B64(p), B64(q) (ii), B66 and B67. Equivalent disclosures must be made in the consolidated financial statements of the group in which the entity is consolidated.
IFRS 5 *Non-Current Assets Held for Sale and Discontinued Operations*	Paragraph 33(c). Equivalent disclosures must be made in the consolidated financial statements of the group in which the entity is consolidated.
IFRS 7 *Financial Instruments: Disclosures* (see below)	All the disclosure requirements in this standard provided equivalent disclosures are made in the consolidated financial statements of the group in which the entity is consolidated.
IFRS 13 *Fair Value Measurement* (see below)	Paragraphs 91 to 99 provided all equivalent disclosures are made in the consolidated financial statements of the group in which the entity is consolidated.

IAS 1 *Presentation of Financial Statements*	Comparative information relating to:
	• Paragraph 79(a)(iv) of IAS 1
	• Paragraph 73(e) of IAS 16 *Property, Plant* and *Equipment*
	• Paragraph 118(e) of IAS 38 *Intangible Assets*
	• Paragraphs 76 and 79(d) of IAS 40 *Investment Property*
	• Paragraph 50 of IAS 41 *Agriculture*
	The requirements in paragraphs 10(d), 10(f), 16, 38A, 38B, 38C, 38D, 40A, 40B, 40C, 40D, 111 and 134 to 136 of IAS 1 *Presentation of Financial Statements*.
	In respect of accounting periods commencing prior to 1 January 2013 paragraphs 38A, 38B, 38C, 38D, 40A, 40B, 40C and 40D should be replaced with paragraphs 39 and 40 of IAS 1 (effective 1 January 2009).
IAS 7 *Statement of Cash Flows*	All provisions in this IAS.
IAS 8 *Accounting Policies, Changes in Accounting Estimates and Errors*	Paragraphs 30 and 31.
IAS 24 *Related Party Disclosures*	Paragraph 17 and the requirements to disclose related party transactions entered into between two or more members of a group (any subsidiary being a party to the transaction must be wholly owned by such a member).
IAS 36 *Impairment of Assets*	Paragraphs 134(d) to 134(f) and 135(c) to 135(e). Equivalent disclosures must be made in the consolidated financial statements of the group in which the entity is consolidated.

It is to be noted that where a qualifying entity has financial instruments that are held at fair value, subject to the requirements of section 36(4) of Schedule 1 to the Regulations, the entity must apply the disclosure requirements of paragraphs 8(e), 9(c), 10, 11, 17, 20(a) (i), 25, 26, 28, 29, 30 and 31 of IFRS 7 and paragraph 93 of IFRS 13 to those financial instruments that are held at fair value. In relation to accounting periods that commence before 1 January 2013, paragraph 93 of IFRS 13 should be replaced with paragraphs 27, 27A and 27B of IFRS 7.

Qualifying entities which are financial institutions reporting under EU-adopted IFRS

For those qualifying entities that are financial institutions reporting under EU-adopted IFRS and that are taking advantage of the reduced disclosure framework, the financial institution must not apply the exemptions in respect of the following:

(a) The disclosure exemptions in IFRS 7 *Financial Instruments: Disclosures.*

(b) The disclosure exemptions relating to IFRS 13 *Fair Value Measurement* to the extent that the disclosures apply to financial instruments (although a qualifying entity that is a financial institution may take advantage in its individual financial statements of the disclosure exemptions from IFRS 13 to the extent that they apply to assets and liabilities other than financial instruments).

(c) The disclosure exemptions from paragraphs 134 to 136 of IAS 1 *Presentation of Financial Statements.*

STATEMENT OF COMPLIANCE

FRS 101 requires a statement of compliance to be included in the notes to the financial statements of qualifying entities that have applied the provisions in FRS 101 as follows:

'*These financial statements were prepared in accordance with Financial Reporting Standard 101 Reduced Disclosure Framework.*'

Ordinarily an entity preparing financial statements under EU-adopted IFRS must also make a statement of compliance that their financial statements comply, in all respects, with EU-adopted IFRS. However, because a qualifying entity would have taken advantage of certain disclosure exemptions, they will not comply with all the requirements of EU-adopted IFRSs and as a consequence a qualifying entity applying FRS 101 should not make the *explicit and unreserved statement of compliance*, which is set out in paragraph 3 of IFRS 1 *First-time Adoption of International Financial Reporting Standards* and IAS 1 *Presentation of Financial Statements* at paragraph 16.

OPTIONS AVAILABLE FOR UK SUBSIDIARIES

In the UK a subsidiary that is a qualifying entity may apply the provisions of UK GAAP, with or without reduced disclosure exemptions in its financial statements, or it may prepare its financial statements under EU-adopted IFRS or prepare them under FRS 101 (i.e. prepare to EU-endorsed IFRS with reduced disclosures). Ordinarily the qualifying entity would choose which framework to apply but would also expect its parent to 'have a say' or authorise such a framework. The parent's involvement would be critical because any reduced disclosures that are applied within the qualifying entity's financial statements should be made within the consolidated financial statements. The idea of the reduced disclosure framework is to reduce the burden on a qualifying subsidiary but equivalent disclosures must be made elsewhere (i.e. within the consolidated financial statements).

A qualifying entity that is wholly owned by an overseas subsidiary might prepare its financial statements to UK GAAP, subject to any reporting requirements imposed by its parent and provided that these are consistent with the Companies Act 2006 requirements, but the options available to the UK subsidiary might be as follows:

(a) As the qualifying entity prepares its financial statements to UK GAAP, it might be more beneficial for the entity to adopt FRS 102 with the disclosure exemptions in paragraph 1.12.

(b) Prepare financial statements to FRS 102 without taking any of the disclosure exemptions that it might otherwise be entitled to take advantage of.

(c) Prepare its financial statements to full EU-adopted IFRS, taking no disclosure exemptions and with the format rules as prescribed in IAS 1 *Presentation of Financial Statements.*

(d) Adopt the provisions in FRS 101 *Reduced Disclosure Framework* and hence apply the recognition and measurement principles contained in EU-adopted IFRS but with the Companies Act 2006 compliant formats.

31 FIRST-TIME ADOPTION OF FRS 102

INTRODUCTION

FRS 102 *The Financial Reporting Standard applicable in the UK and Republic of Ireland* becomes mandatory for accounting periods commencing on or after 1 January 2015. The importance of a thorough programme of planning for the transition across to the new UK GAAP cannot be over-emphasised. Practitioners and company accountants should be considering transitional issues as a matter of priority. The rules in FRS 102 are retrospective in that they must be applied to the comparative period financial statements so that comparability and consistency in financial reporting are achieved. Readers are also encouraged to review Chapter 5 of this book to familiarise themselves with the key differences between the 'old' UK GAAP and FRS 102.

Section 35 *Transition to this FRS* is the vital section that first-time adopters of FRS 102 will need to understand. The section applies to first-time adopters of FRS 102 regardless of the previous accounting framework that was applied in the preparation of financial statements (for example, the old UK GAAP or EU-endorsed IFRS).

First-time adoption can only occur once. This is because, whilst Section 35 may look familiar with the provisions contained in Section 10 *Accounting Policies, Estimates and Errors*, Section 35 contains some special exemptions, simplifications and other requirements that are not inherent within Section 10. In a broad term, Section 35 requires an entity to apply the following rules on first-time adoption of FRS 102:

- Recognise all assets and liabilities where FRS 102 requires such assets and liabilities to be so recognised.
- Not to recognise assets and liabilities where FRS 102 prohibits the recognition of such.
- Reclassify items that were recognised under the previous UK GAAP as one type of asset, liability or component of equity, but which are a different type of asset, liability or component of equity under FRS 102.
- Apply the provisions in FRS 102 from the date of transition in measuring all recognised assets and liabilities.

An entity's *first* set of financial statements prepared under FRS 102 are those financial statements where the entity:

- Did not present financial statements for previous periods (for example, if it is a new start-up company),

- Presented its most recent financial statements under previous UK GAAP or
- Presented its most recent financial statements under EU-adopted IFRS.

IDENTIFYING THE DATE OF TRANSITION

The first step to take on first-time adoption of FRS 102 is to establish the date of transition. The date of transition is the *start date* of the earliest period reported in the financial statements. *Thus, for a year-end of 31 December 2015, the date of transition will be 1 January 2014.* This is because the 2014 financial statements will be the comparative period reported in the current year's financial statements and hence the start date of that comparative period is 1 January 2014. Using quarter-end dates, the following table should help companies to establish their date of transition to FRS 102:

Year-end	Date of transition
31 December 2015	1 January 2014
31 March 2016	1 April 2014
30 June 2016	1 July 2014
30 September 2016	1 October 2014

The fact that the rules are *retrospective* will mean that an opening FRS 102 balance sheet (statement of financial position) must be prepared at the date of transition across and hence essentially for a 31 December 2015 year-end the closing trial balance as at 31 December 2013 will need to be restated in order to generate the opening balances, which are FRS 102-compliant as at 1 January 2014. With the vast majority of accountancy firms using automated accounts production software systems, the use of such programs will inherently help the transition. However, such systems will need to be 'told' information to enable the conversion to be done accurately and hence this is the reason why technical staff involved in the conversion will need to be thoroughly conversant with all aspects of Section 35 and FRS 102 in general.

ACCOUNTING POLICY ALIGNMENTS

Once the date of transition has been established, the next step is to consider the entity's accounting policies. This is important because some accounting policies may be permissible under the old UK GAAP, but not permissible under FRS 102 (for example, the prohibition of the last-in first-out method of stock valuation in FRS 102, which was permissible in SSAP 9 *Stocks and Long-Term Contracts*).

Where accounting policies are not compliant with FRS 102, they will need to be changed to comply and this will result in transitional adjustments being made and hence it will more than likely mean that the 2013 trial balance is amended to form the FRS 102-compliant opening balances as at the date of transition. Alternatively, some automated accounts production systems may allow postings directly into the 2014 opening trial balance as transitional adjustments, although if this is not the case then the only other option will be to amend the 2013 trial balance. Whatever method is required, it is important that the opening figures are FRS 102-compliant.

Example – Accounting policy alignment

A company has a 31 December 2015 year-end and falls under the scope of FRS 102. Under 'old' UK GAAP the following opening balances as at 1 January 2014 have been generated by the company's accounting system:

	DR	CR
Plant and machinery – cost	100,000	
Plant and machinery – depreciation		30,000
Computer equipment – cost	30,000	
Computer equipment – depreciation		20,000
Investment property	140,000	
Stock	45,000	
Trade and other debtors	85,000	
Cash at bank and in hand	60,000	
Trade and other creditors		50,000
Corporation tax		17,000
Ordinary share capital		10,000
Revaluation reserve (Note 1)		25,000
Profit and loss reserves		308,000
	460,000	**460,000**

Note 1
The revaluation reserve account is in relation to the investment property, which is carried at open market value in accordance with SSAP 19 *Accounting for Investment Properties*. This was the only revaluation in respect of this investment property and was carried out on 31 December 2013.

The accounting policy alignments in this example are fairly straightforward. The first issue relates to the investment property.

The investment property is currently accounted for under the provisions in SSAP 19, which required all fair value gains and losses to be taken directly to the revaluation reserve unless a deficit (or its reversal) on an individual investment property is expected to be permanent, in which case it is charged (or credited) to the profit and loss account of the period. Paragraph 16.7 effectively extinguishes the use of the revaluation reserve account for investment properties and under FRS 102, fair value gains and losses are instead taken directly to profit or loss (this treatment is consistent with the *IFRS for SMEs* and the international equivalent, IAS 40 *Investment Properties*). This treatment must be reflected in the opening trial balance at the date of transition and therefore at the transition date the following transitional adjustment will be made:

DR revaluation reserve account	£25,000
CR profit and loss account reserves	£25,000

An important point to flag up is that any revaluation reserve account in respect of property that is not investment property may not need adjustment on transition to FRS 102, as the concept of the revaluation reserve account is still in existence in FRS 102 for property, plant and equipment accounted for under the revaluation model permitted in Section 17 *Property, Plant and Equipment* (see paragraph 17.15E).

Another point to note is that the £25,000 credit to the profit and loss reserve account in respect of the revaluation of the investment property will not be distributable to shareholders in the form of a dividend because it is not a realised gain for dividend purposes. It is therefore advisable for reporting entities to keep a record of the value of undistributable reserves in order to prevent such reserves being distributed as a dividend inappropriately.

The next issue to consider is the deferred tax implications relating to this investment property. Under FRS 19 *Deferred Tax*, provision for deferred tax in respect of non-monetary assets subject to revaluation would only be made if:

1. The asset is revalued to fair value each period with changes in fair value being recognised in the profit and loss account.
2. The entity has entered into a binding agreement to sell the revalued asset, has revalued the asset to its selling price and does not expect to obtain rollover relief.

Section 29 to FRS 102 *Income Tax* deals with the issue relating to investment property in paragraph 29.16. This particular paragraph requires deferred tax to be calculated in respect of investment property carried at fair value using the tax rates and allowances that apply to the sale of the asset. The exception to this rule is where the investment property has a limited useful life and is held within a business model where the objective is to consume (substantially) all of the economic benefits of the property over time.

Section 35 is silent on the treatment of deferred tax, but the transitional procedures in FRS 102 will apply to deferred tax in order to comply with paragraph 35.7, which requires FRS 102 assets and liabilities to be recognised, reclassified and measured according to FRS 102 in an entity's opening balance sheet (statement of financial position).

To arrive at the FRS 102-compliant trial balance, deferred tax will need to be recognised on the investment property gain at the date of transition. If it is assumed that the company pays corporation tax at the rate of 20% (and this rate of tax will essentially apply to the sale of the asset), deferred tax in respect of this investment property gain at the date of transition (ignoring the effects of issues such as indexation) will be £5,000 (£25,000 × 20%).

Transitional adjustments will be:

DR profit and loss account reserves	£5,000
CR deferred tax provision	£5,000

Once the transitional adjustments have been made and the opening FRS 102 balance sheet (statement of financial position) has been prepared, the next step is to consider the effects of the accounting policy alignments on the previous year's comparative figures. For the purposes of this illustration, if it is assumed that as at 31 December 2014 the open market value of the investment property had risen to £160,000 (a £20,000 gain during the year), the accounting treatment under 'old' UK GAAP SSAP 19 would have been:

DR investment property	£20,000
CR revaluation reserve	£20,000

This accounting treatment is inconsistent with the requirements of FRS 102 and, therefore, the 2014 year-end financial statements will need restating to become FRS 102-compliant. At 31 December 2014, the financial statements will be adjusted as follows:

| DR revaluation reserve | £20,000 |
| CR profit and loss | £20,000 |

The next step will then be to provide for the additional deferred tax on the revaluation gain in order to comply with paragraph 29.16 to IFRS 102. Again, ignoring the effects of indexation and assuming that the company continues to pay corporation tax at the rate of 20%, the deferred tax balance is calculated as follows:

	£
Deferred tax on revaluation gain (£45,000 × 20%)	9,000
Deferred tax balance at 1 January 2014	(5,000)
Deferred tax expense to 31 December 2014	4,000 (or 20% × £20,000 gain)

Exemptions from full retrospective application

Section 35 is markedly different than Section 10 *Accounting Policies, Estimates and Errors* because it contains specific exemptions. There are mandatory exemptions relating to:

- Derecognition of financial assets and financial liabilities (see Chapter 17),
- Hedge accounting (see Chapter 17),
- Accounting estimates (see Chapter 7),
- Discontinued operations (see Chapter 9) and
- Non-controlling interests (see Chapter 6).

Financial assets and financial liabilities

When an entity has derecognised financial assets and financial liabilities under previous UK GAAP it cannot restore those financial assets and financial liabilities on transition across to FRS 102. Conversely, where the reporting entity would have derecognised financial assets and financial liabilities under FRS 102 in a transaction that took place before the date of transition to FRS 102 but would not have been derecognised under the previous UK GAAP, there are two choices available:

1. To derecognise them at the date of transition to FRS 102 or
2. To continue recognising the financial assets and financial liabilities until they are either settled or disposed of.

Hedge accounting

In relation to hedging relationships that no longer exist at the date of transition to FRS 102, an entity cannot change its hedge accounting for those hedging relationships. Where hedging relationships do exist at the date of transition then the entity must follow the requirements in Section 12 *Other Financial Instruments Issues* for hedge accounting. This is also the case for discontinuing of hedge accounting in respect of hedging relationships that do not meet the conditions in Section 12.

Accounting estimates

An entity cannot retrospectively change the accounting that it followed for its estimates on transition to FRS 102. The consequence of this exemption is that management's estimates at the date of transition to FRS 102 should be consistent with estimates made for the same date in accordance with previous UK GAAP after adjustments to reflect any difference in accounting policies. This exemption is essentially to prohibit the use of hindsight in order to improve the estimates. When new information comes to light that would have caused the estimate to change, then management must deal with this as a non-adjusting event (see Section 32 *Events after the End of the Reporting Period* and Chapter 27) and account for it in the current accounting period.

Discontinued operations

For first-time adopters of FRS 102, it is not permissible to change the accounting that an entity followed under the previous UK GAAP in respect of discontinued operations. Therefore it follows that an entity will not be able to reclassify or remeasure any discontinued operations that were previously accounted for under the previous UK GAAP.

Non-controlling interests

Section 35 does not allow a first-time adopter to retrospectively change the accounting that it followed under the previous UK GAAP in respect of the measurement of non-controlling interests. Therefore, Section 35 will require first-time adopters to apply the following prospectively from the date of transition to FRS 102 (or from an earlier date when FRS 102 applies to a business combination that needs to be restated):

- Allocate profit or loss and total comprehensive income among both the owners of the parent and the non-controlling interests,
- Account for changes in ownership interest in a subsidiary that does not result in the parent losing control of the subsidiary and
- Account for a loss of control over a subsidiary.

In addition to the mandatory exemptions above, there are 18 optional exemptions and a reporting entity can apply some, none, or all of the exemptions in relation to:

- Business combinations, including group reconstructions (see Chapter 6),
- Share-based payment transactions (see Chapter 19),
- Fair value as deemed cost,
- Revaluation as deemed cost,
- Individual and separate financial statements (see Chapter 6),
- Compound financial instruments (see Chapter 17),
- Service concession arrangements (see Chapter 25),
- Extractive industries (see Chapter 25),
- Arrangements containing a lease (see Chapter 20),
- Decommissioning liabilities included in the cost of property, plant and equipment (see Chapter 13),
- Dormant companies,

- Deferred development costs as deemed cost,
- Borrowing costs (see Chapter 14),
- Lease incentives (see Chapter 20),
- Public benefit entity combinations (see Chapter 25),
- Assets and liabilities of subsidiaries, associates and joint ventures (see Chapters 6 and 23),
- Designation of previously recognised financial instruments (see Chapter 17) and
- Hedge accounting.

Business combinations, including group reconstructions

For business combinations that were effected before the date of transition to FRS 102, a first-time adopter can elect not to apply the provisions in Section 19 *Business Combinations and Goodwill*. However, Section 35 requires that if a first-time adopter restates any business combination in order to comply with the provisions in Section 19, it must then restate all later business combinations.

When a first-time adopter does not apply the requirements in Section 19 retrospectively, the entity must recognise and measure assets and liabilities acquired in a business combination in accordance with FRS 102 (which will also be subject to the exceptions and exemptions contained within Section 25). There are exceptions to this rule, which say that:

- Intangible assets that have been subsumed within goodwill are not separately recognised and
- The carrying amount of goodwill is not adjusted.

Example – Restatement of assets and liabilities acquired in a business combination

A company applies FRS 102 with effect from its accounting period commencing 1 January 2015. It has decided to apply the provisions in Section 19 retrospectively and therefore has made adjustments in recognising and measuring its assets and liabilities, which have been acquired from previous business combinations.

All adjustments relating to previous business combinations will be made against opening reserves on transition to FRS 102. This is because paragraph 35.10(a) to FRS 102 will not allow any adjustment to the carrying amount of goodwill.

Example – Goodwill carried over into FRS 102

A company acquired a wholly owned subsidiary that was accounted for under the previous UK GAAP. On acquisition, the directors concluded that the goodwill arising on this acquisition had an indefinite useful life and therefore performed annual impairment testing.

On transition to FRS 102, the directors must reassess this situation. This is because FRS 102 does not permit goodwill to have an indefinite useful life. As a consequence of this prohibition, reporting entities that previously did not amortise goodwill under the previous UK GAAP will need to determine the remaining useful life of the goodwill and amortise it over that period.

Share-based payment transactions

First-time adopters will not be required to apply the provisions in Section 26 *Share-based Payment* to any equity instruments that were granted prior to the date of transition to FRS 102. The same exemption also applies to liabilities that have arisen from share-based payment transactions that were settled prior to the date of transition to FRS 102. However, first-time adopters that used FRS 20 *Share-based Payment* or EU-endorsed IFRS 2 *Share-based Payment* for its equity instruments that were granted prior to the date of transition to FRS 102 should apply either FRS 20, IFRS 2 or Section 26 at the date of transition.

Fair value as deemed cost

The use of fair values as deemed cost can apply to both fair value as deemed cost and revaluation as deemed cost; hence a first-time adopter that previously adopted the use of the revaluation model for classes of fixed assets can use a previous fair value as deemed cost and then apply the cost model going forward. This can apply to an:

- Item of property, plant and equipment,
- Investment property or
- Intangible asset that meets the recognition criteria and the criteria for revaluation in Section 18 *Intangible Assets other than Goodwill.*

Revaluation as deemed cost

Section 35 also permits a first-time adopter to use a previous GAAP valuation relating to the above items at, or before, the date of transition. However, if a previous GAAP valuation is used before the date of transition, depreciation/amortisation should be taken into consideration between the date of the valuation and the date of transition to FRS 102.

Individual and separate financial statements

The provisions in paragraphs 9.26, 14.4 and 15.9 require entities that have got investments in subsidiaries, associates and jointly controlled entities to account for such investments either at cost less impairment or at fair value.

First-time adopters that measure their investments in such entities at cost are required to measure such investments in its individual or separate opening balance sheet (statement of financial position) at either:

- Cost, which is determined by applying Section 9 *Consolidated and Separate Financial Statements*, Section 14 *Investments in Associates* or Section 15 *Investments in Joint Ventures* or
- Deemed cost, which is taken to be the carrying value of the investment arrived at under the previous UK GAAP.

Compound financial instruments

Paragraph 22.13 of FRS 102 requires a compound financial instrument to be apportioned between that of its debt component and that of its equity component.

First-time adopters of FRS 102 need not use this 'split accounting' when the liability component of the instrument is not outstanding at the date of transition to FRS 102.

Service concession arrangements

When a first-time adopter is an operator in a service concession arrangement, they are not required to apply paragraphs 34.12E to 34.16A to arrangements that had been entered into prior to the transition across to FRS 102. Instead, the operator will continue to account for them using the same accounting policies that the operator applied at the date of transition to FRS 102. However, for grantors, the requirements of FRS 102 may mean that infrastructure assets and liabilities are recognised that were not previously recognised under the previous UK GAAP.

Extractive industries

It may be the case that a first-time adopter accounted for exploration and developments costs in relation to oil and gas properties in the development or production phases in cost centres that included all properties in a large geographical area. Where this accounting treatment was followed, a first-time adopter could elect to measure such oil and gas assets at the date of transition to FRS 102 as follows:

- For exploration and evaluation assets, these can be measured at the amount determined under the previous UK GAAP.
- For assets that are in the development or production phase, these can be measured at the amount determined for the cost centre under the previous UK GAAP.

Where the entity uses the second bullet point above, it should allocate this amount to the underlying assets of the cost centre on a pro rata basis using reserve volumes or reserve values as of that date.

It is also worth pointing out that Section 35 also requires first-time adopters to test the above assets for impairments at the date of transition.

Arrangements containing a lease

First-time adopters may determine whether an arrangement contains a lease at the date of transition to FRS 102 using the facts and circumstances that exist at that date as opposed to the date on which the arrangement was entered into.

Decommissioning liabilities included in the cost of property, plant and equipment

Section 17 *Property, Plant and Equipment* says that the 'cost' of an item should also include any initial estimates of the costs of dismantling an item and restoring the site on which the item is located (for example, a building). First-time adopters can measure this component of property, plant and equipment at the date of transition to FRS 102 as opposed to the date(s) on which the obligation actually arose.

Dormant companies

A dormant company may elect to retain its accounting policies in respect of reported assets, liabilities and equity as at the date of transition to FRS 102 until there is a change to those balances or the company undertakes new transactions.

If there is planned activity for the dormant company, it may be advisable to go ahead with the change.

Deferred development costs as deemed cost

Where a first-time adopter has deferred development costs, it can elect to measure the carrying amount of those costs at the date of transition to FRS 102 in accordance with the previous UK GAAP SSAP 13 *Accounting for Research and Development* as its deemed cost at the date of transition.

Borrowing costs

FRS 102 allows an accounting policy choice for borrowing costs. Where the first-time adopter chooses to capitalise borrowing costs as part of the cost of a qualifying asset, then the first-time adopter can elect to treat the date of transition to FRS 102 as the date on which capitalisation of borrowing costs commences.

Lease incentives

There is an exemption that allows a first-time adopter not to spread the benefits from a lease incentive over the term of the lease on a straight-line or other systematic basis. However, the term of the lease must have commenced before the date of transition to FRS 102. In addition, the first-time adopter will also continue to recognise any residual benefit or cost associated with lease incentives using the same basis as that applied at the date of transition to FRS 102.

Public benefit entity combinations

For public benefit entity combinations that were effected before the date of transition to FRS 102, first-time adopters can elect not to apply paragraphs PBE34.75 to PBE34.86. There is a proviso in that if, on first-time adoption, a public benefit entity restates any combination in order to comply with Section 35, it must restate all later entity combinations.

Assets and liabilities of subsidiaries, associates and joint ventures

Where a subsidiary company becomes a first-time adopter of FRS 102 at a date later than the parent company, the subsidiary company should (in its own separate financial statements) measure its assets and liabilities at either:

- The carrying values that would be included in the consolidated financial statements, which are based on the parent's date of transition to FRS 102. These carrying values are those when no adjustments were made for consolidation procedures as well as for the effects of the business combination in which the acquisition of the subsidiary took place or
- The carrying values that would be used by FRS 102, which are based on the date of transition to FRS 102 by the subsidiary. Differences may arise on those described in the above bullet where:
  - The exemptions available in FRS 102 result in measurements that are dependent on the date of transition to FRS 102 or

- The subsidiary's accounting policies that have been adopted as the basis for preparing the subsidiary's financial statements differ from those in the consolidated financial statements. An example of this could be where the subsidiary accounts for an item of property under the depreciated historic cost model but group policy is to carry properties at revaluation.

Similar choices are available for associates and joint ventures that become first-time adopters later than an investor has gained significant influence or joint control over it.

Conversely, where a parent/investor becomes a first-time adopter later than its subsidiary, associate or joint venture, the parent/investor should (in the consolidated financial statements) measure the assets and liabilities of the subsidiary, associate or joint venture using the same carrying values as those in the individual financial statements as the subsidiary, associate or joint venture. These values are those that have been adjusted for consolidation and equity accounting adjustments as well as for the effects of business combinations in which the parent acquired the subsidiary or where the investor gained significant influence or joint control.

Finally, where a parent company becomes a first-time adopter of FRS 102 in respect of its separate financial statements earlier or later than for the consolidated financial statements, the parent should measure its assets and liabilities at the same amount in both the separate and consolidated financial statements, except for consolidation adjustments.

Designation of previously recognised financial instruments

At the date of transition to FRS 102, first-time adopters are allowed to designate any financial asset or financial liability at fair value through profit or loss provided that the financial asset or financial liability meets the criteria laid down in paragraph 11.14(b) of FRS 102 at the transition date. Certain debt instruments can only be designated at fair value through profit or loss on initial recognition and this exemption can only apply if the instrument was already in existence at the date of transition to FRS 102.

Hedge accounting

Detailed optional exemptions relating to hedge accounting are contained in paragraph 35.10(t).

Other considerations for accounting policy alignments

Preparers of financial statements under FRS 102 must gain an understanding as to whether, or not, the existing accounting policies for a client/company that is planning to report under FRS 102 are permissible under the new regime. There are notable differences in accounting between the previous UK GAAP and FRS 102 and, therefore, preparers should appreciate that the accounting policies a client adopts may not be permissible under the new UK GAAP or may require different accounting treatments. Among other things, preparers need to consider the differing requirements in connection with:

- Accounting policies for transactions/events not covered by FRS 102 (see Chapter 7),
- Cash flow statement (see Chapter 22),
- Deferred taxation (see Chapter 11),

- Defined benefit pension plans (see Chapter 10),
- Employee benefits (see Chapter 10),
- Fair value accounting,
- Financial instruments (see Chapter 17),
- Fixed assets (see Chapters 12 and 13),
- Investment properties (see Chapter 13),
- Leasing (see Chapter 20),
- Prior-period adjustments (see Chapter 7),
- Revenue recognition (see Chapter 8) and
- Stock valuations (see Chapter 18).

Chapter 5 considers the key differences between previous UK GAAP and FRS 102 and readers are advised to be familiar with the differences between 'old' UK GAAP and FRS 102 so as to ensure FRS 102 is applied correctly in the financial statements. However, the above list is not an exhaustive list and there may be other client-specific policies that will need to be considered in the context of FRS 102.

STATEMENT OF COMPLIANCE

Financial statements prepared under FRS 102 must contain an *explicit and unreserved* statement of compliance with FRS 102.

Reporting entities must comply with all the provisions in FRS 102 in order to make this statement of compliance, which is a key principle in the restatement of the opening balance sheet on the date of transition to FRS 102 to ensure that all opening balances that form the comparative financial statements are prepared in accordance with the provisions in FRS 102. A reporting entity cannot make this explicit and unreserved statement of compliance if it does not comply with all its requirements.

Example – Non-compliance with FRS 102 (no explicit and unreserved statement of compliance)

A company has decided to adopt FRS 102 for its financial year-end of 31 December 2015. The directors of the company have not prepared a cash flow statement (statement of cash flows) on the grounds that they do not believe such a statement to be appropriate to their circumstances. There is no explicit and unreserved statement of compliance noted in the financial statements.

The cash flow statement is a mandatory statement and is required to be completed to comply with the provisions in paragraph 3.17(d), which specifically requires a cash flow statement to be prepared in order for the entity to produce a 'complete' set of financial statements. If the entity does not prepare the cash flow statement it will not be able to make the explicit and unreserved statement of compliance. This may also have an impact on the audit report if the entity is subject to a statutory audit.

> **Example – Non-compliance with FRS 102 (explicit and unreserved statement of compliance made)**

A company has decided to adopt FRS 102 for its financial year-end of 31 December 2015 and is a first-time adopter. The directors of the company have not prepared a cash flow statement (statement of cash flows) on the grounds that they do not believe such a statement to be appropriate to their circumstances. They have made an explicit and unreserved statement of compliance with FRS 102 in their accounting policies.

The auditors have qualified their audit report on the grounds that the company had not prepared a cash flow statement as required by Section 3 *Financial Statement Presentation* and prepared in accordance with Section 7 *Statement of Cash Flows*.

In this example, Section 35 will not apply to the company. If the company's financial statements do not fully comply with all aspects of FRS 102 then they are not considered to be a first-time adopter for the purposes of Section 35 in the current year. The disclosed, or undisclosed, departures from FRS 102 would be treated as an error under Section 35, which would trigger the company having to apply the provisions in Section 10 *Accounting Policies, Estimates and Errors*.

An example of how the explicit and unreserved statement of compliance for a first-time adopter may look in a set of FRS 102 financial statements is shown below.

ACCOUNTING POLICIES

Accounting convention and statement of compliance with FRS 102

The financial statements have been prepared under the historical cost convention as modified by the revaluation of certain assets. The financial statements of the company for the year ended 31 December 2015 have been prepared in accordance with the Financial Reporting Standard applicable in the United Kingdom and Republic of Ireland (FRS 102) issued by the Financial Reporting Council. These are the company's first set of financial statements prepared in accordance with FRS 102 (see Note XX for an explanation of the transition).

DISCLOSURE REQUIREMENTS

There are extensive disclosures required, which are covered in paragraphs 35.12 to 35.15 in FRS 102. A first-time adopter of FRS 102 is required to disclose:

(a) Information that explains how the transition from the previous UK GAAP to FRS 102 has affected the entity's reported financial position and financial performance.

(b) A description of the nature of each change in accounting policy the entity has been required to undertake in order to comply with the requirements in FRS 102.

In addition, various reconciliations are required to be presented as follows:

(a) A reconciliation of the company's equity as per the previous UK GAAP to the equity that has been determined under FRS 102 at:

      i. The date of transition to FRS 102 and
     ii. The end of the latest period shown in the company's most recent financial statements that were prepared under previous UK GAAP.

(b) A reconciliation showing the profit or loss calculated under the previous UK GAAP for the latest period in the company's most recent financial statements to the profit or loss calculated under FRS 102 for the same accounting period.

(c) In situations where a reporting entity has not prepared financial statements for previous periods (for example, a new start-up), the entity is required to disclose the fact that it has not prepared financial statements for previous periods in the first financial statements that are prepared under FRS 102.

Finally, it is worth pointing out that during the transition process, if any errors are noted in financial statements that had previously been prepared under the old UK GAAP, then these must be distinguished separately from the transitional adjustments, which are directly related to accounting policy alignments (errors cannot be classed as transitional adjustments).

Disclosure illustrations

The following illustrate how the additional disclosures required under Section 35 may look. It is to be noted that some automated accounts production software programs may produce the required disclosures in a different format. The formats below are for illustrative purposes only.

Reconciliation of equity

	31 December 2014	1 January 2014
	£'000	£'000
Equity under previous GAAP	X	X
Adjustments:		
Amortisation of goodwill	(X)	(X)
Holiday pay accrual	(X)	(X)
Recognition of derivative financial instruments	(X)	(X)
Remeasurement of stock using spot exchange rate	–	(X)
Equity under FRS 102	X	X

Reconciliation of profit or loss

	31 December 2014
	£'000
Profit for the year under previous GAAP	X
Amortisation of goodwill	(X)
Holiday pay accrual	(X)
Recognition of derivative financial instruments	(X)
Remeasurement of stock using spot exchange rate	(X)
Profit for the year under FRS 102	X

INDEX

Index compiled by Terry Halliday